DRUGS AND
THE PERFORMANCE
HORSE

DRUGS AND THE PERFORMANCE HORSE

By

THOMAS TOBIN
M.V.B., M.Sc., Ph.D., M.R.C.V.S.

Kentucky Equine Drug Research Program
Department of Veterinary Science
University of Kentucky
Lexington, Kentucky

With Forewords by

H. R. H. The Prince Philip
Duke of Edinburgh

and

Ernst Jokl, M.D.

Honorary President, Research Committee
UNESCO, International Council of
Sport and Physical Education

CHARLES C THOMAS • PUBLISHER
Springfield • Illinois • U.S.A.

Published and Distributed Throughout the World by

CHARLES C THOMAS • PUBLISHER

Bannerstone House

301-327 East Lawrence Avenue, Springfield, Illinois, U.S.A.

©*1981, by* CHARLES C THOMAS • PUBLISHER

ISBN 0-398-04446-5

Library of Congress Catalog Card Number: 80-28789

*With THOMAS BOOKS careful attention is given to all details of
manufacturing and design. It is the Publisher's desire to present books that are
satisfactory as to their physical qualities and artistic possibilities and
appropriate for their particular use. THOMAS BOOKS will be true to those
laws of quality that assure a good name and good will.*

Library of Congress Cataloging in Publication Data

Tobin, Thomas, 1941-
   Drugs and the performance horse.

   Bibliography: p.
   Includes index.
   1. Veterinary drugs — Physiological effect. 2. Horses
— Physiology. 3. Doping in horse-racing. I. Heard,
Richard, joint author. II. Title. III. Title: Perform-
ance horse. [DNLM: 1. Doping in sports. 2. Horses —
Physiology. SF 338 T629d]
SF917.T63   636.1′089577   80-28789
ISBN 0-398-04446-5

Printed in the United States of America
C-1

To my wife

Anyone who has ever had anything to do with horses knows what a problem it is to keep them healthy and sound. If the horses are to be raced or used in competitive sport there is the added problem of training and preparing them to go faster or better than their rivals. The trouble is that the dividing line between treatment of injury and disease, on the one hand, and the preparation of horses for competition, on the other, is very narrow and not easily defined. In principle it is obviously right to use medications to cure injuries and disease; but it is patently wrong to use drugs to influence the performance of a horse.

If the equestrian sports are to be fair for all competitors, it is vitally important that these principles are expressed in clear, sensible and enforcible rules. This cannot be done without the help and co-operation of specialist and experienced veterinarians and pharmacologists.

The great value of this book is that for the first time the facts about contemporary medications, drugs and analytical techniques are set out in plain unmistakable language by an acknowledged world authority. It is a book that will be welcomed by competitors, trainers, coaches, veterinarians and administrators.

1980.

THE FIRST RECORDED instance of doping is the biblical account of Adam and Eve eating the forbidden fruit; they did so not because they were hungry but because the serpent deceived them into believing that the fruit would render them God-like. Ever since, the belief that magic substances exist capable of imparting supernatural powers has been expressed in fairy tales and folklore: in stories like that of the sickly horse that turned into an enchanted steed after swallowing burning charcoal; of Popeye the sailor who develops miraculous powers after eating spinach; of the African witch doctor who gives his followers pieces of a lion's heart; and of the medieval alchemists' search for the "philosophers' stone" alluded to in Goethe's *Faust.*

Professor Tobin's book presents the available scientific evidence on "doping." It deals with a variety of pharmacological problems of interest to physiology and clinical medicine. Since Lexington, Kentucky, is a leading center of scientific research on horse racing and sports medicine, Professor Tobin's work has received worldwide attention. The Research Committee of the UNESCO International Council of Sport and Physical Education and the Doping Commission of the International Olympic Committee have sought his advice recently in connection with the establishment of the "Doping Control Laboratories" for the 1980 Olympic Games in Moscow.

Professor Tobin's volume includes information on three important questions: on the validity of the belief in the existence of substances capable of improving performances of horses and athletes; on the biochemical procedures for the detection of "dope" in urine; and on toxic effects of inappropriately large doses of "dope." We know most about the third, least about the first. It is quite possible that with the exception of anabolic hormones and of androgenic hormones in females, no substances exist that improve performances.

In 1964 the Research Committee of the UNESCO International Council of Sport and Physical Education held the first International Symposium of Doping in Gent, Belgium, under the Chairmanship of Nobel Laureate Professor Corneille Heymans. Its proceedings were published in 1965. Since then, no comprehensive study of the subject has appeared. Professor Tobin's book thus fills an urgent need.

ERNST JOKL

PREFACE

As I write these words, the field of performance horse medication in the United States is in turmoil. By the end of the 1970s, the days when horses ran on "hay, oats, and water" and little else were all but gone in the United States of America. Essentially alone among the major racing states, New York ran medication-free horses.* Most of the other major racing states, starting with Colorado and spreading from there, allowed some form of permitted or controlled medication in their horses. While as recently as 1968 the calling of a "positive" for the then-prohibited phenylbutazone on DANCER'S IMAGE in the Kentucky Derby triggered a court battle that lasted for years, by 1978 horses could legally run on phenylbutazone in many of the major racing states. More recently, however, federal legislation has been proposed to ban the use of medication in racing horses, and in the light of this proposal many racing jurisdictions are reassessing their medication policies.

Such quantum changes in usage patterns and people's attitudes to the use of drugs in horses has led to an increased demand for information about the effects of drugs in horses. This, in turn, has led to the setting up of research programs, such as the Kentucky Equine Drug Research Program, of which I am director. The mission of this program is to measure, analyze, and report on the detection and actions of drugs in horses. While results from this and other programs are published in scientific journals, these journals are usually not readily available to horsemen or interested members of the public, and neither is the raw data and partly digested information found in such journals particularly useful to horsemen. A further problem is that the average horseman has nowhere to go to get the background information required to understand such articles and put them in perspective. The primary objective of this book, therefore, is to bring together in one volume the necessary background material and published information to present horsemen with an understandable and informative account of the field of performance horse medication. This book is not an academic exercise, of which I have had plenty, but an effort to describe the current state of our knowledge about drugs in performance horses.

This book is likely to be useful to more than the average horseman. The science of pharmacology is of very recent origin, many of the drugs we use and most of the background information required to understand their use having been developed within the last twenty years. Since most people involved in the management of racing, including commission veterinarians, tend to have had little formal education within this period, this book should be particularly useful to them. The probability is that most commission veterinarians will, like myself, have had courses rather quaintly called "Materia Medica" which discussed the medications and carried the intellectual stamp on an earlier, less complex era.

* Medication "free" in that no drugs are permitted to be administered within 48 hours of post time.

xi

Another important goal of this book is to strip away as much as possible of the myth, rumor, and ignorance that surrounds the use of drugs in horses. On the principle that the less people know, the more they suspect, I have chosen to name drugs and to discuss their actions, doses, time to peak effect, and clearance times in a way that some might interpret as aiding individuals who wish to misuse drugs. I do not think this is likely to be the case. As one reads this book it becomes apparent that most of the effective stimulant dopes have been with us for some time, in many cases up to 100 years and longer. Little that I can say about these drugs will help that most astute equine pharmacologist, the horseman knowledgeable in the use of drugs. The goal of this book is to put drugs in horses into accurate perspective. In the hands of the popular press, and more recently television, completely unsupported rumors have unquestionably done more damage to racing's image than all the drugs that have ever been given to horses. Journalism and media presentations that equate drugs like Lasix® (furosemide) and "bute" (phenylbutazone) with apomorphine and Sublimaze® and lump all drugs under the heading of "dope" will, it is hoped, be easier to refute if the actions, effects, and problems with drugs of all classes are clearly laid out. Secrecy and the uneasy feeling that racing has something to hide in its use of medication do more damage to racing's public image than anything else. Further, this book comes at a time when the racing industry, having developed analytical methods for reserpine and fentanyl, has made spectacular advances in its control of prohibited medication and has good reason to be proud of its record.

The medication of performance horses is a complex area, an interface between the fields of veterinary medicine, pharmacology, analytical chemistry, law, business, public relations, and horse breeding, to mention but a few. As an individual trained in the first three of these fields, I am competent to discuss the actions and detection of drugs in horses with some authority and to offer advice and opinions elsewhere. The reader should keep in mind that the further I stray from the first three of these fields, the less sure my grip on the subject is likely to be. As for my command of the first three fields, most of the material on which I base my comments is published and listed in the reference lists, so if the reader is so inclined he can check it out for himself.

In organizing this book, I have chosen to divide it into five sections. The first section deals principally with the background required to understand why people put drugs into horses, how drugs produce their effects in horses, and, in a broad sense, how horsemen control the use of drugs in horses. We then proceed to a discussion of the specific drugs, starting with the drugs of controlled medication (Section II), followed by the illegal drugs (Section III), and then the drugs that are not considered a regulatory problem (Section IV). Finally, then, in the last section (Section V) we deal with medication control from the point of view of the analyst, the regulator, and the lawyer.

Although equine medication is a complex area, the field does have its humorous aspects. In an attempt to capture this lighter side, my good friend Bob Herndon went through the text and sketched some of the incidents described. While many of these sketches carry very valid messages, their primary role is to lighten an often tedious field. None of them, therefore, is meant to be taken too seriously.

This book is, to my knowledge, the first attempt to draw together pertinent information from the various fields of equine medication and present an understandable synopsis. It is my hope that this volume will serve as an introduction to the area for the many people with an interest in drugs in horses but with little background in pharmacology. It should also serve as an up-to-date refresher for those whose formal training in this area may be dated. Finally, with a media battle looming over the possibility of federal legislation in this area, I hope that this book will serve as a stable point of reference in what can, unfortunately, be a highly emotional area. If I succeed in attaining any one of these goals, I will consider this book a success for the reader. As for myself, I have thoroughly enjoyed writing it.

THOMAS TOBIN

ACKNOWLEDGMENTS

WHILE THE WRITING of this book was largely the result of my own efforts, it would not have been possible without the support that I received from many individuals and organizations. First among these organizations must come the Kentucky State Racing Commission and the Kentucky Harness Racing Commission. In the early 1970s, these commissions, in cooperation with the Department of Veterinary Science, College of Agriculture, University of Kentucky, set up the Kentucky Equine Drug Research Program to study the actions and effects of drugs in racehorses. This program was taken from the talking stage to its present status by my Chairman, Doctor John T. Bryans of the Department of Veterinary Science, and he, along with Mr. Clarkson Beard and Mr. Carl Larsen of the Commissions, have nurtured its progress ever since. In addition, the guidance of Senior Steward Keene Daingerfield and the enthusiastic support and interest of Commissioner Anita Madden have been invaluable. Without their support and contributions to this research program, which is a formal expression of the commitment of Kentucky horsemen to the welfare of the horse, this book could not have been written.

Given the environment and wherewithal to do this work, one then needs colleagues to work with, consult with, and learn from. Foremost among my colleagues stands Professor Jerry Blake, who runs the Kentucky Equine Drug Testing Program. To him go my deepest thanks for his unfailing cooperation and support as we tackled the problems of our respective programs. Our success, such as it may be, is due in no small part to his abilities and endeavors. Others among my colleagues at the University of Kentucky who have contributed to this research include Harry Kostenbauder of the College of Pharmacy, John Dougherty of the Veteran's Administration, Wyman Dorough of the Graduate Program in Toxicology, and Ernst Jokl of the College of Human Medicine, all of whose varied contributions are deeply appreciated.

Equine medication control is an international concern. Among my other colleagues with whom I have consulted, cooperated, or argued, as the case may be, are Albert Gabel, Richard Ray and Richard Sams of the Ohio State University, George Maylin and Jack Henion of Cornell, and John McDonald of the Illinois Racing Board Laboratory. North of the border, Gerry Johnston of Montreal, and in Europe, Michael Moss and Douglas Witherington spring to mind. From all of these people and many others, I have learned much and always enjoyed their company.

Much of the original research on which this book is based was carried out by my students, to whom I will always be indebted. To take them in the order in which they joined my lab, they included Brian Roberts and Richard Miller, Connie White, Joan Combie and Eugenie Greene, Ted Shults and Steve Ballard, and Sylvia Chay. At times as important, and almost always carrying a heavy work load, have been my student assistants, including Steve Arnett, Edith Nugent, Sandy Kownacki, Tommy Nugent, and Mark Crisman. For excellent technical assistance and providing the day-to-day backbone of my laboratory, I have to thank Lee Sturma, Roger Valentine, and William Edward Woods. All of these people made their own unique contributions to this program and thus to the completion of this book.

If you must write a book, a university is a good place to do it. Essential support services, such as artwork, photography, and secretarial work, can be begged, borrowed, bootlegged, or just plain stolen on campus more readily than perhaps anywhere else. Further, since the quality of my artwork and handwriting can only be described as dismal, these people had a further load to bear. To Gene Courtney and Bob Herndon, who did the graphs and cartoons, and to Diane Haughey and Virginia Ransdell, who did most of the typing, go my gratitude for taking this project from my pictographs to the finished product.

Finally, the last proofreading of this manuscript was completed in Nine Mile House, County Tipperary, under the eagle eye of my father, Nicholas Tobin. From Tipperary it went to my publisher, Payne Thomas of Charles C Thomas, Publisher, with whom it has been a pleasure to work.

CONTENTS

DRUGS AND
THE PERFORMANCE
HORSE

Section I

THE HISTORY AND PRINCIPLES OF MEDICATION IN PERFORMANCE HORSES

A S THIS BOOK DEVELOPED, it became clear that it divided into five major sections. This first section, of five chapters, consists principally of the background material necessary to understand the subject of performance horse medication. In the first chapter of this section, we present an overview of the field to orient the reader to its broad general outlines. Having done this, we can then start to trace the history of the field from Roman to recent times.

In tracing the history of this field, I have taken the stories, rumors, anecdotes, and so forth as I found them. The fact that I recount these stories is not meant to authenticate them or the pseudopharmacology in them in any way, but merely to present some of the richly human texture of this subject. If any lesson should come from this section, it is probably that the urge to medicate for advantage is strongly woven into human nature, and as such will inevitably always be with us.

Given that the urge to medicate is likely to be with us indefinitely, the third chapter sketches the cast of characters involved in current medication control. This chapter therefore presents the societal framework within which the use of drugs in performance horses is regulated.

Finally, then, we are ready to look at the drugs themselves. Rather surprisingly, most drugs are natural products, or are derived from natural products, and in fact probably existed on this planet long before we did. As such, horses are well adapted to their use, and they absorb, metabolize, and eliminate these agents readily. Along the way, however, the drugs in which we are interested produce very specific effects in the horse, and the remainder of the book is devoted to consideration of these specific effects.

Chapter 1

THE MEDICATION OF PERFORMANCE HORSES: AN OVERVIEW

THE WORD "DOPING" first appeared in an English dictionary about 1899, defined as a mixture of opium and narcotics used for horses. The root of this word does not stem from English but apparently from the Dutch language, where the word "doop" means to dip. It was incorporated from the Dutch into a dialect spoken by the native workers in southeastern Africa, where the word "dop" meant the local schnapps or hard liquor that was used by them as a stimulant at worship. The word is still in use in that part of the world today, where it refers to the wine ration issued to native workers in South Africa by their overseers. According to Crosier, the word also made its way into American slang, where it was used to describe a gypsy habit of using tobacco adulterated with the seeds of *Datura stramonium* to stupefy wayfarers before robbing them. As modern "doping" is apparently an American habit, it became associated with the illicit medication of racing animals. In everyday English the word "dope" has many meanings, mostly connected with its early associations with drugging. Its basic meaning in the horse world concerns any drug used to affect the performance or demeanor of a horse, but most especially with reference to stimulant effects in the horse.

Two other slang words are also widely used to describe the doping of racehorses. In the United States, a stimulatory doping is often referred to as "hopping," with the obvious meaning that the horse will be visibly stimulated by the drug. This word is also found in the drug subculture, where a drug addict is known as a "hophead." In Great Britain the word "nobbling" is used to describe either depressant doping or laming of a horse, and a horse so treated is spoken of as having been "nobbled."

These terms, and most particularly the term "doping," carry sinister connotations of narcotic administration, addiction, insensibility to normal stimuli, and the stimulation of exceptional or unpredictable performances. In his first description of what he took to be "doped" horses racing in England in about the year 1900, the Honorable George Lambton described "horses who were notorious rogues running, and winning as if they were possessed by the devil, with their eyes staring out of their heads and sweat pouring off them" and one horse, "after winning a race dashed madly into a stone wall and killed itself." Because the general public draws no clear distinction between this very disturbing picture of stimulant doping and the beneficial effects of the legitimate medications approved in some states, American racing authorities prefer to avoid the word "dope" as a loaded and misused term. Thus, in North America "doping" is "illegal medication," in contrast with legal or controlled medication, or permitted medication, which encompasses legitimate therapeutic agents whose use on or close to race day may be approved. On the other hand, the racing authorities in Britain, where no medica-

One horse "after winning a race dashed madly into a stone wall and killed itself." (George Lambton in "Men and Horses I Have Known.")

tion whatsoever is permitted, class any substance that is not a "normal nutrient" in equine urine as "dope" and use this pejorative term freely as an indication of their feelings on the matter of medication in racing horses.

Doping, like pornography, is all but impossible to define, and one man's dope may well be another man's controlled medication or may not even merit consideration. The original thought on medication and horses was that horses should run on "hay, oats, and water" only, but this thought is honored more in the breach than the observance nowadays, particularly in the United States. In England, at one time, a "doper" was defined as follows: "any person who administers or allows to be administered or connives at the administration to a horse of a substance (other than a normal nutrient) which could alter its racing performance at the time of racing shall be guilty of a breach of the rules and may be declared a disqualified person or otherwise penalized by the stewards of the Jockey Club in accordance with their powers." This rule is almost all-encompassing, and any substance that is not a normal constituent of a horse's diet, which could possibly influence the performance of a horse, should not be administered in any quantity, no matter how small.

This is a very vague definition. In the first place, what are "normal nutrients" in the horse? Approaching this problem, **Professor George Clarke of the English Horse Race Antidoping Committee, spoke of the** unintentional inclusion in the horse's feed of some substance that, if given deliberately, would be classed as a dope. So not only what you give but how and why you give it would apparently determine whether or not a drug was a dope. As an example, Professor Clarke pointed to a by now notorious incident in English racing where some cocoa husk was added to an animal food and wound up being fed to racehorses. The upshot of this was that a number of positives were called for caffeine and theobromine in horses trained by some very reputable trainers, including trainers for the highest ranks of British society. This created a very embarrassing incident and highlighted a third factor which influences whether or not detection of a drug is perceived as a doping incident, which is the social status and reputation of the individuals involved.

The wording "normal nutrient" also leads to problems in that many things that are not usually considered "normal nutrients" are present in normal diets. In an authoritative interpretation of this portion of the rule, Professor Clarke pointed out that to be a "dope" a substance must be something other than a normal constituent of a horse's diet. In my experience, the problem with this definition concerning the nature of a "dope" came to a head in South Africa, where the racing authorities chose to prosecute a trainer because a high concentration of arsenic was found in one of his horses' urine. Like it or not, arsenic is an unavoidable constituent of both human and horse food and is therefore undoubtedly a "normal" constituent of a horse's diet. There is, furthermore, not a shred of worthwhile evidence or opinion that arsenic is a tonic or might improve the performance of a horse. Nevertheless, the South African racing authorities were of the opinion that the detection of arsenic in horse urine was evidence of an attempt to dope, and the unfortunate trainer involved in this incident found himself at risk of being "ruled off" for life.

In an effort to get around these problems, the British authorities redrafted their definition of doping in the late 1970s. Evidence for doping of a horse under the new definition depended on "the detection in its tissues, body fluids or excreta of any quantity of any substance which is either a prohibited substance or a substance the origin of which cannot be traced to normal and ordinary feeding and which by its nature could affect the performance of the horse." To round off this definition, a prohibited drug was a substance originating externally, whether or not it was endogenous to the horse. In a nutshell, any substance found in a horse which could not be traced to "normal and ordinary feeding" and which could affect the performance of a horse was a "dope." Detection of such a substance was the sole piece of evidence required for sanctions to be brought against the horse and trainer, and, as is usually the case, the regulations were drafted in the broadest of possible terms. The terms were, in fact, a little too broad. Oxygen, for example, is present in all body tissues and fluids, undoubtedly affects the performance of a horse, and is certainly not a part of normal and ordinary feeding. A strict interpreter of this definition must conclude that all horses are doped; certainly, this is contrary to the intention of this rule.

One of the most confused definitions of doping that I have ever encountered is that presented by the International Olympic Committee in the report on the medical controls at the Montreal Olympics. This definition, which was the product of a commission of experts convened by the Council of Europe in 1963, reads as follows:

> Doping is defined as the administering or use of substances in any form alien to the body, or of physiological substances in abnormal methods, by health personnel, with the exclusive aim of attaining an artificial and unfair increase of performance in competition. Furthermore, various psychological measures to increase performance in sport must be regarded as doping.

This definition was obviously written by a large committee of "experts" in an expansive mood. It emphasizes the role of intent, which is all but impossible to prove. The restriction to administration by "health personnel" is inexplicable, as this would exclude self-administration of drugs by athletes or administration by trainers or coaches. The inclusion of psychological measures also opens up a totally uncontrollable area for the Olympic or any other authorities, and in my opinion this definition raises more problems than it solves.

In attempting to define doping I am often reminded of one of the problems that arose during the Watergate scandal, that of defining what constituted an "impeachable offense." The answer that made most sense was that an impeachable offense was whatever the U.S. Congress chose to consider an impeachable offense. The same rule provides the only practical horseman's definition of doping, which is that doping is whatever the racing authority concerned chooses to consider doping. Obviously, implementation of such a flexible rule will vary from jurisdiction to jurisdiction, and this creates the problem for horsemen and veterinarians of deciding just what drugs, vitamins, food additives, and so forth are likely to be considered doping drugs.

The answer to this question is, of course, that anything may be considered a doping drug, depending on the rules of the particular jurisdiction. In almost all jurisdictions drugs classified as stimulants, depressants, local anesthetics, tranquilizers, or narcotics are banned. The principal exception to this rule that I am aware of is California, where horses in the late 1970s could be raced just twenty-four hours after a dose of pentazocine (Talwin®) and might thus be raced with a drug in their systems that is pharmacologically, if not legally, a narcotic analgesic.

The medication rules in Kentucky in the late 1970s were probably typical of liberal medication rules. The rules in force then stated that in Kentucky, "no horse, while participating in a race shall carry in its body any medication, or drug, or substance, or metabolic derivative thereof, which is a narcotic, or which could serve as a local anesthetic, or tranquilzer or which could stimulate or depress the circulatory, respiratory, or central nervous system of a horse, thereby affecting its speed." The rules further went on to state that "also prohibited are drugs which might mask or screen the aforementioned prohibited drugs, or prevent or delay testing procedures." Kentucky thus allowed the use of diuretics such as Lasix®, anti-inflammatories such as phenylbutazone, the other non-steroidal anti-inflammatory agents and salicylates, muscle relaxants such as Robaxin® (methocarbamol), and the anti-inflammatory corticosteroids. Use of these drugs was carefully monitored by blood and urine analysis, so this was a classic controlled medication program. Compared with European rules of racing, which banned all medications and even physiotherapy, these were very liberal medication rules indeed.

The rules of racing in California in the late 1970s were similarly liberal. Drugs recognized as stimulants, depressants, narcotics, or local anesthetics were banned, and none of these drugs could be given within sixty hours of race time. The guidelines for permitted medications were that the drug could not be a prohibited drug, that it could not be given on race day, and that it must be reported on a veterinarian's report to the official veterinarian. The only exceptions to this rule were treatments for bleeders and authorized emergency care. Specific medications permitted in California in 1978 included steroids, such as corticosteroids and the related A.C.T.H.; aspirin; phenylbutazone and oxyphenbutazone; furosemide and other bleeder treatments, such as premarin and vitamin K; analgesics, including a number of non-steroidal analgesics; and pentazocine. Other drugs also permitted were muscle relaxants, such as methocarbamol, and also dimethyl sulfoxide and vitamins.

In an attempt to prevent the race-day administration of phenylbutazone, the California horse racing board had also established that a test result of over 165 µg of phenylbutazone per milliliter of urine was prima facie evidence of administration of race-day medication in violation of the rules. As pointed out above, California was also highly unusual in that the state allowed horses to run just twenty-four hours after a dose of pentazocine, a narcotic analgesic. California was thus the only racing jurisdiction where one could legally run a horse with a narcotic in its system.

Another approach to the problem of doping drugs, taken by the Canadian and Japanese authorities, was to publish lists of prohibited drugs. These lists are large, since, at least in Canada, a "drug" for racing purposes was defined as being one of the items named on the list. Furthermore, a "positive" occurred when one of these listed drugs was identified in a sample. At the time of writing, this Canadian list covered about 750 drugs, and additions to or deletions from this list were made by a group that consisted of a veterinarian, a chemist, and a policy coordinator.

The curious thing about this extensive list was that all other drugs not legal in Canada were also prohibited by virtue of a catch-all section of the schedule. Why one should go to the bother of drawing up a long list and then say that everything that is on or not on this list is prohibited is a classical maneuver whose principal function would seem to be to create work for bureaucrats. This exercise is also both pointless and a losing proposition, since the number of known chemical entities is increasing by, on the average, 6,000 new chemicals per day, while the lists of prohibited drugs are increasing at a much slower rate. A more rational approach might be for racing commissioners, equine veterinarians, pharmacologists, and analysts to come up with a list of permitted drugs, i.e. drugs that are not considered to affect the speed, stamina, courage, or conduct of a race, and which are acceptable to the authority concerned. Foremost among such drugs would, of course, be the antibiotics.

Whatever the rules of medication are in a given racing jurisdiction, compliance with them is enforced principally by the taking of samples of urine (most commonly), blood (less commonly), or, very rarely, saliva or sweat, and analyzing them for drugs. The samples may be taken pre-race, when the sample taken is almost always blood, or post-race, when the sample is usually urine (depending on the cooperation of the horse), occasionally blood, and rarely sweat or saliva. These samples are then tested in a laboratory at the track, if the test is a pre-race test, or are shipped or even flown to a distant laboratory, if the test is a post-race test. The laboratory usually reports on the samples within forty-eight hours of receiving them, although occasionally the delay may be longer. If no infraction of the medication rules is detected, the purses involved are released. If the test is a pre-race test, any horses found to be in violation of the medication rules are scratched and further samples may be taken and an inquiry held.

If certain medications, such as phenylbutazone or Lasix, are permitted, the analyst will check for the presence of these drugs. The presence of these permitted drugs is tested for because they are declared as being in the horse and the horse might run unexpectedly poorly if a drug was suddenly withdrawn. This practice is called a "controlled medication" program. On the other hand, systems where drugs are permitted but where their use is not rigorously controlled or monitored are called "permissive medication" systems. Tests are made, of course, for prohibited drugs because a horse with a prohibited drug in its body may have an unfair advantage over his competitors or may not be fit to race.

When an analyst finds signs of a prohibited drug in a sample, he has what is called a "suspicious" sample. While a suspicious sample has no standing in law, it may under some circumstances lead to a trainer being warned. When an analyst, in his opinion, has sufficient evidence to unequivocally identify a prohibited substance, he "calls a positive" for the identified drug by notifying the stewards. Since there are at this time no universally accepted guidelines as to what kind of analytical evidence constitutes a "positive," the calling of a positive is made largely on the basis of the analyst's own judgement. Once a positive has been called, the stewards will usually hold an administrative hearing on the positive and recommend appropriate action. The horseman involved in the hearing is often represented by an attorney and usually has the opportunity to appeal the ruling to the courts if he so wishes.

An incident of doping or the detection of evidence of illegal medication in equine blood or urine may arise in a number of ways. First, there is doping to win, in which the horse is given a stimulant drug such as amphetamine, caffeine, apomorphine, or fentanyl to increase its speed (Table 1-I). Doping to lose, or depressant doping, occurs when a horse is given a tranquilizer or depressant drug such as acepromazine or reserpine to make it run more slowly. A third form of doping occurs when a horse is given a drug to restore normal performance. Drugs such as phenylbutazone come into this class, and while this is considered controlled medication in most of the United States, it is considered doping in New York and most of western Europe. The fourth form of doping is accidental or inadvertent doping. This form of doping occurs when a food product, or contaminant, or plant product gives rise to a positive in equine urine. It may also occur when a new and more sensitive analytical method for a drug is introduced or when a combination of circumstances results in a drug being retained or excreted in a particular horse's urine for a very long period.

Stimulant doping may be further divided into two forms, which Clarke has chosen to call acute and chronic. Acute stimulant doping occurs when a rapidly acting stimulant such as amphetamine is given to a horse within hours or minutes

TABLE 1-I

VARIOUS CATEGORIES OF MEDICATION IN PERFORMANCE HORSES

1. Medication to Win
   (a) Acute: short-acting stimulants — amphetamine, cocaine, narcotics.
   (b) Chronic: repeated dosing for weeks, such as with vitamins or anabolic steroids.
   (c) "Washy Horses": dosing with a very small dose of a depressant or tranquilizer to "take the edge off" of an excitable horse.
   (d) Always illegal and usually considered to be an "inside job."
2. Medication to Lose
   (a) Depressants: large doses of a tranquilizer, sedative, or depressant.
   (b) Always illegal and usually considered to be an "outside job."
3. Medication to Restore Normal Performance
   (a) Non-steroidal anti-inflammatory drugs, such as phenylbutazone and its congeners. Often permitted under controlled medication rules.
   (b) Corticosteroids: sometimes administered intra-articularly to control joint pain; occasionally permissible.
   (c) Local Anesthesia: nerve or joint blocks to numb or freeze an area; always illegal.
   (d) Fluids and electrolytes: often permissible.
4. Accidental or Inadvertent or Technical Doping
   The accidental occurrence of a positive —
   (a) Procaine from procaine penicillin
   (b) Caffeine from coca husks in food pellets
   (c) "Robaxin" from glyceryl-guaiacolate
   (d) Botanical positives or false positives
5. Medication to "Mask" other Drugs
   Administration of dipyrone and thiamine, thought to interfere with the detection of illegal medication.
6. Medication to "Dilute" other Drugs
   Diuretics: furosemide, ethacrynic acid, hydrochlorthiazide.
7. Miscellaneous Mechanisms
   "Blood doping"
   "Bicarbonate doping"

of the event. This type of doping requires a good knowledge of the horse, an awareness of the way in which the horse responds to the drug in question, and a knowledge of the appropriate dose and time of administration of the drug in the horse. Too small a dose will have no effect; too large a dose may make a horse uncontrollably excited or may even kill him.

Professor Clarke reports on a horse racing at St. Cloud in France which had been "doped" with a mixture of caffeine and heroin and which became uncontrollable on the course. In other cases (one in western Africa and one in South America) horses have reportedly been doped with so much amphetamine that they have collapsed and died on the course. A dose administered too soon may make an animal uncontrollable in the parade ring and lead to the stewards scratching him; a dose administered too late will not act in time to affect the outcome of the race. Because horses learn how to handle and utilize the stimulation produced by drugs, it may even be necessary to familiarize the horse with the drug on a number of occasions before it is actually used. For these reasons and the fact that the owners may stand to win "big" if they can assure that their horse wins, detection of a potent stimulant drug in horse urine is usually assumed to be the result of an "inside job," i.e. a drug administered by the trainer or someone in his employment.

The critical role that timing plays in acute stimulant doping is well known to horsemen, especially in quarter horse racing, where the short 440-yard distance being raced makes a good "explosive" start absolutely vital. In match racing on "bush tracks" in the southern United States, stimulant medications were not uncommonly administered to horses as a routine part of the pre-race preparations. One maneuver open to the opponents of a horse "hopped" in this way was to delay the start of a match race as long as they possibly could, to allow the effects of the medication in their opponent's horse to pass. As will be seen later, many of the popular stimulant drugs have relatively short periods of action. In this circumstance, the horseman who hopped his horse was "hoist with his own petard," as one can sometimes visibly watch the effects of such a stimulant drug peak and decline, after which his horse was exhausted and in the unfortunate position of running against a fresh horse.

Chronic stimulant doping occurs when substances such as anabolic steroids or vitamins are given for weeks or months as part of a conditioning program. Similarly, testosterone is often given to mares or geldings to improve their performance. These drugs improve the appetite, increase aggressiveness, increase the hematocrit, and lead to the laying down of more bone and muscle. Furthermore, administration of these substances may be discontinued within days of racing and the horse raced relatively "clean." This type of doping is very common in human athletes and has also been detected in racing horses in England. By its very nature, chronic stimulant doping is almost always an "inside job."

A good "explosive" start is useful in some types of racing.

Another paradoxical form of medication to win is one that involves the use of tranquilizers or depressants. "Washy" horses are horses that are hyperexcitable and tend to run their races in the paddock, or that may have trouble getting into or out of the starting gate. One approach to this problem is to administer a small dose of a tranquilizer or depressant to these horses, sufficient to "take the edge off" but insufficient to reduce their performances. This effect is essentially equivalent to a human taking a drink to "steady his nerves," and such people were once spoken of as being born "two highballs under par." Such a use of a depressant to improve performance, and indeed stimulant doping in any form, is always illegal by the rules of racing.

Doping to lose may be relatively crude, or it can be a highly skilled and effective procedure. Over the years, with the advent of highly potent and specific tranquilizers, which can be very difficult to detect, doping to lose has become quite sophisticated. Where once horses were given a dose of chloral hydrate (the legendary Mickey Finn) or phenobarbitone and were clearly incapacitated on the morning of the race, it is now possible to simply "take the edge" off a horse with a small dose of a tranquilizer such as acepromazine. This small dose is not clinically detectable, and other than running poorly, the horse will show no clinical signs of being depressed. Because the trainer has many ways of making a horse run slow other than by giving drugs, depressant doping is almost always considered to be an "outside" job, usually by someone who is trying to manipulate the pari-mutuel payoff. One of the most notorious "doping to lose" cases of this century was the nobbling of PINTURISCHIO, the favorite in the English Derby in 1961. This horse had been heavily backed at long odds before the race, but when it became a "hot favorite" the bookmakers stood to lose a great deal of money. Just before the start of the race it was found that PINTURISCHIO had been heavily sedated, and he was withdrawn, no doubt to the great relief of at least some members of the bookmaking profession.

Therapeutic medication consists of administering an agent to a horse which controls a condition that is interfering with the performance of that horse. Thus an animal with joint or muscle pain may be given phenylbutazone, or a corticosteroid may be injected into a joint to control the inflammation and reduce pain. A dose of Lasix may be given to a "windy horse," that is, a horse with respiratory problems, to improve its breathing and thus its running. The justification for this type of medication is that it allows a horse to run "up to his form" but not beyond his "innate ability"; in other words, these drugs simply restore normal performance. Many of these forms of medication have now been approved for use in the United States and are thus not considered "doping" in these jurisdictions. They are, however, most emphatically not approved for use in New York State or in western Europe and are considered doping or illegal medication in these jurisdictions.

Another troublesome medication problem is what is called inadvertent doping, and this can be a very real problem. Procaine, for instance, can be used as a local anesthetic to "block" a nerve or a joint in a horse and allow what may be a dangerously unsound horse to race sound. Because such a "blocked" horse could break the "blocked" leg and kill other horses and jockeys, use of procaine or any local anesthetics in racing horses is prohibited. Unfortunately, procaine is also a major component of long-acting procaine penicillin and may be excreted in urine for up to two weeks after a dose of procaine penicillin. Further, procaine levels in equine urine are highly unpredictable and can vary as much as 10,000-fold depending simply on whether the horse's urine is acidic or basic. Therefore, after a legitimate therapeutic dose of procaine penicillin, procaine may be found in equine urine in quite high concentrations, giving rise to an "inadvertent" or "accidental" positive. Positives of this nature, where all parties concerned are innocent and racing authorities cannot distinguish between "doping" and an "inadvertent positive," are one of the major problem areas of medication control programs.

Another recent cause of some inadvertent doping positives in England has been the inclusion of cocoa husk in horse rations by a feedstuff manufacturer. Trainers who purchased and used this feed were then unwittingly feeding their horses caffeine, which was metabolized to theobromine and turned up in horse urine for days after the feed was withdrawn. In the early 1970s there was a veritable rash of caffeine and theobromine positives in England, which were traced to accidental feed contamination. Other causes of accidental "positives" include contamination of urine samples with nicotine and/or caffeine during sampling by the urine collector. Still another mechanism that has given rise to false positives due to nicotine and caffeine has been urine collectors losing patience with their equine clients and providing a personal sample in lieu of the equine sample for the analysts!

"Doping" to "mask" other substances or to delay, reduce, or accelerate the excretion of drugs is sometimes attempted. Thiamine was often given in large doses to horses to be excreted in some quantity in the urine and confuse (mask) the chemical detection of other more useful medications. Dipyrone, an analgesic drug, was once used for this effect, although today most analysts should not have any problems with it. Diuretics such as furosemide (Lasix®) may be administered, which will "dilute" other drugs or drug metabolites in urine and may render them less detectable. Lasix clearly dilutes phenylbutazone in equine urine, and likely also dilutes glucuronide metabolites of narcotic drugs such as morphine and pentazocine. Firmly implanted in the minds of track people, many human athletes, and *Playboy®* magazine, however, is the idea that Lasix acts to accelerate the clearance of drugs, i.e. it "flushes drugs out" of horses. Unfortunately for those who use Lasix hoping for this effect, no amount of Lasix can significantly accelerate the elimination of drugs from the bodies of horses. One can, however, alter the pH (acidity or alkalinity) of urine with drugs like sodium bicarbonate and in this way reduce the concentrations of certain drugs in urine.

Another form of doping that is reputedly both potent and widely used is blood doping. In blood doping a volume of blood is withdrawn from a horse a number of days before a race, and the red blood cells are separated out and stored under refrigeration. Then a few hours before the race the horse's own blood cells are infused back into him and he is ready to race. The theory is that because his circulatory system is "supercharged" with red blood cells he will be able to run that much better. Some scientific evidence in support of this proposed mechanism exists, but the amounts of blood that would have to be transfused to improve the performance of a racehorse are very substantial and quite cumbersome to handle.

Yet another approach to the improvement of performance is to render a horse's blood more alkaline than usual by administration of sodium bicarbonate. This method is effective because formation of lactic acid by working muscle and its accumulation in the blood (development of a metabolic acidosis) plays an important part in the development of signs of fatigue. If, on the other hand, the blood is rendered alkaline with bicarbonate before a race, the time for which a given performance can be maintained is extended, especially if exhaustion is a limiting factor in the performance. There appears to be a sound scientific basis to this approach to improving performance, particularly endurance performance.

The final question that one might ask is, What is the actual incidence of doping or improper medication? The answer to this question has to be that nobody knows, as it seems likely that not more than a fraction of the actual attempts at doping are detected. It is my opinion, however, that the vast majority of doping attempts violate nothing more than the spirit of the doping rules, for few dopes are likely to be effective. Thus fentanyl or Sublimaze®, for years the most notorious drug in American racing and, as will be shown later, undoubtedly an effective drug, was being used on the racetrack in a very inefficient way and apparently at doses too low to have any effect. Similarly, not only was this drug not being used effectively on the track, but when a number of University-based programs decided to investigate its properties, they also used these ineffective doses and came up with conflicting and largely negative results. Similarly, Strophanthin K, a cardiac glycoside, was at one time a very popular drug at the Chicago tracks. While Strophanthin K might be useful in a horse with a failing heart, there is no evidence that this type of drug would have any effect on cardiac output in a healthy horse and so it appears highly unlikely to have been an effective "doping" drug under any circumstances.

The only solid figures that one has on the incidence of illegal medication come from the incidence of "positives." Thus, in Kentucky, even with a fairly liberal medication rule, about one prohibited drug per 300 samples tested turns up. Most racing jurisdictions show a rate of prohibited positives of about one positive per 500 to 1,000 samples tested (see Tables I-IV and I-V). Pre-race blood testing, which currently picks up about half the "positives" of post-race urine testing, yields a smaller number of positives. Strangely enough, these rates of positive detection have remained stable over the years, with no substantial variations, despite huge changes in patterns of drug use and improvements in analytical methodology.

The most complete statistics on drugs detected in horses are those of the Association of Official Racing Chemists, which has records of all drugs reported detected in horses by members of this group from 1947 on. As shown in Table 1-II, procaine is the most commonly reported positive, no less than 661 procaine positives having been called to date. Procaine almost always heads doping lists, and it is probably reasonable to assume that most of these positives are inadvertent or accidental positives. Caffeine and amphetamine are the two next most common drugs on the 1947-73 list and were also similarly placed in the 1949-64 list (Table

"Hydromel," an innocuous mix of honey and water, was a favorite illegal medication in Roman times.

1-III). Phenobarbital, a depressant, appears in fourth place in the 1949-64 list, but on the 1947-73 list it had slipped to tenth place. This change points up the fact that though the incidence of positives may not vary much from year to year, the types of drugs detected will, depending entirely on the drugs available to horsemen and the availability of good analytical methods to the chemists.

The last point to be made in this overview, and one that I cannot emphasize too much, is that the actual incidence of medication violations is very small, running at about one tenth of one percent of horses tested. When one deducts from this very small percentage the proportion of inadvertent positives and the incidence of detection of drugs that are likely to be totally ineffective, one comes up with estimates of improper drug use that are much less than one in 1,000, and for harness racing possibly less than one in 10,000. By any standards, these are astonishingly small rates of regulation violation and strongly support the position of most racing authorities that the problem of medication in racing horses is, in the final analysis, very well controlled.

Despite these very low rates of drug detection, racing has always had problems

TABLE 1-II

DRUGS REPORTED BY MEMBERS OF THE ASSOCIATION OF OFFICIAL RACING
CHEMISTS, 1947-1973*

Drug	Times Reported	Drug	Times Reported
Procaine	661	Mephenesin	6
Caffeine	482	Pemoline	6
Amphetamine	452	Pyrilamine	6
Phenylbutazone	267	Acetylsalicylic acid	5
Methylphenidate	193	Butacaine	5
Theobromine	127	Imipramine	5
Methamphetamine	121	Methoxamine	5
Dipyrone	116	Propiomaxine	5
Polyethylene glycol	111	Tetracaine	5
Phenobarbitone	86	Chloroquine	4
Oxyphenbutazone	66	Hydrocortisone	4
Morphine	62	Levorphanol	4
Ephedrine	59	Prednisone	4
Strychnine	50	Mefenamic acid	4
Thiamine	50	Meperidine	4
Pentazocine	49	Cinchonidine	3
Nikethamide	44	Propoxyphene	3
Barbiturates	43	Sulphanilamide	3
Promazine	38	Sulphaphenazole	3
Methapyrilene	35	Thiabendazole	3
Nicotine	33	Acepromazine	2
Indomethacin	26	Antipyrine	2
Ethylaminobenzoate	23	Barbitone	2
Atropine	22	Codeine	2
Pipradrol	21	Chloral hydrate	2
Phenothiazine (derivative)	18	Dibucaine	2
Lignocaine	16	Doxapram	2
Chlorpromazine	15	Guaiacol	2
Prednisolone	13	Phemitone	2
Theophylline	12	Meprobamate	2
Mephentermine	11	Naphazoline	2
Leptazole	10	Pangamic acid	2
Acetophenetidin	9	Sulphonamide [sic]	2
Cocaine	9	Acetophenazine	1
Methocarbamol	9	Amydricaine	1
Phenylpropanolamine	8	Berberine	1
Salicylic acid	8	Bromide	1
Hyosine	8	Camphor (rectal swab)	1
Amylocaine	7	Capsaicine	1
Brucine	7	Chlorbutanol	1
Quinine	7	Cinchonine	1
Thozalinone	7	Cincophen	1
Apomorphine	6	Danthron	1
Alcohol	6	Dapsone	1

* These and subsequent statistics from the Association of Official Racing Chemists (AORC), while the best statistics available, are not absolute. Not all racing jurisdictions around the world report to the AORC, and even in the United States some major racing states used laboratories that had no AORC affiliation. Because of this, and while these figures likely reflect trends, the data base on which they were developed is not complete.

SOURCE: Personal communication, Mr. Gerry Johnston, President, AORC.

TABLE 1-III

DRUGS REPORTED BY MEMBERS OF THE ASSOCIATION OF OFFICIAL RACING
CHEMISTS, 1949-1964

Drug	Times Reported	Drug	Times Reported
Procaine	392	Phenylpropanolamine	3
Caffeine	332	Prednisone	3
Amphetamine	316	Antipyrine	2
Phenobarbital	84	Barbital	2
Phenylbutazone	84	Chloroquine	2
Theobromine	69	Dibucaine	2
Dipyrone	53	Guaiacol	2
Ephedrine	50	Mephobarbital	2
Morphine	49	Meprobamate	2
Thiamine	46	Naphazoline	2
Methamphetamine	44	Pangamic acid	2
Barbiturates	42	Prednisolone	2
Nikethamide	38	Thozalinone	2
Methylphenidate	38	Acetylsalicylic acid	1
Strychnine	36	Amydricaine	1
Methapyrilene	26	Camphor (rectal swab)	1
Nicotine	20	Cinchonidine	1
Atropine	18	Cinchonine	1
Ethyl aminobenzoate	17	Cinchophen	1
Pipradrol	17	Codeine	1
Promazine	17	Dapsone® (trade name)	1
Oxyphenbutazone	11	Dexamethasone	1
Acetophenitidin	9	Dihydrocodeinone	1
Pentylenetetrazol	9	Dihydromorphinone	1
Lidocaine	8	Ethyl isobutrazine	1
Scopolamine	8	Hydantoins	1
Amylocaine	7	Hydroxymethamphetamine	1
Chlorpromazine	7	Meclizine	1
Cocaine	7	Menthol	1
Mephentermine	7	Meperidine	1
Alcohol	6	Mescaline	1
Mephenesin	6	Methylsalicylate	1
Pemoline	6	Methyprylon	1
Quinine	6	Nylidrin	1
Brucine	5	Phenacaine	1
Butacaine	5	Phenazocine	1
Salicylic acid	5	Piperocaine	1
Tetracaine	5	Propoxyphene	1
Theophylline	5	Triprolidine	1
Phenothiazine	3	Yohimbine	1

TABLE 1-IV
JOCKEY RACING

Year	Number of Localities	Number of Samples	Drugging Violations	
			Number	Percent
1949*	30	——	103	——
1950*	39	37,518	73	0.195
1951*	26	45,865	60	0.131
1952*	49	51,106	56	0.110
1953*	55	56,246	55	0.098
1954*	56	55,819	77	0.138
1955*	51	62,158	65	0.105
1956*	53	68,017	69	0.101
1957*	50	71,276	60	0.084
1958*	56	85,153	78	0.092
1959*	45	79,343	94	0.118
1960*	51	84,092	105	0.125
1961*	56	90,800	169	0.186
1962*	61	99,809	126	0.126
1963*	63	103,920	148	0.142
1964*	67	119,131	132	0.111
1965	56	88,380	66	0.075
1966	58	88,498	81	0.092
1967	65	87,489	67	0.077
1968	81	98,254	95	0.097
1969	68	113,499	137	0.121
1970	68	115,377	198	0.172
1971	60	113,000	140	0.124
1972	49	126,643	191	0.151

* Includes thoroughbred, steeplechase, hunt, and quarter horse racing up to 1964. Statistics from quarter horse racing for 1965 to 1972 are tabulated separately, but many quarter horse meets are still includes under Jockey Racing.
SOURCE: AORC statistics.

with the area of medication. From the earliest Roman times, where what can only be considered a totally innocuous mix of water and honey called "hydromel" was used, humans have had a powerful urge to "do something" to improve the performance of their horses. As will be pointed out in the next chapter, the concept of powerful effects being available from minute amounts of potent drugs is deeply rooted in the human psyche and easily played upon. Because of this, individuals who claim that drugs are being used to manipulate horses and races and provide lucrative payoffs for unscrupulous individuals have a ready-made audience for their charges. The credibility of these charges, however, is rooted more in people's beliefs and expectations about drugs than in the facts. In the next chapter I will trace the history of these beliefs and show how they are fundamental to people's beliefs about drugs and are the major reason that, despite excellent drug control, racing always has had, and will have, problems within the area of medication.

TABLE 1-V
HARNESS RACING

Year	Number of Localities	Number of Samples	Drugging Violations	
			Number	Percent
1949	3	—	6	—
1950	12	9,390	5	0.053
1951	14	13,852	9	0.065
1952	16	14,715	4	0.027
1953	23	18,561	8	0.043
1954	21	21,146	4	0.019
1955	23	23,569	19	0.081
1956	23	28,109	12	0.043
1957	20	29,161	11	0.038
1958	26	30,944	15	0.048
1959	23	37,329	27	0.072
1960	19	40,891	12	0.029
1961	25	40,340	23	0.057
1962	25	48,625	35	0.072
1963	28	54,168	31	0.053
1964	25	60,156	37	0.002
1965	25	56,633	28	0.049
1966	25	62,942	18	0.029
1967	31	82,191	40	0.049
1968	44	81,328	40	0.049
1969	29	92,274	39	0.042
1970	30	92,422	45	0.049
1971	29	108,452	90	0.083
1972	26	103,964	74	0.071

Source: AORC statistics.

SELECTED REFERENCES

Association of Official Racing Chemists: *The Chemical Laboratory and its Role in Racing*, 2nd Revision, 1974.

Clarke, E. G. C.: The doping of racehorses. *Med Leg J, 30:*180-191, 1962-63.

———: Dope and doping. *Medicine, Science and Law, 9:*218-223, 1969.

Moss, M. S.: Horse doping: Laboratory and forensic aspects. *Criminol, 8:*39-49, 1973.

———: Dope testing in racing animals. *Vet Rec,* April 27, 1974, pp. 389-394.

Pugh, D. M.: Pre-race medication: A case of Hobson's choice. In Tobin, T., Blake, J. W., and Woods, W. E.: *Proc Third International Symposium on Equine Medication Control*, Lexington, KY, Dept. of Veterinary Science, University of Kentucky, 1979, pp. 475-481.

Rules of Racing. The Commonwealth of Kentucky, 1975 Edition.

The Report of the Duke of Norfolk's Committee to the Stewards of the Jockey Club and the National Hunt Committee, May 1961. Weatherby & Sons, Ltd.

Tobin, T., Blake, J. W. and Woods, W. E.: *Proc Third International Symposium on Equine Medication Control*, Lexington, KY, Dept. of Veterinary Science, University of Kentucky, 1979.

Chapter 2

HORSES, HEROES, AND OTHER ATHLETES: HOW THE CURRENT MEDICATION SITUATION DEVELOPED

THE BASIC HUMAN DRIVES, beliefs, and superstitions that are behind efforts to improve the performance of athletes through medication are as old as the human race and form a recurring theme in history. The Bible, reporting on an early attempt at doping, records that Adam and Eve ate the forbidden fruit not because they were curious, but because the serpent, a typical drug pusher, deceived them into believing that the forbidden fruit would render them God-like. Even in the Garden of Eden man was attracted by the advantages supposedly offered by doping, so it is little wonder that he remains susceptible in his current, somewhat less fortunate surroundings.

Classical mythology is replete with incidents of doping being used to produce useful effects for competent dopers. Diomedes, son of Aries and Cyrene, fed his horses on human flesh to make them savage and unbeatable, an effect the "hop" artists are still trying to reproduce. Medea, the first reported "nobbler," used an opiate to stupefy the dragon that guarded the golden fleece. Although the reference in the book of the Maccabees to use of the juice of grapes or mulberries to rouse war elephants is probably an incorrect translation, there seems little doubt that these animals were given wine for this purpose. From these examples it appears that both the concept and practice of pharmacological modification of animal behavior were well established in ancient times.

Accessibility to unusual or supernatural powers by virtue of special foods is a theme of the legends of most societies. In many primitive societies people ate the flesh of their conquered enemies to avail themselves of their talents, courage, and strength. One of my own earliest school lessons in Ireland was about Finn MacCumail,* the legendary Irish hero. Finn, then a young boy, was cooking a salmon for his master, an old magician. What Finn did not know was that he was cooking a magic salmon, and that the first person to taste its flesh would have all the knowledge of the world and be able to see into the future. During cooking, a blister rose on the salmon, which the careful Finn pricked with his thumbs. In so doing, he burnt his thumb, which he immediately placed in his mouth. Finn, therefore, became the first person to taste the flesh of the magic salmon and gained the knowledge of the world. Furthermore, any time that Finn wanted to see into the future, he had only to suck his thumb, which presumably always contained traces of the fish. As with the best of mankind's drugs, the basic mythological concept is that of potent effects induced by minute amounts of a special substance.

My experience with this Celtic legend and its message is common to all children.

---

* Spelled and pronounced Finn MacCool in English.

21

In the Victorian fable Alice in Wonderland, Alice continually finds bottles labelled "drink me," which she does without the least hesitation and which produce remarkable changes in her size. Similarly, she eats the magic mushroom willingly and again is rapidly changed. In popular American mythology, Popeye the Sailor eats his spinach in moments of crisis and is promptly able to outperform his heavily muscled opponent, Brutus, who looks as though he has grown up on anabolic steroids. In this decade, the miracles of modern technology have been pressed into service in the modern fables of The Six Million Dollar Man and The Bionic Woman. The concept of exceptional performance available to anyone who knows the appropriate secret is woven into the human psyche, and drugs constitute one of the traditional keys to this magic world.

Given this background, it should come as no surprise that the use of drugs in attempts to improve performance in sports is as old as competitive sports them-

The punishment for using honeyed water, a favorite Roman dope, was crucifixion.

Eighteenth-century doping was generally depressant, with the objective of stopping the horse.

selves. Athletes at the ancient Olympic Games held in the third century B.C. were reported to have tried to improve their performance by any means possible. In the racing world, Roman chariot horses were reportedly doped for speed with a mixture of honey and water called "hydromel." It is far from clear how effective this medication was, but the punishment for its use, which was crucifixion, suggests that at least the Roman chariot racing commissioners were impressed with it.

The first report of doping in racing horses in England occurred at Worksop, where an edict in 1666 banned the use of "exciting substances." Concern about stimulant doping at this early date is unusual, as most early doping efforts involved depressant doping or nobbling. In May of 1792, a horse called ROSE-BUD was fancied for a race at York, when "some villains broke into the stable where ROSEBUD stood and gave him a dose of poison." Similarly, in September of the same year "some malicious persons got into the stable where TOSSPOT stood and gave him a dose of physic the night before he was to run." Six years later a horse called MISS NIGHTINGALE died on the Sunday before the races at Boroughbridge. On postmortem, they found "in her stomach about two pounds of lead shot, made up with putty into balls." These efforts are typical of early nobbling attempts, where relatively unsophisticated poisoning of horses competed with outright laming as a method of stopping favorites. The first well documented trial of a horse doper in England occurred during the Cambridge Assizes in 1812, where one Donald Dawson was tried for the poisoning of horses with arsenic and was reportedly hanged.

The earliest reports of doping with what has since come to be regarded as a stimulant drug are attributed to contemporary accounts from the great jockey Sam Chifney. Sam claimed that the Prince of Wales' training groom, Casborne, was "concerned with those breaking into noblemen's stables, the night before running, to give a horse, as was supposed opium balls." While the breaking into stables sounds suspiciously like an "outside job" with the goal of nobbling or depressing the horse, the use of opium suggests a stimulant action. In any event, nobbling was still common a century or so later, and poisoning, along with laming, were the favorite methods of stopping a horse.

Serious stimulant doping awaited development of the pharmaceutical industry and the availability of potent central nervous system stimulants. Since time immemorial horses had been dosed with whiskey before races, but toward the end of the nineteenth century the pace accelerated. Stimulating doping as we know it today was apparently born and bred in the New World and came to the Old World about the year 1900, most notably in the form of an American-financed trainer called Wishard. Wishard was financed by a colorful pair of Americans, one by the name of William "Betcha-a-Million" Gates who had made his fortune in the manufacture of barbed wire, and his accomplice, a horseman and heavy gambler by the name of James Duke. With them, they brought something that they believed would be the key to instant success in England — drugs.

Wishard was reportedly a first-class horseman in his own right, and his horses always looked wonderfully well, but from contemporary accounts he was first and foremost a master at the drugging of horses. While other trainers galloped their horses to put condition on them, Wishard, like the good pharmacologist he was, galloped his horses to determine how much dope was needed to yield a good performance.

According to contemporary accounts, the usual routine for this group was to buy a moderate horse that was "fully exposed," run it for a while way above its class, then fill it with dope and back it off the board. It was thought at the time that Gates, Duke, and the rest of them took approximately two million pounds out of the ring between 1897 and 1901. Their horses were ridden by two brothers, Lester and Johnny Rief. This pair apparently wore knickerbockers and Eton collars and looked as innocent as choirboys, but they were prepared to stop any horse if it was in the best interest of the gang that employed them.

Gates and Duke apparently operated for about three years, and at the end of this period the way the Americans were bringing off coups and doping horses was a crying scandal. One of the last coups brought off by this gang was with a horse called ROYAL FLUSH. At this time ROYAL FLUSH was six years old and

A trainer called Wishard, financed by "Betcha-A-Million" Gates, reportedly brought stimulant medication to England.

appeared to be well over the hill when he came up for sale. Wishard bid 450 guineas for him and took him home to his Red House Stable in Newmarket.

Following in the medicated footsteps of his predecessors, ROYAL FLUSH finished first to win the Royal Hunt Cup at Ascot and, with a slightly increased dose, won the Steward's Cup at Goodwood a couple of months later. This was the last coup that Wishard and his cronies were able to pull off, however, for they soon departed en bloc for France. The reason that they left was that George Lambton had finally convinced the stewards of the Jockey Club that something was amiss. In retrospect, this period was known as the era of the "Yankee alchemists"; Wishard trained fifty-four winners in England in 1900, which made him the leading trainer in races won in England that year.

The dope that Wishard was using was the newly introduced cocaine. The veterinary profession was the first to notice that something was amiss and suggested that that the practice of doping would ruin the horse breeding industry and should be stopped. The stewards of the Jockey Club, however, did not think that there was anything to it, and it was up to George Lambton, the leading English trainer of the time, to take action. His approach was to quite openly dope his own horses and demonstrate to all what cocaine could do.

The first horse that Lambton doped was a chestnut gelding called FOLK-STONE. This horse had always refused to do anything in a trial or a race, always coming in last and neighing. Lambton first doped him in a trial when "he fairly astonished me, for he jumped off in front and won in a canter. I sent him to Pontefract, where he beat a field of 16 very easily, and nearly went around the course a second time before his jockey could haul him up. He won a race again the next day, was sold, and never won again." In another episode, Lambton obtained six dopes from a veterinary surgeon. Surprisingly, these dopes were not injected with a needle but just given out of a bottle. With five of these dopes, Lambton had four winners and a second, and he got these performances out of horses that had not shown any form throughout the year. The last dope Lambton gave to Lord Charles Montague, who wanted it for a horse called CHEERS, a winner of the Eclipse Stakes, which had run badly all year. In the following week CHEERS, with the dope in him, beat a big field for the Makerton Plate. By this time, the Jockey Club needed no further convincing, and doping was made a criminal offense the following year in 1903.

In France, the Societe d'Encouragement also forbade doping in 1903, following the English lead. This embargo, however, had little effect, and by 1906 French trainers had taken to doping en masse, not wanting to lose every race to the Americans. The practice spread like wildfire throughout the continent and by 1910 had become so bad that the Austrian racing authorities had called in the services of a Russian chemist, Bukowski.

Bukowski readily demonstrated that it was possible to detect the presence of drugs in horse saliva, but he refused to disclose his methods. The Austrian authorities thereupon turned to Professor Frankel in Vienna, who confirmed Bukowski's findings. Neither of these analysts, however, showed whether or not the presence of the detected drug was due to actual secretion of the drugs in saliva or just to contamination from oral dosing. In any event, the tests were adequate for the relatively few drugs (strychnine, morphine, cocaine, caffeine) then in use, and the situation was brought under control. Shortly thereafter, in 1912, a horse called BOURBON ROSE won the Gold Cup at Maisons Lafitte in France but was disqualified because it yielded the first positive dope test. Following a pattern that has since become all too familiar, the owners sued, but they lost their case. Dope testing had arrived and had been supported in the courts.

Meanwhile, in the United States, the homeland of stimulant doping, things were relatively quiet. Until 1932 betting on a racecourse was legal in only eight states, but in this year a change in the law permitted it in another twenty states. This led to a great revival in racing and to an equivalent increase in the amount of stimulant medication being used. Because whatever rules there may have been against doping were certainly not being enforced, a very large proportion of the horses running had been administered a wide variety of drugs. Tack rooms were reportedly equipped like pharmacies, complete with scales, weights, measures, test tubes, and an astonishing selection of drugs. One of the prescriptions from this era survives, and it gives some idea of the thought and amount of preparation that went into administering one of these dopes. This particular one contained —

Heroin	1½ gr.
Strychnine	2½ gr.
Nitroglycerine	10 minims
Tinct. Digitalis	5 minims
Cola nut	2 oz.

One half of this dose was to be given fifty minutes before the race, and the other half thirty minutes later. Another prescription called for heroin, cocaine, strychnine, caffeine, and nikethamide. All of these dopes appear to contain two principal and, as we will see later, useful ingredients: heroin to limber up a sore horse and cocaine or caffeine (cola nut) as a stimulant. Because the medication rules were not enforced, an honest trainer had no choice but to adopt the same tactics in self defense, as they said they could not compete with "drugstore" trainers without using their methods. Eventually the problem reached scandalous proportions, and it was left to a famous editorial in *THE BLOOD-HORSE* to point out the magnitude of the problem. At this point the authorities acted, but it was the federal authorities and not the racing authorities. The "Feds" swooped on the tack rooms, and over 100 trainers and horsemen were arrested for breaches of the United States narcotic regulations. A considerable number of convictions were obtained, but the only effect was to make the dopers more secretive. Finally, the Florida Racing Commission took the matter in hand and sent Doctor Catlett, a veterinarian, and Doctor Charles Morgan, a chemist, to France to learn about saliva testing. Upon their return, routine drug testing was started in Florida, later in other states and Canada, and doping was gradually brought under control. Eventually most racing states in the United States came to have their own Racing Chemistry Laboratory, and after World War II these men formed a group called the Association of Official Racing Chemists, or A.O.R.C.

For reasons that are still not clear and which do not appear to have been well chosen, the Association of Official Racing Chemists chose to remain a very closed society. Membership was limited to official racecourse analysts, and members were barred from disclosing the methods by which they had obtained their results. New discoveries, instead of being published in scientific journals, were circulated to members as confidential documents. The only reason given for all this secrecy was that to disclose the methods of the analysts would help the dopers. However, the maxim that "not only should justice be done, but it should be seen to be done" applies to dope testing as much as to any other judicial area, and the secret nature of the tests only served to undermine public confidence in the process. Affairs first came to a head in England.

In England there was a considerable resurgence in dopings after World War II, due in no small part to the use of amphetamines by the military during the war. These drugs were at first quite difficult to detect, and the English Jockey Club reacted ruthlessly. If a horse was believed to be doped, the trainer was "warned off the turf" and forbidden to train again. This meant that the man's livelihood was gone, even though it could be shown that it was physically impossible for him to have doped the horse. The whole system resembled nothing so much as a kangaroo court, for none of the accused were allowed legal representation, none of the rules of evidence were observed, and no one was under oath. The analyst, of course, used his secret methods, and his findings could not be challenged. Expert witnesses were usually not allowed, and if they were, their testimony was quietly ignored. Duplicate samples and independent analysis of duplicate samples were not allowed. The result was that whether or not justice was done, the whole spectacle was that of an inquisition. In one case a horse was reported as giving a "general positive for alkaloids" but the analyst was unable to further identify any drug. This "general reaction for alkaloids" was likely a nonspecific reaction and could not be construed as specific evidence for a doping drug. Yet, on this non-evidence, the trainer — a man named Russell — was warned off the turf, his license withdrawn, and the horse disqualified from running again. The trainer, acting on the advice of various people who pointed out that there was no real evidence that the horse had been doped, brought an action against the stewards of the Jockey Club. This case was heard before the Lord Chief Justice and created a great deal of interest, with both sides gathering their expert witnesses. But the Lord Chief Justice avoided the issue by pointing out that the trainer's license could be withdrawn by the stewards at their discretion at any time, and they had no need to prove anything. So Russell lost his case, and the same thing happened to several trainers subsequently on the flimsiest of evidence.

At times the spectacle of medication control has resembled an inquisition.

Because the testing methods were secret, no one understood the tests, least of all the Jockey Club stewards. The discontent with this system grew until in 1960, the Jockey Club appointed a committee to look into the whole affair. This committee reported in 1961 and made several noteworthy recommendations. Among these was the suggestion that there should be an expert committee composed of a veterinary surgeon, an analytical chemist and a pharmacologist to advise the stewards. This group would receive the analyst's report, and the stewards would only take action on the basis of their recommendation. A second recommendation was that the Jockey Club should set up its own laboratory to do both routine analytical dope detection and basic research on the action of these drugs in horses. Directorship of this laboratory was offered to Michael Moss, at that time a forensic chemist with the London Police Department. This laboratory has since grown into Race Course Security Services, Ltd., and has made very substantial advances in both the science of drug testing and in our knowledge of the pharmacology of drugs in the horse.

In the United States, in the meantime, most racetrack testing was in the hands of members of the Association of Official Racing Chemists, which, as in England, did not tend to publish or allow independent scrutiny of their methods. While the English were basically concerned with improving their post-race testing, the Americans were attempting to introduce a pre-race test. A pre-race test is a test done on a body fluid drawn just prior to the race, with any horse that fails the test disqualified from the race. This is the ideal test, the answer to the racing commissioner's prayer, but effective implementation has always been a problem.

The first serious effort at pre-race testing, to my knowledge, took place in Maryland, where professor James Munch introduced a pre-race test in the 1930s. This test was based on what is called the "Straub Reaction in mice." The Straub Reaction is the unmistakable vertical S-shaped curve in which a mouse injected with morphine carries its tail. To apply this test, Straub and his colleagues fitted out a one-ton truck as a mobile laboratory and took it to the race course. A sample of saliva or urine from each horse was then injected into a mouse and the mouse watched. A "Straub tail" reaction was a positive for a morphinelike drug, while untoward excitement or convulsions was evidence for a central nervous system stimulant drug. Any horse giving a positive reaction was automatically scratched, this being the only sanction against the horseman. The principal problem with this method was the nonspecific nature of the test, and no chemical confirmation or verification was performed post-race.

This pre-race testing system in Maryland apparently lapsed during World War II, and no further pre-race testing was performed in this country until the mid-1960s, when the United States Trotting Association approached the Ohio State University with a request that they reexamine the technical feasibility of pre-race testing. Doctor Richard Ray and his coworkers at Ohio State University applied the relatively new technique of gas chromatography with electron capture detection to the problem and soon came up with a workable system. This system was introduced in Ohio in the mid-1960s, and an updated version of this basic method is still in use there.

The New York State racing authorities followed the Ohio State lead in the early

The basis of one early pre-race test was the Straub reaction, where a mouse injected with morphine will hold his tail in an "S"-shaped attitude

1970s, bringing a drug testing program onto the campus of a major university and introducing a pre-race testing program. Since then both the New Jersey and Pennsylvania authorities have introduced pre-race testing, the New Jersey program being run out of the State Police laboratory in Trenton and the Pennsylvania laboratory being a Racing Commission laboratory. In 1974 the racing authorities in Kentucky set up the Kentucky Equine Drug Research program at the University of Kentucky, with the goal of researching the pharmacology and detection of drugs in racing horses. The following year routine racetrack testing in Kentucky was incorporated into this program as the Kentucky Equine Drug Testing program.

The recent history of doping, especially in terms of organized and sustained doping operations, is much better recorded in England than in America. This is likely because the first of these major incidents gave rise to routine dope testing in England and eventually to a group called the Horserace Anti-Doping Committee (H.A.D.C.) and the Race Course Security Services, which will be discussed in a following section.

The incidents of doping that gave rise to the introduction of routine dope testing took place in England between 1960 and 1965. In the first of these cases several attempts were made to dope horses to win by the use of caffeine. It is not clear how effective this operation was, but it is interesting to note that, in a letter written by one of the conspirators to another, when the supply of caffeine had been exhausted, the remark was made that they did not seem to be having too much success with the stuff lately and perhaps they would be better off without it. These unfortunate dopers, who were all convicted and received heavy sentences, were learning the hard way that doping to win is not easy. It is not possible to stimulate any horse so much that he must inevitably win a race, and selection of the correct drug, dose, and time of dosing to give a good horse an edge requires a considerable degree of skill, plus a sound knowledge of the pharmacology of the drug and the behavior of the particular horse in question.

One of the problems that any doper doing an outside job has is how to get the necessary inside information on which horses are stabled in which boxes, so that the medications can be administered to the correct horses. An early team of depressant dopers had a classic solution to this problem. They had an attractive Swiss girl, impeccably dressed, telephone the trainer and ask could she come to see

"People probably fell over each other to give her a conducted tour of the premises."

his yard, as she was considering having some horses in training with him. She was invariably made welcome and arrived in a chauffeur-driven Rolls-Royce to discuss her arrangements with the trainer. As part of her visit she would ask to see the yard and, human nature being what it is, people probably fell over each other to give her a conducted tour of the premises.

As well as being attractive, this young lady had a retentive mind, and within hours the dopers were in possession of the whole layout of the yard. Since at that time in England (early 1960s) the trainers were not security minded, the dopers had only to return at night when all was quiet to get their administrations completed.

The next two incidents of doping were on a pharmacologically much sounder basis. In one series of doping incidents, favorites scheduled to run the next day and heavily backed in the ante-post market were found sedated on the morning of the race and clearly unable to participate. This was a more sophisticated twentieth-century version of the eighteenth-century horse-poisoning episodes, with much less danger of permanent damage to the horse.

In the summer of 1964 it was again suspected that a team of dopers was at work, because well-backed horses, either first or second favorites in small fields, would run unaccountably badly. For some reason, the dope tests were not carried out on these horses, but toward the end of the summer the investigative arm of the British antidoping organization received information concerning a projected doping at Lambourn. The information was passed to the police, and on the night of fifth of September a team of dopers was caught red-handed in a stable in Lambourn. During the subsequent trial it was found that no fewer than twenty-eight horses had been successfully doped that summer. In all cases, acetylpromazine, a simple tranquilizer, was used, administered orally by "physic ball."* The timing of the operation and exact dosage contained in the ball were vital to the success of the operation and apparently were well chosen. Horses were doped during the night before the race, because, among other reasons, security in the trainer's yard was poor at this time. In the morning the horses, though tranquilized, were fit enough to pass veterinary inspection and thus be included in the betting market. The presence of the dope only became apparent when the horse cantered to the starting post or, in some cases, was only evident or suspected from a poor finish. Thus, doping to lose or nobbling had undergone considerable evolution over the years and had reached the point where it was both reliable and only barely detectable in the final result.

Lest anyone think at this point that man's "inhumanity" towards the horse does not compare with his behavior towards his own species and towards himself as an individual, I am going to briefly review some of the highlights of doping in human athletics. Since doping in human events, in contrast to that in equine events, is almost always stimulant in nature, effective doping in human athletics did not really get underway until the nineteenth century. Thus, in 1864, a gentleman by the name of Pini reported the first doping case among swimmers in a canal race in

---

* "Balling" a horse in English horse circles means placing a semisolid ball containing medication in the back of a horse's mouth so that he cannot avoid swallowing it. The word "physic" refers to the ball's medication content.

Amsterdam, though the nature of the dope was not recorded. By 1879, when the first of the famous Six Day Cycle Races was held, cyclists of the various nationalities already had their favorite dopes on hand to insure victory. French racers preferred a mixture based on caffeine, while the Belgians inexplicably placed their faith in ether-soaked sugar. Others used drinks containing alcohol, while nitroglycerine was the favorite of the sprinters. Already the trainer had slipped into his role as chief pharmacist, producing wonder products out of heroin and cocaine. By 1886, the first doping fatality caused by an overdose of "trimethyl" was reported. This occurred during the 600 km Bordeaux-Paris cycle race, in which an English cyclist called Linton died after excessive doping by his manager, the owner of a bicycle firm. Somewhat later, the use of oxygen to improve performance was introduced. In 1910 one of the few accusations of doping to lose, or nobbling, appeared. After his defeat by Jack Johnson, James Jeffries asserted that his tea had been doped, probably not the first incident in which a boxer had attempted to nobble his opponent, or in which the vanquished claimed that he was nobbled.

Doping in competitive athletics became a substantial problem after World War II. At the Winter Olympics in Oslo in 1952, many broken ampoules and syringes were found in the changing rooms of the speed skaters. Cycling continued to be a hotbed of doping, and doping testing was first introduced in human athletics in this event in 1955 in France. In this first dope test, five of the twenty-five urine tests were positive. Doping with amphetamines continued, and racers were found with up to eighteen amphetamine tablets in their jerseys. Despite this flagrant violation of the rules, racers such as Scheepers of Holland, who were disqualified for doping, were treated as heroes and martyrs in their homeland, while the analysts who conducted the drug tests were maligned.

By the end of the 1950s stimulant doping was widespread in human athletics. In 1958 the American College of Sports Medicine reported on an examination of 441 trainers, coaches, and assistants, in which it was found that 35 percent had

Broken ampoules and syringes were reportedly found in the changing rooms of the speed skaters.

personal experience with benzedrine, while only 7 percent knew nothing about its use. Then in 1960, the Danish cyclist Knut Enemark Jensen collapsed at the Olympic Games after a fatal dose of an amphetamine and nicotinic acid was given him by his trainers. In another incident the British cyclist Simpson, after taking amphetamines, collapsed during the Tour de France and died. Human athletes were prepared to dose themselves with stimulants to the same extent as the most ruthless trainer might dope his horses.

An interesting first-hand account of the spread of medication and doping among Olympic-class athletes has been given by Harold Connolly. Mr. Connolly, a four-time Olympian, has set two world records for the hammer throw and is now an English teacher and a track and field coach at Santa Monica High School, California. Testifying before a Senate subcommittee on the use of drugs in athletics, Mr. Connolly stated that he was for eight years what he described as a "hooked" athlete, who used anabolic steroids as an integral part of his hammer throwing training.

Mr. Connolly was first exposed to drugs at the 1960 Olympic Games in Rome, where he heard rumors concerning a body-building program being used by the Russians. When he came home, he asked his physician to find out what it might be, and the physician said that the only drugs he knew of that would fit the description were the anabolic steroids. For one month, under a doctor's direction, he took "anabolics" but noticed no changes and abandoned them. It may well be that the dosage used in this particular instance, particularly if the doctor followed the manufacturer's recommendations, was too low to produce an effect in a healthy male.

At the Rome Olympics Mr. Connolly became aware of the increasingly widespread use of amphetamines. He was offered some amphetamines by a roommate and, not wanting to do his first experimenting with a drug in actual competition, declined. However, after his competitive event a German athlete friend of his suggested that he had looked lethargic during the event and asked him if he had taken any stimulants. When he replied that he had not, his friend suggested that he was a fool. Connolly subsequently experimented with the amphetamines himself but found that they tended to make him hyperexcited and lose control and coordination. For this reason Connolly himself never took amphetamines during competition, but he was aware of many others who did.

By the time of the 1968 Olympics, athletes in every event were reportedly using anabolic steroids and stimulants. To come down from the amphetamine highs, tranquilizers and marijuana were widely used. One world record holder was combining methamphetamine and Darvon® (a narcotic). The methamphetamine was used to "get him up," the narcotic to control skeletal pain and to keep him from being too agitated by the amphetamine. In 1968 many athletes traveled with their own medicine kits and assisted each other with their injections. Many of the athletes of the 1968 Olympic teams had so much scar tissue and puncture holes in their backsides that it was difficult to find a fresh spot to inject.

The athletes were obviously prepared to do just about anything short of killing themselves to improve their athletic performance. Connolly felt fortunate that in the eight years that he had dosed himself and experimented with drugs he had not experienced any painful or debilitating side effects. But he was at pains to emphasize that athletes are sufficiently single minded about their sport and their quest for fame and victory that they are prepared to try almost anything. In his own words, "they will want to be assured that they will not drop dead from it, of course, but they will try it even though there are warnings about side effects." Among themselves, athletes joked about these side effects. One athlete told him that "maybe when I am forty-five years old my wife will turn to me when we are watching television some night and I will shrivel up to a raisin and fall on the floor, but I don't care." This athlete was a long way from forty-five years old, wanted his record, and was prepared to take very substantial risks to get it. No trainer would inject or dope his horses any more ruthlessly than a highly competitive athlete would dope himself, and the positions of the racing horse and the human athlete when it comes to medication are remarkably similar.

The realities of competitive sports, the wear and tear that they induce in human athletes, and the high stakes involved have led to the emergence of the discipline of sports medicine. The drugs, surgical maneuvers, and medications taken by human athletes parallel those that we will be speaking about in the horse, and it is appropriate, before we discuss this, to see what a modern human athlete and his doctor will do to keep the athlete in action.

Sports medicine in the United States is devoted largely to the care and treatment of some 3,000 highly skilled professional athletes. The role of sport medicine, as with equine medicine, is to keep the "down time" or "time off play" of

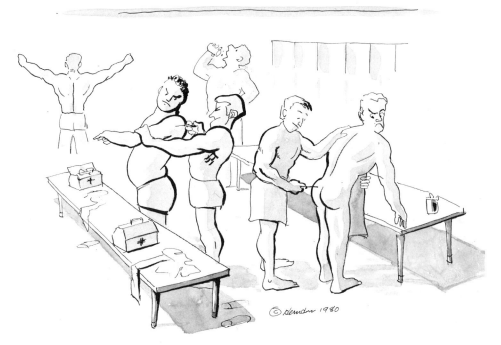

At the 1968 Olympics, many athletes reportedly assisted each other with their injections.

The positions of the racing horse and the human athlete when it comes to medication are remarkably similar.

these athletes to a minimum. As with racehorses, the doctor : patient ratio is low, some professional football teams having one to two doctors and four trainers for about forty players. Whereas twenty years ago a player played until he could play no more and then was replaced, now the players are cared for like kings and their professional lives carefully maximized and extended. Because an athlete must be in peak form to play, the medicine that he gets is at the leading edge of medical science. Research in this area of sports medicine has led to faster and more effective recovery from surgery for all patients and has thus benefitted medicine and humankind as a whole.

Pain is an occupational hazard in sports, and most athletes play with some degree of discomfort, if only from the previous day's injuries. The pressures that make them play may be internal, such as pride, external, such as pressures from the team manager and "team spirit" or pressures from fellow players. Nevertheless, whatever the reasons, most athletes accept considerable levels of pain in their profession, and it is usually only when it begins to interfere with their actual play that they become concerned.

Another reason athletes play in pain is the Wally Pipp syndrome. Wally Pipp was the New York Yankees' first baseman from 1915 to 1925, when he unfortunately got a headache and was replaced by Lou Gehrig. Pipp never again started in a game as first baseman for the Yankees, while Gehrig, who often played in pain, went on to set records. One reason, therefore, for staying in the game is that absence may lead to discovery of an understudy. According to Dallas Cowboy

"Most athletes play with some degree of discomfort."

football coach Tom Landry, the unwritten code is that "if a player will not be hurt so that his injury would be aggravated to the point where it would keep him out of play for a long period, then he is going to have to play."

Medication to control pain is often used in professional sports. The local anesthetic block, illegal in horse racing, has been commonly used in basketball. Willis Reed of the New York Knickerbockers was injected with 250 mg of carbocaine to numb a ruptured muscle in his right thigh, so that he could play the last minutes of the 1970 NBA playoff against the Los Angeles Lakers. The injection of local anesthetic was sufficient to gain victory for Reed's team and established for him a reputation for toughness. The other side of the local anesthetic coin, however, is also seen. For example, Bill Walton, then of Portland, was injected with Xylocaine® and Decadron® (a corticosteroid anti-inflammatory) in his left foot. Walton played fifteen minutes of the first half of the game and then left the game in pain. X-rays the next day showed a broken bone in his foot, and this injury resulted in seven months in a cast and disappearance of most of the musculature in his left foot; it kept him sidelined the entire 1978-1979 season.

According to Walton, he was first injected with a local anesthetic in his leg during a game in 1976. Walton said that he had experienced pain in his leg during warm-ups but decided to play anyway. At halftime he was told that a shot of Xylocaine would do the trick, so he took the shot. He limped through the rest of the game and when he came off had the leg X-rayed. The X-rays revealed a stress fracture of the left foot, which put him on crutches. When asked whether or not he would take injections again, Walton says yes, he would, but he makes it clear that they would be what he calls "therapeutic injections." Walton defined a therapeutic injection as an injection that a doctor gives and then tells you to go home and rest for two weeks, as against an injection "where they numb an area that allows you to play."

Another classic example of an athlete taking an injection to play is that of Billie Jean King, who reportedly went to her doctor in the summer of 1978 and asked him for a shot of cortisone in her heel so that she could try for her twentieth Wimbledon title. According to Mrs. King, "when he shot me before I left, he said 'you know this isn't good for you,'" to which Mrs. King gave the classic athlete's reply "I know, but I just want to get to Wimbledon." In England, Mrs. King requested further shots, presumably to enable her to play. However, as will be pointed out later, the injection of cortisone into joints may be associated with long-term, damage to the joints, and some physicians will not even use it for tennis elbow today.

Why do athletes play in pain? The answer to this is relatively straightforward — that pain is an occupational hazard for athletes. Further, an ability to cope with pain and overcome it is highly regarded in all branches of human endeavor and nowhere more than in athletics. Most athletes are prepared to play with considerable levels of pain, and they are also aware that their colleagues and fans want them to perform, so that they are prepared to push themselves to the limits of their capabilities. Although such peer pressures are part of life for everyone, they are much more compelling for the average athlete, whose career is so much shorter and to whom any individual performance may be critical. This is particularly so for young athletes, who have reputations to build and who cannot afford to be sidelined or to put in a substandard performance. As pointed out previously, the unwritten law is that "if a player will not be hurt so that his injury would be aggravated to the point where it would keep him out for a long period of time, he is going to have to play."

Pain is part of the life of an athlete, an occupational hazard, and a fact of life. Hockey players get cut up all the time, but the tradition among hockey players is that when you get cut, you get stitched and you go back and play. Athletes also, like racehorses, carry their season's trauma from day to day, and once the season starts they are always aching. Their aches and pains may be hidden from their doctors and teammates, but usually not from **their wives**. According to one athlete, "once the season's started, not one time, not one week do you feel fresh, really ready to go. You're always aching. If you're not, then you're not playing."

The critical question in human athletics, as in racing, is where do you draw the line? The team doctor in human athletics is not just the athlete's physician, he is paid by managment in the same way as the veterinarian and, like the veterinarian, may occasionally be the team's owner. This creates special problems for both the doctor and the patient. What is best for the patient and what is best for the athlete may not necessarily be one and the same approach to a problem. Further, the doctor may identify with the more glamorous aspects of his athlete's career and push him beyond what is medically prudent in an effort to keep him in and on top of the game. The doctor's primary role is to keep his athletes in the game. However, since this is often the athlete's aim also, the tendency to push athletes to the maximum is obviously substantial. The bottom line on these aspects of the problem was probably best expressed by Bill Walton when explaining his decision to accept injections of local anaesthetics in the 1978 NBA playoff. The problem, according to Walton, is that the line between getting back too soon is "not a solid, straight line — it's a curvey dotted line, a line players may cross without even knowing it." As Walton says, "I think it's an incredibly tough position for everybody involved. I believe the doctors are trying to do their best and the players are trying to do their best, but given the circumstances under which these decisions are made, mistakes happen."

SELECTED REFERENCES

Association of Official Racing Chemists: *The Chemical Laboratory and Its Role in Racing.* 2nd Revision, 1974.

Clarke, E. G. C.: The doping of racehorses. *Med Leg J, 30:*180-191, 1962-63.

Csaky, T. Z.: Doping. *J Sports Med Phys Fitness, 12:*117-123, 1972.

Kater, J. A.: Horse doping, still a blot on racing. *Life Magazine, 38*(5):93-164, 1955.

Lambton, George: *Men and Horses I Have Known.* London, Butterworth, 1924.

Leavy, Jane: Sports medicine: Healing the athletes. *New York Times,* July 22, 23, 24, 25, 1979.

Longrigg, Roger: *The History of Horse Racing.* New York, Stein & Day, 1972.

Mack, William: Playing hurt: The doctors dilemma. *Review,* 99-103, Sept. 1979.

Pharmacology and the punter. *Nature, 222:*111, 1969.

Proceedings of the International Symposium on Dope Detection in Race Horses, *Br J Sports Med 10* (October), 1973.

Prokop, L.: *The Problem of Doping.* Lausanne, International Olympic Committee Medical Commission Publication, 1972.

U.S. Senate Committee on the Judiciary: Proper and improper use of drugs by athletes. Hearings, 93rd Congress, 1st Session, 1973.

Wright, J. G.: Doping. *Med Leg J, 20:*66-70, 1952.

Chapter 3

THE MODERN MEDICATION SCENE: THE CAST OF CHARACTERS

THE CAST OF CHARACTERS involved in the problems of drugs and the performance horse is substantial. The rules by which the game is governed are made by racing commissioners or other regulatory bodies and enforced by their stewards, hearing committees, veterinarians,and chemists. In making the rules the racing commissioners listen to horsemen, trainers, veterinarians, their own staff, and public opinion. When formulated, the rules are enforced by the commission's staff, which includes stewards, commission veterinarians, and chemists. The medication rules are generally broken by horsemen, trainers, or veterinarians, and sometimes by horse players, who either inadvertently or sometimes less than inadvertently become associated with "positives" called by the regulatory people. If the arguments about guilt or innocence get serious, attorneys and eventually the courts system may be called in. Among these various groups it is the horsemen and the regulatory people who are most concerned with equine medication on a day-to-day basis.

Occasionally, vocal groups from the general public become interested in horse racing, which has a slightly risque image, and will demand that some aspect of the industry be cleaned up. As of this writing, in the spring of 1980, humane society groups are bringing a bill before Congress, initially called the Drug Free Horse Racing Act and later the Corrupt Horse Racing Practices Act of 1980, which would make the medication of racing horses illegal and a federal offense. Other members of the general public who are involved include the horse players, who, although vitally concerned are perhaps the least vocal of all groups. Finally, as bit players, one has the chemists and pharmacologists, occasionally called on by any of the parties involved when they think they may be helpful to their interests.

The pivotal position in this whole structure is held by the racing commissioners. They are usually gentlemen of some prominence in the community, who serve on the commission as political appointees for a definite term. They may or may not have had any substantial previous experience in the racing industry. Since the racing commissioners have the power to make the rules of racing, they should, ideally, consider the points of view of all the parties concerned and affected by the rules and should formulate rules that are in the best interests of racing.

When it comes to formulating medication rules, commissioners usually need much more guidance than they may in other areas. The science of pharmacology, which describes the actions of drugs in man and animals, has developed principally in the last twenty years, which means that most commissioners and commission veterinarians, who tend to be men of mature years, will have had little or no formal education in this area. Much of their information about the actions and effects of drugs in horses comes to them from their chemists, who also usually have little formal training on the actions and effects of drugs, or via the news media and turf writers, which is an excellent way to get confused.

In an attempt to solve this problem, the American Association of Equine Practitioners has set up a Veterinary Chemists Advisory Committee to the National Association of State Racing Commissioners (NASRC), which reports on an aspect of equine medication and drug detection each year to the National Association of State Racing Commissioners convention. The first reports covered phenylbutazone and furosemide (Lasix®), and subsequent reports have dealt with prerace testing, performance studies, and narcotic drugs in the horse. These reports are designed to keep commissioners abreast of developments in the medication area and are, as much as possible, written for the lay public.

Nevertheless, despite this effort on the part of the professions involved, commissioners sometimes get confused. I once appeared before a midwestern racing commission and presented, in point form, the actions and the diuretic effects of Lasix® (furosemide) almost word for word from the committee's report to the National Association of State Racing Commissioners. When I had finished my presentation, one commissioner asked me why my statements were "the opposite of everybody else's." When I recovered from my surprise, I asked him to select any one of the points that he thought was incorrect. He then came up with the popular misconception "Doesn't Lasix flush drugs out of horses?" Well, Lasix of course, does not "flush" drugs out of horses, and when we had convinced him of that, we had his attention.

Another singular example of the lack of exposure of racing commissioners to the basics of biology and pharmacology occurred when a West Coast racing commission decided to take the medication problem in hand. These commissioners had apparently decided to be aggressive, and to sort the medication problem out once and for all. Their incredible approach to this problem, however, was an outright ban on all feed additives, vitamins, minerals, medications, and domestic remedies. In one sweeping action they tried to roll veterinary medicine, nutrition, and horsemanship back to at least the time of Attila the Hun, if not further. The fact that these proposed rules were absolutely unenforceable did not seem to bother anyone on the commission. In their misguided efforts to protect racing, this commission would have harmed the industry in this state greatly. The task of educating this commission as to just what would be fair and effective in this area fell to the state's horsemen, and was eventually successful, but as a statement of attitude and appreciation of the problems of racing on the part of a commission, this incident was remarkable.

Despite these and other incidents, however, it would be fair to say that most racing commissioners, and particularly those hardworking members who actually formulate and draft the rules, are thoughtful men who do their best with a difficult problem. Then, after the commissioners have developed a medication policy, it is up to the commission stewards to see to it that the rules are enforced. In addition to stewards, the racing commission has commission veterinarians, commission chemists, investigative officers, attorneys, and other professionals and personnel as may be required by the commission's circumstances. For some commissions, such as the Illinois Racing Board, these can amount to a very large force indeed.

The executive power of the commission is implemented primarily through the stewards. The stewards exercise immediate supervision, control, and regulation of racing at each association racetrack, on behalf of and responsible only to the commission. They have authority over all horses and persons, licensed and unlicensed, on the racing association grounds during the race meeting. They can investigate, hold hearings on, and rule on all questions, disputes, protests, or objections that arise during a racing meet, and they are empowered to interpret and enforce the rules of racing. Their authority usually starts at midnight on the day before the meeting and ends after the last day of racing of the meeting, except in the event of a dispute, when their authority may be extended to allow resolution of the dispute. In Kentucky, the senior steward and chief administrator are responsible to the commission for the supervision of all matters pertaining to racing. Among those reporting to the senior steward are the commission veterinarian and the commission chemist.

The primary responsibility of the commission veterinarian is the supervision and control of the detention area where the horses go after the race to be sampled and the collection of samples for the commission chemist. The commission veterinarian usually has a number of employees to assist him with the collection of urine samples, which can be a relatively prolonged procedure. If blood samples are collected, they are collected personally by the commission veterinarian, who verifies the identification of the horse and may take note of any unusual clinical signs. He will usually take samples from horses that finish first in any race, and up to the first three horses in a stakes race. He will also test any horse that, in the opinion of the stewards, may have had its performance altered by a prohibited substance.

The commission veterinarian is also custodian of the written medical reports of treatments of all horses racing at a meet. He reviews these and may elect to discuss the medication records on a confidential basis with the treating veterinarian. He is further empowered to make scratches from the daily racing cards when it is his opinion that medication has proceeded to the point that it would be detrimental to the horse, or to the wagering public's interest, for the horse to run. These reports are confidential and, beyond being used for the compilation of medication statistics, are not released from the commission offices.

The compilation of medication statistics is an important job, which at this time is performed voluntarily by some conscientious commission veterinarians. As medication rules change the question arises as to what the incidence of "bleeders" or breakdowns or of "pulling up lame" is on a given track and whether or not it is affected by changes in the medication rules. These questions do not lend themselves to laboratory study, and the best and most satisfactory way to answer them is to keep good records. Unfortunately, with the exception of a few farsighted commissioners and commission veterinarians, these statistics are all too rarely collected and an important source of information is lost.

As a further part of his duties, the commission veterinarian may, from time to time in some states, publish a list of medications by brand or generic name that are specifically prohibited for racing. These lists are not considered exclusive and are only a guide for owners, trainers, and veterinarians. He may also advise owners, trainers, and veterinarians on the likely clearance times for drugs and how close to race time they might be administered. He may further advise trainers, veterinarians, and his own stewards and commissioners as to the probable effects of different medications in horses and as to whether or not the commission should consider medication with such drugs a violation of their rules of racing.

Finally, the commission veterinarian is responsible for insuring the identity and security of the samples taken and also for insuring that the race test laboratory staff does not know the identity of the horse from which the samples came. If a horse fails to urinate, the commission veterinarian may, under some circumstances, administer a diuretic to a horse or else allow it to return to its own barn and have a specimen taken there. Again, the commission veterinarian is responsible for the identity and security of these samples until they come into the care of the commission chemist.

The commission chemist, professionally called a "racing chemist," is the individual responsible for the chemical analysis of the saliva, blood, or urine samples collected by the commission veterinarian. He is usually trained in chemistry to the bachelor's level or beyond, with doctoral level training becoming increasingly common. Most commonly, he is a member of the Association of Official Racing Chemists.

The Association of Official Racing Chemists (AORC) was formed in Chicago in 1947 by the racing chemists from various states in the United States and from Canada, France, and Mexico. The following year it became an associate member of the National Association of State Racing Commissioners and since then has held its annual meetings in association with this group. At these annual meetings, the racing chemists get together to discuss their approaches to mutual problems and to hear invited speakers. The discussions in these meetings are published as a Proceedings; although contrary to the usual rules of science, these proceedings are regarded as being strictly confidential and for circulation to members only. The primary purpose of the AORC is considered to be to "increase the knowledge and skill of its individual members by mutually sharing in research and advances in techniques made by fellow members, and, as a result, perform a more effective service for racing."

Membership in the AORC is limited to those who are concerned with the detection of drugs in racing samples. To become a full member, an analyst must pass a test on his ability to detect drugs added to urine samples. Currently, the test consists of twelve samples, of which eleven contain detectable quantities of important drugs selected from the list of drugs reported by AORC members. To help the member make his identifications he is provided with a list of drugs from which the eleven test samples were selected. To be accepted for membership the candidate must successfully identify these drugs, and beyond this requirement, a candidate also needs to be voted on favorably by 75 percent of the AORC body to attain membership.

The Association of Official Racing Chemists has had, for the longest time, a policy of restricting the flow of information, as outlined in their 1974 booklet *The Chemical Laboratory and Its Role in Racing.*

> The association has established a specific policy which provides that no member may furnish information pertaining to laboratory methods and related topics to any individual until he has been properly certified as the official racing chemist by a racing authority. This action is not meant to perpetuate the professional interest of members, but to safeguard against the transmittal of confidential, specialized information into the hands of those who could use it to the detriment of the sport of racing, rather than for its improvement. After an official has been designated as an official chemist by a racing authority, the AORC is glad to assist him in establishing his procedures for carrying on a reliable testing program.

The reason for this stipulation is far from clear and, as pointed out by Professor Clarke, in the long run only stands to hurt the image of racing chemistry. The adage that "not only should justice be done, but it should be seen to be done" applies just as much in racing chemistry as in any other forensic area.

The type of testing carried out by the commission chemist is entirely at his discretion, and he is specifically charged with detecting prohibited substances or their metabolites in blood, saliva, or urine samples from the horse. The tests are almost invariably carried out blind, which means that the chemist has only a code number to identify the samples and does not know the name of the horse, trainer, or owner involved. He is expected to report all substances that he may find in these tests that are not normal in the body of a horse, and his duties, at least in Kentucky, are limited to these reports and need not include possible effects on the physiology of the horse. If he finds a sample to be negative, he may discard the remainder of the sample. If, on completion of his tests for a positive substance, some sample remains, he is charged with protecting and preserving the remains of the sample until such time as the stewards rule that it may be discarded. The commission chemist's reports are usually due within twenty-four to forty-eight hours after the conclusion of the last race of the preceding day, and the racing association will not distribute any purses until given a clearance on chemical testing by the stewards.

While most chemists discard the remains of the blood or urine sample when it has been judged negative, the chemists for at least one racing commission simply report that the preliminary tests were negative and thereby allow the purses to be released. Instead of being discarded, however, the remains of the urine samples go into the freezer, there to be stored with thousands of other samples for up to three years. Then, if a new analytical method is developed, or the chemist is alerted to a particular pattern of drug use, he can pull all the samples for that particular horseman. The rationale behind this approach is that patterns of drug use over a period of time can be developed and associated with certain individuals. Such patterns of drug use, maintained over a period of time and associated with certain individuals, are much more compelling evidence than a single incident of drug identification. With a single incident of drug identification, there is always the possibility of someone else maliciously administering a drug days ahead to a horse, or even of a simple test tube mixup, which possibilities are much less likely to account for a pattern of drug use.

In the regulatory structure the racing chemist will usually advise the commission about technical advances in his field and how these may be incorporated into the testing procedure. As well as performing routine tests, he will also, as the individual who performed the tests, be both a factual and expert witness for the commission in proceedings concerning drug identification in horses. This is often the most difficult portion of his job, as his technical evidence or his qualifications to draw such conclusions as he may wish from his technical evidence may on occasion be vigorously challenged. He must be capable of presenting his evidence and conclusions clearly, effectively and, most importantly, convincingly, to either hearing committees, judges, or juries who will have little technical expertise in this area. This combination of talents is unusual and, under the direction of an attorney experienced in the area, can make a very potent regulatory tool.

The quality of the expert testimony offered in hearings and adversary proceedings can vary from first class to the totally ludicrous. Hearings usually bring forward classic examples of anecdotal evidence and outright old wives' tales, along with that hardy perennial "common knowledge." Even in more rigorous adversary proceedings, I have heard people testify that they could tell from a urine level, or sometimes the mere presence in urine of a drug, when, where, how, and in what quantity it was administered, which is highly improbable. Others have testified that drug levels in horse urine do not vary significantly, whereas the actual range extends into the thousandsfold. Again, I have heard testimony that the pH scale (acidity measure) was arithmetic, whereas in actual fact the scale is logarithmic. Such testimony from arithmetic minds, lost in logarithmic worlds, is usually perceived by impartial adjudicators for what it is worth, which is nothing. A severe problem arises, however, if the adjudicating body has compelling reasons not to believe but to accept one side's story. Under such circumstances, the uninformed and the improbable may well carry the day, and adjudicators have been known to accept and profess themselves satisfied with testimony that rendered those presenting it physically ill. Such circumstances only reinforce the perception that people believe what they want to believe, and individuals with even good grounds to appeal medication rulings are well advised to keep this fact in mind.

Before we leave the analysts, I must tell you about one particular positive that has been called that appears to defy all reason. According to the Association of Official Racing Chemists, somewhere in the world during 1979 a "pangamic acid" positive was called. "Pangamic acid" has an interesting history (see Chapter 17). It is supposedly present in all seeds and has been *trade named* vitamin B_{15}. No one, however, is quite sure of its chemical structure, and as far as the Food and Drug Administration is concerned, it does not exist. Nevertheless, despite the fact that the very existence of the substance is questionable, a horse urine has been found positive for this substance. One might also point out that "pangamic acid," as a substance supposedly present in all seeds, is the sort of thing that one might reasonably expect to find in horse urines.

This finding of a non-substance, plus the very large number of substances that have been reported found in horse urine, leads me to propose what I will call Tobin's law. Tobin's law is a direct adaptation to the racing world of Murphy's Law. Murphy's law states that *"whatever can go wrong will go wrong,"* and its corollary holds that *"when things do go wrong, they will go wrong in the worst possible way."* In keeping with Murphy's dicta, Tobin's law holds that *"any drug that can be found in horse urine will be found in horse urine,"* and its corollary, based on the pangamic acid positive, holds that *"drugs will be found in horse urines quite independently of whether or not they actually exist."*

The attorneys involved in the medication field come in two types: those experienced in the field, who know its ins and outs and understand the technical jargon, and those who do not. Usually the commission attorney, who may have worked with the jurisdiction's racing chemist frequently, will have a good grasp of the technical apsects of the case and will know which points will appeal to hearing committees, judges, and juries. The defendant's attorney, on the other hand, may be handling a medication violation for the first time and has to learn the intricacies of testing techniques, drug elimination, and pharmacological effects for the first time. Often the outcome of the case depends on how diligently and rapidly the defending attorney sorts out the important from the trivial in his own mind and develops a presentation strategy. Good lawyers may be expensive, but a person who can make such a synthesis and then sell his synthesis to possibly hostile adjudicators is more than worthy of his hire to the person in trouble.

The people who tend to get into trouble with medication rules are most commonly trainers and horsemen and, much less commonly, veterinarians. The cause of their problems may be either misadventure, or they may have been trying to estimate the time and dosage factors too closely. The duty of a trainer, and indeed his economic well-being, depends on keeping his horses in top running form. If the trainer is established and has a first-class national reputation, he will not have much problem with this, as he will have first-class horses to begin with. If, however, the trainer is young, new to the game, and making his way with average horses, he will need to practice his profession keenly, and, particularly with average horses, proper medication can be a critical factor. Under the circumstances, the primary concern of both the trainer and his veterinarian is to keep their horses racing sound and in as close to top form as they can. If they use anything other than permitted medications at any time on their horses, and even with permitted medications, unless they are ultraconservative in their withdrawal times, the chances are that they will, at some time or another, get into trouble with the medication rules, which are drawn up for the average horse under average circumstances.

As will be made clear in later chapters, it is essentially impossible to tell from urinary concentrations of a drug when it was administered, and conversely, it can be quite difficult to tell when a given dose of a drug will clear the urine. The rates at which most drugs are absorbed, distributed, and eliminated by the horse are not known, which is only part of the problem. Most drug testing is by means of urine samples and, for some drugs in particular, their concentrations in urine can be highly dependent on urine volume and pH (acidity). Finally, and most importantly, one often does not know the sensitivity of the analyst's methods, and one cannot in some cases be sure whether or not he will be able to detect it. Even with the best of intentions and reasonable care and precautions, therefore, a horseman may suddenly find himself charged with a medication violation when he may not have done anything he and other horsemen had not been doing for years.

When a "positive" is called, the first person outside of the authorities to find out about it is the trainer. This is because the trainer bears primary responsibility for the proper health, care, training, and protection against the administration of prohibited drugs or medications of the horses in his care. If a horse is found to have been medicated, it immediately becomes the trainer's primary responsibility to show that he took all reasonable precautions to avoid the medication problem. This presumption of either guilt or negligence is spoken of as the "trainer insurer rule," as it is the trainer who insures the condition of the horse. One of the principal "outs" for a trainer under these circumstances would be that he relied on the professional advice of his veterinarian in administering a drug or drugs to his horses.

The veterinarian, duly licensed by the racing commission, is the only person permitted to possess a hypodermic needle, hypodermic syringes, or drugs within the confines of the stable area. He is, by law, the only person allowed to advise about and treat, either medically or surgically, the trainer's horses. The veterinarian has within his power the whole therapeutic armamentarium, and he is bound by his professional responsibility to "promote the welfare of animals entrusted to his care."

If a veterinarian diagnoses a condition in a horse for which drug treatment is appropriate, he has a professional responsibility to recommend that treatment for the horse. Because of this, under "no medication rules" such as those that are in force in New York and England, he must recommend that the horse not be raced until the drug clears the horse. How soon the veterinarian can clear the horse to be raced is often little better than a guessing game, as he — or for that matter everyone concerned — may have only the most approximate idea of when the drug will no longer be detectable in the horse's urine. One way around this problem is a controlled medication program.

The goal of a controlled medication program is to smooth out the minor health and musculoskeletal problems that are common to all athletes and to insure that horses are presented at the starting gate fit to race at their best. By allowing specific therapeutic medications to be used, controlled medication programs avoid driving trainers and veterinarians to more extreme, difficult, and damaging measures, such as freezing, denerving, nerve blocking, and intra-articular corticosteroid injections without rest. Controlled medication programs also monitor the amount of drug allowed in the urine, so that laboratory work is not interfered with and may be able to insure that no medications are given close enough to race time so that untoward side effects influence performance. A number of states in the United States operate such systems, and when well run, they can apparently hit a happy medium between being too permissive and unnecessarily restrictive. For these programs to work well and efficiently, the commission veterinarian is of central importance, as he must have the confidence of the horsemen, the chemist, and the racing commissioners.

The role of the general public in the equine medication picture is sporadic but can at times be critical. Racing commissions, as politically appointed bodies, are sensitive to public opinion and respond promptly to any popular outcry. The usual sequence of events is that a journalist picks up on a story about the drugging of racehorses and presents a scrappy story, short on facts but long on perceived evils. This is then echoed by other journalists and used as ammunition by groups who believe that race horses, as a group perhaps the most pampered beasts on earth, are being mistreated. This refrain may then gather strength around the country, and currently such a coalition of groups is drafting a bill to put the federal government in charge of racehorse medication control.

Last, but not least, one has the horse player. The horse player, who in many ways is the lifeblood of racing, is perhaps the least complaining member of the whole crew, taking medication in his stride. Some racing jurisdictions feel they have a duty to let the horse player know what medication the horses are on and prominently post the medication lists. Others feel that the medication lists are no business of the horse players and do not post any lists. Whichever approach is taken, the horse players turn out and bet faithfully and, apparently, aproximately the same dollar amounts. Sporadically, racing page stories appear that claim that medication has ruined the ability of the horse player to bet accurately, but such stories are rare and do not appear to represent any compelling feeling on the part of the mass of horse players.

The backdrop against which these characters play out their roles is equally impressive (Table 3-I). In 1978 there were 127,000 races in the United States, spread over 13,000 racing days. These races were watched by about 75 million people, who bet approximately 10 billion dollars, or an average daily turnover of about three quarters of a million dollars. Of this 10 billion dollars, a little over half a billion (673 million) went to state government, as admission taxes, parimutuel taxes, and so forth. These are substantial figures, and they are the basic reason why the medication of racing horses is such a politically sensitive area.

A minor but important figure is the pharmacologist, the man who actually studies the actions of drugs in horses. The science of pharmacology as we know it today has only developed within the last twenty-five years, and the pharmacology of the horse in general and with respect to drugs used in medication has scarcely been touched. There are now a number of good research programs on various aspects of the pharmacology and detection of drugs in horses underway around the world, and a group called the International Equine Medication Control Group has been formed to provide a structure for information exchange in this group. Under the direction of the author, this group held its Third International Symposium in Lexington in the summer of 1979, and this meeting was widely regarded as the coming of age of this discipline.

TABLE 3-I
RACING STATISTICS IN THE UNITED STATES

Racing days	13,160
Number of races	128,866
Attendance	72,783,076
Parimutuel handle	$10,727,919,798
Revenue to state government	$ 68,750,126
Revenue to state of Kentucky	$ 15,750,126

SOURCE: NASRC 1979 Report.

The pharmacologist, then, is the man who studies what these drugs actually do in horses. His role is to try and give a balanced description of the benefits that drugs bring to the horse, for they surely do this, and the risks that they may create for the horse, rider, spectators, and others involved in the horse industry. His job is not helped by the emotional responses that the mere mention of the word "drug" brings forth in many, nor by the substantial body of myth and misinformation that surrounds drug use.

Nevertheless, the objective of this book is to describe as clearly and understandably as possible the actions, uses, effects, and detection of drugs in performance horses. To do this our next step must be a general overview of where drugs come from, how they act in the body of the horse, and how they are eliminated by the horse.

SELECTED REFERENCES

Association of Official Racing Chemists: *The Chemical Laboratory and Its Role in Racing*, 2nd Revision, 1974.

Baker, R. O.: *The Misuse of Drugs in Horse Racing*. Barrington, IL, The Illinois Hooved Animal Humane Society, 1978.

Corrupt Horse Racing Practices Act of 1980. Draft of a Proposed Bill.

National Association of State Racing Commissioners: 43rd, 44th, 45th, and 46th Annual Conventions. Executive Vice President's Office, PO Box 4216, Lexington, KY.

Rules of Racing. The Commonwealth of Kentucky, 1975 Edition.

Tobin, Thomas, Blake, J. W., and Woods, William E. (Eds.): *Proceedings of the Third International Symposium on Equine Medication Control*. Dept. of Veterinary Science, University of Kentucky, 1979.

Chapter 4

THE DRUGS: WHERE THEY COME FROM AND HOW THEY PRODUCE THEIR EFFECTS IN HORSES

THE QUESTION OF WHERE the drugs used in horses come from is relatively easy to answer. Most of our oldest and best-known drugs are plant products, which evolved on earth long before man, although not, perhaps, before the horse appeared on earth. Another important and relatively recent source of drugs has been the chemical industry, which screens many of its products for drug action. A third and even more recent source has been man's increasing knowledge of his own chemistry, which has led to the development of drugs based on the bio-chemicals involved in his own metabolism. The rarest type of drug, however, is a drug developed "off the drawing board" by chemists. At the moment, scientists do not know enough about drugs or drug actions to design useful drugs, and I know of only two drugs in clinical use that were developed in this way.

Most plant drugs have been known by man since antiquity, even though their introduction into modern medicine may be relatively recent. Among drugs from this group with which horsemen are concerned are reserpine, morphine and the other opiates, cocaine, ephedrine, caffeine, and nicotine, to mention but a few. These drugs all have highly selective and specific actions in horses, and they are among the most potent drugs we have. It is not clear why drugs that have such potent and specific effects on animals evolved in plants. One suggestion is that "drugs" evolved in plants to discourage or modify grazing by herbivorous animals such as the horse. In any event, plants have been one of the major contributors to our drug compendiums and will no doubt continue to contribute in the future.

The growth of the chemical industry in western Europe since the latter half of the nineteenth century provided man's next major source of drugs. In many cases mankind often simply followed leads provided by plant drugs, such as the model provided by cocaine, which led to the development of procaine and other local anesthetics. In the mid-1930s, however, German researchers found that the red dye prontosil had potent antibacterial effects in mice. Development of this lead gave rise to the sulfonamide family of antibacterial agents. From observations on the side effects of the sulfonamides, which include diuresis (increased urine flow) and hypoglycemia (reduced blood sugar), a number of diuretics and antidiabetic agents were developed.

Another effect of the sulfonamides was that they led to a complete rethinking of the approach to therapy of bacterial disease. Whereas previously vaccines and sera were the only useful weapons against bacterial disease, the sulfonamides showed clearly that direct attack by drugs on bacterial pathogens was possible. This thought, in the late 1930s, stimulated Florey at Oxford University to reex-amine some of the bacterial products that inhibit the growth of other bacteria.

Many of our drugs are plant products and likely evolved to influence the grazing of plants by herbivores such as the horse.

One of the first substances he chose to test was a product of the penicillium mold, which had been reported on some years earlier by Alexander Fleming. Florey, of course, "hit the jackpot" with penicillin, the most potent, most selective, and least toxic of all the antibiotics known, and a major breakthrough in drug research. A worldwide effort in this field then started, and by the 1960s most of the major antibiotics in use today were discovered. Since bacteria are actually microscopic plants, the antibiotics must be classified as plant drugs, whose discovery had to await development of the science of bacteriology.

Another major source of drugs that has opened up in this century has been our increased understanding of how our own bodies work. As the chemical basis of our own life processes is worked out, we discover key molecules that, by themselves or with modification, are very useful drugs. The corticosteroids and the anabolic steroids are good examples of drugs discovered and developed in this way. Similarly, the prostaglandins, triidothyronine, and other hormones and chemical messengers have turned out to be useful drugs, either directly or after suitable chemical modification.

The next question that one might ask is how these diverse chemicals, which we call drugs, produce their effects in the body. Whatever their origin, drugs produce their effects in the body by binding to specific receptors at their sites of action. These receptors are located either on or in the cells where the drugs produce their effects, and the drugs must get to these sites before they can produce their effects. Thus, if administered orally, they need to be well absorbed from the stomach and intestines and distribute well in the body. If given intravenously, they must distribute well to their sites of action, which may be in the brain, heart, or kidneys. Once they reach their sites of action they must bind to and activate the specific drug receptors that produce the responses associated with that drug. Thus, given a potent drug, the thing that determines how rapidly a drug will work and how effective it will be is how well it is absorbed and how rapidly it distributes in the body.

The principal characteristic that determines how well a drug is absorbed, how widely and rapidly it distributes in the horse, and how it is eliminated is its lipid (fat) solubility. This is because the cell membranes in the horse that separate all the compartments in the horse's body are the lipid outer membranes of cells. To get through these cell membranes, to be absorbed from the gut, to pass into the brain from the blood, in fact to pass almost anywhere in a horse, a drug must be lipid soluble.

If a drug is highly lipid soluble, and it is given by intravenous injection, it distributes rapidly in the body, and as we will see later with fentanyl (Sublimaze®), one can see clear-cut signs of its action on the brain within minutes. On the other hand, if a drug is only partly lipid soluble it may take hours to get into the brain. If

THE ABSORBTION AND DISTRIBUTION OF DRUGS
DEPENDS PRIMARILY ON HOW LIPID (FAT)
SOLUBLE THEY ARE.

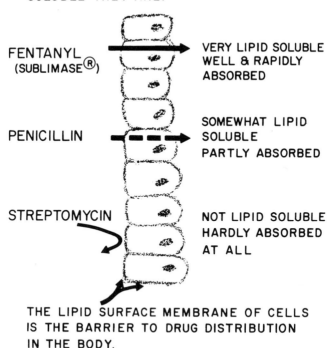

FENTANYL (SUBLIMASE®) — VERY LIPID SOLUBLE WELL & RAPIDLY ABSORBED

PENICILLIN — SOMEWHAT LIPID SOLUBLE PARTLY ABSORBED

STREPTOMYCIN — NOT LIPID SOLUBLE HARDLY ABSORBED AT ALL

THE LIPID SURFACE MEMBRANE OF CELLS
IS THE BARRIER TO DRUG DISTRIBUTION
IN THE BODY.

Figure 4-1. Schematic representation of drug absorption. The fatty (lipid) outer membrane of cells is the principal barrier to the movement of drugs through the body. Fentanyl (Sublimaze®) is a highly lipid soluble drug which readily passes through cell membranes and gets to its receptors in the brain. Penicillin is of intermediate water solubility, passing through cell membranes with some difficulty and thus taking some time to be absorbed and distribute. Streptomycin is very poorly lipid soluble, is very poorly absorbed, and does not distribute well in the body.

a drug is poorly lipid soluble, like the antibiotic streptomycin, it may hardly enter the brain at all. Thus lipid solubility is the most important determinant of how fast drugs can get around the body of the horse and produce their pharmacological effects (Fig. 4-1). Drugs that get into and act in the brain must all be quite lipid soluble, for if they were not they would not be effective drugs.

Let us now follow what happens to a lipid-soluble drug molecule after it is injected intravenously into a horse. We will take as our typical example the drug procaine, both because this is the most commonly reported drug found in horse urine and because it is a drug that has been well studied in the horse. As we follow it through the body of a horse, we will also have occasion to refer to other drugs whose actions and movement through the body differ somewhat from those of procaine.

When a veterinarian wishes to study the movement of a drug through a horse (i.e. its pharmacokinetics*), the first step is to give a fairly large dose of the drug by intravenous (IV) injection. Immediately after injection, the drug goes through a rapid mixing phase in the blood, which takes about three minutes. At the end of this period the drug is evenly distributed in the bloodstream and is moving into organs such as the brain and kidneys. If one draws a blood sample at the end of this period, i.e. at about three minutes, one finds the highest blood levels of drug to which that particular dose can give rise (Fig. 4-2).

The next process, and the first one that we are really interested in, is that of movement of the drug out of blood into the tissues where it will produce its effects. This is technically known as the distribution phase. In it, the drug moves from the blood into the tissues until the tissues are saturated with the drug. This process can occur very rapidly with some drugs, slowly with others, and hardly at all for drugs that are poorly lipid soluble. Usually this process takes somewhere between five and thirty minutes. At the end of this distribution period the tissues are as saturated as they can be with the amount of drug that was administered.

From this point on, the rate at which blood levels of the drug fall depends only on the rate at which the drug is metabolized or eliminated. This is usually much slower than the distribution phase and is called the metabolic or elimination phase. This phase continues until the drug can no longer be detected in the body of the horse, and for a very long time thereafter.

Some typical blood levels obtained after procaine was injected intravenously in horses are presented in Figure 4-2. The first plasma sample was drawn right after the mixing phase and shows about 0.6μg/ml of drug in plasma. As the drug distributed out of plasma and into the tissues, the plasma levels fell very rapidly, and this portion of the curve is marked "distribution" phase. This was then followed by the metabolic phase, during which time the blood levels were reduced by excretion and metabolism of the drug only. If one looks carefully at this curve, one sees that it is declining very slowly and that it looks as though it is never going to reach zero. As a practical matter, this is close to what actually happens — *after you give a drug to a horse, the drug concentrations in that horse can take weeks or months to reach zero!*† This is, of course, a very important concept because it means that

---

* From Pharmacon = drug, and kinein = to move

† See appendix A for calculations of the actual clearance times for drugs.

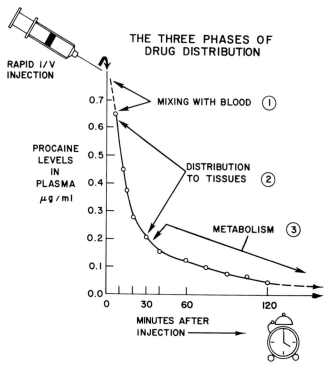

Figure 4-2. After rapid IV injection of procaine (2.5 mg/kg), blood levels of the drug fall rapidly at first, then more slowly. This curve may be divided into three distinct phases. The first phase is the mixing phase, which occurs in the three minutes after injection of the drug. The second phase is the distribution phase, which takes about twenty minutes to complete, during which the drug is distributing to the tissues. The third and final phase is the metabolic phase, during which the drug is eliminated. The metabolic phase can last for months. Reproduced with permission from Tobin, *J Equine Med Surg*, 2:262, 1978.

drugs are only very slowly "cleared" by a horse. What happens in real life when the analyst says that a drug has "cleared," of course, is that the concentration of the drug in the horse has dropped to the point where he can no longer detect it.

Now one might ask, how can anyone tell from the type of data in this illustration when the phase of distribution stops and when metabolism begins, and how can one be sure of the time that it will take for the drug concentration to approach zero? These questions can be easily answered by plotting this data in a slightly different way, that is, by making the vertical axis logarithmic, i.e. change in tenfold units. Since only one axis of the plot is logarithmic, it is called a semi-logarithmic (semi-log) plot.

If one puts the drug levels of Figure 4-2 on this type of plot (see Fig. 4-3), it turns out that the metabolic phase becomes as straight as an arrow, and the metabolic phase is usually defined as that portion of the curve which plots linearly on a semi-log plot. We know that mixing takes about three minutes, so the period between mixing and metabolism becomes the distribution phase. Because there is no zero on a log scale, which simply decreases in tenfold units forever, the blood levels of the drug can theoretically never reach zero and will continue to decline

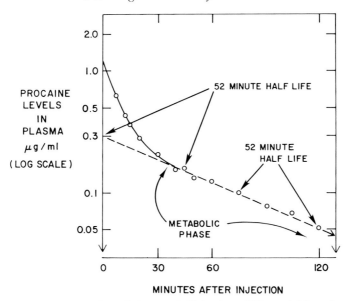

Figure 4-3. Semi-log plot of the data of Figure 4-2. If the data of Figure 4-2 is replotted so that the vertical axis is logarithmic, one gets the type of plot represented here. Because only one axis is logarithmic, this is called a semi-logarithmic plot. It should be noted that there is no zero on the logarithmic scale, but that it simply goes on decreasing in tenfold units for as long as one cares to follow it. On this type of plot, the metabolic phase plots linearly and so decays at a constant rate. Because of this, the time required for the drug concentration to halve is about fifty-two minutes at any point along this line. This time period, fifty-two minutes, is then the plasma half-life of this drug in the horse. Reproduced with permission from Tobin, *J Equine Med Surg*, 2:262, 1978.

forever. In addition, there are a number of very practical things to be learned from the semi-log plot, all of which are based on this "log-linear" relationship between drug concentrations and time.

This "log-linear" nature of the relationship between drug levels and time is very important. In the first place, it turns out that the time required for a drug concentration to halve, i.e. to fall to 50 percent of its original value, is constant, no matter what point on the straight portion of the curve one picks. Thus, the "half-time" or "half-life" of procaine in the horse is about fifty-two minutes, as shown in Figure 4-3. Each drug has its own individual plasma or blood half-time in the horse, and this half-time is, by and large, reasonably constant from horse to horse. Thus, if you know this half-time and the drug concentration in plasma for any given time on the curve, it is easy to estimate what the drug levels were previously or will be in the future in a given animal. This calculation is simple, because you know that one half-time back they were twice what they are now, and one half-time later the drug concentrations will be half what they are now. Then, if you know the relationship between plasma levels of a drug and its pharmacological effects, you can estimate what the pharmacological effects of the drug at the given time would or would not have been.

This relationship between the plasma level of a drug and its pharmacological effects can be very close under some circumstances. Figure 4-4 shows some of the best data I know of illustrating this relationship. In these experiments horses were

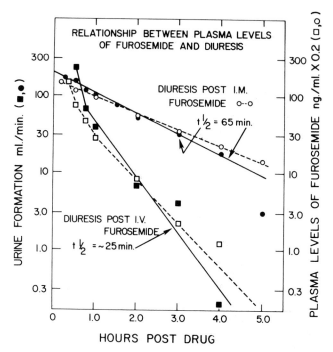

Figure 4-4. Blood levels of a drug and pharmacological effect. The dotted lines (-----) show the plasma (blood) levels of furosemide (Lasix®) after 1.0 mg/kg was given either intravenously or intramuscularly to horses. The solid lines (——) show the diuretic effect after these doses. There is clearly a close relationship between plasma levels of furosemide and the pharmacological effect, with the diuretic response decaying just a little faster than the blood levels of the drug. Reproduced with permission from Tobin et al., *J Equine Med Surg*, 2:216, 1978.

given the diuretic* Lasix® (furosemide) intravenously and intramuscularly and plasma levels of the drug determined. The dotted lines show the plasma levels of the drug, which declined much more slowly after intramuscular injection than after intravenous injection, as is sometimes the case. These two very different rates of decline of blood levels, however, are very closely matched by the rate of decline of the diuretic response (urine flow), which in each case declined just slightly faster than blood levels of the drug. The reason that the diuretic response declined a little faster than blood levels of the drug is likely that these horses did not have access to water. Because of this, the fluid lost during diuresis was not replaced, which made it progressively more difficult for furosemide to produce its diuretic effect as the experiment went on. This experiment shows clearly how closely related plasma levels of a drug and the effects of that drug can be.

While the relationship between plasma levels of the drug and the pharmacological effect can be very close, there are a few drugs for which the relationship is much less clear-cut. These are usually drugs whose blood levels change very rapidly and in such a way that the blood levels get out of step with concentrations of drug at the all important sites of action. One drug that has been studied in our

---

* Diuretic — a drug that greatly increases the volume and flow of urine.

laboratory for which there is only an approximate relationship between blood levels and the trotting response is the narcotic fentanyl (Sublimaze®) (Fig. 4-5). To produce good pharmacological effects with fentanyl, this drug must be given by rapid IV injection. Blood levels of fentanyl thus start high and fall rapidly and continuously, while trotting activity rises, peaks at about five minutes after drug administration, and then declines. Thus in the first few minutes after injection, plasma levels of fentanyl are falling rapidly, while trotting activity and, presumably, brain levels of the drug are increasing. Then, from about three minutes on, plasma levels are still falling rapidly, but trotting activity and presumably brain levels of the drug are declining much more slowly. At the end of the experimental period, however, the trotting activity has declined to control while blood levels of the drug are still present. The experiments suggest no clear-cut relationship between plasma levels of fentanyl and the trotting response to this drug. On the other hand, however, it is very likely that a good correlation exists between brain levels of fentanyl and its behavioral effects.

Drugs may also be given by routes other than intravenously. Many drugs for example, are given by subcutaneous injection, which means injecting them just under the skin. Another common route of drug administration is by intramuscular injection, when the drug is given deep into a muscle mass, usually in the neck or rump. If the drug is in a form in which it may be used intravenously, it will usually be rapidly absorbed after its intramuscular or subcutaneous injection, and absorption is usually, though not always, complete.

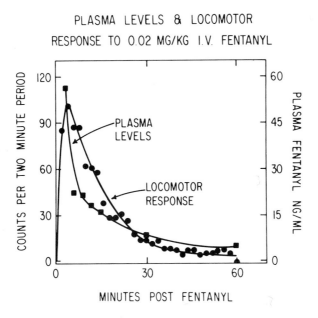

PLASMA LEVELS & LOCOMOTOR
RESPONSE TO 0.02 MG/KG I.V. FENTANYL

MINUTES POST FENTANYL

Figure 4-5. Blood levels of a drug are not always related to pharmacological effects. After fentanyl is given IV to a horse, plasma levels of the drug fall continuously, as indicated by the squares (■—■). The trotting or locomotor response (circles, ●—●), however, rises rapidly, peaks while the blood levels are falling, and then falls more slowly than the motor response. There is thus at best only an approximate relationship between blood levels and pharmacological activity in this case.

The data of Figure 4-6 shows plasma levels of a hypothetical drug after its intravenous and intramuscular injection. After its intravenous injection, blood levels start high and fall linearly (solid circles), with a half-life of about ninety minutes. If this same drug is given intramuscularly in a form in which it is rapidly absorbed, blood levels climb rapidly, usually peak within an hour, and then decline with about the same half-life as after IV injection of the drug (open circles). If the drug is completely absorbed from its injection site, the areas under the two curves will be about the same and the effects of dosing by either route broadly similar. However, by administering drugs IM one does avoid the very high blood levels that one gets immediately after IV injection of the drug. It is also important to note that if the drug is rapidly absorbed from an intramuscular or subcutaneous injection site, its "clearance" from the body is not delayed by administration by these routes as compared with IV administration.

On the other hand, if the drug is administered in a form that is not rapidly absorbed after IM injection, a completely different pattern of distribution is seen. Under these circumstances the peak blood levels obtained after administration of the drug are very low, but the plasma half-life of the drug may be greatly prolonged (Fig. 4-6). This "new" half-life is, in fact, the half-life of the rate of absorption of the drug from its injection site; the classic example of a drug preparation of this type is procaine penicillin.

A major problem with penicillin in therapeutics has been the speed with which it is eliminated. In a very successful maneuver to prolong blood and urinary levels of penicillin, it has been combined with procaine to give a poorly soluble procaine-penicillin salt. This salt dissolves very slowly in water, taking days for the process to complete, and so absorption of the penicillin from its IM injection site is very slow. Peak blood levels of penicillin are much reduced when this preparation is used, but much longer blood levels of penicillin are obtained (see Chapter 18).

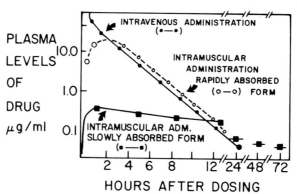

Figure 4-6. Typical plasma levels of a drug after its intravenous or intramuscular administration. The data points show the different rates of absorption and elimination of a hypothetical drug when administered in different ways. If the drug is given intravenously (solid circles, ●—●), plasma levels of the drug start high, drop rapidly, and then drop more slowly. If the drug is given intramuscularly (open circles, o—o), plasma levels climb to close to the IV levels and then fall at about the same rate if the drug is fully and rapidly absorbed from its injection site. If the drug is slowly absorbed from its injection site, another pattern is seen (solid squares, ■—■). In this case, the peak blood levels are much lower than previously, but the blood levels decline much more slowly, with small blood levels of the drug present for days.

Sometimes drugs have been injected subcutaneously under the saddle area for the jockey to squeeze during the race and so aid their absorption.

Because the penicillin is only slowly absorbed from its IM injection site, it trickles into the bloodstream from its "depot" in the muscle. This is very beneficial for all concerned, not least of all the horse. The problem with this approach, however, is that the other half of the salt, procaine, is also being trickled into the bloodstream and, unfortunately, trickled into the urine, too. This, of course, is the major problem with procaine and is the most likely reason why procaine headed the list of positives called since the introduction of procaine penicillin. Slow absorption, then, can delay the elimination of a drug and give rise to long "clearance times" for certain drugs.

If a drug is given orally, as is commonly done, it is likely that the drug will be absorbed slowly and perhaps not completely. For an animal with a complicated intestinal system, such as the horse, the drug will remain in the gastrointestinal tract and continue to be absorbed. As long as the drug is being absorbed, the horse will continue to have blood levels, and blood levels will, in all likelihood, decline much more slowly than after IV injection. The result of this situation is that after a drug is give orally, the blood levels will tend to be lower and more erratic than after its IV injection, and the drug is also likely to take longer to clear in the urine. Giving a drug orally has a number of advantages, principally related to convenience. On the other hand, one can never be sure that the horse has taken all his drug, and some horses can be "picky" eaters. Sometimes this works to the advantage of both the horse and his owner, as for instance with phenylbutazone, where horses who are developing toxicity to this drug will cease to take it orally and thus automatically prevent the toxicity from worsening.

Another mechanism by which drugs were once reputedly administered was by injection in an oily solution subcutaneously. Adrenalin was a favorite drug to be administered in this way, being injected as a subcutaneous "bleb" under the edge of the saddle. This injection would be given some time before the race, and the oily solution of adrenalin would remain in position as a little bleb, without much of the drug being absorbed. Then, as the jockey cantered out to the starting gate, he would lean forward with his knees and give a good massage to the oily drug bleb. The massage would disperse the oil and accelerate the absorption of the adrenalin. Whether or not this unlikely scheme actually worked in practice will remain forever unknown.

Other ways drugs are administered include nerve and joint "blocks." Nerve blocks may be produced by injecting local anesthetics into the area of a nerve, which temporarily blocks the nerve and gives relief for period of hours. On the other hand, one can inject alcohol or other irritant solutions that produce substantial damage to the nerve and which may last for weeks or longer. Nerve blocks of this sort, which are always illegal in racing horses, are usually done to block pain in the extremities. The danger, of course, is that by blocking pain from a weakened limb, the risk of a breakdown on the track and serious injury to horses and riders is increased.

A local anesthetic or a corticosteroid may also be injected directly into a joint. Injection of a local anesthetic into a joint will block pain in that joint for a short period, and like nerve blocks, such blocks are routinely used by veterinarians in the diagnosis of lameness. Despite what one might think, the local anesthetics, which are all highly lipid-soluble drugs, are well absorbed after injection into a joint, and good urinary levels of drugs are obtained, which makes control of this type of maneuver easier than one might think.

When a corticosteroid is injected into a joint, its primary action is to reduce the inflammatory response in the joint; secondarily it will reduce pain in the joint and allow the animal to race sound. Again, the corticosteroids will be absorbed from the joint and appear in the urine, although the effectiveness of detection and control of these small doses of steroids is not clear.

Finally, drugs may simply be applied topically to the skin of the horse, and such drugs are absorbed in varying amounts. In many cases, however, the drugs are applied in DMSO (dimethyl-sulfoxide), a drug that apparently has the ability to greatly increase the absorption of other drugs through the skin. Under these circumstances, detectable blood and urine levels of drugs that were only applied to the skin can occur. Because of this, care should be taken with skin preparations containing DMSO and drugs that are likely to cause problems if detected in the urine after application of such preparations.

The next question one may ask is how do drugs produce their effects in the brain or elsewhere in the body once they get there? The thinking in this area for a very long time has been that drugs produce their pharmacological effects by interacting with specific receptors. The concept of receptors first arose because very minute amounts of potent drugs can produce very dramatic effects. This concept of specific receptors is even further reinforced by the observation that even smaller amounts of specific antagonists can very rapidly and completely reverse the effects of some drugs.

Fentanyl is a good example of a potent drug producing dramatic stimulation in a horse. About 5 mg of fentanyl in a 1,000 lb horse will make the horse trot briskly around his stall within three minutes of administration, with the effect lasting for about thirty minutes. On the other hand, 5 mg of reserpine can depress a horse for up to ten days. Now, 5 milligrams of a drug is a very small amount, being about the amount that would cover this capital O when arranged in a conical pile. Even more remarkable, a more specific narcotic stimulant exists, of which 50 micrograms, or one-hundredth of this amount, can produce equivalent effects. When one further considers that most of these very small amounts of drug distribute to places like the liver, lungs, muscles, and fat, where they have no effect, it becomes apparent that only very small amounts of drug ever get to the sites where they act.

Intuitively, then, one can assume that these very small amounts of drugs do not produce their effects by just floating around in the brain but must act by triggering very precise responses in the brain. Their interaction with their receptors is obviously, therefore, very specific; receptors are defined by the ability of very small amounts of drugs to interact specifically with them and produce characteristic effects called the pharmacological response. By definition, then, a drug receptor is a specific area on a cell with which a drug interacts to trigger its pharmacological effect.

These drug receptors, which scientists are now beginning to isolate, are quite precise in structure, and only specific chemical structures will interact with them to produce the pharmacological effect. Drug receptors may therefore be thought of loosely as a type of lock, in which only a certain key will produce the desired effect (Fig. 4-7). They are usually found only in certain areas of the body, are limited in number, and always have a clearly defined role to play in the body. In most cases the interaction of a drug with a receptor is quite reversible, the drug molecule binding to its receptor for less than a minute, changing the configuration of the receptor, and then moving away, to be replaced by another drug molecule. This rapid turnover of drugs on their receptor sites means that the effects of drugs can be rapidly reversed if one has specific blocking agents to occupy the sites and prevent the active form of the drug from getting to its receptors.

It is characteristic of our thinking about drug receptors that the drug is thought of as inducing a specific change in the shape of the receptor to trigger the response. This concept is presented schematically in Figure 4-7. In it, the drug exists in a specific shape, and when it binds to a receptor the drug induces or stabilizes that shape in the receptor. Once this change in shape is induced in the receptor, the receptor triggers a series of events, which results in the drug response. In the case of apomorphine or morphine, as will be shown later, this response is to make a horse want to run flat out.

There is good experimental evidence for this type of drug-receptor interaction with the many classes of drugs. It has been shown that the narcotic receptor that binds morphine and fentanyl exists in two forms in the horse brain. The normal "relaxed" shape of the receptor is not associated with any of the effects of the narcotic drugs. Therefore, drugs that bind the receptor in this form have no effect of their own but will prevent the actions of injected narcotics and are therefore called narcotic antagonists. On the other hand, if one gives a narcotic drug, it

NARCOTIC DRUGS IN THE HORSE

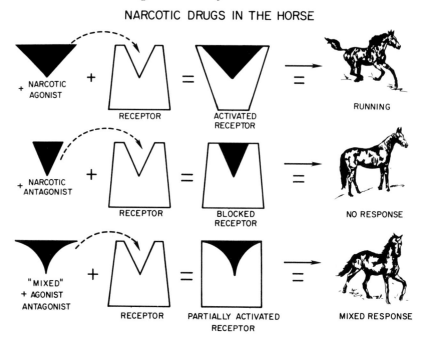

Figure 4-7. Schematic representation of drug-receptor-response interactions in the different classes of narcotic drugs. A narcotic agonist (upper row) binds to the receptor, changes its configuration, and produces the pharmacological response, which is a brisk running. In the center row, an antagonist interacts with the same receptor and produces no change in the receptor or the animal's response. In the lower row, a mixed agonist-antagonist interacts with the receptor and produces an intermediate change in the receptor and a mixed response in the horse.

induces the "active" form of the receptor and one gets all the pharmacological actions of narcotic analgesics. Drugs that produce this "active" form of the receptor are technically called "agonists," after the Greek word meaning "to strain for effect" (Fig. 4-7).

We have now described two principal classes of drugs, the agonists, which activate receptors and responses, and the antagonists, which block them. Obviously, drugs can exist in intermediate forms that are only partially effective in activating receptors, and these drugs are technically called partial agonists. Because of the great potency and potential to produce addiction of narcotic analgesics, many of the narcotics on the market, such as Talwin® (pentazocine) and Stadol® (butorphanol) are actually partial agonists at the narcotic receptor. Similarly, in the horse, these drugs only produce a limited trotting response and likely limited analgesia as well. In fact, the limited analgesic response to drugs of this group is probably the reason for their popularity, since their potential to produce addiction in humans is small and they are therefore not *legally* Class II narcotics and subject to narcotic controls.

As will be detailed later, it turns out to be very easy to measure a trotting response to the narcotic analgesics in the horse. If one gives morphine to a horse he starts trotting immediately, and on a large dose of morphine he will trot for about twelve hours, as shown in Figure 4-8. What, then, happens if you give the proper blocking agent to a horse trotting on morphine? As shown in Figure 4-8, if you give the right dose of a blocking agent, you can stop the action of morphine within minutes. After you have given the blocking drug, the rate at which the horse trots drops from about 100 steps/2 minutes to about 10 steps/2 minutes. If the horse has been given too big a dose of narcotic, has become incoordinated, and has gone down, naloxone can reverse these effects and the horse will stand up and be normal within minutes. This is one of the most dramatic reversals that a pharmacologist can perform, and it depends entirely on drug and antagonist effects on the configuration of receptor molecules in specific areas of the brain.

The receptors with which morphine and fentanyl interact to produce their effects are the same receptors with which the endogenous opiates, the enkephalins, interact to produce their effects. Likewise, almost all the potent drugs produce their effects by interacting with specific receptors, pumps, or other systems that exist in the body to perform a certain function. Apomorphine, for example, produces its effects by interacting with the receptors at which the neurohormone dopamine produces its effects. Some drugs produce their effects on specific pumping systems in the body. Such a drug is Lasix®, which specifically blocks pumps that reabsorb chloride ions in the kidney. Other drugs produce their effects by blocking the actions of enzymes; for example caffeine, which blocks an enzyme called phosphodiesterase. In this case, the receptor for the drug is an enzyme. In any event, whatever the nature of the receptors, one can be sure that the receptors for potent drugs usually have highly specific and important roles to play in the body.

The last characteristic of the action of drugs in the body that must be discussed

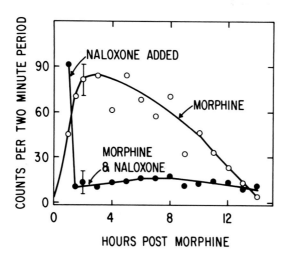

Figure 4-8. Ability of naloxone to reverse morphine-induced trotting activity. The open circles (o—o) show the time course of the twelve hours of trotting induced in four horses by a dose of about 1 gm of morphine. The solid circles (●—●) show the trotting activity induced in another set of four horses, which were treated after one hour with an IV injection of 200 μg/kg of naloxone. The experiment shows rapid and relatively complete reversal of the locomotor response to morphine by naloxone. Reproduced with permission from Combie et al., *Am J Vet Res*, 42:1981.

is what is called the dose-response relationsip. In simple terms, what this describes is how much of a drug one needs to give to produce a measurable threshold, how the effect increases with dose, and what the maximum response is. A theoretical set of dose response curves is shown in Figure 4-9, and a similar family of real curves from racehorses is presented in Chapter 12. The dose-response curve is useful because it immediately allows you to estimate the potency and efficacy (effectiveness) of any drug.

In a dose-response curve, the drug response or effect is plotted on the vertical axis against dose on the horizontal scale. The vertical scale is always arithmetic and may be expressed as a percentage of the maximal response obtainable. The dose of the drug is plotted on the horizontal axis, and always in logarithmic units, as dose-response curves can cover a 100,000-fold range of doses. The dose is always plotted as increasing from left to right, and therefore the more potent a drug, the further to the left it is found. The dose of drug required to produce a 50 percent response is the dose used in comparing potencies, and in Figure 4-9, drug A is 100 times more potent than B. Drugs A and B are both full agonists, since both can produce a full drug response. Drug C, however is a partial agonist, as it can only produce a partial response, and its potency is also about 500 times less than that of A. The action of a potent antagonist is indicated by the solid circles. Since antagonists produce no effects of their own, these effects are demonstrated by the blockade of responses to other drugs, as shown in Figure 4-8.

Another phenomenon sometimes seen in dose-response data is that indicated by the dotted portion of the line for drug A. With some drugs, and particularly with central stimulants, the response increases only up to a point. Beyond this point, if the dose of drug is further increased, the excitation gives way to confu-

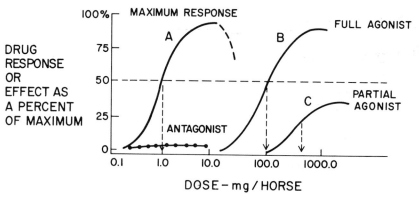

Figure 4-9. Classical dose response curves. In this series of dose response curves, the response to the drug is plotted as a percentage of the maximal response observed on the vertical axis, against the dose of drug on the horizontal axis. On this plot the horizontal axis is the logarithmic scale. Drug A produces a 50 percent response at a 1 mg/horse dose and a maximal response at 10 mg/horse. It is thus a relatively potent full agonist. Drug B requires 100 mg/horse to produce a 50 percent response and about 1000 mg or 1 gm/horse to give a full response. Drug B is therefore a full agonist but is about 100 times less potent than drug A. Drug C cannot produce a full response no matter how big the dose. It is therefore a partial agonist and is also less potent than B. The solid circles indicate the binding of a potent antagonist. An antagonist binds and produces no effect, other than to block receptors. Therefore, its presence is only seen when it is used to block or reverse the effects of drugs such as A, B, or C.

sion and the response begins to fall away. This effect is well known in behavioral work in laboratory animals; it occurs in humans who get jittery after too much coffee, and similar effects in horses are well known to astute horsemen. This falling off in response if the dose is increased too much is indicated by the dotted line in Figure 4-9. This dose-response relationship and its upper limit is of great practical importance for the horsemen and researchers working with stimulant drugs on horses, because it means that there is only a relatively small dose and time response "window" within which useful stimulant effects of drugs will be found.

In summary, then, while drugs may be of plant or animal origin, they must be lipid soluble to get around the body and produce their effects. Once in the body, their blood levels decline at a fairly constant rate for each particular drug. For many drugs there is usually a good relationship between blood levels of the drug and the response that the horse shows, but this is not always necessarily true. Drugs produce their pharmacological effects by interacting with highly specific receptors, and sometimes the interaction of drugs with their receptors can be blocked by specific antagonists. The response that one gets to a drug is always related to the dose given, and if a very small amount (by weight) of a drug produces a good response, the drug is thought of as being "potent." Last, but not least, the potent drugs are the drugs that are important in illegal medication, as the smaller the amount of a drug you put into a horse, the less likelihood there is of anybody ever finding it again.

SELECTED REFERENCES

Baggott, J. Desmond: *Principles of Drug Disposition in Domestic Animals: The Basis of Veterinary Clinical Pharmacology.* Philadelphia, Saunders, 1977.

Brodie, B. B.: Distribution and fate of drugs. Therapeutic implications. In Binns, T. B. (Ed.): *Absorption and Distribution of Drugs.* Baltimore, Williams and Wilkins, 1964.

Combie, J.: *Studies on the Locomotor Responses and Pharmacokinetics of Fentanyl and Other Narcotic Analgesics in the Horse.* M.Sc. Thesis, University of Kentucky, 1979.

Goldstein, A., Aronow, L., and Kalman, S.: *Principles of Drug Action: The Basis of Pharmacology,* 2nd ed. New York, Wiley, 1974.

Goodman, L. S. and Gilman, A.: *The Pharmacological Basis of Therapeutics,* 5th ed. New York, Macmillan, 1975.

Remington's Pharmaceutical Sciences, 15th ed. Easton, PA, Mack Pub., 1975.

Tobin, T.: Pharmacological review: Plasma and urinary drug concentrations, drug "clearance times" and pharmacological effects. *J. Equine Med Surg 2:*262-267, 1978.

Tobin, T., Blake, J. W., Sturma, L., Arnett, S., and Truelove, J.: The pharmacology of procaine in the horse. IV. Pharmacokinetics and behavioral effects. *Amer J Vet Res, 38:*637-647, 1977.

Chapter 5

HOW HORSES ELIMINATE DRUGS, AND THE PROBLEM OF "CLEARANCE TIMES" FOR DRUGS IN HORSES

As POINTED OUT in the previous chapter, a drug must be fat soluble to be absorbed and distribute well in the body, and only drugs that can do this are likely to be pharmacologically active. However, the easier a drug is to absorb, the more difficult it is for the horse to eliminate it, and it has been calculated that the effects of a dose of pentobarbital in man would last for up to 100 years if termination of its action were dependent on excretion of the parent drug alone. Both man and the horse, however, long ago solved this problem, and horses, as hervibores, which are constantly exposed to unusual plant molecules, have very efficient and effective enzymatic systems that convert drugs into forms in which they can be excreted. Since these enzymatic systems are an aspect of the horse's metabolism, they are usually called drug metabolizing systems.

Because it is the characteristic of lipid (fat) solubility that renders drugs difficult to excrete, the basic maneuver in drug metabolism is to modify the drugs in such a way as to render them more water soluble and less lipid soluble. Then, in its newly water soluble form, the drug can be passed out of the body through the kidney or in the bile and will not be reabsorbed. The modification of molecules into more water soluble, less lipid soluble forms is therefore the central theme in drug metabolism.

Although the terms "drug metabolism" or "drug biotransformation" were once considered synonymous with the term "drug detoxification," detoxification is not always what happens. Many drugs exist that are metabolized by the body to more active or toxic forms. Perhaps the best example in equine medicine is the anesthetic chloral hydrate,* which is rapidly metabolized in the liver to its active form, trichlorethanol. The diuretic ethacrynic acid, which was specifically synthesized as a diuretic, produces its diuresis not as ethacrynic acid, but instead only after the horse links it to cysteine as a cysteine "conjugate" or metabolite. Similarly, codeine is thought to produce its pharmacological effects not as codeine, but only after metabolism to morphine, and oxyphenbutazone, an important metabolite of phenylbutazone, shares many of phenylbutazone's pharmacological effects. It is thus apparent that although drug metabolism most commonly means drug inactivation, this is not always the case, and "drug metabolism" will sometimes serve to make drugs more pharmacologically active or toxic.

In most animals in which drug metabolism has been studied, it occurs predominantly in the liver. Some metabolism occurs also in the kidneys, lungs, and intestinal wall. In the horse, which has relatively active blood plasma "esterase"

---

* Chloral hydrate, added to an alcoholic drink, was the classic "Mickey Finn" or knockout drink of Gold Rush days.

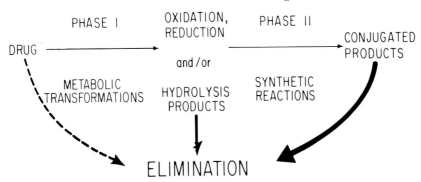

Figure 5-1. Drug biotransformation is the conversion of a drug into a form in which it is more readily eliminated. In phase I, small metabolic transformations are made that either increase the water solubility of the drug per se or else set the drug up for phase II. In phase II, the modified drug is linked with (conjugated) large endogenous water-soluble molecules. These water-soluble conjugates are very readily excreted. Reproduced with permission from Tobin and Woods, *J Equine Med Surg, 3:*150, 1979.

enzymes, substantial metabolism of drugs such as procaine occurs in the blood plasma. Another source of unusual drug metabolites in the horse is the intestinal tract, where microbial degradation of drug molecules probably gives rise to some very unusual drug metabolites.

Drug metabolism has been studied in most detail in the liver, where it is thought of as occurring in two distinct phases (Fig. 5-1). In the first phase the usual effect of the metabolic changes is to attach small groups, such as an OH, NH_2, or COOH

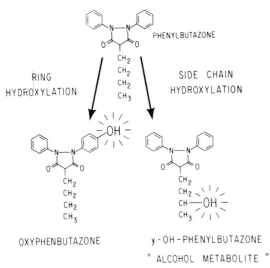

Figure 5-2. Ring and side chain hydroxylation of phenylbutazone. The hydroxylation of phenylbutazone is characteristic of phase I metabolism. Hydroxylation on the ring gives rise to oxyphenbutazone, which has much the same pharmacological activity as phenylbutazone. Hydroxylation on the side chain gives rise to γ-OH phenylbutazone, the so-called "alcohol" metabolite. This metabolite is less active pharmacologically than the parent drug and is more rapidly excreted. It is likely that either of these hydroxylated metabolites may form conjugates. Reproduced with permission from Tobin and Woods, *J Equine Med Surg, 3:*150, 1979.

groups, to the drug molecule (Fig. 5-2). These changes usually serve to increase the water solubility of the molecule, at the same time reducing its lipid solubility, and will usually alter its pharmacological activity. While the pharmacological activity is usually reduced by these changes, it will occasionally be increased as outlined above. Sometimes, too, the toxicity of these metabolites may be much greater for the horse than the toxicity of the original drug. As a general rule, however, the net effect of phase I of drug metabolism is to produce small changes in the drug and to increase the ease with which the drug can be excreted. A further and more important effect of phase I metabolism, however, is that it sets the drug up for phase II.

While the small changes in molecules produced by phase I metabolism do tend to increase the ease with which drugs are excreted, this effect is completed in phase II. In phase II the approach is to link the modified molecule that comes out of phase I to any one of a number of large water-soluble molecules that are found in the body. This process is called "conjugation," and the products of conjugation are almost invariably highly water soluble and, with one known exception, have no pharmacological activity. A common pattern of conjugation is conjugation with glucuronic acid as shown in Figure 5-3. As can be seen, glucuronic acid has a large number of OH groups and also carries an acidic COOH group. All of these groupings confer water solubility on the drug-glucuronide complex, and such drug conjugates are excreted readily in the bile or urine without being reabsorbed to any extent.

By far the simplest pattern of drug metabolism is that found with the local anesthetic procaine, where plasma and liver esterases simply split the drug into two fragments, *p*-aminobenzoic acid (PABA) and diethylaminoethanol (Fig. 5-4). This process occurs quite rapidly in blood, so that at 37°C in equine blood, procaine has a half-life of about eight minutes. In the horse, however, most procaine is distributed outside of the bloodstream, so the actual half-life of procaine in the horse is about fifty minutes — much longer than in the blood. It is important, therefore, to add specific enzyme poisons such as oxalate and fluoride to blood samples if one wishes to find procaine in them, for if this is not done the

DRUG – GLUCURONIDE COMPLEX

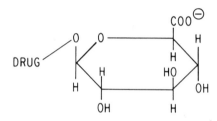

Figure 5-3. In drug conjugation, either the parent drug or its phase I metabolite is linked directly to a large endogenous water-soluble molecule. Conjugation with glucuronic acid is a typical conjugation mechanism. Drug conjugates almost invariably are pharmacologically inactive and are usually rapidly excreted. Reproduced with permission from Tobin and Woods, *J Equine Med Surg, 3:*150, 1979.

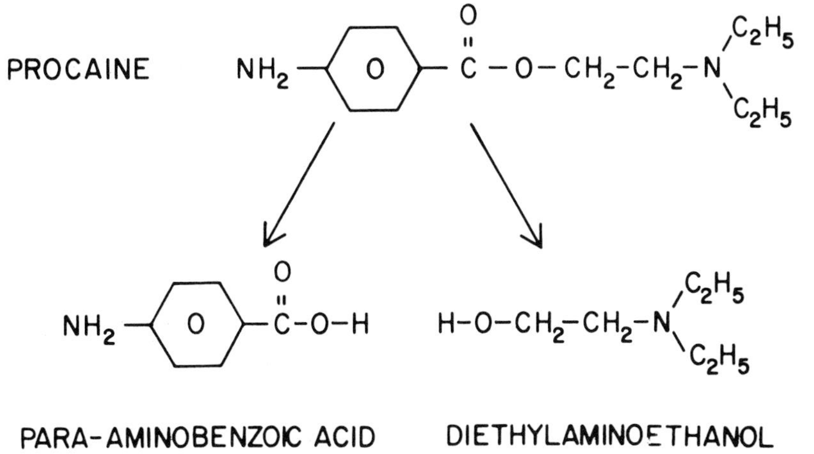

PROCAINE

NH_2 —⟨O⟩— $\overset{\overset{O}{\|}}{C}$ —O— CH_2–CH_2–$N\overset{C_2H_5}{\underset{C_2H_5}{}}$

NH_2 —⟨O⟩— $\overset{\overset{O}{\|}}{C}$ –O–H

H–O–CH_2–CH_2–$N\overset{C_2H_5}{\underset{C_2H_5}{}}$

PARA-AMINOBENZOIC ACID   DIETHYLAMINOETHANOL

Figure 5-4. Hydrolysis of procaine. Procaine is metabolized primarily by splitting the molecule into two fragments, *p*-aminobenzoic acid and diethylamino ethanol. This is one of the simplest and fastest metabolic reactions in the horse.

procaine present will be rapidly hydrolyzed by plasma procaine esterases. The same likely holds true for other drugs that contain ester bonds. A further point of importance is that since procaine is largely hydrolyzed by liver and plasma esterases, and these enzymes are, to a greater or lesser degree, susceptible to inhibition by certain anthelmintics and insecticides, it is possible that the plasma half-life and rate of excretion of procaine in the horse are prolonged by exposure to these drugs. This possibility should be considered by horsemen and racing authorities when estimating "clearance times" for procaine or procaine penicillin in horses.

The metabolism of phenylbutazone in the horse provides good examples of ring and side chain oxidation. The addition of an OH group (hydroxylation) on the ring gives oxyphenbutazone, which shares many of the pharmacological actions of phenylbutazone and is the most persistent of the phenylbutazone metabolites in urine. Hydroxylation on the side chain gives rise to γ-hydroxyphenylbutazone, which is the major metabolite of phenylbutazone found in urine for the first ten hours after dosing. This side chain oxidized molecule is much less tightly bound than phenylbutazone and is excreted in high concentrations in urine during the first twenty-four hours after a dose of phenylbutazone. Together, these two metabolites account for about 25 percent of a dose of phenylbutazone administered to a horse, with the remaining 75 percent of the dose currently being unaccounted for.

A good example of deamination by the horse is provided in the metabolism of amphetamine, where the amine (NH_2) group on the side chain is changed to either an OH group to yield an "alcohol" metabolite, or an oxygen atom to give a "keto" metabolite. Together these two metabolites make up about 40 percent of the known metabolites of amphetamine in the horse (Fig. 5-5).

While these typical phase I metabolic transformations usually increase the water solubility of a drug and accelerate its excretion, the conjugation reactions of

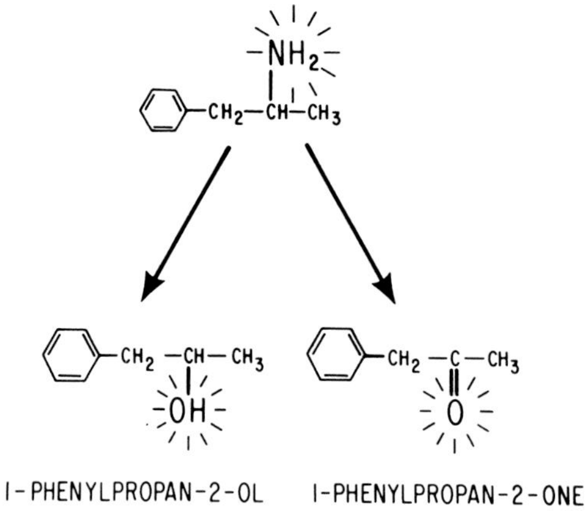

Figure 5-5. Metabolism of amphetamine in the horse. Amphetamine is metabolized principally by deamination, to give rise to two major products, 1-phenylpropan-2-ol and 1-phenylpropan-2-one. Reproduced with permission from Tobin and Woods, *J Equine Med Surg, 3:*150, 1979.

phase II invariably increase the rate of excretion of a compound. In glucuronide formation the parent drug, if it has a suitable acceptor group, or a drug molecule at the end of stage I transformation is linked to glucuronic acid. Glucuronides constitute a major proportion of the metabolites of many phenols, alcohols, and carboxylic-acid-containing drugs in the horse. Further, many drugs, such as morphine, apomorphine, and pentazocine, are likely directly glucuronidated by the horse because of their ring OH groups. Other drugs, such as acepromazine, must first have an OH added on their ring structures in a phase I type of reaction before they can be linked to glucuronic acid.

Inspection of the glucuronic acid molecule as shown in Figure 5-3 shows it to carry a free COOH (carboxyl group) and numerous OH groups. These structures render a drug glucuronide complex highly water soluble and greatly facilitate its excretion. Once a drug-glucuronide complex has entered the renal tubule, it is highly unlikely to be reabsorbed from the renal tubules. Further, by virtue of their free carboxyl group, all glucuronides may be excreted by a special transport system in the renal tubules, which further accelerates their excretion. Glucuronide conjugates may also be excreted by the liver, in the bile, and this can be an important route of excretion if the drug-glucuronide complex has a molecular weight above 300 or so.

The same properties that make drug-glucuronide complexes so easy for the horse to excrete also make it difficult for the chemist to recover glucuronides from plasma and urine. Even though the charge on the acidic carboxyl (COO^-) group can be eliminated by extracting under acidic (i.e. excess H^+) conditions, the numerous OH groups on the glucuronide molecule prevent movement of the drug-glucuronide complex into organic solvents. In experimental work with radioactive drug metabolites, the fraction of radiolabel in urine that the analyst cannot get to move into organic solvents is usually assumed to represent conjugated drug. If a large proportion of a drug is excreted as glucuronide complex, the normal extraction techniques that an analyst uses will not serve to recover sufficient drug-glucuronide complex from plasma or urine for him to detect the drug.

The analyst's approach to this problem is to expose the plasma or urine sample to a glucuronide-splitting enzyme called β-glucuronidase or highly acidic or alkaline conditions. Under these conditions, the drug-glucuronide bond is split and the parent drug or phase I metabolite, which is a slightly modified drug, is recovered. Most analysts carry out this splitting procedure for about two to three hours, which means this test cannot be used in pre-race testing.* At the end of this period the analyst "extracts" the hydrolyzed urine with solvents in the normal way and examines his extracts for drugs. After acidic or enzymatic hydrolysis for about three hours, it is likely that only a fraction of the conjugated drug present is released, and acidic hydrolysis of horse urine is particularly likely to release extraneous material, which does not make the analyst's job any easier.

It turns out that, for reasons that are not clear, glucuronide drug metabolites are often detectable in urine for relatively long periods after drug administration. Thus, the glucuronide metabolite of pentazocine (Talwin®) has been found in horse urine for up to five days, the glucuronide metabolite of apomorphine for up to forty-eight hours, and the glucuronide metabolites of phenothiazine tranquilizers for several days.† Horsemen should be aware of these prolonged excretion times for drug-glucuronide complexes and be careful about the use of drugs detected as glucuronides before competitive events.

Once the drug has been transformed by the horse into a water-soluble form suitable for elimination, the horse then begins the business of excreting the drug. The principal route of drug excretion in the horse is via the urine, and drugs may be considered to enter the urine in three ways (Fig. 5-6). The first, and probably the most important, is glomerular filtration, and all drugs and drug metabolites enter the urine in this way. The second is by being pumped into the urine by specific pumps for organic acids, which pump acidic drugs into the urine, and a pump for organic bases, which pumps basic drugs into the urine. The third method by which drugs enter the urine is by simply diffusing. The difference between the first two methods and diffusing is that diffusing allows drugs to enter and leave the urine, while glomerular filtration and transport just move drugs into the urine.

At the renal glomerulus, where urine is first formed, all drugs and drug metabolites enter the urine by a process of filtration through the glomerulus, which is therefore called glomerular filtration. Once in the newly formed urine in the renal tubule, one of two things may happen to a drug or drug metabolite. If it is poorly lipid soluble, it is now essentially trapped in the urine, and it will inevitably be eliminated with the urine. As the kidney reabsorbs water and essential nutrients from the newly formed urine, these trapped drug and drug metabolite molecules are concentrated, and their final concentration in urine depends only on the degree to which the urine is concentrated.

If the animal is conserving water and the volume of urine is small, the concentrations of these drugs in urine will be very high, theoretically up to 100 times their plasma levels. This is a very important consideration for the analyst, as there are a

---

* Alkaline Hydrolysis, which is rapid, is, however, adaptable to pre-race testing.
† Doctor J. W. Blake, University of Kentucky, Lexington; personal communication.

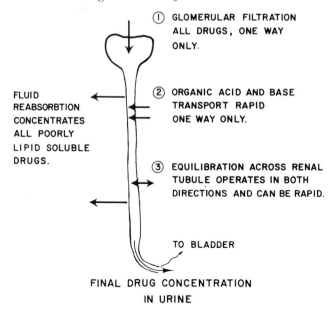

① GLOMERULAR FILTRATION ALL DRUGS, ONE WAY ONLY.

② ORGANIC ACID AND BASE TRANSPORT RAPID ONE WAY ONLY.

FLUID REABSORBTION CONCENTRATES ALL POORLY LIPID SOLUBLE DRUGS.

③ EQUILIBRATION ACROSS RENAL TUBULE OPERATES IN BOTH DIRECTIONS AND CAN BE RAPID.

TO BLADDER

FINAL DRUG CONCENTRATION IN URINE

Figure 5-6. All drugs or drug metabolites free in the plasma enter the urine by filtration through the small pores in the renal glomerules. Drugs that are organic acids, such as penicillin and furosemide, are pumped into the urine by specific transport systems. Any lipid-soluble drug can enter the urine simply by diffusing across cell membranes in the kidney. Once in the urine, all water-soluble drugs are essentially trapped and are concentrated as the kidney concentrates the urine. Lipid-soluble drugs may diffuse back and forth, and their final concentration in urine depends primarily on the pH of the urine and the nature of the drug. Reproduced with permission from Tobin, *J Equine Med Surg, 2*:262, 1978.

number of drugs that cannot currently be detected in plasma and which are only detectable in urine as their water-soluble, highly concentrated metabolites. The best example of a drug such as this is apomorphine. Apomorphine is difficult to detect in equine plasma with current analytical techniques. In urine, however, it is excreted as a water-soluble glucuronide metabolite, which is greatly concentrated in urine. This renal concentrating effect is very important in that it enables most analysts to detect apomorphine in equine urine.

Other drugs that are excreted in this way and concentrated in urine are metabolites of narcotic drugs such as morphine and pentazocine and the phenothiazine tranquilizers. The concentration of all of these drugs in urine is very important for the analyst in that it enables him to detect these drugs in urine. On the other hand, any drug or maneuver that increases the volume of urine (such as a diuretic) will act to dilute the concentration of these drugs in urine, and several examples of this have been reported and will be presented in detail in the chapter on bleeder medication and Lasix® (see Chapter 7).

The second major mechanism by which drugs enter urine is the organic acid and organic base transport system. These are relatively nonspecific pumps, which actually secrete certain drugs into the urine. By far the best known drug that is secreted in this way is penicillin. Penicillin (an organic acid) is very rapidly secreted into the renal tubules and is found in very high concentrations in urine. In fact, in the early days of penicillin therapy, when the drug was extremely valuable, it was sometimes recrystallized from human urine for reuse! Though this is no longer done, penicillin is still excreted largely unchanged in high concentrations in urine. Another drug of particular interest to equine veterinarians that is secreted into urine is furosemide. Sixty percent of a dose of furosemide is excreted unchanged into equine urine, and it is found there in concentrations up to 1,000 times those observed in plasma. It is also found in urine for up to three days after it has been administered to the horse and for long after its pharmacological effects have dissipated.

The third way in which drugs can enter urine is simply by diffusing through the walls of the renal tubules. To do this, the drug must be relatively lipid soluble. If this is the case the drug can easily move from the kidneys into urine, and also just as easily from urine back into the kidney. For such lipid-soluble drugs, the final concentrations of the drug in the urine appear to be primarily dependent on the acidity (pH) of the urine and whether or not the drug is acidic or basic. For these reasons, urinary concentrations of lipid-soluble drugs may vary substantially, depending on the pH of the urine, and are apparently not readily affected by changes in urine volume.

The concentration of any drug in equine urine, therefore, can depend to a large extent on urine volume and pH. Since these factors are varied by the horse, depending on its hydration and acid-base balance, *urinary concentrations of a drug are much more likely to be variable than plasma concentrations of a drug, which will tend to be relatively stable or predictable.* This is only reasonable, as it is by varying urine volume, acidity, and ion content that the horse maintains his own internal environment within the narrow limits that are necessary if he is to function properly. Therefore, the first problem with urinary concentrations of drugs is that they are likely to be much more variable than plasma levels.

Just how variable urinary levels of drugs can be is shown by some data and experiments with the drug procaine. Procaine is a basic drug, that is, a drug that will pick up a positive charge under acidic conditions. It will thus tend to concentrate in acidic urines and be reabsorbed by the horse from basic urines. The question then is, by how much does urinary pH vary in the horse, and how do these variations affect urinary procaine concentrations?

Urinary pH or acidity in the horse shows close to a millionfold range between the lowest (most acidic) and highest (most basic) urinary pH values observed. Examination of the pH of urine samples from racehorses in Japan and England has shown a range of urinary pH values from pH 4.5, which is relatively acidic, to pH 10.0, which is quite basic (Fig. 5-7). In each case, the curve of urinary pH values showed two peaks, with the largest number of urines having a pH on the acidic side at about 5.0, but another group on the basic side showed that a large proportion of the urines had a basic pH of about 8.0.

Because urinary pH is measured on a log scale, the range extends from 10^{-4} M hydrogen ions (pH 4.0, acidic) to 10^{-10} M hydrogen ions (pH 10.0, alkaline). Based on this range of possible urinary pH values and assuming a certain plasma level of drug such as procaine, one can calculate the possible range of procaine concentrations in equine urine using a well-known equation.* It turns out that because of the

---

* See Appendix B for the details of this calculation.

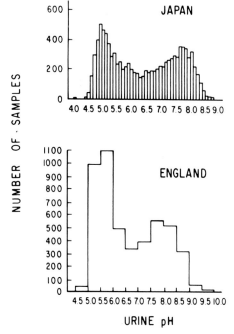

Figure 5-7. These figures show frequency distribution curves for the pH values of racehorse urines received at the National Testing Laboratories in England and Japan. The data show that a small number of racehorses have urines with a pH of 4.0, but that a large number of horses have post-race urines in the order of pH 5.0 or so. A smaller number of horses yield a neutral urine, while a substantial number of horses yield basic urines. Because the pH scale is logarithmic, there is a 100,000-fold difference in the hydrogen ion content (pH) of urines at each end of these curves. These very large acidity (pH) differences can result in massive differences in drug concentrations in urine, depending on urine pH. Reproduced with permission from Tobin and Woods, *J Equine Med Surg, 3:*150, 1979.

urinary pH factor there is a rather mind-boggling *9,000-fold possible range in urinary procaine concentrations, given a single, fixed plasma level of the drug.* This huge range of possible drug concentration in urine leads me to the conclusion that anyone who tries to estimate a precise time of drug administration from a urinary drug concentration is at the very least guessing against tremendous odds.

These theoretical predictions concerning procaine concentrations in horse urine were tested by Evans and Lambert, who showed that the laws of chemistry extend to racehorse urines. Evans and Lambert dosed horses with procaine or procaine penicillin and followed urinary concentrations of procaine. They then treated their horses with ammonium chloride to change their urine pH to an acidic pH and followed the changes in urinary pH and urinary levels of procaine. They found that a decrease in urinary pH was associated with an increase of about tenfold in urinary procaine concentrations (Fig. 5-8). Further, one must remember that these pH-induced increases in urinary procaine concentrations were occurring in the face of rapidly declining urinary levels of procaine. It appears, therefore, that this mechanism of highly pH-dependent urinary levels of the drug also operates in the horse *in vivo*, and there is certainly absolutely no reason that I am aware of to believe that it does not.

Although the actual concentrations of procaine in horse urine may vary markedly, it does not appear likely that changes in urinary pH affect the plasma half-life of procaine. This is because procaine is very widely distributed in the horse and its plasma levels are reduced primarily by drug metabolism. As far as the kinetics of procaine are concerned, one might view the horse as a very large compartment in which procaine is hydrolyzed by enzymes, in equilibrium with a very small pool, the bladder, in which the concentration of procaine is highly pH dependent. Because so little (less than 1%) of a dose of procaine ever appears in the urine, relatively large variations in urinary concentrations of the drug can occur without any significant changes in the plasma half-life of the drug. This, however, is largely hypothetical and should ideally be checked by some rigorous calculations or, more satisfactorily, by experimentation.

Despite this clear evidence for massive variability in urinary levels of procaine in horses, I have heard people testify that urinary procaine concentrations did not vary more than ±25 percent between horses and have heard others testify that they could identify the time and form (i.e. procaine or procaine penicillin) of drug administration based on a single urinary level of procaine. Whatever factual evidence may exist to support these statements remains unknown to me, and they fly in the face of published information on the physical and pharmacological characteristics of procaine in the horse.

Although these pH-dependent changes in urinary concentrations of drugs can be quite large, they do not appear to affect the plasma half-life of drugs. For example, Moss and Haywood administered radioactive phenylbutazone to horses and followed the excretion of radioactivity. Since phenylbutazone is almost completely metabolized in the horse, most of the radioactivity that they found in the urine must have been phenylbutazone metabolites. They found that excretion of these metabolites was slower into an acidic urine, which is consistent with the fact that an acidic drug is better reabsorbed from an acidic urine. However, work by Piperno and coworkers in Michigan has shown that urinary pH has no effect on the rates at which plasma levels of the drug decline. As with procaine, metabolism is the primary factor that determines the plasma half-life of a drug, and although the concentration of the drug or drug metabolites in urine may vary, the amounts of parent drug lost by this route are apparently not large enough to influence the plasma half-life of the drug.

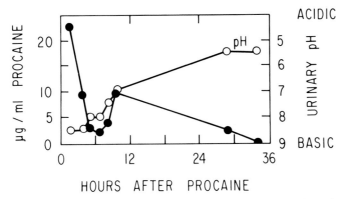

Figure 5-8. Effect of urinary pH on urine procaine concentrations. Evans and Lambert dosed a horse with 4.5 million units of procaine penicillin and followed urinary concentrations of the drug. During this experiment the horse was administered ammonium chloride to change his urinary pH from about 8.5 at the beginning of the experiment to about 5.5 at the end (open circles). The experiment shows that decreasing urinary pH was associated with increasing urinary concentration of procaine. Reproduced with permission from Tobin and Woods, *J Equine Med Surg*, 3:150, 1979.

Experiments by Baggot and his colleagues have shown similar results with amphetamine, where changing the pH of horse's urine did not affect the plasma half-life of the drug but may affect its urinary levels. The message at this point appears to be that, as a general rule, the rates of decline of plasma levels and drug action in the horse are determined by drug metabolism, and while urinary drug concentrations may change, dependent on urine volume or pH, they probably have little affect on the rate of decline of plasma levels of drugs.

The presence of other drugs has been considered as a factor that might affect the metabolism of drugs in horses. The antibiotic Chloromycetin® (chloramphenicol) and oxyphenbutazone have been shown to be potent inhibitors of drug metabolism in other species, and we thought that they might also inhibit the metabolism of other drugs in the horse. This could be very important in a racing situation, where administration of drugs that inhibit drug metabolism might give rise to prolonged urinary levels of other drugs. However, of three likely drug inhibitors tested, none inhibited the metabolism of phenylbutazone to any significant extent, so with perhaps a few exceptions, inhibition of drug metabolism in the liver by other drugs does not seem likely to be a problem in racing horses.

Another factor that might change the rate of metabolism of drugs in the horse is a decrease in blood flow to the liver, which would reduce the rate of delivery of drugs to the drug-metabolizing enzymes. Studies in man have shown that exercise can lead to reduced liver blood flow, and it seemed likely that similar effects occur in the horse. This possibility led Snow and his coworkers to study the effects of exercise in the horse on plasma levels of propanolol, a drug that is primarily cleared by hepatic metabolism. Powis and Snow found rather large increases in plasma levels of propanolol occurring with exercise, and the changes observed were too great to be accounted for by reduced drug metabolism. These workers further found that approximately similar changes were produced by adrenaline, at doses of adrenaline that produced an increase rather than a decrease in hepatic blood flow. Snow was unable to explain the marked alteration in plasma levels of propanolol seen in his experiments. As a practical matter, however, the plasma levels and half-life of propanolol returned to control rapidly after exercise. Because of the very brief period of exercise in which most racing horses are involved, there is no evidence that exercise is likely to affect drug metabolism in a way that would significantly affect pre- or post-race drug testing.

Another problem with using urinary levels of drugs for drug testing is the fact that urinary levels of drugs are often very much higher than plasma levels of drugs. While these high urinary concentrations of drugs are usually not a problem at first, they become so with time, because urinary concentrations of the drugs or their metabolites can be maintained long after the drug has "disappeared" from plasma. Thus, furosemide can be found in urine at 1,000-fold higher concentrations than it is found in plasma, and it can be found there for three days without too much difficulty.

The pharmacological effects of furosemide, however, are notoriously brief and only last between two and four hours. Similarly, the major metabolite of pentazocine is found in equine urine for up to five days after the drug is administered, though it appears highly unlikely that pentazocine's therapeutic effects last for more than four hours. Procaine is always found in equine urine long after its pharmacological effect has dissipated, no matter by what route it is given. These drugs are all legitimate therapeutic agents, but they can give rise to "positives" for many days after their therapeutic effects have dissipated. There is no evidence, therefore, for any correlation between urinary levels of drugs and their metabolites or urinary "clearance times" and the duration of the therapeutic effects of most drugs. This is, from everyone's point of view, the major problem with urine testing for drugs.

The last and most important subject to discuss is "clearance times." A "clearance time" is the period following drug administration that must be allowed to elapse until a drug is no longer detectable in equine urine. The impression exists that this period is in some way related to the metabolism of the drug in the horse and the rate at which horses eliminate a drug. This impression, however, is absolutely incorrect. If any one thing is true for all drugs given to the horse, it is that the concentrations of any drug (or its metabolites) in plasma or urine simply get lower, and lower, and lower, until the drug is "cleared." The analyst's "clearance time," however, does not depend on the drug or its rate of metabolism; it depends on the time elapsed until the analyst can no longer detect it, and on nothing else. For those drugs that analysts cannot detect, the "clearance time" is zero; for all other drugs, the effective "clearance time" is when the analyst loses track of it. If the analyst's methods improve, the "clearance time" extends. Good analysts give rise to long "clearance times." Poor analysts result in "clearance times" approaching zero and an unusual number of drugs for which the "clearance time" is zero.

I am often asked to suggest "clearance times" for drugs in horses, but the only drugs for which a "clearance time" can be cited with confidence are those that the analyst cannot detect, for which the "clearance time" is zero. For any drug that the analyst can or should be able to detect, one can only offer guesses, no matter how much one knows about the drug in the horse. The reason for this is that one never knows how good the analyst is. At least part of the reason for this is that the analyst himself may not know how good he is. He is usually concerned only with detecting the drug and can only guess at the lower limit of sensitivity of his methods for any particular drug. Because of this situation, none of the research on drugs in horses now coming out of research laboratories can be applied to the very practical problem of "clearance times."

To demonstrate the overriding importance of the analyst's methods in determining drug "clearance times," let us inspect Figure 5-9, which shows some data on the clearance of furosemide from equine urines taken from work in our laboratory. After 1 mg/kg of furosemide (IM), urinary concentrations of furosemide peaked at about 28 μg/ml, six hours after dosing, by which time the pharmacological effects of the drug were over. Thereafter, the urinary concentrations of furosemide fell, with a half-life of about 5.3 hours, and were followed in this experiment for three days. In this situation, if the analyst was only able to detect 5 μg/ml, the "clearance time" would be about eighteen hours, i.e. twelve hours after the drug had any pharmacological effect. If the analyst could detect 0.5 μg/ml, the "clearance time" would be thirty-six hours. This is about the sensitivity of the routine analytical procedure used in Kentucky, and it appears to

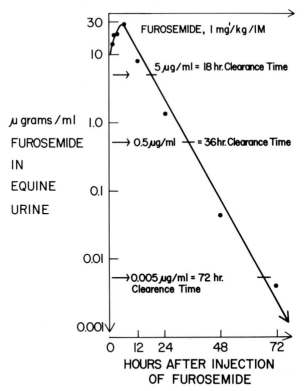

Figure 5-9. Clearance times for furosemide in equine urine. The solid circles (●—●) show urinary concentrations of furosemide after 1 mg/kg was administered IM to four horses. If the detection method of the analyst is good down to about 5 µg/ml, furosemide will have an eighteen-hour clearance time under those circumstances. Another analyst with a tenfold better method will report thirty-six-hour clearance times for furosemide, while an analyst using the method used in these experiments will report a seventy-two-hour clearance time. An analyst with even more sensitive methods will report still longer clearance times. The data show that "clearance times" are dependent on the sensitivity of the analytical method used and may vary between analysts, depending on the methods that they use. Reproduced with permission from Tobin, *J Equine Med Surg*, 2:262, 1978.

be more than adequate for routine work. However, an analyst who wanted to use the methods from these experiments would have increased the "clearance time" to seventy-two hours. If a highly sensitive radioimmunoassay was used, such as is sometimes used for steroids, the "clearance time" could go up to 100 hours. Obviously, all other things being equal, the most important determinant of "clearance times" is the analyst's methods.

Analysts often argue that because of the inherent differences between horses due to sex, age, build, urinary pH, size of dose et cetera, "clearance times" are likely to be so variable that mean "clearance times" such as those presented in Figure 5-9 are not likely to be applicable in specific instances. This argument ignores both the fact that the veterinarian adjusts his dose to take these factors into account and that in any event, changes in dose have only a miniscule effect on "clearance times." While it is true that urinary volume and pH can produce very real effects on drug concentrations in urine, these effects will, in general, be small compared with the 10,000-fold range in drug concentrations demonstrated in Figure 5-9. Route or form of dosage can also be important, but these factors can be specified. Under most circumstances, the effect of increasing or decreasing dose on the urinary "clearance times" of drugs is marginal, as shown in Figure 5-10. The sensitivity of the analyst's methodology is thus the primary and most important factor in determining drug "clearance times." As pointed out earlier, until analysts make known the sensitivity of their tests for legitimate therapeutic agents, none of the research now being done on these agents can be applied to the very practical problem of drug "clearance times." Until then, drug "clearance times" will continue to be handled on a trial and error basis, with veterinarians, trainers, and owners making the errors and going to trial.

As analytical methods improve, medication rules, as currently formulated, will become even more troublesome. To draw a parallel from everyday life, the veterinarian who treats an animal pre-race with a drug is in the position of a man driving into a very strange state. In this state, none of the speed limits are posted because nobody knows what they are (i.e. no one knows how good the analyst's methods are). The speed limits may also be changed without notice (the analyst may change his methods). Further, these unknown and variable speed limits bear no relationship whatsoever to the highway conditions (the "clearance time" is in no way related to the pharmacology of the drug, only to whatever the methods the analyst happens to use). No court that has any pretensions to being a court of justice could enforce speeding tickets issued under these circumstances. Yet, this is the situation in which veterinarians and trainers find themselves daily and will

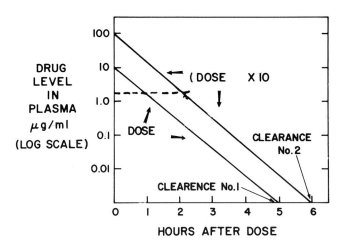

Figure 5-10. Clearance times can be almost independent of dose. This illustration compares the hypothetical clearance times of a dose of drug "X" and a tenfold greater dose of drug "X." Dose "X" when administered yields a peak plasma level of 1.0 μg/ml and clears the plasma by five hours. Administering ten times the dose, however, only increases the clearance time by one hour, or 20 percent. The dose must thus be increased by a factor of 10 to produce relatively small changes in clearance times. This holds if the analytical method for the drug is good and can detect the drug for long periods. If, however, the analytical method can only barely detect the drug (dotted line), then the effect of increasing the dose may be significant. Reproduced with permission from Tobin, *J Equine Med Surg*, 2:262, 1978.

A veterinarian who treats a horse pre-race is like a man driving in a state with unknown but changeable speed limits.

continue to do so until they can encourage the racing community to decide on drug levels that may be considered irrelevant.

SELECTED REFERENCES

Baggott, J. B.: *Principles of Drug Disposition in Domestic Animals: The Basis of Veterinary Clinical Pharmacology.* Philadelphia, Saunders, 1977.

Evans, J. A. and Lambert, M. B. T.: Estimation of procaine in urine of horses. *Vet Rec,* October 5, *95:*316-318, 1974.

La Du, B. N., Mandel, H. G., and Way, E. L.: *Fundamentals of Drug Metabolism and Drug Disposition.* Baltimore, Williams & Wilkins, 1971.

Moss, M. S.: The metabolism and urinary and salivary excretion of drugs in the horse and their relevance to the detection of dope. In *Drug Metabolism — From Microbe to Man.* D. V. Parke and R. H. Smith, Eds. London, Taylor and Francis, 1976.

Moss, M. S. and Haywood, P. E.: Persistence of phenylbutazone in horses producing acid urines. *Vet Rec, 93:*124-125, 1973.

Nakajima, R. and Matsumoto, T.: Doping control in Japan: An automated extraction procedure for the doping test. *Br J Sports Med, 10:*163-169, 1976.

Piperno, E., Ellis, D. J., Getty, S. M., and Brody, T. M.: Plasma and urine levels of phenylbutazone in the horse. *J Am Vet Med Assoc, 153:*195-202, 1968.

Powis, G. and Snow, D. H.: The effects of exercise and adrenaline infusion upon the blood levels of propanolol and antipyrine in the horse. *J Pharmacol Exp Ther, 205:*725-731, 1978.

Tobin, T., Blake, J. W., Tai, C. Y., and Arnett, S.: The pharmacology of procaine in the horse. III. The procaine esterase activity of equine plasma and synovial fluid. *Am J Vet Res, 37:*1165-1170, 1976.

Tobin, T., Blake, J. W., and Valentine, R.: Drug interactions in the horse. I. Effects of chloramphenicol, quinidine, and oxyphenbutazone on phenylbutazone metabolism. *Am J Vet Res, 38:*123-127, 1977.

Tobin, T. and Woods, W. E.: Pharmacology review: Drug metabolism and elimination in horses. *J Equine Med Surg, 3:*150-156, 1979.

Section II

THE DRUGS OF CONTROLLED MEDICATION

THE DRUGS COVERED in this section include phenylbutazone, furosemide (Lasix®), the corticosteroids, and the anabolic steroids. These are the drugs that many racing commissions in the 1960s and 1970s chose to allow to be used in performance horses under controlled conditions. All of these drugs are extremely valuable therapeutic agents in performance horses when correctly used. Under the proper circumstances, they have the ability to enable a horse to perform both more consistently and closer to something that is referred to in racing circles as his "innate ability." On the other hand, however, they all carry with them problems, some real and many imagined.

The drugs dealt with in this section have been suggested by some to be of very great economic importance in racing. For example, proponents of the use of agents such as phenylbutazone suggest that if their use was restricted the number of horses fielded would be markedly reduced. On the other hand, opponents of the use of these drugs maintain that horses that need phenylbutazone to run should not be running under any circumstances, and to run horses on these drugs is inhumane.

Furosemide (Lasix®) is another medication that is considered to help horses with a specific medical problem, bleeding in the respiratory tract, and with other respiratory or "wind" problems. Again, horsemen feel that furosemide helps them to keep their horses running, while the opponents of drug use maintain that horses running on furosemide are pulmonary cripples and should be retired. Usage control for both phenylbutazone and Lasix® is relatively easy, since good analytical methods are available for these agents.

The corticosteroids and anabolic steroids are drugs of controlled medication to some extent by default. Good analytical methods for these drugs are not available in North America, so control is difficult. Because of these technical difficulties, therefore, and because these drugs clearly do not fall into the forbidden "stimulant, depressant, local anesthetic, and tranquilizer groups," use of agents from both of these groups is commonly permitted in North American racing.

As we discuss these individual drugs, we will outline their pharmacology and their therapeutic actions in the horse. We will also outline the other side of the coin with these drugs, which is the adverse effects associated with their use. As we discuss the adverse responses to these drugs, the reader should keep clearly in mind that the bulk of the information that we have on adverse responses to drugs in horses is qualitative. While the therapeutic effects of these drugs are well characterized and occur in essentially all horses, the adverse responses are much less common and only occur in occasional horses. Further, the adverse responses

83

presented in this text are the end points of severe overuse and are extreme examples rather than common occurrences.

It is important for the reader to keep this balance in mind while reading the text and not get carried away with the fear of adverse reactions. When correctly used, all the drugs of this group are therapeutically very useful in the horse, and the adverse responses are minimal. This point, of course, is unfortunately missed by many purists who present the supposed toxicity of many relatively innocuous drugs as gounds for their prohibition in racing horses.

Chapter 6

PHENYLBUTAZONE AND ITS BROTHERS: THE NON-STEROIDAL ANTI-INFLAMMATORY DRUGS

THE AVERAGE RACEHORSE starts about nine times a year and is breezed and galloped "flat out" countless more times than this. At full speed the average race horse hits speeds of over 35 miles per hour and places forces on the order of 2,000 foot-pounds, or about twice his body weight, on his lead foreleg with every stride. The forelegs of a racehorse are remarkably economical structures to carry such massive loads on the straightaway, and on turns the areas over which such loads are distributed are further reduced, thereby increasing the load/unit area and the likelihood of damage.

Further, some researchers have shown that bones have a honeycomblike microstructure and that the shocks of an extended gallop are absorbed by a microcrushing of this structure. Then, at the end of a stressful bout of exercise the bone remodels, regenerates, and extra bone grows in the areas of greatest stress and micro-crushing. As the animal matures and the bone stiffens, more of the micro-crush load is carried by the cartilage, and if the injury is repeated, long term damage to the articular cartilages and surrounding surfaces is suffered.

Another event that occurs inescapably during exercise is that the bone becomes weakened as the micro-crushing process progresses. To break a normal cannon bone at the start of a race it takes about 16,000 foot-pounds of force, but the amount of micro-crushing that can take place in a race can reduce this force to about 9,000 pounds. The final result of this is that the stress of a fast race causes substantial changes in bones, joints, and ligaments in all horses, and it is not surprising that the horse, like any other athlete, is likely to turn up with tissue damage post-race. If the racing process is repeated, if the racing process has taken place on unusually hard surfaces, if the banking of the surface at the turns is less than optimal, or if the conformation of the horse makes it susceptible to particular types of trauma, then there is a substantial probability that the damage to the horse will increase to the point that the animal will come up lame. The lameness will be due to the pain and inflammation associated with the specific injury from which the animal suffers, and one of the time-honored approaches to this problem is to treat the animal with anti-inflammatory drugs.

The classic signs of inflammation were described by the Greeks: heat, redness, swelling, pain, and loss of function, all of which are quite familiar to anyone who has suffered anything as simple as a common sprain. The anti-inflammatory drugs used in equine medicine in the direct treatment of this problem fall into two principal groups, the corticosteroids, which we will be dealing with in the next chapter, and all the others. This other group of drugs is known collectively and rather logically as the non-steroidal anti-inflammatory drugs (NSAIDs).

The original member of the non-steroidal anti-inflammatory group of drugs is

85

aspirin. The second oldest member of this group is phenylbutazone, which was introduced into human medicine around the time of World War II and shortly thereafter into veterinary medicine. Phenylbutazone was widely used in human medicine for a number of years, but it soon became apparent that its use was associated with a small incidence of specific and serious toxicities. Because phenylbutazone has caused deaths in people from aplastic anemia and agranulocytosis, its use in human patients is now restricted. With the realization of the therapeutic limitations of the corticosteroid derivatives and phenylbutazone, and the huge market for a good anti-inflammatory drug, drug companies have researched the non-steroidal anti-inflammatory field thoroughly in the last ten years or so. As a result, a large number of new non-steroidal anti-inflammatory drugs have been developed and recently become available in both human and equine medicine. A partial list of these agents is presented in Table 6-I.

The non-steroidal anti-inflammatory drugs all share a number of properties that seem to be required for their anti-inflammatory action (Fig. 6-1). All are acidic drugs, with a pKa of 4.5 or less. The acidic nature of these drugs means that they are all between 95 and 99 percent bound to plasma proteins. This plasma protein binding is important because it means that drugs of this group do not pass into saliva, and saliva testing is essentially useless for detection of this important group of drugs. Their acidic nature also seems to be important for their action and has led to suggestions that their acidity enables them to accumulate in inflamed tissues, which also tend to be acidic. This accumulation would then allow them to have more effect in inflamed areas than in normal tissue. However, these

TABLE 6-I

SOME NON-STEROIDAL ANTI-INFLAMMATORY DRUGS*

Generic Name	Popular or Trade Name
Phenylbutazone	Butazolidin
Oxyphenbutazone	Tandearil
Salicylates	Aspirin
Thiosalicylate	
Quinine	
Naproxen	Equiproxen
Meclofenamic Acid	Arquel
Indomethacin	Indocin
Ibroprofen	Motrin
Aminopyrine	
Flunixin	Banamine
Niflumic Acid	Nifluril
Flufenamic Acid	
Fenamic Acid	
Mefenamic Acid	Ponstel
Sulindac	Clinoril
Tolmetin	Tolectin
Fenoprofen Calcium	Nalfon
Ketoprofen	Orudis

* These drugs are all classified as non-steroidal anti-inflammatory drugs. They all appear to share the same basic mechanism of action as phenylbutazone and also the same general pattern of toxicity. Some, such as quinine and aspirin, are centuries old, but the clinical use of most is relatively recent.

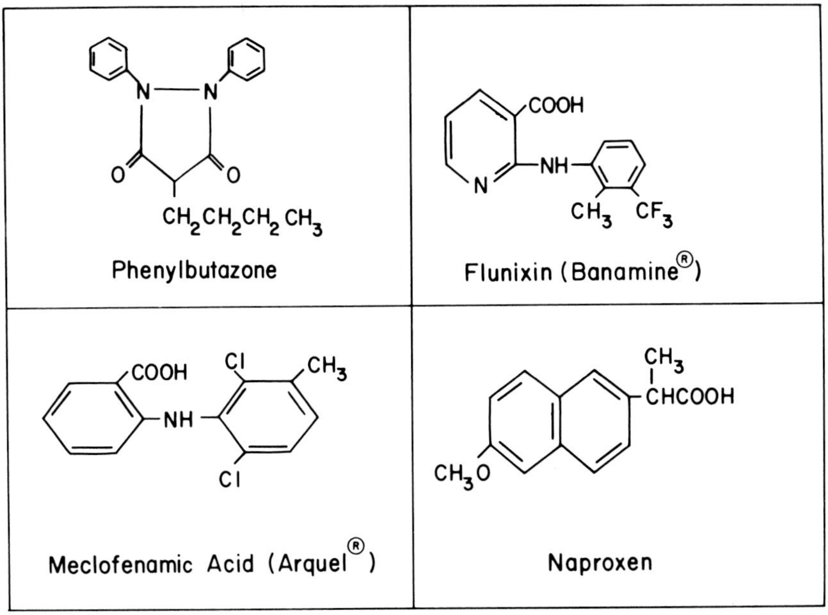

Phenylbutazone

Flunixin (Banamine®)

Meclofenamic Acid (Arquel®)

Naproxen

Figure 6-1. Non-steroidal anti-inflammatory drugs (1) are highly acidic drugs, (2) are highly protein bound in plasma, (3) are difficult to detect in saliva, (4) act by inhibiting prostaglandin synthesis, (5) are likely to be diluted in urine by furosemide.

agents also tend to accumulate in the stomach, small intestine, and kidney, and we will see later that the toxicities produced by these agents are usually associated with these tissues (Fig. 6-2). Also, because prostaglandins are involved in the generation of fever, all these drugs are antifever, or antipyretic, agents (Fig. 6-2).

Among the non-steroidal anti-inflammatory agents, phenylbutazone remains the most popular and most widely used in equine medicine. After its introduction into equine medicine, phenylbutazone established itself as a very effective anti-inflammatory agent. It soon made its appearance on the racetrack, and pressure from horsemen for permission to use it during racing increased. In late 1959, Colorado approved phenylbutazone for use in racing, and the era of controlled medication was born.*

Phenylbutazone and the other non-steroidal anti-inflammatory drugs produce their anti-inflammatory effects by inhibiting the production of chemicals called prostaglandins. Prostaglandins are produced in large amounts in inflamed tissues and are involved in the blood vessel and tissue changes that cause the reddening, heat, swelling, pain, and loss of function that we associate with inflammation. They also have another peculiar action, in that they act to supersensitize pain receptors in the inflamed area to agents that cause pain. Anyone who has had anything as simple as a good sunburn is familiar with the great increase in sensitivity to even the lightest touch that occurs in sunburned tissue. Thus hypersensitivity to pain is a typical effect of certain prostaglandins. In fact, if

---

* G. H. Bierhaus, Colorado Racing Commission veterinarian; personal communication, 1979.

Non-steroidal anti-inflammatory drugs —

(1) inhibit enzymes that form prostaglandins and therefore slowly reduce tissue prostaglandins

(2) Reduce pain hypersensitivity in inflamed tissues by reducing tissue prostaglandin levels

(3) Reduce fever (are antipyretic)

(4) Accumulate in stomach, kidney, and small intestine and tend to produce lesions in these tissues.

Figure 6-2

minute amounts of prostaglandins are injected into a normal joint, that joint soon becomes excruciatingly painful to move. This sensitizing action of the prostaglandins is represented schematically in Figure 6-3. It is clear from this mechanism of action that if the concentration of prostaglandins in inflamed tissues can be reduced, the signs of inflammation, swelling, and particularly the perception of pain in that area will also be reduced. It is important to remember, however, that this is a reduction in a hypersensitivity to pain, and that normal pain perception will be left in the area.

When phenylbutazone is injected intravenously, it takes about thirty minutes to distribute throughout the horse and begin to block formation of the prostaglandins. There are, however, unusually large amounts of prostaglandins already present in an inflamed tissue. Therefore, even though the formation of new prostaglandins is blocked, phenylbutazone will not appear to take effect until these high prostaglandin levels have been reduced. This process usually takes about three to four hours, and once the excess prostaglandin has dissipated, the supersensitivity to pain reduces and the swelling and heat in the area begin to decline. Loss of these signs of inflammation will require a further period of time, so it can take up to twelve hours or more for the full pharmacological action of phenylbutazone to become apparent.

Since most of the non-steroidal anti-inflammatory agents produce their effects in more or less the same way, they take a period of at least several hours to begin to produce effects, even when they are given by intravenous injection. On the other hand, when blood levels of these drugs decline, the concentration of the prostaglandins in the inflamed tissues build back up again, and the pain and other signs of inflammation begin to return. It is then time for another dose of phenylbutazone. It is clear from this mechanism of action that the therapeutic effects of phenylbutazone are directly related to its effects to reduce inflammation, and that any analgesic action it may have is secondary to and dependent on the anti-inflammatory effect. Phenylbutazone has no anesthetic actions and is not an anesthetic. It is simply a very effective anti-inflammatory drug and as such blocks or prevents hypersensitivity to pain, which is one of the cardinal signs of inflammation.

In an average-sized horse (1,000 lb), a dose of 2 to 3 grams per day of phenylbu-tazone intravenously, or about 4 grams orally, should produce optimal anti-inflammatory effect. Two grams daily should then maintain the effect. As the dose of the drug is increased, the blood levels increase and the plasma half-life of the drug is also increased (Fig. 6-4). If the drug is given orally instead of in-travenously, it takes about five hours for peak blood levels to be attained and the time to attain peak pharmacological effect will be further delayed (Fig. 6-5). Urinary levels of phenylbutazone are usually higher than plasma levels of the drug, and urinary levels are detectable for at least twenty-four hours after a 2 gm/1000 lb dose IV (Fig. 6-6). Since the anti-inflammatory effect is not good for much more than about twenty-four hours, daily dosing with phenylbutazone is required.

For a long time the only way to assess the anti-inflammatory and lameness-alleviating efficacy of phenylbutazone was simply by observing a treated horse. This led to some confusion about how effective the drug really was, how long it took to act, and for how long a period it was effective. Recently, however, Professor Pratt and his coworkers at the Massachusetts Institute of Technology have developed an instrument called a "force" plate, which can provide an

PROSTAGLANDINS

I. SENSITIZE PAIN RECEPTORS TO PAIN AGONISTS

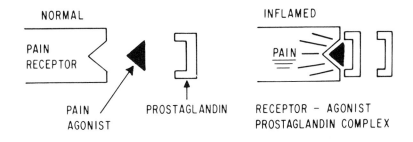

2. INCREASED PROSTAGLANDIN LEVELS (INJECTION OR WITH INFLAMMATION) CAUSES HYPERALGESIA.

3. BLOCK PROSTAGLANDIN SYNTHESIS: TISSUE RETURNS TO NORMAL (SLOWLY — PROSTAGLANDINS FORMED MUST BREAK DOWN.)

Figure 6-3. Schematic representation of pain-sensitizing action of the prostaglandins. Pain is mediated by certain chemicals which interact with pain receptors. The prostaglandins appear to act by increasing the sensitivity of pain receptors to pain agonists, here represented as a locking of the pain agonists onto the pain receptors. In an inflamed tissue the increased levels of prostaglandin cause the hypersensitiv-ity characteristic of inflamed tissues. Once prostaglandin formation is blocked, the high tissue levels of prostaglandin have to decay over a number of hours before the tissue comes back to normal. This is the reason many NSAIDs often take several hours to act. Reproduced with permission from Tobin, *J Equine Med Surg, 3:*253, 1979.

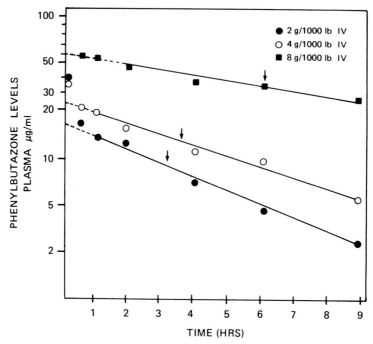

Figure 6-4. Plasma levels of phenylbutazone after administration of different doses. The symbols show plasma levels of phenylbutazone after administration of 2, 4, and 8 gm of phenylbutazone/1000 lb. to horses. At the lower dose, the half-life of phenylbutazone was approximately three hours, while at the higher dose, and half-life was six hours. This is an unusual response and is likely due to oxyphenbutazone, which appears to block the metabolism of phenylbutazone. If high dose levels of phenylbutazone are continued, the blood levels of phenylbutazone increase after every dose (cumulate), the metabolism of phenylbutazone essentially stops, and phenylbutazone toxicity and death may ensue. From Piperno et al. (1968).

objective measurement of lameness and the effects of drugs on lameness. The instrument that does this measures small variations in the load on a horse's leg. It turns out that a horse is very unsteady on a lame leg and that this unsteadiness, in the form of constant small readjustments of weight on this leg, can be measured by means of the "force plate." Then, after phenylbutazone is administered, the horse becomes much more comfortable and thus steadier on his sore leg, which begins to be comparable with his good leg (Fig. 6-7). Using this instrument, Pratt showed that 3 grams of phenylbutazone takes several hours to act after oral administration and its effects are largely over by twenty-four hours. If the dose is given intravenously the onset of action is a little faster, but probably not much faster, because the reduction of tissue prostaglandins by phenylbutazone and other NSAIDs takes some time to develop.

Other ways of measuring the anti-inflammatory actions of the NSAIDs include inducing lameness either chemically or surgically and then measuring the effects of drugs on the lameness. While lameness may be estimated by an experienced clinician, who then scores the animal on a numerical system based on the severity of the lameness, these methods are highly subject to observer bias and are

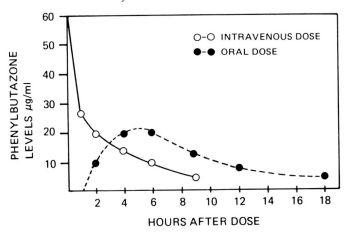

Figure 6-5. Plasma levels of phenylbutazone after oral and IV administration. The open circles (o—o) show plasma levels of phenylbutazone after intravenous administration of 4 gm/1000 lb., while the solid circles (●—●) show plasma levels after oral administration of the same dose. After oral administration, blood levels peak later and lower than after intravenous administration, and blood levels also remain higher longer. From Piperno et al. (1968).

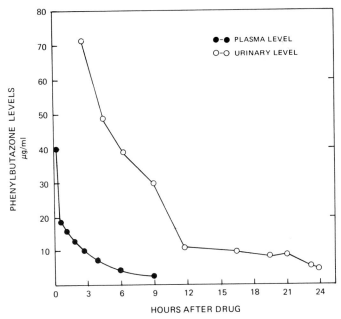

Figure 6-6. Urinary excretion of phenylbutazone. The solid circles (●—●) show plasma levels of phenylbutazone after 2 gm/1000 lb. IV, while the open circles (o—o) show urinary levels of the phenylbutazone in the same horse. From Piperno et al. (1968).

sometimes referred to as the win, place, and show method of evaluating pharmacological effects. Recently, however, stride length has been shown to be very sensitive to the action of these drugs and is now being used to quantitate the effects of drugs on lameness. Stride length may be accurately measured by trotting horses over a freshly raked sanded area and measuring the changes in stride length by the distance between the footprints. Other methods include simple tape measuring of the diameter of an inflamed joint and recording the effects of different drugs on the diameter.

The therapeutic effects that may be expected from phenylbutazone in a horse are perhaps most clearly characterized by the DANCER'S IMAGE case. DANCER'S IMAGE, the champion Candian two-year-old, finished first in the 1968 Kentucky Derby. After the race, however, Kenny Smith, the Kentucky State Racing Commission chemist, reported to the stewards that the urine sample taken from DANCER'S IMAGE contained a medication known as phenylbutazone, and/or a derivative thereof. This finding precipitated a court battle which lasted for years and during which the Kentucky State Racing Commission produced a statement of findings of fact. These findings constitute a classic example of the type of therapeutic response that may be expected from phenylbutazone and other members of the non-steroidal anti-inflammatory group of drugs; it reads as follows:

DANCER'S IMAGE had prominent ankles before he began his racing career, that is, ankles prone or predisposed to trouble under the strain and stress of racing. They were carefully watched and treated from the inception of his racing career by Louis C. Cavalaris, his trainer. The right ankle had begun swelling in early 1968 at Bowie Race Course in Maryland. It was X-rayed at the time of the Wood Memorial in New York by Dr. Girard and prior to and after the Kentucky Derby by Dr. Harthill. It was swollen on Saturday, April 27, 1968, and Sunday, April 28, 1968, and successfully treated by Dr. Harthill with the concurrence of Mr. Cavalaris upon the latter date with a four-gram dose of Butazolidin® (the trade name for phenylbutazone). There was dramatic improvement on April 29, 1968, and the horse was in racing condition and worked out well. However, the condition of the right ankle had again deteriorated by Thursday morning, May 2, 1968, so much so that it was the worst it ever had been up to that time. The ankle was swollen and engorged, a condition known as a red-hot osselet. Dr. Scanlan, the track veterinarian at Churchill Downs, observed DANCER'S IMAGE that day and noticed the horse was so lame and sore that had his condition been the same on Saturday, May 4, 1968, Dr. Scanlan would have recommended to the Stewards that DANCER'S IMAGE be scratched. The ankle began dramatic improvement Thursday afternoon, was in good condition on Friday, May 3, 1968, and on Saturday morning and at the time of the race was in excellent condition and racing sound. The ankle remained sound after the race and through Sunday and Monday. However, by Tuesday, May 7, 1968, the ankle had reverted to its condition of the previous Thursday.

→

Figure 6-7. Measurement of the time course of action of phenylbutazone by force plate. A lame horse constantly readjusts his weight on his sore leg, and the magnitude and frequency of these readjustments are thought to be a measure of the levels of discomfort that the horse is experiencing. The "spread" of distribution of these readjustments by the sore leg in a lame horse is presented in illustration 1 and has a quantitative value (standard error) of about 77. This horse was then dosed with 3 gm of phenylbutazone orally and the spread of the readjustments measured. By twelve hours after dosing with phenylbutazone (illustration 5), the spread of the readjustments was reduced to 30.5, and inspection of the data shows the shape of the distribution curve to be much more compact. Similarly, illustrations 2 through 8 show the development and decay of the antilameness effect of phenylbutazone. The data suggest that the action of phenylbutazone peaks at between eight and twelve hours after an oral dose of the drug and is over between twenty-four hours and thirty-six hours after dosing. Courtesy of Professor Pratt, Massachusetts Institute of Technology.

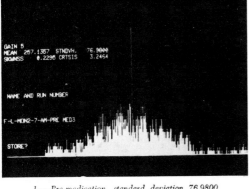

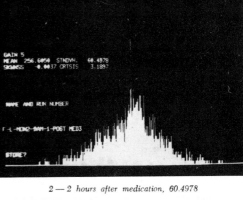

1 — Pre-medication, standard deviation 76.9800

2 — 2 hours after medication, 60.4978

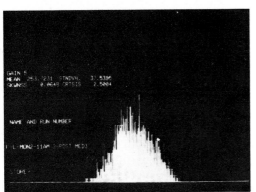

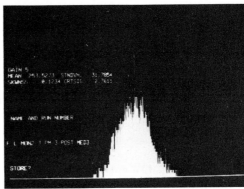

3 — 4 hours after medication, 37.5395

4 — 8 hours after medication, 31.7854

5 — 12 hours after medication, 30.5331

6 — 18 hours after medication, 66.4027

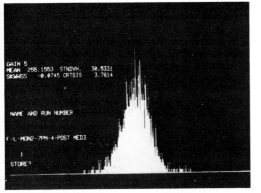

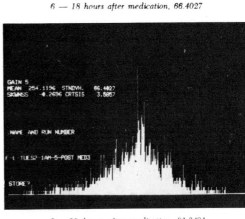

7 — 24 hours after medication, 61.0721

8 — 36 hours after medication, 81.3491

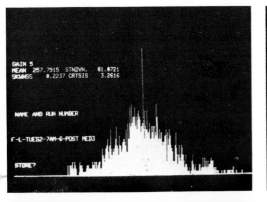

Effective use of phenylbutazone will dramatically improve the condition and health of a horse with a phenylbutazone treatable condition. It affects the speed of a horse to the extent that it enables him to race when he would not otherwise be able to do so. It enables him to perform to his full potential when otherwise he would not be able to do so. Prohibition of the use of phenylbutazone is necessary in order to preserve honesty and integrity in racing because the indiscriminate use and withdrawal of the medication with many horses would vary their performance in racing. The rules of racing are designed to prevent use of medications and other devices for such a purpose.

Regardless of the amount of phenylbutazone and/or derivative thereof in the urine of DANCER'S IMAGE on Saturday, May 4, 1968, its presence in any amount shows that the administration affected the health and speed of the horse by enabling him to run racing sound.

The basic description of the condition of DANCER'S IMAGE and its improvement is what one may expect with drugs of the phenylbutazone type. DANCER'S IMAGE was apparently prone to musculoskeletal problems in his ankles, and this condition responded well to phenylbutazone. The ankles were X-rayed to check for skeletal problems, and the X-rays were apparently negative. Phenylbutazone was capable of rendering DANCER'S IMAGE racing sound and is capable of enabling horses with phenylbutazone-treatable conditions to perform to their full potential.

In addition to osselets (such as were involved in the DANCER'S IMAGE case), other conditions that Professor Gabel of the Ohio State University considers to respond well to phenylbutazone include sore feet (pedal osteitis), cunean tendon bursitis (jacks), spavins, minor sprains and muscle soreness, splints, navicular disease and ringbones. Further, it is common practice for many horsemen to administer phenylbutazone after a race, as this will often prevent a horse from "cooling out sore." Under all of these circumstances, the use of phenylbutazone appears beneficial and, as pointed out by the Kentucky State Racing Commission, allows a horse to run up to his best form.

It is important to differentiate between the actions of phenylbutazone and those of other classes of drugs that might also be used in lieu of it. As pointed out earlier, the primary action of phenylbutazone is to block the inflammatory response and the hypersensitivity to pain that accompanies inflammation. Once this has been accomplished, the treated area is essentially normal with normal pain perception and also normal proprioception, which is the awareness that the leg is in a given position and carrying a certain amount of weight. This normal feedback from the affected area is important because it is what enables the horse to run properly on the treated leg.

On the other hand, if a horse is treated with a local anesthetic block, as outlined in Chapter 16, there is no perception of pain whatsoever, either normal or abnormal, from the joint. While this in itself is not a problem, there is also no proprioception, or sense of place, position, or presence from the limb. If a horse runs on a "numbed" leg, it is generally considered that his chances of making a misstep and thus causing a breakdown are greatly increased. However, it should be quite clearly understood that neither phenylbutazone nor any of the other non-steroidal anti-inflammatory drugs block either normal pain perception or proprioception in an area, and a horse therefore races in an essentially normal way when it is treated with phenylbutazone or other non-steroidal drugs.

Another mechanism of reducing the perception of pain in an area is to administer a centrally acting narcotic such as morphine. What morphine and the other narcotic analgesics do is reduce the perception of pain in the brain. The narcotics therefore do not reduce the formation of pain impulses at the site of the lesion as does phenylbutazone, and neither do they block the transmission of pain along a nerve, as do the local anesthetics. What the narcotic analgesics do is reduce the sensitivity of the central nervous system to pain, which is a true analgesic effect. So far as is known, phenylbutazone and the other non-steroidal anti-inflammatory drugs have no significant effects on pain perception in the brain and thus no narcotic-like effects. Another and entirely distinct problem with the narcotic analgesics, however, is that they are powerful stimulants, as we will see later.

Although the pharmacological action of phenylbutazone is over within twenty-four hours, the time for the animal to "eliminate" phenylbutazone is much longer, as it is with any drug given to a horse. Since phenylbutazone is relatively easy to detect, it can be detected for a very long period indeed if the analyst so desires. Figure 6-8 shows some of the best data on plasma levels of phenylbutazone in the horse that have come to my attention. In this experiment, horses were given varying doses of phenylbutazone for up to three days, and plasma and urinary levels of the drug followed. Plasma levels started at about 20 to 30 µg/ml, declined with a half-life of about one day, and were still detectable in plasma eight days after dosing and in some urine samples on the ninth day after dosing. This experiment, when taken in conjunction with the previous data, emphasizes the

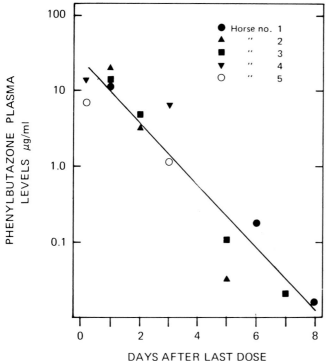

Figure 6-8. The symbols show plasma levels of phenylbutazone in horses that had been dosed with 2.4, and 6 gm phenylbutazone for up to three days before measurement of plasma levels. Phenylbutazone was detectable in plasma for eight days and in urine for up to nine days. After Norheim et al. (1978).

point that while the pharmacological actions of phenylbutazone may be over within twenty-four hours, detection of phenylbutazone in plasma and urine after treatment with this drug is possible for very long periods indeed.

Although the "clearance time" for phenylbutazone in plasma and urine obviously depends on the methods that the analyst elects to use, it is usually safe to assume that plasma and urine are clear by forty-eight to sixty hours after the last dose. Judging from the data of Figure 6-8 and what we know about the pharmacology of phenylbutazone, there appears to be little need for a phenylbutazone positive to be called when plasma or urinary levels of the drug are less than 1μg/ml.

At the other end of the scale, some racing authorities have rulings designed to discourage race-day medication of horses with phenylbutazone. These rulings state that if certain levels, often 165 μg/ml, of phenylbutazone and/or metabolites are found in post-race urine, this level indicates race-day medication and that a "no medication on race day" rule has been infringed. In the absence of published data, the scientific status of these claims is somewhat uncertain, and rulings based on this information should be treated with caution.

As far as the horse is concerned, phenylbutazone, when used in the recommended doses and for the recommended periods of time, is a very safe drug. Over the years the number of doses administered to horses must be astronomic, while the incidence of reported side effects is small. The principal dangers with phenylbutazone are associated with its improper injection. If phenylbutazone is injected around the jugular vein by mistake, it may cause severe inflammation, abscessation, and eventual loss (sloughing) of the vein. This, however, can occur with many drugs and is a problem with injection technique rather than with phenylbutazone. Phenylbutazone may also be injected directly into the carotid artery in the neck by accident. If this happens the horse immediately becomes excited, falls prostrate, and may die. Some veterinarians and trainers report that phenylbutazone will occasionally depress a horse, especially with large doses in Standardbred horses. However, to judge from the number of horses running on phenylbutazone at some tracks, this effect must either be very rare or else horses get over it rapidly.

Reviewing the data available on phenylbutazone toxicity up to March 1977, the Veterinary Chemist's Advisory Committee to the National Association of State Racing Commissioners concluded that the side effects and toxicities of phenylbutazone at *usually used* clinical doses are minimal. While this statement still stands, data has recently become available on adverse reactions after higher doses of this drug over longer periods of use than recommended by the manufacturer. Because of the widespread use of this drug, it is appropriate for us to review this data so that veterinarians and horsemen may become aware of the circumstances under which these toxicities appear and the signs of toxicity when they occur.

The published and in-press reports of phenylbutazone toxicity both occurred when researchers elected to give higher than usual doses of phenylbutazone to horses to study its effects on liver metabolism of drugs. Working in Scotland, Snow gave 10 mg/kg (about 4.5 gm/1,000 lb) orally for from seven to fourteen days to ten ponies, while Gerber, in Switzerland, gave about 3.4 gm/1000 lb IV to three horses for eight days. Clinical signs of toxicity were seen in most of these horses, and a number of deaths were recorded. These data emphasize the need for careful monitoring of horses maintained on high therapeutic doses of phenylbutazone.

In Snow's studies, the ponies stopped taking phenylbutazone orally by the sixth day and the drug had to be administered IV. Of the ten ponies in Snow's studies, only two showed no clinically recognizable side effects, while two showed a slight decrease in appetite. For four ponies, treatment was stopped because of the severity of the clinical signs, while three ponies died during the course of therapy. On postmortem, all of these animals had ulcerations in the mouth, peritonitis, and edema of the bowel, while one had a small stomach ulcer.

Clinical signs seen in these animals included dullness, listlessness, and inappetence, with diarrhea developing later. If the treatment was stopped, the ponies gradually returned to normal.

Blood tests showed that most of these horses showed a decrease in plasma protein concentration and increased plasma urea. Marked depressions in plasma calcium and potassium were also seen. These changes were interpreted by Snow as indicating marked water and sodium retention, which is a common side effect of phenylbutazone therapy in man. Snow felt that the critical event leading to death was the development of submucosal edema in the large intestine, leading to shock and then to death.

An essentially similar but less extensive study by Gerber produced broadly equivalent results. Gerber was also studying drug metabolism in horses, but he elected to give his horses 7.5 mg/kg of phenylbutazone IV. In two of three horses, he saw signs of extreme depression, anorexia, fever, and impaired liver function. While one horse recovered, one had to be put down, as peritonitis developed following a liver biopsy. As in Snow's experiments, one horse did not develop any significant clinical signs throughout the experiment.

In conclusion, it appears clear that high doses of phenylbutazone, maintained for more than five days, caused toxicity problems in approximately two out of three horses. While the precise basis of this effect is not clear, it is self-limiting if the drug is given orally, as the horse will refuse to eat and the drug will clear the horse. If the drug is given parenterally, it should not be given at these doses beyond five days and the horse should be carefully watched for signs of toxicity. While there are suggestions in the experimental work that the effect may be due to drug cumulation, horsemen are well advised to cut back or discontinue high doses of phenylbutazone at the first signs of inappetence, fever, edema, or leucopenia.

The pattern of minimal toxicity due to *therapeutic* doses of phenylbutazone in the horse contrasts sharply with the serious toxicities seen in man. In man, some type of side-effect is seen in from 1 to 40 percent of patients; these include peptic ulcer, liver and kidney problems, and, most seriously, inability to form red or white cells in the blood. A number of phenylbutazone-dependent deaths have been recorded, and for this reason its use is restricted in man and it is best used only in short-term therapy.

Because a dose of phenylbutazone persists a long time in the blood of man (half-life about 3 days) compared with its relatively short plasma half-life in the horse (6 to 8 hours), it has been suggested that its lack of toxicity in the horse is due to its rapid metabolism by the horse. This theory ignores observations that drug toxicities are very often due to drug metabolites rather than to the drug itself, which metabolites are, of course, formed at a much greater rate in the horse than in man.

The question about the effect of phenylbutazone on the performance of horses has often been raised. Reviewing the subject of phenylbutazone and Lasix® in racing horses, the Veterinary Chemists Advisory Committee to the National Association of State Racing Commissioners concluded that phenylbutazone does not change the innate ability of a horse to race but, by relieving inflammation, may enable him to race nearer to his maximum capacity. Studying the effects of phenylbutazone in time trials in horses, Sanford and his colleagues found that phenylbutazone administered intramuscularly twenty-three hours before "time" trials improved performance in their horses. These workers were apparently rather surprised by this result and concluded that phenylbutazone had acted to relieve subclinical lameness rather than to stimulate the horses. This interpretation is well supported by some experiments from our laboratory, which show no effect of phenylbutazone on fentanyl-stimulated trotting in horses, minimizing suggestions that phenylbutazone either stimulates or depresses horses at the usually used clinical doses.

Another important question with phenylbutazone is whether or not it interferes with the detection of other drugs, the popularly called "masking" effect. While there is no doubt that the presence of any drug must make the detection and unequivocal identification of another drug somewhat more difficult, the consensus of the Veterinary Chemists Advisory Committee was that the usual doses of phenylbutazone given on race day may or may not interfere with the detection of other medications, depending on the analytical methods used.

As pointed out earlier in this chapter, the drug industry has been vigorously researching the area of non-steroidal anti-inflammatory drugs and in recent years has devleoped a number of new non-steroidal anti-inflammatory drugs. Pharmacologically, these are all closely related to phenylbutazone. Because of their recent introduction they are not as well characterized clinically as phenylbutazone, but it appears at this point that their basic pharmacology and actions in the horse are broadly similar to those of phenylbutazone.

Equiproxen (Naproxen®)*

Equiproxen is another non-steroidal anti-inflammatory agent with analgesic and antipyretic actions. It is recommended for the relief of pain, inflammation, and lameness associated with "tying up" and soft tissue disease of the horse. Its therapeutic effects in the horse have been studied in some detail by Wynn-Jones and coworkers. These workers induced "tying up" in horses by injecting lactic acid into the back muscles of horses and then studied the effects of equiproxen on length of stride, pain, lameness, and tissue swelling in these horses.

Length of stride in the horse is a sensitive measure of lameness, and Kilian and Wynn-Jones were able to show that equiproxen greatly reduced the lameness

---

* Naproxen®, Diamond Laboratories, Des Moines, IA

caused by the lactic acid injections. In the untreated horses lameness peaked two days after the injury was induced and persisted for up to fourteen days, while in equiproxen-treated horses the lameness was greatly reduced and virtually eliminated within three days. Comparison of the areas under the curves for the treated and nontreated horses suggests that equiproxen treatment was at least 80 percent effective in reducing lameness. Similarly, equiproxen treatment had marked effects to reduce the amount of swelling, and other data showed that it also reduced pain equivalently. These data constitute the best and most clear-cut experimental work demonstrating the therapeutic effects of a non-steroidal anti-inflammatory drug that I am aware of, and clearly delineate the therapeutic efficacy of equiproxen.

Based on this experimental model, a study in which phenylbutazone and Naproxen® were directly compared led Jones and Hamm to conclude that, in the equine myositis model, equiproxen was superior to phenylbutazone for the more rapid relief of inflammatory swelling and associated lameness.

In other work, the response to equiproxen obtained in these studies was compared with the response in naturally occurring "tying up" disease. In the natural disease the average time for remission was found to be about five days and a favorable response was observed in more than 90 percent of the animals.

Hamm also evaluated the effects of continuous administrations of equiproxen during training to fifty yearling Quarterhorse colts. These colts were assigned to two equal groups at the beginning of a four-month training season, the yearlings assigned to the untreated (control) groups receiving standard medication for musculoskeletal disease as required. The test horses received about 5 gm daily of equiproxen in the feed during the training session. Hamm observed a marked and highly significant reduction in time lost during training and in the racing season in the horses on equiproxen, who lost only 3 percent of their training time, compared with a 13 percent loss in training time in the control group. The appearance of musculoskeletal problems was delayed in the equiproxen-treated group, and when musculoskeletal problems did appear their duration was reduced compared with the control group. The horses treated with equiproxen raced significantly more often than the control horses, and the overall frequency of musculoskeletal injuries was dramatically reduced, by fourfold during the training phase and by thirtyfold during the racing phase, for the horses on continuous equiproxen. These are very provocative data and, if independently confirmed, make a clear case for the benefits of anti-inflammatory medication of young horses in training and in racing.

After oral administration of equiproxen the drug is about 50 percent absorbed. The recommended dose is 10 mg/kg or about 5 mg/lb. After oral administration, plasma levels of the drug peak at about 25 μg/ml between two and three hours after dosing and then decline to less than 1 μg/ml between two and three hours after dosing and then decline to less than 1 μg/ml at twenty-four hours. If the drug is given twice a day, as recommended, one would then get a second peak of drug, which should decline to less than 5 μg/ml by twenty-four hours. Equiproxen thus apears likely to have little tendency to accumulate in the horse (Fig. 6-9).

Equiproxen is a very easy drug to detect in the horse. It is easily detectable by

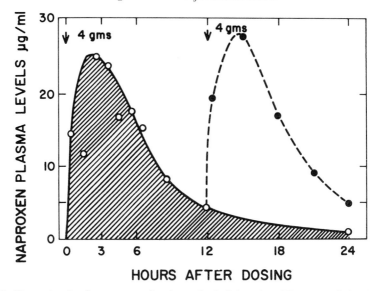

Figure 6-9. Plasma levels of naproxen after its oral administration. The open circles (o—o) show plasma levels of naproxen after dosing with 4 gm orally. The solid circles (●—●) show the calculated blood levels of naproxen if this dose is repeated at twelve hours.

ultraviolet spectrophotometry, either as the parent drug or as its major metabolite, 2-(6-hydroxynapthyl) propionic acid, both of which are excreted in high concentrations in the urine. The approximate half-life of these compounds in equine urine is about six hours, and it appears that at least sixty hours should be allowed for equiproxen to clear the urine of the horse.

Equiproxen appears to be a relatively safe drug in the horse in that three times the recommended dose can be given for up to forty-two days with no lesions attributable to equiproxen. In mares, equiproxen was administered in late pregnancy without apparent effect on the mare or the foal, and these mares were subsequently rebred and conceived normally.

Flunixin Meglumine (Banamine®)*

Flunixin is another member of the NSAID family that has recently been approved for use in equine practice. It appears to be more potent than other members of this group in that a dose of about 1.0 mg/kg produces good clinical effects. The pharmacology and pharmacokinetics of flunixin in the horse have been reported by Houdeshell and Hennessey. These workers reported that an intravenous dose of flunixin improved lameness by 55 percent and swelling by 34 percent at thirty hours postinjection, compared with a 52 percent and 23 percent improvement due to phenylbutazone. While these results might seem to suggest that flunixin is more effective than phenylbutazone, the apparent comparison of these drugs at thirty hours postdosing may be misleading, as phenylbutazone was only effective for twenty-four hours in these particular studies. A more appropri-

---

* Banamine®, Schering Corporation, Kenilworth, NJ

ate period for evaluating the relative merits of phenylbutazone and flunixin would be the times of peak drug effect, or after the horses had been on both drugs for a period. Because of the uncertainty of the times at which the actions of phenylbutazone and flunixin were compared in these studies, it is difficult to evaluate the relative effectiveness of these drugs. Flunixin produced approximately the same response whether it was given orally, intravenously, or intramuscularly.

Field trials with flunixin for a typical clinical spectrum of musculoskeletal disorders showed that remission of clinical signs occurred after two to three days of therapy. Overall, 40 percent of the horses were rated as having an excellent response, 34 percent as having a good response, 14 percent as fair, and 12 percent as poor. Unfortunately, no control data or positive control information with a well-characterized drug such as phenylbutazone were presented for comparative purposes.

It is characteristic of the NSAIDs that individual members of this group are more effective in some conditions rather than others. Both the literature and clinical experience suggest that flunixin is particularly useful in the treatment of colic and rapidly alleviates pain and distress associated with this condition. In studies on the use of this drug in animals with predominantly spastic and flatulent colics, Vernimb and Hennessey found an excellent or good response in 93 percent of flatulent colics, in 72 percent of spastic colics, 52 percent of statis colics, and 60 percent of other types. Fifteen percent of horses showed a fair response, and another 25 percent showed no response. The onset of the response to flunixin was also remarkably fast; about 40 percent of horses showed improvement in 15 minutes, and some evaluators reported favorable changes in four to eight minutes. These are remarkably rapid changes to be induced by an antiprostaglandin agent, which, as pointed out previously, generally must reduce existing tissue prostaglandin levels to normal before acting. In fact, a response within four minutes, which is not more than two circulation times for the horse, must be accounted a very rapid response indeed. The duration of relief after flunixin was more in keeping with the known time course of action of this drug and averaged six to eight hours after a single dose.

While flunixin is effective at 1.0 mg/kg, and 4.4 mg/kg of phenylbutazone is needed to produce an equivalent effect, this potency of flunixin should not in any way be taken as a particular advantage for flunixin. As far as the clinician and horseman are concerned, potency is primarily an academic concept. What counts in the clinical setting is the quality of the clinical response and the ratio between the dose producing a good clinical response and that which produces a toxic effect. The actual number of milligrams of a chemical required to produce the clinical effect is of little practical significance as long as its use in effective doses is not associated with side effects or toxic effects. The greater potency of flunixin may, however, have regulatory importance. Because flunixin is more potent than phenylbutazone, it is found in blood and urine samples of much lower concentrations than phenylbutazone or its metabolites. Because of this, flunixin may, under some circumstances, be more acceptable in medication programs than less potent drugs such as phenylbutazone because of its lesser potential for "masking."

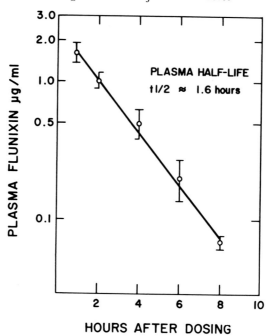

Figure 6-10. The open circles (o—o) show plasma levels of flunixin after 1.1 mg/kg was administered IV to five horses. Unpublished experiment reproduced courtesy of Professor George Maylin, Cornell University, Ithaca, NY.

The plasma half-life of flunixin in the horse is remarkably short, being only about 1.6 hours after its intravenous injection (Fig. 6-10). After this dose, plasma levels peaked at 1.6 μg/ml, while urinary levels of the drug peaked at 60 μg/ml two hours after injection and then declined. After dosing horses with 1.1 mg/kg daily for four days, plasma levels of 2.9 μg/ml were observed, and traces of flunixin were still observed in urine forty-eight hours after the last dose (Fig. 6-11).

Although the plasma half-life of flunixin in the horse is very short (1.6 hours), the peak pharmacological response to flunixin occurs at twelve hours after dosing and the effect persists for thirty hours. This is an unusually long period of action for a drug with such a short plasma half-life, and it may raise some questions about the mechanism of action or the active species of flunixin.

Flunixin appears to be a relatively safe drug in the horse, with doses up to five times the recommended dose for five days producing no drug-related problems or toxicities.

Meclofenamic Acid (Arquel®)*

Meclofenamic acid is another member of the non-steroidal anti-inflammatory group of drugs. It is available as oral granules and is reportedly quite palatable and can be mixed with the grain ration once a day. The usual dose rate is about 1.0 mg/lb of body weight for from five to seven days.

---

* Arquel®, Parke Davis & Co., Detroit, MI

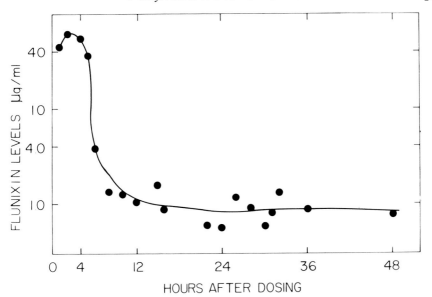

Figure 6-11. Urinary "clearance" of flunixin after 1.1 mg/kg of flunixin IV. The solid circles (●—●) show urinary levels of flunixin after administration of 1.1 mg/kg IV to four horses. Unpublished experiment reproduced courtesy of Professor George Maylin, Cornell University, Ithaca, NY.

Meclofenamic acid is an unusual drug among the NSAIDs in that its onset of action can be relatively slow, taking from thirty-six to ninety-six hours to develop. After dosing with 1 gm/1000 lb of Arquel® in the horse, plasma levels of the drug peak within one to four hours at a little more than 1 μg/ml. They then decline with an apparent half-life of about six hours to clear the plasma by twenty-four hours. Because the plasma is essentially cleared after twenty-four hours there is no tendency for meclofenamic acid to accumulate in plasma in the normal horse (Fig. 6-12).

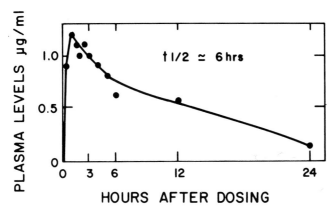

Figure 6-12. Plasma levels of meclofenamic acid after 1.0 mg/lb of Arquel®. The solid circles (●—●) show plasma levels of meclofenamic acid after oral administration of 1.0 mg/lb of Arquel® to horses. After Connor et al., *AAEP Proceedings*, 1973.

If meclofenamic acid is fed orally for five days, urinary concentrations of the drug run at about 25 μg/ml throughout the dosing period. After the last dose of meclofenamic acid, the drug is reportedly detectable in urine for ninety-six hours, although the levels are very low from forty-eight hours on (Fig. 6-13). Again, since meclofenamic acid does not tend to accumulate in the body, the same rate of decline for meclofenamic acid in urine should be followed after single or multiple dose regimens. About 10 to 24 percent of the drug administered is eliminated in the urine, and it is thought that a good proportion of the drug is eliminated via the bile and feces. No data is available on the metabolism of meclofenamic acid in the horse.

In clinical trials on 304 horses suffering from osteoarthritis, navicular disease, laminitis, and soft or bony tissue conditions, it was found that 78 percent of the cases with navicular disease improved, 76 percent with laminitis improved, and 61 percent of the cases with osteoarthritis improved. Since all these cases were carefully screened to exclude horses that might improve with stall rest, these improvements are difficult to compare with reported improvements on other drugs. These workers also reported that it was not possible to predict which horses would improve on meclofenamic acid and which would not.

Signs of toxicity to meclofenamic acid appear at high dose levels (6 to 8 mg/lb) and include mouth ulcers, loss of appetite, depression, edema, and loss of weight. If the dosage rate is kept low (1 mg/lb), however, meclofenamic acid is a safe drug and useful in the treatment of musculoskeletal disease in the horse.

Aspirin

The oldest and best known of the non-steroidal anti-inflammatory group of drugs is aspirin, or acetylsalicylic acid. The fact that aspirin is a household remedy and very readily available should not delude one into thinking that it is anything but a very effective drug. Aspirin has long been the drug of choice in the

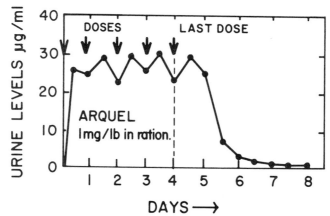

Figure 6-13. Urinary "clearance times" for meclofenamic acid. The solid circles (●—●) show urinary clearance times for meclofenamic acid in four horses after daily oral dosing with 1 mg/lb of Arquel®. Arquel® was still detectable in urine four days after the last dose. After Connor et al., *AAEP Proceedings*, 1973.

treatment of human arthritis, but it is unfortunately not nearly as effective a drug in the horse.

Where aspirin is concerned, nature has played a number of tricks on horsemen. The first of these is that the urine of horses and other herbivores normally contains small quantities of salicylate. This salicylate either comes from the grass and hay that the horse ingests or is a product of the horse's metabolism. Whatever its origin, however, the result is that it is difficult for a chemist to call a salicylate "positive" because salicylate is a natural constituent of horse urine.

While salicylate might thus seem to be an answer to the horseman's prayer, the drug is, unfortunately very rapidly excreted by the horse. It turns out that as an acidic drug, salicylic acid is rapidly eliminated in the basic urine of the horse. The half-life of salicylate in the blood of horse with basic urine is less than one hour, so it is very difficult to maintain plasma levels of the drug. Thus, if you want to use salicylate effectively in the horse, you must give large doses of the drug and give them relatively close to the time at which you want the drug to take effect.

It would help considerably with the effects of salicylate if one could give aspirin intravenously or intramuscularly and in this way obtain a high blood level of the drug. However, since salicylate itself is not available as an injectable, this approach cannot be taken. On the other hand, a close relative of acetylsalicylic acid, thiosalicylate, is available and can be administered by injection.

Thiosalicylate is chemically a slightly different molecule from salicylic acid, in which an oxygen atom has been replaced with a sulfur atom. This chemical change results in this particular salicylate being available in an injectable form, which means that higher blood levels and thus effective concentrations of the drug are readily attained. No information is available on the half-life of thiosalicylate in the horse. However, it is presumably much like that of salicylate itself. Thiosalicylate was once much used in some racing jurisdictions as a substitute for phenylbutazone, particularly in those states that have upper limits on post-race urinary concentrations of phenylbutazone. Unfortunately, because of the presence of the sulfur atom, it is possible to distinguish this drug from normal salicylate, and a number of thiosalicylate "positives" have been called. Even though it makes little pharmacological sense to allow phenylbutazone and aspirin and ban thiosalicylate, this apparently is the status of thiosalicylate in racing chemistry at the moment.

Dimethyl Sulfoxide (DMSO)

Dimethyl sulfoxide (DMSO) is a colorless liquid with a weak odor, which leaves a bitter taste in the mouth shortly after its application to the body by any route. Chemically, DMSO is unusual in that it mixes well with both water and lipid-soluble compounds, and these chemical characteristics enable it to penetrate rapidly through cell membranes. DMSO also accelerates the movement of other substances through cell membranes and is thus useful in increasing the transcutaneous absorption of drugs. It is approved for use by the FDA in the dog and horse, but it should be used only in the medical or pure form, usually at between 80% and 90% strength.

As well as aiding the transcutaneous penetration of drugs, DMSO has been reported to have many other pharmacological effects. Among these effects are anti-inflammatory actions, local anesthetic properties, antibacterial effects, and effects on diuresis and vasodilation. DMSO is also hygroscopic, absorbing up to 70 percent of its weight of water from the air. Similarly, when it is added to water, heat is released, and this effect may be produced locally when high concentrations of DMSO are applied to the skin. Most of the clear-cut effects of DMSO appear to require high concentrations of this agent, which means that its most marked pharmacological effects are associated with its local application.

In human medicine, DMSO has been reported by some investigators to be very effective in musculoskeletal disorders. Local treatment with DMSO resulted in marked improvement in about 50 percent of patients with chronic osteoarthritis, bursitis, periostitis, and tendinitis, while partial improvement was obtained in about 35 percent. The duration of treatment was rarely longer than three weeks, the response to DMSO was considered to compare favorably with that of intra-articular corticoids, and treatment with DMSO was associated with a reduction in areas of calcification in some patients.

In the horse, Teigland and Saurino have studied the action of DMSO on an inflammatory model and in clinical practice. In their experimental studies with induced inflammatory responses, the DMSO-treated sites never became as swollen and indurated as the untreated sites. Further, in the DMSO-treated sites the inflammation and edema dissipated more rapidly and the horses appeared to experience less pain and discomfort from the DMSO-treated lesions.

In their clinical studies, Teigland and Saurino reported on the use of DMSO on open wounds with subcutaneous edema and hemorrhage. When DMSO was painted onto these lesions twice a day, the wounds were apparently less painful, the edema reduced, and the limb returned to normal more rapidly. Similarly, bursitis and synovitis responded well to these drugs, and osteoarthritic lesions also responded well. DMSO was also useful in the treatment of bucked shins, acting to reduce the discomfort of the animal markedly, but it did not, of course, change the requirement for rest in this condition. Because the lower limbs of the horse are very prone to edema and swelling, DMSO appears to be particularly useful in limb injuries in this species.

Along with its own pharmacological properties, DMSO markedly accelerates the absorption of other drugs, in some cases up to 100-fold. It is therefore often combined with steroids, where it aids their penetration into tissues, or with antibiotics, whose penetration into bacteria and thus antibacterial action it appears to accelerate. DMSO is also occasionally combined with steroids and furacin as a topical wound dressing.

When used in small amounts, the toxicity of DMSO appears to be minimal. Not more than 100 ml per day is the recommended topical dose for a horse, and the drug should not be used in horses treated with cholinesterase-inhibiting anthelmintics. While prolonged use of DMSO has been associated with changes in the lens of the eye in dogs and other mammals, there appears to be little likelihood of this occurring in the horse at the recommended dose rates.

DMSO is one of the few stubstances that an analyst can detect in a urine sample the moment that he opens the urine jar. This is because DMSO is transformed in the body to metabolites that yield a garlic odor, and this odor may be readily detectable in urine samples.

Although DMSO is not difficult to test for, it requires special testing techniques, and since it is a topical medication, most racing jurisdictions do not test specifically for it. Horsemen should be aware, however, that because of the ability of DMSO to accelerate the transcutaneous absorption of other drugs, its topical use in conjunction with agents such as benzocaine or corticosteroids may lead to increased blood or urine levels of these drugs and thus to inadvertent positives for these agents.

Orgotein (Palosein®)*

Orgotein is the generic name adopted for drug versions of a copper- and zinc-containing metalloprotein called superoxide dismutase. In 1964 it was discovered to be a potent anti-inflammatory agent, and it was soon shown to be an enzyme and was named superoxide dismutase. Beyond this, little was understood about the mechanism of its anti-inflammatory action, other than that it was different from most of the other anti-inflammatory drugs then in current use.

Superoxide dismutase has recently been shown to be an intracellular enzyme that is part of the body's defense against the highly toxic O_2^- of superoxide radical. Blood cells such as neutrophils and macrophages generate significant amounts of the superoxide radical as a killing agent in their attacks on bacteria, but these superoxides can also kill the phagocytes themselves. When administered as a drug, superoxide dismutase apparently scavenges this excess superoxide radical and prolongs phagocyte life.

Superoxide dismutase also mobilizes polymorphonuclear leukocytes and increases their numbers at the site of inflammation. When administered by intra-articular injection it preserves or restores the viscosity of synovial fluid and does not interfere with the activity of host defense cells. In spite of the fact that it is a foreign protein, it appears to be very poorly antigenic, and it is essentially nontoxic. It may be administered by any route, but the safest and most economical route would appear to be intra-articular.

Clinical trials in humans have reportedly shown that orgotein is a safe, effective nonanalgesic anti-inflammatory drug. Its effects apparently take from two to six weeks to develop and persist for up to one month after termination of treatment. Orgotein may be administered systemically or, when the pathology is localized, injected into and around a site of a chronic inflammation.

In Sweden, Ahlengard and coworkers studied the efficacy of intra-articular orgotein in a series of cases of noninfective traumatic arthritis in horses. These workers concluded that intra-articular orgotein produced beneficial results, the effects being most marked (94% recovery) in horses that had shown lameness for less than two months, and less marked (49%) in horses that had been lame for more than two months before treatment.

Decker and coworkers also reported on the treatment of seventy horses with local and/or intra-articular injection of Palosein®. These workers considered the response obtained excellent, with fifty-three of the horses returning to racing

---

* Palosein®, Diagnostic Data, Inc., California

within a few days and some winning their races. Of twenty horses with fetlock problems, sixteen responded to treatment and most of these after only a single dose of the drug.

As a naturally occurring metalloprotein of high molecular weight, Palosein® is not likely to enter equine urine in significant amounts. Even if it did, it would be difficult to recover, detect, and prove to be of exogenous origin by currently used drug testing techniques.

Hyaluronic Acid

Hyaluronic acid is an essential component of synovial fluid and also of articular cartilage, which has recently been introduced as an intra-articular therapy for joint problems. High molecular weight hyaluronic acid, which is the form injected into joints, inhibits lymphocyte migration and phagocytosis and also reduces the permeability of the synovial membrane. Usually between 20 and 40 mg* of the sodium salt of hyaluronic acid (10 mg/ml) is injected into the joint, with an equivalent volume of synovia being removed. Reporting on a study of the effects of hyaluronic acid treatment in racing horses, Asheim and Lindblad saw "frequently very good effects" with hyaluronic acid. These good effects were seen in horses that had previously been point fired, blistered, and sometimes treated with intra-articular corticosteroids. These authors considered it remarkable that in most cases injection of 1 to 2 ml of hyaluronic acid was sufficient to cure the lameness. The only factors that appeared to predictably interfere with therapy were pronounced bony changes in the joint or prior treatment with corticosteroids.

The mode of action of hyaluronic acid is not clear, but it appears to persist in the joint for days after an injection. One theory is that hyaluronic acid has good surface-protecting properties. Because of its high molecular weight and the large number of electrical charges carried by hyaluronic acid, diffusion of hyaluronic acid out from an intra-articular injection site and its detection in urine by current routine screening methods is highly unlikely.

In summary, reviewing the properties of the non-steroidal anti-inflammatory drugs, it is apparent that phenylbutazone is still the standard against which other drugs are compared. All these drugs share a number of broadly similar characteristics in that dosages are approximately equivalent from drug to drug, their time course of action is broadly similar, and their detection in blood or urine is not particularly difficult. There are, however, subtle differences in their clinical effectiveness against certain conditions, which makes certain agents the drugs of choice for specific conditions. In this way flunixin is apparently more effective against colic than other members of this group and is the drug of choice in this area. Similarly, Naproxen® appears to be the drug of choice for muscle soreness and is reported to be particularly effective in young horses with minor muscle problems. Meclofenamic acid has acquired a reputation for being useful in foot and hoof problems, and other specific strengths of individual members of this group will doubtless become apparent as clinical experience with these drugs

---

* More recent work suggests that smaller doses may be used.

increases. Therefore, despite the basically similar mechanism of action of the NSAIDs, they are all far from clinically equivalent, and it is a good idea to try different NSAIDs on clinical conditions that might be expected to respond to these drugs if the response to one member of this group is poor.

SELECTED REFERENCES

Ahlengard, S., Tufuesson, G., Petterson, H., and Andersson, T.: "Treatment of traumatic arthritis in the horse with intra-articular orgotein (Palosein®)." *Eq Vet J, 10:*122-124, 1978.

Ashelm, A., and Lindblad, G.: "Intra-articular treatment of arthritis in race horses with sodium hyaluronate." *Acta Vet Scand, 17:*379-394, 1976.

Clofalo, V. B., Latranyl, M. G., Patel, J. B., and Taber, R. I.: "Flunixin meglumine: a non-narcotic analgesic." *J Pharm Exp Ther, 200:*501-507, 1977.

Conner, G. H., Riley, W. F., Beck, C. C., and Coppock, R. W.: Arquel (Cl-583), "A new non-steroidal anti-inflammatory drug for horses." *Proc AAEP, 19:*81-90, 1973.

Davis, L. E., and Westfall, B. A.: Species differences in biotransformation and excretion of salicylate." *Am J Vet Res, 33:*1253-1262, 1972.

Decker, W. E., Edmonson, A. H., Hill, H. E., Holmes, R. A., Padmore, C. L., Warren, H. H., and Wood, W. C.: "Local administration of orgotein in horses," *MVP, 9:*773-774.

Ferreira, S. H., and Vane, J. R.: "New aspects of the mode of action of nonsteroid anti-inflammatory drugs." *Ann Rev Pharmacol, 14:*57-73, 1974.

Gabel, A. A., Tobin, T., Ray, R. S., and Mayling, G. A.: "Phenylbutazone in horses." A review. *J Eq Med Surg, 1:*221-225, 1977.

Gabriel, K. L., and Martin, J. E.: "Phenylbutazone short term versus long term administration to Thoroughbred and Standardbred horses." *JAVMA, 140:*337-341, 1962.

Goodman, L. S., and Gilman, A.: *The Pharmacological Basis of Therapeutics.* 5th ed., Macmillan Publishing Co., New York (1975).

Hamm, D.: "Continuous administration of naproxen to the horse during training." *J Eq Med Surg, 2:*125-128, 1978.

Houdeshell, J. W., and Hennessey, P. W.: "A new nonsteroidal anti-inflammatory analgesic for horses." *J Eq Med Surg, 1:*57-63, 1977.

Jones, E. W., and Hamm, D.: "Comparative efficacy of phenylbutazone and naproxen in induced equine myositis." *J Eq Med Surg, 2:*341-347, 1978.

Kilian, J. G., Jones, E. W., Hamm, D., Riley, W. F., and Averkin, E.: "The efficacy of equiproxen (Naproxen) in a unique equine myositis model." *Proc AAEP, 20:*201-215, 1974.

Linton, J. A. M.: "The use of orgotein in the treatment of soft tissue injuries of the horse." *Irish Vet J, 30:*53-46, 1976.

Maylin, G. A.: "The disposition of phenylbutazone in the horse." *Proc AAEP, 20:*243-248, 1974.

Norheim, G., Hoie, R., Froslie, A., and Bergsjo, T. H.: "Gas chromatographic determination of small amounts of phenylbutazone and oxyphenbutazone in horse plasma and urine." *Fresenius Z Anal Chem, 289:*287-288, 1978.

Piperno, E., Ellis, D. J., Getty, S. M., and Brody, T. M.: "Plasma and urinary levels of phenylbutazone in the horse." *JAVMA, 153:*195-198, 1968.

Pratt, G.: "Breakthrough on understanding lameness." *The Blood-Horse, 103:*3758-3760, 1977.

Riley, W. F., Romane, W. M., Ellis, D. J., and Haury, K. W.: "Preliminary report on a new nonsteroidal anti-inflammatory agent in the horse." *Proc AAEP, 17:*293-300, 1971.

Salin, M. L., and McCord, J. M.: "Free radicals and inflammation protection of phagocytosing leukocytes by superoxide dismutase." *J Clin Invest, 56:*1319-1323, 1975.

Sanford, J.: "Effects of drugs on performance of the horse." In *Symposium on Large Animal Therapeutics,* University of Surrey, Guildford, Surrey, 1978.

Snow, D., and Bogan, J. A.: "Phenylbutazone toxicity in ponies," *Vet. Rec., 105:*26-30, 1979.

Teigland, M. G., and Saurino, V. R.: Clinical evaluation of dimethyl sulfoxide in equine applications. *Ann NY Acad Sci, 141:*471-477, 1967.

Tobin, T.: "Pharmacology Review: The nonsteroidal anti-inflammatory drugs. I. Phenylbutazone." *J Eq Med Surg, 6:*253-258, 1979.

Tobin, T.: "Review: The nonsteroidal anti-inflammatory drugs. II. Equiproxen, meclofenamic acid and others." *J Eq Med Surg, 7:*298-302, 1979.

Vernimb, G. D., and Hennessey, P. W.: "Clinical studies on flunixin meglumine in the treatment of equine colic." *J Eq Med Surg, 1:*111-116, 1977.

Wanner, F., Rollinghoff, W., Gerber, H., and Preiny, R.: "A preliminary report; demethylations, hydroxylation and acetylation in the horse. Side effects of repeated phenylbutazone medication." Proceedings of the Third International Symposium on Equine Medication Control, Tobin, T., Blake, J. W. and Woods, W. E., Eds. Dept. of Veterinary Science, University of Kentucky, 1979.

Wigren, A., Falk, J., and Wik, O.: "The healing of cartilage injuries under the influence of joint immobilization and repeated hyaluronic acid injections." *Acta Orthrop Scand, 49:*121-133, 1978.

Chapter 7

BLEEDER MEDICATION: LASIX® (FUROSEMIDE) AND OTHER DRUGS

THE HISTORY OF BLEEDERS is at least as old as Thoroughbred racing itself. Bleeders have been recorded among the earliest Thoroughbred horses and are still with us to this day. Bleeding, known technically as "epistaxis," consists of hemorrhage from the nostrils of a horse, usually either during or after severe exercise.* In racehorses, bleeding is almost always bilateral and from the lungs; this is what is considered the classic "bleeder."

The loss of blood from classic exercise-induced epistaxis is rarely severe, and death in association with exercise-induced epistaxis is essentially unknown. There is apparently no defect in blood coagulation in these horses, and the bleeding stops shortly after the exercise is stopped. The problem with bleeding of this type is that horses that bleed severely may slow down abruptly or stop in the stretch. This can lead to accidents and injury to other horses and jockeys. In addition, the sight of horses pulling up covered with blood and blood-spattered jockeys is not considered good for the image of racing, and for these reasons most racing authorities have regulations and restrictions on the running of bleeders.

The true bleeder bleeds not from the head area but from the lungs. Because of the horizontal layout of the horse's respiratory tract, the blood comes up from the lungs as a trickle or stream and appears at the nostrils as a stream. This is in contrast to the situation in man, where blood brought up from the lungs comes as a foam, as this is the only way it can be moved up the vertical human trachea. If a horse bleeds from one nostril, the chances are that the blood is coming from the head area and he is not a true or pulmonary bleeder.

Because a bleeder is unsightly on the track and under some circumstances can rack up a whole field of horses, most racing authorities have strict regulations about bleeders. In New York, a first-time bleeder is put on the "vet's list" for a minimum of two and one half weeks. At the end of this period the horse is worked ⅝ of a mile, and if the horse does not bleed he is permitted to race again. If the horse bleeds a second time he is stopped for three months, and if he bleeds a third time he is stopped for six months. The fourth time a horse bleeds in New York, he is barred as a chronic bleeder.

Because of these stringent regulations for bleeders, there has long been a search for a drug that, when administered pre-race, will prevent bleeding. Among the drugs that have been used for this have been drugs that are thought for various reasons to increase blood coagulability, even though there is no known coagulation defect in bleeders.

Oxalic and malonic acids, which bind calcium ions in the blood, have been used

---

* Since the classic pattern of pulmonary bleeding occurs after exercise, this syndrome is now known as Exercise-Induced Pulmonary Hemorrhage, or E.I.P.H.

111

The sight of blood-spattered horses pulling up is not considered good for the image of racing.

historically for bleeders. The rationale behind this approach was that if one produced a small reduction in free calcium ion in the blood, one could accelerate the clotting process and thus prevent bleeding. While small amounts of oxalic and malonic acid will indeed tie up calcium ions, there is no good reason to think that this will affect the incidence of bleeders in any way, and Cook regards the success reported by some workers with these drugs as surprising. Similarly, the approach of treating horses with Vitamin K would appear to be an exercise in futility, as Vitamin K deficiency is associated with a clotting defect and there is no reason to suppose that there is a clotting defect in these animals.

Other preferred and used therapies have included bloodletting, presumably on the hypothesis that reducing blood volume will tend to reduce blood pressure. Premarin®, which is a preparation of conjugated estrogens (principally oestrone sulfate) from mare's urine, has also been used. This drug has been reported to accelerate blood clotting in dogs and is presumably used in horses for this reason, again despite the fact that there is no evidence for a clotting defect in bleeders.

Another approach to the bleeding problem that has been used for a long time is the withholding of water from the horse for about nine hours before a race. This will have the effect of reducing fluid volume in the horse, and reports from trainers suggest that this approach is successful. It is likely that it is the reported success with this approach that first gave rise to the use of Lasix® in an attempt to control the bleeder problem.

Next to Butazolidin, Lasix® is the most controversial drug in racing. Lasix is a potent diuretic drug, which causes up to a fiftyfold increase in the amount of urine voided in horses and man (Fig. 7-1). It produces this effect within minutes after its intravenous or intramuscular injection. Lasix is, in general, a safe drug. It is about the fifth most commonly prescribed drug in human medicine, a tribute to safety and efficacy. As will become apparent as this story unfolds, Lasix is just as effective in the horse as in man, and there is no reason to think that it is any less safe in the horse than it is in the human.*

Lasix was introduced into equine medicine by Doctor Marvin Beeman and his colleagues in Colorado. It is useful in edema (excess fluid in the tissues) from all causes. It is particularly useful in cases of pulmonary (lung) edema, because it acts to move this fluid out of the lungs within minutes, even before it causes any increase in the rate of urine formation. Lasix is now standard emergency therapy in the human in cases of pulmonary edema.† Its ability to increase the volume of urine may also be used to dilute substances and prevent kidney damage. Thus, when a horse "ties up," the released muscle pigment may deposit in and damage his kidneys. In situations such as this, the increased urine volume due to Lasix acts to dilute the pigments and greatly reduces the possibility of renal damage. As we will see later, Lasix can produce the same effect with some drugs, diluting them "out" in urine and rendering their detection more difficult.

---

* NOTE: All the work reported from the Kentucky Equine Drug Research program refers to injectable Lasix®, 50 mg/ml, from National Laboratories Corp., subsidiary of American Hoechst Corp., Somerville, NJ. Most of the research on furosemide reported here was done in my laboratory in cooperation with Brian Roberts, whose MSc thesis was on the pharmacology of furosemide in the horse.

† Pulmonary edema = increased fluid in the lungs

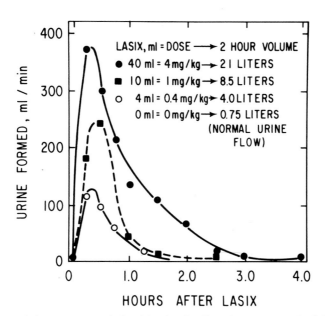

Figure 7-1. Dose and time response relationships for the diuretic response to Lasix®. The symbols show the time course of the diuretic response to an antiepistaxis dose of Lasix (open circles, o—o), a typical clinical dose of Lasix (solid squares, ■—■), and a very large dose of Lasix (solid circles, ●—●). Note that for the antiepistaxis (antibleeding) and the clinical dose, the bulk of the response is over well within one hour of dosing. All doses were administered by intravenous injection in four horses.

When our research started there were a multitude of theories about what Lasix did to horses.

Based on clinical experience with the drug, a large number of veterinarians and trainers came to believe that Lasix was an effective drug in the treatment of epistaxis. According to such clinical reports, about 200 mg (4 ml) of Lasix given intravenously or intramuscularly within one to three hours before racing either prevents epistaxis or reduces the risk of epistaxis. Based on this knowledge and the known small incidence of bleeders, many racing commissions approved furosemide for use in racing horses as prophylaxis against epistaxis.

It turned out, however, that while only a small percentage of horses suffer from epistaxis, much larger proportions of horses were being run on Lasix in jurisdictions where Lasix was a permitted medication. Many racing jurisdictions that had approved Lasix for use in bleeders found upwards of 50 percent of their horses were at times being run on Lasix. Therefore, among the questions that we hoped to answer when we studied the pharmacology of Lasix in the horse was the question of why is the use of Lasix so popular in horses that are not bleeders?

Backstretch gossip can suggest an enormous number of reasons for the use of any drug, and it was not short of suggestions about Lasix. Lasix, it was said, could "move horses up" — it would improve their performance, and this was the reason that it was widely used in horses. It was supposed to be very potent in this regard and could make "pulmonary cripples" run like the wind. Lasix also "flushed drugs" out of horses, so that the chemist would not be able to find them in blood. As well as flushing drugs out of horses, it "masked" them and diluted them in urine, so the chemist could not find them in urine. Lasix increased the blood pressure in horses, which, as everyone knows, makes horses run better. Lasix concentrated the blood in horses, which, as eveyone knows, makes horses run better. Lasix also calmed horses, which helped them to run better. This multitude of suggestions about Lasix indicated the need for a careful study of its pharmacology in the horse.

In our initial studies on Lasix in the horse, Brian Roberts and I elected to simply characterize its diuretic effect in the horse. If you give a 1000 lb horse 4 ml of Lasix (which is about 200 mg), the horse will produce about four liters of urine, mostly within the next forty minutes (see Fig. 7-1). This is about the dose that veterinarians on the track use in horses to prevent bleeding. At this dose, and if the horse is denied access to water, he will run about 8.8 lb lighter than he normally would. Some individuals believe that this is all Lasix does to a horse, and that it will, therefore, both improve his performance and explain the improvement.

A 10 ml dose of furosemide, which is a common clinical dose, produces about 9 liters of urine, mostly within the first hour after dosing. This cannot be considered a large dose of the drug, and it produces only very transient changes in the blood picture. If the dose is increased to 40 ml (4 mg/kg), the horse will lose about 21 liters of urine within two hours after dosing. One finds that if one gives 40 ml of Lasix either as a single dose intravenously (IV) or in repeated doses every hour, one still gets only about the same response (see Fig. 7-4). This and other data suggest that the maximum yield of urine in a normal horse after Lasix is about 20 to 22 liters of fluid and that the diuretic response is self-limiting.

RENAL TUBULE

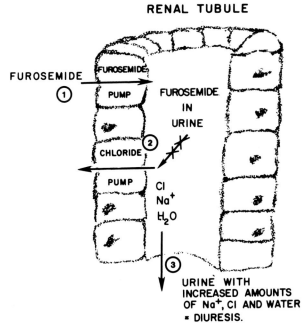

Figure 7-2. Mechanism of action of furosemide. Furosemide is actively pumped (1) into the freshly formed urine in the renal tubules by the organic acid transport system (furosemide pump). Once in the urine, furosemide blocks the reabsorption of chloride from the urine by blocking the chloride pump (2). Since sodium and water reabsorption depends on chloride reabsorption, furosemide administration leads to the elimination of increased amounts of sodium, chloride, and water, or technically, naturesis, chloruresis, and diuresis (3).

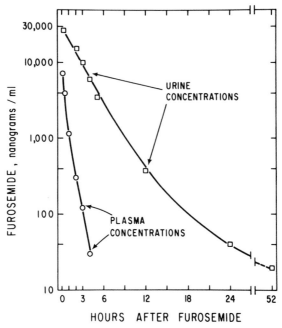

Figure 7-3. Plasma and urinary concentrations of Lasix® after intravenous administration of 1 mg/kg. The open circles (o—o) show plasma levels of Lasix after intravenous administration of 1 mg/kg of Lasix, while the open squares (□—□) show urinary concentrations of the drug. Plasma levels of furosemide fall very rapidly because it is pumped into the urine, where high concentrations of urine are found for long periods of time.

Lasix produces its diuretic effect in the horse directly in the urine by preventing the reabsorption of water in the kidney (Fig. 7-2). Lasix is a strongly acidic drug and is actively pumped out of the blood and into the newly formed urine. In the urine it acts to specifically inhibit another pump, which moves chloride ions from the urine back into the body. Chloride ions (Cl^-) are negatively charged, and positively charged sodium ions (Na^+) and water normally follow the chloride ions back into the body. By blocking the chloride pump, Lasix prevents the kidney from reabsorbing both salt (Na^+Cl^-) and water. Lasix is a particularly potent drug. Whereas normally 99 percent of the water in newly formed urine is reabsorbed during the process of urine formation, in the presence of Lasix only 50 percent may be reabsorbed. Lasix can thus produce, for a short period, a fiftyfold increase in the volume of urine being formed in horses (see Fig. 7-1).

Despite the fact that Lasix is a very potent drug, its action in the horse is very short-lived, especially if it is given by intravenous injection. The most important reason that its action is short-lived is that it is very rapidly pumped into the urine and eliminated. If one looks at the plasma levels of Lasix after it has been injected IV, one finds that they drop very rapidly indeed, with a half-life of a little over thirty minutes. On the other hand, one finds that the concentrations of the drug in urine are high, and that they fall much more slowly than the plasma levels, which one might expect if the drug was being pumped directly into the urine (Fig. 7-3).

The fact that one can get a good response to a second 10 ml dose of furosemide within one hour of a first dose further supports the idea that it is a lack of blood level of the drug that terminates the diuretic response to Lasix (Fig. 7-4). Further, if you plot the rate of decline of the plasma levels of the drug and compare them with the rate of decline of the diuretic effect, you will find a very good relationship whether the drug is given intravenously or intramuscularly. Based on these observations we concluded that the principal reason for the short action of Lasix after its intravenous injection was that it was rapidly excreted in the urine.

Because furosemide is secreted rapidly and directly into urine, it is found there in quite high concentrations and for a much longer period than it can be detected in blood. Lasix fluoresces strongly under ultraviolet light and under acidic conditions gives a good color reaction in the Bratton-Marshall test. Chemists use both of these reactions to detect Lasix on thin-layer plates. If the Lasix molecule is methylated it runs well on gas-liquid chromatography, and this derivative of the molecule can also be analyzed by mass spectrometry. A good analyst can easily detect furosemide in equine urine for twelve hours after a 10 ml dose, and we were able to detect it in our experiments for up to fifty-two hours (see Fig. 7-3). Because none of the effects of furosemide are likely to last longer than about six hours or be associated with a urinary level of the drug of less than 0.5 µg/ml of furosemide, there appears to be no need for detection of Lasix more than twelve hours after its administration. Racing chemists should bear this in mind when setting the levels of sensitivity of their test systems and not use unduly sensitive tests for this drug.

This rapid excretion of Lasix also means that a very large proportion of a dose of Lasix is excreted unchanged in the urine. While for most drugs in the horse only a very small (5% or less) proportion of the parent drug is excreted unchanged in the urine, at least 60 percent of a dose of Lasix is excreted in the urine. This means that there is no tendency for Lasix to accumulate or build up in the horse,

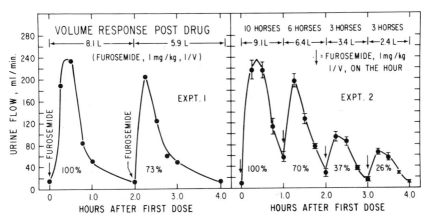

Figure 7-4. Diuretic response to repeated doses of furosemide. To test the hypothesis that it is the rapid elimination of furosemide that terminates its pharmacological effect, repeated doses of the drug were administered. The data show that a second dose within one hour after the first produced a good diuresis, showing that the horse is still able to respond to furosemide. While consistent with the idea that it is drug elimination that terminates the diuretic action after a single dose, the effects of repeated doses show that under some circumstances the availability of fluid to eliminate can be the critical factor. Reproduced with permission from Tobin et al., *J Equine Med Surg*, 2:216, 1978.

TABLE 7-I

CUMULATIVE WATER AND Na$^+$ LOSS AFTER 1 mg/kg FUROSEMIDE INTRAVENOUSLY
AND INTRAMUSCULARLY

Time After Administration	1.0 mg/kg IV		1.0 mg/kg IM	
	Urine Vol. (liter)	Na$^+$ Excretion (mEq)	Urine Vol. (liter)	Na$^+$ Excretion (mEq)
1 hour	8.2	732	8.4	621
2 hours	9.0	744	12.6	887
4 hours	10.5	748	16.2	994

so the drug is not toxic and doses can be safely repeated at daily intervals. Further, since many drug toxicities are due to drug metabolites rather than to the drugs themselves, the small metabolism and rapid excretion of Lasix makes it that much safer as a drug.

One way of getting partly around the rapid excretion of Lasix is to give it intramuscularly. When given in this way the drug is apparently slowly released from the injection site in muscle into the bloodstream. Its half-life in the blood is therefore about eighty minutes instead of thirty minutes, and the diuretic effect lasts longer. If one gives a 10 ml dose of Lasix by IM injection rather than by IV injection, one gets about a 50 percent greater response and the response is spread over three hours instead of one hour after IV administration. All other things being equal, then, IM administration is probably the most effective way to use Lasix (Table 7-I).

The effects of Lasix on the heart and blood vessels are also transient, peaking within ten minutes and then declining. After IV injection, furosemide reduces blood pressure in the lungs within minutes. This effect occurs independently of the diuretic effect and has been seen in experimental animals in which no urine was being formed. Curiously, however, this effect seems to require furosemide to release a prostaglandin from the kidney. Antiprostaglandin drugs such as phenylbutazone, therefore, may act to block the pulmonary effects of Lasix, a rather surprising finding in view of the frequency with which these two drugs are used together in racing horses.

In the general circulation, Lasix does not affect or reduce blood pressure, despite "off the cuff" comments by people who should know better. Furosemide, however, produces a small increase in heart rate but reduces the actual amount of blood pumped by the heart. After IV injection of the drug at 1 mg/kg (10 ml, more than the usual dose used in epistaxis) the effects of Lasix on the heart and blood vessels are usually over within two hours.

In the bloodstream a dose of Lasix produces an increase in total plasma solids of about 10 percent and an increase in the concentration of red blood cells (hematocrit) of about 5 percent. Despite the fact that sodium is the major cation lost in urine after Lasix, there is never any change in plasma sodium concentrations. Lasix, however, rapidly reduces plasma potassium by about 25 percent. All of these effects occur between ten and thirty minutes after an IV dose, and all values are back to control levels by two hours postdosing (Fig. 7-5).

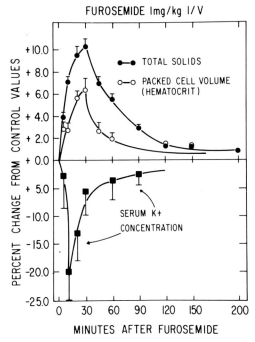

Figure 7-5. Effects of furosemide on some blood parameters. The solid (●) and open (○) circles show the effects of 1 mg/kg of furosemide IV on blood hematocrit (red cell fraction) and total plasma solids. The solid squares (■) show the depression of serum potassium levels produced by this same dose. The effects all peak within thirty minutes after dosing and by two hours postdosing are back to control levels. Reproduced with permission from Tobin et al., *J Equine Med Surg*, 2:216, 1978.

There is a widespread belief that Lasix has an effect on the detection of drugs in horses and that this effect might possibly account for its widespread use in racing horses. One of these is the thought that Lasix might, by increasing the volume of urine, cause a "flushing" of drugs out of the body of the horse. Another is that Lasix might mask or interfere with the detection of other drugs. A third and more likely effect is that the increased volume of urine produced by Lasix simply dilutes some of the drugs normally found in urine. Typical of these views are the following comments cited in a book entitled *The Misuse of Drugs in Horse Racing*, which read as follows:

> Lasix® binds itself to other drugs that may be circulating freely in the horse's system and washes the other drugs out. There is no doubt that some trainers are using Lasix to mask other (illicit) drugs that may be administered before a race. Whether Lasix actually prevents bleeders is iffy. It lowers the blood pressure through dehydration and this may help. But the real interest is in flushing and masking. There is no question that it gives horses a competitive edge.

These comments are particularly surprising. There is no evidence whatsoever that Lasix binds itself to other drugs. There is not a single shred of evidence in the scientific literature that Lasix "washes" or "flushes" drugs out of a horse's body. In a number of studies carried out in Kentucky, Lasix did not act to reduce plasma half-lives ("clearance time") of either procaine (Fig. 7-6) or phenylbutazone (Fig. 7-7) or methylphenidate, and these studies have been confirmed and extended by other laboratories. All one can say, in block letters, is that **LASIX DOES NOT FLUSH DRUGS OUT OF THE BLOODSTREAM OF HORSES, PERIOD.**

The reason that Lasix does not flush drugs out of horses (i.e. reduce their blood levels) is quite simply that Lasix does not move very much fluid out of horses.

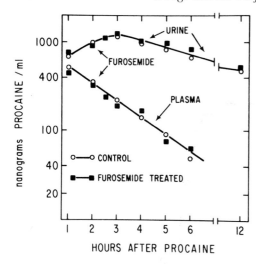

Figure 7-6. Lack of effect of furosemide on plasma and urinary levels of procaine. The open circles (○) show plasma and urinary concentrations of procaine after 10 mg/kg of procaine was given by IM injection. The solid squares (■) show plasma and urinary levels when the same dose of procaine was followed by 1 mg/kg of furosemide IV. The data show that the administration of procaine had no significant effect on plasma or urinary levels procaine. Reproduced with permission from Roberts et al., *J Equine Med Surg*, 2:185, 1978.

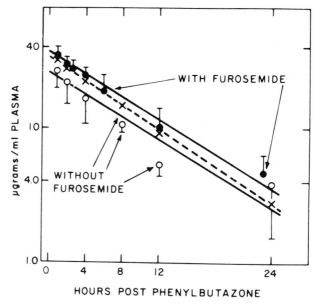

Figure 7-7. Lack of effect of furosemide on plasma levels of phenylbutazone. The open circles (○—○) and crosses (×—×) show plasma levels of phenylbutazone after 6.6 mg/kg (about 3 gms/1000 lb.) of the drug was administered IV. The solid circles (●—●) show the plasma levels of phenylbutazone when the phenylbutazone was followed by 1 mg/kg of furosemide IV at 2.5 hours. The data show that furosemide did not significantly reduce the plasma levels of phenylbutazone. Furosemide, therefore, did not "flush" phenylbutazone out of these horses. Reproduced with permission from Roberts et al., *J Equine Med Surg*, 2:185, 1978.

Although the diuretic response looks very dramatic to the casual observer, the actual volume of urine is only about 2 to 3 percent of the body fluid of the horse. Thus, in its brief period of action, Lasix would be unlikely to lead to the loss of more than 3 percent of the drug in the horse, and for most drugs the effect will be a lot less than this. This inability of Lasix to lead to the elimination of more than a very small percentage of a drug from a horse accounts for its lack of effect on the blood levels of drugs in horses.

Lasix does not reduce the concentrations of certain classes of drugs in equine urine. In studies at the University of Kentucky we administered procaine, a local anesthetic, and methylphenidate, a brain stimulant, to horses and studied the effects of Lasix on urinary concentrations of these drugs. Lasix had no significant effect on the urinary concentrations of these drugs, indicating that their detection in urine is not likely to be significantly affected by Lasix. Experimental work on amphetamine using a closely related diuretic shows that this effect likely also holds for the amphetamines. Thus, it turns out that for these basic, lipid-soluble drugs, Lasix is not able or likely to interfere with urinary detection.

Treatment with Lasix can have marked effects on the urinary detection of other drugs. For example, if a horse is treated with phenylbutazone, the urinary concentration of the drug measured, and then Lasix administered, one finds that Lasix can reduce the urinary concentration of phenylbutazone up to fiftyfold. This is a very substantial reduction in the urinary concentration of phenylbutazone, and it is sufficient to interfere with routine screening for phenylbutazone (Fig. 7-8). This can create problems when both Lasix and phenylbutazone are permitted medications. The answer to this problem, however, is relatively straightforward. Because Lasix *does not change the plasma levels of any drug,* one can readily (and more accurately) determine the presence of phenylbutazone from a blood sample, and this is now routinely done in Kentucky.

Although the specific experimental work has not been done, it appears very

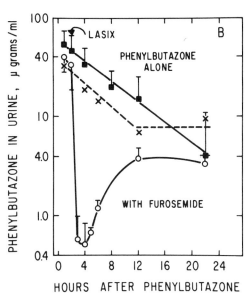

Figure 7-8. Effect of furosemide on urinary phenylbutazone concentrations. The crosses (×—×) and solid squares (■—■) show the urinary concentrations of phenylbutazone after horses were administered 3 gms/1000 lb. (6.6 mg/kg) at zero time. The open circles (o—o) show urinary concentrations of phenylbutazone when 1 mg/kg furosemide was administered IV at 2.5 hours after the Lasix®. The experiment shows that treatment with furosemide can reduce urinary concentrations of phenylbutazone up to fiftyfold or more for a short period after administration of the drug. Reproduced with permission from Roberts et al., *J Equine Med Surg,* 2:185, 1978.

likely that Lasix will similarly dilute urinary levels of other non-steroidal anti-inflammatory drugs such as Equiproxen, Banamine®, Tolectin®, et cetera. Another group of drugs whose detection in urine is highly likely to be influenced by Lasix is water-soluble glucuronide drug metabolites. These drug metabolites enter urine either by glomerular filtration or are pumped into it by the organic acid transport system. Once in the renal tubule, these highly water-soluble drug metabolites are not about to pass back into the blood. Their final concentration in urine, therefore, depends on the degree to which the urine is concentrated. Since Lasix can dilute equine urine up to fiftyfold, it is likely to dilute some water-soluble drug metabolites such as glucuronides by up to fiftyfold.

We have experimentally demonstrated this effect on drug metabolites with Talwin® (pentazocine), a narcotic analgesic often used in the horse. After a dose of Talwin in the horse, relatively large amounts of pentazocine (Talwin) glucuronide are found in the urine. Glucuronides are one of the most important types of water-soluble drug metabolites formed in the horse, and they are not likely to be reabsorbed in the renal tubules. The experiment of Figure 7-9 shows that the glucuronide metabolite of pentazocine is diluted up to fiftyfold after Lasix and that as the effect of Lasix wears off, the urinary concentrations of the drug return to control values.

Because fentanyl is a very potent narcotic that has been used in racing horses, we also tested the effects of furosemide on its urinary detection. We elected to carry out this experiment with the dose of furosemide usually used in the treatment of epistaxis, as the diluting effect of this dose should be both smaller than and of shorter duration than the effect of a 1 mg/kg dose. As shown in Figure 7-10, furosemide produced about a fifteenfold dilution of urinary fentanyl at peak effect, and the effect was over within about 2.5 hours after dosing. The experiment suggests that when a diluting effect of furosemide does occur, the extent of the dilution is closely related to the diuretic response and therefore is dose related.

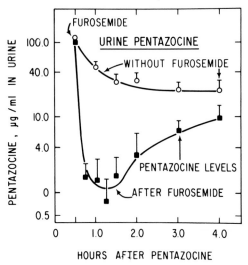

Figure 7-9. Dilution of the glucuronide metabolite of pentazocine by furosemide. The open circles (o—o) show urinary concentrations of pentazocine as pentazocine glucuronide after administration of 0.33 mg/kg of pentazocine (Talwin®). The solid squares (■—■) show urinary concentrations of this metabolite in horses treated with 1 mg/kg of furosemide thirty minutes after the pentazocine was administered. The experiment shows that furosemide transiently dilutes urinary levels of the major glucuronide metabolite of pentazocine. Reproduced with permission from Roberts et al., *J Equine Med Surg*, 2:185, 1978.

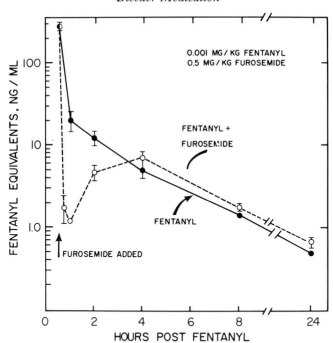

Figure 7-10. Urinary levels of fentanyl after 0.5 mg/kg furosemide. The solid circles (●—●) show urinary concentrations of fentanyl as fentanyl equivalents after administration of 0.5 mg of fentanyl to three horses. The open circles (○—○) show urinary levels of fentanyl equivalents when 0.5 mg/kg of furosemide was administered at thirty-one minutes after the fentanyl. The data show that this dose of furosemide reduced the urinary concentrations of fentanyl about fifteenfold and that the effect lasted for about two and one-half hours.

Because of this shorter period for which the smaller, antiepistaxis dose of Lasix acted to dilute fentanyl in urine, we elected to repeat this dilution experiment with phenylbutazone as the test drug. In the experiment of Figure 7-11 we dosed three horses with 2 gm/1000 lb of phenylbutazone IV and then treated them with 3.5 ml of furosemide (0.33 mg/kg) at two hours after the dose of phenylbutazone. As before, treatment with Lasix produced an immediate and rapid dilution of the phenylbutazone in the horse's urine, but the dilution was very short-lived. By four hours after dosing with furosemide the urinary levels of phenylbutazone were not significantly different from the controls. Comparison of the data of Figure 7-11 with the data of Figure 7-8 therefore shows that the diluting effect of Lasix is much shorter-lived when the dose is reduced to the antiepistaxis dose, and it appears that the duration of the dilution effect is therefore dose related.

This dilution of the major water-soluble metabolite of pentazocine and fentanyl may also occur with other drugs. Thus, apomorphine, morphine, and related narcotics and the phenothiazine tranquilizers are all detected in equine urine as water-soluble glucuronides. Since these are potent drugs that produce their pharmacological effects at quite low doses, the concentration of these glucuronide metabolites in urine can be quite important for their detection. Their dilution by Lasix may be a problem for the analyst and appears to be the only potential problem associated with approval of furosemide for use in racing horses.

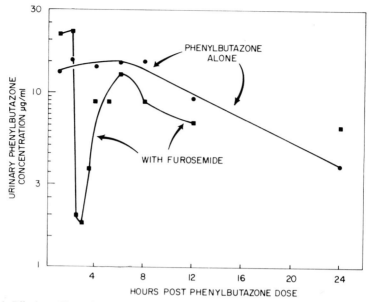

Figure 7-11. Diluting effect of an antiepistaxis dose of furosemide on uinary phenylbutazone. Four horses were dosed with 2 gms/1000 lb. of phenylbutazone IV at indicated zero time and then with either saline or 0.33 mg/kg (3.5 ml) of furosemide at two hours. The solid circles (●—●) show the urinary concentrations of phenylbutazone in the horses receiving saline, while the solid squares (■—■) show urinary levels of phenylbutazone in the horses treated with furosemide.

On the other hand, from what we know about the glucuronide metabolites of both pentazocine, apomorphine, and the phenothiazine tranquilizers, they are excreted over particularly long periods — apparently up to five days in some cases. If this prolonged excretion holds for other glucuronide metabolites, then simply holding horses for three to four hours after the injection of furosemide should yield a reasonably concentrated urine sample and detectable quantities of glucuronides. In this way it may be possible to get around the only potential problem with the approval of Lasix for use in racing horses, which is it diluting effects for some drugs in equine urine.

Another major area of contention about Lasix concerns its effect on equine performance. As suggested earlier, some uncomplicated minds have put forward the simple theory that Lasix treatment just makes a horse eight pounds lighter and therefore eight pounds faster. This proposal ignores the many other known effects of Lasix or perhaps assumes that they conveniently cancel each other out. Theoretical concepts of this caliber do not belong in serious scientific discussions.

A commonsense approach to problems such as this is first to determine whether or not the problem actually exists. Does Lasix actually improve the performance of horses? Performance trials in which horses were raced with and without Lasix have been carried out at both the Ohio State University and the University of Kentucky. These trials were on healthy horses and were conducted double-blind, that is, the people handling and clocking the horse did not know which horses were getting the drugs and which ones were getting the nondrug injections. Both of these trials showed no statistically significant effects of Lasix on the performance of Standardbred horses.

While these results were encouraging, the number of horses used in the tests was small, and one could reasonably suggest that a bigger study might show a significant improvement of performance in horses on furosemide. At the prompting of Mr. Carl Larsen of the Standardbred Commission in Kentucky, we did a retrospective study on the effect of Lasix on the track times of horses racing at Louisville Downs in the summer of 1977. At this meet, Lasix was the only permitted medication, and its use was monitored by drug testing. Horses could elect to go on furosemide at any time throughout the meet, but once on Lasix they had to stay on Lasix. From this group of horses whose trainers elected to put them on Lasix during the meet, we found 58 horses for whom we had 160 times before they went on furosemide and 232 after they were on furosemide. We thus had a large number of times for 58 horses before and after they went on furosemide. These horses were presumably "put on" furosemide because their owners, trainers, or veterinarians thought that it would improve their performance. When the figures were analyzed, it turned out that the horses were actually 0.14 second slower on Lasix than without Lasix (Table 7-II). This very small difference was not significantly different statistically from the control or pre-Lasix time. From these figures it appears that Lasix does not improve the performance of a horse and, if anything, is likely to add a tenth of a second to his time.

The only conclusion from this study seems to be that the horsemen at Louisville Downs in the summer of 1977 were not, on the whole, able to improve the performance of their horses with furosemide, and it would seem reasonable to extend this experimental result to other horses and horsemen. Lengthy speculations such as one hears, and occasionally sees published, about possible mechanisms by which furosemide improves the performance of horses are therefore not valid.

As well as not improving performance in the horse, Lasix is relatively nontoxic and appears to be a very safe drug in the human as well as in the horse. The usual

TABLE 7-II

LACK OF EFFECT OF FUROSEMIDE ON THE PERFORMANCE OF HORSES RACING AT LOUISVILLE DOWNS, SUMMER, 1977*

	# of Horses	# of Trials	Mean Times	S.E.M.	
Prefurosemide	58	160	128.5925	0.2031	F = <0.00
With furosemide	58	232	128.7366	0.1594	(F for significance should be >3.0)

* At this meet, furosemide was the only permitted medication, and its use was checked by urinalysis. Horses could elect to go on furosemide at any time throughout the meet but once on furosemide had to stay on it. Performance times for horses pre- and postfurosemide treatment were obtained from the meet programs and compared. Only times on good or fast tracks were taken. Of the 58 horses selected, 160 prefurosemide times were available and 232 postfurosemide times. A randomized block design was used where each horse represented a block. After adjusting for blocks (i.e. differences between horses) there was no significant difference between treatments (i.e. times on and off furosemide). Furosemide therefore had no significant effect on the performance of this group of horses.

dose administered in the treatment of "bleeders" is a small dose, and when administered IV, its action is brief. If the horse is given access to water and salt, any drug-induced fluid or salt losses should be rapidly replenished.

In another series of experiments we dosed horses daily with 10 ml (1 mg/kg) doses of furosemide for four consecutive days, and a series of blood values over the four-day test period were observed. No cumulative changes in the blood picture of these horses during this four-day study were observed. However, if these same four doses were given at hourly intervals, a 40 percent drop in serum K^+ was observed. Thus, the only acute problem with large and repeated doses of furosemide would appear to be the possibility of inducing hypokalemia (lowered serum potassium levels) with repeated doses, a situation that is not likely to occur in racing horses.

How furosemide might act to prevent "bleeders" is currently unclear, due at least in part to the fact that no one knows what causes bleeders in the first place. While "true bleeders" are usually assumed to bleed from the lungs, the lung has two blood supplies, and no one knows which blood supply is involved in incidents of bleeding. The lung has a low pressure blood supply to the tissue where the gas exchange takes place and a higher pressure (normal body blood pressure) supply to the supporting structures of the lung such as the tracheobronchial tree and connective tissue. Which of these two circulations is involved in "bleeders" is unknown.

One often suggested cause of bleeding is pulmonary hypertension (i.e. high blood pressure) in the pulmonary circulation, leading to rupture of a blood vessel. The problem with this hypothesis is that high blood pressure in the pulmonary circulation is much more likely to cause massive pulmonary edema than hemorrhage. In other words, the increased blood pressure would cause the horse to drown in his own pulmonary fluids before breakdown of a blood vessel and bleeding from the lungs might be expected. Similarly, upper airway obstruction can be ruled out as a cause of bleeders, since pulmonary edema rather than hemorrhage is the most likely end result of upper airway obstruction.

Giving further consideration to this problem, Robinson* suggests that local lesions in the lung tissue, such as airway obstruction, scar tissue, or pleural adhesions, are critical factors in the incidence of bleeders. Under these circumstances these locally lesioned portions of lung would not expand, while the rest of the normal lung would expand considerably. The horse is among animals that have very poor collateral ventilation in their lungs, and their alveoli thus very easily become blocked off. Under these circumstances a strong inspiratory effort expands all but the lesioned portion of the lung, and capillary rupture occurs at the interface of the normal and affected tissue.

It is also clear that if furosemide does anything in the lungs, it acts to reduce pulmonary edema. As pointed out earlier, this action is rapid, is independent of the diuretic effect of this drug, and appears to be due to a furosemide-induced release of prostaglandins from the kidneys. If Robinson's model is correct and a local lesion in the lungs is the fundamental cause of epistaxis, then furosemide

---

* N. E. Robinson, Professor of Large Animal Surgery and Medicine, Michigan State University, East Lansing, MI

may act by relieving pulmonary edema, eliminating local blockade of airways in damaged lung tissue, and thus preventing hemorrhage. Similarly, Robinson points out that E-prostaglandins are bronchodilators, and their release by furosemide may act by dilating bronchi to reduce localized airway obstruction and thus the incidence of epistaxis (Fig. 7-12).

Another question that is often asked about Lasix is why, if there are not more than 200 racehorses in California that bleed in any one year, are much higher percentages, reportedly sometimes up to 80 percent of horses at some meets, running on Lasix? The answer to this question that veterinarians give is that Lasix helps a large number of horses with their breathing and therefore helps these horses to perform up to their best form.

Until very recently, there was no experimental evidence to support this clinical impression of practitioners and horsemen. Recently, however, Doctor John Pascoe of the University of California has been studying hemorrhage in the upper respiratory tract of horses post-race and has come up with some results that throw a completely new light on the incidence of bleeding in racing horses.

Doctor Pascoe and his colleagues have been examining the upper respiratory tracts of horses in the test barn immediately post-race with a fiberoptic endoscope. These studies have been carried out in California, Illinois, and Florida, in both Thoroughbred and Standardbred horses, and the basic observations have been essentially similar in each case. What Doctor Pascoe found was that the incidence of overt bleeding from the nostrils post-race was about that which has been reported over the years, i.e. 2 to 3 percent or so. However, fiberoptic endoscope

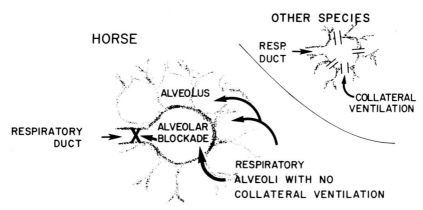

Figure 7-12. Schematic representation of Robinson's equine epistaxis hypothesis. Robinson has suggested that the reason the horse suffers from epistaxis more than other species is anatomical. In the lungs of most species, the small delicate organs called the alveoli, where gas exchange takes place, communicate readily with one another. These communications (inset) are technically called collateral ventilation and make it very difficult to prevent air from entering the alveolus. In the horse, however, there is little collateral ventilation, as indicated by the heavy stippling around the alveolus. Under these conditions, if blockade of the respiratory duct occurs, the alveolus will not expand with the rest of the lung when the animal breathes in. It is thought that the pressure differences between the blocked and unexpanded alveolus (indicated by the dark lines) cause rupture of the alveolar wall and bleeding into the lung tissue, which may appear at the nostrils as epistaxis. Furosemide, by dilating respiratory ducts and reducing pulmonary edema, is thought to reduce alveolar blockade and thus the incidence of epistaxis. Species other than the equine tend to have good collateral ventilation between alveoli (inset), so alveolar blockade and epistaxis in the equine pattern is much less likely to occur.

While some people have the idea that huge amounts of Lasix are used in horses, in actual fact the dose used in the treatment of bleeders is quite small.

Use of the endoscope to examine the windpipe of horses post-race has thrown a great deal of light on the incidence of epistaxis.

examination of the upper respiratory tract has shown about 10 percent of horses post-race have very substantial amounts of blood in their windpipes (trachea, Fig. 7-13), that about 10 percent show flecks of blood, and that another 20 percent show intermediate amounts of hemorrhage. Thus, in all, between about 30 and 40 percent of horses show signs of hemorrhage in the upper respiratory tract post-race, although only 1 to 3 percent ever show overt bleeding at the nostrils. It appears likely, therefore, that the small percentage of bleeders seen historically only represents the "tip of the iceberg" with regard to pulmonary hemorrhage, and that pulmonary hemorrhage is far more widespread in racing horses than previously realized. These observations are, of course, in good agreement with the clinical impression that Lasix helps a much greater proportion of horses than just the classic bleeders.

Finally, one might ask, does Lasix actually prevent bleeding in horses, and if so, how? This is a very difficult question to answer, because since such a small percentage of horses bleed from the nose, and then only sporadically, it is not a problem that it is possible to easily approach experimentally. By and large, therefore, the principal evidence that Lasix actually does help prevent bleeding is the experience of veterinarians, which is a clinical impression. In this regard,

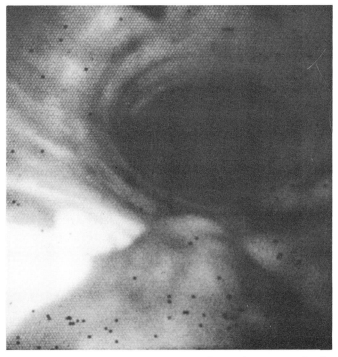

Figure 7-13. Post-race tracheal hemorrhage. In this horse, fiberopticscope examination of the trachea post-race revealed a "river" of blood about one-half inch wide on the floor of the trachea. No hemorrhage was visible at the nostrils in this horse. The black dots are due to damaged fibers in the endoscope. Courtesy of Doctor John Pascoe, University of California, Davis.

recent studies* by Doctor John Pascoe of the University of California have shown that the incidence of E.I.P.H. or pulmonary bleeding in furosemide-treated horses varies between about 40 and 60 percent. What is not known, however, is what the proportion of hemorrhage would have been in these horses in the absence of furosemide treatment. Nevertheless, these results do suggest that, at best, furosemide treatment cannot be more than about 50 percent effective in the treatment of E.I.P.H. or pulmonary bleeding.

To summarize the research findings with this drug, it is clear that Lasix is a very safe and effective diuretic in the horse. It is approved for use in the treatment of epistaxis by many racing authorities and is widely used in horses for this effect. However, the evidence that suggests that it is an effective treatment for this problem comes primarily from clinical observations. Lasix has been very widely and also very incorrectly reported to "flush" drugs out of horses. *Lasix does not flush drugs out of horses.* "Masking" of drugs by Lasix is a problem that has not been studied or reported on and does not appear to be significant. Lasix will act to dilute some drugs and drug metabolites in horse urine. This appears to be the only potential problem with the approval of Lasix for use in racing. It can be overcome by waiting about four hours for the diluting effects of Lasix to pass and then taking the urine sample.

Lasix is widely rumored to improve the performance of racing horses. As with most rumors, it is not clear whether or not the horses helped are healthy horses, whom Lasix enables to perform better than their normal ability, or horses with respiratory problems, whom Lasix brings up to normal performance. Many veterinarians have speculated about these rumored performance effects and have proposed mechanisms by which Lasix might improve performance. Unfortunately, all studies on the effects of Lasix on performance in horses have shown no effect, both in healthy horses in University-sponsored studies or in retrospective studies on track times. *The conclusion that Lasix does not improve the performance of horses under racing conditions seems at this time to be inescapable.*

Finally, concluding a remarkably complete compendium of opinions on the effects of Lasix in horses, Robert Baker levelled the accusation against the racing community that it is "now using Lasix to keep pulmonary cripples racing." If Lasix were indeed a "wonder drug" that could keep "pulmonary cripples" racing, one might reasonably expect to see at least some small improvement in performance in a study such as the Louisville Downs study. No trace of such an effect was observed, which strongly suggests that current patterns of Lasix use in horse racing do not represent an abuse of this drug.

SELECTED REFERENCES

Bourland, W. A., Day, D. K., and Williamson, H. E.: The role of the kidney in the early non-diuretic action of furosemide to reduce left atrial pressure. *J Pharmacol Exp Ther, 202:*221-229, 1977.

Burg, M. and Stoner, L.: Renal tubular chloride transport and the mode of action of some diuretics. *Ann Rev Physiol, 38:*37-45, 1976.

Cook, W. R.: Epistaxis in the racehorse. *Equine Vet J, 6:*45-58, 1974.

---

* Pascoe, J.R. Exercise induced pulmonary hemorrhage in racing horses: Current status. Presented at the Invitational Workshop on Viral Respiratory Diseases and Complications, May 19-21, The Ohio State University, Columbus, OH, 1980.

Gabel, A. A., Tobin, Thomas, Ray, Richard S., and Maylin, G. A.: Furosemide in horses: A review. *J Equine Med Surg*, *1:*215-218, 1977.

Muir, W. W., Milne, D. W., and Skarda, R. T.: Acute hemodynamic effects of furosemide administered intravenously in the horse. *Am J Vet Res, 37:*1177, 1976.

Roberts, B. L., Blake, J. W., and Tobin, T.: The pharmacology of furosemide in the horse. II. Its detection, pharmacokinetics, and clearance from urine. *J Equine Med Surg, 2:*185-194, 1978.

Robinson, N. E.: Functional abnormalities caused by upper airway obstruction and heaves: Their relationship to the etiology of epistaxis. *Vet Clin North Am: Large Animal Practice, 1:*17-34, 1979.

Tobin, T.: Pharmacology review: A review of recent research on furosemide in the horse. *J Equine Med Surg, 2:*314-321, 1979.

Tobin, T., Roberts, B. L., and Miller, R. W.: The pharmacology of furosemide in the horse. I. Effects on the disposition of procaine, phenylbutazone, methylphenidate, and pentazocine. *J Equine Med Surg, 1:*402-409, 1977.

Tobin, T., Roberts, B. L., Swerczek, T. W., and Crisman, M.: The pharmacology of furosemide in the horse. III. Dose and time response relationships, effects of repeated dosing and performance effects. *J Equine Med Surg, 2:*216-226.

Vail, C. D., Beeman, G. M., and Johnson, H. W.: Furosemide in equine practice. *Vet Med, 62:*881-884, 1967.

Chapter 8

STEROIDAL ANTI-INFLAMMATORY AGENTS: THE CORTICOSTEROIDS AND ACTH

THE CORTICOSTEROIDS are drugs that are chemically classified as steroids and were originally identified in the cortex of the adrenal glands. The adrenals are two small glands that lie just above the kidneys and which have been known for over 100 years to be essential for normal life. By the 1930s, crude extracts of the adrenal glands were being used in human medicine, and over the next twenty years the chemical structure, pharmacological properties, and therapeutic uses of these drugs were worked out. The corticosteroids are classic examples of drugs whose discovery and development were based on man's increasing understanding of his own chemistry.

The corticosteroids may be divided into three subgroups based on their therapeutic effects. The first, and most important group for horsemen, is the glucocorticoids, which predominantly affect protein and carbohydrate metabolism and which produce the powerful anti-inflammatory effects of this group of drugs. The second group is the mineralocorticoids, represented in nature by aldosterone, which give rise to sodium and water retention. The third group consists of the adrenal sex hormones. Since the anti-inflammatory actions of the corticosteroids are those with which horsemen are primarily concerned, this chapter will concentrate on the pharmacology of the glutocorticoid or anti-inflammatory corticosteroids.

Cortisol is the natural anti-inflammatory corticosteroid, but it also has substantial effects on sodium and water retention. Because of this, drug companies have selectively modified the basic cortisol molecule to give rise to analogues with more anti-inflammatory activity and fewer effects on water retention. The drug companies have been very successful in this search, and the synthetic corticosteroid flumethasone, for example, is about 700 times more potent an anti-inflammatory agent than cortisol and has essentially no effect on water or sodium metabolism (Table 8-I).

The precise mechanism of the anti-inflammatory effects of the corticosteroids is not known, although substantial research progress has been made in this area. In the horse, the natural corticosteroids travel from the adrenal in the bloodstream to reach the target tissue. Once they reach the tissue where they are to act, they enter the individual cells and bind to specific receptor proteins in the cells. This corticosteroid-receptor complex then enters the nucleus of the cell, where it gives rise to the synthesis of new protein (Fig. 8-1). The initial action of all steroid hormones, therefore, is thought to be new protein synthesis, even though the results of this new protein synthesis may lead to cellular breakdown and death of cells. The synthetic corticosteroids produce their anti-inflammatory effects locally if injected locally, or over the whole animal if injected systemically.

As well as having a potent anti-inflammatory effect, the corticosteroids have

TABLE 8-I
RELATIVE POTENCY OF CORTICOSTEROIDS

	Sodium Retention	*Anti-inflammatory Action*
Natural Steroids:		
Cortisol	1	1
Corticosterone	15	0.3
Synthetic Steroids:		
Prednisolone	0.8	4
Dexamethasone	0	25
Flumethasone	0	700

equally potent effects on protein and sugar metabolism. So far, it has proved impossible to separate these effects on protein and sugar metabolism from the anti-inflammatory effects of this group of drugs. It appears likely, therefore, that the effects on protein and sugar metabolism and the anti-inflammatory response are different facets of the same fundamental process.

The anti-inflammatory effects of the corticosteroids are seen after both local and general (systemic) administration. Because bursal, tendon, or joint problems

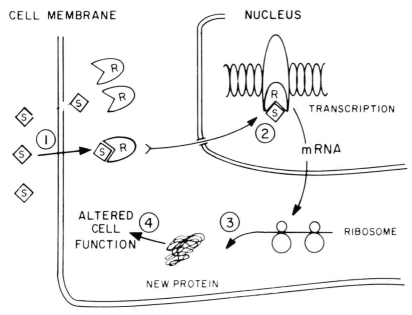

Figure 8-1. Mechanism of action of the corticosteroids. Corticosteroid drugs (S) enter the target cells and bind to specific receptors (R) in the cell cytoplasm (1). In binding they change the shape of these receptors, and the altered drug-receptor complex diffuses into the nucleus of the cell. In the nucleus this complex binds to receptors on the genes and initiates transcription (2). The newly formed mRNA diffuses out of the nucleus, binds to the ribosomes, and gives rise to new proteins, which redirect the function of the cell (4). Although the primary action of the corticosteroids is therefore to cause the synthesis of new proteins, their ultimate effects usually lead to tissue breakdown. Reproduced with permission from Tobin, *J Equine Med Surg, 3:*10, 1979.

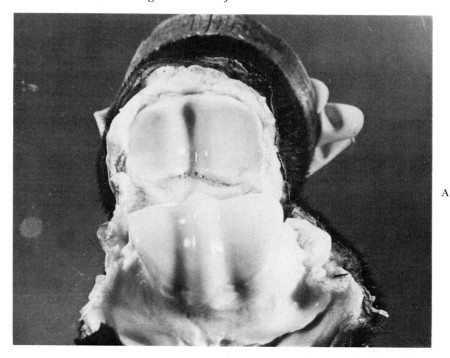

A

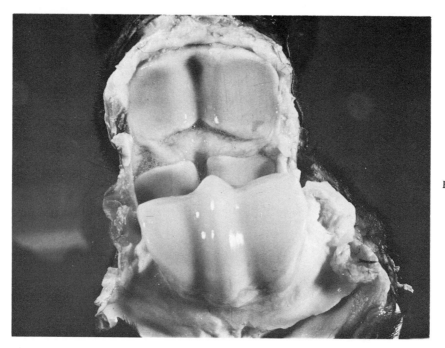

B

Figure 8-2. Articular damage in a corticosteroid-injected joint. A and B. A normal fetlock or pastern (ankle) joint from a mature horse. Note the clear, **smooth,** continuous articular cartilages on which the joint rotates. Small wear lines are visible on the **upper right-**hand surface of the pastern bone, which is

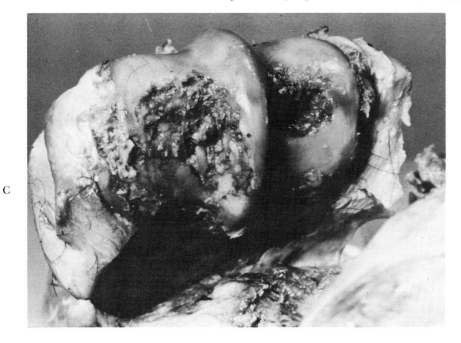

C

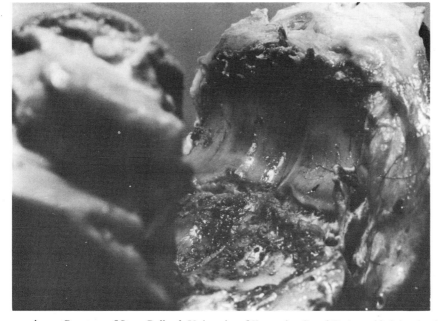

D

the upper bone. Courtesy of Steve Ballard, University of Kentucky. C and D. An ankle joint that had been injected with corticosteroids, showing large erosions penetrating down to the surface of bone through the articular cartilage. Courtesy of Doctor Larry Bramledge, The Ohio State University.

in racing horses are usually limited to one or two specific areas, the anti-inflammatory corticosteroids are very often given locally, usually directly into or adjacent to the inflamed tissue or joint cavity.

When injected either locally or systemically, the synthetic corticosteroids have the ability to prevent or suppress the heat, redness, pain, swelling, and loss of function by which inflammation is recognized. At the microscopic level they inhibit both the early and late phases of the inflammatory process. In the early stages they inhibit fluid formation, capillary dilation, and the migration of inflammatory cells from the blood into the tissues. They also inhibit the later stages of inflammation, such as capillary proliferation and scar tissue formation. The precise mechanisms of these effects are not well understood, but the corticosteroids produce these effects quite independent of the type of agent that elicits the response. The effect is therefore a suppression of the scar tissue response to trauma rather than any direct neutralization of the causative agents.

Because the anti-inflammatory effects of the corticosteroids simply suppress tissue response, treatment with these drugs in no way neutralizes or removes the primary cause of the disease but merely suppresses the clinical signs. This suppression of clinical signs is the most dangerous aspect of corticosteroid therapy. For example, a damaged joint injected with corticosteroids will appear to improve and the horse will be much improved or go sound. In truth, however, the condition may well progress at least at the same rate as it would have in the absence of corticosteroids, and collapse, when it does occur, can be sudden and without warning. This aspect of the action of the corticosteroids has given rise to the grim comment that "a patient on corticosteroids can walk all the way to the autopsy room." Similarly, a horse can wear a joint surface right down to the bone running on a glucocorticoid-injected joint (Fig. 8-2).

The corticosteroids are found in high concentrations in inflamed tissue, and their anti-inflammatory action in any tissue depends directly on their tissue concentration. When applied locally, therefore, they achieve high tissue concentrations and very potent local anti-inflammatory effects. Injection of corticosteroids into joints, tendons, or bursal spaces can give very good relief of pain and return of function, in keeping with the actions of these drugs on inflammation from any cause. The ultimate outcome of such treatment, however, is determined largely by the amount of stress to which the injected area is subjected in the period postinjection. For best results the corticosteroids should be used in conjunction with rest to allow as complete healing as possible, with minimum scar tissue formation around the joint. As a general rule, bursal injections of corticosteroids can be used with a minimum of postinjection rest. Thus, for example, injections into the cunean tendon bursa (jacks), trochanteric bursa (whorl bone), and bicipital bursa can be made and the horse continued in racing. Similarly, bog spavins in young animals, especially if they are due to trauma rather than poor conformation, may be treated with corticosteroids quite successfully.

Injection of corticosteroids into inflamed joints needs considerably more care and judgment than tendon or bursal injections. In keeping with the rule that corticosteroids cannot affect the basic cause of the inflammation, the joint should, ideally, first be examined radiographically and, depending on the circumstances,

For best results the corticosteroids should be used in conjunction with rest.

bacteriologically, for primary causes such as bacterial infections, chip fractures, fractures involving the joint area, or synovial membrane nodules. Correction of such underlying problems greatly improves the prognosis in any joint trouble, whether or not corticosteroids are administered. On the other hand, if chips or other inciting causes are not removed, the continued mechanical trauma will only cause further deterioration, which may result in reinjection of the joint. Continuation of this cycle results in eventual erosion of the joint surface, complete loss of joint function, and possible incapacitation of the animal for use even as breeding stock.

Joint conditions that are especially amenable to corticosteroids therefore include nontraumatic arthritis, osteoarthritis uncomplicated by joint deformities, and traumatic arthritis without fracture or derangement of the joint. The value of intra-articular steroid therapy is much more limited in chronic osteoarthritis and osteoporosis. Steroid therapy is contraindicated where there is erosion of the cartilage and septic arthritis. Damaged or degenerated articular cartilage responds poorly to steroid injection, and useful regeneration of the joint cartilage rarely occurs.

When steroid hormones are injected intrasynovially (i.e. into a synovial sac), they are taken up by the cells of the synovial membrane within two to four hours. Very little is absorbed into the cartilage, and it appears that the major anti-inflammatory effect is exerted via the synovial membrane. The steroid not taken up by the synovial membrane diffuses from the joint into the systemic circulation within hours. When injecting a dose of corticosteroid into a joint, the clinician will often remove a smaller or equivalent volume of synovial (joint) fluid. Since synovial fluid is replaced within twenty-four hours, this usually does not create problems.

Symptomatic improvement of acute arthritis usually occurs within the first twenty-four hours after intra-articular injection of the steroid, although as much as three days may be required for maximal effect. If a rapid onset of action is required, a short-acting steroid should be used, while if a prolonged action is required, a long-acting steroid should be used. For cases where a rapid onset and prolonged duration of action are required, suitable combinations of short- and long-acting steroids are available. Steroids that must be metabolized into active forms are of little use intra-articularly. For example, cortisone and prednisone are apparently not converted to their active forms, hydrocortisone and prednisolone, by the synovial membrane and are thus relatively ineffective if administered intra-articularly.

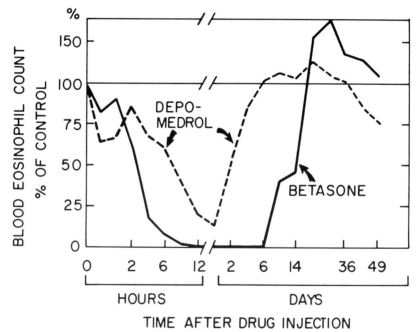

Figure 8-3. Effect of bethamethasone phosphate/diproprionate and dimethylprednisolone acetate on blood eosinophil counts. Three mares were injected intra-articularly with 25 mg of bethamethaxone diprorionate and 10 mg of bethamethasone phosphate as Betazone®, while three other mares were injected with 40 mg of methylprednisolone acetate as Depo-Medrol®. The solid and dotted lines show the average eosinophil count for each group, respectively. The bethamethasone diprorionate/be-tamethasone phosphate combination of a soluble and long-acting steroid gave a more rapid onset combined with a longer duration of action. After Vernimb et al. (1977).

In a careful study of the effects of intra-articular steroids on surgically induced chip fractures of the knee, Meagher found much more rapid deterioration in joints injected with corticosteroids than in noninjected joints. Although the injected joints initially showed less lameness and swelling than untreated joints, the healing process was delayed in the steroid-treated joints. In uninjected joints there was active bone production in the fracture area and the healing process proceeded well. In the injected joints, however, considerable lysis of bone and cartilage was seen, and instead of production of new bone, there was demineralization at the fracture site combined with a periarticular fibrocartilage buildup around the injected joint. This type of response gives rise to the typical "productive-destructive" lesions characteristic of corticosteroid-injected joints.

In the second portion of Meagher's study, the bone chips were removed from both the injected and uninjected joints after the course of corticosteroid therapy. Thirteen days after surgery all of the corticosteroid-injected joints were hot, swollen, and painful, while no reaction was noted in the uninjected joints. Vigorous antibiotic therapy was begun, and the infections were controlled. This susceptibility to inflammation is consistent with the action of corticosteroids to suppress tissue response to injury and infections and emphasizes the risks of performing surgery on joints recently exposed to local corticosteroid therapy.

From this study, Meagher concluded that joint deterioration after chip fracture was accelerated by corticosteroids and that use of corticosteroids in the presence of chip fractures is contraindicated. Intra-articular steroids were considered useful in soft tissue injury of a joint, but a period of at least thirty days rest should follow treatment. These authors also concluded that surgery on a corticosteroid-injected joint should not occur for at least eight weeks after the last treatment with corticosteroids.

In a somewhat less rigorous study on the use of corticosteroids in Thoroughbreds racing in Canada, McKay and Milne reported on a series of twenty-two horses treated intra-articularly with corticosteroids. Unfortunately, these authors failed to detail the clinical conditions that prompted the intra-articular injection of corticosteroids in these horses. Of the twenty-two horses treated, six showed radiographic evidence of deterioration in the joint subsequent to the initial radiographic examination, but in only one horse were signs of diminished joint space and "productive-destructive" lesions of new bone laid down on the lateral aspects of the joints seen (Fig. 8-4). While these lesions were considered characteristic for intra-articular corticosteroid injection, changes in the other six joints could not be distinguished from the normal progression of joint disease. The remaining sixteen horses showed no radiographic evidence of joint deterioration. The authors interpreted these results as supporting a role for the careful and judicious use of intra-articular corticosteroids in racing horses.

Consistent with the conclusions of McKay and Milne, other workers hold that when rationally employed the corticosteroids are effective in prolonging the performance career of carefully selected equine patients. Among the classes of horses helped by the corticosteroids are included those with irreversible pathology of their musculoskeletal systems, such as progressive degenerative joint disease. In these horses, in which surgical intervention or rest will not be of benefit,

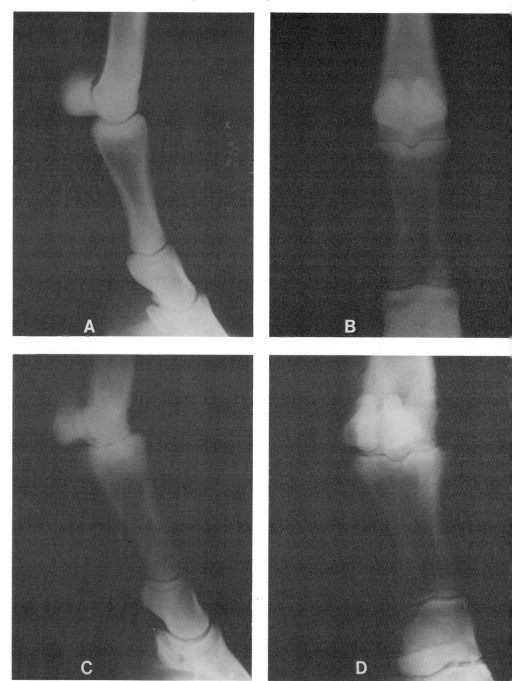

Figure 8-4. Corticosteroid-induced joint damage. Improper use of corticosteroids in joints can lead to loss of joint space, destruction of the articular cartilage, and the formation of diffuse and poorly organized new bone around the joint. If the condition progresses, loss of the articular surfaces leads to the formation of what is popularly called a dry joint. A and B shows a normal "ankle" joint in a horse with clean, well-defined bone structure and good joint cavity. C, D, and E show a corticosteroid-

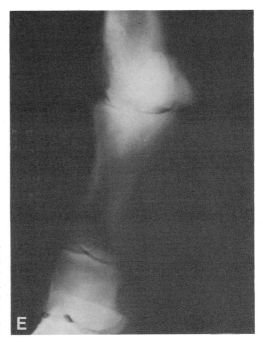

injected joint. Note the erosions on the anterior surface of the bone, the poorly defined and irregular joint surfaces, and the poorly organized proliferation of new bone. The structural changes observed in these radiographs are referred to as "productive-destructive" lesions. Radiographs courtesy of Doctor Paul Thorpe, Hagyard, Davidson & McGee, Lexington, KY.

intra-articular corticosteroid administration can be the most effective measure to return the animals to productivity. A different category includes those in which a favorable response to surgical intervention or rest is anticipated. In these cases of reversible joint pathology, other avenues of approach are available, and the attainment of immediate racing goals have to be balanced against the risk of abbreviating the horse's racing career. Finally, this author adds the one point about the intra-articular corticosteroids that should be kept in mind above all else, i.e. that they should be used in minimum doses and as infrequently as possible.

In a detailed laboratory study of the effect of intra-articular corticosteroids, Behrens and his coworkers observed gross and microscopic damage to articular cartilage after twelve weekly injections of hydrocortisone in rabbit knee joints. In these animals, the non-weight-bearing surfaces were not distinguishable from normal specimens, but the weight-bearing surfaces of the knee joints showed multiple yellowish lesions in 50 percent of the animals.

These observations led these authors to propose a sequence of changes in joint cartilage in response to intra-articular injection of steroids. The first step in this sequence was thought to be a massive decrease in the synthesis of all major cartilage components. Among these components a loss of proteoglycan content in a particular joint was thought to lead to a loss in cartilage stiffness. In non-weight-bearing areas, the cartilage was able to maintain its structural integrity. However, the mechanical stress in weight-bearing areas caused death of cells, followed by disruption and loss of articular cartilage and eventual destruction of the joint structure and function (Fig. 8-5).

In a review on the intra-articular use of steroids, four distinct patterns of

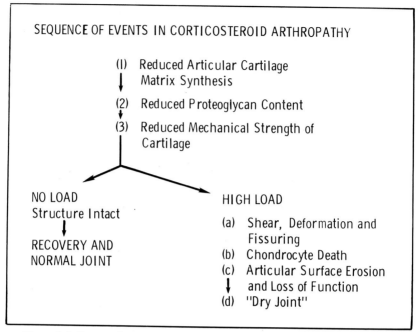

SEQUENCE OF EVENTS IN CORTICOSTEROID ARTHROPATHY

(1) Reduced Articular Cartilage Matrix Synthesis

(2) Reduced Proteoglycan Content

(3) Reduced Mechanical Strength of Cartilage

NO LOAD
Structure Intact

RECOVERY AND
NORMAL JOINT

HIGH LOAD

(a) Shear, Deformation and Fissuring
(b) Chondrocyte Death
(c) Articular Surface Erosion and Loss of Function
(d) "Dry Joint"

Figure 8-5. Proposed sequence of events in corticosteroid-induced arthropathy.

detrimental effects after intra-articular corticosteroids in the horse have been identified. These are listed as (1) postinjection "flare-up," (2) osseous metaplasia, (3) septic arthritis, and (4) steroid arthropathy.

Acute postinjection "flare-ups" begin a few hours after injection of corticosteroids and last for up to twenty-four hours. The cause is unclear and may be due to irritation caused by microcrystalline injections of corticosteroid esters or simply due to the volume of material injected. The problem is usually mild and transitory, although local anesthetic injection has been recommended in severe cases.

The second syndrome that has been described is "osseous metaplasia," which means the formation of new bone in areas adjacent to the joint. This most commonly occurs after the inadvertent injection of long-acting steroid preparations into the soft tissues around a joint. Since this problem is associated only with the long-acting corticosteroids, it appears to be a tissue reaction to the constituents used to make these preparations long acting. These lesions take a long time to develop postinjection and may not be evident to the touch for at least four months after injection. These lesions may grow quite large and cause lameness merely due to their size and position, since they will usually be located close to a joint. Surgical removal usually does not result in marked improvement. Because of the possibility of this complication developing, particular care should be taken with intra-articular injection of long-acting corticosteroids.

Septic or bacterial arthritis is a potentially disastrous complication of any intra-articular injection in the horse, and it is especially dangerous after corticosteroid therapy because of the ability of corticosteroids to reduce the resistance of the joint to infection. Infection may be due to direct contamination of the joint occurring during the injection process, or it may be due to bacteria carried in the bloodstream. Signs of infection may not appear for several weeks. Infections due to gram-positive organisms tend to be acute in onset and produce severe swelling and lameness. On the other hand, infections due to gram-negative organisms produce lameness of gradually increasing severity, with swelling more often in the structures around the joint than in the joint itself.

Following multiple corticosteroid injections, and especially if adequate rest is not allowed, severe steroid arthropathy may be seen. The clinical signs of advanced degenerative joint disease include lameness, joint enlargement from both capsular distension and new bone growth around the joint, crepitation (grating noise) on moving the joint, and a reduced range of joint movement. Advanced cases show a narrowed joint space due to loss of articular cartilage, areas of bone erosion below the cartilage, and increased new bone growth around the joint itself. There is no effective treatment for advanced steroid arthropathy.

When used systemically, the corticosteroids have a number of pharmacological effects that might be considered useful in a horse about to compete in a performance event. They stimulate the utilization of fat and amino acids and thereby increase blood glucose levels, which glucose is presumably available as extra energy to the horse. The glucocorticoids also stimulate appetite and in man have clear-cut euphoriant or stimulant effects, which has led to people becoming emotionally dependent on them. Thus, because of these reasons and the difficulty in detecting them, corticosteroids have reportedly occasionally been used as a "pre-race shot" in performance horses. Further, they are also likely to be quite valuable in horses that have been severely stressed and need to be able to perform again shortly, such as a three-day event horse.

Multiple corticosteroid injections can give rise to severe joint problems.

There are a number of problems associated with the systemic use of corticosteroids that need to be kept in mind. While a single large dose can be used in a healthy animal with essentially no fear of a significant adverse reaction, repeated doses or use in a less-than-healthy animal can be dangerous, as large or repeated doses of corticosteroids can leave a horse wide open to generalized infections. This effect is so predictable that in experimental work, injections of large doses of corticosteroids are routinely used to render animals susceptible to infections. If large doses of the corticosteroids are maintained for any sustained period of time (2 weeks), atrophy of the adrenal cortex occurs. One way of avoiding this problem is to administer short-acting corticosteroids intermittently every second or third day. This pattern of intermittent administration allows plasma levels of the steroid to drop, which stimulates natural ACTH release, which in turn will stimulate and maintain normal function in the adrenal cortex. For these reasons, corticosteroids are rarely used systemically in large doses over long periods unless the disease involved is both life threatening and not amenable to other therapy.

Horsemen who routinely do blood picture analyses on their horses should be aware of the very special effects of the corticosteroids in this area, producing what is called the glucocorticoid hemogram. The glucocorticoids tend to increase the hematocrit and the number of polymorphs in the blood, while the number of eosinophils, lymphocytes, and basophils declines rapidly (Fig. 8-6). The corticosteroids have a marked effect on lymphatic tissue, causing marked destruction of lymphocytes, which leads to their use in certain types of lymph gland cancers.

The corticosteroids also have marked effects on both growth and the nervous system. Their antianabolic effect appears as a suppression of growth, which is a widespread effect of the glucocorticoids. In the fully grown animal this same effect is seen as a delay in wound healing. The glucocorticoids also increase the rate of demineralization of bone, and prolonged administration can lead to osteoporosis and compression fractures. In humans, use of the corticosteroids during pregnancy has been associated with an incidence of cleft palate in infants. One case of cleft palate in the foal of a Purebred Arab mare has been reported in

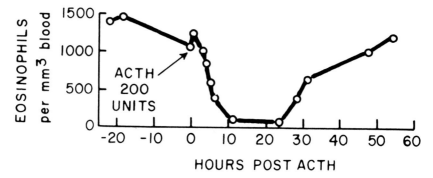

Figure 8-6. Effects of corticosteroids on eosinophil count in the horse. Horses were injected with 200 units of adrenocorticotrophic hormone, which stimulates the release of endogenous corticosteroids. The open circles (o—o) show the sharp and transient drop in the eosinophil blood count induced by this treatment. Reproduced with permission from Tobin, *J Equine Med Surg*, 3:10, 1979.

which the dam was treated with large doses of an oral corticosteroid by her owners during early pregnancy.

Another unusual toxicity of the corticosteroids that is unique to hooved animals is an ability to precipitate laminitis. Studies in horses have shown that in animals dosed with large doses of corticosteroids or maintained on corticosteroids for long periods, the incidence of laminitis is markedly increased. In this regard, it turns out that large doses of corticosteroids are believed to have a calming (tranquilizing) effect on animals, and an increased incidence of laminitis has been reported in show horses due to increased use of corticosteroids in an effort to produce tranquilization in these horses.

Outside of their use in joints and to affect equine behavior, corticosteroids have other uses in equine medicine. They have marked effects on allergic responses, and certain allergic states are often dramatically reduced by the corticosteroids. They are, therefore, often used in allergic skin conditions, in cerebral edema, and in selected cases of respiratory disease. Endotoxin shock in the horse also responds well to massive doses of corticosteroids, which should be administered along with large quantities of fluids.

The various corticosteroid preparations available to the veterinarian differ from each other in regard to their potency, pharmacokinetics, and therapeutic effects. Cortisol, cortisone, prednisolone, and prednisone possess both mineralocorticoid and glucocorticoid activity. The newer synthetic corticosteroids, such as methylprednisolone, betamethazone, and triamcinolone, are all potent anti-inflammatory steroids, with few mineralocorticoid actions. The plasma half-lives of all the adrenal steroids are relatively short, with an apparent plasma half-life for cortisol of about eighty minutes. Long-acting steroid preparations are therefore slowly absorbable forms and are given intramuscularly. Absorption of corticosteroids after intramuscular injections may be delayed either by adding an ester group or by injecting them in a microparticulate form.

The period for which corticosteroids are likely to turn up in urine vary. The most detailed studies on the "clearance times" of corticosteroids in the horse were published by Chapman and his coworkers in England. Using a radioimmunoassay (RIA) technique, these workers detected dexamethasone in urine for 155 hours after intramuscular (IM) administration of about 20 mg of a long-acting dexamethasone preparation. Similarly, depot preparations of flumethazone were detected for up to ninety hours after 10 mg doses IM. Most other steroid preparations tested by these workers were not detected for longer than about forty-eight hours. Racing chemists in the United States, however, generally use less sensitive thin-layer chromatographic (TLC) screening techniques for the corticosteroids. Our experience with this method in Kentucky suggests that corticosteroids rarely appear in TLC systems more than twenty-four hours after dosing. Similarly, in one experiment where Chapman et al. gave dexamethasone 21-sodium phosphate intra-articularly, it was detected in urine by RIA for only twenty-four hours, the same period for which it was detected after IM injection. On the other hand, Moss and Rylance found prednisolone and its metabolites in equine urine for up to three days after its IM administration as the trimethylacetate. Of particular forensic interest was one instance in which excretion did not start for two days after the drug was administered and then continued for three more days, which led to the suggestion that the drug had inadvertently been injected into fatty tissue, which delayed both its absorption and excretion by forty-eight hours.

Unpublished observations by Horner and Moss on the metabolism of dexamethasone in the horse showed that about 1 percent of an intravenous dose was excreted unchanged in the urine in the first twelve hours, with about 4 percent of the dose eliminated as the glucuronide or ethereal sulfate. In the first twenty-four hours about 44 percent of the administered radioactivity was excreted, and a further 13 percent up to sixty hours. The same rate of excretion of radioactivity was seen after its intramuscular administration. After prednisolone administration in ponies, Moss and Rylance reported detection of prednisolone and prednisone and their respective 11-deoxycortisol metabolites. Administration of prednisone gave essentially the same metabolite pattern as did prednisolone, with urinary excretion of the drug and its metabolites being complete within three days.

Another way in which the typical còrticosteroid effects may be obtained is to administer adrenocorticotrophic hormone (ACTH), the hormone that controls the activity of the adrenal gland. Administration of this hormone brings about a prompt increase in plasma cortisol which is equivalent to systemic injection of corticosteroids (Fig. 8-7).

ACTH is also directly involved in one of the principal problems of corticosteroid therapy, which is the withdrawal syndrome. If a horse has been administered systemic corticosteroids over a long period of time, the high blood levels of steroid suppress the release of ACTH from the anterior pituitary. Since it is ACTH that stimulates and controls the function of the adrenal glands, suppression of its release results in atrophy of the adrenals. This is a classic "feedback inhibition" loop, where high levels of a hormone (either natural or synthetic) act to inhibit its own formation. If corticosteroid therapy is then abruptly terminated, the horse is left with reduced or no natural corticosteroids, which, in a serious case, can be fatal (Fig. 8-8). In a milder form this may be manifested in the "turning out" syndrome, which is seen when horses are "turned out" after a racing season during which

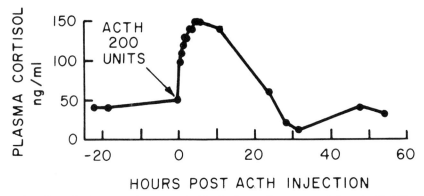

HOURS POST ACTH INJECTION

Figure 8-7. Effect of ACTH on plasma cortisol in the horse. Horses were injected with 200 units of ACTH at the indicated times. The solid circles (●—●) show plasma levels of cortisol prior to and after IM injection of this drug. Reproduced with permission from Tobin, *J Equine Med Surg, 3*:10, 1979.

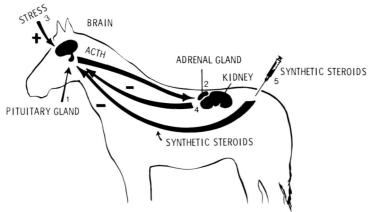

Figure 8-8. Control of plasma corticosteroid levels in the horse. Adrenocorticotrophic hormone (ACTH) is secreted by the pituitary gland (1) and travels in the blood to the adrenal, where it regulates the activity of this gland (2). Various forms of stress (3) can increase the rate of release of ACTH and thus the activity of the adrenal gland. The blood levels of corticosteroid either from the adrenal (4) or administered by injection (5) act to inhibit the release of ACTH by a feedback inhibition mechanism. Administration of prolonged high levels of steroids (5) can lead to atrophy of the adrenal gland by suppressing the release of ACTH. Abrupt cessation of steroid therapy can then lead to a corticosteroid withdrawal crisis and possibly death of the animal.

they received large doses of corticosteroids. These horses tend to be unthrifty, dull, and depressed and to show mild anemia despite good care. Several months may be required after prolonged treatment with corticosteroids for the adrenal glands to recover fully. One way of avoiding this problem of feedback inhibition is to administer short-acting corticosteroids intermittently every second or third day. This pattern of intermittent administration allows plasma levels of the steroid to drop, which stimulates natural ACTH release. An alternative maneuver that has been suggested is to administer injectable ACTH with the steroid, which will stimulate and maintain normal function in the adrenal cortex.

ACTH disappears rapidly from plasma in man, and "none" of it reportedly turns up in human urine. This nonappearance of ACTH also presumably occurs in the urine of the horse, and even if it did appear, it would be very difficult to distinguish from natural ACTH.

In summary, therefore, the corticosteroids are classical examples of drugs that have been developed based on man's investigation of his own chemistry. Powerful synthetic analogues of the natural hormones have been developed, in which the anti-inflammatory action of this group of drugs has been separated from their actions on sodium and water metabolism. These anti-inflammatory corticosteroids are strongly antianabolic, that is, in general they tend to give rise to tissue breakdown. When administered locally into joints they are strongly anti-inflammatory, but their effects to suppress tissue metabolism means that they leave the joint open to damage if it is overused in the presence of corticosteroids. Corticosteroids should be used in joints with great care.

In addition, the corticosteroids, when used systemically, produce an elevation of "mood" and increased blood sugar levels. These actions make these agents useful in animals that are under severe stress and are probably the effects that have led to the use of these drugs as pre-race shots. The same response can also be obtained by injecting ACTH. While large doses of corticosteroids can be given systemically on a very short term basis, prolonged use of these agents systemically is best reserved for life-threatening disease.

SELECTED REFERENCES

Balch, H. W., Gibson, J. M. C., and El-Ghobarey, A. F.: Repeated corticosteroid injection into knee joints. *Rheumatol Rehabil, 16:*137-140, 1977.

Behrens, F., Shepard, N., and Mitchell, N.: Alteration of rabbit articular cartilage by intra-articular injection of glucocorticoids. *J Bone Joint Surg, 57-A:*70-76, 1975.

Chapman, D. I., Moss, M. S., and Whiteside, J.: The urinary excretion of synthetic corticosteroids by the horse. *Vet Rec* (May) *100:*445-450, 1977.

Goodman, L. S. and Gilman, A.: *The Pharmacological Basis of Therapeutics,* 5th ed. New York, Macmillan, 1975.

James, V. H. T., Homer, M. W., Moss, M. S., and Ripon, A. E.: Adreno-cortical function in the horse. *J Endocrinol, 48:*319-335, 1970.

McKay, A. G., and Milne, F. J.: Observations of the intra-articular use of corticosteroids in racing Thoroughbreds. *Am J Vet Res, 168:*1039-1042, 1976.

Meagher, D. M.; The effects of intra-articular corticosteroids and continued training on carpal chip fractures of horses. *Proc AAEP, 16:*405-42, 1970.

Moss, M. S.: The metabolism and urinary and salivary excretion of drugs in the horse and their relevance to detection of dope. In *Drug Metabolism — From Microbe to Man.* D. V. Parke and R. L. Smith, Eds. London, Taylor and Francis, Ltd., 1976.

Moss, M. S., and Rylance, H. H.: A thin layer chromatography study on the metabolism of prednisolone in the horse. *J Endocrinol, 37:*129-137, 1967.

Nickels, Frank A., Grant, B. D., and Lincoln, S. D.: Villonodular synovitis of the equine metacarpophalangeal joint. *Am J Vet Res, 168:*1043-1046, 1976.

O'Malley, B. W. and Buller, R. E. E.: Mechanisms of steroid hormone action. *J Invest Dermatol, 68:*1-4, 1977.

Short, C. R. and Beadle, R. E.: Pharmacology of anti-arthritic drugs. *Vet Clin North Am, 8:*401-417, 1978.

Tobin, T.: Pharmacology review: the corticosteroids. *J. Equine Med Surg, 3:*10-15, 1973.

Vernimb, G. D., VanHoose, L. M., and Hennessey, P. W.: Equine arthropathies. *VM/SAC, 72:*241-244, 1977.

Chapter 9

BUILDING MUSCLE, BONE, AND MAYBE WINNERS: THE ANABOLIC STEROIDS

E VERYONE IS FAMILIAR with the marked changes that occur in the human male at about the time of puberty. During this period the male increases in height and shows increased muscle development, thickening of bones, and the changes in voice, body hair pattern, and aggressiveness that are associated with the adult male. All these effects are due to increased secretion by the testis of the androgenic* or "male-making" hormones.

In the horse, the androgens, of which testosterone is the primary example (Fig. 9-1), produce both the increase in bone and muscle mass (the anabolic effect) and changes in the secondary sexual characteristics, such as changes in voice, crest, and aggressiveness of the stallion. These changes in secondary sexual characteristics are known as the androgenic actions.

Because the anabolic effect, as a simple increase in muscle mass, was relatively easy to measure, and it appeared that there might be a good market for a pure anabolic drug, research chemists working in various drug companies modified the natural testosterone molecule in attempts to produce such a pure anabolic drug. Various groups succeeded to varying degrees in separating the body-building from the androgenic effects (Fig. 9-1), but none was completely successful. Therefore, all the anabolic steroids on the market today retain some of the androgenic action of the original testosterone molecule, and it is this residual androgenic action that gives rise to many of the side effects of this group of drugs. It is also appropriate to mention at this point that very little work has been done on anabolic steroids in the horse and that most of the work reported here is derived from experience in humans or experimental animals.

The most clear-cut and easily demonstrated action of the androgens is to literally produce a "red-blooded male," since they act to increase an animal's production of red blood cells and thus its hematocrit. In most species the entire male usually has a higher hematocrit than the female, and the hematocrit of the castrated male is lowest of all. Testosterone injection in the castrated male can produce up to a 20 percent increase in the red blood cell count. This effect also occurs in the female and to a lesser extent in the entire male, which, of course, already has considerable circulating testosterone. Nevertheless, the effect of the androgen-anabolic steroid group on the formation of red blood cells is sufficiently clear-cut to render them the drugs of choice in most forms of anemia, and in human medicine they are considered the most useful nonspecific stimulants of red blood cell formation.

As well as stimulating red blood cell formation, the anabolic steroids stimulate growth. In the young, prepubescent male, growth is stimulated at once, appetite is

---

* From the Greek *andros* = man + *gen* = make

149

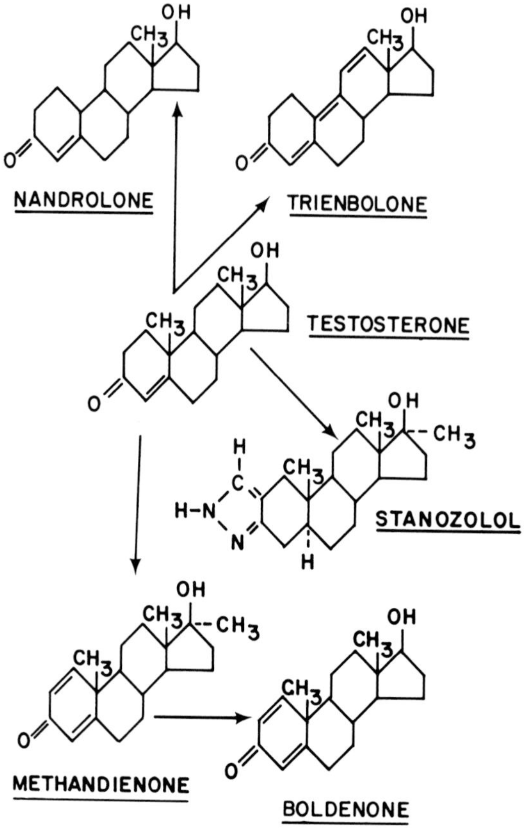

Figure 9-1. Structure of testosterone and some anabolic steroids commonly used in equine medicine. After Snow et al. (1977).

increased, muscular strength and physical vigor is increased, and a feeling of well-being prevails. If the weight increases are plotted against time, it can be shown that the spurt in growth occurs right at the start of treatment. As well as increasing growth, the androgen-anabolic steroids cause genital development, with scrotal reddening, penile development, and sometimes frequent erections.

The androgen-anabolic steroids also have very clear-cut effects on bone growth. They act to increase the retention of calcium in bones, giving rise to thicker bone and greater bone growth. However, greater growth of bone in length can occur only if the epiphyseal plates are still cartilaginous and able to grow. Unfortunately, administration of large quantities of these agents to young animals can hasten closure of the epiphyseal plates at which growth occurs and thus prevent growth in length of these bones. In the human, eunuchs, the castrated male guardians of eastern harems, always grew considerably taller than the normal male because their lack of testosterone delayed closure of their epiphyseal plates. Therefore, any use of the androgen-anabolic steroid group of drugs in young horses before closure of the epiphyseal plates carries with it the danger of accelerating closure of these plates and preventing further growth.

As well as stimulating growth, the anabolic steroid-androgen group of drugs gives rise to increased muscle mass, and the significance of their actions on muscle mass and athletic performance is also a hotly argued area. The simplest and perhaps the "purest" use of the anabolic or muscle-building action of these drugs is in the body building field. At a recent "Mr. America" contest in Detroit, one of the former Mr. Americas, John Grimek, estimated that "somewhere between 99 and 101 percent" of the entrants in the contest had experimented with this group of drugs, and that a high proportion of the competitors were using these drugs in massive doses. Other estimates suggest that 80 to 90 percent of weight lifters use these drugs, about 75 percent of football players, and about 33 percent of athletes in general. It seems that the body builders at least know exactly what they are doing, for most of the scientific work to date supports their conviction that the anabolic steroids produce considerable increases in muscle mass and body weight. This increase in muscle mass is not due to an increase in the number of muscle fibers but rather to an increase in the size of individual fibers, causing an overall increase in muscle mass. This marked effect on muscle mass has led to horsemen and athletes to refer to these drugs as "muscle puffers."

While the anabolic drugs may produce clear-cut increases in muscle mass,

The anabolic steroid-androgen group of drugs gives rise to increased muscle mass in both man and horses.

whether or not this increase in muscle mass is accompanied by increased or improved performance remains unclear. Some scientists hold that the increased muscle mass is simply due to increased fluid retention and that no increase in muscle power occurs. These statements, however, contradict the everyday experience, which clearly suggests the average male mammal is much stronger, more heavily built, and athletically more competitive than his female or gelded counterpart. This tendency toward athletic superiority of the male would seem to be borne out by the fact that no filly has ever won the Triple Crown. However, with the advent of anabolic steroids, this bastion of equine male supremacy may not remain intact much longer.

Other studies have shown that when the anabolic steroids are combined with a high-protein diet and vigorous training, an increase in muscle strength does occur. The weight of the reports and the experience (and conviction) of the athletes who use them seem to suggest that athletes who use the anabolic steroids and who train and diet accordingly may expect to increase their body weight up to 5 percent and their muscle strength up to 18 percent.

In some human athletic events, such as the hammer throw, a simple increase in body mass is thought to be helpful. In racing horses, an increase in muscle mass might help improve the performance of sprinting horses and is also thought likely to improve the stamina and endurance of horses. However, no experimental evidence in support of these beliefs is available at this time. Furthermore, because of the longer time period and training required to develop the anabolic effect in horses, it is likely to be very difficult to experimentally demonstrate an effect on performance horses.

Very closely interwoven with the effects of the androgen-anabolic steroids on body mass and performance are their psychological effects. Thus, the androgen-anabolic steroid group acts to produce a marked feeling of well-being and confidence; these drugs also increase appetite and are important in the development of characteristic male aggressive behavior. These effects are clearly seen in horses that become much more difficult to handle and control when given androgens. The relationship of testosterone to aggressiveness had long been suspected, and one of the first reported uses of androgens to improve performance occurred during World War II, when German troops were supposedly given testosterone injections before going into battle to enhance their aggressiveness. How much these psychological effects on mood, aggressiveness, and confidence influence athletic performance is not clear, but a strong feeling exists among athletes and trainers that anabolic steroids are a great help to the mediocre performer, giving him "winner's" confidence along with the will to win. There is no reason to suppose that these psychological effects do not occur in animals, and the consensus among horsemen is that the anabolic steroids improve general vigor and muscle tone, produce a more alert and more aggressive attitude, and also brighten the hair coat.

While most of the effects of the androgen-anabolic steroids on growth, bone mass, and muscle strength require treatment over a period of weeks for full effect, this is apparently not so for the psychological effects of these agents. It appears that the psychological effects of the androgen-anabolic steroids group of drugs appear within hours and, if the drug is a short-acting drug, can dissipate just as rapidly. This has led some racing authorities to the conclusion that the anabolic steroid-androgen group of drugs could be used to run horses hot and cold. Fillies and geldings, as horses with little androgen of their own, are likely to be particularly susceptible to this pattern of drug use.

The side effects of the anabolic steroids are almost all related to their residual androgenic actions, for none of these agents are purely anabolic. Thus, in young, growing horses, premature epiphyseal closure and the resultant cessation of growth would seem to be the most serious problem. In this regard, oxandrolone has been reported to favor bone growth over epiphyseal maturation. Another somewhat less serious problem would be the tendency of the increased body weight to produce epiphysitis. Rooney has outlined how muscular young quarterhorses are predisposed to this problem, and the anabolic steroids could presumably produce the same effect simply by increasing the body mass of young horses above that which their forming bones can carry. What happens is that under the incluence of anabolic steroids, young horses may put on too much weight for their still growing bones to carry. The first signs will usually appear on the lower inside portion of the radius in horses nearing two years of age. The problem is that the weight crushes the sensitive growing epiphyseal cartilage plate and the animal becomes lame. In "natural" cases the lameness usually disappears rather quickly, while the enlargement may persist as a blemish for some time. In anabolic steroid induced cases, appearance of this problem would indicate immediate cessation of steroid therapy.

For mature horses, a possible problem suggested by some authors is that the increase in muscle mass may occur without a corresponding increase in bone strength. Since the weakest point in any tendon is its point of insertion into bone, an increased risk of bone/tendon rupture appears to be a possibility. Other possible problems in fillies involve overt masculinization and interference with future breeding performance due to the androgenic action remaining in most anabolic steroids. While the changes induced in human females by prolonged androgen therapy of prominent musculature, body hair, enlargement of the clitoris, and male pattern baldness are all largely irreversible phenomena, no data yet exists for horses on the effect of anabolic steroid treatment on the future fertility of fillies.

A paradoxical effect of the androgen-anabolic steroid group of drugs in the male is that they act to reduce sex drive, potency (the ability to maintain an erection), testicle size, and sperm count. Thus the animal or the athlete on anabolic steroids possesses all the muscle mass and secondary sexual characteristics of a super male, except that his sexual performance is likely reduced. The reason for this effect is that testosterone produced in the testicle is the signal that tells the brain that all is well and functioning in the testicle and surrounding areas. Thus, when high levels of the anabolic steroids come in the blood to the brain, the brain assumes that the testicle is overproducing testosterone and commands (through the gonadotrophins) the testicle and associated departments to cease production. The result of this is that if the dosage of the androgen-anabolic steroid is maintained, the testicle shrinks and sex drive, potency, and fertility can reportedly be lost.

The effect of high doses of androgen-anabolic steroids has been a problem for some human athletes on anabolic steroids, and what may be a related condition has been seen in horses. Since 1970, in the Kentucky area, there has been a large increase in the number of immature germ cells seen in stallion semen samples submitted to our Department for analysis. Recently, the accidental death of one of these stallions gave a colleague the opportunity to microscopically examine the testes of one of these horses. In this particular animal the testes showed focal areas of degeneration and loss of ability to form normal spermatozoa. This condition had existed for at least three years in the particular horse in question. The cause of this irreversible effect on the testicles and spermatogenesis in these stallions is not known, but the anabolic steroids must be prominent among the possible causes.

The most clear-cut data on the actions of the anabolic steroids on reproductive function are those reported by Pickett and his coworkers at Colorado State University. Pickett administered Equipoise® and Decadurabolin® to four groups of eight stallions each, once every three weeks for eighteen weeks. In all his test stallions, Pickett found reduced spermatozoal motility, spermatozoal concentration, and numbers of spermatozoa per ejaculate. Some of these effects were considered particularly dramatic, and at the end of the study the stallions receiving Decadurabolin were ejaculating only 10 percent of the spermatozoa that they were ejaculating at the beginning of treatment (Fig. 9-2). Further, total scrotal width and testicular weights in all treated stallions were reduced (Figs. 9-3 and 9-4), but no increase in body weight was seen in any of these stallions.

Despite these marked effects on spermatozoal numbers and testicular size, the animals' behavior was not affected. The time required for these horses to attain

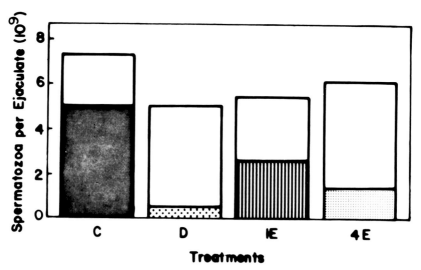

Figure 9-2. Billions of sperm per ejaculate in control and anabolic steroid treated stallions. Stallions were treated with no drug (control, C), Decadurabolin® (D, 0.5 mg/lb.), and Equipoise 1 (1E, 0.5 mg/lb.) or Equipose 4 (4E, 2 mg/lb.) every three weeks for eighteen weeks. The upper bars show the average number of sperm per ejaculate prior to treatment, while the lower bars show the number of spermato-zoa-ejaculate after fourteen weeks of treatment. Spermatozoal output of the Decadurabolin-treated stallions was reduced to only 10 percent of the control value, with smaller reductions being observed in the other groups. Reproduced with permission from Pickett et al. (1979).

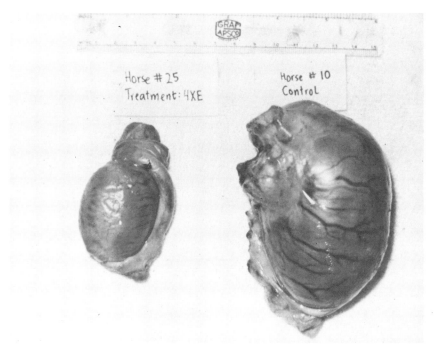

Figure 9-3. Testicle size in control and anabolic steroid treated stallions. The testicle to the left is from a horse treated with the "4E" Equipoise dose, while the testicle to the right is from a control horse. In some treated horses, testicular weight was reduced to around 40 percent of control weights. Reproduced with permission from Pickett et al. (1979).

erection, the time to first mount, the time to ejaculation, and the number of mounts per ejaculate were not affected by these treatments. Pickett therefore concluded that the anabolic steroids had profoundly detrimental (from a breeding point of view) effects on seminal characteristics, with no apparent beneficial effects, such as increased sex drive or weight gain. Based on these observations, Pickett concluded that the use of anabolic steroids in stallions is contraindicated.

The only group of anabolic steroids with toxic effects not directly related to their androgenic action are the methyl-substituted anabolic steroids. These methylated derivatives were introduced to prolong their action in the body but have wound up producing a number of slowly developing and quite serious liver toxicities. The simplest of these include mild hepatitis and an inability of the liver to eliminate bile. A more serious effect associated with this group of drugs is the induction of precancerous liver changes, which return to normal if the administration of drugs is stopped. If administration continues, liver cancer can appear after a number of years. Because nonmethylated anabolic steroids apparently do not produce these hepatic effects, use of the methylated steroids should be avoided in all species.

A more satisfactory mechanism of prolonging the action of this group of drugs is to esterify the compound, suspend it in oil, and inject it intramuscularly, and this is the type of anabolic steroid now in use. The nature of the ester group deter-

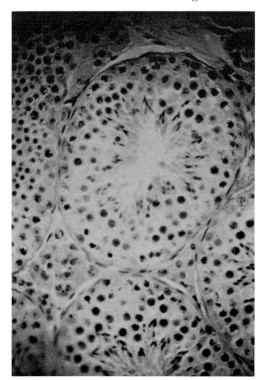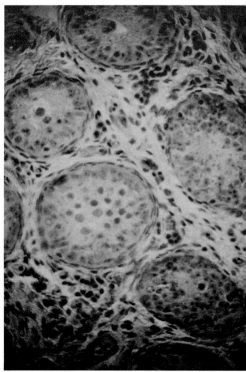

Figure 9-4. Seminiferous tubules from control and anabolic steroid treated stallion. The illustration at the left shows a cross section of seminiferous tubules from a control stallion, with an abundance of germ cells in the seminiferous tubules. The illustration at the right shows a section from one of Pickett's 4E horses. The seminiferous tubules are greatly reduced in size, and the number of developing germ cells is severely reduced. Reproduced with permission from Pickett et al. (1979).

mines the duration of action (Fig 9-5). Some of these derivatives are quite long acting and may only require administration at intervals of up to one month.

The anabolic steroids have been used in a large number of clinical conditions in both man and horse. In surgery, an important use of the anabolic steroids is in treatment of delayed healing, where they promote a laying down of calcium and aid in the repair of tendon injuries. They may also be used postsurgery simply to assist the animal in recovering from the stress of surgery. It has also been suggested that in cases of prolonged corticosteroid therapy, intermittent treatment with anabolic steroids should be considered. It appears that the anabolic steroids do not interfere with the anti-inflammatory properties of the corticosteroids but will block the tendency of the corticosteroids to cause weight loss. In addition, the anabolic steroids may be indicated in debilitation from most causes because of their general stimulant effect.

In a number of equine studies it has been suggested that anabolic steroids can lead to an improvement in the performance of horses. Stihl and coworkers in Germany found that mares treated with anabolic steroids had higher weight gains than stallions, and that the greatest increases were found in young horses. Other workers, using 500 mg of nandrolone decanoate (500 mg monthly for 10 months in both Thoroughbreds and Standardbreds), found, in general, a greater increase in muscle mass in treated animals compared with control animals. Again the effect was more pronounced in mares than in stallions and greater in young animals than in older ones. Although the anabolic steroid treated horses showed better racing records, the authors stressed that this finding was not conclusive because the treated and control horses may have had differing initial performance abilities.

At the moment, to my knowledge, no racing jurisdiction in the United States is testing for anabolic steroids, but in the spring of 1976 testing started in England, and disciplinary action was taken against a number of trainers. The basis for the screening test against the anabolic steroids is called a radioimmunoassay (RIA) and depends on binding of the anabolic steroid in urine to a specific antibody. While these tests are highly sensitive, they are not specific. Any anabolic steroid, metabolite of an anabolic steroid, or endogenous steroids or their metabolites could possibly give rise to a positive test. For this reason, RIA assays in no way identify the drug administered, and RIA data alone should not be taken as evidence of anabolic steroid administration. The International Olympic Committee requires definitive identification of all drugs before invoking disciplinary

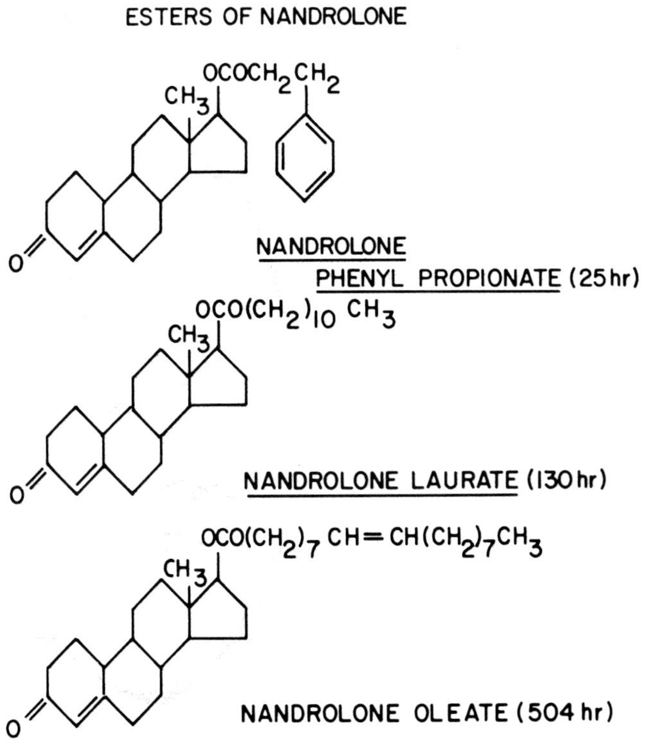

ESTERS OF NANDROLONE

NANDROLONE
PHENYL PROPIONATE (25 hr)

NANDROLONE LAURATE (130 hr)

NANDROLONE OLEATE (504 hr)

Figure 9-5. The effect of different esters on the duration of blood levels of nandrolone, the figures in parentheses indicating the half-life of the compounds in rat plasma. After Snow et al. (1977).

action, and for this, gas chromatographic-mass spectrometric analysis is required. The absolute sensitivity of the mass spectrometer is not clear, but the Race Course Security Services Laboratory in England reports being able to detect nor-testosterone in urine by radioimmunoassay for up to forty-four days after the administration of 200 mg of 19-nor-testosterone laureate intramuscularly. This is a very long time to be able to detect the effects of a relatively small dose of drug, and the only question that remains is how long after administration its presence can be confirmed by mass spectrometry.

The length of time for which the presence of an anabolic steroid can be confirmed in urine is critical. For instance, it is possible for a horse or other athlete to be "on" an anabolic steroid until two to three weeks before an event. The anabolic steroids can then be discontinued, but the horse will still have the increased bone and muscle mass for the competitive event. The critical question then becomes which declines more rapidly, the drug's anabolic effect or the chemist's ability to identify and confirm the drug? At the moment, we do not have the answer to this question. However, one approach to this problem now reportedly widely used in human athletics is to substitute testosterone for the anabolic steroid, which is, of course, difficult for an analyst to distinguish from natural testosterone.

SELECTED REFERENCES

Barragry, T. B.: Anabolic steroids: A review. *Ir Vet J, 28*:28-33, 1974.

Casner, S. W., Early, R. G., and Carlson, B. R.: Anabolic steroid effects on body composition in normal young men. *J Sports Med, 11*:98-103, 1971.

Frasier, S. D.: Androgens and athletes. *Am J Dis Child, 125*:779-780, 1973.

Goodman, S. and Gilman, A.: *The Pharmacological Basis of Therapeutics,* 5th ed. New York, Macmillan, 1975.

Johnson, F. L., Lerner, K. G., Siegel, M., Thomas, E. D., Feagler, J. R., Majerus, P. W., and Hartman, J. R.: Association of androgenic anabolic steroid therapy with development of hepatocellular carcinoma. *Lancet, 2*:1273-1276, 1972.

Jondorf, W. R. and Moss, M. S.: On the detectability of anabolic steroids in horse urine. *Br J Pharmacol, 60*:297-298, 1977.

Lamb, David R.: Androgens and exercise. *Med Sci Sports, 7*:5, 1975.

News and Comment, Anabolic steroids — Doctors denounce them but athletes aren't listening. *Science, 176*:1399-1401, 1972.

Pickett, B. W., Squires, E. L., Todter, G. E., and Berndtson, W. E.: Effect of anabolic steroids on reproduction function of stallions. *Proc Third Intl Symposium on Equine Medication Control,* Lexington, KY, 1979.

Rooney, J. R.: *The Lame Horse: Causes and Treatment.* Cranbury, NJ, A. S. Barnes, 1974.

Snow, D. H., Munro, C. D., and Nimmo, M.: Anabolic steroids in equine practice. *Proc AAEP, 23*:411-418, 1977.

Stihl, H. G.: Use of an anabolic steroid in veterinary practice for horses. *Tierarztl Wochenschr, 81(19)*:378-382, 1968.

Swerczek, T. W.: Immature germ cells in the semen of Thoroughbred stallions. *Reprod Fert (Suppl.), 23*:135-137, 1975.

Tahmmdjis, A. J.: The use of anabolic steroids by athletes to increase body weight and strength. *Med J Aust, 1*:991-993, 1976.

Wynn, V.: Metabolic effects of anabolic steroids. *Br J Sports Med, 9*:60-64, 1975.

Section III

THE "ILLEGAL" DRUGS

THE "ILLEGAL" DRUGS are drugs whose actions are considered to render them unsuitable under any circumstances for use in horses that are being raced, and whose use is therefore banned. They are most commonly listed as the stimulants, depressants, local anesthetics, narcotics, and tranquilizers. Because these drugs are considered to clearly influence the performance of a horse, or to make the horse more dangerous to ride or handle, they are banned in essentially all racing jurisdictions around the world.

Because these drugs produce their effects in the horse by acting on nervous tissue, this section opens with a brief description of the brain of the horse and how these drugs act there. Having outlined the theoretical basis for the actions of these drugs, we then point out the problems of studying these drugs in practice. In particular the problems with the usual horseman's approach to the study of drug effects in horses are highlighted, and more specialized methods are shown to be necessary.

Having outlined the basic mechanisms of action of these agents and outlined how they can be studied, we then begin a consideration of individual agents. Chapter 11 deals with the classic central nervous stimulants of the amphetamine-caffeine type, drugs whose pharmacology is unexpectedly difficult to study in the horse. The second group of drugs studied are the narcotic analgesics, the drugs whose actions are easy to study in the horse but whose detection can be troublesome. The last group of stimulant drugs that we will discuss are the so-called dopaminergic stimulants, of which apomorphine is the best known and most dramatic example.

Among the tranquilizers, acepromazine, a typical phenothiazine tranquilizer, and reserpine, a long-acting tranquilizer, are the most widely used. Other agents whose use in the horse are less well characterized, such as the minor tranquilizers, are also discussed. The section ends with a chapter on the various ways of producing local anesthesia used in racing, including local anesthetic drugs, neurectomies, and icing.

Chapter 10

STIMULANTS, DEPRESSANTS, NARCOTICS, TRANQUILIZERS: HOW THEY ACT IN THE HORSE

THE BRAIN OF THE HORSE is, like our own brains, composed of about 100 billion nerve cells or neurons all intercommunicating in very definite and specific ways. Each gram of a horse's grey matter contains about 200 million of these neurons, and a typical neuron has a cell body ranging in size from about 5 to 100 micrometers (thousandths of a millimeter) in diameter. Emerging from this cell body is one major fiber, the axon, and a number of fibrous branches, the dendrites (Fig. 10-1). In general terms, the dendrites receive the incoming signals, the cell body combines and integrates them, and the outgoing signals run down the axon to pass to other neurons or to directly activate muscle or gland structures.

The number of other neurons that a nerve cell can interact with may be very great, and a large neuron in the cerebral cortex may interconnect with as many as 3,000 to 4,000 other nerve cells. These nerve cells are organized into "neuronal pools," which include structures such as the basal ganglia, the cerebellum, the pons, and the medulla. The primary functions of these nerve cell pools are to receive, store, and modify and transmit information in the brain. There are two principal ways in which nerve cell pools perform their function of transmitting information.

The basic structure of a nerve cell or neuronal pool is shown in Figure 10-2. Information in the form of nerve impulses enters the pool along the input fibers (solid fibers), which divide, spread over a large area in the pool, and finally synapse or make contact with the dendrites or cell bodies of the neurons in the pool. Information coming into the pool thus passes along the axons of the input cells until it reaches the terminal junctions, or synapses, where the axons of one cell make contact with the dendrites of another nerve cell. It is at these terminal junctions that a nerve cell transmits its information to another cell. The synapse seems to be one of the fundamental structures in the functioning of the brain, and a rough estimate as to the number of synapses in a brain would be about 100 trillion, or 1,000 times more than the number of neurons. Experiments in simple animals have shown that synapses form or are obliterated as the animal learns and forgets, and it may be that the functions of learning and memory so characteristic of the brain reside in the development of specific synaptic patterns.

While nerve cells transmit information along their length electrically, transmission of information across synapses is, in almost all cases, chemical (Fig. 10-3). Electrical transmission is apparently not suited to this task, perhaps because it may be difficult to modulate. For any nervous system that is to function above the level of a "knee jerk response," subtle modulating mechanisms that allow messages to be selectively suppressed or amplified are required. In mammalian brains this

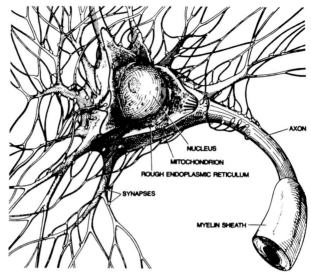

Figure 10-1. The neuron. Like cells in the body, the neuron has a distinct cell body containing a nucleus. Projecting from one end of the neuron, however, are a large number of branched structures called dendrites which make contact with projections from other cells. Also arising from the cell body is the main projection of the neuron, the axon, which may extend for several feet before making contact with another nerve cell, or perhaps a muscle or a gland. From *The Neuron*, Charles F. Stevens. Copyright © 1979 by Scientific American Inc. All rights reserved.

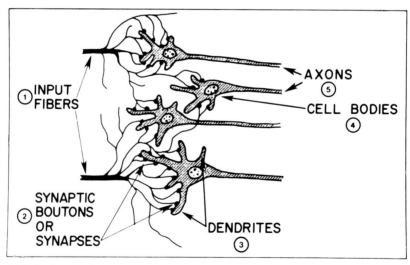

Figure 10-2. Basic organization of a neuronal pool. Nerve impulses enter the neuronal pool as electrical signals traveling down the axons of the input cells (1). These axons divide and make contact (2) at synapses with many of the neurons in the pool. A chemical signal (neurohormone) is passed across the synaptic cleft, electrically activates the dendrites, and the impulse is passed on down the cell bodies (4) and axons (5). Reproduced with permission from Tobin and Woods, *J Equine Med Surg, 3*:60, 1979.

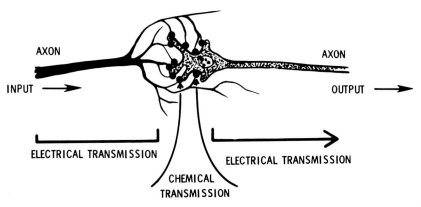

TRANSMISSION IS ELECTRICAL ALONG THE LENGTH OF A NERVE, BUT IS CHEMICAL OR NEUROHORMONAL BETWEEN THEM. THE POINT WHERE TWO NEURONS MAKE CHEMICAL CONTACT IS CALLED A SYNAPSE.

Figure 10-3. The dual roles of chemical and electrical transmission in nerve impulse transmission.

suppression or amplification of messages takes place primarily at synapses, and it is here that we find all the sites of subtle drug effects.

At the synapse the nerve impulse is carried from one cell to the other by the release of certain small charged molecules from one cell and their recognition by the neighboring cell. Since the structure is called a "synapse," the chemical that transmits the message is the "synaptic transmitter," or neurotransmitter, or neurohormone. At this point no one knows how many neurotransmitters there are in the mammalian brain, but a list of known or suspected neurotransmitters is presented in Table 10-I. This list of about twenty neurotransmitters is thought to be not more than perhaps 5 percent of the total number of neurotransmitters remaining to be identified in the brain.

What makes these neurotransmitters so exciting and useful for horsemen is that particular neurotransmitters are often associated with relatively specific functions in the brain. Thus, the neurotransmitter norepinephrine in the brain is broadly associated with mood, and in the human, mood-elevating drugs appear to be associated with increased norepinephrine levels. The neurotransmitter dopamine appears to be associated with running activity, and dopaminergic drugs such as apomorphine and Sublimaze® can dramatically increase running activity in the horse. Finally, and perhaps most clear-cut of all, the "endorphins" are opiatelike neurotransmitters that are formed in the brain and are associated with pain suppression. This endorphin-containing synapse system is, of course, the synaptic system that provides the pharmacological receptors for opium and all the opiate drugs. From these few examples it is clear that many of our useful drugs produce their effects by acting on synapses. Because of the central importance of the synapse in understanding the pharmacology of stimulant drugs, it will be useful first to look at the structure of the synapse in some detail.

Microscopically, a synapse appears as a swelling on the end of a nerve where it

TABLE 10-I
KNOWN OR PROBABLE NEUROHORMONES

1. Acetylcholine	12. DOPAMINE*
2. γ-Aminobutyric acid	13. β-ENDORPHIN*
3. Glycine	14. Angiotensin II
4. Taurine	15. Oxytocin
5. β-Alanine	16. Vasopressin
6. Glutamic acid	17. LH-RH
7. Aspartic acid	18. Substance P
8. Cysteic Acid	19. Neurotensin
9. Homocysteic Acid	20. Somatostatin
10. NOREPINEPHRINE*	21. SEROTONIN*
11. ENKEPHALIN*	

* The capitalized neurohormones are involved in drug effects of particular interest to horsemen. The adrenergic drugs produce their effects via norepinephrine (Chapter 11), the narcotic analgesics produce their effects via the enkephalins (Chapter 12), and apomorphine and pemoline produce their effects by mimicking the actions of dopamine (Chapter 13). The phenothiazine tranquilizers (Chapter 14) produce their effects by blocking dopaminergic receptors, while reserpine produces its effects by depleting either norepinephrine or serotonin from nerve cells.

makes contact with another nerve (Fig. 10-4). It consists of a pre-synaptic portion, which is the end of one nerve, a synaptic cleft, which is the space between the nerves, and a postsynaptic portion, which is the beginning of another neuron. The presynaptic portion will have the necessary enzymes to synthesize the neurohormone, a mechanism for storing it, and a method for releasing it. Once released, the neurohormone moves across the synaptic cleft and activates its specific receptors on the postsynaptic portion, which is the beginning of the next nerve cell. After the neurotransmitter has activated the receptors on the next nerve cell it must be disposed of, usually either by being split by specific enzymes or sometimes by re-uptake into the presynaptic portion by a special pumping mechanism.

This fairly complex mechanism and the fact that there are a large number of known neurotransmitters obviously allows for a very large number of possible sites of drug action. Examples of the points on synapses where drugs of particular interest to horsemen act include the following. Reserpine produces its tranquilizing effect by blocking storage of the neurohormone norepinephrine in nerve terminals. In the reserpinized animal, only about 20 percent of the normal norepinephrine stores are found in the storage granules, and this depletion of an excitatory neurohormone accounts for the tranquilization found after administration of reserpine (Fig. 10-5).

Once norepinephrine is released from the presynaptic terminal, its function is to activate the norepinephrine receptors on the postsynaptic membrane. Amphetamine, metamphetamine, and methylphenidate (Ritalin®) all produce their pharmacological effects by accelerating the release of norepinephrine from the presynaptic terminal. This increased release of norepinephrine produces the excitement seen after administration of amphetamine and metamphetamine. Some drugs, on the other hand, act by directly stimulating the postsynaptic receptors. The best example of a drug that does this is apomorphine, which directly stimulates the postsynaptic receptors for dopamine in dopaminergic synapses and

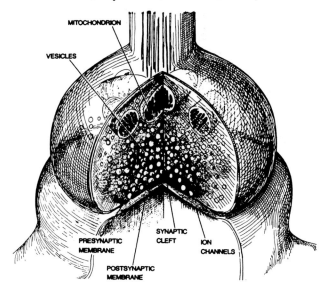

Figure 10-4. The synapse is the relay point where information is conveyed by chemical transmitters from neuron to neuron. A synapse consists of two parts: the knoblike tip of an axon terminal and the receptor region on the surface of another neuron. The membranes are separated by a synaptic cleft of some 200 nanometers across. Molecules of chemical transmitter, stored in vesicles in the axon terminal, are released into the cleft by arriving nerve impulses. The transmitter changes the electrical state of the receiving neuron, making it either more likely or less likely to fire an impulse. From *The Neuron*, Charles F. Stevens. Copyright © 1979 by Scientific American Inc. All rights reserved.

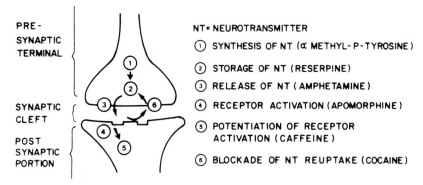

Figure 10-5. The synapse as a site of drug action. The presynaptic portion of the terminal contains biochemical pathways for the synthesis (1), storage (2), and release (3) of the neurotransmitters. In the adrenergic neuron, synthesis and storage are blocked by α-methyl-*p*-tyrosine and reserpine, which, therefore, are both tranquilizers. Release of norepinephrine (3) is stimulated by amphetamine and methylphenidate, which are thus stimulant drugs. Apomorphine directly stimulates dopaminergic receptors in the dopaminergic synapse (4), resulting in locomotor stimulation. In the noradrenergic synapse, caffeine acts postsynaptically to (5) potentiate receptor activation by norepinephrine and is thus a stimulant. In the synaptic cleft, cocaine (6) acts to prevent presynaptic uptake of norepinephrine, increasing its concentration at the receptor level and thus producing its stimulant effects. Reproduced with permission from Tobin et al., *J Equine Med Surg, 3*:60, 1979.

produces the running activity so characteristic of apomorphine in the horse. The phenothiazine tranquilizers such as acepromazine produce their tranquilizing effects by directly blocking postsynaptic adrenergic and dopaminergic receptors, and preventing the normal release of neurohormones from having any effect.

Another point of action for drugs on the adrenergic synapse is on the mechanism by which the neurohormone is removed from the cleft. As pointed out earlier, norepinephrine is pumped out of the cleft back into the presynaptic terminal. This process is very specifically blocked by cocaine, and cocaine therefore gives rise to increased concentrations of norepinephrine on the post-synaptic receptors and thus gives rise to brain stimulation.

This, then, is how the drugs whose actions are well understood at this time produce their effects in the horse's brain. The next question, and an intensely practical one, is how can we study the actions of these drugs in the horse in a way that will be useful to people who want to understand their actions and effects in racing and performance horses?

The most commonly suggested answer to this question is to run a performance experiment. A performance experiment is done by taking a number of horses in training, running them on a drug, timing their performance, and then comparing these times with their performance times without the drug. If their times are improved (i.e. reduced) after drug X, then you can say that drug X is a stimulant, and if they are not, you can then say that drug X is not an important drug in racehorses.

While this sounds like a simple, logical, and effective approach, in actual fact it is a difficult, expensive, time-consuming, and almost invariably futile approach to the study of the actions and effects of stimulant drugs in horses.

In the first place, this type of study is an extremely expensive proposition. From my own experience, the maintenance, care and feeding of a stable of horses is, in comparison with the research budgets available for such work, very expensive. Further, the soundness of the horses that most research programs can afford to buy is marginal, so just keeping the horses at anything approaching racing soundness is a problem in and of itself. Since you are experimenting with drugs, you cannot use other drugs to keep the horses "sound" without compromising the design and interpretation of the experiment. For economic reasons alone, therefore, the maintenance of an experimentally useful number (at least 10) of horses sound and ready to go when the experimenter requires it is very expensive, and by itself, a full-time job.

Now, let us suppose that you had sufficient money to put together a stable that could field ten horses racing sound once or twice a week. The selection of the drugs to test is usually no problem, since they are the drugs that are causing public relations problems in racing and which the racing community wants tested. Another problem, however, arises when you try to determine the dose of drug to give, the route by which you should give it, and how long you should wait before you test the horses. Where does the equine pharmacologist go to get this information? He can listen to trackside rumor, if he is not very particular about the quality of information on which he is going to base his experiments and expend his funds. In the last analysis, however, there is only **one** answer to this question. If his work

The maintenance of a racing research program can be a very expensive proposition.

is to be scientifically sound, he must develop this information for himself and demonstrate clearly why he picked the dose, route of administration, and the time postdosing to run the tests on each drug that he studies.

Information about the appropriate dose, route of administration, and time of peak drug effect is critical, because without this information, one cannot interpret one's experiments with confidence. For example, studying the effects of furosemide on performance in racing horses, colleagues of mine at another university elected to use a dose of 1 mg/kg and test the performance of their horses two hours and fifteen minutes after dosing. The results of this study were negative, furosemide under these conditions having no effect on the performance

Where does the equine pharmacologist go to get his information on doses? He can listen to trackside rumor, if he is not very particular about the quality of his information.

of these horses. So can one conclude that furosemide has no effect on the performance of horses? Not really, because one can show that most of the pharmacological effects of a dose of furosemide are over by two hours postdosing, which means that furosemide might have produced an effect earlier, and a study that waited for 2¼ hours after dosing might miss this effect. Investigating the effects of about 0.5 mg/kg of furosemide at thirty minutes after dosing (about the time for peak drug effect), I and my coworkers also found no effect on performance in time trials. We, however, were also in the position to study track times from a Louisville Downs harness racing meet and, based on the results of a retrospective study of almost 400 times from 58 horses and the previous time trial data, concluded that there was no evidence that furosemide improved the performance of horses.

Similar problems with dose, route of administration, and time postdosing to conduct the test were encountered in studies with fentanyl. Track gossip suggested that a useful dose of fentanyl in a horse was 0.25 mg, given intramuscularly about thirty minutes before a race. Testing this dose on harness horses in training, I found no effect whatsoever of fentanyl either on behavior or, in limited studies, on the times of harness horses to race one mile. Good reason for the lack of effect of these doses became apparent later when it was discovered that for a stimulant effect, fentanyl must be given by rapid IV injection, that the dose should be at least five times the 0.25 mg dose suggested by track rumor, and that the action of this particular drug peaks at five minutes after dosing. Therefore, in the case of fentanyl, studies based on doses and routes of administration rumored to be used on the track would be highly likely to be negative, as these doses cannot produce a stimulant effect. Other people have also performed pharmacological studies on fentanyl, using doses suggested by "track rumor" and have, not surprisingly, also found negative effects.

Another problem with stimulant drugs is that the dose needed to produce useful stimulation varies from horse to horse, and, as will be shown later, these differences can be quite large. Like some individuals who cannot function in the morning without two cups of coffee, and others whom coffee makes hyperactive, some horses respond well to small doses of stimulants, while other horses may need ten times the dose to produce the same effect. Therefore, it would not be particularly helpful to go to a pharmacology text and pull out an average dose, for this dose might be too high for one horse but too low for another, and thus eliminate whatever improvement in performance that the correct dose might produce in a third horse.

This problem of identifying the dose, route of administration, and time post-dosing to determine drug effect has given rise to what I like to think of as a "window" concept for optimal drug effect. This is the area in the dose and time response curves for a drug response where a beneficial effect on performance may be expected. This "window" must be defined before any kind of pharmacological trials may even be attempted with a drug. For example, with any stimulant drug there is a dose that will not produce any significant stimulation, a dose that will produce just the right effect, and a dose that is too large to produce a useful stimulation and on which the animal becomes incoordinated or otherwise does not perform effectively. This concept of a dose and time-dependent period postdosing when significant effects on performance may be expected is presented in Figure 10-6. As well as being dose sensitive, this "window" is time sensitive, occurring within five minutes of dosing for a rapidly acting drug like fentanyl and likely much later for long acting drugs like morphine or reserpine.

Another major problem in the time trial approach is that the animal is working at very close to its maximal effort and any drug-induced response can only add a very small percentage on top of this effort. Further, the closer the horse is to producing his maximal response, the less room there is to see a drug effect (Fig. 10-7). In essence, therefore, the closer the experimenter's horses are performing to "maximal" racing performance, the less likely the experimenter is to be able to show a drug-dependent stimulation, which defeats the purpose of the exercise. This problem of the magnitude of the effect that the experimenter is trying to measure is further compounded by its very small size. Good harness horses will run the mile in two minutes, or 120 seconds, but a difference in time of 0.1 seconds

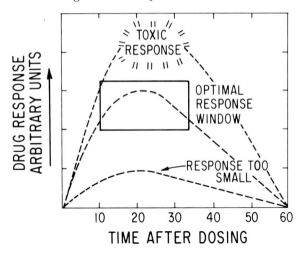

Figure 10-6. Concept of an optimal response "window" for testing drug responses. For any stimulant drug there is a dose that is too small to produce an effect, a dose that produces a useful effect, and a dose that produces an ineffective response. The time postdosing at which the optimal effect occurs is also critical if effective pharmacological studies such as time trials are to be carried out, as both the correct dose and time postdosing to run the study are critical. The dose and time slot within which a useful response can be found is referred to as the optimal response window.

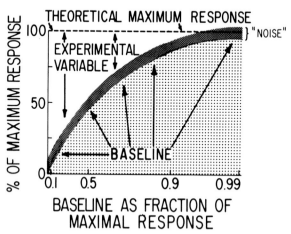

Figure 10-7. "Performance tests" are unsatisfactory experimental models because the objective is to run the horse as close to his maximum speed as possible, then administer a drug and look for an improvement. On this model, indicated to the right side of the illustration, the baseline constitutes about 99 percent of the measured response, and the drug effect is very difficult to distinguish. If, however, the experiment starts with a standing horse, both baseline and the random variation of the baseline called noise are very small compared with the maximal response. Under these circumstances, it is relatively easy to measure a drug effect, as the experimental variable is large. Experiments are thus best set up with a large variable to measure, rather than with a miniscule variable and massive baselines.

Performance trials require large numbers of horses and may not be very useful scientifically.

or half a length can make the difference between a winner and third place. This difference in time of less than 0.1 percent is far too small to be scientifically testable with the small numbers of horses used in performance trials, given the day-to-day variability caused by track conditions, weather, the animal's form, the driver's form, and so forth. In a nutshell, performance trials are of marginal scientific use for the determination of drug effects of horses, and to attempt time trials without carefully characterizing the pharmacology of the drugs in question in the horse is to make very elaborate, expensive, and almost certainly futile efforts.

Despite these problems, however, it is very important that we characterize and quantitate the actions of drugs in horses accurately, for in the last analysis it is these actions that are at the center of the medication problem. Working on this problem in Kentucky, we are in the process of developing a number of simple models, which we believe will allow us to measure and quantitate the actions of stimulant and depressant drugs in horses accurately and economically. To date, we have come up with two powerful methods in this area and are in the process of developing others.

After about two years of fumbling about with expensive and useless electronic behavioral instrumentation, we were fortunate enough to discover what we call the step-counting method. This simple procedure provides an extremely sensitive and reproducible method of quantitating the pharmacological response to certain drugs in the horse. The development of this method started with experiments on the track with doses of fentanyl rumored to be effective. We administered a number of these 0.25 mg doses of fentanyl to Standardbred horses, saw no consistent effects on performance or times, and more or less abandoned this research approach.

Somewhat later, we started some analytical experiments on fentanyl and, to assist us in this detection work, we increased the dose of fentanyl about ten times to 5 mg. One of my students, Joan Combie, injected a horse in a box stall with this intravenous dose and watched in amazement as the horse started to trot around the stall. Observing this response, we immediately repeated the dose and got the same effect. At this point I enlisted Mark Crisman, then a summer student in my

Fumbling about with expensive electronic equipment is not necessarily the best experimental approach with horses.

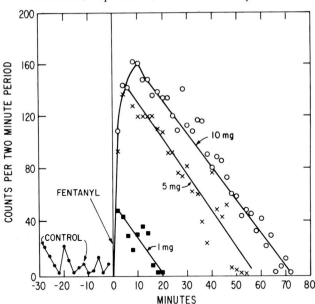

Figure 10-8. The step-counting method: effects of fentanyl on spontaneous motor activity in the horse. A horse in a quiet box stall was injected with 1, 5, and 10 mg of fentanyl per 1000 lb. by rapid IV injection. Every time it lifted its left foreleg from the ground and completed a step, it was scored for one step. The number of steps for each two-minute period was recorded and plotted on the vertical axis against time in minutes on the horizontal axis. The control portion shows stepping after an injection of saline. The method shows consistent baseline levels and large and clear-cut responses to drugs. Reproduced with permission from Tobin, *J Equine Med Surg,* 2:379, 1978.

lab, handed him a stopwatch, a hand-held counter, and a legal pad, and told him to count the number of steps the horse made with its left front leg every two minutes for the next hour.

At the end of the hour the experiment was over and Mark brought me the data. When plotted, the data from these first experiments showed a classic time-response curve, the action of the drug peaking rapidly and then declining back to baseline (Fig. 10-8). After repeating this experiment a couple of times it was quite clear that we had stumbled onto something very useful. When carefully performed, the step-counting method is a classic experimental model in that the baseline values are low, with small variability, and the peak responses are large, up to twenty-five times baseline values. The experiments are rapid, easy to perform, yield a large number of data points, and require no sophisticated instrumentation with malfunction problems. Extensive work with this method, outlined in Chapters 12 and 13, has allowed us to characterize the actions of drugs such as apomorphine and the narcotics, which stimulate running in the horse. While this method does not work particularly well with drugs such as caffeine, amphetamine, cocaine, and methylphenidate, these drugs will accentuate the response to fentanyl and their effects can be demonstrated in this way. Certain drugs such as phenothiazine tranquilizers also block the trotting response and their time course and duration of action can be measured in terms of their ability to block this trotting response.

Stimulated by our success with this simple step-counting method, we examined a number of other drug-induced behaviors in an attempt to develop other methods of measuring drug effects on behavior. Among the effects that we spent some time investigating were the effects of cocaine and amphetamine on head shaking behavior. Casual inspection had suggested to us that use of these drugs was associated with increased head shaking, and this response was investigated in some detail. Unfortunately, it proved difficult to unambiguously define the activity, and the behavior did not appear reliably in all the horses tested. In some individuals, however, the head shaking or bowing response could be quite marked, as shown in Figure 10-9.

In the experiment of Figure 10-9, a horse was dosed with a large dose of cocaine

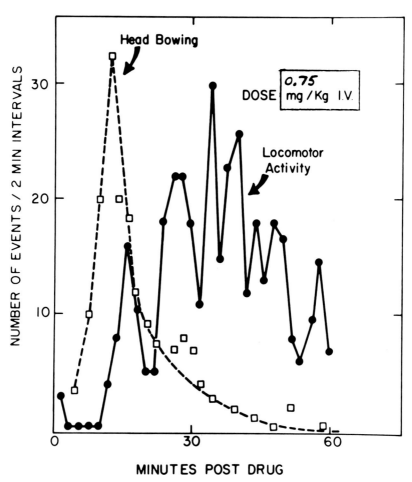

MINUTES POST DRUG

Figure 10-9. Effect of cocaine on head bowing and locomotor activity in the horse. An adult gelding was dosed with 0.75 mg/kg of cocaine by rapid IV injection, and his rate of head bowing and locomotor activity was monitored. Head bowing was defined as a complete movement of the head from the horizontal position to below the knee and back to the horizontal position. The open squares (□—□) show the number of head bowing events per two-minute period, while the solid circles (●—●) show the spontaneous locomotor activity over these same periods.

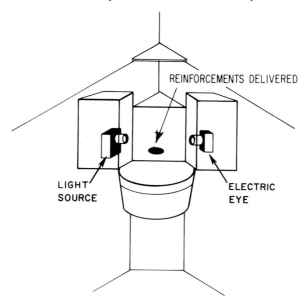

REINFORCEMENTS DELIVERED

LIGHT
SOURCE

ELECTRIC
EYE

Figure 10-10. Behavior apparatus feeding console. An oaken console was built around a feed tube installed in the corner of a box stall. Just above the feed tube is a light source and an electric eye. When the horse breaks the light beam, an audible click is sounded, and after a certain number of breaks he is rewarded for his efforts through the small tube just above the feed tub. Reproduced with permission from Shults et al., *Am J Vet Res, 42:*1981.

IV, and both its head bowing and locomotor activity were monitored. Head bowing, as shown by the open squares, appeared within minutes, and the rate of bowing increased rapidly, to peak at about twelve minutes after dosing and then rapidly decline. Locomotor activity, however, was low at first but increased as the head bowing activity declined. The data suggest that head bowing activity in this horse was associated with high blood levels of cocaine, and it also appears that head bowing inhibits locomotor activity. Unfortunately, despite a number of interesting and provocative experiments like this, we have yet to develop a useful experimental method based on monitoring head shaking.

After a period spent studying the effects of drugs on head bowing and other nervous mannerisms of the horse, one of my students, Ted Shults, began to investigate another methodology, widely used in pharmacological studies, called operant behavior. In this type of study the horse is trained to break an electric eye, for which he gets a food reward, and the effects of drugs on the rate at which he works the machine are studied. It has turned out in our hands to be a very successful method of studying the action of stimulants and depressant drugs in horses.

The operant apparatus consists of a special console above the horse's feed bucket in the corner of a box stall. Just above the feed bucket is an electric eye, placed so that the horse cannot get into the feed bucket without breaking the electric eye. Breaking the electric eye triggers the release into the feed bucket of about half a cup of oats and also sounds an audible click (Fig. 10-10). Most of the apparatus which operates this console is, of course, behind the console in the control room, being monitored by a student (Fig. 10-11). Once the horses get used to the apparatus, they work it diligently, and pretty soon they are eating all the oats that the machine will provide.

At this point we play a trick on the horses. The machine is re-programmed so that it only responds at random intervals to the horse's breaking of the light beam. Pretty soon the horses find that if they keep breaking the light beam at a certain rate they will get fed, so each horse figures out his own rate and works the machine at that rate. These rates are individual to each horse and remarkably stable. As shown in Figure 10-12, horses will hold with their individual light beam-breaking rates for months on end and, in our work, these rates have been stable for as long as we have tested them.

Once this experimental system has been set up we are dealing with a specific response which is relatively stable and is quite individual to that horse. The data of Figure 10-13 shows how a typical experiment with this apparatus is set up to determine whether or not phenylbutazone is a behavioral stimulant in horses. The responding rate of the three horses was determined on three individual days, and on each of these days the horse received an injection of saline. Then on the fourth day the horses received a dose of phenylbutazone instead of saline and were tested again. As shown in Figure 10-13, treatment with phenylbutazone produced no increase or decrease in the responding rate and thus does not appear to be a behaviorally active drug in the horse.

Data from the responding apparatus may be presented in a number of ways. In one series of experiments with this method we dosed a horse with reserpine and

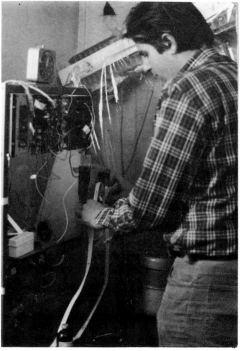

Figure 10-11. Behind the scenes in operant conditioning. In the tack room behind the feeding console is the apparatus to operate it. This consists of (1) a battery of electronic apparatuses to monitor the number of beam-breaking events and randomly reward the horse, (2) a multi-chamber oats dispenser from which the reward is dispensed, (3) a Harvard recorder which makes a hard record of all the events, and (4) Theodore Shults, graduate of the Rube Goldberg School of Engineering and mastermind of the whole apparatus.

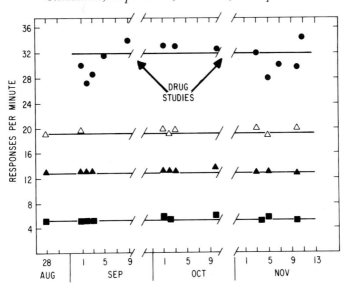

Figure 10-12. Control responding rates in behavioral apparatus. Each symbol represents a different horse and shows his responding rate over a four-month period. One horse, indicated by the solid squares, only made about five responses per minute, while others responded at about thirteen, eighteen, and thirty-two responses per minute. If the experimental conditions are carefully controlled, these responding rates are quite stable and become a very sensitive measure of drug effects. Reproduced with permission from Shults et al., *Am J Vet Res, 42*:1981.

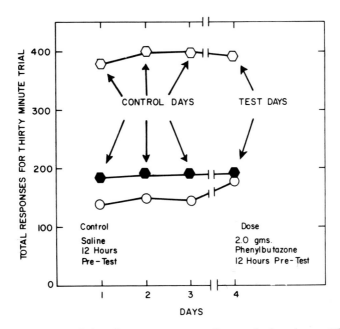

Figure 10-13. Lack of effect of phenylbutazone on responding rate in three horses. The symbols for days one, two, and three represent the responding rates twelve hours after intravenous injection of saline, while the symbols on day four show the responding rates in the same horses twelve hours after 2 gm of phenylbutazone was injected intravenously to each horse.

ran the test the following day. We were surprised and delighted to find that the responding rate of all our horses was markedly reduced, that this effect took between three and five days to peak, and that it lasted for up to ten days. The method allows us to very clearly delineate the actions of a long-acting tranquilizer such as reserpine, as outlined in Chapter 15. This method can also be used to study the actions of stimulant drugs, and it turns out to be very sensitive to them, very small doses of stimulants producing a significant increases in responding rate (see Chapter 11).

Another factor that appears clearly in this model is the difference in sensitivity of different horses to drugs. Thus, as we will see later, some horses are quite sensitive to cocaine and are stimulated by small doses of the drug, while other horses require much larger doses to produce the same effect. This individual difference in doses necessary to produce a stimulation is also encountered in the doses required to depress activity, which are higher in the horses less sensitive to cocaine than in those that are sensitive to the drug.

In the next three chapters we will discuss the central stimulants used in the horse under three separate headings. The first group, which consists primarily of drugs that produce central nervous system stimulation in the horse without any clear-cut signs of behavioral stimulation, is called "horses just stimulated." Typical of this group of drugs are amphetamine and caffeine, which stimulate a horse without producing any clear-cut behavioral patterns to characterize their actions. The next group of drugs discussed are the narcotic analgesics, which produce very clear-cut trotting behavior and which, to judge from their actions on horses and humans, likely make the horses "happy" while they trot. The last group of drugs discussed are those related to apomorphine, which also produces clear-cut running behavior in horses and which, again to judge from the horses' behavior, makes them run scared.

Having completed our discussion of the stimulant drugs, we then close out our study of the illegal drugs with chapters on transquilizers and depressants, followed by a final chapter on the local anesthetics and their uses in the performance horse.

SELECTED REFERENCES

Cooper, J. R., Bloom, F. E., and Roth, R. G.: *The Biochemical Basis of Neuropharmacology.* New York, Oxford University Press, 1978.

Guyton, A. C.: *Basic Human Physiology: Normal Function and Mechanisms of Disease.* Philadelphia, Saunders, 1971.

Iversen, S. D. and Iversen, L. L.: *Behavioral Pharmacology.* New York, Oxford University Press, 1975.

Julien, R. M.: *A Primer of Drug Action.* San Francisco, W. H. Freeman, 1975.

Shepherd, G. M.: *The Synaptic Organization of the Brain.* New York, Oxford University Press, 1974.

Shults, T.: *The Behavioral Effects and Pharmacokinetics of Cocaine in the Horse.* M.Sc. Thesis, University of Kentucky, 1980.

Shults, T., Combie, J., Dougherty, J., and Tobin, T.: Variable interval responding in the horse: A sensitive method of quantitating the effects of centrally acting drugs. *Am J Vet Res*, submitted for publication, 1980.

Tobin, T., Combie, J., and Dougherty, J.: The pharmacology of narcotic analgesics in the horse. III. Characteristics of the locomotor effects of fentanyl and apomorphine. *J Equine Med Surg, 3:*85-90, 1979.

Chapter 11

HORSES JUST STIMULATED: AMPHETAMINE, COCAINE, CAFFEINE, METHYLPHENIDATE, AND OTHER DRUGS

THE STIMULANT DRUGS that will be discussed in this chapter in general produce their stimulant effects by either mimicking or accentuating the actions of a neurohormone called norepinephrine in the horse's brain. Although they can be readily shown to stimulate horses, they do not produce the clear-cut type of trotting activity associated with the narcotic analgesic drugs and apomorphine. Rather, their effect seems to be more of the character of a subtle general stimulant effect, and this effect is often not easy to define or measure. The actions of this group of drugs in the horse are therefore consistent with what is known of the actions of norepinephrine in the human, as this hormone is primarily associated with mood elevation in humans. The best known and perhaps most widely used of this group of drugs, in both humans and horses, is amphetamine and its close relative, methamphetamine.

Amphetamine and Methamphetamine

Amphetamine has a long history of use in racing, dating from its introduction into human and veterinary medicine prior to World War II. Amphetamine was widely used by the military forces on both sides during World War II, primarily due to the fact that it increases wakefulness and alertness and decreases the sense of fatigue. Prolonged use in humans, however, is always followed by fatigue, depression, and psychosis.

The amphetamines began to appear in post-race equine urines soon after World War II and enjoyed a period of popularity that may still continue in some racing jurisdictions around the world. More recently, however, with the development of sensitive TLC and GC methods for their detection, their use has become relatively easy to control, and because of this, racing jurisdictions with good laboratories no longer have a problem with amphetamine abuse.

The amphetamines produce their brain-stimulating effects by stimulating the release of norepinephrine and dopamine from nerve terminals. Thus, in animals in which formation of these neurohormones has been blocked by use of experimental drugs, amphetamine does not produce its characteristic stimulant effects. Which of these two neurohormones is most important for the brain-stimulating effect of amphetamine, however, is not clear. In horses, the response to amphetamine, which is subtle and visible primarily as restlessness, is quite clearly distinct from the powerful running response induced by apomorphine (see Chapter 13). Since the apomorphine response is generally considered to be a pure dopaminergic stimulant effect, it seems likely that, in the horse at least, the response to amphetamine must be mediated primarily by norepinephrine rather than dopamine.

179

The amphetamines are among the most potent of the amine drugs with respect to brain stimulation. Animals given amphetamine show tremor, restlessness, increased motor activity, agitation, and sleeplessness, which effects are thought to be due to stimulation of the cerebral cortex. In the human, amphetamine increases the duration of performance before fatigue sets in, and the effects of fatigue are reversed, particularly when performance is reduced due to lack of sleep. These actions led to their use by airmen during World War II and account for their more current use by truck drivers and by students cramming for exams.

Methamphetamine is closely related chemically to amphetamine and ephedrine. Small doses of methamphetamine have prominent effects on the brain without significant effects on the heart and blood vessels, while larger doses produce marked effects on the heart and blood vessels.

We have studied the actions of methamphetamine on spontaneous motor activity in the horse in our laboratory (Fig. 11-1). Unlike the clear-cut trotting response that one sees after administration of fentanyl or apomorphine, the trotting response to methamphetamine alone is very small. However, if the animal is injected with small doses of fentanyl (see Chapter 12) and methamphetamine

Amphetamines delay the onset of fatigue and have been used for this by airmen, truck drivers, and students, as well as in horses.

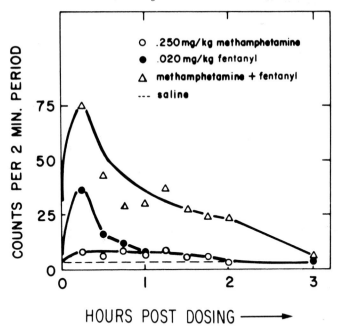

Figure 11-1. Accentuation or potentiation of the trotting response to fentanyl by methamphetamine. The dashed line (-----) shows the spontaneous motor activity of three horses injected with normal saline, and the open circles (o—o) show the small increase in spontaneous locomotor activity produced by an IV dose of 0.25 mg/kg of methamphetamine. The solid circles (•—•) show the response of these horses to the IV injection of 0.02 mg/kg of fentanyl, while the triangles (▲) show the response to the doses of methamphetamine and fentanyl combined. As can be seen, the combination of methamphetamine and fentanyl produced a greater response than the sum of the individual responses. Technically, these drugs are said to "potentiate" each other. Reproduced with permission from Tobin et al., *J Equine Med Surg*, *3*:63, 1979.

together, the methamphetamine augments the fentanyl-induced trotting response and the trotting response persists for a period after the response to fentanyl would normally have disappeared (Fig. 11-1). This prolonged trotting response after methamphetamine suggests at least a two-hour course of action for methamphetamine after its intravenous administration.

In the circulatory system, the amphetamines generally raise blood pressure, which in turn causes a reflex slowing of heart rate, so cardiac output is not increased by therapeutic doses of these drugs. Studying the cardiovascular actions of amphetamine in the horse, Smetzer and his coworkers at the Ohio State University found that amphetamine alone caused a small but significant increase in heart rate and blood pressure. In the exercised horse, these workers found a much greater incidence of irregular heartbeats in amphetamine-treated horses after exercise. Smetzer concluded that in the exercised horse the release of norepinephrine by amphetamine probably caused many of the irregular heartbeats by increasing the excitability of the heart muscle. Other actions of the amphetamines include relaxation of bronchial muscle, which increases the diameter of airways in the lungs, but this effect is not large enough to be useful. The respiratory center is usually stimulated by amphetamines, and though this effect is small in normal animals, amphetamine stimulation of respiration can be substantial and useful in animals with respiratory depression.

Therapeutic doses of amphetamine cause a modest increase in metabolic rate (10 to 15%) and Gabel* and coworkers report a significant increase in body temperature in horses dosed with 250 mg of amphetamine and paced for one mile under racing conditions.

The clearance of amphetamine by the horse has been studied in some detail by both Baggot and Chapman. Baggot injected Shetland ponies with a dose of amphetamine equivalent to about 300 mg/1000 lb and drew his first blood samples thirty minutes after dosing, at which point plasma levels of amphetamine of about 200 ng/ml were observed. By six hours after dosing these levels had declined to less than 15 ng/ml to give a plasma half-life for this drug in the horse of about 1.4 hours, somewhat faster than an apparent half-life of about two hours seen in later experiments by this same group. Unfortunately, Baggott and his coworkers did not report any clinical signs or behavioral changes in these animals.

In studies on the metabolism of amphetamines in the horse, Chapman's group found that 84 percent of the radiolabel from C^{14} amphetamine was excreted within twenty-four hours, of which about 4 percent was amphetamine. Because amphetamine is extensively metabolized in the horse and only a small portion of the drug is excreted in the urine, its plasma half-life is not affected by urinary pH. On the other hand, as a basic drug, a much higher proportion of both amphetamine and its basic metabolites are found in acidic urine, which probably makes the drug easier to detect in acidic urine. The main excretion products are 4-hydroxyamphetamine (free and conjugated), free and conjugated amphetamine, and 1-phenylpropan-2-ol (12%) and 1-phenylpropan-2-one (28%). However, Chapman's results on the metabolism of amphetamine were in contrast with those of Karawya, who reported that up to 55 percent of a dose of amphetamine was excreted as amphetamine in the urine over forty-eight hours. Karawya's horses, however, were producing an acidic urine (pH 6.0) in contrast with the alkaline urine (pH 7.8) of Chapman's horses, which may account for the differences.

Ray and his coworkers at the Ohio State University have studied the disposition of methamphetamine in the horse and its "clearance times" in plasma and urine. After 150 mg methamphetamine administered intramuscularly (IM) in six horses, these workers found plasma levels of methamphetamine peaked at about 43 ng/ml within twenty minutes of drug administration and then declined in a complex fashion to be no longer detectable in plasma about eight hours after dosing (Fig. 11-2). Salivary levels of methamphetamine were always somewhat less than plasma levels of the drug, as is usually the case with basic drugs.

The urinary levels of methamphetamine reported by Ray and his colleagues were remarkably high after this dose, peaking at 7 µg/ml four hours after dosing and then declining rapidly to about 500 ng/ml at twelve hours after dosing. Thereafter, the decline in urinary levels was relatively slow, and traces of methamphetamine were still detectable in urine at forty-eight hours after dosing. It seems prudent, therefore, to allow at least forty-eight hours after dosing with amphetamine or methamphetamine for the urine to clear, particularly in the case of

---

* A. A. Gabel, The Ohio State University; personal communication, 1978.

methamphetamine, where what can only be described as massive urinary levels of this drug are observed.

Studying the performance effects of amphetamines in horses, Stewart and his colleagues in Australia dosed three Thoroughbred horses with about 100 mg of amphetamine intravenously (IV) thirty to sixty minutes before exercising them. Prior to exercise he found that amphetamine caused an increase in the respiratory rate but had no significant cardiac effects. He then galloped these horses over distances of between 800 and 1600 meters and found that the gallop speed was improved in each of five trials. The improvement in speed ranged from 0.4 percent to 8.3 percent, with a mean improvement of 2.4 percent, which he did not consider to be statistically significant.

Sanford and his coworkers in Scotland studied the effects of methamphetamine on horses doing timed circuits at the collected and extended trot and the canter, using between three and four horses in each study. Methamphetamine was given IV at a dose of about 45 mg (0.4 mg/kg) one hour before testing. At this dose, methamphetamine was found to increase speed at all paces tested (P < 0.02) without affecting coordination. A dose of about 20 mg increased speed at the trot

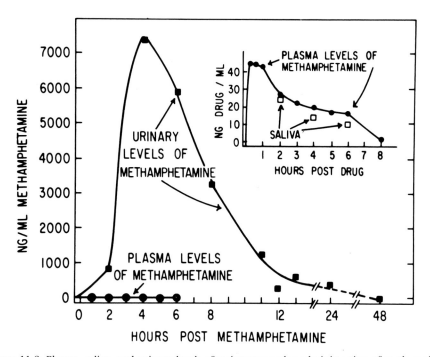

Figure 11-2. Plasma, saliva, and urinary levels after intramuscular administration of methamphetamine in the horse. Horses were dosed with 150 mg of methamphetamine IM at indicated zero time. The solid squares (■—■) show mean urinary levels of methamphetamine, which ranged up to 200 times the levels observed in plasma (solid circles, ●—●). The inset in the upper right-hand corner shows the relationship between plasma levels of methamphetamine (solid circles, ●—●) and salivary levels of methamphetamine (open squares, □—□) on an increased scale. All data points represent means of experiments on eight different horses and are replotted from the work of Ray et al. Reproduced with permission from Tobin et al., *J Equine Med Surg*, 3:64, 1979.

TABLE 11-I

GALLOP TEST 2 × 200 M. COMPOUNDS INCREASING SPEED SIGNIFICANTLY P < 0.05

Compound	Dose (mg/kg)	Route	No. Tested
Methylamphetamine	0.1	IM	3
	0.2	IM	1
Methylphenidate	0.25	SC	4
	0.5	SC	4
Pemoline	4.0	Oral	4
	8.0	Oral	4
Caffeine	2.0	Oral	3
	4.0	Oral	3
	8.0	Oral	1
Phenylbutazone	6.6	IM*	4

* Injection made twenty-three hours before test.

NOTE: In these gallop tests, horses were run singly over a 200 meter course from a flying start. After an interval of about five minutes, during which period the horse returned to the start at a trot or slow canter, this gallop was repeated. No data on the dosing times, the actual performance times, or the variability in the performance times on which these conclusions were drawn was presented.

SOURCE: Sanford, Symposium on Large Animal Therapeutics, University of Surrey, Guildford, Surrey, 1978. Courtesy of Blackwell Scientific Publications.

only. On the gallop test, however, the effect of methamphetamine was variable, with only one horse showing an increase in speed at a dose of 0.2 mg/kg (Tables 11-I and 11-II).

Outside of their stimulant action in fatigued or perhaps moribund patients, there are relatively few indications for amphetamine and methamphetamine in equine medicine. The amphetamines are potent respiratory stimulants and have been recommended for treatment of anesthetic respiratory collapse. Recommended doses in the horse are between 100 and 500 mg subcutaneously (SC). It is suggested that if amphetamine must be given in large doses IV that it be given

TABLE 11-II

PERFORMANCE TEST. EFFECT OF CNS STIMULANTS ON SPEED AT TROT AND CANTER

Compound	Dose (mg/kg)	Route	No. Tested	Effect on Speed at Trot and Canter
Methylamphetamine	0.05	IM	4	+ in 2/4 at extended trot
	0.01	IM	4	+ in 2/4 at collected trot
				+ in 4/4 at extended trot
				+ in 2/4 at canter
Methylphenidate	0.25	SC	4	+ in 4/4 at all paces
	0.5	SC	4	+ in 4/4 at all paces
Pemoline	4.0	Oral	3	+ in 3/3 at all paces
	8.0	Oral	3	+ in 3/3 at all paces
Caffeine	2.0	Oral	3	No consistent effect
	4.0	Oral	3	No consistent effect

+ = increased speed

SOURCE: Sanford, Symposium on Large Animal Therapeutics, University of Surrey, Guildford, Surrey, 1978. Courtesy of Blackwell Scientific Publications.

slowly, as death in the human has followed rapid IV injection of 120 mg. Symptoms of amphetamine toxicity in the horse have not been described but might be expected to include convulsions, fever, circulatory collapse, coma, and death, with cerebral hemorrhage as the main pathological finding. The phenothiazine tranquilizers would be expected to effectively control the CNS symptoms and may also help reduce an elevated blood pressure. Chronic amphetamine intoxication, which causes vivid hallucinations and delusions in the human, is unlikely to be seen in the horse.

Ephedrine

Ephedrine occurs in certain plants of the genus *Ephedra*, a family of small shrubs distributed widely throughout the world. The species of plants containing ephedrine are native to China and Tibet, and the plant has been used in Chinese medicine for over 5,000 years. During the 1930s the plant was grown in the Middle West of the United States, but most ephedrine now used is prepared by organic synthesis.

Ephedrine is closely related pharmacologically to the amphetamines. It both stimulates the release of norepinephrine from storage sites in the nerve terminals and also directly stimulates the receptors for norepinephrine. Its brain stimulant actions are less marked than those of the amphetamines, but its effects on the heart, blood vessels, and lungs are greater.

The actions of ephedrine in horses were studied in Japan by Fujii and his coworkers. These investigators dosed three Thoroughbred horses with 100, 300, and 500 mg of ephedrine subcutaneously and tested them about one hour after injection. They reported performance-stimulating effects of ephedrine, which were apparently less marked and easier to control than those observed after caffeine. They also reported that ephedrine induced very frequent irregularities in the heart rate. In their hands, ephedrine also brought about an increase in the respiratory rate during the period of standing before exercise and caused restlessness in some of the horses after exercise. The restlessness was not so serious, however, as to make the horses unmanageable. The authors concluded that ephedrine was inferior to caffeine in improving performance and that its use was likely to be associated with more risk to the horse than with caffeine.

Studies in man have shown that the heart and blood vessel effects of ephedrine are smaller than those of epinephrine but that they persist up to ten times longer. In man, the strength of the heartbeat is increased by ephedrine, and blood pressure is usually raised. Relaxation of the bronchial muscles and airways also occurs with ephedrine, which improves breathing in "windy" horses, but the effect is less marked than with epinephrine. Similarly, brain stimulation after ephedrine in man is less marked than after epinephrine.

In an unpublished English study by Chapman and Marcroft, 87 percent of the C^{14} in a dose of $[C^{14}]$ ephedrine was excreted in the urine within twenty-four hours. These workers identified norephedrine, 4-hydroxynorephedrine, and 4-hydroxyephedrine, both free and conjugated, which comprised about 18 percent of the radioactivity. These metabolic patterns and "clearance" rates suggest a clearance time for ephedrine of not greater than forty-four hours in the horse.

Methylphenidate

Methylphenidate (Ritalin®) was first introduced into human medicine in 1959, some fifteen years after its synthesis and five years after it had been demonstrated to be a central nervous system stimulant. Since then it has been the drug of choice in the treatment of minimal brain dysfunction (MBD) in children, or "hyperkinetic children." Its pharmacological effects are essentially the same as those of amphetamine, but it is considered to have more prominent effects on mental than on motor activity. It is available in tablet or injectable form, and it shares the same abuse potential in humans as the amphetamines. Methylphenidate is well absorbed after oral administration and is almost completely metabolized, less than 1 percent of the parent drug being eliminated unchanged in the urine.

Studying the disposition of methylphenidate in the horse, we found a plasma half-life for this drug in the horse of about 3.4 hours, which half-life corresponded well with the rate of urinary excretion of the drug. After subcutaneous (SC) or intramuscular (IM) injection of the drug, plasma levels peaked at about one hour postdosing (Fig. 11-3) and were no longer detectable after six hours. Urinary levels of the drug peaked between one and three hours postdosing and remained detectable for up to thirteen hours postdosing, suggesting that at least twenty-four hours should be allowed after a dose of methylphenidate for the drug to "clear" the urine. These observations on the pharmacokinetics of methylphenidate in horses are in good agreement with some experiments previously published by Ray and his colleagues at the Ohio State University.

In our studies with methylphenidate, no clear-cut and easily quantifiable signs of brain stimulation were seen. Gabriel and his coworkers, however, have re-

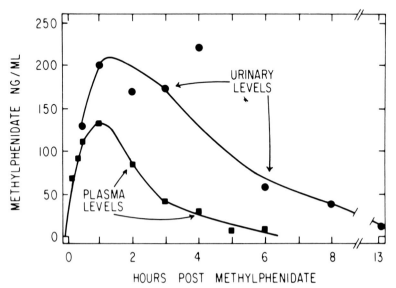

Figure 11-3. Plasma and urinary levels after intramuscular administration of methylphenidate in the horse. The solid squares (■—■) show plasma levels of methylphenidate, and the solid circles (●—●) show its urinary levels after IM administration of 0.35 mg/kg of methylphenidate to four Thoroughbred horses. Reproduced with permission from Shults et al., *Am J Vet Res*, 42:1981.

ported clinical signs after administration of up to 600 mg of methylphenidate intramuscularly to horses. In these studies, doses of methylphenidate as small as 50 mg doubled the respiratory rate of horses within fifteen minutes after dosing. When the dose was increased to 400 mg, the respiratory rate peaked at about sixty movements per minute, and if the dose was further increased the respiratory rate became too rapid to count. No effect on heart rate was seen until 400 mg was administered, but the heart rate was more than doubled after 600 mg. Along with the increase in heart rate, signs of brain stimulation were seen, the horses becoming quite restless. Gabriel considered the behavior of his horses to be so affected by large doses of methylphenidate that it would be relatively easy to pick out methylphenidate-medicated horses. He did not, however, make clear how he would distinguish a methylphenidate-stimulated horse from a spontaneously nervous horse. This ability of methylphenidate to make a horse "excitable" in a way difficult to distinguish from spontaneous excitement has apparently led to the more than occasional use of this drug in show horses, where such behavior is apparently sometimes considered desirable.

While it may be difficult to detect clinical signs of methylphenidate treatment simply by inspecting a horse, methylphenidate turned out to be a spectacularly effective drug in experiments with the responding or "feeder" apparatus described in Chapter 10. In these experiments, horses were dosed with methylphenidate IV at the indicated doses and introduced into the "feeder" apparatus twenty minutes later. Since the experiments ran for thirty minutes, the horses were thus tested over a period estimated to produce peak drug effects. As shown in Fig. 11-4 and as will be seen later with other stimulants, each horse showed a distinctly individual response to this drug. BALLARD, a horse whom in our experience is responsive to most drugs, was most sensitive to methylphenidate, showing maximal stimulation in responding rate at doses of between 0.2 and 0.4 mg/kg. MULIE, however, showed only a very small maximal response to methylphenidate compared with any of the other horses tested, and further increasing the dose of methylphenidate reduced her responding rate. NOELLE and DOC responded well to methylphenidate and showed maximal stimulation in responding at about 1 mg/kg, although again much higher doses reduced their responding rates.

These data highlight a number of important points about stimulant drugs in horses. First, they show that for at least some classes of stimulant drugs, each horse must be considered an individual. In the same way as some humans require two cups of coffee to function and others become agitated and disorganized after the same amount of coffee, the horses of Figure 11-4 responded differently to methylphenidate. While if one had to pick one "stimulant" dose for all four horses, 0.4 mg/kg would be the dose to pick, such a dosage schedule would clearly miss the maximal effects of methylphenidate in NOELLE and DOC, who yielded their best responses after a 1 mg/kg dose. Thus, in selecting the dose of a stimulant drug such as methylphenidate with which to perform a performance trial, both the dose and the time postdosing would have to be optimized for each individual horse, and ideally some poor responders such as MULIE should be identified and culled from the experimental group.

The second characteristic of stimulant drugs demonstrated by this data is that

Drugs and the Performance Horse

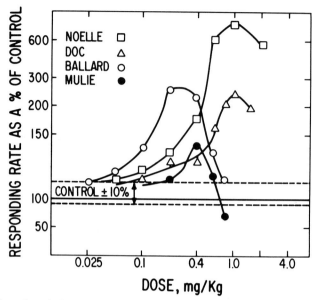

Figure 11-4. Effect of methylphenidate on responding rate in four horses. Four horses were dosed with the indicated amounts of methylphenidate intravenously and introduced to the responding apparatus twenty minutes later. The symbols show the percent change in rate for each thirty-minute session after administration of the indicated dose of methylphenidate to each horse. Each experiment was performed between 10 and 12 AM on consecutive days, and horses were treated with saline and allowed to return to their control responding rates between tests. Reproduced with permission from Shults et al., *Am J Vet Res, 42:*1981.

too large a dose of a stimulant will depress a given activity. This, of course, is the result of the overstimulation of the animal, interfering with its making the appropriate responses required by the stimulation. As shown in Figure 11-4, the dose at which this shift from stimulation to inhibition occurs is again an individual characteristic of the horse. This effect will be seen with other central stimulant drugs, and for some drugs such as cocaine there is a very wide range between horses in the doses at which this effect occurs.

Finally, these data with methylphenidate are consistent with the clinical characteristics of methylphenidate in humans. Methylphenidate seems to improve the ability of human children to concentrate and perform more effectively desired behaviors. The very large stimulation of responding rate observed after methylphenidate, much larger than any observed to date with other drugs in the horse, is consistent with the idea that methylphenidate both stimulates animals and aids their concentration. This is because an effect of methylphenidate on concentration could allow the horse to continue to increase its responding rate at dose levels that with other drugs would lead to aberrant and nonproductive behavior. Thus, the unusually high stimulation rates produced by methylphenidate are likely a reflection of the drug's ability to both stimulate a performance and concentrate the animal's attention on that performance.

The only reports on effects of methylphenidate on athletic performance in horses are those of Sanford, who reported that methylphenidate increased speed in doses that had little effect on coordination (see Tables 11-I and 11-II). It appears that methylphenidate produced this effect in short gallop screening tests, but no details as to magnitude of dose or effect were given. While suggestive of an effect on performance, a more detailed report on these experiments would be useful.

The clinical indications for methylphenidate in the horse are likely to be similar to those for amphetamine, with the difference being that methylphenidate appears to allow the animal to concentrate more on a desired behavior and is therefore probably a superior drug. One interesting reported use for methylphenidate in central Kentucky* concerns a stallion that had difficulty in serving and was restored to normal performance by 100 mg of injectable methylphenidate IV one hour before his services were required, thus improving a specific performance desired both by the owners and presumably also by the horse himself.

Cocaine

Cocaine is a plant alkaloid obtained from the leaves of *Erythroxylon coca* and related species. These plants are indigenous to Peru and Bolivia, where their

---

* G. Priest, D.V.M., The Woodford Veterinary Clinic, Versailles, KY; personal communication.

The difference between the behavioral response to cocaine and apomorphine in the horse may be *loosely* described as the difference between a fast run (apomorphine) and horses attempting to foxtrot.

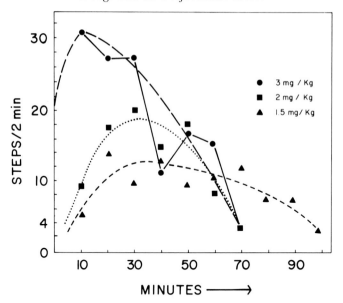

Figure 11-5. Locomotor response to cocaine in the horse. The symbols show the locomotor response to 1.5 (▲), 2.0 (■), and 3.0 (●) mg/kg of cocaine IV. Locomotor activity was measured as described by the step-counting method, and spontaneous activity after a saline injection was about 4 steps/2 minutes. Reproduced with permission from Tobin et al., *J Equine Med Surg*, 3:102, 1979.

leaves have been used for centuries for their stimulant effects. As well as its central stimulant actions, cocaine has local anesthetic effects and was the first local anesthetic to be introduced into medicine. Because of its toxicity and addicting properties, however, cocaine was soon supplanted as a local anesthetic by the more specific and less toxic procaine. Later, after a period during which cocaine was a common additive in wines and soft drinks, it was quite incorrectly declared a narcotic* drug, which remains its current legal classification.

Cocaine produces its brain-stimulating effects by specifically blocking the enzyme that pumps norepinephrine out of the "synaptic cleft" and back into the presynaptic nerve termina. The net result of this effect is to increase the amount of norepinephrine at the norepinephrine receptors, which results in an increased level of brain stimulation. In man, this excitation first appears as a stimulation of the higher centers, and the individual becomes garrulous, restless, and excited. In laboratory animals, this effect appears as an increase in spontaneous movement, and increased movement is also seen in the horse. The effect on locomotor activity in the horse is not, however, as marked or as clear-cut as that due to narcotic analgesics or apomorphine (see Chapters 12 and 13). Thus, although the spontaneous activity of horses can be raised far above that of baseline activity, quite large amounts of cocaine are required to produce these effects and the responses are far from being clear-cut and dose related. Figure 11-5 shows some spontaneous locomotor (trotting) activity obtained after administration of the indicated doses of cocaine IV. This pattern of responses is erratic and clearly less

---

* Narcotic = Sleep inducing and pain relieving

reproducible than the responses to fentanyl presented in Chapter 12. In addition, the movement response after cocaine is characteristically different from that produced after narcotics or apomorphine in that it appears primarily as a restlessness rather than as coordinated, purposeful running activity. This qualitative difference has been loosely described in our laboratory as the difference between a fast trot (apomorphine or fentanyl) and a horse attempting to dance the foxtrot in a straw-covered stable (cocaine).

An easily measured physiological response that responds readily and reproducibly to cocaine is the respiratory rate. As shown in Figure 11-6, the respiratory rate of untreated horses is about twelve respirations per minute, and these rates are rapidly increased by IV injection of cocaine. The data also show that the onset of action of cocaine is very rapid after its IV injection. The horses' respiratory rates in all cases peaking within fifteen minutes of injection of the drug. The duration of the respiratory response to cocaine, however, was quite variable and appeared to be highly dependent on the dose administered. Thus, after the lowest dose tested (about 60 mg/horse), the respiratory stimulation lasted less than an hour, but increasing the dose increased both the magnitude and the duration of the response (Fig. 11-7). Whether or not these prolonged responses at higher doses are associated with delayed "clearance" of the drug is not clear at this time and awaits further experimentation.

As pointed out earlier with methylphenidate, it is characteristic of the effects of stimulant drugs on animals that their actions are biphasic, producing stimulation at low levels and, if the dose is increased beyond a certain point, inhibition. Figure 11-8 shows that this same effect occurs with cocaine. In this experiment horses were dosed IV with between 2 and 1000 mg of cocaine per horse and ten minutes

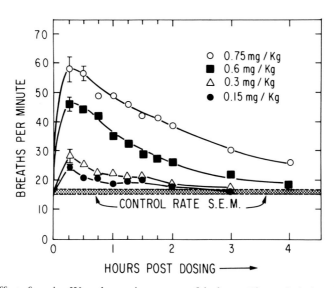

Figure 11-6. Effect of cocaine IV on the respiratory rate of the horse. The symbols show the respiratory rates of four horses after IV administration of the indicated doses of cocaine. Note the rapid onset of drug action, with peak drug effect in each case obtained within fifteen minutes of drug administration. Reproduced with permission from Tobin et al., *J Equine Med Surg, 3*:107, 1979.

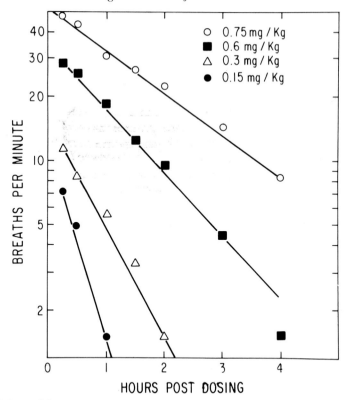

Figure 11-7. Rate of decay of cocaine-induced increases in respiratory rate. In this plot, the control respiratory rate was deducted from the respiratory rates of the data of Figure 11-6 and the remaining cocaine-induced increase in respiratory rate plotted against time. On this plot, the rate of decay of the respiratory stimulation is clearly dose related, with the response to the larger doses decaying more slowly than the response to the smaller doses.

later put into the "feeder" apparatus. Among the horses tested, MULIE was most sensitive to cocaine, the very small dose of 4 mg/horse producing maximal stimulation and increasing the dose produced inhibition. BALLARD, on the other hand, required about 300 mg of cocaine to reach his peak response, which is almost 100 times the dose that MULIE required. The other horses tested, DOC and T-3, yielded peak responses after doses of cocaine intermediate between these two levels. The experiment shows the variability in the response of different horses to cocaine, and it shows that overdosing with the drug depressed the responding rate of all horses. The experiment also shows that as far as this type of test is concerned, methylphenidate was by far the most superior stimulant, producing up to a 700 percent increase in responding rate (see Fig. 11-4) compared with only a 170 percent increase after cocaine (Fig. 11-8).

These same effects of individual variation in sensitivity to drugs and the detrimental effects of too large doses are well known to human athletes. Harold Connolly, the Olympic hammer champion, reports trying amphetamines at one point in his career and then abandoning them when he found that they interfered with his coordination. There is no reason to suppose that this classic type of biphasic response to cocaine does not occur with other central stimulant drugs in the horse and does not also occur "on the track." This biphasic response to simulant drugs and the variabilty between horses in the dose that produces peak stimulation makes the selection of the correct dose of stimulant drugs on a horse-by-horse basis critical for one to have any hope of success in performance work.

In the cardiovascular system, small doses of cocaine may depress the heart rate but higher doses stimulate it. Blood pressure tends to rise due to the increased heart rate and vasoconstriction. There is no evidence that cocaine increases the intrinsic strength of muscular contraction, and the relief of fatigue from cocaine which has been seen so clearly in man seems to result from brain stimulation, which masks the sensation of fatigue.

Cocaine is markedly fever inducing and appears to have a direct action on the heat-regulating centers, for the onset of "cocaine fever" in man is associated with a "chill," which indicates that the body is adjusting its temperature to a higher level. The increased muscular activity due to cocaine and vasoconstriction also tends to increase body temperature. Cocaine fever is usually a striking feature of cocaine poisoning; it can easily be elicited in animals, and heatstroke would seem to be a particularly likely problem in horses running "on cocaine" in warm climates.

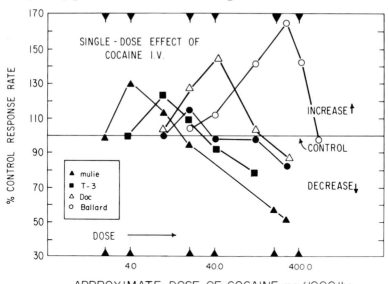

Figure 11-8. Stimulant effects of IV cocaine on operant behavior of horses. The 100% line across the center of the figure represents the mean control responding rate of each horse. Each symbol represents the responding rate of the individual horses after the indicated doses of cocaine ten minutes before the horses were put in the apparatus. The solid triangles (▲) show that MULIE was maximally stimulated by a cocaine dose of 4 mg/1000 lb., and that increasing the dose beyond that level depressed her responding rate. On the other hand, BALLARD (○) required about 300 mg for maximal stimulation, and the doses for maximal stimulation of T-3 (■) and DOC (△) were intermediate. The data show that there is almost a 100-fold range in the doses required for an optimal stimulatory effect of cocaine between these four horses. The data also show that cocaine was a much less effective stimulant than methylphenidate (see Fig. 11-4), producing a maximal responding rate of only 170% (cocaine), as compared with up to 700% (methylphenidate). Reproduced with permission from Shults et al., *Am J Vet Res*, 42:1981.

Cocaine is well absorbed from all sites of application, including mucous membranes. Cocaine is a local anesthetic in concentrations as low as 0.02%, which blocks sensory nerve endings; higher concentrations block nerve impulse conduction in nerve trunks or produce anesthesia on application to mucous membranes or the eye. Cocaine is recommended only for topical anesthesia in veterinary medicine and should not be injected into tissues. Doses as low as 600 mg have been reported to cause toxic effects in the horse. Although cocaine has been reported to be hydrolyzed in the gastrointestinal tract and thus to be inactive by the oral route, at least 2,000 years of experience of leaf-chewing Indians and some recent experimental work has shown that good blood levels of cocaine are attained after oral administration.

After intravenous injection in the horse, cocaine is eliminated with an apparent plasma half-life of about forty-five minutes (Fig. 11-9). The period for which cocaine or its metabolites appear in urine is not clear, but preliminary work from our laboratory suggests that, under some circumstances at least, very little appears in urine as unchanged cocaine. Blake and his coworkers have reported an analytical method for cocaine in which a fragment of the drug is split out and derivatized for electron capture detection. The yields in this reaction procedure are unknown, and it should always be kept in mind that this method only identifies a fragment of the cocaine molecule, which fragment may possibly occur in plant alkaloids other than cocaine.

Caffeine

Mankind has known about caffeine, like most plant drugs, since earliest times, and use of caffeine in tea, coffee, and soft drinks is widespread throughout the

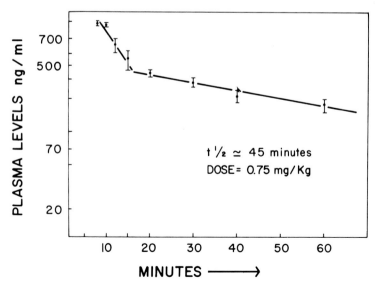

Figure 11-9. Plasma levels of cocaine in the horse after its IV administration. The solid circles (●—●) show plasma levels of cocaine after IV administration of 0.75 mg/kg cocaine to four horses. Reproduced with permission from Tobin et al. *J Equine Med Surg*, 3:108, 1979.

In Ireland, the tradition of giving greyhounds tea before a race long antedates the advent of analytical chemistry.

world. Caffeine has an unusual position in sports medicine in that its use is permitted in human athletes if it is taken as a beverage but not if it is taken in an abnormal way or in abnormal amounts. Caffeine is also "legal" in greyhound racing in Ireland, where the tradition of dosing greyhounds with tea before racing long predates the advent of analytical chemistry. No such subtle distinctions are made in horse racing, however, and traces of caffeine or any of its metabolites in equine urine can cause plenty of problems if reported in a post-race sample by an analytical chemist.

The precise mechanism of action of caffeine is not clear, but it appears reasonably certain that its site of action is both postsynaptic and intracellular. Caffeine appears to act by potentiating the actions of norepinephrine, most likely via its action on levels of a substance called cyclic AMP. When norepinephrine activates its postsynaptic receptors, its effect is to increase the level in the postsynaptic cell of a second messenger substance, cyclic AMP. Cyclic AMP, is, in turn, broken down by an enzyme called phosphodiesterase. It turns out that caffeine inhibits these phosphodiesterase enzymes. Inhibition by caffeine of these phosphodiesterase enzymes therefore causes increased levels of cyclic AMP in the postsynaptic cell. The effects of a dose of caffeine are thus broadly equivalent to an increase in the amount of norepinephrine at the postsynaptic receptors, which leads to a general brain stimulant effect.

Drugs and the Performance Horse

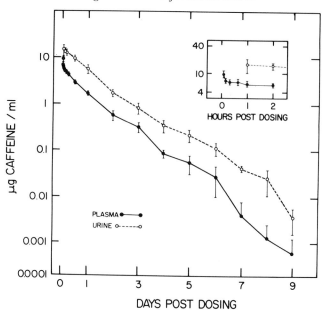

Figure 11-10. "Clearance times" for caffeine after its IV administration to horses. The solid circles (●—●) show plasma levels of caffeine after about 2 gm each (4 mg/kg) was administered IV to four horses. The open circles (○—○) show urinary levels of caffeine in these same horses. Note that the blood and urinary levels of the drug fall in parallel, with a half-life of about twenty-two hours, and that caffeine took nine days to clear the horses in this experiment.

Studying the effects of caffeine on cardiovascular parameters in humans, Robertson and coworkers found that 250 mg of caffeine administered orally increased the respiratory rate and blood pressure. Only small changes in heart rate were seen. Blood levels of the stimulatory neurohormones epinephrine and norepinephrine increased sharply after caffeine and remained elevated for the three hours of the experiment. Urinary volume was also increased in all subjects, with an increase of about 30 percent above control being observed. Since caffeine has a plasma half-life of between four and ten hours in man, these effects can persist for quite some time in the human, accounting for the difficulty that some people have in sleeping after even modest amounts of coffee.

In studies on the effects of caffeine on three Thoroughbred horses, Fujii and coworkers injected horses with 2.5 and 5 gm (between 5 and 10 mg/kg) of caffeine and sodium benzoate. These workers found that caffeine enhanced the running performance of all horses, especially at the canter, and that the amount of stimulation observed made it difficult to monitor motor activity on the small track available. In one horse, cardiac arrythmias were seen after caffeine, and in all horses, caffeine increased the heart rate after exercise and delayed return of the heart rate to normal. The authors interpreted these results to indicate that caffeine markedly enhanced the running performance of horses but tended to increase the frequency of cardiac arrhythmias. In agreement with Fujii's work on performance, Sanford found that caffeine at 2, 4, and 9 mg/kg increased speed significantly ($P < 0.05$) in gallop tests.

The metabolism and elimination of caffeine in the horse has been studied most extensively in England, where the accidental inclusion of cacao husk in horse rations has given rise to a number of inadvertent and embarrassing drug positives. Among the reasons that caffeine can be a forensic problem are its ease of detection, its long plasma half-life, and its tendency to metabolize into other easily detectable drugs such as theobromine. Working in my laboratory, Eugénie Greene has shown that the plasma half-life of caffeine in the horse is about seventeen hours, and that the drug is detectable in plasma or urine for up to nine days after an IV dose (Fig. 11-10). As a "neutral" drug, or one that does not carry any predominant charge, the distribution of caffeine into horse urine is little affected by urinary pH changes, which accounts for the fact that its concentrations in urine closely parallel its concentrations in plasma. Because caffeine or its metabolites can be detected for such a long period in urine after the animal is exposed to caffeine, the chances of finding a caffeine positive are relatively greater than for other more rapidly excreted drugs.

The most extensive studies on the metabolism of caffeine in horses have been carried out in England by Moss and his coworkers at the Racecourse Security Services' Laboratory. Working with radioactive caffeine, these investigators reported a plasma half-life of caffeine of greater than twelve hours, with the excretion of detectable radioactivity continuing for up to eight days, in good agreement with the figures reported above. Various methyluric acid derivatives accounted for about 30 percent of the caffeine administered, while caffeine itself accounted for 4 percent or less of the dose. The remaining 15 percent of the dose accounted for was found as paraxanthine, and also theophylline and theobromine, both of which are considered drugs in their own right. No evidence for conjugation of caffeine either as glucuronides or arylsulfates was found, but traces of theobromine sufficient to "call a positive on" have been found in horse urine for up to ten days after a dose of caffeine.

Theobromine

As well as being a metabolite of caffeine, theobromine is a drug in its own right, having a small diuretic action. Theobromine, along with salicylate, is one of the major constituents of Doan's Pills®. Doan's Pills have been a favorite pre-race medication of some trainers, presumably because of their salicylate (aspirin) content. When a chemist picks up a theobromine "positive" in the absence of caffeine, the chances are that it was given as theobromine. Since theobromine is virtually devoid of CNS or cardiovascular actions, its presence in urine is not likely to be a factor in influencing the outcome of a race.

SELECTED REFERENCES

Baggot, J. D. and Davis, L. E.: A comparative study of the pharmacokinetic of amphetamine. *Res Vet Sci, 14:*207-215, 1973.

Baggot, J. D., Davis, L. E., Murdick, P. W., Ray, R. S., and Noonan, J. S.: Certain aspects of amphetamine elimination in the horse. *Am J Vet Res, 33:*1161-1164, 1972.

Blake, J. W., Ray, R. S., Noonan, J. S., and Murdick, P. W.: Rapid, sensitive gas-liquid chromatographic screening procedure for cocaine. *Anal Chem, 46:*288-289, 1974.

Chapman, D. I. and Marcroft, J.: Studies on the metabolism of symphathomimetic amines: the metabolism of (±)-[^{14}C]amphetamine in the horse. *Xenobiotica, 3:*49-61, 1973.

Fujii, Senji, Inada, Shichiro, Yoshida, Shigeru, Kusanagi, Chiyoko, Mima, Kyosuke, and Natsuno, Yoshihiro: Pharmacological studies on doping drugs for racehorses. III. Ephedrine. *Jpn Vet Sci, 36:*9-18, 1974.

Gabriel, K. L., Henderson, B., and Smith, W. F.: Studies on the physiologic effects of methylphenidate in Thoroughbred horses. *Am J Vet Res, 142:*875-877, 1963.

Karawya, M. S., El-Keiy, M. A., Wahba, S. K., and Kosman, A. R.: A note of a simple estimation of amphetamine, methylamphetamine and ephedrine in horse urine. *J Pharm Pharmacol, 20:*650-652, 1968.

Moss, M. S.: The metabolism and urinary and salivary excretion of drugs in the horse and their relevance to detection of dope. In *Drug Metabolism — From Microbe to Man.* D. V. Parke and R. L. Smith, Eds. London, Taylor & Francis, Lts., 1976.

Moss, M. S., Jackson, R. J., Woodhead, S., Houghton, E., and Horner, M. W.: The metabolism and excretion of caffeine in the horse. In *Proc Third International Symposium on Equine Medication Control,* Tobin, T., Blake, J. W., and Woods, W. E., Eds. Dept. of Veterinary Science, University of Kentucky, 1979, pp. 347-351.

Oettinger, L. and Majovski, L. V.: Methylphenidate: A review. *South Med J, 69:*161-164, 1976.

Ray, R. S., Noonan, J. S., Murdick, P. W., and Tharp, V.: Detection of methylphenidate and methamphetamine in equine body fluids by gas chromatographic analysis of an electron capturing derivative. *Am J Vet Res, 33:*27-31, 1972.

Robertson, D., Fromich, J. C., Carr, R. K., Watson, J. T., Hollifield, J. W., Shand, G. G., and Oates, J. A.: Effects of caffeine on plasma renin activity, catecholamines and blood pressure. *N Engl J Med, 298:*181-186, 1978.

Sanford, J.: Drugs and their effects on performance in the horse. *HBLB Conference of Research Workers,* 40-41, April, 1973.

Sanford, J.: Medication affecting the performance of racehorses and its control. *Proc 19th World Vet Cong,* 382-385, 1971.

Smetzer, D. L., Senta, T., and Hensel, J. D.: Cardiovascular effects of amphetamine in the horse. *Can J Comp Med, 36:*185-194, 1972.

Stewart, G. A.: Drugs, performance and responses to exercise in the racehorse. 2. Observations on amphetamine, promazine and thiamine. *Aust Vet J, 48:*544-547, 1972.

Tobin, T., Combie, J., and Dougherty, J.: The pharmacology of narcotic analgesics in the horse. III. Characteristics of the locomotor effects of fentanyl and apomorphine. *J Equine Med Surg, 3:*284-288, 1979.

Shults, T., Kownacki, A. A., Woods, W. E., Valentine, R., Dougherty, J., and Tobin, T.: Pharmacokinetics and behavioral effects of methylphenidate in Thoroughbred horses. *Am J Vet Res,* submitted for publication, 1979.

Weiss, B. and Laties, V. G.: Enhancement of human performance by caffeine and the amphetamines. *Pharmacol Rev, 14:*1-36, 1962.

Chapter 12

HORSES RUNNING HAPPY: FENTANYL, MORPHINE, AND THE OTHER NARCOTIC ANALGESICS

THE OPIATE NARCOTIC analgesic drugs have been known since the dawn of history as the most effective medication available for the relief of pain. In addition, in man, they produce sedation (narcosis) and depressed breathing. In the horse they also depress pain and breathing, but instead of sedating a horse they stimulate him to move at a pace somewhere between a brisk trot and a gallop. This stimulant effect in horses is common to all the narcotic analgesics, including fentanyl.* This stimulant effect is easily measured, since it is a clear-cut trotting or running activity. The message in this chapter is that narcotic analgesics make horses run, and, insofar as one can make such judgements about horses, they appear to make them run happy.

The opiate or narcotic analgesic drugs are chemically and pharmacologically related to morphine, the principal narcotic found in the opium poppy. Since morphine was identified as the active principle of opium, many synthetic drugs with morphinelike activity have been developed. In our work on these drugs we have studied the effects of the natural opiate, morphine, the synthetic opiates fentanyl, pentazocine, and butorphanol, and a number of other narcotics. As mentioned above, all of these drugs turned out to be potent locomotor (trotting) stimulants in the horse.

As pointed out in Chapter 10, it is very easy to demonstrate the stimulant actions of narcotic analgesics in the horse. All one has to do is to take a horse, put a white bandage on his left foreleg and put him in a quiet stall for about twenty-four hours. The white bandage is just to help you keep your eye on the left foreleg. As the horse adjusts to the stall, his spontaneous movement (motor activity) will settle down at about four steps per two minutes with his left foreleg. If you log the number of steps the horse takes, and if it is an average horse in a quiet stall, this baseline activity will hold steady at this value over a number of hours (Fig. 12-1).

To demonstrate the trotting effect of the narcotic analgesics, one takes an appropriate dose of a narcotic drug and injects it rapidly intravenously. We find that between 4 and 8 mg of fentanyl (Sublimaze®) produces a very good effect in a 1,000 lb. horse (Fig. 12-1). At the 8 mg dose, which is about as high as one wants to go with this drug, the horse will begin to trot in his stall within two minutes. The effect peaks at about 100 steps/2 minutes between four and six minutes after the syringe has been withdrawn from the vein and then begins to decline. Simply plotting the number of steps for every two minutes against time yields a very smooth curve of this trotting (locomotor) response to fentanyl. After about one

---

* Fentanyl (Sublimaze®) — a potent synthetic relative of opium

While narcotic analgesics make man drowsy and want to sleep, the right dose makes horses want to run.

hour the horse is back down to control levels, and we have found that if you repeat the dose you will get almost exactly the same response again.

The speed of the trotting response obtained is directly related to the dose of fentanyl you inject into the horse. If you increase the dose from 1 to 2 to 4 to 8 mg the rate at which the horse trots increases from just about nothing in a smooth "dose-response" fashion to give a peak at about 100 steps/2 minutes at the 8 mg dose. If you increase the dose to 16 mg, the trotting does not increase, but instead the animal becomes incoordinated, staggers, and may fall. Because of this, in making a horse trot with a narcotic analgesic, it is difficult to push him beyond about 100 steps/2 minutes. We will see later, however, that horses stimulated with apomorphine will run scared, will run a lot faster than horses on narcotics, and will not become incoordinated.

If carried out in a quiet box stall with well-trained personnel and horses used to their surroundings, this trotting response to fentanyl (Sublimaze®) can only be described as remarkably reproducible. The same horse will respond in just about the same way to a given dose of fentanyl every time one tests him. In other experiments we dosed horses every ninety minutes with fentanyl four times in succession, and their trotting response peaked at between 100 and 103 steps per two-minute period every time. This is an exceptionally reproducible response to a drug, and there appear to be at least two good reasons why this is the case.

The first reason is that the action of fentanyl in the horse's brain is most likely ended by fentanyl being carried away in the blood. When fentanyl is given by rapid intravenous injection (the way it is supposed to be given in the human), a highly concentrated "slug" of fentanyl hits the brain initially and diffuses into the brain receptors, where the drug acts (Fig. 12-2). When it hits these receptors, the horse starts to trot. The trotting peaks at about five minutes after dosing, which almost certainly corresponds with peak fentanyl levels in the brain. Then the fentanyl begins to diffuse out of the brain, is carried away in the blood, and one gets the rapid decline in trotting activity. Since the movement of fentanyl into and out of the brain is determined primarily by the blood flow carrying the fentanyl into the brain and then carrying it away, the effect is very similar from horse to horse and from time to time.

If the above mechanism of action is correct, one might expect to get a poor response to fentanyl from subcutaneous or intramuscular injections, which will not give high initial blood levels of the drug. Our experience has been consistent with this, in that trotting responses after subcutaneous and intramuscular injections of fentanyl have been much smaller and more erratic than those after intravenous administration of this drug. What is surprising, however, is that IM is the route by which fentanyl was reportedly given "on the track" and at only 0.25

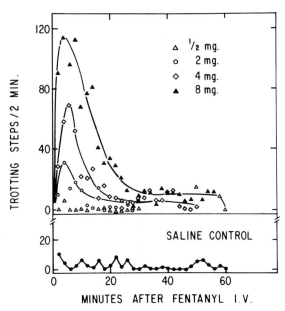

Figure 12-1. Horses trot faster after increased doses of fentanyl. The lower panel shows the normal activity of a horse at rest in his stall, about four steps in two minutes. The top panel shows the trotting response produced in horses by injection of about ½, 2, 4, and 8 mg of fentanyl/1000 lb. by rapid IV injection. Note the short, sharp time course of the fentanyl stimulation of trotting activity. Reproduced with permission from Tobin et al., *J Equine Med Surg, 3*:286, 1979.

If the dose of a narcotic is increased beyond the "trotting" dose, the horse becomes incoordinated and will fall.

mg doses. How fentanyl given by this route at these doses could produce any effect is not clear, as the only conclusion that can be drawn from our studies is that the drug is ineffective by this route and at these doses.

It is likely that other factors also contribute to the reproducibility of the fentanyl-induced trotting response. The most important of these is probably the very nature of the narcotic-induced state, which seems to make the animal much less responsive to external distractions. A horse on a high dose of a narcotic has a glazed appearance and seems largely unaware of his environment. On high doses of morphine they avoid the walls of their boxes poorly and tend to bump into them. The horses appear to be responding to internal stimuli and are obviously interacting poorly with their environment. This is a big advantage in behavioral work, as it means that the horses are not responding to external variables that the experimenters may have difficulty in controlling, such as farm tractors running past the stalls in which we do our experiments.

Because fentanyl rapidly enters and leaves its site of action in the brain, plasma levels of the drug correspond poorly with the intensity of the trotting response. However, plasma levels of fentanyl are detectable by RIA for at least twelve hours after an intravenous dose of 8 mg of fentanyl, and for four hours after a dose of 0.5 mg (Fig. 12-3). Urinary levels of the drug, on the other hand, are detectable for up to four days after a dose of fentanyl (Fig. 12-4). While the nature of the material in urine that reacts with the fentanyl antibody in radioimmunoassay has not been fully identified, a material identified as despropionylfentanyl has been suggested as a metabolite of fentanyl found in horse urine, and fentanyl "positives" have been called on the basis of this metabolite. Despite the fact that for a long period fentanyl was a very difficult drug to detect in horse urine, this despropionylfentanyl test now appears well established and also not unduly difficult to perform.

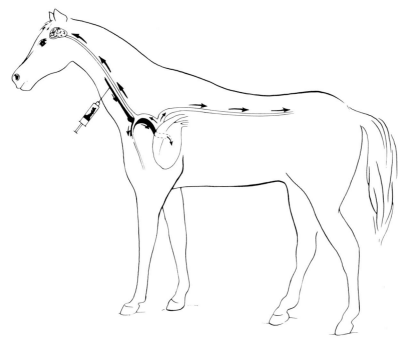

Figure 12-2. Bolus effect of rapid IV injection of a drug. When a drug is given into the jugular vein by rapid IV injection, it first travels along the jugular vein to the heart. It is then pumped by the heart through the lungs (not shown), back to the heart and out into the general circulation. If the injection is administered rapidly, quite high concentrations reach the brain within thirty to sixty seconds of the injection. If the drug is very fat soluble, it enters the brain rapidly, and behavioral effects may be seen within minutes. These effects, however, do not last very long, because drug levels in the brain and blood drop rapidly as the drug distributes to the body. This pattern of a short, sharp action of a drug after its IV injection is called a bolus effect, and fentanyl appears to be a typical drug of this type.

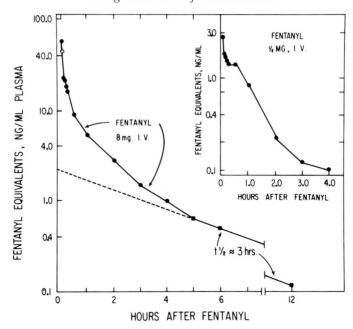

Figure 12-3. Blood levels of fentanyl after its IV injection.

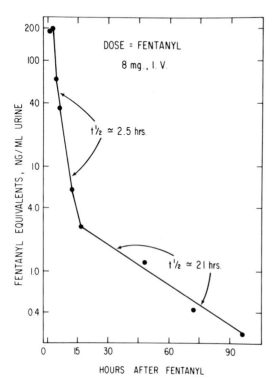

Figure 12-4. Fentanyl takes four days to "clear" urine. The circles (●—●) show urinary levels of fentanyl or fentanyl metabolites after administration of about 8 mg of fentanyl intravenously to horses. Urine can, therefore, take up to four days to clear after a dose of fentanyl.

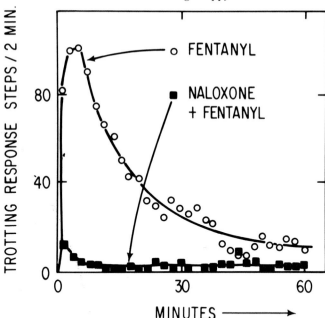

Figure 12-5. Blockade of the trotting response to fentanyl by naloxone. The open circles (o—o) show the trotting response of horses to 8 mg of fentanyl, while the solid squares (■—■) show the lack of response to fentanyl in horses pretreated with about 7 mg of naloxone.

The trotting response to fentanyl is clearly due to occupation of the same type of receptors in the brain at which narcotic drugs produce their analgesic effects. We know this because we have highly specific blocking drugs for the narcotic analgesics, whose only known action in the brain is to block for narcotic drugs. If a horse is pretreated with a very small amount of naloxone, one of the specific blockers referred to in Chapter 4, and then given fentanyl, no trotting response is seen (Fig. 12-5). This specific blockade is very convincing evidence to a pharmacologist that fentanyl produces its trotting response via receptors that are not distinguishable from narcotic analgesic receptors. Further evidence in support of this idea is presented by other observations showing that all the narcotic analgesics produce good motor stimulation in the horse.

As a narcotic analgesic, fentanyl is also likely to have analgesic actions in the horse, and a number of investigators have reportedly studied this problem using a colic model in the horse. In this model, a balloon is introduced into a horse's caecum and inflated. This produces an immediate colic in the horse, which can be relieved by drugs. In another model these workers fractured a bone in the knee of horses (a slab fracture) and studied the effects of fentanyl on the resulting lameness. However, the dose that these workers used was apparently the 0.5 mg/horse dose reportedly used on the track. Little analgesic response to fentanyl was seen in either of these models at the doses used, in good agreement with the work reported here.

Fentanyl, of course, was at one time rumored to be the hot "stimulant" drug used in American racing, a miracle drug, when doses of 0.25 mg of the drug were given intramuscularly anytime up to one hour before the race. To my knowledge, there was no clear-cut feeling among the racing fraternity as to what these doses were supposed to do to a horse or his performance in a race. For example, both the California Horse Racing Board and the American Horse Shows Association have listed fentanyl as a depressant. Three things, however, appear clear from the work performed on fentanyl in our laboratory. First, fentanyl is indisputably a stimulant drug in performance horses, despite anything that certain rule books may say. Second, a 0.25 mg dose of fentanyl is far too small to produce any stimulant effect, and likely also too small to produce an analgesic effect, in agreement with the work at other universities referred to above. Third, the intramuscular route of administration is wrong, as fentanyl must be given by rapid intravenous injection for good effect. These thoughts and observations on the actions of fentanyl are in good agreement with the dose used in humans, where 0.1 to 0.2 mg administered intravenously is a normal dose. Multiply this by ten for the body weight of a horse and you get a 2 mg dose, which fits right into the stimulant dose range for fentanyl in the horse. The result of all this is that fentanyl was almost certainly being used ineffectively in performance horses, if it was being used at the doses and by the routes that backstretch druggists apparently recommended.

On the other hand, since fentanyl produces both a running response and analgesia in a horse, it has the potential, if used in the correct doses and by the right route, to be a very useful medication in sore horses, helping to "move them up" in two distinct but complementary ways. In using fentanyl as a stimulant medication in horses, horsemen are following a long tradition of opiate use to stimulate horses. The principal advantage with fentanyl is the very small amount of drug (3 mg or less) likely to be useful, which made detection difficult. Further, if used properly, the action of fentanyl is brief, unlike the actions of some of the other narcotics, which can last for hours.

The only study on the performance effects of fentanyl of which I am aware is that reported by Professor Gabel and his coworkers at the Ohio State University.* In a pilot study on the performance effects of fentanyl on Standardbred trotters, these workers saw no effects of a 3 mg dose of fentanyl intravenously on performance in a small number of Standardbred horses.

The next drug that we tested in the step-counting model was morphine. The trotting response to morphine turned out to be particularly prolonged, taking up to three hours to peak after an intravenous injection and then remaining effective for up to fourteen hours. Once the response got to about 80 to 100 steps/2 minutes, the horses became dreamy and less well coordinated. They tended to brush walls and just trotted in a dazed fashion hour after hour. Reducing the dose reduced the top speed and the duration of the trotting, so again the rate at which they trotted was clearly dose related (Fig. 12-6). If we plotted the peak response versus dose of morphine on a mg/kg basis, we got a curve parallel with the fentanyl curve, but requiring about eighty times more drug to produce the same effect. This is the exact ratio between the potencies of fentanyl and morphine as analgesics in man (Fig. 12-7).

---

* A. A. Gabel, personal communication

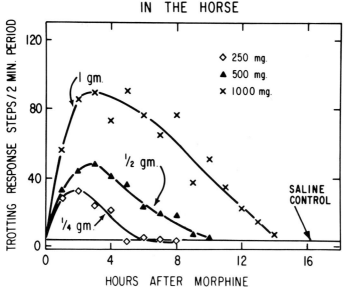

EFFECT OF MORPHINE ON TROTTING
IN THE HORSE

Figure 12-6. Morphine can make a horse trot for more than half a day. The symbols and lines show the trotting response in horses following the indicated doses of morphine per horse IV. After the high dose, horses will trot for up to twelve hours on morphine. Reproduced with permission from Combie et al., *J Equine Med Surg*, 3:379, 1979.

We also tested a number of other narcotic drugs occasionally used in perform-ance horses, such as Dilaudid®, methadone, anileridine, and pethidine. All pro-duced the same characteristic trotting response, and all the dose-response curves were parallel to the morphine and fentanyl curves (Fig. 12-7). High doses of some of these drugs were not tested because only relatively small amounts of these drugs were available to us at the time that these experiments were being done. Neverthe-less, the same clear pattern of trotting activity was seen throughout all the experi-ments, with fentanyl being the most potent of the drugs commonly available and producing a brief response, while morphine was one of the least potent but produced the most prolonged response. An experimental drug was also made available to us, and this drug turned out to be about 100 times more potent than fentanyl, again emphasizing the great specificity and range of potency available among the narcotic drugs.

The data of Figure 12-7 demonstrates many of the dose-response characteris-tics of drugs that we referred to conceptually in Chapter 4. First, all the drugs tested had about the same maximal response, about 100 steps/2 minutes, so they all produced about the same pharmacological effects. The only exceptions to this rule were apomorphine, which we will see later acts by an entirely different mechanism, and pentazocine and meperidine, which are classed as only partially effective drugs (partial agonists). For all the other drugs the action was the same, and only the dose required to produce the effect was different. Thus, it took about

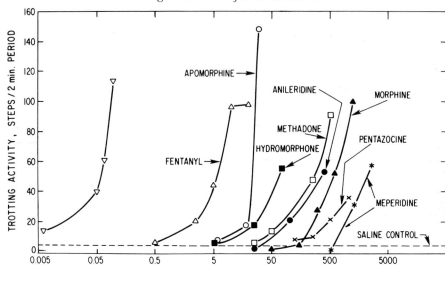

Figure 12-7. Trotting responses in horses after different narcotic drugs. Horses were injected IV with the indicated number of milligrams of each drug and the trotting response counted. The peak trotting response to each drug was then plotted against dose. An unnamed experimental drug was the most potent drug tested, being about 100 times more potent than fentanyl. Fentanyl was the next most potent drug, as 8 mg was enough to produce a peak response. After fentanyl, the next most potent drug was apomorphine, followed by hydromorphone, methadone, anileridine, morphine, pentazocine, and meperidine. This is the same order as their potency as narcotic analgesics in man. Note in particular the poor response to pentazocine (Talwin®) in this test.

0.5 gm of morphine to produce the same effect as 5 mg of fentanyl, or only 50 µg of the nameless experimental drug. This, of course, pinpoints the importance of potency in medication testing, which is that the more potent the drug, the more difficult it is for the chemist to find. On the other hand, when these drugs are being used medically, potency is not a serious concern, as the clinician is usually not concerned whether it takes one or a hundred milligrams of a drug to do the job.

Pentazocine (Talwin®) is an unusual member of the narcotic analgesic family that enjoys widespread use in the horse and deserves special mention. Scientists were long intrigued by the existence of specific opiate-blocking drugs such as naloxone, which could occupy the opiate receptor and block the actions of addicting narcotics. They therefore started to modify these blocking drugs in the hope of making a molecule that would produce analgesia (a desired response) without the addicting potential that all narcotic analgesics possess. Pentazocine is the result of such a research program, and it is probably fair to look on it as a receptor-blocking drug that the chemists have rearranged to give it some analgesic properties.

It appears that along with analgesic properties in the horse go trotting-stimulating properties, and pentazocine has some trotting-stimulating properties, although not a great deal. In our first series of experiments all we could get a horse up to with pentazocine was about 40 steps/2 minutes, less than half the response one gets with morphine, even though these horses were getting the same number of milligrams of drug as our largest dose of morphine. Pentazocine was also clearly different from the other narcotics in that the slope of the dose response curve was much shallower (see Fig. 12-7) and the trotting response was qualitatively different, the animals trembling much and moving poorly.

One explanation for the partial response to pentazocine is that pentazocine might only occupy about one third of the receptors available to other drugs and thus produce only one third of the effect. An alternative explanation might be that pentazocine has occupied all the narcotic receptors in the brain, but in a way that is only partially effective. A simple way of deciding between these alternatives was for us to dose a horse with fentanyl "on top of" or after dosing with pentazocine. We reasoned that if 30 percent or so of the opiate receptors were free to interact with fentanyl, one might expect to see a good response to the extra fentanyl. On the other hand, however, if all the receptors were occupied in an only partially effective way by pentazocine, we should expect no response to fentanyl. The

Scientists have long tried to rearrange the basic narcotic molecule to produce an analgesic drug without addicting properties. Partial agonists, such as pentazocine (Talwin®) and butorphanol (Stadol®), are typical results of these efforts.

experiment presented in Figure 12-8 shows that in the presence of a high dose of pentazocine no extra response due to fentanyl was seen, leading us to conclude that pentazocine had occupied all the narcotic receptors in the horses in an only partially effective fashion.

Butorphanol (Stadol®) is another drug that has recently appeared in racing and seems to be a "partial agonist" in its pharmacology. Like pentazocine, it is a poor trotting stimulant; horses on butorphanol are not trotting at above 20 steps/2 minutes on any dose tested by us to date. These doses, however, blocked the response to fentanyl completely, showing that Stadol, like Talwin, occupied all the narcotic receptors but only very poorly activated them (Fig. 12-9).

This poor trotting response to pentazocine is in good agreement with the findings of Lowe on the analgesic effects of pentazocine in his colic model. Lowe found that even though high doses of pentazocine were used, only poor relief of pain was obtained, in the same way as only a poor trotting response was obtained in our experiments. Pentazocine and butorphanol, chemically closely related to the narcotic antagonists, are at best weak narcotic analgesics (pain relievers) and poor trotting stimulants in the horse. Like fentanyl, however, pentazocine lingers in horse urine, and it can still be found in urine samples for up to five days after an intravenous dose, a fact of which all horsemen should be aware (Fig. 12-10).

During all these experiments a number of other behavioral effects due to the narcotic analgesics were observed. At low doses they tended to stimulate eating behavior, and if the dose used was low this was the only effect seen (Fig. 12-11). If the animals had access to hay, they would stand in front of the hay rack and eat,

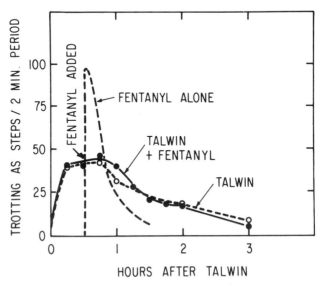

Figure 12-8. Pentazocine (Talwin®) blocks narcotic receptors and thus the trotting response in horses. The open circles (o—o) show trotting after about 1 gm of pentazocine IV. The solid circles (●—●) show that no increase in trotting was observed if 8 mg of fentanyl was injected "on top" of the Talwin®. Talwin® thus acts to occupy all the narcotic receptors in the brain but to only partially activate them, and also to prevent their activation by fentanyl. Reproduced with permission from Combie et al., *Am J Vet Res, 42:*1981.

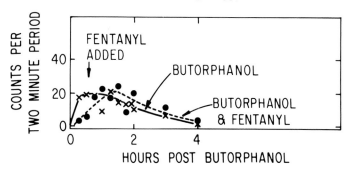

Figure 12-9. Blockade of trotting response to fentanyl by butorphanol (Staphol®). The crosses (×—×) show the locomotor response of the horse to 0.4 mg/kg butorphanol. The solid circles (●—●) represent activity when 0.020 mg/kg fentanyl was added on top of 0.4 mg/kg butorphanol. There was no difference between the response induced by butorphanol alone and that induced by butorphanol plus fentanyl. Thus, butorphanol appears, like pentazocine, to be a partial agonist, which acted to prevent receptor occupancy by fentanyl. Reproduced with permission from Combie et al., *Am J Vet Res,* *42:*1981.

which depressed their trotting activity. If, however, they were put in a bare stall, they always walked, even on very low doses of morphine. Throughout all of these experiments we saw no good evidence for any sedative effects of the narcotic analgesics in horses!

As the dose of narcotic was increased the trotting response increased, but the urge to eat remained (Fig. 12-11). Horses on the high doses of morphine, however, were so busy running that they just swiped a wisp of hay from the hay rack as they trotted past and held it in their mouth for hours. If the dose was further increased, the animals became uncoordinated and tended to bump the walls and injure themselves. The relationships among these narcotic-induced behaviors in the horse are presented schematically in Figure 12-11.

The locomotor stimulation produced by narcotic analgesics in the horse can be blocked by tranquilizers such as acepromazine and promazine, which do not inhibit the analgesic response to these drugs. If the doses of both drugs are carefully chosen, very good analgesia and sedation in a horse can be obtained. A combination of etorphine, a very potent narcotic, and acepromazine has been commercially available in England for some time, where it is used for the immobilization of horses for minor surgery. The combination may be injected intravenously or subcutaneously, and the onset of action takes from thirty seconds to four minutes. At this point, the animal goes down and is ready for surgery. When the surgical interference is over, a narcotic antagonist of the naloxone type is injected intravenously. Within thirty seconds the narcotic effect is reversed and only the tranquilizing action of acepromazine remains. Because of its rapid action and ready reversibility, this combination of drugs can be very useful in handling fractious animals.

The principal side effect seen with this combination of drugs is muscle tremors, presumably associated with the ability of narcotic drugs to produce increased motor activity, and respiratory depression, which appears to be inherent in the action of all narcotic drugs. Both of these effects are rapidly reversed by the

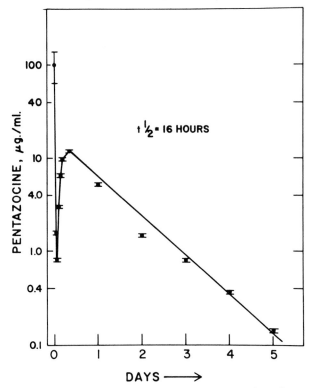

Figure 12-10. Pentazocine (Talwin®) takes up to five days to "clear" equine urine. In this experiment, horses were dosed with ⅓ mg/kg of pentazocine IV, which dose was followed by 1 mg/kg of furosemide IV. The data points show urinary concentrations of the major glucuronide metabolite of pentazocine in this experiment. It was five days before the pentazocine was undetectable in the urine of these horses. Reproduced with permission from Tobin et al., *J Equine Med Surg, 3:*196, 1979.

antagonist, which gives the clinician a good measure of control when using this combination of drugs. Great care, however, should be taken by the clinician not to accidentally inject himself with any of these very powerful narcotic drugs, as accidental self-injection of small quantities of these very potent drugs has caused death among veterinarians in England.

The next question that one might ask is, What is the nature of the receptors in the brain at which these narcotic drugs produce their effects? The nature of the specific receptors in the brains of man and horses for narcotic drugs has long been an enigma, as well as why there should be receptors in the brain for a drug found principally in the opium poppy. Over the last few years, with the advent of radioactive drugs, some very interesting answers to these questions have become available. Using radioactive narcotics and narcotic antagonists like naloxone, both of which are thought to bind to the same receptors in the brain, groups of workers in New York and at Johns Hopkins have directly demonstrated the existence of the specific narcotic receptors whose presence had long been inferred from the remarkable potency of narcotic drugs.

It was soon discovered that all vertebrates (including the horse) possess these narcotic receptors, and they are found in the brain and spinal cord in areas known to be involved in pain perception or in emotional responses to pain. This then raised the question of why should man and all vetebrates have specific receptors for drugs that are found primarily in the opium poppy? The most logical answer to this question is that all vertebrates must also possess in their own brains "opiate" type molecules and that the opiate narcotics are a chance interaction with this system. A search for these "endogenous opiates" was immediately instituted, and they were soon identified as two closely related "opiod" molecules called leucine and methionine "enkephalin." These enkephalins are found in the same areas of the brain as the opiate receptors, but once released from nerve terminals they are rapidly broken down by the body. Because of this rapid breakdown, they are not very active pharmacologically when given intravenously. However, if given intracerebrally they produce good analgesia, and, insofar as one can tell with rats, they also produce addiction. More recently, nonmetabolizable analogues of the enkephalins have become available, and these presumably produce all the pharmacological actions of the enkephalins for longer periods. Rumors also abound that astute track veterinarians, ever abreast of the latest advances, have been found with large quantities of these synthetic enkephalins in their possession. What use these enkephalins could possibly be to these veterinarians, however, is not clear, since these drugs have to be injected directly into the brain for significant pharmacological effect.

These enkephalins or endogenous opiates, however, may be the reason that acupuncture produces its reported effects. It has long been known that one can produce a sort of anesthesia by passing an electric current through a dog's brain. What is surprising, however, is that it was found that this electrically induced anesthesia could be antagonized by narcotic antagonists such as naloxone. This strongly suggests that the endogenous opiates are involved in electrically induced

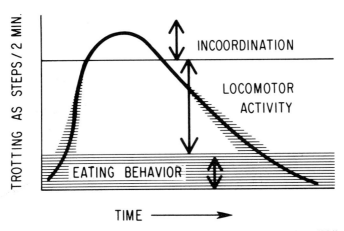

Figure 12-11. Relationships among opiate-induced behaviors in the horse. The solid line represents a typical trotting response to a large dose of a narcotic drug in a horse. At lower dose rates, or at the beginning or end of a response, eating behavior predominates. As the blood levels of the drug increase, trotting becomes predominant, with traces of eating behavior remaining. At very high blood levels of drug, incoordination occurs and limits the trotting response. Reproduced with permission from Combie et al., *J Equine Med Surg, 3:384,* 1979.

anesthesia, and it also appears likely that they are involved in acupuncture-induced analgesia and anesthesia as well.

As well as being found in the central nervous system, both the opiate receptors and the enkephalins are found in high concentrations in the gastrointestinal tract. This distribution of opiate receptors accounts for the well-known constipating effects of opiates, since propulsive movements in the gut are reduced by opiate drugs. However, the tendency of opiates to increase tension in the gastrointestinal tract may create problems in the treatment of colic in horses, as the increased tension may increase pain and counteract the analgesic effect of these drugs.

The last point of concern about narcotic analgesics in the horse is why would these drugs, which so clearly produce sedation in man, be so markedly stimulant in the horse? In this regard it is interesting to speculate on the evolutionary pressures on the horse that might have favored a close linkage between the pain-suppressing (analgesic) and running responses to opiate drugs. The endogenous opiates or enkephalins apparently function as a natural pain "override" mechanism. They therefore probably serve to prevent a horse's escape or other self-preservation responses from being incapacitated by pain.

The classic example of this effect occurs with soldiers in battle, who may be severely wounded but are often not aware of any pain until they are removed from the battle situation. In the horse, which evolved into an animal that utilized escape as its principal defense against predators, a close linkage between the animal's natural analgesic mechanism and its motor "urge" to run and escape would obviously be beneficial. From the work reported here and that in progress, it appears possible that activation of opiate receptors in the brain enables the horse to both ignore pain and get moving rapidly. Both of these abilities must have been strongly selected for as the horse evolved into an animal for whom escape was a major defense mechanism. Correctly used, therefore, the narcotic analgesics would potentially seem to be highly effective medications for a sore racehorse, as it gives him almost immediate freedom from pain and a sharp urge to "go." An intravenous shot of a narcotic in a horse apparently turns to full "on" an innate escape mechanism that is part of the evolutionary heritage of the horse and which is also likely to be very useful to him in the modern racing situation.

As a practical matter, the work reported here has shown that all the narcotic analgesics, fentanyl included, are potent motor stimulants in the horse. This is despite the fact that both the California racing authorities and the American Horse Shows Association in the past listed fentanyl as a depressant drug. Recognition of this aspect of the pharmacology of fentanyl was apparently delayed by the use of small doses and incorrect routes of administration. The locomotor stimulant actions of morphine are apparently well known, and morphine, heroin, and other narcotics have been widely used in horse racing for at least 100 years. Because these drugs combine an analgesic effect with a powerful urge to run, they could be particularly useful drugs in sore horses. However, other than the pilot study at the Ohio State University the only work that I am aware of on the performance effects of narcotic analgesics in the horse is that of Sanford, who reported that stimulation due to the narcotics was variable and that coordination was impaired. This impairment of coordination suggests that Sanford was using relatively large doses, but no details of his experiments are available.

SELECTED REFERENCES

Combie, J. E.: *Studies on the Locomotor Responses and Pharmacokinetics of Fentanyl and Other Narcotic Analgesics in the Horse.* M.Sc. Thesis, University of Kentucky, 1979.

Combie, J., Dougherty, J., Nugent, E., and Tobin, T.: The pharmacology of narcotic analgesics in the horse. IV. Dose and time response relationships for behavioral responses to morphine, meperidine, pentazocine, anileridine, methadone and hydromorphone. *J Equine Med Surg, 3:*377-385, 1979.

Davis, L. E. and Knight, A. P.: Review of the clinical pharmacology of the equine digestive system. *J Equine Med Surg, 1:*27-35, 1977.

Hughes, J., Smith, T., Morgan, B., and Fothergill, L.: Purification and properties of enkephalin — the possible endogenous ligand for the morphine receptor. *Life Sciences, 16:*1753-1758, 1975.

Lal, Harbens: Narcotic dependence, narcotic action and dopamine receptors. *Life Sciences, 17:*483-496, 1978.

Lowe, J. E.: Pentazocine (Talwin-V) for the relief of abdominal pain in ponies — a comparative evaluation with description of colic induced for analgesia evaluation. *Proc AAEP,* 34-46, 1969.

Lowe, J. E.: Xylazine, pentazocine, meperidine, and dipyrone for relief of a balloon induced colic: A double blind comparative evaluation. *J Equine Med Surg, 2:*286-291, 1978.

Pert, C. and Snyder, S. H.: Opiate receptor: Demonstration in nervous tissue. *Science, 179:*1011-1019, 1973.

Sanford, J.: Drugs and their effects on performance in the horse. *HBLB Conference of Research Workers,* 40-41, April, 1973.

Tobin, T., Combie, J., Crisman, M. W., and Blake, J. W.: Narcotic analgesics in the horse: Studies on the detection, pharmacokinetics, urinary clearance times and behavioral effects of pentazocine and fentanyl. *Ir Vet J, 33:*169-176, 1979.

Tobin, T. and Miller, J. R.: The pharmacology of narcotic analgesics in the horse. I. Detection, pharmacokinetics and urinary clearance times of pentazocine. *J Equine Med Surg, 3:*191-198, 1979.

Tobin, T. and Sen, A. K.: Stability and ligand sensitivity of [^{3}M] ouabain binding to Na$^+$ K$^+$-ATPase. *Biochim Biophys Acta, 198:*120-131, 1970.

Chapter 13

HORSES RUNNING SCARED: APOMORPHINE, PEMOLINE, AND STIMULANTS OF THE DOPAMINERGIC SYSTEM

T HE CLEAR-CUT STIMULATION of trotting or running activity seen with the narcotic analgesics outlined in the previous chapter is now usually considered to be associated with an indirect stimulation of nerve tracts in the brain in which dopamine is the neurohormone. It would seem reasonable, therefore, that a drug that directly mimicked the actions of the neurohormone dopamine in the brain of horses might be a very powerful locomotor (running) stimulant. The most potent dopaminergic drug known is apomorphine, and horsemen have been using apomorphine for quite some time as a powerful stimulant drug in racing horses.

Apomorphine is obtained from morphine by treating it with a strong acid, which causes a quite substantial rearrangement of the morphine molecule (Fig. 13-1). These changes result in loss of the typical narcotic analgesic properties of morphine and in the appearance of pharmacological activity resembling the actions of the neurohormone dopamine. Apomorphine is now thought by most authorities to be a pure dopaminergic activator, i.e. a drug whose effects are to mimic the actions of dopamine and directly stimulate dopaminergic receptors. Although derived from morphine, apomorphine is not thought of any longer as a narcotic, and it was recently removed from the Schedule II list of drugs. Further, the pharmacological actions of apomorphine are apparently not in any way blocked by naloxone, one clear-cut test for narcotic actions of a drug.

In man, the pharmacological activity of apomorphine appears as stimulation of vomiting, which has been its principal use in human and small animal medicine. However, in some animals, and particularly in the horse, apomorphine is a powerful locomotor stimulant that induces a very specific running pattern of activity. This running action induced by apomorphine has been studied extensively in small laboratory animals, and we have recently extended these studies to the horse.

Apomorphine produces its "running" stimulant actions by directly stimulating dopaminergic receptors. Cell groups located in a part of the brains called the mesencephalon give rise to most of the dopamine-containing nerves. These nerves fulfill all the criteria for "dopaminergic" nerves in that the necessary machinery to synthesize, store, and release dopamine is present in them. Apomorphine acts to mimic the action of naturally released dopamine at the dopamine receptors, and it is this direct receptor activation that gives rise to its pharmacological effects.

The role of dopamine in the running response to apomorphine has been very neatly demonstrated by one of my colleagues at Michigan State University, Doctor Ken Moore. What Doctor Moore did was to cut the dopaminergic nerves on one side of the brain of a mouse, allow the animal to recover, and then administer

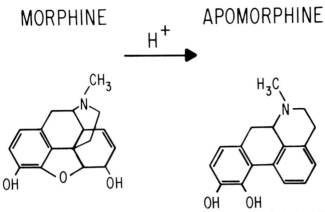

Figure 13-1. Structures of morphine and apomorphine. Apomorphine is derived from morphine by exposing it to strong acid. Despite the fact that it is derived from morphine, apomorphine is not a narcotic drug and is not any longer legally classed as a narcotic drug. Apomorphine produces pharmacological effects that are entirely different from those of morphine and interacts with a different receptor system from that used by morphine. Reproduced with permission from Tobin et al., *J Equine Med Surg*, 3:102, 1979.

apomorphine (Fig. 13-2). Since these mice had many more dopaminergic receptors on one side of their brain than on the other, they were stimulated to run on one side only and therefore ran faster on one side than the other. This, as horsemen are well aware, leads to turning, and Moore simply counted the number

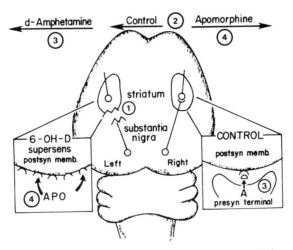

(From Moore et al, 1974)

Figure 13-2. Unilateral locomotor stimulation in mice by apomorphine and amphetamine. Dopaminergic nerves in the brain are cut on the left side (1) and a period of a few days allowed. Because dopamine is now only released on the right side of the brain, these animals are only stimulated to run on their right sides and thus spontaneously circle to the left (2). If amphetamine is administered, it stimulates dopamine release only on the right side and the animal turns faster to the left (3). If apomorphine is given, it finds more dopaminergic receptors that have developed on the left side to directly stimulate (4), so the apomorphine-stimulated mouse circles to the right (4). Reproduced with permission from Tobin et al., *J Equine Med Surg*, 3:102, 1979.

of circles that the mice made to get a very simple measure of the response of his mice to apomorphine.

One can imagine that if apomorphine is a direct locomotor stimulant in brain-damaged mice, its effects in Thoroughbred horses are likely to be dramatic, and this is certainly the case. While horses, for reasons that are not clear, do not respond reliably to apomorphine, when they do respond the effect is dramatic. As shown in Figure 13-3, 60 mg of apomorphine in a 1,000 lb. horse can increase the locomotor response up to about 160 steps per 2 minute period, or 80 steps per minute. Peak running activity occurs at about five to six minutes after an intravenous (IV) dose and declines rapidly thereafter. By forty minutes after dosing, all of the horses tested had returned to their baseline activity of about 4 steps/2 minutes and were apparently normal. Apomorphine is a very potent drug in the horse, a dose of less than 0.1 mg/kg (50 mg) producing a running response at up to forty times the normal spontaneous walking activity.

While apomorphine produces a running response that in many ways resembles that produced by the narcotic analgesics, there are a number of quite clear-cut differences between the actions of these drugs. Apomorphine-treated horses remained well coordinated at all doses tested, and the dosages that we tested were limited only by our horses' ability to maneuver at speed in the confines of a box stall. On high doses of apomorphine our horses "got up" to rates of 160 steps/2 minutes, at which point they appeared to be moving as rapidly as they could in the stall. In contrast, as the dose of fentanyl or other narcotic was increased and the horses surpassed rates of about 100 steps/2 minutes, the horses began to show

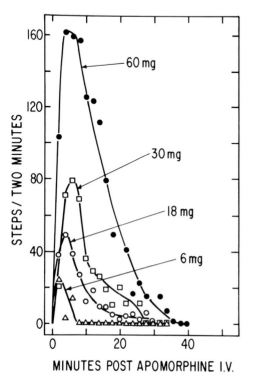

Figure 13-3. Stimulation of running activity by apomorphine in the horse. A horse was injected intravenously with the indicated doses of apomorphine and its trotting activity measured by the step-counting method. Note the very rapid increase in trotting after injection of the drug, and the fact that trotting activity is much faster after apomorphine than after narcotic drugs. Also, the rate of decline of the trotting response to apomorphine is unusually fast and appears to be faster than that observed after fentanyl. Reproduced with permission from Tobin et al., *J Equine Med Surg*, 3:103, 1979.

On apomorphine horses may get extremely excited and apprehensive; they appear to lunge toward the ceiling on high doses of this drug.

impairments in coordination and occasionally bumped into the walls of the stall. If the dose of fentanyl was further increased, the animals became incoordinated and fell. This incoordination was a direct effect of the fentanyl and not due to the small size of the loose boxes, because animals on apomorphine showed very much greater running responses with no signs of incoordination.

Unlike the dreamy, dissociated appearance of horses on high doses of narcotics, horses on apomorphine appeared apprehensive and uncomfortable with the presence of the observer. While horses on fentanyl or morphine circled, horses on apomorphine always kept a distance from the observer at the door of the box. The running activity on apomorphine invariably took place along the wall of the box distant from the observer, the horse pacing back and forth repeatedly. If the animal was extremely excited and apprehensive, it lunged up toward the ceiling as it reached each corner, as though seeking to escape out of the loose box over the far corner. At this point it would abruptly change direction, pace back along the wall to the other distant corner of the box, and repeat the process. All these maneuvers were carried out at speed, as the trotting-running rate of up to 160 steps/2 minutes suggests, and the horses were well coordinated throughout. If the dose of apomorphine was further increased, though, the horses tended to injure themselves on the loose box walls, and this limited the doses of drug that we could use in our tests.

In addition to these remarkable increases in running activity, horses dosed with apomorphine emitted a typical snort or snore during the period of drug action. This sound was so characteristic that it came to be referred to in the laboratory as the "apomorphine snort." This same snort has been reported and commented on from New Zealand by Mackay. Although horses dosed with fentanyl and other narcotic analgesics showed many behaviors suggestive of dopaminergic stimulation, they never emitted this typical "apomorphine snort."

Another characteristic of the apomorphine response that became apparent as our work progressed was its unreliability. While the running response of horses to fentanyl and other narcotic analgesics was always highly predictable, and repeatable within ninety minutes, the response of any horse to apomorphine could never be predicted or reliably repeated. As shown in Figure 13-4 and seen repeatedly in other work, the peak locomotor response to fentanyl in our hands was always found at 20 µg/kg and was always very close to 100 steps/2 minutes and encompassed by a relatively small "window" as shown by the dotted line. On the other hand, a peak response to apomorphine, or no response at all to apomorphine, might be found after doses of between 18 and 30 mg, while on other occasions, 60

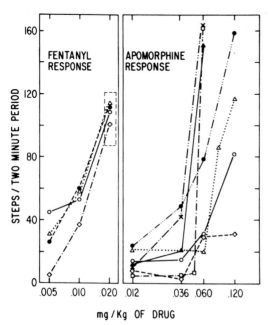

Figure 13-4. Individual dose response curves to fentanyl and apomorphine in the horse. The left panel shows four individual dose response curves to fentanyl obtained in a sequence of experiments. The consistent nature of the response to fentanyl is indicated by the dashed "window" and has been seen repeatedly in other experimental work. The right panel shows all the dose response data obtained with apomorphine, demonstrating the very wide scatter in responses and the sometimes very steep dose response curves obtained after treatment with apomorphine. Reproduced with permission from Tobin et al., *J Equine Med Surg,* 3:103, 1979.

mg was not enough to elicit more than a small response. Obviously, the predictability of a response to apomorphine is very small, which makes it a difficult and unreliable drug to use under any circumstances in the horse.

As with fentanyl, the onset of action of the response to apomorphine in the horse after IV injection was also very rapid (see Fig. 13-3). It appears likely, therefore, that apomorphine is also a highly lipid-soluble drug which enters the brain rapidly. The rate of decline in the running response to apomorphine, however, can also be very rapid, and the decline may be too rapid to be easily accounted for by redistribution out of the brain in the bloodstream. The running response to fentanyl, which peaked even sooner than that to apomorphine, invariably declined in a smooth and slower fashion. The running response to apomorphine, however often declined sharply from 130 to 5 steps/minute within minutes. Since apomorphine is very susceptible to oxidative breakdown, it may be that oxidation of this drug as it distributes *in vivo* can account for its variable effectiveness and the sometimes very rapid decline in its pharmacological response. In any event, this rapid onset and decline of action of apomorphine may be related to the unpredictability of its action and, as pointed out earlier, make it a difficult drug to work with, either experimentally or in a more practical context.

Of further interest is the fact that the dose of apomorphine reportedly used "on the track" was 60 mg of apomorphine subcutaneously, thirty to forty-five minutes prior to a race. While the dose selected in this case would appear to be in the right range, whether or not the right route of administration has been chosen is not clear. The rapid onset and decline of the action of apomorphine seen in our experiments may suggest that the drug has to be given IV at this dose for good effect, and like fentanyl, apomorphine may be much less effective by the subcutaneous route.

The locomotor response to apomorphine in the horse is blocked by tranquilizers such as haloperidol and is also likely to be blocked by phenothiazine tranquilizers such as acepromazine. In studies on the kinetics of apomorphine in the horse, one of my students, Richard Miller, routinely dosed horses with 90 mg apomorphine in an attempt to obtain consistently measurable blood levels of apomorphine. All Miller's horses were pretreated with 15 mg of haloperidol, and no difficulty in handling or obtaining blood samples from any of these horses was experienced. Naloxone, however, was unable to block the trotting response to apomorphine, showing that apomorphine does not produce its effect on narcotic receptors (Fig. 13-5).

In our kinetic experiments, we found plasma levels of apomorphine difficult to detect reliably, consistent with the variable response of our horses to apomorphine. In horses dosed with about 90 to 100 mg of apomorphine, Miller found plasma levels of apomorphine of about 25 ng/ml or less, and plasma levels of the drug tended to be erratic. Urinary levels of the drug could not be successfully quantitated, but Maylin reports detection of apomorphine in equine urine for up to forty-eight hours after its IV administration. Apomorphine is excreted in equine urine at least partly as a glucuronide metabolite, which may be expected to persist in urine for at least forty-eight hours after dosing and is also likely susceptible to dilution by diuretics such as furosemide.

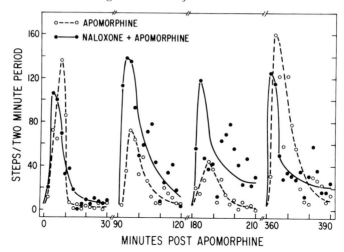

Figure 13-5. Naloxone and apomorphine-stimulated motor activity. The dotted lines and open circles show the response of an individual horse to doses of 30 mg of apomorphine administered intravenously every ninety minutes. Note the erratic response and compare it with the very consistent responses obtained after repeated doses of fentanyl in Figure 14-2. The solid circles show the response to apomorphine in naloxone pretreated horses. In each case, full trotting response to each dose of apomorphine was obtained. The experiment shows the erratic nature of the horse's response to apomorphine and clearly shows that the effect is not blocked by naloxone. Reproduced with permission from Tobin et al., *J Equine Med Surg, 3:*104, 1979.

As of this writing, I am not aware of any other published work on apomorphine in the horse beyond Mackay's paper, nor of any clinical uses for apomorphine in the horse; neither am I aware of any studies in which this drug has been used in performance trials. Apomorphine was until recently classified with morphine as a Schedule II drug but is no longer so classified.

Apomorphine has apparently been widely used in racing horses, and in 1952 the National Association of State Racing Commissioners organized a racing research fund to foster research on drug detection in horses. One of the drugs that was selected for study was apomorphine, and Doctor E. L. Way of the University of California was selected to tackle the problem of detecting apomorphine in horse urine. Doctor Way soon showed that apomorphine could be detected in horse urine as a glucuronide metabolite, and many racing chemists incorporated this test for apomorphine into their testing systems. Up to 1972, only ten apomorphine positives had been reported by AORC members, but this figure was soon to increase dramatically.

In early 1975, the Illinois Racing Board charged twelve trainers with illegal medication violations, and shortly thereafter six more trainers and a veterinarian were added to this list. The drug in question was apomorphine, and the reason for the number of "positives" and the large number of tracks involved was in part related to the "modus operandi" of the Illinois Racing Board laboratory.

At the beginning of the 1974 racing season, Mr. John MacDonald, the chief chemist in the Illinois Racing Board laboratories, decided that so much money was being spent collecting, identifying, and splitting each sample into "laboratory" and "referee" samples that a portion of each sample should be saved for future use.

This collection of frozen samples grew to 25,000 samples by the end of the 1974 season. In this new procedure, when the usual post-race test was completed in Illinois, the chemists would simply report "preliminary examination completed" and the purses would be released. The remainder of the urine sample, however, went into the freezer to be held in case of further developments.

The further developments in the apomorphine cases were reportedly precipitated by a particular practitioner gaining an unusually large number of clients in a short period. Further, the brother of this particular individual, a trainer in Florida, was discovered with "three white tablets which were not bute" and a note as how they should be used. The tablets were apomorphine, and this, apparently, was the secret of the practitioner's expanding clientele. The laboratory was "tipped off" and began to carefully examine horse urines from certain trainers. Soon the apomorphine positives came rolling in, and from here it was only a short step to the freezer and a step back in time through the 1974 racing season urines. Checking the freezer samples yielded evidence that suggested patterns of repeated violations, and one particular individual was reportedly charged with about sixty separate instances of improper medication, all for apomorphine, with approximately a half-million dollars in purse money involved.*

Although these positives were called in early 1975, these cases are still not resolved and at the time of this writing are before the Supreme Court in Illinois. Even though a large number of positives were called on one individual and witnesses were produced who reportedly saw the pre-race shots of 18 mg of apomorphine being given subcutaneously fifteen minutes before the race, grounds for appeal in the "chain of evidence" were found and some of the cases are still unresolved.

In summary, apomorphine is a clear-cut locomotor stimulant in horses, producing the most powerful running response that we have ever seen a drug produce in our hands. It produces this running without any sign of incoordination at high doses, in sharp contrast with the narcotic analgesics. The drug, however, appears to make horses apprehensive and fearful, and it is in addition quite the most unreliable drug that we have worked with to date, in that we can never predict the response that we are likely to get to a given dose. While apomorphine was a problem drug in racing for a number of years, it is no longer so, as good analytical methods for its detection in urine have been worked out and applied by analytical chemists.

The only other clear-cut locomotor stimulant of the apomorphine class apparently being used in racing today is pemoline. Pemoline is a central nervous system stimulant which is structurally distinct from the amphetamines and methylphenidate. It is very poorly soluble in water, which creates problems with its IV administration. My colleague Doctor Blake, in experiments with pemoline, chose to make it up for IV injection in dimethylsulfoxide (DMSO), in which pemoline is relatively soluble.

In experiments with small laboratory animals, pemoline has been shown to stimulate locomotor activity at doses of about 10 mg/kg. Similarly, preliminary experiments in horses have also shown that pemoline is a locomotor stimulant with

---

* John MacDonald, Chief Chemist, Illinois Racing Board; personal communication.

the ability to increase spontaneous locomotor activity in horses between ten- and twentyfold (Fig. 13-6). Unfortunately, because of the relatively large doses of drug required to produce these effects, it was not possible to complete these experiments, but all the data currently available indicates that pemoline is a locomotor stimulant in horses of the same general type as apomorphine.

In studies on the effects of drugs on the performance of horses, Sanford reported that pemoline significantly ($P < 0.05$) increased speed over a 200-meter gallop test at doses of 4 gm per horse by an unspecified route. No details on times or percent improvement in performance were presented. Nevertheless, it seems clear that pemoline is a potential performance-improving drug in the horse, although the doses required to produce these effects are extremely large compared with those of other CNS stimulants.

Preliminary work on "clearance times" for pemoline have shown this drug to have one of the longest half-lives of any drug studied in the horse. After IV administration of 1 gram of pemoline, its plasma half-life is on the order of 150 hours, and blood levels of this drug can still be found for *one week* after dosing. To further complicate the picture, urinary levels of pemoline are up to ten times higher than blood levels of this drug, and pemoline can readily be detected at the microgram level in urine for four days after dosing (Fig. 13-7). Although these experiments are not complete, the data indicates that pemoline may be detectable in urine by the techniques used in this study for up to fourteen days after a dose. These "clearance time" characteristics make pemoline one of the most persistent

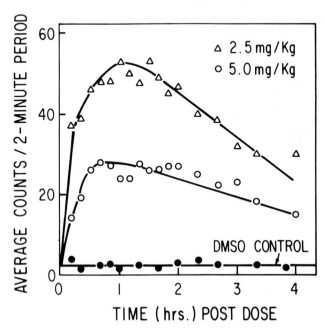

Figure 13-6. Trotting response after intravenous administration of pemoline. The curves show the trotting response of three horses after intravenous administration of the indicated doses of pemoline. After Igwe (1979).

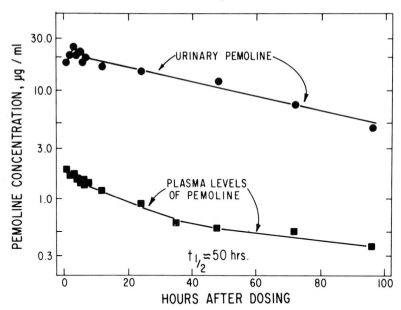

Figure 13-7. "Clearance times" for pemoline in the horse. The solid squares (■—■) show plasma levels of pemoline after intravenous administration of 1 gm/1000 lb. of pemoline to four horses. The solid circles (●—●) show urinary levels of pemoline in these horses. The urinary half-life of pemoline, at about 150 hours, is one of the longest half-lives measured for any drug in the horse (Igwe, 1979).

drugs that we know of in horse urine, comparable with that major bugbear of racing chemistry, procaine penicillin.

A number of other miscellaneous stimulants are used in racing horses which fall into no clear-cut category. Among these are camphor and strychnine, which are commonly used in equine tonics, and each of which will be discussed briefly.

Camphor

Camphor (*d*-camphor) is the chief constituent of oil of camphor and is obtained from the wood and bark of *Cinnamomum camphora*, which is grown in Japan and Taiwan. Camphor was once used in human medicine as both a "cerebral" and respiratory stimulant, but these uses are now considered obsolete. Camphor, however, is still used widely in equine track practice as a respiratory stimulant, and Fujii and coworkers have studied its pharmacology in the horse in some detail. These authors considered camphor to be a heart stimulant and reported that it is commonly detected in post-race testing in Japan.

In their studies, Fujii et al. administered trans-π-oxycamphor in 200 and 2,000 mg doses IV to horses. They saw no behavioral changes in these horses, with the exception of spasmodic extensions of the head and neck in one horse immediately after a 2,000 mg injection IV. Regardless of the dose of oxycamphor administered, this drug did not appear to affect the speed of the horse. Oxycamphor, however, tended to reduce the heart rate both during and after exercise. It slowed the heartbeat in these horses and caused it to fluctuate greatly, in combination with disturbances in cardiac rhythm. Reviewing the results of their experiments, Fujii et al. concluded that the actions of oxycamphor that they observed in the horse suggested intoxication of the heart muscle due to this drug. It appears that camphor in the horse is not likely to have any useful stimulant actions, and its standing as a drug in equine medicine should probably be close to that accorded it today in human medicine, which is just about zero!

Strychnine

Strychnine is an alkaloid obtained from the seeds of the tree *Strychnos nux-vomica*. Strychnine is bitter tasting and has been used in the past as a "bitter" stimulant for the digestive trace. Strychnine is well absorbed from the gastrointestinal tract and is a potent convulsant in both animals and man. It is apparently this ability to produce what can be lethal stimulation in animals and man that led in the past to the use of strychnine as a stimulant tonic.

Strychnine produces its stimulant effects by directly blocking the actions of the inhibitory neurotransmitter γ-aminobutyric acid. This neurohormone controls the overall level of excitability in the brain and spinal cord and acts as a "squelch" on the level of activity of the animal. When its action is inhibited by strychnine, the slightest stimulation or sound stimulates the animal and may throw him into a convulsion, with all the muscles in the body becoming tense. This interferes with respiration, and eventually the animal dies of respiratory failure. Because it is primarily a convulsant, there is no rational use for strychnine as a tonic or stimulant in equine medicine, and its use as a tonic must be considered obsolete.

In conclusion, a number of facts emerge from these reviews and the work in our laboratory on the actions of stimulant drugs in horses. It appears that clear-cut locomotor stimulation as an unmistakable tendency on the part of the horse to trot or run is primarily associated with dopaminergic stimulation. Apomorphine is clearly the most effective drug known in this area, but its effects are very erratic. Because of the highly variable response and the short period for which the horse responds to it, apomorphine is a most difficult drug to study in performance trials. It was apparently clearly identified by pharmacologically inclined horsemen as a potent stimulant of running behavior long before academic pharmacologists became aware of its value, and although apomorphine has apparently been widely used on the track, to my knowledge no performance trials have been done with it. A final comment might also be that the apparent fear and clear-cut stimulation observed in animals on apomorphine appears to constitute sufficient reason to ban the use of this drug in racing horses, as it seems very likely that use of this drug could lead to injuries to horses and people.

Next to apomorphine, the narcotic analgesics were the most clear-cut locomotor stimulants tested. Fentanyl produced a brief but intense locomotor stimulation, and our horses remained reasonably alert and well coordinated unless the dose was about 8 mg/1,000 lb. or higher. This stimulant action of fentanyl is of particular interest because no signs of depression were seen in any of our experiments with narcotic drugs. Despite this, both the California Rules of Racing and the American Horse Shows Association have listed fentanyl as a depressant drug, and their basis for this classification remains unclear. Again, despite the fact that morphine has been known as a stimulant drug in horses for many years, the only studies on the performance effects of narcotics in horses are those of Sanford, who noted that morphine and a combination of etorphine and acepromazine (Immobilon®) increased speed in performance tests when given in low doses. However, no experimental details or data are available. In other experiments, Gabel reports that 3 mg of fentanyl administered IV to three Standardbred horses produced no significant improvement in their times to pace one mile. Again, however, these are preliminary results and difficult to evaluate.

The classical central stimulants such as amphetamine, methamphetamine, caffeine, and cocaine do not appear to specifically stimulate running activity in the horse in the same way as apomorphine and the narcotics. Rather, they appear to increase the general level of excitability of the horse and may thus secondarily increase his running ability in the same way as methamphetamine potentiated the motor response to fentanyl. Further, these drugs may very well affect the aggressiveness, courage, or demeanor of a horse in a race in ways that might not show up on performance tests but that might very well affect the outcome of a race, though this is a question that is unlikely to be answered in the near future. Strangely, these less clear-cut "motor" stimulants have been much more thoroughly studied in the horse than apomorphine or the narcotics. The general consensus of these studies seems to be that these classical central nervous system stimulants either can or are likely to improve performance in horses, although whether all the data on which these conclusions are based would withstand rigorous statistical analysis is far from clear.

SELECTED REFERENCES

Di Chiara, G. and Gessa, G. L.: Pharmacology and neurochemistry of apomorphine. In Garrattini, S., Goldin, A., Hawking, F., and Kopin, I. J. (Eds.): In *Advances in Pharmacology and Chemotherapy*, Vol. 15.

Goodman, L. S. and Gilman, A.: *The Pharmacology of Therapeutics*, 5th ed. New York, Macmillan, 1975.

Fujii, S., Yoshida, S., Kusanagi, C., Mima, K., and Natsuno, Y.: Pharmacological studies on doping drugs for race horses. Trans-oxocamphor. *Jpn J Vet Sci, 32:*307-317, 1970.

Igwe, O. J.: *Analytical Protocol, Pharmacokinetics and Time-Response Relationships of Pemoline in the Horse.* M.Sc. Thesis, University of Kentucky, 1979.

Mackay, A.: Some effects of drugs in the "doping" of race horses. *NZ Vet J, 9:*129-135, 1961.

Moore, K. E.: Behavioral effects of direct and indirect-acting dopaminergic agonist. In Usdin, E. (Ed.): *Neuropsychopharmacology of Monamines and Their Regulatory Enzymes.* New York, Raven, 1974.

Sanford, J.: Drugs and their effects on performance in the horse. *HBLP Conference of Research Workers,* 40-41, April, 1973.

Sanford, J.: Medication affecting the performance of racehorses and its control. *Proc 19th World Vet Cong,* 382-385, 1971.

Tobin, T. and Woods, W. E.: Pharmacology review: Actions of central stimulant drugs in the horse. I. *J Equine Med Surg, 2:*60-66, 1979.

Tobin, T., Combie, J. D., and Shults, T.: Pharmacology review: Actions of central stimulant drugs in the horse. II. *J Equine Med Surg, 3:*102-109, 1979.

Chapter 14

CALMING HORSES FOR SHORT PERIODS:
ACEPROMAZINE AND ITS COUSINS

U NTIL THE EARLY 1950s, the only drugs available to calm nervous horses were depressant drugs like chloral hydrate and the barbiturates. While these drugs would calm nervous and fractious animals, they only did so at doses that clearly rendered them drowsy and affected their motor ability and coordination. With the introduction of reserpine and the phenothiazine tranquilizers in the early 1950s, a class of drugs became available that would render animals less reactive to environmental stimuli with minimal effects on their consciousness, motor ability, and coordination. Technically, these drugs were found to block learned (conditioned) responses and not affect innate or unlearned responses, and the term "tranquilizer" was coined to describe this new group of drugs. It subsequently developed, however, that the major action and use of this group of drugs in humans were for the treatment of psychotic individuals. They are therefore now known in human medicine as the antipsychotic or neuroleptic drugs, and "tranquilizer" is considered obsolete. The term tranquilizer, however, is still widely and rather loosely used in equine circles to describe any drug that allows a horse to remain conscious and standing but enables a veterinarian to take substantial liberties with it. It is not, however, in this equine usage, in any way a precise term.

Perhaps the subtlest use of this rather heterogenous group of depressant or tranquilizing drugs is to "take the edge" off a horse. This is primarily a horseman's use of these drugs. What the horseman requires in this circumstance is a drug that will allow a somewhat nervous horse to perform in a relaxed manner in an unusual or challenging environment. Thus, a "washy" horse, which gets excited and "runs his race" in the paddock before the actual race, might benefit from being "touched" with (i.e. administered a small dose of) a tranquilizer pre-race. The idea in this case is to give a horse a dose that will keep him from being hyperexcitable in the paddock but will allow him to run "up to form" in the actual race. Other circumstances where a small dose of a tranquilizer might help is for a horse that does not take readily to starting gates, for horses that tense up and "ease over jumps" better on a small dose of tranquilizer, and for show horses. Similarly, trainers will sometimes use a small dose of a tranquilizer when first saddling a horse or teaching him to load or use a starting gate. All of these uses require very subtle drug effects and are outside the usual "clinical" uses of "tranquilizers" as drugs. Another area where "tranquilizers" have been used is, of course, in the "nobbling" or stopping of horses. In this case, a slightly larger dose of "tranquiliz-er" is used, the objective being to reduce the speed of the horse to the point at which he must lose the race, without affecting him to the point that he is clearly tranquilized and scratched from the race.

A somewhat more substantial "tranquilizing" effect is that which is required for

228

Small doses of tranquilizers are sometimes administered prior to the air transportation of horses.

transport of an animal. The goal here is to reduce the amount of stress experienced by the horse and thus the likelihood of injury or of the horse being stressed to the point that he leaves himself open to a shipping pneumonia. Also, one might hope with judicious medication to avoid the possibility of uncontrollable excitation occurring during transportation, with the unwelcome outcome, in air transport, of having to destroy a valuable horse in midflight.

The third and perhaps most clearly veterinary use for this group of drugs is for restraint in a clinical situation. Here, the veterinarian wishes to perform some minor interference on an animal, and what he is interested in is his personal safety and degree of control of a conscious standing animal rather than a subtle drug effect. However, because animals are easily aroused from, for example, phenothiazine-induced "tranquilization," these drugs alone are not the most satisfactory drugs for this rather specialized type of chemical control or restraint. There are now a number of other useful drugs or drug combinations available in this area that appear to be fundamentally quite different from and more effective than the classical "tranquilizers" and which will be dealt with later in some detail.

Reserpine, a plant alkaloid, was the first drug of this group to be reported on, and Yonkman coined the term "tranquilizer" to characterize the psychic effects of reserpine on humans. At about the same time, a group of French workers synthesized chlorpromazine, the prototype member of the phenothiazine group of tranquilizers. This group has since been expanded to include a very large number of tranquilizers based on the phenothiazine nucleus, only a few of which are used in veterinary medicine. Another family of tranquilizers, called the butyrophenones, has recently been developed; although chemically distinct from the phenothiazines, these drugs are pharmacologically quite closely related to them.

Other drugs that are usually grouped with these agents are the so-called minor tranquilizers, Librium® and Valium®, whose mode of action is quite distinct from that of either reserpine or the phenothiazines. A relatively recent introduction to veterinary medicine is xylazine or Rompun®, which is a very potent though relatively short acting depressant. Lastly, there are a number of other drugs, such as the corticosteroids and thiamine, which are believed, rightly or wrongly, to produce "tranquilizing" effects at certain doses and which are used under some circumstances in an attempt to obtain this effect.

The Phenothiazine Tranquilizers

The prototype of the phenothiazine tranquilizers is chlorpromazine, which is chemically related to the anthelmintic phenothiazine. It was first synthesized in France in 1950 and its pharmacological effects investigated. Like all the phenothiazine tranquilizers, chlorpromazine has a very large number of pharmacological actions, which property is reflected in one of the first trade names for this drug, Largactil®. Chlorpromazine, however, is not widely used in equine practice, as it reportedly produces undesirable side effects in many cases. According to Booth, after a few minutes of initial sedation following administration of the drug, the animal may become unsteady, sink backward on its hocks, and lunge forward in an uncoordinated manner. The horse may stumble and fall but then will stand up with continued lunging and rearing. This violent reaction reportedly alternates with periods of sedation.

Acetylpromazine (acepromazine), an acetylated derivative of promazine (Fig. 14-1), is one of the most commonly used phenothiazine tranquilizers in equine medicine. It is recommended for use in horses at doses of between 0.05 and 0.1 mg/kg (2 to 4 mg/100 lb.) for a spectrum of effects that cover the area popularly referred to as "tranquilization" in horses. All the phenothiazine derivatives, including acepromazine, appear to produce at least part of their central effects by blocking dopaminergic receptors in the brain. These dopaminergic receptors are the receptors on which apomorphine and the narcotic analgesics act to produce the trotting response that we detailed previously. Therefore, it would seem reasonable that if the phenothiazines block these receptors, they should also act to block the narcotic-induced trotting response, and this indeed turns out to be the case. If one pretreats horses with acepromazine, the trotting response to fentanyl

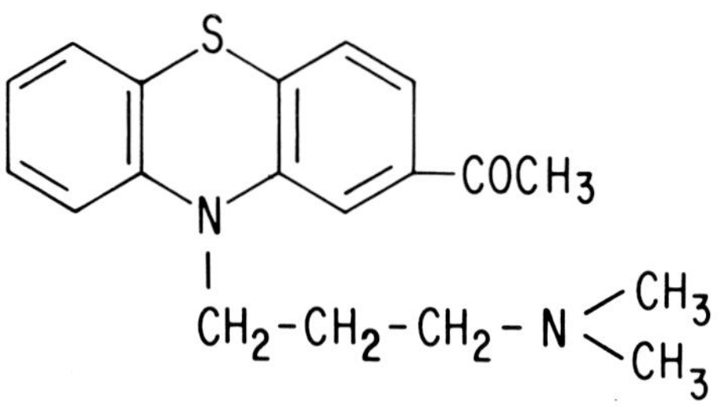

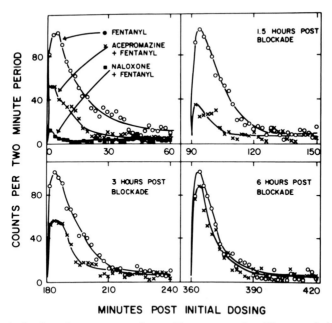

Figure 14-1. Chemical structure of acepromazine (acetylpromazine).

is reduced, and one can use the data to develop both dose response and time response data on the pharmacological response to acepromazine in the horse.

If one pretreats a horse with acepromazine, his trotting response to fentanyl is very rapidly blocked, and one can use this response to measure the time course of action of acepromazine. In the experiment of Figure 14-2, horses were dosed every ninety minutes with fentanyl, and in each case their response to fentanyl was about the same. When these horses were pretreated with acepromazine, however, the effect of fentanyl was blocked, by about 50 percent at fifteen minutes after dosing, and about 65 percent at ninety minutes after dosing. Thereafter the blockade declined, and the horses were almost back to control by six hours after

Figure 14-2. Blockade of trotting response to fentanyl by acepromazine. The open circles (o—o) in the left panel show the trotting response of three horses dosed with about 8 mg/1000 lb. of fentanyl by rapid intravenous injection every ninety minutes. The crosses (×—×) show the trotting response in these horses when they were dosed with 0.1 mg/kg of acepromazine. The experiment shows the reproducibility of the fentanyl-induced trotting response and the time course of the action of acepromazine on this effect. Reproduced with permission from Combie et al., *Proc 2nd Equine Pharmacology Symposium*, 188, 1978.

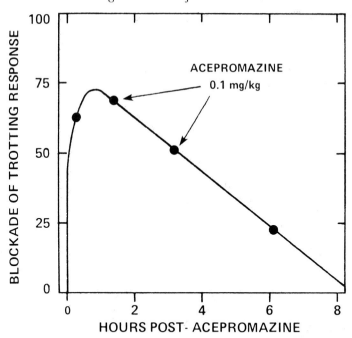

Figure 14-3. Time course of the acepromazine blockade of fentanyl-induced trotting. The peak effects of acepromazine on fentanyl-induced trotting from Figure 14-2 are replotted as blockade of trotting against time. The curve and solid circles thus show the time course of action of acepromazine in these horses. Reproduced with permission from Tobin et al., *J Equine Med Surg*, *3*:461, 1979.

the acepromazine. Figure 14-3 shows those data replotted as blockade of the trotting response, which plot clearly shows the time course of action of acepromazine on motor activity in these horses. Those data provide good evidence for occupation of dopaminergic receptors by acepromazine in the horse and show that the blockade lasts for about eight hours after a dose of this size in the horse. If the dose of acepromazine was reduced, both the extent and time course of the response were reduced, although the time of peak effect remained approximately the same.

Working in Scotland, MacKenzie and Snow used 0.5 mg/kg of acepromazine, about five times the dose used in our experiments, as a chemical restraining agent when performing muscle biopsies in seven horses. At these doses, MacKenzie and Snow considered that the tranquilizing effects of acepromazine lasted for twenty-four hours, considerably longer than the eight-hour response seen at the manu-facturer's recommended dose.

In other studies we used our variable interval responding apparatus to study the actions of acepromazine on the central nervous system of horses. In these experiments we administered the acepromazine intravenously ten minutes before allowing the horse to enter the responding apparatus and followed the horse's response rate for thirty minutes. As shown in Figure 14-4, 0.01 mg/kg aceproma-zine had relatively little effect on the responding rate of these horses, and doses in the region of 0.04 to 0.1 mg/kg were needed to obtain clear-cut central effects.

These results contrast with the marked sensitivity of penile extension and blood hematocrit to acepromazine, and they show that the central nervous system may be relatively resistant to the depressant actions of this agent.

Along with a reduction in spontaneous locomotor activity, the phenothiazine tranquilizers markedly reduce respiratory rate, both in the standing horse and after strenuous exercise. Figure 14-5 shows the effects of increasing doses of acepromazine IV on the respiratory rate of horses in our laboratory. The mean respiratory rate in control horses was about seventeen respirations per minute, which rate remained constant over the two-hour control period. The smallest dose that we tested, 0.01 mg/kg, had little effect on the respiratory rate and is therefore a subthreshold dose for a pharmacological response. The next dose tested, 0.04 mg/kg (about 20 mg to a 1,000 lb. horse), produced a modest respiratory depression, peaking at about fifteen minutes and returning to control within one hour of dosing. This response presumably parallels the "tranquilizing" response to this dose of acepromazine IV. If the dose of acepromazine was increased, the depression in respiratory rate observed became more profound and took longer to develop. Thus, after 0.08 mg/kg, respiratory depression peaked at around thirty minutes postdosing and then returned toward control. After 0.1 mg/kg, the higher end of the manufacturer's recommended dose, the effect peaked after forty-five minutes and then slowly declined, not having returned to control by three hours postdosing. At the highest dose tested, 0.4 mg/kg, respiratory depression took one hour to peak and then declined even more slowly, the respiratory rate being still markedly depressed three hours after dosing.

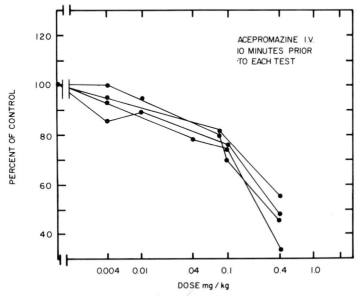

Figure 14-4. Effects of acepromazine on the variable interval responding rate of four horses. The one solid circle (●) at 100% represents the mean control responding rate of four horses, while the remaining solid circles show the depression in responding rate produced by the intravenous administration of the indicated doses of acepromazine.

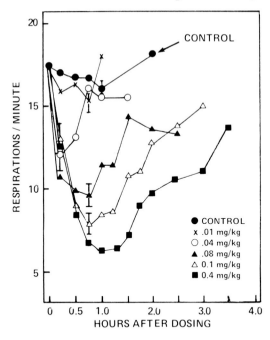

Figure 14-5. Effect of acepromazine IV on respiratory rate in the horse. The solid circles (●—●) show the respiratory rate in control horses, while other symbols show the respiratory rates observed in these horses after the indicated doses of acepromazine IV. All data points are the means of determinations on four horses, and the vertical bars represent standard errors of the means. Reproduced with permission from Tobin et al., *J Equine Med Surg, 3:*462, 1979.

The family of dose and time response curves presented in Figure 14-5 allow some conclusions of interest to the veterinarian and horseman to be drawn. If, as is usually the case, the practitioner wants to work on the horse for about ten minutes within about fifteen minutes after dosing, there is not much point in giving more than 0.05 mg/kg. This is because "tranquilization" will apparently be maximal for this time period at this dose. You can produce more "tranquilization" with a higher dose, but you also have to wait longer to allow the effect to develop. Therefore, increasing the dose of a phenothiazine tranquilizer does not appear to accelerate the onset of tranquilization but just means that the effect becomes more profound if you are prepared to wait for it to develop.

Muir and his coworkers at the Ohio State University have studied the effects of acepromazine on ventilatory variables in the horse in some detail. It turns out that although acepromazine depresses the respiratory rate as breaths per minute, the volume of air respired is increased to compensate and thus ventilation is maintained at approximately the same level. While such a depression of respiratory rate is not particularly surprising in standing horses, it turns out that essentially the same effect is seen in phenothiazine-treated horses after strenuous exercise. This effect was demonstrated clearly by Carey and Sanford, who showed that pretreatment with small dose of acepromazine (0.02 to 0.08 mg/kg) inhibited the exercise-induced increase in respiratory rate up to 50 percent. Similar results have also been observed by Fujii with chlorpromazine, by Stewart with promazine, and by Courtot with acepromazine. Depression of the respiratory rate, therefore, is a clear-cut and consistent effect of the phenothiazine tranquilizers, even in the face of substantial exercise stress.

Another very obvious and consistent indication of the action of phenothiazine tranquilizers is extension of the penis in stallions and geldings. Figure 14-6 shows the time course of penile extension in four geldings after treatment with various doses of acepromazine IV. In most cases penile extension was essentially complete within fifteen minutes after dosing and at the highest dose tested remained maximally extended for up to four hours after dosing. At lower doses full extension was apparently not obtained and the penis was rapidly withdrawn. The lowest dose tested, 0.004 mg/kg, had no effect, although 2½ times this dose produced a sharp though short-lived response. As suggested by this data and the work of Fujii and coworkers, who detailed the clinical signs of chlorpromazine administration in horses, penile extension appears to be a relatively sensitive indicator of the action of these drugs.

Extremely rarely following acepromazine, but apparently more commonly with propiopromazine, a long-lasting paralysis of the retractor penis muscle resulting in long-term extension of the penis has been observed. This phenomenon is apparently dose related and is thought to be more common in stallions than in geldings. With propiopromazine, erectile penile paralysis has been observed for up to eighteen months after dosing, and even after castration the penis had failed to retract completely two years later.

Other clinical signs of phenothiazine tranquilization were detailed by Fujii and coworkers. These investigators reported lowering of the upper eyelids, penile protrusion, and postural sway as the most sensitive signs of chlorpromazine administration in horses, appearing after doses of 0.25 mg/kg. As they increased the dose to 0.5 mg/kg, drowsiness, dulling of responses to external stimuli, and

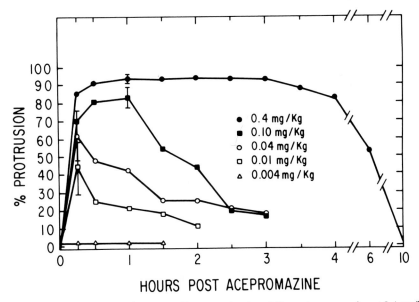

Figure 14-6. Effect of acepromazine on penile protrusion in geldings. Acepromazine at 0.4 mg/kg was administered to four geldings and the maximal length of penile protrusion measured. The symbols show the penile protrusion measured after each dose of acepromazine, expressed as a percentage of the maximal protrusion seen in each horse.

Extension of the penis in stallions is a very obvious indication of the action of the phenothiazine tranquilizers.

restlessness became apparent, and the restlessness increased when the dose was increased to 1.0 mg/kg. A decrease in tail tension never became apparent in the work of Fujii et al., and it seems reasonable to assume that essentially the same sequence of signs holds for all the phenothiazine derivatives. Drooping of the head is also one of the common signs of phenothiazine action in the horse, and at high doses sweating is commonly seen.

The increased restlessness reported by Fujii et al. is of interest, as a number of workers have reported excitement occurring in the horse after high doses of tranquilizers. Thus, Carey and Sanford report that after a few minutes of initial quiet following the injection of tranquilizers, the horse may become unsteady, sink back, and plunge forward in an uncoordinated manner. In their hands the horses may stumble, fall, and get up, and bouts of sedation may alternate with bouts of excitement. In a somewhat similar vein, MacKenzie and Snow reported a violent hyperexcitability reaction in a horse after 0.5 mg/kg of acepromazine intramuscularly (IM). This reaction was accompanied by sweating, trembling, and restlessness, which lasted about forty minutes. The cause of these reactions is not known, although both a sudden drop in blood pressure and a fear response to drug-induced muscular weakness have been suggested as probable causes. However, the work of Hall et al., who measured blood pressure during this response in a Welsh pony, suggests that a drop in blood pressure is not a likely cause of this response.

This response is of particular interest in light of a response observed in our laboratory after administering 0.4 mg/kg of acepromazine by rapid IV injection. Studying the effects of large doses of acepromazine on heart and respiratory rates, we were surprised to find a marked though transient locomotor response. This response peaked at about 60 steps/2 minutes about five minutes after the IV injection of the drug and was seen in four of five horses. Qualitatively, however, this response did not resemble the fentanyl- and apomorphine-stimulated trotting but rather suggested that the animal was falling forward and moved forward just to keep his feet under him! This response is being further investigated but was initially a most surprising response from a dopaminergic-blocking drug.

Another clear-cut central group of actions of the phenothiazine tranquilizers is that found in the hypothalamic or brain stem area. This area controls body temperature, respiratory rate, and the releasing factors for the pituitary hormones, all of which are affected to varying degrees by the phenothiazine tranquilizers.

The hypothalamic mechanism controlling body temperature is affected in such a way by the phenothiazines that the body temperature of the horse tends to approach environmental temperature. Thus, under normal conditions horses on the phenothiazines become hypothermic, but if ambient temperature is higher than body temperature, they can become hyperthermic. However, the usual pattern of response is a degree or two of hypothermia, elevating during exercise but still remaining a degree or two below the body temperature of untreated controls.

In humans and laboratory animals, high doses of the phenothiazine tranquilizers produce marked effects on the release of hypothalamic hormones. They can block FSH and LH release and thus suppress ovulation and the estrous cycle and cause infertility and pseudopregnancy. These effects, however, do not appear to be a serious problem with single doses, and tranquilizers are often used to facilitate the breeding of mares, apparently without any substantial effects on their conception rates.

As well as blocking dopaminergic receptors and thus motor responses, the phenothiazine tranquilizers also have potent blocking effects on adrenergic and cholinergic receptors. Blockade of alpha-adrenergic receptors in the vascular system leads to a rapid drop in mean arterial blood pressure, as shown in Figure 14-7. In this experiment, 0.066 mg/kg of acepromazine IV produced a drop in arterial blood pressure from 130 mm Hg to about 90 mm Hg, and a larger dose (0.1 mg/kg) has been reported to reduce mean arterial blood pressure to about 50 mm Hg. These are substantial drops in blood pressure and in the normal horse are usually associated with compensatory increases in heart rate. These hypotensive effects, however, lead to the almost absolute contraindication of phenothiazine tranquilizers in cases of shock, in which condition their action to reduce blood pressure is almost certain to exacerbate the clinical problem.

Another little-known circulatory effect of the phenothiazine tranquilizers is to reduce the hematocrit, and in our hands this has been one of the most sensitive indicators of the action of this group of drugs in the horse (Fig. 14-8). As is well known, the hematocrit in hot-blooded horses increases very rapidly in response to

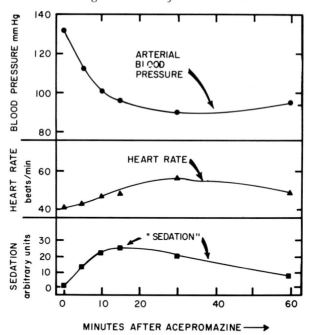

Figure 14-7. Effect of acepromazine on blood pressure, heart rate, and sedation in horses. Three horses were dosed with 0.066 mg/kg of acepromazine maleate IV. The solid circles (●—●) show the reduction in arterial blood pressure observed in these horses, while the solid triangles (▲—▲) show the corresponding increase in heart rate observed. The solid squares (■—■) show the amount of "sedation" observed in these horses, as determined by an arbitrary scoring method. Modified from Kerr et al., *Am J Vet Res*, 33:779, 1972.

excitement, apparently due to the rapid adrenalin-induced release of red blood cells sequestered in the spleen. It appears that in the presence of acepromazine the opposite occurs, and very small doses of acepromazine (0.002 mg/kg) are sufficient to produce a marked reduction in the hematocrit of treated horses and presumably also lead to an accumulation of red blood cells in the spleen.

Phenothiazine tranquilizers such as acepromazine have also been suggested to be useful in cases of mild colic, where they appear to relax the gastrointestinal tract and aid in the expulsion of flatus. The basis for this pharmacological effect is not known, but it is likely associated with the cholinergic blocking activity of this drug. In any event, acepromazine has been recommended by a number of authors for use in mild colics, although it should be kept in mind that it must be used with caution in colics that are likely to develop a component of shock.

The effects of the phenothiazines on performance are likely to be among the most subtle effects of this group of drugs, and a number of workers have investigated this aspect of their pharmacology. Thus, Fujii and his coworkers in Japan have studied the actions of chlorpromazine on Thoroughbred horses at doses of 0.25, 0.5, or 1.0 mg/kg. They found that at these doses chlorpromazine showed pronounced performance-decreasing effects, and the horse administered 1.0 mg/kg could not change his pace from a canter to a trot but continued to run at a canter. Like acepromazine, chlorpromazine increased the heart rate, and horses ran with the penis protruded. Chlorpromazine also decreased the respiratory rate, which decrease was evident immediately after exercise. Fujii and his coworkers interpreted their results to mean that medication with chlorpromazine, even at very small doses, was likely to interfere with the performance of the horse.

In Australia, Stewart investigated the effects of 0.2 mg/kg of promazine hydrochloride on gallop tests in three racehorses. At these doses the horses were clinically tranquilized, with a sleepy, lethargic appearance, lowering of the head and neck, protrusion of the penis, and slight dragging of the hind legs when walking. He reported small decreases in heart rate after injection of promazine but noted that the usual marked increase in heart rate occurred when the horses were walked onto the track prior to work.

In ten gallop tests at this dose of promazine, the speed of Stewart's horses was decreased between 0 and 15 percent, with a mean decrease of 4 percent. There was little effect of promazine on heart rate at any time throughout these tests, but respiratory rate was markedly reduced, both before galloping and immediately after the galloping test. The decrease in speed produced by promazine was statistically significant and clearly shows that promazine at these doses will interfere with racing performance. However, from the clinical signs shown by these animals, it does not appear likely that either Stewart's or Fujii's horses would have passed a pre-race examination, so the practical significance of these results is not clear.

Sanford and his coworkers carried out some rather elaborate but preliminary studies on the actions of promazine and acepromazine on speed and coordination in horses. In their trials, horses were injected IM with promazine or acepromazine and then held one hour to allow the drug to act. After this one-hour period,

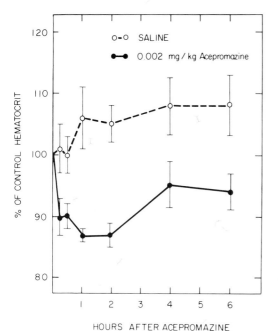

HOURS AFTER ACEPROMAZINE

Figure 14-8. Effect of acepromazine on hematocrit in horses. Four horses were dosed with 0.002 mg/kg of acepromazine at indicated zero time. This is about 1 mg of acepromazine to a 1,000 lb. horse, and is therefore about one tenth the strength of the standard 10 mg/ml acepromazine preparation. The open circles (o—o) show the hematocrits of control horses, while the solid circles (●—●) show the effects of acepromazine. This is the most sensitive pharmacological response to acepromazine in the horse yet reported, and correspondingly greater effects were observed as the dose was increased. The zero time hematocrits in these horses averaged about 32.5%.

respiratory rate, pulse rate, and rectal temperature were measured before sad-dling the horse. The horse was then ridden 1,500 meters to the paddock and taken four times at the walk and four times at the trot over six cavaletti, which process took about thirty minutes. The cavaletti were about 12 inches high and 12 feet apart, and a fault was scored if the crossbar was knocked, yielding a total possible fault score of 192. After the cavaletti (coordination) test, the physiological param-eters were again recorded and the horse circled around the paddock, twice at the trot on the right rein, twice at the trot on the left rein, and then twice at the canter the same distance on both reins. The horse was then galloped 220 meters and the physiological parameters again measured. The horse then returned the 1,500 meters to the barn, was unsaddled, and the parameters were again measured. The total distance covered by the horse in these tests amounted to about 4,620 meters.

Sanford found that in general the control values on the cavaletti test were quite resistant to changes in ground condition, weather, and other variables that horse-men might tend to blame for erratic performance. One horse, SHANE, had a mean number of errors on the cavaletti of about 11 faults, which number of faults was increased to 17 by doses of from 0.04 to 0.06 mg/kg of acepromazine and was more than doubled by 0.08 mg/kg. The canter test was found to be very insensitive to drug effects, and all the other tests were found to be approximately similarly sensitive to drugs. For one horse on the gallop, Sanford noted control times for the 200 meter gallop of about 19.5 ± 2.4 seconds, which was increased by promazine to about 22.5 seconds after 0.4 and 0.6 mg/kg, and to about 27.5 seconds after 0.8 mg/kg. While these are very interesting and suggestive results, the small number of horses used in these studies makes it difficult to draw specific conslusions from these studies.

The changes in the physiological parameters found by Sanford were in good agreement with the known pharmacology of the phenothiazines. Thus, acepro-mazine was found to reduce rectal temperature in the one horse tested by about 1 degree, and the body temperature tended to increase with exercise as in the control horse. The pulse rate was little affected after acepromazine, but the respiratory rate was markedly reduced, peaking at about 25 respirations/minute after the gallop test in control horses but at only about half of this level after treatment with acepromazine (Fig. 14-9).

In other studies, Aitken and Sanford measured heart rates in horses in an attempt to quantitate the effects of these drugs on fear and excitement. In these experiments the heart rates were recorded by radiotelemetry from unrestrained horses in box stalls. The experimenters then challenged the horse with stimuli such as presenting the horse with a whip, opening an umbrella, bursting a balloon, and sounding a horn, to which unmedicated horses responded with an increase in heart rate. The drugs studied were acepromazine, azaperone, and xylazine. Acepromazine was used at the very substantial dose of 0.2 mg/kg, while azaperone was investigated at 0.4 and 0.8 mg/kg, and xylazine at 2.0 and 3.0 mg/kg. Of seven horses screened for cardiac response in this testing system, four of the most nervous Thoroughbreds were selected for testing.

In general, Aitken and Sanford found that at the doses used, xylazine was the most effective drug, essentially completely eliminating or abolishing the cardiac

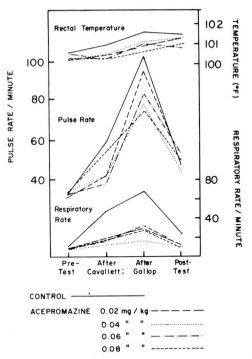

Figure 14-9. Effects of acepromazine on pulse and respiratory rates and rectal temperature in a horse during exercise tests. Reproduced with permission from Carey et al., *Br Equine Vet Assoc Bull*, 1965/1966.

response to visual stimuli and also the response to an examiner entering a box with an electric clippers. Azaperone reduced the response, but of the three drugs at the doses tested, acepromazine was clearly the least effective. Furthermore, these workers reported that xylazine was the most consistently effective drug with an absence of undesirable side effects in all horses tested.

Recent studies by Steve Ballard in my laboratory have provided the first data on blood levels of acepromazine in horses (Fig. 14-10). In these experiments, the initial blood (plasma) levels of the drug seen after dosing with about 0.3 mg/kg IV were about 100 ng/ml, which levels fell rapidly in the first 30 minutes to about 25 ng/ml. Thereafter, plasma levels of the drug fell more slowly, with an apparent half-life of about 4.5 hours, to become undetectable in plasma after about 8 hours. These data correlate reasonably well with the data available on the pharmacological effects of this drug and suggests that behavioral effects of acepromazine are associated with plasma levels of this drug of above 10 ng/ml.

Urinary clearance times have long been a problem with the phenothiazine tranquilizers and are likely to remain so for some time. To my knowledge, there are no published data on the urinary clearance times of phenothiazine tranquilizers or their metabolites using modern testing technology. Using UV analysis and colorimetric methods, Weir and Sanford studied the urinary clearance of promazine, chlorpromazine, and acepromazine about ten years ago. These studies

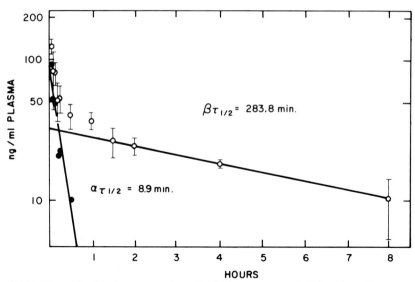

Figure 14-10. Plasma levels of acepromazine after its intravenous administration. The open circles show plasma levels of acepromazine after intravenous administration of 0.3 mg/kg to four horses. The drug has a distribution half-time of about 9 minutes and an apparent plasma half-life of about 4.5 hours.

showed that after the very large dose of 1 mg/kg of acepromazine, less than 5 per cent of the dose was recovered in the urine. Metabolites of acepromazine could no longer be detected in the urine thirty-two hours after IM injection and forty hours after oral dosing. Similarly, after a 10 mg/kg dose of promazine, about 10 per cent of the dose administered was eliminated in the urine, the bulk as glucuronide metabolites and small amounts as sulfates and unconjugated drug. After this dose of promazine, metabolites were detected in urine for up to seventy-two hours in one experiment.

After administration of chlorpromazine (2.5 mg/kg), up to 20 per cent of the dose administered was detected in the urine, and metabolites were detectable in urine for up to ninety-six hours. However, in assessing this data, one must keep in mind that the gas chromatographic analytical techniques currently in use in many jurisdictions are likely to be much more sensitive than the techniques used by Weir and Sanford and that the appearance of traces of phenothiazine tranquilizers in the urine for long periods after administration of the last dose has been reported.

In conclusion, the phenothiazine tranquilizers clearly block a wide range of central and peripheral effects in horses. Although their central effects are marked, it appears that their actions on the circulatory system and particularly on hematocrit are the most sensitive of their effects. In the male horse, penile protrusion is also a highly sensitive indicator of drug effect, and it appears to occur in the absence of measurable central nervous system depression. At higher doses, the central effects are marked, and at clinically used doses the phenothiazines substantially depress alertness and responsiveness in horses and make them easier to handle.

Horses on some tranquilizers may rouse readily and kick vigorously as an unconditioned response.

There are, however, three characteristics of the pharmacology of the phenothiazine tranquilizers that the horsemen would do well to bear in mind when they use these drugs. The first is that horses are easily aroused from their depressed or tranquilized state. This was perhaps most clearly shown by Stewart's horses, which, though clinically "tranquilized," still showed the anticipatory rise in heart rate when led on to the racetrack. The second is that tranquilizers block conditioned (learned) responses. What this means to the practicing veterinarian is that the horse will not be afraid of you when you enter the stall to work on him (a learned response), but when you tweak that sore spot you are going to work on he will arouse readily (typical of the phenothiazines) and may kick your head off (an unconditioned or innate response). The third and last point to remember is that no one has yet published good clearance data for the phenothiazine tranquilizers in urine, so when you give that tranquilizer shot to help loading, transport, or minor surgery, it is prudent to ensure that the horse is not likely to be urine tested for at least the next four days.

SELECTED REFERENCES

Aitken, M. M. and Sanford, J.: Comparative assessment in the horse. *Proc Assoc Vet Anaesthesiol,* *33:*20-28, 1972.

Bogan, J. A., MacKenzie, G., and Snow, D. H.: An evaluation of tranquilizers for use with etorphine as neuroleptanalgesic agents in the horse. *Vet Rec, 18:*471-472, 1978.

Booth, N. N.: Psychotrophic drugs in veterinary medicine. In *Principles of Psychopharmacology,* Clark, W. and Delguidice, J., Eds. New York, Academic Press, 1978, 655-687.

Carey, F. M. and Sanford, J.: Tranquilizers and equine practice. *Proc Brit Equins Vet Assoc,* 18-25, 1963.

Combie, J., Dougherty, J., Shults, T., and Tobin, T.: Quantitation and selective blockade of response to narcotic analgesics in the horse. *Proc 2nd Equine Pharmacology Symposium,* The Ohio State University, 1978, p. 188.

Courtot, D., Roux, L., Mouthon, G., and Jeanin, E.: Incidence duopage par le tranquillisants sur l'activité musculaire du cheval de sport. *Ann Rech Vet, 6:*102-116, 1975.

Fujii, S., Inada, S., Yoshida, S., Kusanagi, C., Mima, K., and Natsuno, Y.: Pharmacological studies on doping drugs for racehorses. IV. Chlorpromazine and phenobarbital. *Jpn J Vet Sci, 37:*133-139, 1975.

Gabel, A. A., Hamlin, R., and Smith, C. R.: Effects of promazine and chloral hydrate on the cardiovascular system of the horse. *Am J Vet Res, 25:*1151, 1964.

Goodman, L. S. and Gilman, A.: *The Pharmacological Basis of Therapeutics,* 5th ed. New York, Macmillan, 1975.

Hall, L. W.: The effect of chlorpromazine on the cardiovascular system of the conscious horse. *Vet Rec, 72:*85, 1960.

Klavano, P. A.: The pharmacology of the tranquilizers used in equine practice. *Proc AAEP, 21:*145-147, 1975.

Kerr, D. D., Jones, E. W., Holbert, D., and Huggins, K.: Comparison of the effects of xylazine and acetylpromazine maleate in the horse. *Am J Vet Res, 33:*777-784, 1972.

Limont, A. G.: Clinical observations on the use of promazine hydrochloride in horse practice. *Vet Rec, 73:*691-692, 1961.

MacKenzie, G. and Snow, D. H.: An evaluation of chemical restraining agents in the horse. *Vet Rec, 101:*30-33, 1977.

MacLeod-Carey, F. and Sanford, J.: A method for assessing the effects of drugs on performance in the horse. *Br Equine Vet Assoc Bull,* 1-10, 1965-1966.

Muir, W. W. and Hamlin, R. L.: Effects of acetylpromazine on ventilatory variables in the horse. *Am J Vet Res, 36:*1439, 1975.

Raker, C. W. and English, B.: Promazine — its pharmacological and classical effects in horses. *J Am Vet Med Assoc, 134:*19-23, 1959.

Soma, L. R.: Tranquilizers. *Proc Symp Equine Pharmacology and Therap,* The Ohio State University and AAEP, 1969, 29-31.

Stewart, G. A.: Drugs, performance and response to exercise in the race horse. II. Observations on amphetamine, promazine and thiamine. *Aust Vet J, 48:*544-547, 1972.

Tobin, T. and Woods, W. E.: Pharmacology review: Actions of central stimulant drugs in the horse. *J Equine Med Surg, 2:*60-66, 1979.

Weir, J. J. R. and Sanford, J.: Urinary excretion of phenothiazine tranquilizers by the horse. *Equine Vet J, 4:*88-93, 1972.

Chapter 15

CALMING HORSES FOR LONGER PERIODS: RESERPINE, THE MINOR "TRANQUILIZERS," AND SOME OTHER DEPRESSANTS

V ERY OFTEN HORSEMEN need a tranquilizer that will "take the edge" off a horse for longer periods of time than those for which the relatively short-acting phenothiazine tranquilizers are useful. Such circumstances might include naturally hyperexcitable horses, which are hard to catch and handle, horses that do not adjust to strange circumstances such as starting gates well, or horses that are in the process of developing disruptive habits. In all of these circumstances a relatively long acting tranquilizer that can assist in training or produce a substantial modification in behavior without harming the horse can be very helpful.

Under such circumstances, where a subtle but long-lasting effect is required, one of the oldest tranquilizers known to man, reserpine, is likely to be useful. The drug has a plasma half-life of about eleven days in man, and its pharmacological effects can last about as long after a single dose in the horse. It also has the further advantage that it is a remarkably potent drug in the horse, since doses of 5 mg or less to a horse will produce these effects.

Reserpine is another plant drug, being the principal alkaloid of a climbing shrub of the Apocynaceae family, *Rauwolfia serpentina,* which is indigenous to India and neighboring countries. It was described in ancient Hindu writings and medieval Western medicine as the "insanity herb" and was widely used in traditional Indian medicine for treatment of high blood pressure, insomnia, and insanity. These uses of the reserpine plant went unnoticed by modern Western medicine until 1931, when two Indian doctors, Sen and Bose, described its use for the treatment of psychoses ("madness") and high blood pressure in the Indian medical literature. This report attracted attention to *Rauwolfia,* and pure reserpine was isolated from the crude plant material in 1952. When reintroduced in this form, reserpine was the first of the modern major "tranquilizers" and in the 1950s and early 1960s was widely used in the treatment of mental illness and hypertension. It soon became apparent, however, that its use was associated with a small incidence of severe side effects. Thus, parkinsonism, severe depression, suicide, and epileptic seizures have been related to its use in humans and reserpine is currently recommended for use primarily in patients with high blood pressure resistant to other forms of therapy. In equines, however, reserpine has enjoyed a wide use as a tranquilizer, because of its efficacy and long duration of action after a single dose, its remarkable absence of side effects when used at low doses, and, until recently, its difficulty of detection.

Reserpine is a remarkably potent drug in the horse, and very small doses (<5 mg) can produce considerable biochemical and behavioral effects. Reserpine is active in such low doses and is so difficult to detect that it was first thought to be a

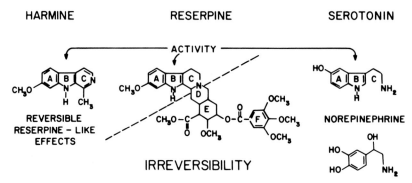

Figure 15-1. Structure of reserpine and related neurohormones. The A, B, and C rings of the reserpine molecule are structurally related to the neurohormones norepinephrine and serotonin, whose storage in nerve terminals reserpine blocks. Harmine, which is structurally similar to the A, B, and C rings of reserpine, produces the same pharmacological effects of reserpine, but its action is very short-lived. It therefore appears that the prolonged action of reserpine is associated with its D, E, and F rings. Reproduced with permission from Tobin, *J Equine Med Surg*, 2:434, 1978.

"hit-and-run" drug, i.e. a drug that when administered produced a biochemical change that persisted for days after the drug was eliminated from the body. This concept is now known to be incorrect, and the current thinking of most pharmacologists is that reserpine is very tightly bound at specific sites in the body and remains bound at these sites for at these sites for at least as long as it produces its pharmacological effects and possibly for much longer (Fig. 15-1).

Like all highly potent drugs, reserpine has a very specific mechanism of action. Reserpine produces its tranquilizing effects by acting on the storage granules for the neurohormones norepinephrine and serotonin in the brain. Reserpine acts by destroying the brain's storage capacity for these neurotransmitters, and if brain tissue from a reserpine-treated animal is analyzed for these neurohormones, they are found to be greatly depleted. Only about twenty reserpine molecules are needed to bind to each storage granule to destroy it, and the horse apparently does not return to normal until these granules are regenerated (Fig. 15-2).

The clinical signs seen after a large dose of reserpine are quite dramatic. After a 10 mg dose (a large dose) little change is seen for the first two hours, after which period the first signs of reserpinization appear. These signs usually consist of sweating over the shoulders, back, stifle, and between the legs, which effects are quite clear-cut by three hours after dosing. Soon the horse begins to pass increased amounts of gas, and then diarrhea commences. The feces become soft, liquid, and cowlike and remain like this for from two to three days. Within the first few hours, drooping of the upper eyelid appears and remains apparent for the duration of most of the clinical signs, being one of the most sensitive signs of reserpinization. If the horse is male, penile extension starts at about five hours post-dosing; it is maximal for this particular dose at about twelve hours, and the penis may be almost completely retracted by twenty-four hours postdosing. At about four hours after dosing, the animal has a glazed appearance and by eight hours may be standing relatively immobile and apparently depressed. If the animal is particularly sensitive to reserpine (and there are suggestions that males are more sensitive to reserpine than females), it may show signs of acute colic and go down for a period. More commonly, however, the animal simply appears depressed and may appear so for up to forty-eight hours. By sixty to seventy-two hours postdosing, however, an animal dosed with 10 mg of reserpine will appear clinically normal and may be difficult for an observer not familiar with the horse to distinguish from an untreated animal.

In our hands, lower doses of reserpine produced correspondingly less marked pharmacological effects. A dose of 5 mg IV produced droopy eyelids at three hours with passage of gas and some diarrhea at about eight hours. A dose of 0.5 mg to a horse produced little observable change beyond the passage of some very loose stool at about ten hours. At these low doses (0.5 to 1 mg) the animals were indistinguishable from untreated horses within twenty-four hours. These dose-response relationships agree well with the dose-response relationships reported in the horse by the first workers who studied reserpine in the horse in the early 1950s.

In other experiments in our laboratory, we studied the effects of dosing with reserpine on spontaneous locomotor activity in horses. Despite the substantial clinical signs of the action of reserpine in these horses, it took very large doses of reserpine to depress locomotor activity in our horses. As shown in Figure 15-3, doses of 12 mg/horse, about as large a dose of reserpine as we could routinely give to our horses, produced a depression of locomotor activity for only about three days, in good agreement with the reported duration of clinical signs after such a dose of reserpine. Further, another horse, which we had dosed with reserpine and then challenged with fentanyl, we found to be fully responsive to fentanyl, trotting as though it were untranquilized (Fig. 15-4). Locomotor responses, then, do not appear to be particularly susceptible to inhibition by reserpine, and reserpine does

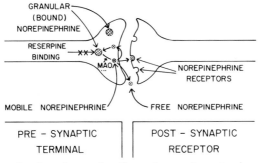

Figure 15-2. Mechanism of action of reserpine. Reserpine produces its pharmacological actions by interfering with the metabolism of the neurohormones norepinephrine and serotonin. Norepinephrine (or serotonin) is stored tightly bound in storage granules in the presynaptic terminal. Reserpine binds to these granules, disrupts them, and thus displaces these neurotransmitters from the neurons and produces the resulting tranquilization. Elimination of the reserpine from the storage granules must occur before the reserpine-induced tranquilization wears off. Reproduced with permission from Tobin, *J Equine Med Surg*, 2:434, 1978.

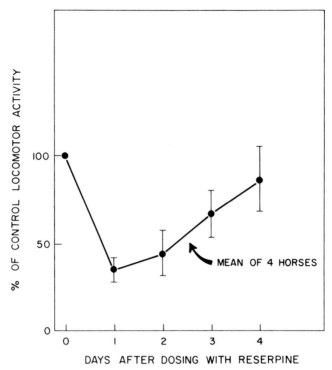

Figure 15-3. Effect of reserpine on spontaneous activity in the horse. The solid circles (●—●) show the decline in spontaneous motor activity of four horses with 12 mg/1000 lb. of reserpine IV. Locomotor activity was determined by counting all steps by the left front foot of these horses over a thirty-minute period and expressing the total as a percentage of that observed in two thirty-minute periods predrug. Despite the large dose of reserpine administered, the horses were apparently clinically normal, and their locomotor activity had returned to normal by the fourth day after dosing.

not act to block locomotor responses to fentanyl in anything like the clear-cut way that can be easily demonstrated with the phenothiazine tranquilizers.

Although the overt clinical signs of reserpinization are almost always over within two to three days, horsemen, trainers, and veterinarians who are familiar with the uses of reserpine in horses have long known that its subtle effects last for much longer than this. It was not, however, possible to measure these effects until very recently, when we applied the operant conditioning or "feeder" apparatus described in Chapter 10 to the study of reserpine. In these experiments, we dosed horses with 5 mg of reserpine intravenously at 9 PM in the evening and then tested them in the operant conditioning apparatus at 10 AM the following morning and on each of the following mornings until their rate of light beam breaking (responding) returned to pre-reserpine levels.

As shown in Figure 15-5, the effects of reserpine when tested in the operant or "feeder" apparatus showed some variation between the horses tested, but the effect was, in each case, remarkably prolonged. In the most sensitive horse the effects took about five days to reach maximum, at which point the animal's responding rate was about 60 percent inhibited, and it took more than than ten days for this horse to return to control. While none of the other horses tested were as sensitive to reserpine as this particular horse, all showed the same slow onset of action of the pharmacological effect and a duration of action that varied from about six to ten days in each horse (Fig. 15-5).

Apart from the prolonged duration of action of reserpine, the time course of these effects is also unusual. While the clinical signs of reserpinization peak within the first day or so and are over within three days, the subtle effects of reserpine on the CNS develop slowly, peak at between two and five days, and then decline. This apparent dissociation between the central effects of reserpine and its clinical signs was quite unexpected, and it is a unique aspect of the pharmacology of this drug in the horse.

These subtle behavioral effects are apparently similar to the effects that horsemen report. In our hands, no overt signs of reserpinization in these horses were seen after the third day, in good agreement with reports by other clinicians. However, these subtle and prolonged behavioral effects are also in very good agreement with what is known of the "persistence" or slow "clearance" of reserpine in most species. Reserpine, for example, has an approximately eleven-day half-life in man, which is a very long half-life for a drug, and there is no reason to think that the half-life is substantially different in the horse. For example, reporting on a simple thin-layer test for the reserpine in horses, investigators at the Ohio State University have reported detection of reserpine in equine plasma samples for 144 hours after a dose of only 2 mg of reserpine, a dose that these workers

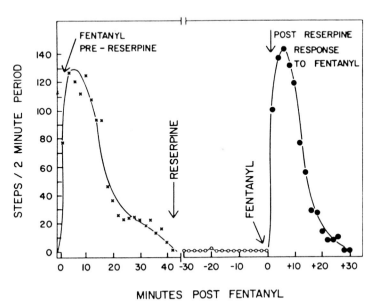

Figure 15-4. Lack of effect of reserpine on fentanyl-induced trotting in horses. The solid squares (■—■) show the locomotor response of a horse after rapid IV administration of 8 mg of fentanyl. The horse was then treated with 10 mg of reserpine IV and three hours later challenged with another 8 mg dose of fentanyl. The solid circles (●—●) show the response to fentanyl after pretreatment with reserpine and suggest no diminution of the fentanyl response by treatment with reserpine. Reproduced with permission from Tobin, *J Equine Med Surg, 2:*435, 1978.

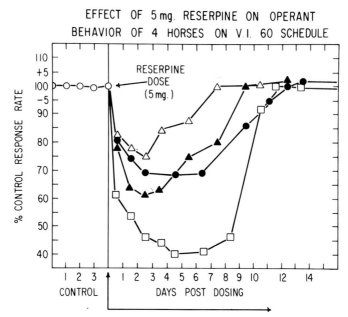

Figure 15-5. Inhibition by reserpine of variable interval responding in horses. The open circles (o—o) show operant behavior, normalized as 100% for four horses for five days prior to dosing. The open squares (■), solid circles(●), and open (Δ) and solid (▲) triangles show the inhibition of operant behavior (tranquilization) in these horses after a single dose of 5 mg per horse of reserpine IV on indicated day zero. Reproduced with permission from Shults et al., *Am J Vet Res, 42:*1981.

reported produced no clinical signs of reserpinization. While there are unexplained differences between the colors reported for reserpine in these tests and those reported by other workers, a prolonged half-life for reserpine is certainly consistent with what is known about the pharmacology of reserpine in the horse and other species.

As well as interfering with the metabolism of norepinephrine in the brain, reserpine treatment also interferes with its metabolism in the cardiovascular system and in the gastrointestinal tract. In the cardiovascular system, reserpine lowers blood pressure and causes slowing of the heart rate, which actions lead to its use in the treatment of high blood pressure in humans. In the gastrointestinal tract, the reduction in the content of norepinephrine leads to increased activity and diarrhea. If the dose of reserpine is large enough, the horse will show signs of colic and may go down. Although early reports suggest that as little as 5 mg of this drug can produce violent colic in a horse, we have routinely used doses of 10 mg and higher in our studies with no problems. The recommended antidote to reserpine is methamphetamine, which makes good pharmacological sense, as methamphetamine mimics the action of norepinephrine, the substance depleted by reserpine.

For a long time there was no useful analytical test for reserpine, and because of this it was reportedly used in racing and show horses to "take the edge" off them. One of the problems with the use of reserpine in this way, and indeed for any clinical use of this drug, is individual variation in the response of horses to it and therefore the difficulty in predicting how a horse will respond to it. Nevertheless, one interesting aspect of reserpine's pharmacology is its very long period of action. Thus, if small doses of reserpine are given daily, or indeed at intervals of several days, its pharmacological effects will tend to accumulate and one can gradually approach a useful level of tranquilization for the particular animal and problem involved. At any point during this slowly increasing effect, the effect may be maintained simply by increasing the interval between doses. If dosing is abruptly stopped, the drug effect will decay at its maximum rate, the same as that observed after an acute intravenous dose of the drug.

At the time of this writing, the only tests available for reserpine are plasma tests, with no tests adaptable to urine testing being reported. A further item of interest that should be borne in mind by this testing for reserpine is the fact that this drug is a plant product. Plants growing in the southeastern United States that have been reported to contain reserpine include the periwinkles, members of the genus *Vinca*, such as *Vinca herbacea* and *Vinca rosea*. In addition, there are about ten to twelve species of the Apocynaceae growing in the southeastern United States, but knowledge concerning the reserpine content of these plants is limited. In view of the possibility of "positives" in equine plasma from reserpine or related alkaloids of botanical origin, particular care should be taken by analysts when testing for reserpine in equine plasma.

The Minor Tranquilizers: Librium® and Valium®

Clearly distinct from the phenothiazine tranquilizers and reserpine, we have another important group of "tranquilizers," the so-called minor tranquilizers, represented by Librium® and Valium®. Librium®, or chlordiazepoxide, was the first member of this group synthesized, and it was found to have very interesting muscle-relaxing and taming properties in animals. Its clear-cut "taming effects" in monkeys soon led to its clinical trial in humans and to the discovery of its potent "antianxiety" effects. While the antianxiety effects of these drugs are extremely difficult to characterize and quantitate in either experimental animals or humans, the widespread acceptance and use of these drugs in human medicine speaks for their efficacy in this area.

Like the pharmacological effects of reserpine, the effects of Librium® and Valium® (diazepam) on horses can be clearly distinguished from those of the phenothiazines by the responses of treated horses to fentanyl. In some of our experiments with diazepam on horses we administered about 50 mg of Valium® to horses and then tested their response to fentanyl. After we administered this dose of diazepam by intravenous injection, the horses showed substantial signs of CNS depression. For example, the legs of one particular horse became shaky immediately after injection, and he sank toward the floor and, with his head down, appeared to be sniffing at the floor, with muscle tremors and labored breathing. For the next ten to fifteen minutes the horse remained extremely unsteady while walking and tended to stagger, although he looked relatively normal when standing still.

Despite these substantial early signs of CNS depression, a depressed respiratory rate, and an apparent interference with motor activity, these acute effects passed

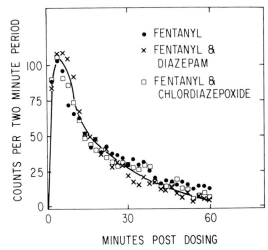

Figure 15-6. Lack of effect of Valium® and Librium® on fentanyl-induced trotting in horses. Horses were dosed with 0.1 mg/kg (250 mg/1000 lb.) of diazepam (Valium®) or 0.2 mg/kg (200 mg/1000 lb.) of chlordiazepoxide (Librium®) and then challenged with about 8 mg of fentanyl. The solid circles show the trotting response to fentanyl, while the crosses (×) show the response in the presence of Librium® and the open squares (□) the response in the presence of Valium®. Valium® did not affect the trotting response to fentanyl, while a small but statistically significant inhibition was seen after Librium®.

and the horses were well coordinated within thirty minutes after the intravenous injection of Valium®. At this point we challenged these horses with the usual 8 mg dose of fentanyl, expecting the trotting response to fentanyl to be markedly inhibited. However, as shown in Figure 15-6, this dose of diazepam had no inhibitory effects whatsoever on the locomotor response to fentanyl, and neither did an approximately equivalent dose of chlordiazepoxide. The experiment shows clearly that the pharmacological action of this group of drugs is quite distinct from that of the phenothiazine tranquilizers, which very effectively block the trotting response to fentanyl.

The precise mechanism of action of the Valium® group of drugs is still unknown. Recently, Braestrup and Squires in Denmark have demonstrated the existence in nerve cell membranes of specific receptors for members of the Valium® type group of drugs. While it was at one time thought that these drugs acted by interfering with the inhibitory neurotransmitter GABA,* this does not now appear to be the case, and the Danish workers believe that an unknown neurotransmitter must be involved in the action of this group of drugs. What this means, of course, is that, as with the endogenous opiates, there may exist in man and horses a neurohormone that is intimately involved in what can only be called "anxiety" and whose actions are blocked by the Valium® group of drugs.

In man, the time course of action of the benzodiazepines is remarkably long, Valium® having a plasma half-life of from two to three days. It is not clear how long the half-life of the drug in the horse is. Ray and his coworkers at the Ohio State University have detected Valium® in equine plasma for twenty-four hours after a single IV dose of 40 mg/horse, and at the end of this period it did not appear to have reached the metabolic phase or terminal elimination phase. No unchanged Valium® was found in the urine of these horses. After hydrolysis of the urine sample to release glucuronide metabolites, however, three Valium®

---

* γ-aminobutyric acid

metabolites were found. According to Ray, Valium® metabolites could be found in horse urine for forty-eight hours following administration of the Valium®, and from what is known of its pharmacokinetics in the horse and other species, it appears likely that this is a conservative estimate for the "clearance times" of Valium® in horses.

The pharmacology of the Valium® group of tranquilizers is characterized by a number of clear-cut and distinct pharmacological effects. At the lowest doses used they are potent antianxiety agents, which action appears in animals as a taming effect. At higher doses, drugs of this group are powerfully anti-convulsant, and drugs of this group are the treatment of choice for "status epilepticus" or continuous seizure in humans and other animals. As the dose of the drug is further increased, these agents become sedative and muscle relaxant. Their sedative action appears as a reduction in reactivity and a tendency to sleep, and these actions are potentiated by other central nervous system depressants. These drugs do not have marked analgesic effects at any doses. While these actions of the benzodiazepines are well characterized in man and other animals, information on their expression in the horse is limited.

An unusual clinical use for Valium® that highlights its antiepileptic action occurred when a horse was admitted to a local veterinary clinic with a history of repeated bouts of colic. Careful clinical examination revealed no obvious cause of the colic, and the horse responded poorly to conservative medical treatment. Since the colics continued, an exploratory laparotomy was carried out and again no cause for the recurrent colic found. After recovery from surgery, the intermittent colics continued and were apparently more severe after medication with acepromazine, a phenothiazine tranquilizer.

There occurs in humans a rare form of epilepsy in which the clinical signs and symptoms of the epileptic attacks are severe abdominal pain. Although the pain is central in origin and responds to antiepileptic medication, it is usually perceived by both patient and physician as occurring in the abdomen. Such patients may undergo a number of exploratory laparotomies before the pain is found to respond to antiepileptic medication and the diagnosis of abdominal epilepsy made.

Because of the similarity between this case and the typical human case of abdominal epilepsy, it was considered that this might be an equine case of abdominal epilepsy, and therapy with Valium® was recommended. The dose of Valium® selected to commence therapy was 100 mg every second day, later reduced to 50 mg every second day. Once therapy with Valium® was started, the colic episodes ceased. Thereafter, the horse was returned to his home farm, where he was maintained on Valium® every two days for an extended period, after which the underlying condition apparently spontaneously resolved.

This case also highlights an important difference between the benzodiazepine minor tranquilizers and acepromazine, which is their actions on epileptic patients. While Librium® and Valium® are strongly antiepileptic and Valium® is one of the drugs of choice in treating epileptic conditions, the phenothiazine tranquilizers will precipitate epileptic incidents in predisposed patients and should not be used in patients with symptoms of epilepsy.

In studies on the action of benzodiazepines on exercised horses, Courtot administered diazepam IM at a dose of 0.1 mg/kg twenty-five minutes prior to exercising his horses. He considered that this time period was necessary for the tranquilizer to produce its effect. Courtot was able to detect diazepam in plasma at between 10 and 30 ng/ml at sixty-five minutes later but was not able to detect diazepam in plasma at ninety minutes after injection. He found that diazepam depressed respiratory rate in his horses, although the effect appeared small. He also found an increase in CPK levels in serum samples from these horses, although whether or not the increases were clinically significant is not clear. Unfortunately, Courtot did not report whether or not diazepam treatment had any effect on the performance of his horses.

In summary, the benzodiazepines or minor tranquilizers are a group of drugs about which little is currently known in the horse. They appear to have a relatively long plasma half-life in the horse, and it appears likely that their pharmacological effects persist for longer than those of the phenothiazine tranquilizers. They are relatively easy to detect in plasma and urine, and clearance times of at least forty-eight hours should be allowed after their use. A very interesting use for these drugs in equine medicine relates to their antiepileptic activity, and the antiepileptic activity of the benzodiazepines might well be kept in mind by practitioners dealing with obscure central nervous system syndromes in the horse.

Xylazine

It is clear from the description of the actions of the phenothiazine tranquilizers, reserpine, and Valium® that their effects can be quite subtle and that the treated horse may still retain considerable offensive and locomotor ability. What the horseman or veterinarian often needs, however, is a drug that will reduce a horse to a "dummy" that will just stand there and allow itself to be manipulated. This requirement is more nearly filled by a drug called xylazine (Rompun®), alone or in combination with other drugs, than any other drug on the market today, and this drug is now widely used in equine medicine.

Xylazine hydrochloride (Rompun®) was first synthesized in 1967 in Germany and introduced into equine practice in Europe. It soon became enormously popular for the control or chemical restraint of large animals and was introduced into the American market. Xylazine is now approved for use in the horse in the United States and Canada and is widely used for what is called "chemical restraint" in equine practice.

When xylazine is given intravenously or intramuscularly in a horse, the animal is rapidly sedated and muscle tone drops dramatically. The horse willingly stands in one place with a drowsy attitude, lowers his head and neck, his lower lip hangs loose, and he rests a hind leg. The extreme relaxation of the neck muscles and lowering of the head allows blood to pool in the nasal mucosa, and hypostatic congestion may occur. In the male, prolapse of the penis may occur, but according to McCashin, the prolapse is less marked than with promazine. The animal is unconcerned about events in his environment and may be so relaxed that he has difficulty in standing and walking. It has been suggested that because of this relaxation, animals should not be kept on a smooth surface because in their relaxed condition they may lose their footing easily.

BEST TRANQUILIZER IN THE WHOLE WORLD. TURNS THE HORSE INTO A REAL DUMMY.

What the veterinarian usually needs is a tranquilizer that will reduce a horse to a dummy.

A particular advantage of xylazine is that its onset of action is very rapid and its time course of action short, which makes it particularly useful for the practitioner who wants to perform a brief, minor surgical interference. When the drug was given intravenously at about 1 mg/kg, the average time to onset of action was about two minutes, with the peak effect occurring at about 7.5 minutes. The sedative effect was also short lived, being about 50 percent gone after thirty-four minutes. On the other hand, if the drug was given intramuscularly, the time to onset of action was a little less than five minutes, with peak drug effect at about fifteen minutes after intramuscular administration. The average time until 50 percent of the drug effect had worn off was fifty minutes. McCashin preferred the intravenous route where possible because the onset of action was so much faster. These workers also noted that even by the intramuscular route the onset of action of xylazine was as rapid as that of promazine intravenously. These observations all suggest very rapid absorption and distribution of xylazine, and in good agreement with this it has been reported that two thirds of an intramuscular dose is absorbed from the injection site within ten minutes. After intravenous injection of xylazine, blood levels of the drug fall rapidly at first and then more slowly, with an apparent plasma half-life of about forty-five minutes, to "clear" plasma in about four hours. Unchanged xylazine is also easily detected in urine for a period after dosing, although no estimated clearance times for this drug in urine are yet available.

When used clinically in the context of "chemical restraint," xylazine seems markedly superior to the phenothiazine tranquilizers. Its rapid onset and short duration of action make it very useful for the practitioner seeking useful control of an animal for a short period. Because of the marked relaxation of the neck muscles, it is ideal for use with an endoscope, the horse often resting his head on the observer's shoulder. If painful manipulations are required, however, further precautions are required. Local anesthesia is still required for anything other than very minor surgery, and a number of people use xylazine in combination with other drugs such as methadone.

The basic mechanism of action of xylazine is unclear. Although it is reputed to have a number of pharmacological characteristics in common with morphine, it certainly does not produce effects like morphine or any of the narcotic analgesics that we have tested in the horse. Whereas in our hands narcotic analgesics consistently and markedly stimulate locomotor activity in the horse, xylazine, given by intravenous injection, rapidly and dramatically depresses a horse. No one who had ever witnessed the rapid, clear-cut, and diametrically opposed actions of these two drugs on the horse would be impressed with suggestions that xylazine produces its depressant effects in the horse by mimicking the action of morphine.

In one rather dramatic experiment in our laboratory we administered a sedating dose of xylazine to a horse and followed it with a full locomotor-stimulating dose of fentanyl. The rationale behind this approach was that if xylazine was indeed a partial agonist at the narcotic receptor, it would block the action of fentanyl, in much the same way as we have seen earlier with Talwin® and Stadol®. What happened in this experiment, however, was that the horse went down in a heap and appeared quite distressed. Rapid administration of a narcotic antagonist blocked the fentanyl effect and left just the xylazine effect. The experiment did not suggest any "morphinelike" actions of xylazine to us but rather highlighted one of the principal actions of xylazine in the horse, which is to dramatically reduce his muscle tone. In other studies using electroencephalographic techniques on cats, xylazine has been shown to produce brain wave patterns similar to those of sleep, but from which the animal is readily aroused. The muscle relaxation appears to be due to a "suppression of interneuronal transmission of impulse," but xylazine does not block neuromuscular junctions.

Although xylazine is often reported to have analgesic effects in the horse, whether or not it actually possesses these properties is unclear. Studying the response to pinpricking in the horse, Kerr reported that he considered quantitation of analgesia in the horse difficult. However, he believed that "analgesia" due to xylazine in the horse, which he apparently estimated from a reduced response to pinpricks, was directly related to the degree of sedation. In laboratory animals, some of the early work suggests that the analgesic action of xylazine is comparable to that of morphine or pethidine. Other workers, however, consider that the evidence for analgesic actions of xylazine is small, and some practitioners have elected to combine xylazine with morphine (xylazine 1.1 mg/kg IV, followed IV by morphine, 0.6 mg/kg). As a practical matter, however, horses treated with xylazine indicate less disturbance when manipulated in painful ways than horses on tranquilizers such as promazine and acepromazine, and it matters little to the practitioner whether the effect is due to suppression of the perception of pain or simply that the animal is physically unable to respond.

One proposed mechanism of action of xylazine is that it produces its analgesic actions by blocking central adrenergic receptors. In a detailed study of this mechanism of action of xylazine, Schmitt and his coworkers showed clearly that the analgesic actions of xylazine are more readily demonstrated in some types of analgesic tests than in others. They concluded that xylazine may act by blocking central adrenergic receptors, which are broadly similar to the peripheral receptors, but are still structurally distinct from these receptors. Other actions of xylazine that are consistent with its pattern of action on adrenergic receptors are a marked hyperglycemia produced by this drug and an increased urinary output, possibly due to an increased output of glucose in the urine.

Outside of its effects on the central nervous system, xylazine has marked effects on the cardiovascular system, especially if it is given by rapid intravenous injection. It appears that xylazine has a direct effect to rapidly constrict blood vessels, which leads to sharply increased blood pressure. Instead of actually increasing heart rate, however, the carotid body — vagal reflex acts to depress heart rate, from about 45 beats/minute in control horses to just above 30 beats/minute in treated horses (Fig. 15-7). This depression of heart rate is mediated via the vagus and can be blocked by premedication with atropine.

Because of this increased vagal activity, xylazine sedation is typically associated

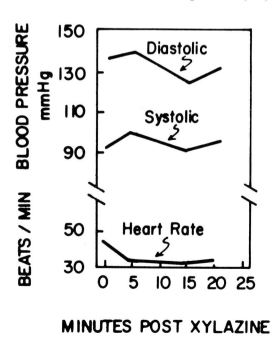

Figure 15-7. Effect of intravnous xylazine on heart rate and blood pressure in the horse. After intravenous injection of 1 mg/kg of xylazine, blood pressure showed a small rise, but heart rate dropped rapidly and significantly within five minutes after injection of the drug. Reproduced with permission from McCashin et al., *Am J Vet Res,* 36:1423, 1975.

with an increased incidence of cardiac arrythmias. Normal horses, particularly young horses in good condition, can have a rate of dropped (missed) heart beats of as high as 16 percent. Of twelve horses in a series of experiments with xylazine, five developed disturbances of cardiac rhythm within minutes of intravenous xylazine. It appears very likely that these rhythm disturbances were due to increased blood pressure depressing the heart rate. The incidence of these arrythmias can be greatly reduced by pretreatment of the horses with atropine. Alternately, since they are transient and of little consequence, they may simply be ignored.

Following intravenous xylazine, a fall in respiratory rate to as low as 50 percent of the pretreatment rate may accompany the onset of sedation. The reduction in respiratory rate is associated with an increase in the depth of breathing. No significant changes in blood oxygen or carbon dioxide levels were noted, indicating that the drug had minimal overall effect on the respiratory rate.

Traditionally, xylazine has been regarded as a drug that makes a horse safe about the head and neck but not a drug to take risks with behind a horse. Xylazine has also been used in colics, and here it is again reported as an effective "sedative analgesic," although whether all it does is simply suppress the signs of colic pain is not clear. While its short duration of action is not helpful in cases of colic, its ability to maintain blood pressure may be useful. A further use for xylazine that has been suggested is in capture guns, because of its very rapid action after intramuscular injection.

Glyceryl-Guaiacolate (G.G.E.)

Glyceryl-guaiacolate is a guaiacol derivative which has been used as an expectorant (aid to coughing) in human and veterinary medicine for over 100 years. It has for a long time been a popular constituent in cough medicines, and the familiar smell of many old cough remedies was due largely to their glyceryl-guaiacolate content.

When administered to the horse in large doses intravenously, glyceryl-guaiacolate can produce profound muscle relaxation and central nervous system depression. However, the anesthesia and analgesia produced are minimal. Glyceryl-guaiacolate is usually classified as a restraining drug, and it is most commonly used in association with other drugs, such as xylazine. When used in combination with xylazine, the onset of anesthesia takes about three minutes, and the anesthesia lasts slightly longer (22 minutes) than that due to xylazine and ketamine. The principal disadvantage with G.G.E. as a sedative and anesthetic is that it must be given in very large volumes and is therefore cumbersome to prepare and administer.

A glyceryl-guaiacolate is also a component of many proprietary "wind" medicines, and some trainers routinely dose their horses with these "wind" preparations pre-race. Glyceryl-guaiacolate is apparently included in these "wind" preparations for its expectorant actions, but recent work suggests that the expectorant effects of glyceryl-guaiacolate at the usually administered doses are not likely to be significant. Thus, although glyceryl-guaiacolate has turned up in post-race urines and trainers have been disciplined on the basis of such findings, there is no evidence to suggest that this agent is likely to affect the performance of racing horses.

The Dissociative Anesthetics: Phencyclidine and Ketamine

Phencyclidine was the first of the dissociative anesthetics and was synthesized by Parke-Davis and Company in the late 1950s. Early human trials showed that the drug produced an unresponsive state when administered intravenously, even though the subjects seemed to be awake, with open eyes and a blank stare. The patient, however, does not respond to painful stimuli and on recovery has no memory of the events, thus meeting the minimal requirements for an anesthetic agent. These agents are called dissociative anesthetics because their basic action appears to be to dissociate the patient's awareness or consciousness from his body and in this way produce anesthesia. When used in small doses in humans they cause a state of excitement or mild agitation, and since these drugs are also potent analgesics, the patient does not respond to painful stimuli.

The principal problem with this group of drugs in the human is that they produce a state of postanesthetic confusion, including agitation, excitement, disorientation, and hallucinatory phenomena. For these reasons these drugs are not often used as anesthetics in adult humans, although some members of this group may sometimes be used in children, and ketamine, another member of this group, is approved for use in the cat and primates.

Currently, in equine medicine, ketamine is primarily used in combination with xylazine to produce brief episodes of general anesthesia. When used together these agents give a fast, quiet induction, a short period of anesthesia with good analgesia and a fast, quiet recovery. This combination of properties make this drug combination very useful in equine medicine.

When used alone in horses, ketamine can produce excitement, hyperthermia, and incoordination. Similarly, studies in the dog have shown that ketamine alone stimulates the metabolic rate in the brain, increasing cerebral blood flow and oxygen tension. In this regard it is of interest that phencyclidine, under its street name of "angel dust" has reportedly been used as a stimulant medication in horses in the Southwest. How effective agents of this group might be remains unclear, but at adequate doses they certainly may be expected to produce at least impressive signs of central nervous system stimulation in horses.

SELECTED REFERENCES

Alpers, H. S. and Shore, P. A.: Specific binding of reserpine association with norepinephrine depletion. *Biochem Pharmacol, 18:*1362-1363, 1969.

Ashworth, B.: Antidote for reserpine. *Vet Rec, 100:*458, 1977.

Braestrup, C. and Squires, R. F.: Brain specific benzodiazepine receptors. *Brit J Psychiatry, 133:*249-260, 1978.

Brodie, B. B. and Beaven, M. A.: Neurochemical transducer systems. *Medna Exp, 8:*320-351, 1963.

Burgi, H.: Changes in the fiber system and viscosity of the sputum of bronchitis during treatment with bromhexine and guaiphenisen (guaiacol glyceryl ether). *Scand J Respir Dis [Suppl], 90:*81-85, 1974.

Butera, T. S., Moore, J. N., Garner, H. E., Amend, J. F., Clarke, L. L., and Hatfield, D. G.: Diazepam/xylazine/ketamine combination for short term anesthesia in the horse. *VMSAC, 73:*490-499, 1978.

Clarke, E. G. C. and Clarke, M. L.: *Garner's Veterinary Toxicology,* 3rd ed. Baltimore, Williams & Wilkins, 1967.

Cooper, J. R., Bloom, F. E., and Roth, R. H.: *The Biochemical Basis of Neuropharmacology,* 3rd ed. New York, Oxford U Pr, 1978.

Costa, E., Gessa, G. L., Hirsch, C., Kuntzmann, R., and Brodie, B. B.: On the current status of serotonin as a brain neurohormone and in action of reserpine-like drugs. *Ann NY Acad Sci, 96:*118-131, 1962.

Courtot, D., Mouthan, G., Roux, L., and Jeanin, E.: Incidence du dopage par les tranquillisants sur l'activité musculaire du cheval de sport. *Ann Rech Vet, 6:*117-129, 1975.

Davis, L. E., and Wolff, W. A.: Pharmacokinetics and metabolism of glyceryl guaiacolate in ponies. *Am J Vet Res, 31:*469-473, 1970.

DaPrade, M. and Pletscher, A.: Isolated 5-hydroxytryptamine organelles of rabbit blood platelets: Physiological properties and drug induced changes. *Br J Pharmacol, 34:*591-597, 1968.

Ellis, R. G., Lowe, J. E., Schwark, W. S., and Taylor, J. I.: Intravenously administered xylazine and ketamine HCl for anesthesia in horses. *J Equine Med Surg, 1:*259-265, 1977.

Funk, K. A.: Glyceryl guaiacolate: A centrally acting muscle relaxant. *Equine Vet J, 2:*173-178, 1970.

Funk, K. A.: Glyceryl guaiacolate: Some effects and indications in horses. *Equine Vet J, 5:* 15-19, 1973.

Kerr, D. D., Jones, E. W., Holbert, D., and Huggins, K.: Comparison of the effects of xylazine and acetylpromazine maleate in the horse. *Am J Vet Res, 33:*777-784, 1972.

Kerr, D. D., Jones, E. W., Huggins, K., and Edwards, W. C.: Sedative for horses and cattle. *Vet Rec, 85:*512-516, 1969.

Maas, A. R., Jenkins, B., Shen, Y., and Tannebaum, P.: Studies on the absorption excretion and metabolism of [^{3}H] reserpine in man. *Clin Pharmacol Ther 10:*366-371, 1969.

McCashin, F. B. and Gabel, A. A.: Further evaluation of xylazine as a sedative and pre-anaesthetic agent in horses. *Am J Vet Res, 36:*1421-1429, 1975.

Morgan, J. P. and Solomon, J. L.: Phencyclidine: Clinical pharmacology and toxicity. *NY State Med, 78:*2035-2038, 1978.

Pletscher, A., Shore, P. A., and Brodie, B. B.: Serotonin release as a possible mechanism of reserpine action. *Science, 122:*375-376, 1955.

Ray, R. S., Sams, R. A., and Huffman, R.: Detection, identification and quantitation of reserpine and diazepam. In *Proceedings of 2nd Equine Pharmacology Symposium,* J. T. Powers and T. E. Powers, Eds. Columbus, OH, 1978, pp. 209-215.

Roberts, W. D., Rosborough, J. P., Garner, N. E., and Tillotson, P. T.: Glyceryl-guaiacolate (panel). *Proc AAEP,* 297-307, 1968.

Schmitt, H., LeDouarec, J. C., and Petillot, N.: Antagonism of the antinoceptive action of xylazine, a gamma sympathomimetic agent, by adrenoceptor and cholinoceptor blocking agents. *Neuropharmacology, 13:*295-303, 1974.

Schwartz, B. F.: *Pulmonary and Vascular Effects of Glyceryl Guaiacolate in the Absence of Detectable Secretory Changes.* Ph.D. Thesis, Department of Pharmacology, University of Kentucky, Lexington, 1973.

Sen, G. and Bose, K. C.: Rauwolfia serpentina, a new Indian drug for insanity and high blood pressure. *Indian-Med World, 2:*194, 1931.

Slotkin, T. A.: Reserpine. In Simpson, L. L. and Curtis, D. R. (Eds.): *Neuropoisons: Their Pathophysiological Actions,* Vol 2. New York, Plenum Pr, 1974.

Stahl, S. and Meltzer, H. Y.: A kinetic and pharmacologic analysis of 5-hydroxytryptamine transport by human platelets and platelet storage granules: Comparison with central serotonergic neurons. *J Pharmacol Exp Ther, 205:*118-132, 1978.

Stahl, S.: The human platelet: A diagnostic and research tool for the study of biogenic amines in psychiatric and neurologic disorders. *Arch Gen Psychiat, 34:*509-516, 1977.

Stein, Bruce, Laessig, Ronald H., and Indriksons, Andris: An evaluation of drug testing procedures used by forensic laboratories and the qualifications of their analysts. *Wis Law Rev, 3:*727-789, 1973.

Stevens, M. E., Roman, A. K., Sourkes, T. S., and Boyd, E. M.: On the expectorant action of creosote and the guaiacols. *Can Med Assoc J, 48:*124-127, 1943.

Tobin, T.: Narcotic analgesics and the opiate receptors in the horse. *J Equine Med Surg, 2:*397-399, 1978.

Tripp, S. L., Williams, E., Wagner, W. E., and Lukas, G.: A specific assay for subnanogram concentrations of reserpine in human plasma. *Life Sci, 16:*1167-1178, 1975.

White, C. G., Woods, W. E., and Tobin, T.: The pharmacology of reserpine in the horse. I. Effects of reserpine and imipramine on platelet uptake of serotonin in vitro. *J Equine Med Surg, 3:*325-330, 1979.

White, C. G., Woods, W. E., and Tobin, T.: The pharmacology of reserpine in the horse. II. Biochemical and behavioral effects of reserpine. *J Equine Med Surg, 3:*446-451, 1979.

Chapter 16

LOCAL ANESTHESIA: FREEZING, NUMBING, NERVING, OR BLOCKING SPECIFIC AREAS

THE APPROACH TO PAIN represented by phenylbutazone and the other non-steroidal anti-inflammatory agents is to treat the whole animal with a drug to control a source of pain that may, under some circumstances, often be localized in a specific joint, tendon, or muscle. An alternative approach to a localized problem, however, is to "block" the nerve, joint, or portion of a limb with a local anesthetic. Because a small amount of local anesthetic can be injected directly into a nerve or joint (Fig. 16-1), the area affected by the drug can be quite localized. If the veterinarian has correctly pinpointed the source of pain and the area to inject, the horse will "go sound" after the injection, the local anesthetic blocks of this type are widely used in the diagnosis of lameness in veterinary practice.

A local anesthetic block that will allow a horse to "run sound" in a diagnostic test will also allow a horse to run sound in a race. For example, if a horse has a sore foot, such as may be caused by navicular disease, the posterior digital nerve can be blocked and the animal will run and race sound for the duration of the block. There are, however, two problems with this type of block. The first is that a good laboratory can readily detect most of the classical local anesthetics, and the second is that the duration of action of most local anesthetics is short, not lasting for longer than a couple of hours at most. This can be a problem if the lameness involved is chronic and long lasting, as the blocks have to be repeated each time that the horse performs.

As well as injecting the local anesthetic into a nerve, a veterinarian may inject any other structure that gives rise to pain. Thus a sore joint, a joint with chip fractures, or even a slab fracture of the carpus may be injected, and the animal will run sound. Similarly, painful tendons, tendon sheaths, bursae, and so forth may all be injected with local anesthetics, and the horse will run sound and perform at his best for the period during which the area is "blocked."

While the blockade produced by a local anesthetic is always relatively short lived, a much more prolonged local blockade can be obtained by injecting alcohol into the area of a nerve. When injected in this way absolute alcohol causes substantial nerve damage, which lasts for months, and the nerve fibers only slowly regenerate. Thus, the injection of alcohol (or quinine or urea) into the area of a nerve will produce a long-term "block" in the area supplied by the injected nerve and will allow that animal to run sound while the block lasts. Because alcohol is rapidly eliminated within hours and in any event is rarely searched for in drug detection programs, the possibility of detecting a properly performed alcohol block in a drug screening program is minimal. These semipermanent alcohol- and phenol-induced nerve blocks have a long tradition of use in human medicine, being for a long time the principal therapy available for facial neuralgia, a spontaneous, recurring, and very painful condition of the fifth facial nerve.

261

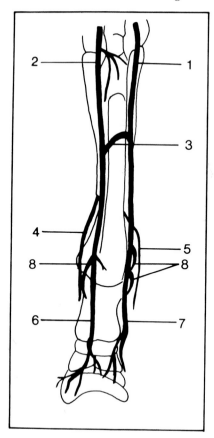

Figure 16-1. The nerve supply to the forelimb of a horse. This illustration shows the distal part of a left foreleg of a horse, viewed from behind. The nerves represented by the solid black lines are (1) medial palmar nerve, (2) lateral palmar nerve, (3) communicating branch, (4) lateral palmar metacarpal nerve, (5) medial palmar metacarpal nerve, (6) lateral palmar digital nerve, (7) medial palmar digital nerve, and (8) dorsal branches. Modified from Derksen (1980).

Another form of blockade very similar to an alcohol block is cryosurgery. In cryosurgery, a disc of metal cooled with liquid nitrogen to about $-196°C$ is placed on the skin over the nerve for a short period. The skin and nerve are frozen by this maneuver, and again a temporary nerve block is obtained. As with the alcohol block, the nerve recovers slowly over a period of weeks and sensation gradually returns to the area. The damage to the skin, however, shows up as a spot of white hair, which remains white for the life of the animal, and horses that have been "nerved" in this way may be recognized by grey spots over the site of the block.

A more complicated but much older method of blocking a nerve permanently is by neurectomy or "nerving." In this operation, the surgeon opens the skin and dissects down to the nerve. Then he cuts a segment of about an inch out of the nerve, carefully ties off and sutures the cut ends of the nerve, and closes the skin incision. Done correctly, this operation permanently interrupts the nerve supply to an area and desensitizes it. Two common neurectomy operations are the so-called low neurectomy, which desensitizes the heel area, and the high neurectomy, which desensitizes a larger area of the foot (Fig. 16-2).

In the United States most racing jurisdictions appear to permit low neurectomy, sometimes loosely called a heel nerve neurectomy. This relieves pain coming from the heel area or any area to the rear of the foot. It is not permitted in New York to run a horse whose nerves have been severed at or above the sesamoid bones or the level of the ankle. It is relatively easy to tell whether or not a horse has been nerved, as both the skin scar and the cut end of the nerve can easily be felt by careful examination of the leg. Many excellent horses have been low nerved early in their career and have gone on to be very successful, both on the track and in stud. Nerving at a level higher than the sesamoids, however, is not permissible, as such animals lose sensation in a much larger portion of their foot and are thought to be more susceptible to breakdown.

One of the simplest ways of all to "numb" a joint or a limb is to "ice" it. To "ice" a limb it is placed in water containing ice cubes for a period of about two hours, until the limb is numb. The numbing "holds" for about thirty minutes after the horse comes out of the ice bucket and, under some circumstances, can help a horse run up to his potential. This method is very commonly used in racing in North America, although such procedures are considerably less acceptable in Europe.

Once any of these blocks has been induced and the blocked portion of the limb

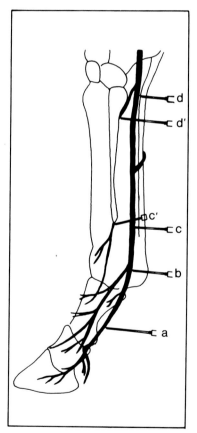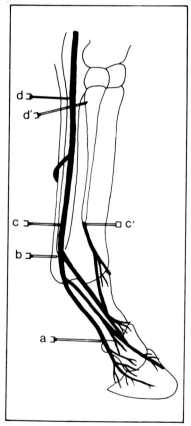

Figure 16-2. Nerves of the forelegs of the horse and the location of nerve blocks. The solid lines show the nerve supply to the foreleg of the horse from the lateral view (left) and medial view (right). The "a" indicates the point of low digital or heel block, "b" the point of base sesamoid block, "c" and "c¹" the point of block desensitizing the metacarpophalangeal region, and "d" and "d¹" the points of a block partially desensitizing the metacarpal region. Modified from Derksen (1980).

The simplest way of all to "numb" a joint or limb is to "ice" it.

is no longer painful, the horse will run sound for as long as the block lasts. Blocks induced in this way are quite humane, in that the horse feels no pain while he is performing and, indeed, would not put in a good performance unless the pain was adequately controlled. One of the principal arguments against these types of blocks, however, is that by enabling a horse to perform on a damaged limb, the probability of injury to the limb, joint, or so forth may be increased, which means that blockade induced performances could be detrimental to the horse's future health. An equally important argument is that the risk of breakdown in such horses may be increased, with the possibility of serious injury and death to both horse and jockey. A further argument against the use of local anesthetic blocks is that large concentrations of some of these drugs are stimulant to the CNS and will produce excitement in horses given in large enough doses.

Blockades by "icing" or low digital or "heel" neurectomy are permitted in many jurisdictions. The principal problem with nerving or blocking an area is not that the pain from the area is eliminated (which may be a problem) but what is called proprioception from the area is also blocked. The word proprioception is used to describe all the non-pain sensations from, for example, a limb, which informs the brain as to the position of a limb, the pressures on it, the tension in its muscles and tendons, and so forth. This feedback of information from a limb is blocked out by most of the nerving, numbing, or blocking methods described, and therefore an animal running on a "blocked" limb is deprived of this important information. If the blockade is extensive, it is considered that the lack of proprioceptive feedback increases the probability of the animal making a misstep and thus the likelihood of a breakdown, although, needless to say, no good scientific evidence is available on this problem.

Given these circumstances, the reason that "low" or "heel" or posterior digital nerving is acceptable is that the localized area of the lesion makes it unlikely that breakdown or serious injury will occur. Because the area supplied by the posterior digital nerve is small, being restricted primarily to the heel area, the interference with proprioception from the limb is negligible. If the "nerving" is done properly, it is essentially irreversible, and the horse's form is consistent and cannot be manipulated at will to affect the outcome of the race. Whether or not the horse has been nerved may easily be determined by palpating for the surgery scar and feeling for the missing portion of the nerve. The extent of the area affected by the nerving can be estimated from the position of the nerving or directly tested for by pricking the skin of the foot. For these reasons, therefore, "low" neurectomies have been acceptable in many performance horses for a long time, although there is little difference in principle between a nerved horse and a horse with a heel problem treated with phenylbutazone. In practical terms, however, the major difference is that with a low digital neurectomy the extent of the desensitization is precise and irreversible, while with phenylbutazone neither the location of the lesion, its extent, or the quality of the drug effect is precisely known.

"Icing" a limb is accepted because icing produces only minimal desensitization of the limb. The principal effect of "icing" is to delay or impede the inflammatory process, so the process of icing is in many ways similar to the action of the anti-inflammatory drugs. Secondly, the action of "icing" an area interferes with, but is not likely to block completely, nerve conduction from an area. Therefore, the loss of sensation and proprioception is at best only partial in this process, in contrast with the complete loss of sensation and proprioception that follows nerving or local anesthetic block. The third factor with "icing" is that its effects on nerve conduction will begin to reverse rapidly when the limb is removed from the ice and the horse begins to warm up for the race. Under these circumstances, blood flow to the limb increases, the temperature of the tissues rises, and nerve conduction rapidly returns toward normal. The inflammatory process, however, takes a longer period to return to normal than nerve conduction, so "iced" horses are, in effect, running primarily on an anti-inflammatory effect of the icing and not on limbs that are in any significant way "blocked."

When a veterinarian wants to produce a local anesthetic nerve block, the first thing he has to do is determine the location of the lesion he wishes to block. Having done this he then considers the nerve supply to the area and selects a suitable point on the nerve supply to the area as close as possible to the lesion at which to perform his block. Because the nerve supply below the knee and hock in the horse is readily accessible and can easily be palpated under the skin, he will usually have little trouble in accurately depositing a small volume of local anesthetic right beside the nerve. Since local anesthetics are highly lipid-soluble drugs, they diffuse rapidly into the nerve and produce a local blockade of nerve transmission.

The mechanism of action of the local anesthetic is simplicity itself. It turns out that the electrical activity of a nerve consists of a very rapid exchange of charged particles of sodium and potassium between the inside and outside of the nerve. These charges flow through very narrow channels in the cell membrane, and if the cell membranes swell, these channels are blocked and with them the electrical activity of the nerve. What a local anesthetic does is simply insert into the cell membrane in much the same way as water soaks into wood, causing the membrane to swell, producing blockade of the small channels in the membrane and thus blocking the electrical activity of the cell (Fig. 16-3).

Because the local anesthetics act on both sensory and motor nerves, both sensation and the ability to use muscles in an anesthetized area are lost. For the horse, however, which is almost all bone and tendon below the knee, the loss of motor function associated with most local anesthetic blocks in the lower part of the foot is minimal.

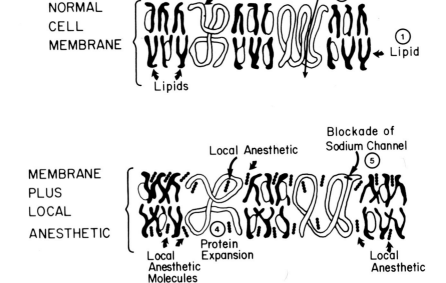

Figure 16-3. Mechanism of action of local anesthetics. The upper panel shows a normal cell membrane with its constituent lipid (1) and protein (2) molecules. One of the protein molecules contains a sodium channel (3), which is required for propagation of the nerve impulse. When a local anesthetic is added to this system, it leads to an expansion of the membrane. This expansion occurs most readily in the protein section (4) and leads to blockade of the sodium channel (5). Blockade of the sodium channel leads to nerve block and thus to local anesthesia of the area supplied by the nerve. Modified from Seeman (1974).

As pointed out earlier, all the clinically useful local anesthetics are very lipid soluble, which enables them to diffuse into the nerve, cause it to swell, and block it. However, they do not stop diffusing when they hit the nerve but diffuse right on past it, for diffusion is a characteristic of these drugs. What happens, therefore, is that immediately after a local anesthetic is injected around a nerve, there is a high local concentration of anesthetic and a rapid and effective nerve block. As the local anesthetic diffuses away from the nerve, however, the intensity of the block declines, and usually within about two to four hours the block has dissipated and sensation in the nerve returns to normal. In some preparations of local anesthetics a little adrenaline (1 part in 200,000) is included to constrict the local blood vessels and thus prolong the action of the local anesthetic for a period. One of the characteristics of a good local anesthetic is that it does little or no permanent damage to the nerve, and essentially full function of the nerve is recovered.

In contrast with the reversible action of the local anesthetic, the action of an alcohol nerve block is to kill the nerve cells and more or less permanently block an area. High concentrations of alcohol, urea, or phenol are directly toxic to nerve cells and will kill them within a short period. Then, when the alcohol or phenol has been removed, nerve function is lost until regeneration of the nerve trunk occurs. Regeneration of the nerve will take a period of weeks and may never be complete. A nerve block produced in this way, then, is a long-term block, and recovery of sensation in the area depends primarily on regrowth of the nerve.

Injection of a local anesthetic into the vicinity of a nerve is also known as a "nerve block." Depending on the site chosen for the injection, the area blocked by the nerve may be small and localized, or it may be considerably larger. A common nerve block used in horses is the posterior digital nerve block, which blocks out the heel area in the foot only. This is the block that is used in the diagnosis of navicular disease. Higher up the leg the volar nerves may be blocked at the level of the sesamoids for a low volar nerve block, or about four inches below the knee for a high superficial volar nerve block. Both of these blocks anesthetize large portions of the foot, but to completely anesthetize the foot, five individual nerves have to be anesthetized. A simpler way of blocking the leg below a certain level, however, is to inject a "ring" of local anesthetic into the skin and nerves around the leg, which maneuver is rather logically known as a "ring block."

As well as being used to block nerves, local anesthetics may be injected directly into joint spaces, tendon sheaths, bursal sacs, and other areas. Injected in this way they act to directly anesthetize the inflamed surfaces and allow a horse to run sound. Although the fiction persists in racing circles that drugs injected into joints remain localized, are not absorbed into the bloodstream, and do not appear in the urine, this is usually not the case. Local anesthetics of the commonly used clinical types are all well absorbed after injection at any site, and they distribute throughout the body and appear in the urine almost as readily as if they had been injected subcutaneously or intravenously. The experiment of Figure 16-4 shows some data from our laboratory in which procaine hydrochloride, a typical local anesthetic, was injected into the knee joints of horses. While the blood levels of procaine after the injection of these small quantities of local anesthetic were quite low, easily detectable levels of drug were found in the urine for a period of up to thirty hours

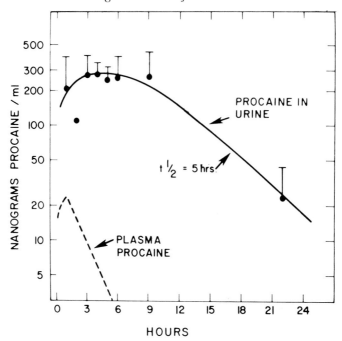

Figure 16-4. Blood and urine levels of procaine after intra-articular injection of procaine hydrochloride. The dotted line (-----) shows the plasma levels of procaine after intra-articular injection of 8 ml of procaine hydrochloride as Novocaine®. The solid circles (●—●) show urinary concentrations of procaine after this same dose. The data show that substantial levels of procaine are detectable in urine after intra-articular injection of procaine. Reproduced with permission from Tobin et al., *J Equine Med Surg, 1*:91, 1977.

after dosing. The data clearly shows that local anesthetics are well absorbed after intra-articular injection and can give rise to good urinary levels of the drug.

In veterinary practice, local anesthetics are often used to "block" an area for minor surgery. For example, to probe and suture a skin wound, to suture a mare, or to fire a horse, a veterinarian will usually infiltrate a local anesthetic into the tissues, which allows these maneuvers to be performed. However, if the area of surgery is extensive, substantial quantities of local anesthetic may be injected. After such injection of local anesthetics, procaine may turn up in the urine for long periods. Thus, after about 4 gm of procaine hydrochloride were injected intramuscularly, it took three days for procaine to clear from the urine in our experiments. The experiments suggest that after large doses of procaine hydrochloride have been used for infiltration anesthesia, at least three to four days should be allowed for procaine to clear from equine urine (Fig. 16-5).

Another problem with local anesthetics, and one of the reasons that their use in performance horses is banned, is that they can, under some circumstances, cause marked excitement in horses. This phenomenon is very well known in humans and was first reported in horses by Jones. It further turns out that horses are particularly susceptible to the central stimulant effects of local anesthetics, for reasons that are not at all clear.

While it is paradoxical that a drug that can produce a block of nerve function locally should produce stimulation of the brain, this is indeed what happens. The usual explanation for this is that the local anesthetics act by inhibiting inhibitory mechanisms in the brain, although why inhibitory pathways should be blocked but not stimulatory pathways is not at all clear. In any event, whatever its basis, the ability of local anesthetics to produce stimulation of the central nervous system in both horses and man is well characterized and is one of the reasons given for the essentially absolute ban on these drugs in racing.

In our hands, the first signs of central nervous system excitation seen with procaine were deep blowing expirations, which occurred even when the blood levels of procaine were relatively low. If the blood levels of procaine rose higher than this, signs of pacing and excitation were seen. If the horses were restrained, the pacing took the form of rapid shifting from leg to leg and occasional pawing with the forefeet. In unrestrained horses, pacing took the form of either to-and-fro weaving movements or circling. Pacing and circling were reasonably well coordinated in some animals but poorly coordinated to the point of staggering in others. As the blood levels of the drug were increased, all the horses showed hypersensitivity to stimuli and fine muscle twitching along their backs and haunches. As pointed out earlier, Thoroughbred horses are particularly suscepti-

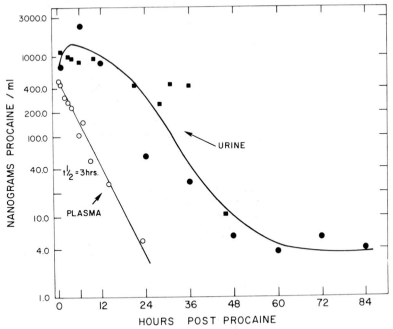

Figure 16-5. "Clearance" of procaine from plasma and urine after intramuscular injection of procaine hydrochloride. The open circles (o—o) show plasma levels of procaine after the intramuscular administration of 10 mg/kg of procaine HCl. The solid circles (●—●) and solid squares (■—■) show urinary concentrations of procaine in two separate experiments. All urinary data points are the means of experiments on at least three (●) and five (■) horses, respectively. Reproduced with permission from Tobin et al., *J Equine Med Surg*, 1:191, 1977.

ble to the central stimulating effects of procaine, being about twenty times more sensitive to these effects than are humans (Fig. 16-6).

While the central nervous system stimulating characteristics of procaine can be a problem for owners and racing authorities, by far the most important problem with procaine in performance horses is its use in procaine penicillin. As discussed earlier, penicillin is pumped directly from the blood into the urine in the kidney tubules and is therefore very rapidly excreted by the horse. One way around this problem is to inject a large amount of penicillin into a muscle and arrange that the penicillin is only slowly released from the muscle. The reason for the procaine in procaine penicillin is to insure that the penicillin is only slowly released and absorbed from its intramuscular injection site.

Injection of the penicillin as procaine penicillin insures that the penicillin is released slowly because procaine penicillin is a very poorly water-soluble salt. Thus, after injection into the muscle, the procaine penicillin slowly dissolves in the

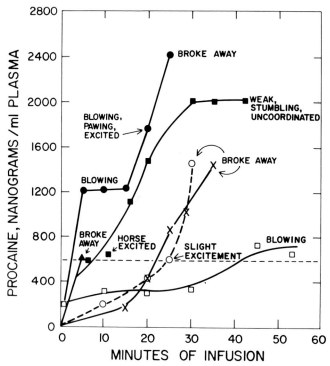

Figure 16-6. Blood levels of procaine and signs of central nervous system excitation in the horse. In this experiment, horses were infused with procaine HCl, their behavior watched, and blood samples drawn approximately every five minutes when the behavior of the horse permitted it. No signs of central nervous system excitation were seen until blood levels of the drug reached about 600 ng/ml, at which time "blowing" expirations were noted. When blood levels of procaine reached 1000 ng/ml, or 1μg/ml, the horse was quite excited, showing pacing, circling if he was free, fine muscle tremors, and hypersensitivity to sound. The animal may also be quite poorly coordinated and easily stumble. If the blood level of the drug was further increased, the animal became uncontrollable and usually broke away from the infusion apparatus. Reproduced with permission from Tobin et al., *Am J Vet Res,* *38*:641, 1977.

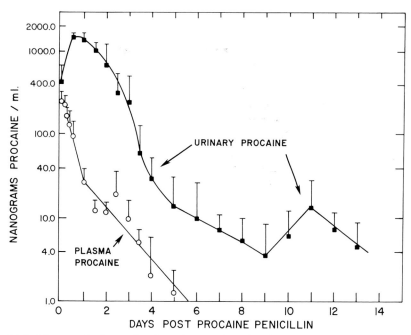

Figure 16-7. "clearance" of procaine from horse urine after intramuscular injection of procaine penicillin. The open circles (o—o) show plasma concentrations of procaine after the intramuscular administration of 33,000 I.U./kg of procaine penicillin to Thoroughbred horses. The solid squares (■—■) show urinary concentrations of procaine in these experiments. All data points are means ± SEM of experiments on four different horses. Reproduced with permission from Tobin et al., *J Equine Med Surg, 1*:191, 1977.

muscle fluids and is released into the circulation. Once dissolved, the procaine and the penicillin go their own separate ways in the body. However, because the dissolving process takes a long time, the procaine and penicillin trickle out from the injection site and into the blood and urine over quite long periods.

Just how long these periods can be is shown in Figure 16-7. Here, horses were dosed with about 15 million units of penicillin, a dose at the high end of the range of the "normal" clinical doses of procaine penicillin. We then followed both plasma and urinary levels of procaine for as long as we could detect them with a gas chromatographic detection method commonly used for procaine. It turned out that procaine was detectable in plasma for five days postdosing and in urine for thirteen days postdosing. It is this ability of procaine to turn up in equine urine for the better part of two weeks after a dose of procaine penicillin that leads to procaine being the drug that has been the most commonly called "positive" since racing began.

To further complicate the picture, procaine is a classic example of a drug whose concentration in urine depends almost entirely on whether the horse's urine is acidic or basic. As detailed in Appendix B, a single plasma level of procaine can theoretically give rise to a 9,000-fold different range of urinary procaine concentrations, depending on whether the urine is acidic or basic. Because of this vast possible range in urinary procaine concentrations, it is not possible to deduce from a urinary procaine concentration when,* in what form,† or in what way‡ the procaine was administered, notwithstanding the fact that one will often hear testimony to the contrary in disciplinary proceedings. I have, on occasion, reviewed proceedings in which it was claimed that there is only a 25 percent variation in the urinary concentrations of procaine between various horses, an absolutely incredible statement to anyone who has the vaguest knowledge of experimental biology, let alone racehorse urines.

This problem of the persistence of procaine from procaine penicillin in horse urine has been a serious problem for racing chemistry for a long period, and a number of approaches to the problem have been suggested. At one point the hypothesis was put forward that the procaine and penicillin molecules circulated in the body as a pair of molecules bound together and could be detected and identified as such. Unfortunately, careful experimentation in our laboratory revealed no evidence whatsoever in support of this rather unlikely hypothesis, and this particular approach to the problem appears to have come to naught.

The only possible approach that I am aware of is to determine the plasma half-life of the procaine. If the procaine is slowly cleared from plasma, with a half-life of greater than eight hours, the chances are that the horse has been treated with procaine penicillin. On the other hand, if the procaine has a short plasma half-life, on the order of about two hours, the chances are that the procaine was administered as procaine hydrochloride. While not a particularly practical solution, this is apparently the only basis for distinction between these two forms of procaine that can be offered at this time.

Procaine has always been a relatively easy drug to detect in horse urine because of its chemical structure. It reacts well to give a bright red color in a simple color test, which is very useful for screening. In addition, it is easily labeled with marker chemicals for gas chromatographic detection and thus can be picked up in very low concentrations in blood or urine. For a long time other local anesthetics such as Carbocaine® (mepivacaine), which do not react in these tests, were not readily detectable. However, with the development of a new gas chromatographic detector called the nitrogen detector, it became possible to pick up Carbocaine® in quite low concentrations in equine urine. The result of this was that the introduction of nitrogen detectors into our laboratory in Kentucky was associated with the sudden appearance of a number of Carbocaine® positives before it became clear that Carbocaine® would no longer "go through" the laboratory tests. However, after the first few incidents of detection, the use of Carbocaine® apparently stopped and few Carbocaine® positives have appeared since then.

In contrast with the ease of detection of procaine in urine, procaine was for the longest time difficult to detect in blood. The reason for this is that procaine is very rapidly metabolized in blood, being split by enzymes in the blood into two major fragments, as shown in Figure 16-8. As a result, if one drew a blood sample of procaine and did not have an enzyme poison in the sample, the procaine in the

---

* Within a period of days.
† Procaine or procaine penicillin.
‡ Intra-articularly, intramuscularly, or as a nerve block.

sample was very rapidly broken down. As a matter of fact, procaine in a horse is metabolized more slowly than procaine in a blood sample, as most of the procaine in a horse will locate in fatty tissue, where it is protected against the blood enzymes. Until this problem was understood, no one had identified procaine in horse blood, but with the addition of enzyme poisons to blood samples, procaine is relatively easy to detect in blood.

While procaine has been widely used as a local anesthetic, the ease with which it is hydrolyzed by blood enzymes (Fig. 16-8) has to some extent limited its usefulness. Its usual duration of action is only about an hour, and it has the further disadvantage that it penetrates mucous membranes poorly, so it is not good for topical anesthesia. Further, according to Adams, procaine is not useful for intra-articular injection, since it does not produce an effective joint block.

Cocaine was the first of the local anesthetics to be discovered and was introduced into medicine as a local anesthetic by a student of Sigmund Freud. While cocaine has the advantage that it is absorbed well after topical application to mucous membranes, it is considered too toxic to be injected into tissues and has a considerable abuse potential. These problems led to the synthesis of a synthetic analogue, procaine, and since then many other local anesthetics have been introduced into medical practice.

Lidocaine (Xylocaine®) is a more recently introduced local anesthetic, which has the advantage of giving good topical anesthesia and a longer action than procaine.

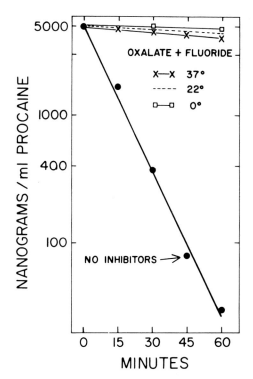

Figure 16-8. Hydrolysis of procaine by equine plasma and the effects of enzyme inhibitors. The solid circles (●—●) show the rate of hydrolysis of procaine added to freshly drawn equine plasma at 37°, while the rates of hydrolysis of procaine in blood drawn into tubes containing potassium oxalate and sodium fluoride and incubated at 0°, 22°, and 37° are shown by the squares (□—□), dotted line (-----), and crosses (×—×), respectively. Reproduced with permission from Tobin et al., *Am J Vet Res, 38*:643, 1977.

It is also reported in humans to produce sedation along with the local anesthetic effect, although whether or not it produces these effects in horses is not clear. Mepivacaine (Carbocaine®) is another local anesthetic with a slightly longer duration of action than lidocaine, but which is also more expensive.

Benzocaine is a chemical relative of procaine, which differs from it primarily in being very poorly water soluble. Benzocaine is, therefore, not used systemically, but it may be applied topically either as a dust to abraded areas or in oily preparations commonly called freezes in the horse world. As it is slowly absorbed, it gives rise to local surface anesthesia, and its slow absorption leads to a long duration of action. It is cleared in the urine and after topical application to abraded areas can give rise to benzocaine "positives" in urine, which some racing authorities have chosen to call.

In summary, a variety of maneuvers may be used to produce a local blockade of pain in performance horses. One of the oldest and a well-accepted method under some circumstances is simply to cut the nerves to an area. If this is done only for the heel area (low digital neurectomy) it is often considered an acceptable procedure. Neurectomy higher up is not approved for use in performance horses because a larger area is desensitized and the risk of breakdown of the horse is thought to be increased. If performed properly, neurectomy permanently desensitizes the area supplied by the cut nerves. A temporarily equivalent effect to neurectomy is produced by freezing (cryosurgery) the area of the nerve that would be cut in a neurectomy. The effect of freezing, however, is reversible, and at least partial recovery of sensation is apparent after a few weeks. Another method of producing a slowly reversible blockade of a limb is to inject the nerve supply to the area with a substance such as absolute alcohol or quinine. These injections severely damage the nerve and numb the area, which then only slowly recovers. Blockade by this method may not be readily detectable.

Transient blockade of a limb, joint, tendon sheath, or bursa may be provided by injecting a local anesthetic or by cooling the area. Cooling, usually by placing the limb in ice water for a period, produces a partial local block that lasts for about thirty minutes or so and also has anti-inflammatory effects. This method is traditional in equine circles in North America, is well accepted by the various authorities involved, and does not involve the use of drugs.

Blockade by local anesthetics, such as procaine, may, under some circumstances, be an effective though transient method of making a sore horse sound. However, the amounts of local anesthetics used can give rise to quite high urinary levels of drugs, which may be readily detected in urine. Blockade in this way is, in principle, therefore, relatively easy to control. Blockade in this way is always considered illegal because it is thought that it increases the risk of injury to horse and rider in competitive events. The clearance times for procaine vary, depending on the dose of the drug used and the form in which it is administered. After injection of a small amount of this drug for a local block, at least thirty hours should be allowed for the urine to clear. After a large dose, such as might be used for infiltration anesthesia, four days are required. After a large dose of procaine penicillin, up to two weeks may be required. While clearance times for other local anesthetics are not available, it appears unlikely that they are cleared more rapidly than procaine, and the same clearance times as are used for procaine hydrochloride should be considered.

The final forensic problem in the local anesthetics concerns the role of procaine penicillin. Procaine penicillin is a long-acting penicillin compound, which unfortunately releases the procaine just as slowly as the penicillin. After procaine penicillin, procaine may be found in equine urine for up to two weeks, and the actual amounts of procaine in the urine vary considerably, depending on whether the urine is acidic or basic. It is not possible, therefore, to tell from a single urinary level of procaine in what form, by what route, or when the procaine was administered to a horse.

SELECTED REFERENCES

Adams, O. R.: *Lameness in Horses*, 3rd ed. Philadelphia, Lea and Febiger, 1974.

Derksen, F. J.: Diagnostic anesthesia of the equine front limb. *Equine Pract, 2:*41-47, 1980.

Evans, J. A. and Lambert, M. B. T.: Estimation of procaine in urine of horses. *Vet Rec, 95:*316-318, 1974.

Jones, L. M.: Miscellaneous observations on the clinical effects of injecting solutions and suspensions of procaine hydrochloride into domestic animals. *Vet Med, 46:*435-437, 1951.

Seeman, P.: The actions of nervous system drugs on cell membranes. *Hosp Prac, 9:*93-101, 1974.

Tobin, T.: Pharmacology review: A review of the pharmacology of procaine in the horse. *J Equine Med Surg, 2:*209-214, 1978.

Tobin, T. and Blake, J. W.: A review of the pharmacology, pharmacokinetics and behavioral effects of procaine in the Thoroughbred horse. *Br J Sports Med, 10:*109-116, 1976.

Tobin, T. and Blake, J. W.: The pharmacology of procaine in the horse. Relationships between plasma and urinary levels of procaine. *J Equine Med Surg, 1:*188-194, 1977.

Tobin, T., Blake, J. W., Sturma, L., Arnett, S., and Truelove, J.: The pharmacology of procaine in the horse: Pharmacokinetics and behavioral effects. *Am J Vet Res, 38:*637-647, 1977.

Tobin, T., Blake, J. W., Tai, C. Y., and Arnett, S.: The pharmacology of procaine in the horse. II. The procaine esterase activity of equine plasma and synovial fluid. *Am J Vet Res, 36:*1165-1170, 1976.

Tobin, T., O'Leary, J., Blake, J. W., Tai, C. Y., Sturma, L., and Arnett, S.: The pharmacology of procaine in the horse. III. The "procaine penicillin" complex and its forensic significance. *Am J Vet Res, 38:*437-442, 1977.

Tobin, T., Roberts, B. L., and Miller, J. R.: The pharmacology of furosemide in the horse. I. Effects on the disposition of procaine, methylphenidate, phenylbutazone and pentazocaine. *J Equine Med Surg, 1:*402-407, 1977.

Section IV

VITAMINS, MINERALS, FLUIDS, ANTIBIOTICS, AND OTHER DRUGS

MOST OR ALL OF THE DRUGS that we have dealt with up to this point have been either natural or synthetic chemicals, clearly foreign to the horse. There are, however, many other substances that are given to horses either in their food, as food supplements, or by injection shortly before racing. Sometimes, as a matter of fact, horses are treated pre-race with an intravenous injection of about a liter or so of an amino acid-sugar-vitamin-mineral mixture, the whole popularly known in the United States as a "jug." The objective of "jugging" a horse is to make sure that his mineral-amino acid-vitamin status is as good as it can possibly be pre-race, and it may be considered the horse's equivalent of an athlete's steak dinner. Since most of the substances used in such "jugs" are normally found in the body of the horse, have no known pharmacological effects at the doses at which they are usually administered, and in any event cannot be distinguished in drug testing from normal body constituents, the pre-race use of these "jugs" is not regulated to any extent.

A number of vitamins have long been thought to influence the performance of horses when administered pre-race. Thus, for example vitamin B_1, or thiamine, has been thought to have a tranquilizing action on horses, and vitamin B_{12} has been thought to put an edge on a horse. Similarly, vitamin B_{15} has been claimed to stimulate performance in horses, and in the first chapter of this section we examine the actions of all the known and some rather questionable vitamins on horses.

Another enormously important group of drugs for both the horseman and the horse is the antibiotics, and these are dealt with next. These drugs, so important for the health of the horse, are often found in the urine of horses after racing, and are not usually considered to contravene the rules of racing. Similarly, many hormones are obviously found in equine urine, and because of this most hormones are not called by racing chemists. In this section of the book we will discuss the pharmacology of a number of these agents and describe what is known of their pharmacology and detection in the horse.

Chapter 17

THE VITAMINS

A VITAMIN MAY BE very broadly defined as a substance that is required for normal body function but which is not synthesized in the body and which must therefore be obtained from an exogenous source. Under normal conditions they are not regarded as drugs, but if the danger of a deficiency exists, then vitamins are commonly administered in much the same fashion as drugs, and they are sometimes in this circumstance regarded as drugs. In this chapter we will describe the actions of the common vitamins in horses, present their normal daily requirements where known, and discuss the signs of either a deficiency or excess of these agents. In discussing the vitamins, we will follow their natural division into two major groups, the water-soluble vitamins of the B and C groups, and the fat-soluble vitamins, A, D, E, and K.

THE FAT-SOLUBLE VITAMINS

Vitamin A

The signs and symptoms of vitamin A deficiency were first recognized as night blindness in poorly nourished slaves in Brazil and, curiously enough, among orthodox Russian Catholics who fasted during the Lenten period. Later, during World War I, it became apparent that xerophthalmia* (thickening and drying of the cornea) was a result of a decreased butterfat in the diet, which observation paved the way for the discovery of vitamin A.

Vitamin A has a number of very important functions in the body. As is suggested by its involvement in night blindness, it is important in the visual function of the retina. It is essential for normal embryonic development and growth, especially of bone, and reproduction. Finally, and most readily seen in the adult, it is very important for the integrity of the skin and other epithelial cells, and a lack of it is associated with an unusual susceptibility to infection.

In the horse, the most common source of vitamin A is carotene from the forage. Different forages contain different levels of carotene, due at least in part to the way they are handled during processing. In this regard, alfalfa hay appears to maintain its vitamin A content more effectively than other hays. Practically all concentrates, with the exception of corn, are low in vitamin A.

The National Research Council has set 25 I.U. vitamin A/kg body weight as the maintenance requirement for mature adult horses. In weanlings, which are growing and lack liver stores of vitamin A, 40 I.U. of vitamin A/kg is the suggested daily intake rate. Pregnant or lactating mares require 50 I.U. vitamin A/kg body weight. It has been suggested that colostrum is an important source of vitamin A for the

---

The assistance of Sandy Kownacki, D.V.M., in researching and drafting this chapter is gratefully acknowledged.
* *Xeros* = dry; *ophthalmia* = eye

neonate, as carotene was not thought by some workers to cross the placental barrier. As a fat-soluble vitamin, however, it seems highly unlikely that vitamin A from the mare does not readily pass to the fetus, and a more than adequate supply should be provided to the fetus *in utero*, providing the broodmare's level of vitamin A is satisfactory.

Pastured broodmares show marked seasonal fluctuation in plasma vitamin A and carotene levels, which correlate well with the levels available in the pasture. In addition, the horse appears to be relatively resistant to reduced carotene or vitamin A levels in pasture. Vitamin A deficiency has been reported in the horse, however, and is characterized by progressive weakness and death. As in the human, the most consistent sign is night blindness, followed by different degrees of keratinization of the cornea and lacrimation. Other signs include loss of appetite, poor bone growth, dry, scaly, abnormal hooves that are increasingly brittle, respiratory infections, and poor coat condition.

Because vitamin A is involved in the integrity of connective tissue, Abrams in Cambridge has studied the racing performance of horses with and without vitamin A supplements. Abrams considered that the diet of these horses, which consisted of oats, bran, and rather poor hay, to likely be low in vitamin A. Since studies showed that his horses' vitamin A status was indeed marginal, he chose to supplement the diets of four of his horses with weekly dietary supplements of

TABLE 17-I

EFFECT OF DIETARY VITAMIN A SUPPLEMENTS ON RACING PERFORMANCE AND CLINICAL COMMENTS

Horse	1974 Season	1975 Season
Golden Ensign (A)	Intermittent lameness; swelling of fore tendon sheath; 4 races	Fit and well all season; 8 races (1 win; once 4th)
Kilbaigie (A)	Contused fetlock; lame after shoeing; 3 races	Fit and well all season; 6 races (1 win; twice 5th)
Desiroyal (A)	Swollen flexor tendon and suspensory ligament; no races	Fit and well, but uncompetive; 5 races
Trackers Request (A)	Lame, fore and hind limbs; tender fetlock; 1 race	Fit and well all season; 7 races (once 4th)
Balaton	Swollen check ligament; slight lameness; 1 race	Did not race; strained flexor tendon
Solamba	Lame; tender suspensory ligament, 1 race	Lame in off hind limb; poor hock conformation; 4 races (once 3rd)
Buttery	Lameness in fore and hind limbs; poor leg conformation; 1 race	Ruptured flexor tendon during race; 3 races
Craigie Burn	A temperamental horse; leg damaged in horse box; no races	Swollen tendon; nervous and difficult to exercise; 3 races

(A) = Dietary vitamin A supplement.

NOTE: Four yearlings were supplemented with 50,000 I.U./day of Retinol (A), while control horses received no supplementation. These horses were trained and raced over two seasons, with the results indicated above.

SOURCE: After Abrams, *Bibl Nutr Dieta*, 27:113-120, Karger, Basel, 1979.

vitamin A at a rate equivalent to about 50,000 I.U. per day. According to his data, both the physical condition and the performance of the horses improved when supplemented with vitamin A. This study suggests that the vitamin A levels in the diets of horses with tendon problems might well be increased to obtain the beneficial effects of vitamin A on connective tissue integrity and repair (Table 17-I).

Vitamin A toxicity is occasionally seen in children and adults, usually as the result of overdosage with supplements. Historically, vitamin A toxicity was most commonly seen among Arctic explorers, who dined too heavily on the livers of fish-eating Arctic carnivores, such as the seal, polar bear, and even the Husky! Signs of toxicity include drowsiness, headache, vomiting, and a generalized peeling of the skin after twenty-four hours. In chronic toxicity, hyperostosis (swelling) of the long bones and lameness are the most common lesion having been reported in humans and calves but not, so far, in horses.

In summary, vitamin A is a vitamin that may well need to be included as a dietary supplement if horses are on a traditional hay, oats, and water type of fare. While night blindness is the most common sign in humans, the possibility that subacute tendon problems might be associated with vitamin A deficiency should be considered in horses showing such symptoms. Vitamin A is not screened for in most drug testing systems and is not considered a prohibited medication by most racing authorities.

Vitamin D

Horses and other mammals may synthesize sufficient vitamin D for their daily needs simply by being exposed to direct sunlight for about sixty minutes each day. Under these circumstances, sterol molecules in the skin are changed by the ultraviolet light to vitamin D_3. Alternatively, the process also occurs in sun-cured hay, where the same reactions occur in the presence of UV light. The importance of vitamin D is that it plays a central role in calcium and phosphorus metabolism and therefore in bone growth and strength.

Because of the ease with which a horse's vitamin D requirements can be met, simple vitamin D deficiency in foals is quite rare, although it has been produced experimentally and one clinical case has been reported. It should be noted, however, that young age, rapid growth, excess carotene intake, indoor stabling, smoke-laden atmosphere or overcast climates, and modern haymaking techniques all tend to keep vitamin D levels at a minimum. These circumstances should be kept in mind if symptoms in horses suggestive of vitamin D deficiency are observed.

Vitamin D serves two important physiological functions in the body. It is required for normal mineralization of bone, and it plays an essential role in the regulation of plasma calcium concentrations. It acts to stimulate the absorption of calcium and phosphate in the intestine, and it also acts to promote the movement of calcium from bone. It also appears to affect the elimination of calcium and phosphate by the kidney. Vitamin D deficiency in horses is characterized by reduced bone calcification, stiff and swollen joints, stiffness of gait, and reduced serum levels of calcium and phosphorous. Deficiencies can be prevented by supplementation with 6.6 I.U. of vitamin D/kg.

Horses synthesize sufficient vitamin D simply by being exposed to direct sunlight for about sixty minutes each day.

A more likely occurrence than vitamin D deficiency is vitamin D toxicity. Oral vitamin dosing with 500 times the suggested N.R.C. standards was lethal to ponies in four months. Similarly, horses that received eight weekly treatments of 4 million I.U. of vitamin D from misguided owners showed loss of appetite, weight loss, polydipsia, polyuria, and stiff gait. Extensive mineralization of cardiovascular and other soft tissues from increased calcium and phosphorous blood levels were also evident. One case of hypervitaminosis D was successfully treated with 30 mg of intravenous dexamethasone, followed by thirty days of 5 mg of the steroid orally, with the addition of sodium phytate to the diet to discourage calcium absorption.

Ingestion of *Solanum malacokylon* by horses in Argentina and Brazil is associated with diseases called "enteque seco" and "epischamento." Recently, certain analogous plants in Florida *(Cestrum diurnum)* and possibly Hawaii *(Solanum sodomaeum)* have been shown to contain substances similar to vitamin D and capable of producing signs identical to vitamin D toxicity in the horse.

Since acute doses of vitamin D have no known effect on the performance of horses and vitamin D is not tested for in drug testing, it is not a forensically significant substance in performance horses.

Vitamin E

Vitamin E, or alpha-tocopherol, is a vitamin found in cereal grains but not in mature grasses. Aside from relieving symptoms of its deficiency, vitamin E appears to have no significant pharmacological activity. Deficiency symptoms due to a lack of vitamin E appear to be associated with its antioxidant abilities. In the absence of sufficient vitamin E or other antioxidants, peroxidation (breakdown) of lipids occurs, with resultant damage to cell membranes. Clinical signs of such damage appear within the first few months after birth and include failure to suck, difficulty in standing, unsteadiness, muscular tremors, and death from acute cardiac failure. In such animals, most major muscles undergo "lipid peroxidation," leading to hyaline degeneration and calcification of muscle fibers. Dietary deficiency of vitamin E and/or selenium is the major cause of nutritional muscular dystrophy in foals and other domestic animals.

The mineral selenium is able to some extent to compensate for a low vitamin E level in the diet. Thus, typical vitamin E deficiency is most likely to appear where selenium levels are low in the diet, which is largely dependent on soil type. In these circumstances, increased levels of selenium in the diet will make up for the relative vitamin E deficiency. While attempts to measure blood and serum levels of vitamin E and selenium have been difficult, what data there is suggests that mares with muscular dystrophic foals appear to be selenium low or deficient.

In the horse, one of the signs of muscle damage is creatine phosphokinase, where serum levels increase in a variety of conditions associated with muscle damage, such as azoturia, nutritional muscular dystrophy, tetanus, and physical exertion. Treatment with vitamin E and selenium has been reported to return elevated C.P.K. levels to normal in foals otherwise clinically normal but in herds where nutritional muscular dystrophy was present.

Vitamin E deficiencies were originally shown to cause reproductive deficiencies in rats, which led to it being hailed as the "antisterility" vitamin and to a huge demand in health food stores for wheat germ oil. There is, however, only the most marginal of evidence to suggest that it may be involved in fertility in the equine. On the other hand, supplementation of vitamin E to horses in the tropics has been suggested to lead to a 90 percent cure rate in correcting "anhidrosis" or dry coat.

Finally, the most popular and most common use of vitamin E is in combination with selenium for the treatment of azoturia or "tying up." Although there is no evidence that the occurrence of "tying up" is related to a vitamin E or selenium deficiency, this combination is popular for both its prophylaxis and treatment. It is commonly given to racing and other performance horses and occasionally creates problems because of its polyethylene glycol content. While the polyethylene glycols have no pharmacology of their own, at high levels in urine they may interfere with (mask) thin-layer analysis for drugs. As with any "masking" agent, the severity of the problem depends to a large extent on the methods that the analyst uses, and unless the problem is particularly severe, it can usually be circumvented.

Vitamin K

Vitamin K is a dietary principle that is required for the synthesis of several factors required in the clotting of blood. It is plentiful in most plants as the vitamin and is also synthesized in the gastrointestinal tract of ruminants. Because of this widespread occurrence, direct dietary deficiency is rare in horses.

In the absence of this vitamin, or, more commonly, in the presence of vitamin K antagonists such as the rat poison warfarin, or as are found in sweet clover hay, the clotting factors that are synthesized using vitamin K are not formed. In their absence the animal hemorrhages readily from the mouth, anus, minor abrasions, and bruises, and it soon bleeds to death. Bleeding, therefore, is the cause of death when warfarin is used as a rat poison and in sweet clover disease of cattle. Vitamin K antagonists such as warfarin and dicoumarol are often used in human medicine to reduce the probability of blood clots forming in patients who have suffered heart attacks and in other conditions in which increased blood clotting is a problem.

The most recent and unusual use for warfarin and other vitamin K antagonists has been in the treatment of navicular disease in horses. Navicular disease is a chronic condition of the navicular bone and its attachments and most commonly is found in the forelegs. The changes associated with this condition include ulcerations and erosions of the fibrocartilage and bone, and the lesions sometimes involve the deep digital flexor tendon.

Because of the chronic progressive nature of the disease and the lack of understanding of its cause, therapeutic measures have almost always been palliative and not directed at reversing the basic cause. Most commonly, animals with navicular disease are denerved or are put on long-term phenylbutazone therapy. The long-range prospects in navicular disease have always been poor, and in a study of 580 cases treated in a variety of ways, one investigator reported only 10 percent alive a year later and 4.5 percent described as sound.

Recently, however, Colles, in Newmarket, has proposed that the basic lesion in navicular disease is thrombosis (clotting) in the navicular arteries and periosteal blood supply to the navicular bone. Based on this proposed cause, Colles suggested that therapy with an anticoagulant such as warfarin might inhibit or reverse the clotting process and allow revascularization of the bone from the periosteum, thereby halting or reversing the course of the disease and the resulting lameness.

Testing this hypothesis, Colles identified twenty horses with navicular disease and administered sufficient warfarin orally each day to slow the blood clotting time, as assessed by an increase of the "one stage prothrombin time," by two to four seconds. Of the twenty horses treated, seventeen became sound after an average of seven weeks of treatment, and the remaining three showed marked improvement. Colles noted that while it was too early to comment on the long-term results of this therapy, at the time of writing two horses had been sound for over a year and the other horses had been sound for an average of six months. Furthermore, no horse that had gone sound on warfarin had redeveloped lameness while on warfarin. While the general applicability and long-term response to this treatment remains to be determined, warfarin therapy represents a stimulating and apparently promising approach to a previously intractable disease.

One of the problems with warfarin or other anti-vitamin K therapy is that once the clotting factors are depleted, it takes at least a couple of hours to reverse the process and reform the clotting factors. Administration of vitamin K in sufficient amount will overcome the warfarin blockade and allow synthesis of new clotting factors. This, however, may take up to twenty-four hours to occur, which is not very useful in an acute hemorrhagic episode.

Because vitamin K is one of the few drugs that are known to increase the coagulation of blood under any circumstance, vitamin K is often prescribed for clinical conditions in which there is unusual or unexplained hemorrhage. Among these conditions are epistaxis or "bleeder" horses. Since there is usually no evidence of a deficiency of clotting factors that respond to vitamin K therapy in the horse, such therapy must be considered irrational.

These, then, are the fat-soluble vitamins. Vitamin A would seem to be of concern in performance horses primarily for its possible role in tendon strength, and there is some evidence to suggest that horses with tendon problems may benefit from vitamin A supplements. Vitamin K is an unlikely vitamin to be deficient in the horse, with the exception of horses poisoned with warfarin or being treated for navicular disease. In horses with navicular disease, a recently suggested mode of therapy is treatment with sufficient warfarin to induce a partial clotting defect and thus reverse the disease. Finally, with vitamin D the possibility of toxicity due to overgenerous supplementation would seem to be the most likely concern for horsemen.

THE WATER-SOLUBLE VITAMINS

Vitamins B and C are the most important of the water-soluble vitamins in equine medicine. The B complex is considered to consist of thiamine (B_1), riboflavin (B_2), niacin or nicotinic acid, pyridoxine, pantothenic acid, and cyanocobalamin (B_{12}). As a group the B vitamins may be divided into two major subgroups, (1) those that act as cofactors in the release of energy from food, and (2) those that act in the formation of nucleic acids and red blood cells.

Abundant synthesis of the B complex vitamins appears to take place in the microflora of the equine cecum and colon. Further, in addition to synthesis in the gastrointestinal tract, the B vitamins are commonly found in large amounts in the hays, grasses, and grains commonly fed to horses. High quality diets with concentrate supplementation further favor B vitamin synthesis by increasing the numbers of bacteria in the gastrointestinal tract.

While it seems unlikely, therefore, that a B vitamin deficiency would occur naturally in the horse, the higher requirements of performance horses and horses operating under stress must be kept in mind. Since the B vitamins are directly involved in either energy release or red blood cell formation, the supplementation of these vitamins to horses in training seems reasonable. Veterinarians, therefore, routinely recommend B vitamin supplements to horses in training or other stressed horses. Further, no toxicities due to B vitamins are known, which makes the risks associated with such supplementation minimal.

The Energy-Releasing B Vitamins: Thiamine, Riboflavin, Nicotinic Acid, and Pantothenic Acid

Vitamin B₁ (Thiamine)

Thiamine is a complex organic molecule containing a pyrimidine and thiazole nucleus, and it functions in the body as a phosphate derivative, thiamine pyrophosphate. Its essential function in the body is as a coenzyme in sugar metabolism. Thiamine itself is considered by pharmacologists to be essentially devoid of pharmacological actions in the therapeutic dose range.

The N.R.C. has set the daily dietary requirement for thiamine at 3 mg/kg of feed, and based on these levels the rations of some pregnant mares late in gestation may be inadequate in thiamine, requiring supplementation.

Deficiencies of thiamine most commonly occur not due to a lack of thiamine in an animal's diet but to the presence of an enzyme called thiaminase, which breaks down thiamine. The Pacific Coast plants bracken fern* and mare's tail† contain high levels of thiaminase, and horses eating these plants rapidly develop signs of thiamine deficiency. These include incoordination to the point of falling and bracycardia due to cardiac irregularity. When standing, the legs are placed well apart and crouching of the back is evident. Muscle tremors develop, and eventually the horse is unable to rise and dies in convulsions. The response to I.V. thiamine, 5 mg/kg of body weight every three hours is dramatic and should be followed up by oral thiamine every three days. Since horses rarely graze either bracken fern or mare's tail, the problem usually occurs when they are fed hay containing these plants.

Thiamine deficiency has also been suggested to be involved as a causative agent in "roaring" in horses. This suggestion was apparently based on reports of left laryngeal nerve paralysis in humans who were suffering from thiamine deficiency and on "roaring" in bracken-fern-poisoned cattle. The left recurrent laryngeal nerve is the longest motor nerve in the horse and, as such, is likely the most susceptible to damage induced by nutritional deficiencies, such as a thiamine deficiency. However, other nerves are spared in horses with roaring, and considering the chronicity of "roaring," this is not consistent with it being due to a nutritional deficiency. Since the incidence of roaring in the Thoroughbred is about 5 percent, the nutritional status of most Thoroughbreds would also have to be very poor indeed to accommodate this hypothesis. In order to definitely link thiamine deficiency with roaring, controlled experiments would have to show that horses on B₁-deficient diets had a higher incidence of the disease or that thiamine supplementation could prevent roaring in a predisposed group of horses. Studies of such massive proportions are unlikely to emerge in the near future.

The medication of racehorses with thiamine is not an uncommon practice.

---

* *Pteridium aquilinum*
† *Equisetum arvense*

Between the years 1947 and 1973, the Association of Official Racing Chemists reported fifty "positive" urine determinations for thiamine in samples taken from racing horses. Thiamine is apparently used in racing horses for three reasons, namely its supposed abilities as a masking agent, its supposed actions as a tranquilizer, and its possible actions in the treatment of azoturia or "tying up."

The ability of thiamine to mask the presence of other drugs presumably depends on its ability to absorb ultraviolet light, thus interfering with UV scanning for drugs. Nowadays, however, UV screening for drugs plays a relatively minor role in most drug testing systems, and the ability of thiamine to mask in the face of modern detection methods is likely minimal.

The origin of the hypothesis that thiamine can tranquilize unruly horses is unknown, unless it comes from the reversal of the nervousness and excitability of thiamine-deficient horses by thiamine. The first work in this area was done by Mackay, who reported a tranquilizing effect in all horses dosed with parenteral thiamine in doses of as low as 1000 mg. The primary parameter used as an index of tranquilization by Mackay was a slowing of pulse rate. In a subsequent paper, however, Irvine and Prentice refuted this work by running double blind studies on horses dosed with either saline or 2000 mg thiamine on separate days before measuring physiological parameters. Although the changes in pulse rate of the B_1-dosed horses seen by Mackay were also observed by these authors, the same changes were also seen in the horses receiving saline control injections. It was suggested that what Mackay had recorded was the normal settling down of a highly strung horse after the procedure of bringing the animal into a loose box and submitting him to an intravenous injection. In the healthy racehorse, doses of thiamine of up to 50 mg/kg body weight failed to affect pulse rate, the electrocardiogram, or behavior.

In another study, Stewart administered doses of 5 mg thiamine/kg to horses thirty to sixty minutes before exercise. There was no significant alteration in performance or change in cardiovascular or respiratory parameters. Without knowing the nature of the injections, the jockey and trainer did report on three occasions that the horses were less excitable when walking to the racetrack.

On the other hand, recent studies by Sandy Kownacki in our laboratory indicate that doses of thiamine ranging from 5 to 10 mg/kg body weight have no effect on the operant response rate of horses conditioned to break an electric eye for food reinforcements (unpublished data). We have found this operant method to be a very sensitive measure of the actions of many stimulants and depressants in the horse, and if thiamine does indeed alter behavior in the horse, the technique sensitive enough to monitor these changes has not yet been developed (Fig. 17-1).

Thiamine is also routinely used in the treatment of azoturia or "tying up" disease of horses. Because of the role of thiamine in carbohydrate metabolism and the association of azoturia with carbohydrate metabolism, its use in this syndrome may well be justified. In any event, many veterinarians include two 2,000 mg doses of thiamine hydrochloride intravenously in the therapeutic treatment of azoturia in the horse. Similarly, selenium and vitamin E preparations are often administered prophylactically for chronic cases of azoturia.

No adverse effects from administration of 5 mg/kg body weight given every

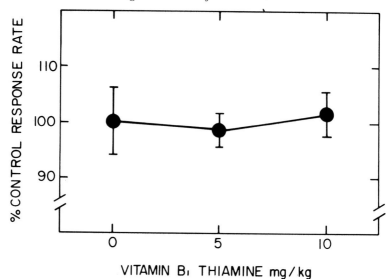

Figure 17-1. Lack of effect of vitamin B₁ (thiamine) administered IV thirty-minutes before operant behavior testing of three horses.

three hours for up to four days were seen in the horse, and the very large dose of 50 mg/kg, a lethal dose for laboratory animals, has been reported as producing no effect in the equine. Therefore, the margin of safety with thiamine in the equine appears to be very large and the possibility of overdosing with thiamine slim.

Vitamin B₂ (Riboflavin)

Riboflavin, or vitamin B₂, was first identified in milk in 1879, but its importance as a vitamin was not appreciated until 1933, when it was found to stimulate the growth of rats on a purified diet. As its name suggests, it is a yellow, crystalline substance, and it is a coenzyme of absolute requirement for many of the energy-yielding reactions (oxidation-reduction) of the body.

According to the N.R.C. report, horses need about 2.2 mg/kg feed of riboflavin. There are, however, wide variations in the absolute levels of any one feedstuff analyzed. Yeast is a very rich source of riboflavin, and hay contains more riboflavin than cereal grains. The possibility exists of deficieneices of riboflavin in performance horses on high grain diets, and some workers have also suggested that riboflavin should also be added to foal rations.

The possible role of riboflavin deficiency as a causative agent for "moonblindness" or periodic ophthalmia in foals is unclear. "Moonblindness" is characterized by tearing from the affected eyes, inflammation of the affected eyes, cornea vascularization spreading through the eyes, an aversion to light, and eventual blindness in both eyes if the attacks continue to recur. These symptoms bear a remarkable similarity to the symptoms of riboflavin deficiency in laboratory animals and have given rise to suggestions that a riboflavin deficiency may be involved in "moonblindness" in horses. Unlike a simple vitamin deficiency, however, moonblindness responds well to phenylbutazone therapy, suggesting a substantial involvement of inflammatory processes in this condition.

It now appears that while nutritional deficiencies may predispose a horse to "moonblindness," other factors, most likely leptospiral infections, may be involved. Studies on one farm have shown that moonblindness occurred in six of sixteen horses with a confirmed history of *Leptospira pomona* infection, despite all horses having been fed 40 mg/day of riboflavin. On the other hand, earlier reports suggest that supplementation with similar amounts of riboflavin has prophylactic value against moonblindness. It appears possible that nutritional deficiencies may predispose horses to "moonblindness" by reducing levels of other substances more directly necessary for normal ocular function.

Nicotinic Acid or Niacin

Nicotinic acid is widely distributed in both plants and animals and serves a vital role in two coenzymes involved in tissue respiration. Although nicotinic acid is distantly related to nicotine, it has none of the pharmacological activities of nicotine. Nicotinic acid, however, has some clear-cut pharmacological effects of its own, acting to produce flushing of the skin and itching. In addition, nicotinic acid acts to reduce cholesterol and triglyceride concentrations in the plasma in man, and it is marketed for this use in human medicine.

Nicotinic acid is unique among the B-complex vitamins in that the amount found in the urine of ponies varies very little, independent of the dietary regimen on which the ponies were kept. These observations are consistent with the idea that ponies get adequate nicotinic acid from their diet and/or rumen microflora, and symptoms attributable to a nicotinic acid deficiency have never been reported in the horse.

There are thirty-three reports of nicotine and forty-four reports of nikethamide being detected in the urine of racehorses over a period of twenty-six years. Nikethamide (Coramine®) is a central nervous system respiratory stimulant that has apparently been used to "treat" performance horses as well as Olympic cyclists. Because nikethamide is very rapidly metabolized to nicotinamide, a metabolite of nicotinic acid and a normal constituent of horse urine, it can be difficult to prove medication with nikethamide. This is so because only about 0.37 percent or less of the dose of nikethamide is excreted unchanged in the urine, which makes detection of the unchanged drug quite difficult. Therefore, detection of N-ethyl-nicotinamide as a metabolite of nikethamide in the horse represents a substantial advance in the control of this drug.

Nicotine

Nicotine is an alkaloid that is chemically related to nicotinic acid and is found in high concentrations in tobacco. Aside from its use as a pesticide (Black Leaf 40®), nicotine has essentially no therapeutic applications, although it has quite a complex pharmacology.

Pharmacologically, nicotine is characterized by stimulant and depressant actions, usually in that order. For example, in the CNS, nicotine first stimulates and then depresses the CNS, with death being due to respiratory paralysis. In the cardiovascular system, small doses of nicotine cause vasoconstriction, but large doses cause vasodilatation, due to ganglionic block. Stimulation of the gastrointestinal system causes increased gastrointestinal motility, leading to vomiting, increased peristalsis, and defecation, as all young people smoking their first cigarettes become aware.

One of the problems that faces the analyst when nicotine is detected in urine samples is to determine whether or not the nicotine was administered to the horse or is due to postsampling contamination. However, recent work has shown that nicotine is metabolized to cotinine in the horse and suggests that the presence or absence of cotinine in a urine sample would enable one to determine whether or not the nicotine present had been metabolized by the horse and thus actually been "through" the horse.

Pantothenic Acid

Pantothenic acid functions in the body as a constituent of coenzyme A. Other than its biochemical function as a part of coenzyme A, it has no pharmacological actions, and it is essentially nontoxic.

Pantothenic acid is essential for the growth of many microorganisms and as such is found in large quantities in the gut flora of herbivores such as the horse. While considered a necessary dietary essential for the horse, most feeds are though to be sufficiently rich in pantothenic acid to meet the horse's requirements, although, according to N.R.C standards, pantothenic acid should make up 0.015 percent of the diet. In experimental animals, pantothenic acid deficiency is manifested by symptoms of neuromuscular degeneration, adrenocortical insufficiency, and death.

The Hemopoietic (Red Blood Cell Forming) Vitamins: Vitamin B_{12}, Pyridoxine, and Folic Acid

Folic Acid

Folic acid is an essential vitamin in man and is required for normal red blood cell formation. In man, "subclinical" deficiencies of serum folate result in mild anemias with lassitude and irritability. In severe folic acid deficiency, anemia due to a reduced number of relatively large red cells is found. In man, folic acid deficiency and resultant anemia may result from pregnancy, hemolytic anemia, or the natural aging process.

Folic acid is richly supplied by fresh green forages and is also synthesized by intestinal bacteria. Based presumably on the assumption that equines may gain adequate supplies from both of these sources, the National Research Council (1978) has set no requirements for folic acid in equines.

In contrast with this lack of requirements by the National Research Council, recent research in England strongly suggests that horses in training will benefit from folate supplementation. These investigations started in 1967, when a group of English workers, investigating cases of anemia in stabled Thoroughbred horses, studied vitamin B_{12} and iron levels in these horses, as well as folate levels in these horses' diets. They found that serum folate levels in grass-fed horses were 11.5 μg/ml, whereas the serum folate levels of the stabled horses were 7.4 μg/ml. This difference was highly significant statistically, and these lower serum folate levels would be considered to be on the borderline of folate deficiency in man.

In an individual case report, a stabled two-year-old gelding was found to have had a hemoglobin of 11.5 gm/100 ml, far below the normal 14.5 gm/100 ml. The horse was also in poor body condition and performed badly during strenuous exercise. This horse had not been fed a diet containing fresh grass for many months. The animal was placed on folic acid, 20 mg/day, and within one month its hemoglobin level had risen to more then 14.0 gm/100 ml, along with increased serum folate levels (Fig. 17-2). These changes were accompanied by parallel improvements in the animal's condition and performance, despite the fact that he continued on a grass-deficient diet. Based on these studies, these authors concluded that "there may well be a case for routine administration of folic acid to horses which are denied access to fresh grass and particularly if such stabling becomes necessary during pregnancy."

Following up on this early work, Allen, at the Equine Research Station in Newmarket, studied the serum folate values of Thoroughbred mares at stud, ponies at grass, and Thoroughbreds in training to race. While the serum folate levels of the mares at stud and the ponies at grass were 10.6 and 10.9 μg/ml, respectively, the values in the Thoroughbreds in training were an amazingly low 3.3 μg/ml and showed a very close distribution about the mean (Fig. 17-3). Allen suggested that the very low levels of serum folate in stabled horses in training was due to the lack of fresh grass in the diet of these horses combined with the increased loss of folate in sweat of horses in training, since the concentrations of folic acid in sweat are about five times those in serum. A further factor was likely to be the increased red blood cell formation and turnover of folate in horses in training. Allen concluded that stabled horses, and in particular stabled racehorses,

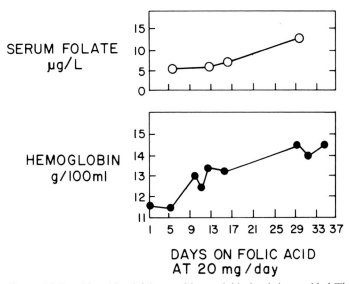

Figure 17-2. Effects of folic acid on blood folate and hemoglobin levels in a stabled Thoroughbred horse. A stabled Thoroughbred horse in poor condition and with low blood hemoglobin was administered folic acid at 20 mg/day, starting on day one. The upper panel shows the resultant increase in plasma folate levels, while the lower panel shows the corresponding increase in blood hemoglobin levels. Adapted from Seckington et al. (1967).

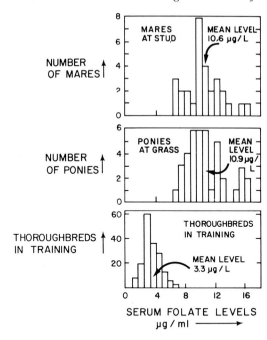

Figure 17-3. Frequency histograms of serum folate levels in mares, ponies at grass, and Thoroughbreds in training. These panels show the number of animals of each group with a given serum level of folate. The lower panel shows that no Thoroughbred in training had a serum level of folate above 7 μg/L, that the mean level was about 3.3 μg/L, and that some Thoroughbreds in training had very low (<2 μg/ml) levels of folate. In contrast, the serum folate levels of the mares and ponies at grass were between 7 and 17 μg/L of folate, with mean folate values on the order of about 10.75 μg/L. Since 3.3 μg/ml is a borderline folate level in the human, the folate levels of many Thoroughbred horses in training are either marginal or below marginal levels. Adapted from Allen, 1978.

required folate supplementation during their period of training. The amount of supplementation would appear to be on the order of 15 to 16 mg/day, and it would appear wise to include this supplement in the diet of any horses that do not have ready access to fresh grass.

With regard to folic acid supplementation, it is important to remember that folic acid is a DNA precursor and that a deficiency may lead to reduced formation of more than just red blood cells. Folic acid supplementation is therefore likely to be important in horses recuperating from surgery, or upper respiratory tract or viral infections, where rapid wound healing and cellular regeneration are important. Of further importance is the fact that anabolic steroids and other "blood builders" such as iron injections are much less likely to be effective in the absence of adequate folic acid levels, since folic acid is one of the basic building blocks for new bood cell formation.

Despite this clear-cut evidence for the importance of folic acid in training horses, most vitamin and mineral supplements do not contain sufficient amounts of this very important vitamin. A notable exception to this rule is the Irish Thoroughbred products preparation Plusvital® Syrups, which are supplemented with sufficient folic acid to meet the requirements of horses under all likely conditions.

Vitamin B_{12} (Cyanocobalamin)

Vitamin B_{12} is synthesized only by certain microorganisms, and all animals are ultimately dependent on bacterial synthesis of this vitamin, although carnivores may obtain their B_{12} from the flesh of other animals. Since the concentration of vitamin B_{12} in the horse's gut increases from the stomach to the rectum, it appears that synthesis of vitamin B_{12} by gut flora of the horse occurs readily.

Vitamin B_{12} is an extremely complex molecule, containing a cobalt atom at its center. It is unique among the vitamins in that its absorption from the stomach requires the presence of another factor, called intrinsic factor, and absence of this factor can result in failure of B_{12} absorption and signs of its deficiency. Its precise role in the body is not clear, but a deficiency of B_{12} appears to result in reduced DNA synthesis. The signs of deficiency include an anemia with enlarged red blood cells and also neurological changes with demyelination of nerves.

Because cobalt is an essential component of vitamin B_{12}, deficiencies of this vitamin occur in cattle and sheep grazing cobalt-deficient soil in many parts of the world. However, horses raised on these same pastures show no signs of vitamin B_{12} deficiency, presumably because intestinal synthesis of the vitamin remains adequate for their needs. The National Research Council does not report on vitamin B_{12} requirements for horses.

Alexander and Davies have shown that intramuscular injection of vitamin B_{12} results in a twenty-four-hour rise of serum B_{12} levels, but that most of the vitamin is excreted in the feces. Injection of vitamin B_{12} is presumed to alleviate parasitic and dietetic anemias. Oral administration of cobalt chloride has little effect on serum levels of vitamin B_{12}, although it will give rise to substantially greater amounts of vitamin B_{12} in the feces.

Treatment of horses on the racetrack with vitamin B_{12} is common, supplemental daily injections of up to 20,000 µg of vitamin B_{12} being thought "to put an edge on a horse" and improve his performance. Studies in our laboratory by Sandy Kownacki, analogous to those reported for vitamin B_1 earlier, have not shown any action of vitamin B_{12} on operant behavior in horses at doses of up to 40

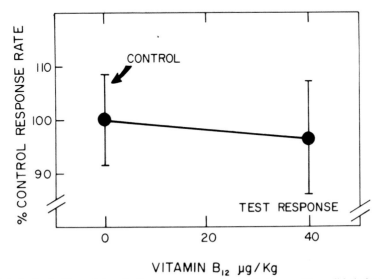

Figure 17-4. Lack of effect of vitamin B_{12} on operant behavior in horses. The solid circles show the operant behavior rates of four horses prior to and after treatment with 40 mg/kg of vitamin B_{12} IV ten minutes prior to testing in the behavioral apparatus.

mg/kg (Fig. 17-4). As was reported with vitamin B_1, any behavioral actions of vitamin B_{12} apparently either do not exist or are not detectable by any tests currently available in equine pharmacology.

Vitamin B_6 (Pyridoxine)

Pyridoxine, as pyridoxal phosphate, serves a vital role in metabolism as a coenzyme for a wide variety of reactions involving amino acids. Symptoms of its deficiency may include anemia, convulsive seizures, and dermatitis. Certain drugs, most notably isoniazid, may interfere with pyridoxine metabolism, and it is routine to supplement pyridoxine in the diet of patients being treated with isoniazid.

Very little investigation of the requirements for pyridoxine in the horse has been done. Evidence has been presented for synthesis of vitamin B_6 by gut flora in the horse, and Stowe has estimated that the adult horse requires 50 to 70 µg/kg body weight/day of pyridoxine. While this amount may be present in the rations of equines it has been suggested that adequate intake of B_6 should be insured during pregnancy, antibiotic therapy, and periods of increased environmental temperatures.

"Vitamin B_{15}" (Pangamic Acid)

In 1943, Ernest Krebs, Senior and Junior applied for a patent for a material isolated from apricot seeds, which they named pangamic acid* and which they *trade named* "Vitamin B_{15}." Since then pangamic acid has been widely promoted both as a food supplement for horses and for the relief of numerous human ailments, including heart disease, diabetes, drug addiction, jaundice, neuralgia, and neuritis, to mention but a few. It has had a considerable following as a health food, and it has been claimed that "pangamic acid has been widely studied and accepted as a necessary food factor with important physiological actions."

The name pangamic acid originally described what may have been a sodium or potassium salt of *d*-gluconodimethyl aminoacetate. However, in actual practice the label more often described a product that is one part gluconate, one part glycine or dimethylglycine, and, often, one part diisopropylamine dichloroacetate. Because of this chemical variety in the materials sold as pangamic acid, some people have held that the substance does not exist, since there is no standard chemical identity for products sold under the pangamic acid label.

Pangamic acid has been reportedly fed by the United States Equestrian Team to its horses, recommended by Doctor Robert Atkins of the "Dr. Atkins Super Energy Diet," and used by Muhammad Ali when he feels below par. It is reported to increase the supply of oxygen in the blood and its uptake in tissues. This action accounts for its tonic and vitamin effects, although quite how it does this is not clear. Several athletes reportedly eat B_{15} like candy, but whether or not it helps them perform is another matter. The dosage recommended has varied from 50 mg/day in Russia to 150 mg/day among American users.

The final word on pangamic acid may well be that of the Food and Drug

---

* Pangamic = in all seeds; from the Greek *pan* = in all, and *gamic* = seed

Administration, which holds that vitamin B_{15} is not an identifiable substance, "is neither a vitamin or a provitamin," that there is no accepted scientific evidence establishing any nutritional properties of the substance or any deficiencies in man or animal, and that no medical nutritional or other usefulness for these substances has been established. The FDA also considers vitamin B_{15} to be food additive for which no evidence of safety has been offered, and it is therefore illegal for the substance to be sold as a dietary supplement. No new drug application for "pangamic acid" has been submitted or approved by the FDA, and the substance cannot legally be marketed as a drug.

Vitamin C (Ascorbic Acid)

It has been known since the 1700s that the juice of fresh vegetables prevents and reverses the symptoms of scurvy, and in the 1800s a compulsory ration of lime juice was issued to British sailors (hence the name "Limey" for a Britisher). The active principle in these juices was, of course, ascorbic acid or vitamin C, and vitamin C is required in the diet of man, the guinea pig, the fruit-eating bat of India, and a rather curiously named avian called the red-vented bulbul bird. All other animals can synthesize vitamin C from sugars, and the horse does not require a dietary source of vitamin C. Horses on a vitamin C-deficient diet can continue to maintain plasma levels of the vitamin and continue to excrete considerable urinary levels of the drug.

Despite this apparent nonrequirement for vitamin C in the diet of the horse, a relationship between breeding performance and ascorbic acid in the equine has been suggested. In 1943, Davis and Cole arbitrarily divided mares into two groups. Good breeders were those that could be bred during one or two heat periods, and poor breeders were those that had to be bred on more than two consecutive heat periods. Good breeders were found to have higher ascorbic acid values than poor breeders, and the difference was most pronounced in draft mares. About one month after daily supplementation of 1 g ascorbic acid, two mares that had previously failed to come into heat were in estrus and bred. The sperm count of a Belgian stallion had dropped dramatically but was shown to improve in number and motility on three separate occasions following injection of 1 g ascorbic acid every three days or feeding 1 g ascorbic acid per day. Whenever vitamin C supplementation was discontinued, the sperm quality again deteriorated rapidly. Feeding vitamin and mineral supplements to subfertile stallions six weeks prior to the breeding season has been suggested to improve spermatogenesis and sperm motility.

Vitamin P (The bioflavonoids)

The bioflavonoids, abundant in citrus plants, are a unique group of compounds that reportedly contribute to the maintenance of blood vessel integrity at the capillary level and have a synergistic effect with ascorbic acid. Although they have no clearly defined nutritional role, they have, nonetheless, become known as vitamin P. In horses, they have been suggested as part of the therapeutic regime in laminitis, and they have also been suggested to be useful in the prophylaxis of epistaxis, for which purpose they have been marketed on the West Coast of the United States.

In summary, therefore, among the fat-soluble vitamins, only vitamin A and D are likely to need supplementation in the normal diet (Table 17-II). It would appear to be prudent to supplement with vitamin A in horses in racing and training because this vitamin is involved in connective tissue integrity, and reduced levels of it may lead to tendon and ligmament problems.

The circumstances under which supplementation with vitamin D is required are less clear-cut. If horses or their food have been exposed to normal sunlight, the need to supplement would appear to be small. If, however, the amount of sunlight to which the animals are exposed is restricted, then supplementation with vitamin D is probably wise. While vitamin D toxicity has been reported in the horse, the amounts needed to produce these effects are apparently large and are not likely to be reached by the feeding of normal vitamin D supplements.

With the water-soluble vitamins, all of which are rapidly excreted, there is little danger of accumulation or toxicity. It is prudent, therefore, to supplement with these vitamins if there is any possibility that the animal may be deficient. Thiamine should probably be supplemented to mares late in gestation, as the amounts of thiamine that these animals get in their diet may not be adequate. Similarly, the diets of performance horses and foals should also be supplemented with riboflavin, particularly in the case of adult horses on a high grain diet.

Among the hemopoietic (red blood cell forming) vitamins, folic acid would appear to be the vitamin most likely to need supplementation. It appears clear that

TABLE 17-II
SUGGESTED DAILY VITAMIN REQUIREMENTS FOR HORSES

Vitamin	Horse	Amount
Fat-Soluble Vitamins		
Vitamin A	Adult	25 I.U./kg/day
	Weanlings	40 I.U./kg/day
	Pregnant mares	50 I.U./kg/day
Vitamin D	Adults	6.6 I.U./kg/day
Vitamin E		No additional required
Vitamin K		No additional required in normal horse
Water-Soluble Vitamins		
Vitamin B_1 (thiamine)	Adults	3 mg/kg/feed
Vitamin B_2 (riboflavin)	Adults	2.2 mg/kg/feed
Nicotinic acid		No additional required
Pantothenic acid	Adults	0.015% of diet
Folic acid	Adults	20 mg/day/horse
Vitamin B_{12}	Adults	None reported
Pyridoxine	Adults	70 μg/kg/day
"Vit. B_{15}" (trademarked vitamin, pangamic acid)		Not recognized by F.D.A.
Vitamin C		No reported requirement
"Vitamin P"		Not recognized

horses in training with restricted access to fresh grass need to have a folate supplement, and supplementation is probably a wise precaution for any stabled horse and particularly broodmares in foal. Supplementation with folic acid is all the more important because in the absence of sufficient folate, other measures commonly used to build up the hematocrit, such as anabolic steroid and iron treatments, are much less likely to be effective.

The only other vitamin likely to need supplementation in adult horses is pyridoxine, or vitamin B_6, which may be needed during periods of pregnancy, antibiotic therapy, or high environmental temperatures. Vitamin C, while a required vitamin in man, is not needed in the horse, and there is no good evidence for the existence of some other "vitamins" that one occasionally finds suggested for supplementation in the diet of horses.

SELECTED REFERENCES

Abrams, J. T.: The effect of dietary vitamin A supplements on the clinical condition and track performance of racehorses. *Bibl Nutr Dieta, 27:*113-120, 1979.

Alexander, F. and Davies, M. E.: Studies on vitamin B_{12} in the horse. *Br. Vet J, 125:*169-175, 1969.

Allen, B. V. (Cited by Allen, B. V.): Serum folate levels in horses, with particular reference to the English Thoroughbred. *Vet Rec, 103:*257-259, 1978.

Blood, D. C., Henderson, J. A., and Radostits, O. M.: *Veterinary Medicine, A Textbook of the Diseases of Cattle, Sheep, Pigs and Horses.* 5th ed. Philadelphia, Lea & Febiger, 1979.

Colles, C. M.: A preliminary report on the use of warfarin in the treatment of navicular disease. *Equine Vet J, 11:*187-190, 1979.

Cymbaluk, N. F., Fretz, P. B., and Lowe, F. M.: Thiamin measurements in horses with laryngeal hemiplegia. *Vet Rec, 101:*97-98, 1977.

Cymbaluk, N. F., Fretz, P. B., and Lowe, F. M.: Amprolium-induced thiamine deficiency in horses. Clinical features. *Am J Vet Res, 39:*255-261, 1978.

Davies, M. E.: The production of B_{12} in the horse. *Br Vet J, 127:*34-36, 1971.

Davis, K. G. and Cole, C. L.: The relation of ascorbic acid to breeding performance in horses. *J Anim Sci, 2:*53-58, 1943.

Delbeke, F. T. and Debackere, M.: Excretion and metabolism of nikethamide in the horse. *Br J Sports Med, 10:*116-123, 1976.

Dodd, D. C. et al (1960): Cited by *N.R.C. Nutrient Requirements of Horses.* Washington, DC, National research Council, 1978, pp. 6-10.

Frape, D. L.: Recent research into the nutrition of the horse. *Equine Vet J, 7:*120-130, 1975.

Garton, C. L., Vander Noot, G. W., and Fonnesbeck, P. V.: Seasonal variation in carotene and vitamin A concentration of the blood of brood mares in New Jersey. *J Anim Sci, 23:*1233, 1964 (abstr).

Irvine, C. H. G. and Prentice, N. G.: The effect of large doses of thiamine on the horse. *New Zealand Vet J, 10:*86-88, 1962.

Jones, T. C.: Equine periodic ophthalmia. *Am J Vet Res, 3:*45, 1942.

Jones, T. C.: Riboflavin and the control of equine periodic ophthalmia. *J Am Vet Med Assoc, 114:*326-328, 1949.

Jones, T. C., Maurer, F. D., and Roby, T. O.: The role of nutrition in equine periodic ophthalmia. *Am J Vet Res, 6:*67-80, 1945.

Lannek, N. and Lindberg, P.: Vitamin E and selenium deficiencies (VESD) of domestic animals. *Adv Vet Sci Comp Med, 19:*127-164, 1975.

Lehninger, A. L.: *Biochemistry, the Molecular Basis of Cell Structure and Function,* 2nd ed. New York, Worth, 1975.

Linerode, P. A.: Studies on the synthesis and absorption of B-complex vitamins in the horse. *Proc AAEP,* New Orleans, LA, 283-314, 1967.

Muyelle, E., Oyaert, W., DeRoose, P., and Vanden Hende, C.: Hypercalcaemia and mineralization of non-osseous tissues in horses due to vitamin D Toxicity. *Zentralbl veterinaermed [A]s, 21:*638-643, 1974.

N.R.C. Nutrient Requirements of Horses. Washington, DC, National Research Council, 1978, pp. 6-10.

O'Moore, L. B.: Nutritional factors in the rearing of the young Thoroughbred horse. *Equine Vet J, 4:*9-16, 1972.

Pearson, P. B. and Luecke, R. W.: Studies on the metabolism of nicotinic acid in the horse. *Arch Biochem,* 6:63-68, 1944.

Pearson, P. B. and Schmidt, H.: Pantothenic acid studies with the horse. *J Anim Sci,* 7:78-83, 1948.

Seckington, I. M. and Huntsman, R. G.: The serum folic acid levels of grass fed and stabled horses. *Vet Rec, 81:*158-161, 1967.

Shults, T., Combie, J., Dougherty, J., and Tobin, T.: Variable interval responding in the horse. I. A sensitive method of quantitating the effects of centrally acting drugs. Submitted for publication, 1979.

Stowe, H. D.: Reproductive performance of barren mares following vitamin A and E supplementation. *Proc AAEP,* 81-94, 1967.

Stowe, H. D.: Alpha-tocopherol requirements for equine erythrocyte stability. *Am J Clin Nutr, 21:*135-142, 1968.

Chapter 18

THE ANTIBIOTICS: THE PENICILLINS AND GENTAMICIN

STRANGLES IS A DRAMATIC infectious disease of young horses in which they rapidly become fevered and develop a purulent mucous nasal discharge. Later the lymph glands in the jaw and neck areas swell up and appear to be about to strangle the horse, from which the disease gets its name. Strangles, caused by *Streptococcus equi,* is a highly contagious disease in young horses, but it may be cured or prevented by early treatment with penicillin, the wonder drug of the twentieth century. How penicillin turns the tables on the strangles organism and other bacteria affecting both man and the horse is an intriguing story, which tells us a great deal about the relationships among microbes, men, and horses.

Pencillin is the most potent, most effective, and least toxic of the very important group of drugs known as the antibiotics. An antibiotic may be defined as a substance produced by microorganisms, which is selectively toxic to other microorganisms. How these substances, with which bacteria and fungi have been fighting each other for hundreds of millions of years, were identified and introduced into medicine is a complete story in itself, which started over fifty years ago with a German researcher by the name of Domagk.

Domagk was a physician working in the German chemical industry, where he was engaged in the routine screening of dyes for antibacterial activity. Domagk was performing his screening experiments in mice, first injecting them with a lethal dose of bacteria and then trying to protect them by injecting the dye that he was testing. During these studies he injected his mice with a red dye called prontosil, and he found that this dye readily protected his mice against normally lethal doses of bacteria. From this discovery sprang the sulfonamide family of drugs, the first agents to show clearly that drugs could be toxic to bacteria without affecting the host animal.

The initial reports of the antibacterial effectiveness of the sulfonamides were greeted with much skepticism, but as their effectiveness became clear, the whole approach to infectious disease therapy changed. This change in attitude led people to look for other substances that might be selectively toxic to bacteria, and one of the substances selected for reexamination was the antibacterial substance produced by the penicillum mold, which had been discovered by Alexander Fleming in the 1920s.

Although Fleming had worked extensively with the antibacterial substance produced by the pencillium mold in the 1930s, he had been unable to purify it and develop it properly. Further, the basic approach of studying microbial toxins had been tried before by quite a number of investigators, but invariably the antibacterial substances recovered from microorganisms had been too toxic to animals for general use. Because of this, the climate of scientific opinion was not receptive for

Bacteria and fungi have been fighting each other with antibiotics for hundreds of millions, possibly billions, of years.

penicillin when Fleming first reported it in the 1920s, and penicillin was simply regarded as a laboratory curiosity.

This climate of opinion, however, changed abruptly after discovery of the sulfonamides, and in the early 1940s, Florey and Chain, at Oxford, set about a systematic reexamination of antibacterial substances produced by microorganisms. One of the first substances they studied was the secretion of the penicillium mold that Fleming had discovered. Chain was a capable chemist, so they soon purified it and showed it to be a potent antibacterial with little or no toxicity for mammals. With this discovery the antibiotic era was born and the way was clearly pointed for the discovery of the other major antibiotics.

In the remainder of the 1940s, the techniques for the mass production of penicillin were worked out and a number of other antibiotics discovered. Streptomycin was discovered in 1944 and the tetracyclines and chloramphenicol in 1948. Thus, within little more than ten years, most of the major groups of antibiotics available to us today were discovered, although their full development continued into the 1950s and 1960s. One should keep in mind, however, that of the thousands of antibiotics that have been discovered by the worldwide screening procedures, the vast majority are too toxic to mammalian systems to be of any clinical importance. Because of this, it took the discovery of penicillin to demonstrate the possibilities of this very effective and likely very old group of plant drugs.

The antibiotics are selectively toxic to bacteria and relatively nontoxic to their hosts because of the basic biochemical differences that have evolved between plants and animals. Most bacteria have strong fibrous cell walls, which serve the very important purpose of protecting the bacterium from damaging agents in its environment. If bacteria are deprived of this strong cell wall, they swell up and die. Penicillin kills bacteria indirectly by blocking formation of their cell walls. However, since mammalian cells do not have strong fibrous cell walls, penicillin has almost no toxicity for the horse.

While penicillin acts on a complex sequence of biochemical steps involved in synthesis of a tough fibrous cell wall, in theory one single difference in a biochemical pathway between a bacterium and the horse should be sufficient to allow a drug to act selectively. As we will see later, the sulfonamide group of drugs inhibit growth in bacteria because bacteria manufacture their own folic acid, while horses and man get folic acid preformed in their diet. This one extra step in a biochemical pathway in a bacterium can render it susceptible to attack by a drug that will not affect the host.

In the last analysis, simple binding site or "receptor" differences can be enough to account for the differences in drug sensitivity between bacteria and mammals. The antibiotic streptomycin acts by binding to the protein synthetic machinery in the bacterial cell and disrupting its function. There are, however, subtle and not very well understood differences between the protein synthetic machinery of bacteria and horses, and streptomycin does not bind to the machinery in the horse and inhibit its function. Streptomycin, therefore, only inhibits protein synthesis in the bacteria and not in the horse, so it is nontoxic for the horse. This difference appears to be due to the fact that the horse does not have the special binding sites or receptors for proteins that the gram-negative bacteria sensitive to streptomycin have.

The antibiotics, then, act to slow the growth of or kill bacteria by being selectively toxic to the bacteria but relatively nontoxic to horses and other mammals. In the next two chapters we will consider how the various antibiotics act in the horse, what they may be expected to do in the horse, how one should best use them, and finally, what one should watch out for with them. The first of the antibiotics that we will discuss is the most potent and least toxic of all the antibiotics, the penicillins.

THE PENICILLINS

Although the first of the true antibiotics to be introduced into medicine, the penicillins remain by far the most potent and effective of the antibiotic group of drugs. Over the years, their mechanism of action has been studied in some detail, and it turns out that their basic structure and mechanism of action determines many of their clinical properties. Figure 18-1 shows the basic chemical structure of penicillin G and points to the β-lactam bond, which is the "active" bond or active site of all members of the penicillin group and the closely related cephalosporins. In this chapter we will review the pharmacology of the penicillins and show how many of the clinical characteristics of the penicillins in horses are determined by its basic pharmacology.

As we have pointed out earlier, the penicillins kill bacteria by robbing them of their cell walls. As illustrated in Figure 18-2, the normal bacterium lives inside its tough cell wall, which protects it from "osmotic" rupture. The last step in the formation of this cell wall is the opening of an alanine-alanine bond and its "cross" linking with special groups on an adjacent chain to complete the cell wall. The action of penicillin is to specifically block the cross-linking enzyme that splits the alanine-alanine bond and in this way block the final step in cell wall formation (Fig. 18-2).

Penicillin blocks the enzyme that splits the alanine-alanine bond by "fooling" the cross-linking enzyme. It turns out that the portion of the penicillin molecule called

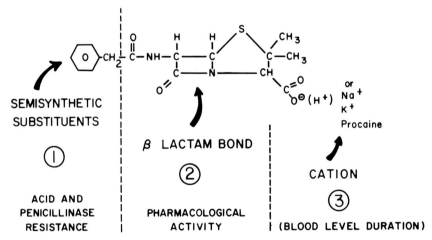

Figure 18-1. Structure and activity of penicillin G. The antibacterial activity of penicillin resides in the CN β-lactam bond (2), which is attacked by, but blocks, the bacterial "cross-linking" enzyme. This lactam bond is sensitive to acidic or penicillinase hydrolysis. Alterations at (1) on the penicillin molecule give rise to the semisynthetic penicillins, which can be acid-stable (oxacillin), penicillinase-resistant (methicillin), or broad-spectrum (ampicillin). In crystalline penicillins, the H at (3) is substituted for by Na^+ or K^+, which gives rise to highly water soluble compounds suitable for intravenous administration. If procaine is substituted for these ions, a slowly dissolving crystal is formed, which is a useful intramuscular "depot" or long-acting preparation of penicillin.

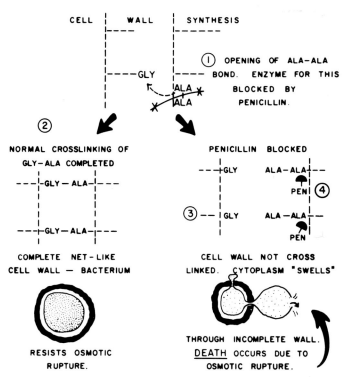

Figure 18-2. Bactericidal action of penicillin. The last step in bacterial cell wall synthesis is the opening of an alanine-alanine bond at (1) and the linking of the remaining alanine to a glycine on the next strand. This cross-linking (2) completes the cell wall, which protects the bacterium from osmotic rupture. In the presence of penicillin, the cross-linking enzyme attacks and attempts to open the β-lactam bond of the penicillin molecule. Penicillin binds covalently to the active site on the enzyme (3) (Pen—▶), blocking its action, with the result that the cell wall is not cross-linked (4) and the bacterium is not protected against osmotic rupture. Bacterial death, when it occurs, is due to osmotic rupture and not to any direct action of penicillin. Reproduced with permission from Tobin, *J Equine Med Surg*, 2:475, 1978.

the β-lactam bond looks just like the alanine-alanine bond of the bacterial cell wall (Fig. 18-3). The cross-linking enzyme binds the penicillin molecule in just the same way as it would bind the alanine-alanine bond and then tries to open the β-lactam bond of the penicillin molecule. The cross linking enzyme gets about halfway and then cannot go any further. The process stops with the penicillin covalently and irreversibly bound to the active site of the cross-linking enzyme. The cross-linking enzyme has in a way "bitten off" more than it can chew, and winds up with a penicillin molecule "stuck in its throat" (Fig. 18-4). Since the penicillin binds irreversibly to the cross-linking enzyme, it can no longer make bacterial cell wall. Without their tough bacterial cell wall, the bacteria swell up, burst, and die.

Many of the clinical actions and effects of penicillin in the horse relate directly to this mechanism of action. Penicillin is categorized as a bactericidal drug, which means that it actually causes bacterial death, rather than simply stopping growth of bacteria. This action of penicillin is illustrated schematically in Figure 18-5. In this illustration, when penicillin is added to a culture of rapidly growing bacteria, it

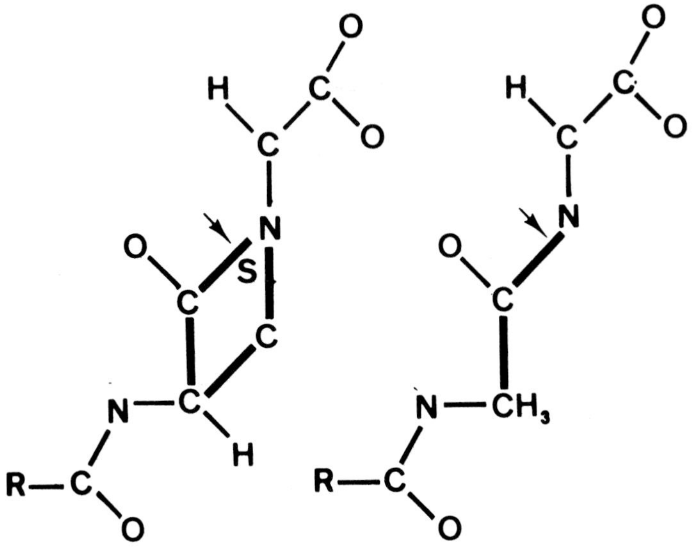

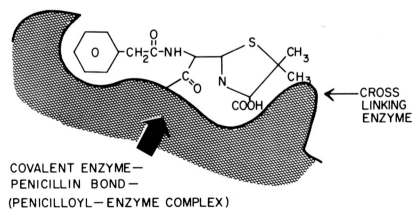

Figure 18-3. Structural similarity of the β-lactam bond and the D-alanyl-D-alanine bond. The β-lactam ring of the penicillin molecule is outlined in the heavy strokes, as is the D-alanyl-D-alanine bond. The arrow shows the point of attack of the cross-linking enzyme on these bonds. The thiazolidine ring of the penicillin molecule has been omitted for clarity.

immediately stops further growth and then causes death of all the bacteria in the culture (or the horse). On the other hand, if an antibiotic that was simply bacteriostatic was added, further growth of the bacteria would stop but bacterial death would not occur. Obviously, in a clinical situation, a bactericidal drug is preferable to a bacteriostatic one, and penicillin is one of the most potent bactericidal agents known.

Figure 18-4. Penicillin irreversibly binds to the active site of the cross-linking enzyme. The hatched surface represents the active center of the cross-linking enzyme to which penicillin becomes chemically linked to form a stable penicilloyl-enzyme complex. This stable chemical linking of penicillin to its receptor means that penicillin is a highly potent antibacterial substance.

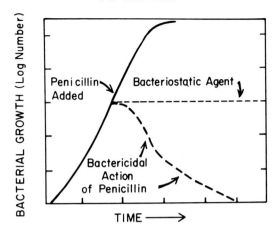

Figure 18-5. Bacteriostatic and bactericidal action of antibiotics. The solid line represents a bacterial culture in which the numbers of bacteria are rapidly increasing. If penicillin is added to such a rapidly growing culture, it first stops further bacterial growth and then proceeds to kill the bacteria in the culture, as indicated by the heavy dashed line. On the other hand, some antibiotics are simply bacteriostatic, and while they will prevent bacterial growth, they will not kill bacteria. This action is indicated by the light dashed line.

Because penicillin only blocks formation of new cell wall, it is primarily effective against "young," rapidly growing populations of bacteria. If the bacteria are "mature" and not forming new cell wall, penicillin is much less effective. This is also the reason that bacteriostatic drugs antagonize the actions of penicillin, because they simply prevent bacterial growth and thus formation of new cell wall and thereby block the action of penicillin.

The very tight or "irreversible" binding of penicillin to the cross-linking enzyme is the principal reason for the potency and effectiveness of penicillin. Unlike penicillin, most other antibiotics, and indeed most drugs, only bind to their receptors for a few seconds and then diffuse away from the receptor. With penicillin, however, the irreversible binding means that once the penicillin has reached the cross-linking enzyme, it stays there. Because of this, relatively little penicillin is required to block the cross-linking enzymes, and penicillin is thus a very potent drug. The irreversible nature of the binding also means that penicillin is one of the few drugs whose blood level you can afford to let drop, since the drug will remain bound to the cross-linking enzyme. While this is not to be encouraged, penicillin is one of the few drugs with which one has this leeway.

Another clinical characteristic of penicillin that relates to its mechanism of action is that it may be ineffective in certain areas of the body. Because penicillin does not kill bacteria directly but just robs them of their cell walls, it is possible for bacteria to "persist" without their cell walls in certain areas of the body. These areas are usually areas of high osmotic pressure, such as the kidney, and possibly in certain abscesses. Bacteria may thus "persist" in these protected areas during therapy and then reinfect the animal when the drug is withdrawn. In the face of such "persisters," another type of antibiotic needs to be selected for good drug action.

Among the various penicillins, penicillin G, or benzylpenicillin (Table 18-I), is

TABLE 18-I
THE SEMISYNTHETIC PENICILLINS

NAME	STRUCTURE	ACTIVITY
PENICILLIN G	—CH$_2$—	CHEAPEST AND MOST POTENT
METHICILLIN	OCH$_3$ / OCH$_3$	PENICILLINASE RESISTANT
OXACILLIN	C—C— N C O CH$_3$	PENICILLINASE RESISTANT
AMPICILLIN	—CH— NH$_2$	GRAM POSITIVE AND GRAM NEGATIVE ACTIVITY
AMOXICILLIN	OH— —CH— NH$_2$	GRAM POSITIVE AND GRAM NEGATIVE ACTIVITY BETTER ABSORBED
CARBENICILLIN	—CH— COONa	GRAM POSITIVE AND GRAM NEGATIVE ACTIVITY INCLUDING ACTIVITY AGAINST PSEUDOMONAS

the most likely penicillin that the veterinarian will be administering, since it is the most potent, most effective, and least toxic of all the penicillins. Penicillin G is available in three different dosage forms, as the water-soluble sodium or potassium salts, as procaine penicillin, and, less commonly, as benzathine penicillin.

Since the sodium and potassium salts of penicillin are water soluble, they may be given intravenously or intramuscularly. When given by either route, one gets a very high blood level of penicillin initially, which then falls away rapidly over the next twelve hours or so. This rapid fall in the blood level of penicillin occurs because as an organic acid, penicillin is pumped directly into the urine, in much the same way as furosemide. This rapid decrease in the blood levels of penicillin is a therapeutic problem, since it means that good blood levels of penicillin are likely to be difficult to maintain.

One solution to this problem of the rapid elimination of penicillin is to inject the drug intramuscularly in a form in which it is only slowly absorbed. When given this way, penicillin trickles into the bloodstream from its IM injection site, and as long as it continues to trickle in, one maintains a blood level of penicillin. The problem with this approach, however, is that one never gets very high blood levels of penicillin (Fig. 18-6).

Procaine penicillin is the most commonly used depot or slowly absorbed form of penicillin, and with this preparation one rarely gets penicillin levels in the bloodstream of above 2 µg/ml. This is a marginal concentration of penicillin to have in the bloodstream if the organism is in any way resistant to penicillin (Table 18-II).

In addition, penicillin is not a particularly good penetrator into tissues, and the

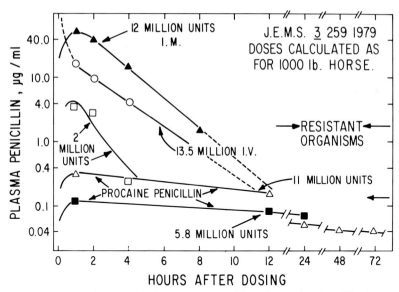

Figure 18-6. Plasma levels of penicillin after sodium penicillin and procaine penicillin. The data show the different rates of absorption and elimination of penicillin when administered in different forms. The open circles (o—o) show plasma levels of penicillin after about 13.5 million units of sodium penicillin IV, while the solid triangles (▲—▲) show plasma levels after about the same dose was given IM. In both cases, peak plasma levels of the drug of about 40 μg/ml were obtained, which decayed rapidly. If about the same dose was given intramuscularly as procaine penicillin, however, 100-fold lower blood levels of drug were obtained initially, but these lower levels declined much more slowly and small blood levels of penicillin were still observed at seventy-two hours after dosing. The arrows (→) marked resistant organisms indicate the blood levels of penicillin required to combat resistant organisms, while the single arrow (→) indicates the blood level required to inhibit susceptible organisms.

TABLE 18-II

PERCENT OF COMMON EQUINE PATHOGENS SENSITIVE TO THE PENICILLINS

Pathogen	Penicillin %	Oxacillin %	Methacillin %	Ampicillin %
Steptococcus zooepidemicus	100	75	100	100
Nonhemolytic streptococci	80	45	—	73
Staphylcoccus aureus	29	94	100	42
Samonella	0	0	—	42
Proteus mirabilis	12	0	—	12
Pseudomonas aeruginosa	0	0	—	0
Pasteurella sp.	90	17	—	95
Klebsiella pneumonia & K. oxytoca	0	0	—	13
Escherichia coli	3	4	—	63
Enterobacter	0	0	—	0
Bordetella bronchiseptica	0	0	—	—
Corynebacterium equi	54	0	13	—
Actinobacillus suis & A. equuli	70	—	—	74

SOURCE: After Knight and Heitala (1978).

high initial blood levels obtained after injection of Na $^+$ and K $^+$ penicillin will yield higher tissue levels of drug than may be expected after procaine penicillin. Therefore, if an infection is located in a protected site, such as a joint, abscess, or in the CNS, it may be better to give frequent large doses of Na $^+$ or K $^+$ penicillin rather than equivalent doses of procaine penicillin. Finally, because procaine penicillin is an insoluble form of the drug, it should never be given intravenously, as administration by this route may cause massive pulmonary embolism and death.

Among the various penicillins that have been developed, penicillin G or benzyl-penicillin is the most potent, most effective, and least expensive of all the penicillins. It is therefore, all other things being equal, the drug of choice from this group. However, penicillin G has a number of disadvantages, and to avoid these disadvantages, the semisynthetic penicillins were developed.

The semisynthetic penicillins were developed to deal with the various problems that one can run into with penicillin G. Penicillin G is broken down in the presence of stomach acid, so acid-resistant forms of penicillin were developed. Penicillin G can also be inactivated by penicillinase-producing organisms, so the penicillinase-resistant penicillins were developed (see Table 18-I). Lastly, penicillin G is almost inactive against gram-negative organisms, so the broad-spectrum penicillins were developed, which are active against both gram-positive and gram-negative bacteria (see Table 18-I).

In performing these modifications, the first step was to grow the basic penicillin nucleus in culture; then, different synthetic chemical groups were added to the left-hand portion of the molecule as shown in Figure 18-1. Because half the molecule is grown in a culture of the penicillum mold and the other half is synthetic, they are called the semisynthetic penicillins. Because these changes are modifications of the potent penicillin G molecule, the semisynthetic penicillins are all less potent than penicillin G. It is a tribute to the great potency of the penicillin molecule that it can be manipulated so much and still retain useful antibacterial activity.

Methicillin is one of the principal penicillinase-resistant penicillins. This drug has been modified such that when it is attacked by the penicillinase enzyme it binds to and inactivates it. It is, however, much less potent than penicillin G, and higher levels of it are required to produce the same antibacterial effect. On the other hand, since methicillin acts to block penicillinase, there is no reason that one cannot combine penicillin G, which is cheap, with methicillin, which is more expensive but which will block any penicillinase present and allow penicillin G to act on the bacteria.

Until the relatively recent development of the broad-spectrum penicillins, the penicillins were essentially inactive against gram-negative organisms. With the advent of ampicillin, however, the first of the broad-spectrum penicillins was introduced into medicine. While ampicillin is only half as potent as penicillin G against various gram-positive organisms, it is up to ten times more potent than penicillin G against various gram-negative organisms. One point to remember about ampicillin, however, is that the ampicillin sodium gives much better blood

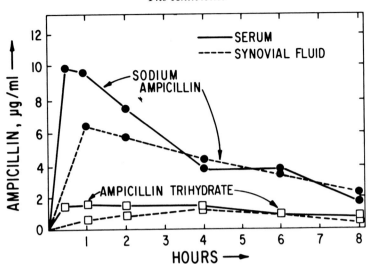

Figure 18-7. Blood levels of ampicillin after sodium ampicillin and ampicillin trihydrate. The solid circles (●—●) show serum and synovial fluid levels of ampicillin after injection of 11 mg/kg of sodium ampicillin, while the open squares (□—□) show levels after injection of the same amount of ampicillin trihydrate. Adapted from Beech et al. (1979).

levels of ampicillin than ampicillin trihydrate and is thus likely to give better clinical results (Fig. 18-7).

Amoxicillin is a recently introduced broad-spectrum penicillin that seems to be more bioavailable than the other broad-spectrum penicillins. When administered systemically, higher blood levels of this agent are obtained than with the other broad-spectrum penicillins. As well as giving better blood levels, amoxicillin also appears to penetrate bacteria more rapidly than the other broad-spectrum penicillins and thus leads to more rapid bacterial death than is the case with other broad-spectrum agents.

As pointed out earlier, penicillin is essentially nontoxic in the horse. About the only direct toxicity associated with penicillin is its ability to cause convulsions if given in very high doses, and, to my knowledge, this problem has never been reported in the horse. A much more likely problem, however, is cation toxicity, for if large doses of potassium penicillin are given IV, the added potassium ion may depress the heart. All other things being equal, therefore, the sodium salt is the penicillin of choice to use intravenously. Occasionally, when large doses of procaine penicillin are given, horses may go through an acute excitement response. A similar sequence is occasionally seen in the human, and its cause remains unclear and is almost invariably self-limiting. As with any drug, allergy or hypersensitivity problems may be seen. The incidence of this is higher with the penicillins than with other drugs. Finally, the major problem with the penicillins in performance horses is the ability of procaine from procaine penicillin to turn up in horse urine for up to two weeks after a dose of procaine penicillin, giving rise to embarrassing "inadvertent" positives due to procaine (see Chapter 16).

In summary, when it comes to using the penicillins in an individual case, it should be remembered that penicillin G is the least expensive and most potent of all the penicillins. Further, because the penicillins are essentially nontoxic, there is no reason to restrict the dose. Currently, doses of procaine penicillin administered IM to humans range up to 5 million units, and 5 million units must be considered a conservative dose for a horse. It is also important to remember that high plasma levels of penicillin aid its diffusion into infected areas, and in an acute situation my own preference would be for frequent high doses of sodium penicillin rather than less frequent doses of procaine penicillin.

If the microorganism causing the problem is penicillinase resistant, methicillin or oxacillin may be used. Full dosage schedules of these agents should be used, and it is probably advantageous to combine these drugs with penicillin G, since these drugs act by blocking the penicillinases and will thereby protect the more potent penicillin G from hydrolysis and allow it to act.

Among the broad-spectrum agents, ampicillin or amoxicillin would appear to be the drugs of choice, with amoxicillin appearing to give better blood levels and more rapid action. Carbenicillin is the agent of choice in treating *Pseudomonas* infections, usually in combination with gentamycin, the most effective antibiotic of the aminoglycoside group.

GENTAMICIN AND THE AMINOGLYCOSIDES

Gentamicin is currently the most important member of the aminoglycoside family of antibiotics, of which streptomycin was the first member discovered. The discovery of streptomycin in 1944 was followed by neomycin (1949), kanamycin (1957), gentamicin (1963), and others. As a group, these agents are known as the aminoglycoside antibiotics, and they share a large number of pharmacological and therapeutic properties in common.

The characteristic that completely dominates the pharmacology of this family of antibiotics is their high water solubility and low lipid solubility. Even casual inspection of the structures of streptomycin or gentamycin (Fig. 18-8) shows them to contain many OH (hydroxyl) and NH groups. These groups interact well with water, and the net result is that streptomycin, gentamycin, and the other members of this family cross the lipid outer membrane of cells with difficulty. They are therefore all poorly absorbed after oral administration and distribute poorly in the body even if given by injection. They cross into the brain with extreme difficulty, enter the eye poorly, and even have trouble getting into red cells. Because they do not enter liver cells, they are not metabolized to any significant extent and are not excreted in the bile. They are therefore excreted largely unchanged by the kidneys, and since they are concentrated by the renal concentrating mechanisms, they are found in high concentrations in urine. Because of the many characteristics that this group of drugs have in common, we will present the pharmacology of gentamicin first and then compare the others with this widely used therapeutic agent.

Like all members of this group, gentamicin is poorly absorbed from the intestinal tract and acts essentially only on the intestinal tract after oral administration. For systemic action, gentamycin must be given parenterally, usually by intra-

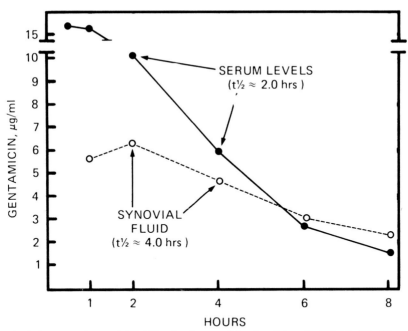

Figure 18-10. Serum and synovial fluid levels of gentamicin after 4.4 mg/kg IM. Modified from Beech et al., *Am J Vet Res*, 1977.

can be very effective in urinary tract infections. Further, if the urine is alkaline, the antibacterial activity of these agents may be substantially increased. As mentioned earlier, the treatment of choice for the very difficult to treat *Pseudomonas* infections is a combination of carbenicillin and gentamicin. When using this combination, however, it should be remembered that these agents should not be mixed up together in solution, as they are chemically incompatible and will inactivate each other.

The use of gentamicin in the treatment of metritis in mares and genital tract infections in stallions has been reported. In a somewhat sketchy study, Morrow and coworkers reported on an investigation in which sixty mares, barren for an average of 3.2 years, were treated with 1 to 2.5 gm (2 to 5 mg/kg) of gentamicin daily in about 300 ml of physiological saline as an intrauterine infusion for from one to ten days. Prior to treatment, about half of these mares cultured positive for *Pseudomonas*, with *Streptococcus*, *Staphylococcus*, and coliforms making up the balance. After gentamicin treatment, 86 percent of these mares reportedly had bacteriologically negative uterine cultures, and 74 percent produced live foals, a substantial percentage of mares to get in foal by any standard. Broadly similar results have also been reported by Houdeshell.

Hamm has reported on the use of gentamicin in the therapy of genital tract infections in three stallions. One of these stallions had bacteriologically confirmed *Pseudomonas aeruginosa* infection in the genital tract with decreased sperm count, reduced percentage motility, "livability," and volume, with an increased number of white blood cells. Another stallion had *Klebsiella* and *Pseudomonas* spp. in his semen in association with impaired semen quality. In these stallions, treatment at 4.4 mg/kg twice a day, either IM or IV (in the event of muscle soreness) for between ten and twenty days, eliminated *Pseudomonas* spp. from the tract of one and returned each horse of breeding soundness.

Hamm and Jones have reported preliminary results on use of gentamicin in the treatment of diarrhea in twenty foals of from two to seventy-five days of age. Thirteen of these foals had severe clinical signs of disease for more than four days, and eight had received treatment with other antimicrobials, including neomicin and streptomicin. All animals were given 250 mg gentamicin IV twice daily until remission of the clinical signs of disease, even though no bacteriological typing of the cause of the diarrhea was attempted. The IV route was selected over the oral route because of the poor absorption of gentamicin from the gastrointestinal tract and the signs of systemic involvement in many of these foals. In all foals, remission, as evidenced by improved stool consistency, had occurred within sixty hours of starting therapy and in some foals had occurred after only one day of therapy. Signs of improved appetite and elimination of dehydration and depression occurred in most of these animals within twenty-four hours of starting treatment, and body temperature also declined to normal within thirty-six hours. No recurrence of diarrhea in any animal was observed during a posttreatment period of fourteen days. Hamm and Jones suggested that these very promising results would justify a more thorough study of the efficacy of gentamicin in the therapy of foal diarrhea.

While these results are impressive, experience in Kentucky suggests that gentamicin should be used with particular care in young foals, as renal function in these animals may not be mature enough to withstand prolonged gentamicin therapy. In one series of fourteen-day-old pony foals, which received high doses of gentamicin for seven to ten days to control diarrhea, good control of the diarrhea was obtained. However, five to six weeks later, a number of these foals became lethargic, showed ventral edema, and died of renal failure. Postmortem examination showed signs of proximal tubular damage, and similar patterns of proximal tubular damage with a history of gentamicin therapy a number of weeks previously had been seen in foal accessions to our postmortem room at the University of Kentucky. It is probably wise, therefore, to use gentamicin sparingly in young foals and not to prolong therapy unduly. Treatment with other drugs that are either nephrotoxic or are excreted vias the kidney is also likely best avoided in young horses on gentamicin therapy.

Streptomycin is now rarely used alone in equine medicine, but almost always as part of a penicillin-streptomycin combination. The principal problem with streptomycin is that resistance to it is both relatively common and occurs readily, which greatly reduces its usefulness (Table 18-IV). Like the other members of this group, streptomycin is relatively rapidly excreted, and it should be given in three daily doses at about 20 mg/kg. Because of its rapid excretion there is little danger of cumulation of this drug if renal function is normal, but if renal function is impaired, high blood levels of streptomycin and toxicity can readily result.

Kanamycin is the second most effective drug in this group but is less active and more toxic than gentamycin. Its plasma half-life is relatively short, with an appar-

TABLE 18-IV

PERCENT OF COMMON EQUINE PATHOGENS SENSITIVE TO
AMINOGLYCOSIDE ANTIBIOTICS

Pathogen	Streptomycin %	Kanamycin %	Gentamycin %	Neomycin %
Streptococcus zooepidemicus	71	83	100	63
Nonhemolytic streptococci	50	38	80	30
Staphylococcus aureus	47	96	100	95
Salmonella	25	33	100	33
Proteus mirabilis	44	67	100	71
Pseudomonas aeruginosa	17	12	92	53
Pasteurella sp.	83	92	100	85
Klebsiella pneumonia & K. oxytoca	69	94	100	87
Escherichia coli	38	75	100	4
Enterobacter	89	90	100	90
Bordetella bronchiseptica	0	95	100	95
Corynebacterium equi	100	90	100	100
Actinobacillus suis & A. equuli	61	91	100	84

Source: Knight and Heitala (1978)

ent half-life of about 1.5 hours, which makes it difficult to maintain blood levels. Knight, in California, suggests a dosage rate of about 5 mg/kg, three times a day, for this agent.

Neomycin is closely related to kanamycin but is even more toxic, which limits its usefulness. In human medicine it is rarely used systemically because of its toxicity. Neomycin is principally used, therefore, as a topical preparation for infections of the eyes, ears, and skin, and to "sterilize" the bowel prior to surgery. Neomycin has been suggested for systemic use in the horse along with ampicillin in the treatment of contagious equine metritis, but its role and efficacy in this therapy remains to be determined.

Spectinomycin is an aminocyclitol antibiotic rather than an aminoglycoside, and thus its actions and toxicities differ substantially from those of a typical aminoglycoside. It is less active on a molar basis than this group of drugs, and data from humans suggest dosage rates of up to 40 mg/kg parenterally. It has been used in the horse with good results as an intrauterine infusion in the treatment of mixed uterine infections and infections due to *Klebsiella*. When administered in this way, the dose to an adult horse is about 2 to 3 g of spectinomycin in a 500 ml volume for three to four days. Because spectinomycin is not an aminoglycoside, it can be used in high doses without fear of inducing eighth nerve damage or renal toxicity. Adverse reactions reported in humans include dizziness, vertigo, malaise, and anorexia. Spectinomycin may also be used parenterally in the horse, and dosage schedules and indications for its use by this route in the horse are now being worked out.

In summary, gentamycin is clearly the aminoglycoside of choice in the therapy of most gram-negative infections in horses. It is currently effective against a wide range of gram-negative organisms and, in combination with carbenicillin, is especially useful in treating deep-seated infections due to *Pseudomonas* spp. Gentamicin should, however, be used with care in young foals, and all horses on gentamicin should be watched carefully for signs of renal damage. Gentamicin has essentially replaced kanamycin in equine medicine and relegated streptomycin to use in penicillin-streptomycin combinations. While a number of new aminoglycoside antibiotics have recently been developed, these, with the possible exception of amikacin and spectinomycin, have at present no readily apparent advantages over gentamicin.

SELECTED REFERENCES

Barza, M. and Scheife, R. T.: Antimicrobial spectrum, pharmacology and therapeutic use of anti-· biotics. IV. Aminoglycosides. *Am J Hosp Pharm, 3:*723-737, 1977.

Beech, J., Kohn, C., Leitch, M., Weinstein, A. J., and Gallagher, M.: Therapeutic use of gentamicin in horses: Concentrations in serum, urine and synovial fluid and elevation of renal function. *Am J Vet Res, 33:*1085-1087, 1977.

Beech, J., Leitch, M., Kohn, C. W., Weinstein, A., and Gallagher, M.: Serum and synovial fluid levels of sodium ampicillin and ampicillin trihydrate in horses. *J Equine Med Surg, 3:*350-354, 1979.

Behrens, E., Beech, J., and Donawick, W. J.: Serum and peritoneal fluid concentrations of gentamicin in horses. *J Equine Med Surg, 3:*484-488, 1979.

Brewer, N. S.: Antimicrobial agents. II. The aminoglycosides streptomycin, kanamycin, gentamicin, tobramycin, amikacin, neomycin. *Mayo Clin Proc, 52:*675-679, 1976.

Burns, S. S., Simpson, R. B., and Snell, J.R.: Control of microflora in stallion semen with a semen extender. *J Reprod Fertil, 23:*139-142, 1975.

Doll, E. R., Wallace, M. E., and Hull, F. E.: Serum levels of penicillin in domestic animals. *Ky Agric Exp Sta Bull,* No. 549, 1950.

Doll, E. R., Wallace, M. E., and McCollum, W. H.: Serum levels of horses following intramuscular injection of aqueous suspension of procaine penicillin. *J Am Vet Med Assoc, 45:*247-309, 1950.

Green, R. L., Lewis, J. E., Kraus, S. J., and Frederickson, E. L.: Elevated plasma protein concentrations after administration of procaine penicillin G. *N Engl J Med, 291:*223-226, 1974.

Hamm, D. H.: Gentamicin therapy of genital tract infections in stallions. *J Equine Med Surg, 2:*243-245, 1978.

Hamm, D. H. and Jones, E. W.: Gentamicin in the treatment of foal diarrhea. *J Equine Med Surg, 4:*159-162, 1979.

Hennessy, P. W., Kohn, F. S., Bickford, S. M., and Loy, J. I.: *In vitro* activity of gentamicin against bacteria isolated from domestic animals. *VMSAC, 66:*1118-1112, Nov. 1971.

Houdeshell, J. W. and Hennessey, P. W.: Gentamicin in the treatment of equine metritis. *VM SAC, 67:*1348-1352, 1972.

Huebner, R. A.: Therapeutic serum concentrations of penicillin. *J Am Vet Med Assoc, 159:*757-759, 1971.

Knight, H. D.: Antimicrobial agents used in the horse. *Proc AAEP, 21:*131-144, 1975.

Knight, H. and Hietala, S.: Antimicrobial susceptibility patterns in horses. *Proc 2nd Conf Equine Pharmacol,* The Ohio State University, 1978, p. 63.

Knudsen, E.: Renal clearance studies in the horse. II. Penicillin, sulfathiazine and sulfadimidine. *Acta Vet Scand, 1:*188-200, 1960.

Morrow, G. I., Jackson, R. S., and Teeter, S. M.: Gentamicin therapy for endometritis in the mare. *Proc AAEP, 18:*411-416, 1977.

Pratt, W. B.: *Chemotherapy of Infection.* New York, Oxford U Pr, 1977.

Raichle, M. E., Knutt, H., Louis, S., and McDowell, F.: Neurotoxicity of intravenously administered penicillin G. *Arch Neurol, 25:*232-239, 1971.

Roberts, M. C. and English, P. B.: Antimicrobial chemotherapy in the horse. II. The application of antimicrobial therapy. *J Equine Med Surg, 3:*308-315, 1979.

Rollins, L. D., Teske, R. H., Condon, R. J., and Carter, G. G.: Serum penicillin and dihydrostreptomy-cin concentrations in horses after intramuscular administration of selected preparations containing these antibiotics. *J Am Vet Med Assoc, 161:*490-495, 1972.

Tobin, T.: Pharmacology review: Chemotherapy in the horse — the penicillins. *J Equine Med Surg, 3:*475-479, 1978.

Tobin, T.: Pharmacology review: Steptomycin, gentamicin and the aminoglycoside antibiotics. *J Equine Med Surg, 4:*206-211, 1979.

Tobin, T., and Blake, J. W.: The pharmacology of procaine in the horse. Relationships between plasma and urinary concentrations of procaine. *J Equine Med Surg, 1:*188-194, 1977.

Chapter 19

THE BROAD-SPECTRUM ANTIBIOTICS

$\mathbf{S}$ OON AFTER THE DISCOVERY of penicillin and streptomycin, the major "broad-spectrum" antibiotics were discovered. The broad-spectrum antibiotics are so called because they inhibit the growth of both gram-positive and gram-negative bacteria. In addition, they also have actions on some other groups of organisms, such as the *Rickettsia,* the mycoplasmas that cause atypical pneumonias, and some other organisms. The drugs that we will consider here include the tetracyclines and chloramphenicol, and in addition we will briefly review the sulfonamides and the nitrofurans.

TETRACYCLINES

The tetracyclines were discovered in 1948 in a soil sample from a field close to the veterinary school on the University of Missouri campus. Chlortetracycline (Aureomycin®) was the first of the tetracyclines to be introduced, and, like the penicillins, there are now a number of chemically closely related tetracyclines on the market (Fig. 19-1). Among the tetracyclines of interest to the equine practitioner are tetracycline itself (Polyotic®), oxytetracycline (Liquamycin®), and tetracycline-containing ointments. These drugs are all closely related both pharmacologically and chemically, and if a bacterium is resistant to one of these agents, it is likely to be resistant to all of them.

Like gentamicin, the tetracyclines produce their antibacterial effect by inhibiting protein synthesis in susceptible bacteria and also by binding to and inhibiting the cellular machinery that synthesizes proteins. The actions of the tetracyclines, however, are not completely specific for bacteria, and they also appear to affect protein synthesis in man and horses. In man, this becomes apparent as what is called an "antianabolic effect," or an inability of individuals on the tetracyclines to put on weight. According to practitioners in the central Kentucky area, a similar phenomenon is seen in foals, and foals on tetracyclines for a period will not "do" as well as might be expected. It is also suspected that the immune response of animals on tetracyclines may be reduced, although clear-cut evidence in this area is lacking.

The tetracyclines are generally considered to be broad-spectrum agents, active against both gram-positive and gram-negative organisms (Table 19-I). They are, however, considered to be bacteriostatic agents, that is, agents that simply stop bacterial proliferation but which do not kill bacteria.

Administration of the tetracyclines to horses can be somewhat of a problem. If given orally, the tetracyclines may be well absorbed, but absorption from the gut is readily interfered with. In the intestinal tract, the tetracyclines readily complex with calcium salts, and milk and iron salts also can interfere with absorption of the tetracyclines. Further, the tetracyclines have an ability to cause gastrointestinal

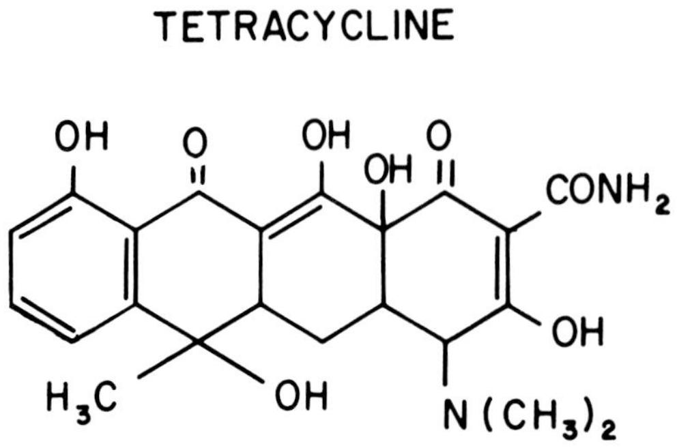

TETRACYCLINE

OH   O   OH   O

OH   OH   CONH$_2$

OH

H$_3$C   OH   N(CH$_3$)$_2$

Figure 19-1. Structure of tetracycline.

upsets in both the human and the horse, so administration to horses by this route should not be undertaken in other than exceptional circumstances.

Intramuscular or subcutaneous administration of the tetracyclines is usually not feasible because most preparations of these drugs are strongly acidic. Given intramuscularly, they may cause pain and tissue swelling, which limits their use by this route. If given IV, they should be given slowly in dilute solution, with care taken not to inject any of these irritant drugs outside the vein, which may cause abscessation of the vein. Because of their irritant properties, the tetracyclines should never be administered into the cerebrospinal fluid, where their administration is likely to cause convulsions, or into joints.

Once they are absorbed, the tetracyclines distribute well in the body and give good blood and tissue levels. Their plasma half-lives are relatively long in the horse, usually in the order of ten to fifteen hours, so the maintenance of blood levels of these drugs is not too difficult (Fig. 19-2). For good antibacterial activity, blood levels of the tetracyclines should be in the 1 to 2 μg/ml range. Data from the University of Pennsylvania suggests that 4.4 mg/kg twice a day is a useful dosage schedule for the tetracyclines in the horse.

TABLE 19-I

PERCENT OF COMMON EQUINE PATHOGENS SENSITIVE TO TETRACYCLINES

Pathogen	% Sensitive
Streptococcus zooepidemicus	71
Nonhemolytic streptococci	74
Staphylococcus aureus	87
Salmonella	33
Proteus mirabilis	33
Pseudomonas aeruginosa	20
Pasteurella sp.	100
Klebsiella pneumonia & *K. oxytoca*	69
Escherichia coli	53
Enterobacter	90
Bordetella bronchiseptica	100
Corynebacterium equi	77
Actinobacillus suis & *A. equuli*	93

Source: Knight and Heitala (1978)

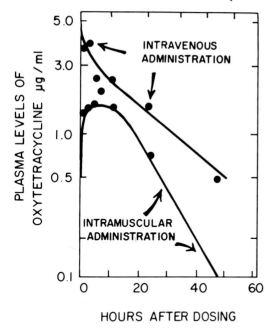

Figure 19-2. Serum levels of oxytetracycline in horses. The solid circles (●—●) show serum levels of oxytetracycline in horses following 2 mg/lb. (4 mg/kg) administered IV and IM, respectively. Adapted from Teske et al. (1973).

There are a number of problems associated with the use of tetracyclines in the horse. If the drug is given in too concentrated solution, or too rapidly, acute collapse can occur. Usually the animal will only go down for a period of from five to forty-five minutes, although death may occur. As part of the ability of the tetracyclines to bind Ca^{++}, they are deposited in growing teeth and bone. Since the tetracyclines readily fluoresce under ultraviolet light, these deposits are easily seen, and this has led to the tetracyclines being used as markers for bone growth in experimental work. Use of the tetracyclines has also been associated with photosensitization, in which white skin areas may react and become ulcerated after exposure to sunlight. Another problem with the tetracyclines is that superinfections are not uncommon after administration of this group of drugs.

An unusual adverse reaction to the tetracyclines that occurs only in horses is a pattern of profuse diarrhea developing after a dose of tetracycline. Usually the animal in question has been stressed, either by travel, surgery, or by a mild infection. Administration of a dose of tetracycline to these animals may result in the development, within about four days, of a profuse diarrhea, with a high probability of death. If this syndrome appears, tetracycline therapy should immediately be discontinued. Because of this problem, some practitioners avoid the use of tetracyclines in the horse, while others use conservative doses and report no problems.

In summary, the tetracyclines are broad-spectrum antibiotics, which are effective against a wide range of bacterial agents but which may be troublesome to administer and use in horses. Although the number of reported adverse reactions to the tetracyclines is small, there is, in the literature, a clear pattern of adverse reactions to these agents under some circumstances. Because of this, some authors consider that the "tetracyclines should not be given to horses, by any route, unless the organisms present are solely sensitive to these drugs and their prophylactic use should not be contemplated." While all practitioners do not follow these rather strict guidelines, any that do elect to use these agents are well advised to keep their doses on the conservative side and take particular care with their intravenous administrations.

CHLORAMPHENICOL

Chloramphenicol (Chloromycetin®) (Fig. 19-3) was discovered in 1947 and introduced into human medicine shortly thereafter. As a broad-spectrum antibiotic it soon found wide use in human medicine and rapidly became very popular. Within a few years, however, it became apparent that use of chloramphenicol in man is associated with a small incidence of a fatal aplastic anemia.* This occurs in about 1 in 50,000 humans on the drug, and these individuals simply stop making some or all of their blood cells. Because the white blood cells are a person's principal defense against infection, these individuals will die, usually after a prolonged illness, from overwhelming infections. Although the incidence of this problem is low, the mortality is very high, and chloramphenicol is not recommended for use in humans for other than life-threatening conditions. No cases of aplastic anemia have ever been reported in the horse, however, and as the horse is rarely used for food, chloramphenicol may be used more readily in the horse.

Chloramphenicol, like the tetracyclines, is bacteriostatic and is considered a broad-spectrum agent. It is active against gram-positive and gram-negative bacteria and also against *Mycoplasma* and *Rickettsia* (Table 19-II). It produces its antibacterial action by inhibiting protein synthesis in bacteria and it also appears to have some action on protein synthesis in mammals. These actions on protein synthesis in mammals show up as a tendency for mammals on high doses of

---

* Aplastic anemia is an anemia in which blood cells, either the white or red blood cells, are not formed.

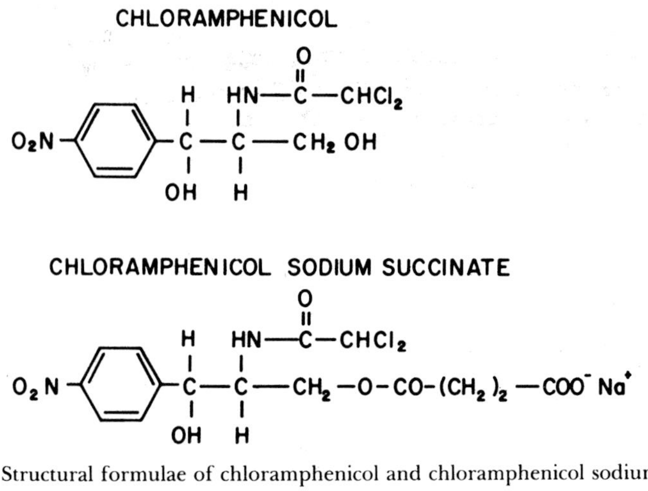

CHLORAMPHENICOL

CHLORAMPHENICOL SODIUM SUCCINATE

Figure 19-3. Structural formulae of chloramphenicol and chloramphenicol sodium succinate.

TABLE 19-II

PERCENT OF COMMON EQUINE PATHOGENS SENSITIVE TO CHLORAMPHENICOL

Pathogen	% Sensitive
Streptococcus zooepidemicus	100
Nonhemolytic streptococci	95
Staphylococcus aureus	100
Salmonella	92
Proteus mirabilis	63
Pseudomonas aeruginosa	12
Pasteurella sp.	100
Klebsiella pneumonia & K. oxytoca	81
Escherichia coli	87
Enterobacter	100
Bordetella bronchiseptica	100
Corynebacterium equi	100
Actinobacillus suis & A. equuli	100

SOURCE: Knight and Heitala (1978)

chloramphenicol to develop simple anemias, and the drug also appears to have some immunosuppressant effects.

Among all the antibiotics, chloramphenicol is by far the most lipid soluble, and it therefore distributes well in the body. Once absorbed, chloramphenicol distributes very widely and gives good concentrations in all body tissues. In fact, if any antibiotic is going to get to the site of a problem, chloramphenicol will, a factor that should be kept in mind when selecting an antibiotic.

Because chloramphenicol is so lipid soluble, this drug is well absorbed after oral administration (Fig. 19-4). It is apparently also completely absorbed, for the incidence of gastrointestinal upsets reported with the tetracyclines does not appear to occur with chloramphenicol. Use of chloramphenicol by the oral route has the further advantage that preparations of the drug for use in this way are quite inexpensive. For example, some preparations of chloramphenicol marketed for use in small animals have been used in horses by practitioners in the central Kentucky area. These workers report good clinical results after oral doses of chloramphenicol of about 5 grams four times a day, which treatments cost less than ten dollars per day.

The lipid solubility of chloramphenicol means that this drug is poorly water soluble, and it cannot be administered parenterally as Chloromycetin®. The solution to this problem was to link chloramphenicol to a succinic acid group to give chloramphenicol sodium succinate. This water-soluble form of the drug can be administered either IV or IM and gives good blood levels of the drug. The only problem, however, is that this can be an extremely expensive form of the drug, and the amounts required to maintain good blood levels in a large horse can quite rapidly amount to substantial sums (Fig. 19-5).

Other problems with chloramphenicol are the differing bioavailability of different forms of the drug and the plasma half-life of the drug, which is quite short. As shown in Figure 19-5, chloramphenicol has a half-life in the horse of about one hour after its IV injection, the shortest plasma half-life of any of the antibiotics,

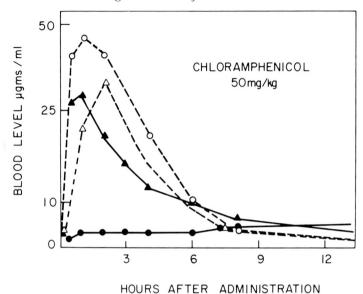

Figure 19-4. Blood levels of chloramphenicol after its oral or intramuscular administration in horses. Chloramphenicol at 50 mg/kg in various forms was administered to horses. The open circles (o—o) show blood levels after oral chloramphenicol, the open triangles (Δ—Δ) after oral chloramphenicol palmitate, the solid circles (●—●) after chloramphenicol IM, and the triangles (▲—▲) after chloramphenicol sodium succinate IM. Adapted from Oh-Ishi (1968).

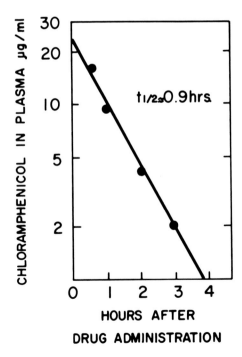

Figure 19-5. Plasma half-life of chloramphenicol in ponies. The solid circles (●—●) show plasma levels of chloramphenicol after its IV injection as chloramphenicol succinate in the horse. Adapted from Davis et al., *Am J Vet Res*, 1972.

which adds to the expense of maintaining blood levels of this drug when it is administered parenterally.

The suggested dose rates for chloramphenicol in horses vary considerably between investigators. Workers at the University of Pennsylvania recommend 12 mg/kg of the succinate IV or IM, four to six times a day, and this dose is used principally in the treatment of salmonella septicemia. Others have suggested dose rates of between 50 and 200 mg/kg, three to four times a day. The suggested blood levels of chloramphenicol to be maintained are 5 μg/ml, but because of the variability in the analytical methods and data reported by different investigators, it is difficult to determine what blood levels are attained after any given dosing schedule.

Reports of adverse reactions to chloramphenicol in the horse are rare. While chloramphenicol has been clearly shown to inhibit the metabolism of other drugs in many species, there is no evidence that it does so in the horse (Fig. 19-6). Chloramphenicol has also been reported to produce a simple anemia in man, this effect appearing in up to one third of individuals on Chloromycetin®. To my knowledge, this effect has not been reported in the horse, perhaps because the dosage levels of chloramphenicol have not been sufficiently high or prolonged enough for this effect to become apparent. In any event, this simple anemia,

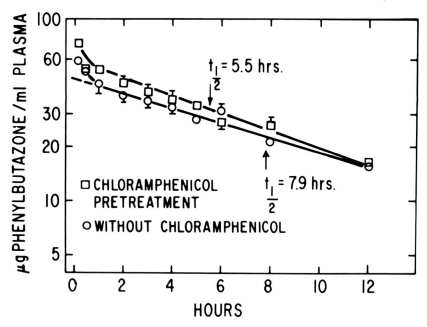

Figure 19-6. Lack of effect of chloramphenicol on the half-life of phenylbutazone in horses. Chloramphenicol (33 mg/kg) or an equivalent volume of normal saline solution was administered IV to Thoroughbred horses. Forty-five minutes later, phenylbutazone (6.6 mg/kg) was administered by rapid IV injection. The open circles (o—o) show the plasma half-life of phenylbutazone in horses pretreated with saline solution, the open squares (□—□) the plasma half-life in horses pretreated with chloramphenicol. By regression analysis, the slope with chloramphenicol pretreatment was significantly (P < 0.01) greater than that without pretreatment. All points are the mean ± SEM of experiments on four different horses. Reproduced with permission from Tobin et al., *Am J Vet Res,* 1977.

which is quite distinct from the aplastic anemia mentioned earlier, is readily reversible on withdrawal of the drug and is not a clinical problem.

Another syndrome that has been reported in the human following chloramphenicol therapy is the so-called "grey baby" syndrome. This occurs in newborn infants, whose ability to metabolize and eliminate chloramphenicol is much less than that of adults. Because of this, both the parent drug and its metabolites can build up in these infants, causing a shocklike syndrome and death. Because of the circulatory problems the the babies turn grey before death, which has given rise to the name of the syndrome. No parallel syndrome has been reported in the horse, but practitioners treating very young foals would do well to dose conservatively and keep this syndrome in mind.

As pointed out earlier, one of the problems with the tetracycline group of drugs has been their tendency to produce gastrointestinal upsets in humans, and similar effects have been seen when these drugs have been given orally to horses. This, however, does not appear to be a problem with chloramphenicol, perhaps because it is rapidly and completely absorbed from the gastrointestinal tract, thereby reducing the likelihood of gastrointestinal upsets.

In summary, therefore, chloramphenicol is a broad-sprectum antibiotic that distributes very well in the horse. Because of this, it is particularly useful in infections in relatively inaccessible locations, such as joint problems, meningitis, or eye infections. One of the principal problems with chloramphenicol in the horse has been the cost of the succinate preparations of chloramphenicol used for parenteral use. Oral preparations of chloramphenicol are available, however, that are quite inexpensive and, to judge from experience in central Kentucky, give very satisfactory results in clinical practice.

THE SULFONAMIDES

Although generally classed with the antibiotics, the sulfonamides are in fact synthetic chemicals that happen to have substantial antibacterial action. As pointed out earlier, they were the first drugs of this general group to be identified, and they have long been used in equine medicine. With the advent of the more potent and specific antibiotics, they are less used now than previously, but they still remain useful and effective antibacterial agents in the horse.

The sulfanomides produce their antimicrobial action by what is called an antimetabolite effect. Bacteria sensitive to the sulfonamides synthesize their own folic acid from a precursor called para-aminobenzoic acid (PABA). The sulfonamides structurally resemble PABA and simply bind to the PABA sites on the folic acid synthesizing enzyme (Fig. 19-7). In this way, they block the formation of folic acid by the bacterium, which eventually stops further growth of the bacterium. However, because each bacterium will already have some preformed folic acid in it at the time that the sulfonamide is injected into the animal, there is "lag" period between the application of the sulfonamide and the cessation of bacterial growth, usually on the order of about four hours or so (Fig. 19-8). Because men and horses get their folic acid preformed in the food as a vitamin, the sulfonamides are only toxic to bacteria and not to horses.

Although there are a large number of different antibacterial sulfonamides

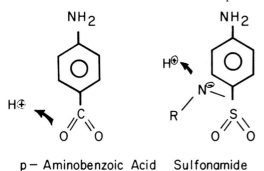

Figure 19-7. Structural similarity between PABA and sulfonamides. The sulfonamide drugs are closely related to *p*-aminobenzoic acid and act by blocking its incorporation into folic acid and DNA in susceptible bacteria.

available, the antibacterial activity of all these agents is approximately equivalent. They are all bacteriostatic, in that they stop bacterial growth rather than kill the bacteria, and the principal differences between the various groups of sulfonamides relate to how they distribute in the horse. Thus some sulfonamides have been designed to act only in the gastrointestinal tract, while others are absorbed well, give good blood levels, and are active against systemic infections. Still others are well absorbed but are also rapidly excreted, giving rise to good antibacterial effects in the urinary tract. All of the sulfonamides have the same spectrum of antibacterial action, being active against both gram-positive and gram-negative agents, and also against some members of the psittacosis-lymphogranuloma group. They are therefore usually considered broad-spectrum agents (Table 19-III). Similarly, if an organism is resistant to one member of the sulfonamide group of drugs, it is resistant to all the members of this group.

The sulfonamides active in the gastrointestinal tract include sulfaguanidine, sulfasuxidine, and sulfathaladine. These sulfonamides are chemically modified in such a way that they must first be hydrolyzed by the bacteria in the intestine before they can act. They are always given orally, and their action is thus largely restricted

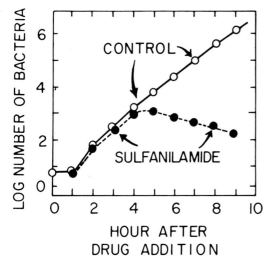

Figure 19-8. Lag period in the action of the sulfonamides. Because bacteria must exhaust their preformed folic acid, there is about a four-hour delay period before the antibacterial action of the sulfonamides becomes apparent. The symbols show growth of hemolytic streptococci in blood without (o—o) and with (●—●) 10^{-5} M sulfanilamide.

TABLE 19-III

PERCENT OF COMMON EQUINE PATHOGENS SENSITIVE TO SULFONAMIDE

Pathogen	% Sensitive
Streptococcus zooepidemicus	—
Nonhemolytic streptococci	0
Staphylococcus aureus	83
Salmonella	67
Proteus mirabilis	50
Pseudomonas aeruginosa	12
Pasteurella sp.	73
Klebsiella pneumonia & *K. oxytoca*	79
Escherichia coli	38
Enterobacter	100
Bordetella bronchiseptica	68
Corynebacterium equi	—
Actinobacillus suis & *A. equuli*	81

SOURCE: After Knight and Heitala (1978)

to the gastrointestinal tract; significant amounts of these drugs are not absorbed.

The second major group of sulfonamides are the systemically active sulfonamides. These drugs are usually administered in their active form intravenously, and they are widely distributed in the body. Blood levels of these drugs are well maintained, and twenty-four hours after administration they are usually in the range of about 30 to 40 μg/ml. After administration of a second dose, blood levels will usually be maintained above the 50 μg/ml considered necessary for a therapeutic effect. The sulfonamides are therefore one of the few antibiotics in the horse with which you only need single daily doses (Fig.19-9) to maintain effective blood levels.

In another variation on the sulfonamide theme, sulfonamides have been developed that are rapidly excreted via the kidneys. These sulfonamides, therefore, give rise to high urinary tract levels of the drug, and they are used in the treatment of urinary tract infections. Sulfisoxazole, or Gantrisin®, is a typical example of this type of sulfonamide. The dose in the human is about 1 gm every six hours, so the dose for the horse is presumably about 8 gm every six hours.

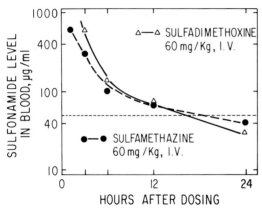

Figure 19-9. Blood levels of sulfonamides and horses. The systemically active sulfonamides sulfamethazine and sulfadimethoxine have relatively long plasma half-lives in horses, and useful blood levels (>50 μg/ml, dotted line) can be maintained by single daily doses of about 60 mg/kg IV.

The recent development of a group of drugs that act on another step in folic acid metabolism has allowed the concept of a sequential inhibition to be applied in antibiotic therapy. Trimethoprim is a drug that inhibits the enzyme dihydrofolate reductase, which catalyzes the change of dihydrofolic acid to tetrahydrofolic acid. Using the sulfonamides in combination with trimethoprim therefore allows a sequential two-point attack on folic acid metabolism in the bacteria. Trimethoprim distributes well in the body but is excreted rapidly in the urine. High urinary concentrations of the drug are attained, and this is where this combination is likely to be particularly effective. These drugs, however, are best avoided in pregnant animals.

The sulfonamides can be quite irritant and painful if given by intramuscular injection and are best administered intravenously. However, if large doses are to be administered intravenously they should be given with care, as staggering tremors and collapse may occur if they are given too rapidly. In the early days of sulfonamide therapy, crystallization of these drugs in the kidney, with renal damage and bloody urine, was a problem. Although this is less of a problem with modern sulfonamides, horses on these drugs should have free access to water and be kept well hydrated to prevent recurrences of this problem.

In summary, the sulfonamides are useful broad-spectrum antibiotics that are available in a number of different chemical forms. They distribute well in the body, and effective levels are found in most body compartments. They also have the advantage that single daily administrations are sufficient to maintain blood levels of these agents. Although reported to be particularly useful in pneumonias, they are not widely used in equine medicine, having been to a large extent supplanted by the more recently developed antibiotic agents.

THE NITROFURANS

The nitrofurans, like the sulfonamides, are synthetic chemicals with a broad spectrum of antibacterial action. They are active against both gram-positive and gram-negative agents, and although they were discovered in 1944, their mechanism of action is not well understood (Table 19-IV).

TABLE 19-IV

PERCENT OF COMMON EQUINE PATHOGENS SENSITIVE TO NITROFURANS

Pathogen	% Sensitive
Streptococcus zooepidemicus	100
Nonhemolytic streptococci	64
Staphylococcus aureus	100
Salmonella	100
Proteus mirabilis	51
Pseudomonas aeruginosa	0
Pasteurella sp.	95
Klebsiella pneumonia & *K. oxytoca*	67
Escherichia coli	100
Enterobacter	100
Bordetella bronchiseptica	0
Corynebacterium equi	75
Actinobacillus suis & *A. equuli*	100

Source: After Knight and Heitala (1978)

The nitrofurans are characterized by their rapid excretion in horses. Because of this, one does not get good blood levels of these agents but high levels in the urinary tract, where they give a good antibacterial action. The nitrofurans are more active in an acidic urine than in an alkaline urine, and they also color the urine brown. Because of the very low blood levels that the drugs give, their use is essentially limited to topical use or in the treatment of urinary tract infections.

Adverse reactions to the nitrofurans are rare, but damage to the peripheral nerves has been reported in man. In equine medicine their most common use is in topical preparations, and the danger of toxicity when they are used in this way is essentially nil.

THE PRINCIPLES OF ANTIBIOTIC USE

While the antibiotics are very potent and useful drugs, like all other drugs they need to be used correctly if maximum benefit is to be obtained from them. The first ground rule in antibiotic use is that they should only be used in circumstances where they are likely to be effective. Using them against resistant bacteria or, worse still, viruses, is a misuse of a vital group of therapeutic agents. Therefore, before an antibiotic is used, one should try to ascertain the nature of the causative organism and whether or not it is susceptible to antibiotics. Sometimes the clinical circumstances, such as an outbreak of strangles, will make the choice of antibiotic clear-cut. More often, however, it will be necessary to sample and culture the

TABLE 19-V

SUGGESTED DAILY DOSAGE RATES AND ROUTES OF ADMINISTRATION OF SOME ANTIMICROBIAL AGENTS

Drug	Daily Dose Rate	Route(s)
Benylpenicillins:		
Sodium or potassium salts	30,000-100,000 u/kg in 3 or 4 doses	IM IV SC
Procaine	15,000-70,000 u/kg in 2 doses	IM
Benzathine	25,000-50,000 u/kg at 4-day intervals	IM
Ampicillin sodium	13-40 mg/kg in 2 or 3 doses	IM IV
Oxacillin	50 mg/kg in 2 or 3 doses	IM IV
Streptomycin	15-20 mg/kg in 2 or 3 doses	IM
Kanamycin	11-15 mg/kg in 2 or 3 doses	IM
Neomycin	20-50 mg/kg in 3 or 4 doses	IV oral
Gentamicin	6-18 mg/kg in 3 or 4 doses	IM
	2-2.5 g/250 ml normal saline	IU*
Erythromycin	10 mg/kg in 3 or 4 doses	IV
Chloramphenicol	100-200 mg/kg in 3 or 4 doses	IM IV oral
Oxytetracycline	4.4-10 mg/kg in 1 or 2 doses	IV
Sulphamethazine	60-150 mg/kg in 1 dose	IV SC oral
Sulphamethylphenazole	110 mg/kg in 1 dose	IV oral
Isoniazid	3-20 mg/kg in 2 doses	oral
Griseofulvin	10 mg/kg in 1 dose	oral
Nystatin	2.4×10 u/250 ml normal saline	IU
Amphotericin B	0.24-0.81 mg/kg in 1 dose	IV
	(>0.58 mg/kg every other day)	diluted in 1 liter 5% dextrose
	100 mg/250 ml normal saline	IU

* IU = intrauterine.
SOURCE: Roberts and English (1979).

Drug	Route, Dose, Frequency	Daily Dose	Daily Cost ($)
Cell Wall Synthesis Inhibitors			
Pro. pen G	IM, 6,600 u/kg, l. 24 hr.	3 Mu	0.34
	IM, 20-50 u/kg, q. 12 hr.	46 Mu	5.03
K pen G	IM, IV, 12.5-50 u/kg, q. 6 hr	91 Mu	33.85
Ampicil. Na	IM, IV, 6.6 mg/kg, q. 12 hr.	6 g	8.00
	IM, IV, 20-50 mg/kg, q. 6 hr	91 g	121.33
Amoxicillin	IM, SC, 2-7 mg/kg, q. 24 hr	Suitable dosage forms unavailable	
	PO, 4-12 mg/kg, q. 12 hr		
Bacteriostatic Inhibitors of Protein Synthesis			
Oxytet.	IV, 5-7.5 mg/kg, q. 12 hr	6.8 g	1.86
	IV, 8.8-22 mg/kg, q. 12 hr	20 g	5.46
Erythro. lactobio.	IV, 2.5 mg/kg, q. 6 hr	4.6 g	32.35
Chloramp.	all, 25-50 mg/kg, q. 6 hr	91 g	
	PO, 12.5 mg/kg, q. 6 hr		
	Powder (0.14/g)		12.74
	Sol — prop. glyc. (1.35/g)		122.85
	Na succinate (6.13/g)		557.83
Bactericidal Inhibitors of Protein Synthesis			
DHSM*	IM, 11 mg/kg, a. 12 hr	10 g	1.14
Kanamycin	IM, 5 mg/kg, q. 8 hr	6,8 g	23.65
	IM, 4.4-11 mg/kg, q. 6 hr	1.82 g	34.78
Gentamicin	IM, 1-2 mg/kg, q. 8 hr	2.73 g	49.14
	IM, 1 mg/kg, q. 6 hr	1.82 g	32.76
Neomycin	PO, 13 mg/kg, q. 24 hr	6 g	0.49
	PO, 12.5-25 mg/kg, q. 6 hr	46 g	3.75
Inhibitors of Intermediary Metabolism			
Sulfadimethoxine	IV, 27.5 mg/kg, q. 24 hr	12.5 g	3.44
Nitrofurantoin	PO, 2.2 mg/kg, q. 8 hr	3 g	1.88
Furazolidone	PO, 4.4 mg/kg, q. 8 hr	5 g	2.12
Isoniazid	PO, 3 mg/kg, q. 12 hr	2.73 g	0.27
	PO, 5-15 mg/kg, q. 12 hr	13.65 g	1.34

* DHSM = dihydrostreptomycin.
Source: Aronson and Brownie (1978).

causative agent to determine its antimicrobial sensitivity, and this should be done if at all possible.

Once the causative organism and its antibiotic sensitivity is known, the appropriate antibiotic may be selected. In making this choice, a narrow-spectrum agent should be selected above a broad-spectrum agent, and a bactericidal agent is preferred above a bacteriostatic agent. Specific toxicities or allergies associated with each drug should be kept in mind and such drugs avoided in situations where the horse may be predisposed to them. Finally, cost of the therapy may have to be borne in mind, as it can be quite expensive to maintain effective blood levels of some drugs for an adequate period of time in animals as large as the horse (Tables 19-V and 19-VI).

It is very important that adequate blood levels of a drug be maintained for an adequate period of time. Again, this can be quite a challenge in the horse, both because of the horse's large size and the speed with which he eliminates drugs. However, if full blood levels of drugs are not maintained long enough, the development of resistant strains is encouraged and the organism will be more difficult to treat with the antibiotic a second time. Blood levels of an antibiotic should therefore be maintained throughout the period of therapy and for a further three to four days after apparent resolution of the problem.

The therapeutic action of an antibiotic should be assisted by mechanically removing as much infected material, bacteria, debris, or foreign bodies from the site of infection as possible. Thus, abscesses should be drained, foreign bodies removed, and catheters, bone plates, or other mechanical items removed if at all practical. The importance of this step cannot be overemphasized, as the removal of as much foreign material as possible greatly assists the action of all antibiotics. If the infection is in the urinary tract, the action of the antibiotic may be aided by changing the acidity of the urine to assist the antibiotic. An optimal route of administration should be used, and it should be remembered that high blood levels of antibiotics favor their penetration in useful concentrations into restricted areas such as abscesses, the CNS, the eye, or joint fluid.

Combinations of antibiotics are usually not good practice unless they are clearly indicated by specific circumstances. If the problem is due to a mixed bacterial infection, such as occurs with peritonitis or urinary tract problems, the results of culture may suggest the use of two or more drugs. A further advantage to the use of two or more drugs is that combinations act to delay the emergence of resistant strains, which can be very useful if one of the drugs is one to which resistance occurs readily. Beyond this, there are only a few specific instances where combinations of antibiotics may be used, but as a general rule the dictum that bactericidal agents may be combined but that bacteriostatic and bactericidal agents should not be mixed should be kept in mind.

RESISTANCE TO ANTIBIOTICS

Drug resistance, or resistance to an antibiotic, is a state of decreased sensitivity or insensitivity to drugs that ordinarily are bacteriostatic or bactericidal. While resistance to antibiotics is becoming an increasingly serious problem in human medicine, it is much less of a problem in equine medicine, probably in large part because horses are rarely kept in the same crowded conditions as other domestic animals or humans. However, while some organisms never become resistant and are as sensitive to antibiotics today as when the drugs were first introduced thirty years ago, many bacteria have developed resistant strains, and multiple-resistant strains of bacteria are fast becoming a problem in some circumstances.

Resistant strains of bacteria have appeared for the simple reason that bacteria, like all living things, adapt to selective pressures placed upon them. The basic mechanism by which resistant strains develop is mutational, i.e. a spontaneous mutation occurs that renders that particular strain of bacterium more resistant to the antibiotic than other strains. Most commonly the amount of resistance conferred by each individual mutation is small, and a number of mutational events are required to confer significant resistance on an organism. Resistance developing in this way is called stepwise resistance.

Because resistance most commonly develops in this stepwise fashion, the use of small doses of antibiotics encourages the development of resistant forms. It does this because although the dosage may be sufficient to kill off most of the bacterial population, a few marginally resistant organisms survive low levels of antibiotics, and in this way a new, more resistant strain develops. Then, if this new, somewhat more resistant strain is exposed to a somewhat higher but still marginal concentration of antibiotic, another slightly more resistant strain develops. In this way, the use of marginal concentrations of antibiotics selects for resistant strains. As a general rule, therefore, one should always use full dosage levels of drugs to minimize these problems.

In another pattern of resistance, as seen with streptomycin, resistance develops very rapidly, in a single step. This form of resistance is associated with a single mutational event and is called the large-step type. Fortunately development of resistance in this way is a rare event and is clinically significant only for streptomycin.

The problem of resistance to the antibiotics is best approached by the careful use of these drugs. The indiscriminate use of antibiotics should be avoided, as this only encourages the development of resistant forms. When selecting an antibiotic to use, the selection should be as specific as possible. If possible, a culture should be taken and a narrow-spectrum antibiotic, which affects a smaller range of bacteria, should be used instead of a broad-spectrum agent. Doses sufficient to give adequate blood levels of drugs should be used, as low blood levels favor the development of resistant forms. As pointed out above, drug combinations may also be justified, as these help delay the appearance of resistant forms. In the last analysis, however, the combatting of drug resistance lies with the organic chemist, who may be able to modify the drug in such a way that the bacteria are no longer resistant to it.

In an emergency, it is considered good practice to first take suitable samples to allow culturing to identify the causative agent and then treat the animal with a broad-spectrum bactericidal antibiotic or combination of antibiotics. The dosages used should be large and continued until the results of the culture are obtained. At this point, treatment should be switched to that indicated by the culture and pursued vigorously.

It is time to change antibiotics when no response or a poor clinical response is obtained after forty-eight to seventy-two hours. It is considered good practice to culture before changing drugs and to select the new antibiotic based on the culture results. In case of an adverse reaction, its potential severity for the patient needs to be judged and, if the indications are severe enough, a switch to a second choice drug made. The clinician should always be on the watch for subtle signs of an adverse reaction and should check any suspicions he may have of a possible adverse reaction with appropriate clinical tests.

A superinfection occurs when signs of a new infection appear in the course of treatment of a previous condition. Under these circumstances, the potential severity of the superinfection and its outcome has to be judged. If the superinfection is more threatening than the original condition, the original therapy should be stopped, the superinfection cultured, and appropriate antibiotic therapy of the superinfection instituted.

SELECTED REFERENCES

Andersson, G., Ekman, L., Mansson, I., Persson, S., Rubarth, S., and Tufvesson, G.: Lethal complications following administration of oxytetracycline in the horse. *Nord Vet Med, 23:*9-22, 1971.

Aronson, A. L.: Absorption in distribution and excretion of antimicrobial agents in the horse. In *Symposium on Equine Pharmacology and Therapeutics.* Am Assoc Equine Pract, Nov. 18-19, 1969, pp. 10-18.

Aronson, A. L., and Brownie, C.: Clinical pharmacology of antibacterial drugs in horses, in *Proceedings of 2nd Equine Pharmacology Symposium,* Powers, J. D. and Powers, T. E., eds., American Association of Equine Practitioners, Golden, Colorado, 1978, pp. 115-128.

Baker, J. R. and Leyland, A. P.: Diarrhoea in the horse associated with stress and tetracycline therapy. *Vet Rec, 93:*583-584, 1973.

Bowen, J. M. and McMullan, W. C.: Influence of induced hypermagnesemia and hypocalcemia on neuromuscular blocking property of oxytetracycline in the horse. *Am J Vet Res, 36:*1025-1028, 1975.

Cook, W. R.: Diarrhoea in the horse associated with stress and tetracycline therapy. *Vet Rec, 93:*15-16, 1973.

Davis, L. E., Neff, C. A., Baggott, J. D., and Powers, T. E.: Pharmacokinetics of chloramphenicol in domesticated animals. *Am J Vet Res, 33:*2259-2266, 1972.

English, P. B. and Roberts, M. C.: Antimicrobial chemotherapy in the horse. I. Pharmacological considerations. *J Equine Med Surg, 3:*259-268, 1979.

Knight, H. D. and Heitala, S.: Antimicrobial susceptibility patterns in horses, in *Proceedings of 2nd Equine Pharmacology Symposium,* Powers, J. D. and Powers, T. E., eds., American Association of Equine Practitioners, Golden, Colorado, 1978, pp. 63-88.

MacKellar, J. C., Vaughan, S. M., Smith, R. J. G., Brooks, N. G., and Warren, C. G. B.: Diarrhoea in horses following tetracycline therapy. *Vet Rec, 93:*583, 1973.

Oh-Ishi, S.: Blood concentrations of chloramphenicol in horses after intramuscular or oral administration. *Jpn J Vet Sci, 30:*25-28, 1968.

Pilloud, M.: Pharmacokinetics, plasma protein binding and dosage of chloramphenicol in cattle and horses. *Res Vet Sci, 15:*231-238, 1973.

Potter, W. L.: Collentrations of chloramphenicol in horses after intramuscular or oral administration. *Jpn J Vet Sci, 30:*25-28, 1968.

Pilloud, M.: Pharmacokinetics, plasma protein binding and dosage of chloramphenicol in cattle and horseimicrobial therapy. *J Equine Med Surg, 3:*308-315, 1979.

Sisodia, C. S., Kramer, L. L., Gupta, V. S., Lerner, D. J., and Taksas, L.: A pharmacological study of chloramphenicol in horses. *Can J Comp Med, 39:*216-233, 1975.

Teske, R. H., Rollins, L. D., Condon, R. J., and Carter, G. G.: Serum oxytetracycline concentrations after intravenous and intramuscular administration in horses. *J Am Vet Med Assoc, 162:*119-120, 1973.

Tobin, T., Blake, J. W., and Valentine, R.: Drug interactions in the horse: Effects of chloramphenicol, quinidine, and oxyphenbutazone on phenylbutazone metabolism. *Am J Vet Res, 38:*123-127, 1977.

Chapter 20

COLICS AND OTHER GASTROINTESTINAL PROBLEMS: THEIR TREATMENT AND CONTROL

THE GASTROINTESTINAL SYSTEM of the horse took a wrong turn during its evolutionary development, and horses in general and horse owners in particular have been paying for that error ever since. One evolutionary pathway, selected by ruminants, was to expand the stomach into a large holding tank that allows for both fermentation and rumination. The other approach, selected by the horse, was to expand the cecum and large colon into the necessary fermentation vat. Of the two approaches, the ruminant model has turned out to be by far the most successful, and the cow's digestive tract is estimated to be 50 per cent more efficient than that of the horse. Ruminants of all sizes and shapes have spread over much of the world, and one ruminant, the goat, is legendary for its digestive capacities. On the other hand, the horse, with its small stomach, relatively narrow small intestine, and complicated cecal-colon arrangement, has been notably less successful and remains particularly susceptible to painful gastrointestinal tract (GIT) problems, popularly called colics.

In the medical approaches to treatment of gastrointestinal problems in the horse, there are relatively few basic maneuvers available to the veterinarian. The principal one is to accelerate the movement of ingesta through the gastrointestinal tract, and historically a wide variety of drugs have been available to do this. Less commonly, he may wish to directly depress the motility of the gastrointestinal tract and slow the movement of ingesta through the tract, and again specific groups of drugs are available to do this. Control of pain from the GIT, which can be severe and result in the animal damaging himself, can be a very acute problem, and a variety of medical approaches to this problem are available, none of which are completely satisfactory. Finally, if the GIT problem is infectious, it may be necessary to administer anti-infective agents whose action is primarily limited to the GIT. Along with such anti-infectives, a class of drugs called demulcents may be administered, whose primary action is thought of as mechanically protecting the inflamed gastrointestinal wall and reducing irritation.

Among these different groups of drugs, it is probably appropriate to first examine those that accelerate the movement of ingesta through the gastrointestinal tract. The most benign members of this group of drugs are the emollient laxatives, or fecal softeners. As a group, these rarely result in more than a slight intensification of intestinal motility and softening of the fecal mass. Slightly more powerful are the bulk-forming laxatives and the saline cathartics, followed by the more powerful and dangerous irritant cathartics. The irritant cathartics cause a marked intensification of intestinal motility and result in the expulsion of the contents of the colon and rectum. Occasionally, in cases of overdosage or in an unusual reaction to these drugs, superpurgation will occur. This is marked by extreme and continued intestinal activity and the painful evacuation of fluid and

The goat is legendary for its digestive capacities, while the horse is particularly susceptible to colics.

blood-stained feces. The resultant dehydration and shock may cause death, and horses are traditionally considered more susceptible to superpurgation and shock than other species.

Approximately equivalent to irritant cathartics are the neuromuscular purgatives, whose use is now on the decline. Finally, and now essentially obsolete, one has the drastic purgatives, a kill-or-cure approach guaranteed to move out what ails a horse's intestines, along with everything else in his gastrointestinal tract, or else remove the horse from the land of living.

The Lubricant or Emollient Laxatives

Fecal Softeners

The simplest way of accelerating the movement of material through the GIT is to add a lubricant. These emollients lubricate and soften the intestinal contents and aid the passage of material, particularly in the case of low-grade impactions. The principal emollient laxatives are dioctyl sodium sulfosuccinate and, almost traditional in the horse, mineral oil.

Mineral oil, or liquid paraffin, is a colorless, nearly transparent, odorless, and close to tasteless mixture of inert hydrocarbons of varying viscosity. At one time, eastern Europe was a common source of this substance, so it was known as Russian mineral oil. Most mineral oil now available in the United States is of local origin and comes in a variety of grades, with the low grades (low viscosity) having some advantage over the heavy grades for horses. The oil is indigestible and is relatively poorly absorbed from the intestines. In the intestinal tract it appears to retard the absorption of water, thus softening the feces and presumably also lubricating and mechanically aiding the movement of the feces or small fecal balls past constrictions in the intestines.

The major advantage of mineral oil is that it is a very safe, conservative treatment. As an inert, poorly absorbed lubricant it is unlikely to do much damage, and it is often, therefore, the first line of therapy in any colic in the horse. About the only disadvantage of "oiling" a horse with colic is that if surgery later becomes necessary, the presence of oil in the inestines can make surgery and suturing more difficult.

The repeated use of mineral oil in a horse or any other animal should be undertaken with care. Mineral oil acts as a fat solvent and reduces the absorption of the fat-soluble vitamins A, D, E, and K. Absorption of these vitamins may be particularly important in pregnant mares, so repeated use of mineral oil in pregnant mares is not particularly advisable.

Despite its inert nature, a certain amount of mineral oil is always absorbed from the gastrointestinal tract and makes its way into the mesenteric lymph glands, where it can set up foreign body reactions. Mineral oil is apparently absorbed as "fatty" droplets, which may suggest that surfactant type laxatives should not be used with mineral oil. This is because the surfactants will break the mineral oil up into readily absorbable droplets and in this way tend to increase the absorption of mineral oil from the gut. On the other hand, emulsified mineral oils are available in human medicine, which apparently penetrate and soften intestinal contents more readily than ordinary mineral oil, so this combination might well be tried in cases of simple impaction. Use of an emulsified oil also reduces leakage of oil from the anus, which can be a problem under certain circumstances, such as with rectovaginal fistulas.

Mineral oil enjoys wide popularity among equine veterinarians, being the laxative of choice among 75 per cent of veterinarians. The usual dose is between one and three quarts. Gentle jogging of the horse after such a dose may help the oil distribute and penetrate the intestinal contents and aid its lubricant action. Mineral oil may also be used as a lubricant on diagnostic and other instruments, such as stomach tubes or catheters. It may also be used post-surgically to reduce straining and may be particularly useful for this purpose following surgery in the anal or vaginal area.

The Bulk-Forming Laxatives

An alternative method of accelerating the movement of material through the gastrointestinal system is to increase the bulk of the intestinal contents, preferably in a fluid form. The increased bulk distends the intestines, which has the effect of reflexly increasing intestinal motility, while the increased fluid volume helps to lubricate and evacuate the contents.

Wheat bran, as the classic "bran mash," is the most commonly used bulk laxative in the horse. The action of wheat bran is slow, not commencing for about twenty-four hours and requiring two to three days for full action. Like mineral oil, bran mashes are useful in patients in whom it is necessary to reduce straining, and they are also useful in horses in the late stages of pregnancy. Further, because of their ability to absorb water, bran mashes may be useful in the treatment of patients with acute diarrhea and who have undergone intestinal surgery. No bulk laxative, however, should be used in patients with adhesions, ulcerations, or intestinal stenosis.

For a bran mash preparation, Seckington recommends 3 lb. of bran, 1 oz. of common salt, and 2½ pints of boiling water. These should be mixed, covered, and allowed to cool for twenty minutes and then fed to the horse. For a linseed bran mash, 1 lb. of linseed and 6 pints of water, brought to the boil and simmered for three hours is recommended. To this residue, Seckington adds 2 lb. bran and 1 oz. common salt. Treacle and liquid paraffin may be added if desired. Other traditional additives, especially in the British Isles, are raw eggs and, for that extra touch, a pint of Guinness stout, of which horses apparently become very fond.

Saline Cathartics

Another type of bulk purgative is the "saline" cathartic or purgative, the classic "dose of salts." The mechanism of the bulk increase in this case is that the poorly absorbable ions of a salt such as magnesium sulfate (Epsom salts) remain in the intestinal tract and will either "hold" or osmotically "attract" water into the gastrointestinal tract. As with the bran mash, the increased fluid volume in the intestines reflexly increases motility in the gastrointestinal tract and an increased volume of fluid feces is eliminated. If the saline cathartic is hypertonic* (more concentrated than blood) when given, it will tend to draw sufficient fluid into the gut to render it isotonic, and in this way the patient may become dehydrated. On the other hand, if the solution is hypotonic, the patient will tend to absorb the fluid. For magnesium sulfate 35 gm/Liter is approximately isotonic, while for sodium sulfate, 30 gm/L is isotonic. These solutions, however, are very dilute, and a more practical approach is to use them at about twice isotonicity or about 60 gm/L.

The saline cathartics are simple, inexpensive, nonirritant, and relatively safe. About the only problems with them can come from absorption of the ions or dehydration of the patient. Usually, only about 20 percent of the magnesium in magnesium sulfate is absorbed, and in the normal animal this is readily excreted through the kidney. However, if renal function is impaired, serum levels of magnesium may increase and give rise to neuromuscular depression and death. Unless the patient is dehydrated, is not drinking, or is perspiring heavily, the water loss associated with a saline purgative should not be a serious problem.

A typical dose of magnesium sulfate or sodium sulfate to horses runs between 250 and 500 gm. Milk of magnesia, which is another saline cathartic and is in

---

* Hypertonic approximately means more concentrated than blood; isotonic (*iso* = equal, *tonus* = strength) means the same strength as; and hypotonic means less concentrated than blood.

addition an antacid, is sometimes used in foals. The usual dose in foals is 30 to 60 ml, and it may be administered in combination with colostrum or mineral oil.

The Irritant Cathartics

The irritant cathartics reportedly act by a direct irritant action on the intestinal wall, which increases motility and secretion in the GIT. In low doses they produce a substantial incease in fluid volume of the feces and straining. In large doses they produce a chemical enteritis* with substantial fluid losses and possibly shock. At all effective doses they cause griping pains, intestinal cramps, and increased mucus secretion. Further, there is considerable individual variability in their action, and doses that produce a small or modest response in one individual may produce little response in another, or occasionally an excessive response. Among this group, castor oil and possibly linseed oil act on the small intestine, and the others, such as aloes, danthron, and cascara, act on the large intestine.

Castor Oil

Castor oil is a triglyceride of ricinoleic acid, which is, in and of itself, a bland, nonirritant oil. However, after administration, castor oil is split in the small intestine to yield ricinoleic acid, which acts as a direct stimulant on the wall of the small intestine. Because it acts on the small intestine, the effects of castor oil develop promptly after its administration. This prompt action also accelerates the movement of the remaining castor oil through the tract, and thus the purgative action of this drug is self-limiting. Usually, therefore, the action of the castor oil is seen after eight to twelve hours in foals and somewhat later in adult horses. The usual dose in a foal is 1 to 6 oz., with 1 to 2 pints being the dose of an adult horse.

Linseed Oil

Another laxative-cathartic that has been widely used in the horse is linseed oil. In doses of 500 to 750 ml, it is most commonly used for impaction of the colon. Linseed oil is lubricant and also has an irritant action, by virtue of its breakdown to linoleic and linolenic acids. A problem with linseed oil is that many preparations may have had lead and other paint additives included to enhance their quality as paints. These paint additives, however, include lead oxide, which renders linseed oil preparations highly toxic to the horse.

The Anthraquinone Cathartics

These cathartics are known as the anthracene or emodin cathartics, and their active principal is closely related to 1-8-dihydroxyanthraquinone. This active agent is bound in glycoside form in plant preparations and is active only after release from the parent compound by bacterial action in the GIT.

The anthraquinone purgatives produce their principal pharmacological effects in the large intestine. They apparently reach the large intestine both directly, by being absorbed through the gastrointestinal wall, and also indirectly, by being absorbed into the bloodstream and reaching the large intestine via the circulation. Precisely how the anthraquinone moiety acts to produce its cathartic effect in the

---

* Enteritis = inflammation of the enteron, or gut

large intestine is not clear. Some suggest that its effect may be via an action on sodium transport and water absorption in the large intestine, while others suggest an action on intestinal motor function. In any event, the horse, with its numerous colon flexures and its decrease in diameter at the pelvic flexure appears to benefit particularly from this type of purgative. However, because of this complex cycle of action, purgation with this group of drugs is delayed for at least eighteen hours.

Aloes is the botanical or crude plant form of aloin and is an obsolete cathartic whose use should be abandoned. Its action tends to be unpredictable, and it may produce griping, pelvic congestion, and inflammation of the kidneys. Aloin is the active principle of aloes.

Danthron is pure 1-8-dihydroxyanthraquinone, which is the free drug rather than the bound glycoside form. Its pharmacological properties are as outlined above, but as the drug is given in its pure form the action is more predictable. Danthron produces its purgative effect within twenty-four to thirty-six hours, and the owner should be warned that danthron may color the urine red.

The Neuromuscular Purgatives

The normal motility and secretory activity of the gastrointestinal tract is under the direct control of a portion of the nervous system called the autonomic nervous system. The principal stimulatory neurotransmitter or neurohormone in the intestine is acetylcholine, and an excess of acetylcholine results in greatly increased motility and secretion in the gastrointestinal tract. Drugs that mimic the actions of acetylcholine, such as Carbachol®, therefore act to stimulate increased motility and secretion in the intestinal tract and as such are purgatives. As well as Carbachol®, another drug that mimics the actions of acetylcholine in the gastrointestinal tract is bethanechol.

Carbachol® is a structural analogue of acetylcholine which is almost completely resistant to cholinesterase, the enzyme that inactivates acetylcholine in just fractions of a second. Carbachol® is best given by subcutaneous injection to avoid the high plasma levels and abrupt onset of action that occur if it is given by intravenous injection. After injection, the first effects that are noted are the classical signs of colic. The horse may kick at his flank, stamp, lie down, get up, and show general signs of uneasiness. The stimulation of salivary secretion results in a drooling of clear watery saliva from the mouth within about five minutes, with patches of sweat appearing on the body after another five minutes. Within about twenty minutes, soft fluid feces are passed and the effects begin to wear off. By one hour postdosing, if there is no impaction or twist, the animal will be back to normal.

The principal problem with Carbachol® is that if the colic is due to impaction, its use may lead to rupture of the intestines or an intussusception.

In an intussusception a part of the intestine becomes "telescoped" over its neighboring intestine and in doing so cuts off the blood supply to that portion of the intestine. If the telescoping or intussusception continues for more than a few hours, the entrapped piece of intestine dies, the intestine ruptures, and the horse, in the absence of prompt and skillful surgery, will also die. Carbachol® should only be used, therefore, after more conservative measures such as mineral oil and saline cathartics have been tried. Carbachol® should be used cautiously, and care should be taken to insure that the colic is not due to impaction or that any weakening of the gut is presented that might lead to rupture. Nowadays, Carbachol® is more rarely used in equine colics than previously. Alexander has suggested that the intestinal activity induced by Carbachol® is incoordinated and hazardous and suggests that if Carbachol® is to be used, its specific antidote, atropine, should always be on hand. Atropine, which binds very tightly and specifically by cholinergic receptors, may be expected to very effectively block the effects of Carbachol® on the intestines, and, if given IV, to reverse its actions rapidly.

Another family of drugs that increases motility and secretion in the gastrointestinal tract are the cholinesterase inhibitors. These act by inhibiting the breakdown of acetylcholine and thus accentuating the action of the acetylcholine that is normally released in the intestinal walls. For actions in the gastrointestinal tract, neostigmine is considered the drug of choice, because it has fewer side effects than the other members of this group. Neostigmine is administered at doses of about 1 mg/100 lb. subcutaneously and acts within ten to thirty minutes. Its action persists for several hours, and like Carbachol®, it should not be used unless atropine, which directly blocks the receptors for acetylcholine, is readily available.

Antispasmodics

Since atropine is the specific antidote of drugs that mimic or potentiate the colic-producing actions of acetylcholine, one might well ask whether Atropine alone would block or reduce the severity of a spontaneous equine colic. This possibility is the rationale behind the use of atropine or drugs structurally related to atropine as anticholinergic agents. However, controlled studies have failed to show any superiority of these newer synthetic agents over atropine, and they are, at this time, little used in equine medicine.

A group of pharmacologically unrelated antispasmodics that are used in equine medicine are the smooth muscle relaxants. These agents act directly on smooth muscle to relax it and are independent of any anticholinergic action. Ethaverine (ethylparaverine), marketed as Myoquin®, is one member of this group that is recommended for use in equine patients. The dose is 200 to 400 mg intravenously. However, evidence for a pharmacological action of papaverine on gastrointestinal spasms at these doses is scanty, and its therapeutic effectiveness in colic remains unclear.

CONTROL OF VISCERAL PAIN

One of the major problems in the treatment of gastrointestinal problems and colic is the control of pain. Control of pain may be necessary just to allow the veterinarian to examine the animal and make a diagnosis. More importantly, a horse in severe colic will thrash and roll to such an extent that he may well injure himself severely or perhaps fatally "twist"* a gut. For humane reasons it is also

---

* A section of the intestine may "twist" into such a position that the blood supply to that section is blocked. If this condition is maintained, that section of the intestine will deteriorate and rupture, again almost certainly causing death to the horse.

desirable to attempt to relieve the horse's pain as much as possible, but given the current state of equine therapeutics, it is not always possible to do this.

Perhaps the most commonly used drugs for the control of visceral pain are the non-steroidal anti-inflammatory drugs, such as dipyrone and Banamine®. Dipyrone is chemically closely related to aminopyrine and has been a very popular treatment for colic in horses. It is claimed to be an analgesic, antipyretic and antispasmodic and to be particularly useful in the treatment of equine colics.

Some doubts have been cast on the value of dipyrone in the treatment of equine colic by workers using a balloon colic model in the horse. In this model a balloon is introduced into the equine cecum through a permanent surgical fistula ("hole") in the animal's flank and the balloon inflated. As soon as a pressure of about 1 pound per square inch is reached, the horse immediately shows signs of colic. These signs include twitching the tail, crouching, stretching out, defecating, urinating, looking at the flank, pawing at the ground, groaning, whinnying, curling the upper lip, and rolling. By increasing or decreasing the pressure on the balloon, Lowe could induce either mild or severe colic at will. Lowe's balloon colic model is thus a very useful model with which to evaluate the ability of different drugs to control the overt signs of colic.

Using this colic model, Lowe and his coworkers administered doses of dipyrone

In the "balloon colic" model for evaluating analgesia, a balloon is placed in the horse's cecum and inflated until he "colics."

of about 15 cc (500 mg/ml) and saw no clear-cut beneficial effects of dipyrone in any of his colic cases. However, this experimental report contrasts sharply with reports by practitioners who claim that dipyrone is effective in many instances at doses of up to 40 cc. The reason for the conflict between the experimental cases and the model is not clear, but the answer may lie in the comments of one practitioner. This individual rather cheerfully reported that if dipyrone does not help them (the horses) they are going to die anyway! Based on this analysis, it may be that practitioners administering dipyrone and getting good responses are observing spontaneous resolutions, while the "serious" cases progress to their fatal outcome anyhow and are also not influenced by dipyrone.

In a careful laboratory study of the action of dipyrone on intestinal function in a number of pharmacological models, Yano and Gray found little evidence for an antispasmodic action of dipyrone, other than to block bradykinin-induced intestinal spasm. This suggests a rather limited spectrum of action for this drug and is consistent with the negative results observed in the balloon colic model.

Another drug that is strongly recommended for the control of colic pain is the non-steroidal anti-inflammatory drug Banamine®. Clinical experience with Banamine® suggests that it is particularly useful in spastic and flatulent colics, with an extremely fast onset of action and a reported duration of action of from six to eight hours. These reports, however, are all based on field trials, where it is very difficult, for instance, to determine the duration of drug action. It would be very interesting, therefore, to see how Banamine® responds in a test such as the balloon colic model, where both the effectiveness and duration of action of a drug can readily be determined.

The role of the narcotic analgesics in the control of pain in colic is also far from clear-cut. In studies on Talwin® (pentazocine) and meperidine, it has been found that both produce analgesia for relatively short periods. Thus, Talwin® at 2 mg/kg, about seven times the manufacturer's recommended dose, produced analgesia lasting for ninety minutes, while meperidine at 1 mg/lb. produced twenty-one minutes of analgesia. In this study, pentazocine was clearly the superior drug, although meperidine almost certainly did not get an adequate trial, the dose selected being much too low to produce the same degree of occupancy of narcotic receptors as is obtained with 2 mg/kg of Talwin® (see Fig. 12-7). This is because meperidine is actually less potent than pentazocine on a mg/kg basis, and the effect of comparing 2 mg/kg of pentazocine with 1 mg/kg of the less potent meperidine was to weight the outcome of the experiment grossly in favor of pentazocine.

In a subsequent study by this investigator, pentazocine and meperidine were compared with the sedative-analgesic xylazine. For reasons that are unclear, the dose of pentazocine was reduced in this second study, and the same low dose of meperidine was compared with the clinically recommended dose of xylazine. Under these conditions, 1 mg/kg of xylazine produced good symptom control for an average of sixty-five minutes, which not surprisingly compared favorably with the symptom control produced by the low doses of pentazocine and meperidine used in this study.

Oxymorphone is a morphine analogue which is ten times as potent as morphine and has been suggested to have few side effects in horses. As reported by Davis and Knight, 10 mg to an adult horse is used in the management of colics at the Colorado State University. This, however, is a threshold dose for clear-cut behavioral stimulation by this drug, and oxymorphone thus is comparable with the other narcotics used for analgesia in the horse.

Studies by Joan Combie and her coworkers in my laboratory have shown that increased locomotor activity is a consistent behavioral response to narcotics in the horse and can be used to characterize both dose response relationships and the time course of action of these drugs (see Chapter 12). Data from Combie's work suggests that there is likely to be little significant difference in the side effects of narcotic analgesics in the horse, as the doses selected for clinical use in colic all appear to fall at the threshold for locomotor stimulation. The data also show that morphine and particularly hydromorphone produce the most prolonged responses in the horse and may thus be expected to produce the longest periods of effective pain control.

A possible role of the endogenous opiates or endorphins in shock may suggest that narcotic analgesics for the control of colic pain should be used with caution. In some species very small doses of morphine will produce hypotension and slowing of the heart rate. Because the endogenous opiates or β-endorphins are stored in the pituitary and hypothalamus along with ACTH, it has been suggested that both ACTH and the endogenous opiates are released in response to stress and as shock. Thus, the hypotension associated with both endotoxin and hypovolemic shock might conceivably be due to the circulatory depressant effect of endogenous opiates released in response to the stress of shock.

To test this hypothesis, Holaday and Faden induced both endotoxic and hypovolemic shock in rats and then administered naloxone, the specific opiate antagonist. The only known pharmacological actions of naloxone are to block the binding of opiates or endorphins to opiate receptors. In both cases, the hypotension associated with both endotoxic and hypovolemic shock was rapidly reversed, suggesting that central opiate receptors are indeed involved in the hypotension that is characteristic of shock.

These observations give rise to two practical suggestions for the treatment of colic pain by narcotic analgesics. First, it is probably prudent that if the narcotic analgesics are to be used, they should be used only in cases of colic that are considered unlikely to develop a component of shock. Secondly, if one is treating a case of colic that shows signs of developing into shock, it would be wise to try a narcotic antagonist. Thirdly, if a colic case develops to the point at which shock therapy is needed, it might also be wise to administer a narcotic antagonist to combat any already existing hypotensive effects due to endorphins.

It seems clear that naloxone will readily antagonize the actions of both endorphins and exogenous opiates. Studying the effects of naloxone on the locomotor responses to large doses of endorphins, Combie and her coworkers found that 0.02 mg/kg (10 mg) of naloxone was able to almost completely antagonize the actions of 2.4 ng/kg morphine, or more than 100 times the dose of naloxone. Further, this reversal persisted for about twelve hours, suggesting a reasonably long period between naloxone treatments.

In summary, therefore, a wide range of drugs are available that accelerate or retard the flow of ingesta through the gastrointestinal tract, and the pharmacology and therapeutics of these agents are well worked out. The control of visceral pain in the horse, however, is an area where clear-cut therapeutic guidelines are still lacking. In mild cases of colic the phenothiazine tranquilizers and Banamine® appear to be effective. In more severe cases, where the horse runs the risk of injuring himself or the veterinarian, more aggressive therapy may be required. One approach to these cases is to use narcotic analgesics in the largest doses that will not produce behavioral stimulation. When this approach is taken, it should be kept in mind that the hypotensive effects of the narcotic analgesics may exacerbate shock if this develops. An alternative approach may be to use xylazine, which gives good control of the symptoms of colic but whose period of action is relatively short-lived.

SELECTED REFERENCES

Alexander, F.: Certain aspects of the physiology and pharmacology of the horse's digestive tract. *Equine Vet J, 4:*166-169, 1972.

Becker, G. L.: The case against mineral oil. *Am J Dig Dis, 19:*344-347, 1952.

Coffman, J. R. and Garner, H. G.: Acute abdominal disease of the horse. *J Am Vet Med Assoc, 161:*1195, 1972.

Combie, J., Dougherty, J., Nugent, E., and Tobin, T.: The pharmacology of narcotic analgesics in the horse. IV. Dose and time response relationships for behavioral responses to morphine, meperidine, pentazocine, anileridine, methadone and hydromorphone. *J Equine Med Surg, 3:*377-385, 1979.

Davis, L. E. and Knight, A. P.: Review of the clinical pharmacology of the equine digestive system. *J Equine Med Surg, 1:*27-35, 1977.

Faden, A. I. and Holaday, J. W.: Opiate anatagonists: A role in the treatment of hypovolemic shock. *Science, 205:*317-318, 1979.

Holaday, J. W. and Faden, A. I.: Naloxone reversal of endotoxin hypotension suggests a role of endorphins in shock. *Nature, 275:*450-457, 1978.

Jones, L. M., Booth, N. H., and McDonald, L. E.: *Veterinary Pharmacology and Therapeutics,* 4th ed. Ames, Iowa State University Press, 1977.

Lowe, J. E.: Pentazocine (Talwin) for the relief of abdominal pain in ponies — A comparative evaluation with description of a colic model for evaluation of analgesia. *Proc AAEP,* 1969, 31-46.

Lowe, J. E.: Rompun, Talwin, Demerol and Novin for relief of a balloon-induced colic: A double-blind comparative evaluation. *J Equine Med Surg,* in press, 1979.

Seckington, I. M.: Treatment of colic from a practitioner's point of view. *Equine Vet J, 4:*188-194, 1972.

Tobin, T.: Pharmacology review: The non-steroidal anti-inflammatory drugs. II. Equiproxen, Meclofenamic Acid, Flunixin and others. *J Equine Med Surg, 3:*298-302, 1979.

Teigland, M. B.: Therapeutic agents currently used in equine practice. *Proc 15th Ann Conv AAEP,* 1969, 299-307.

Yano, B. L. and Gray, G. W.: A study of the actions of methampyrone and of a commercial intestinal extract preparation of intestinal motility. *Am J Vet Res, 36:*201-208, 1975.

Chapter 21

FLUID THERAPY: THE USE OF FLUIDS, ELECTROLYTES, BLOOD, AND BASES IN PERFORMANCE HORSES

FLUID THERAPY is almost unique in equine medicine in that, given proper laboratory backing, one can measure precisely the deficits in a tissue, take steps to correct them, and directly monitor the progress of therapy. Stated in this way, fluid and electrolyte therapy, which is almost always symptomatic, with the goal of adjusting the body's fluid and electrolyte* balance toward normal, sounds simple. In real life, however, given one or more sometimes poorly identified primary causes and the fact that practitioners may not have available to them all the instrumentation needed to identify and monitor changes in plasma and electrolyte levels, fluid therapy remains somewhat of an art.

Fluid therapy is important because a horse suffering from shock, colic, or diarrhea, or one that is simply heat and exercise stressed, can lose from 10 to 80 liters of water, or between 3 and 25 percent of the total body water, in twenty-four hours. Along with these large amounts of water, varying amounts of different electrolytes are lost, depending on the particular pattern of fluid loss. If the fluid loss is large and the condition acute, rapid replacement of the body fluids and electrolytes may be imperative, with the successful outcome of therapy of the basic cause of the problem directly dependent on the correction of the fluid deficit.

In approaching the problem of fluid therapy in the horse, I have chosen to first outline our basic knowledge about the various components involved, then list the clinical signs that may be expected with disturbance of these components, and lastly show how these disturbances may be corrected. This, however, is a somewhat cut-and-dried approach, and it is important to remember that actual clinical conditions are rarely simple but more commonly are complex disturbances of water and electrolyte metabolism. With this proviso in mind, we will start our description of the invidividual analysis of water and electrolyte metabolism and at the end will attempt to develop a useful therapeutic approach to some common fluid and electrolyte problems in performance horses.

Body Water

Total body water in the normal horse averages about 60 percent of the mass of the horse, although in the obese horse this value may be as low as 50 percent. The horse's total water volume is usually divided into two major compartments, intracellular water (ICW), comprising about 50 percent of the total, and extracellular water (ECW), which comprises the other 50 percent. The extracellular water can be further subdivided into a number of compartments, the blood volume at

---

* Electrolyte, from *electron* = charged, and *lyte* = dissolved in: a small charged particle, such as sodium or potassium, dissolved in water. Also called ions.

about 5 percent of body weight and the interstitial fluid at about 15 percent of the total. The bulk of the interstitial fluid is the fluid between the capillary walls and the cells themselves. In addition, there are two other major water pools in the horse, bone water and "transcellular water." Transcellular water comprises fluid in the bladder, body cavities, and, especially in the horse, the approximately 35 liters of fluid in the gastrointestinal tract (Table 21-I). Because of the relatively large volume of fluid in the gastrointestinal tract, some workers believe that this constitutes a reservoir of fluid on which the horse can draw under certain circumstances. Conversely, under other circumstances, such as in a case of colitis X, a horse can "lose" large quantities of water into his GIT and become functionally dehydrated before clinical signs of diarrhea develop.

Plasma Proteins

While water molecules exchange freely throughout the different compartments of the body, the substances dissolved in the fluids of these compartments do not exchange so freely. Because of their relatively large size, plasma proteins are essentially limited to the vascular compartment, where they contribute to the osmotic pressure of the plasma and thus to fluid balance in the body. Plasma protein concentration is normally measured by means of a refractometer and usually averages between 6.6 and 7.5 gm/dl of total plasma proteins (TPP). Total plasma proteins concentrations of greater than 8.0 gm/dl are suggestive of dehydration, while concentrations of less than 6.5 gm/dl are hypoproteinemic and may mean that the animal is dehydrated.

Total plasma protein is not an absolute indicator of gains or losses of fluid from the circulating fluid compartment because protein can apparently be moved into or out of the circulatory compartment, depending on the animal's circumstances. Nevertheless, these changes are usually always smaller than the changes in packed cell volume (PCV), which can occur so readily in blooded horses, and total plasma protein is therefore one of the better indicators of the hydration status of a horse.

Red Blood Cells

The proportion of red cells in a horse's blood may be expressed by centrifuging or spinning down the blood and measuring the volume of the packed red cells as a proportion of the total blood volume. The resultant value is called a packed cell

TABLE 21-I
BODY WATER IN THE HORSE

Total body weight	100%	450 kg
Total intracellular water	30%	135 Liters
Total extracellular water	30%	135 Liters
Total body water	60%	270 Liters
Extracellular Water Consists of		
(1) Blood plasma		22.0 Liters
(2) Interstitial fluid		63.0 Liters
(3) Bone water		10.0 Liters
(4) Transcellular water		40.0 Liters
Extracellular water		135 Liters

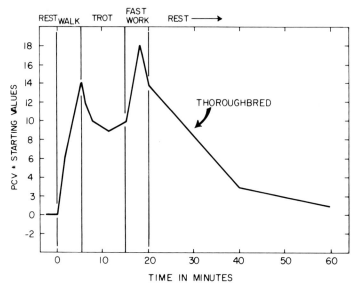

Figure 21-1. Effect of exercise on packed cell volume in a Thoroughbred horse. The solid line shows the increase in packed cell volume in a Thoroughbred horse that was put through a graded series of exercises and then allowed to rest. After Archer and Clabby (1965).

volume (PCV), but in general, a packed cell volume is much less reliable than TPP as an indicator of fluid status. Packed cell volumes in the horse vary between 30 percent and >60 percent, in large part because the horse has a splenic red blood cell reservoir containing up to 30 percent of his total red cells, from which he can increase his packed cell volume. Thus, simple excitement or exercise is sufficient to increase a horse's PCV from a "normal average" of about 38 percent to up to the mid-forties, and the PCV may go even higher after strenuous exercise (Fig. 21-1). On the other hand, after treatment with certain tranquilizers the PCV may drop to as low as 30 percent, which appears to be a baseline PCV value for the normal horse. This variability in the baseline PCV, which is most marked in hot-blooded horses, greatly reduces the reliance that can be placed on PCV as an indicator of fluid status. Further, in view of the interest that the concept of "blood doping" has caused in man, it is interesting to see that the horse, as a master athlete, has evolved a specific mechanism for increasing his hematocrit during periods of exercise.

Blood Doping

Blood doping is a controversial technique where some of an athlete's blood is withdrawn pre-race and the red cells "centrifuged down" and stored. The blood is withdrawn sufficiently early before the athletic event so that he may be able to get his blood hemoglobin back to normal. Then, just before the athletic event, the blood previously withdrawn is infused back into the athlete. In theory, the oxygen-carrying capacity of the blood is increased by the re-infused red cells, and the athlete's performance is correspondingly improved.

A number of studies on blood doping have come up with conflicting results, but one recent study has given apparently clear-cut positive results. In this study, twelve long distance runners (not world-class level) had about 1 liter of blood removed and stored. Then the blood was re-infused one to two days prior to the test. The tests were performed on a treadmill and were the equivalent of a five-mile run.

In the actual test, it was found the hemoglobin level of the infused runners was raised and that the runners subjectively felt better and thought they were running faster. In fact, eleven of the twelve runners in the test showed improved times, and the improvement, at an average of forty-four seconds, or almost nine seconds a mile, was very large. The authors of this work attributed its success to the large volume of blood used. They were, however, careful to point out that these runners were not world-class runners and that it is not clear whether or not the performances of world-class athletes would be improved.

While it might seem that blood doping would be impossible to detect, this is not necessarily the case. In the first place, the amounts of blood with which one would have to infuse a horse would be relatively large, and thus the simple act of collecting, storing, and reinfusing the blood would be difficult to conceal. In the second place, to prevent the blood from clotting while it is stored, one has to add an anticoagulant to it. When the blood is reinfused into the horse, these anticoagulants are likely to be detectable in either blood or urine and thus point toward a recent blood transfusion. In practice, therefore, blood doping is likely to be fairly easy to control, whether or not it turns out to be a valid method of improving performance.

Electrolytes

While the red blood cells and plasma proteins are mechanically restricted to the vascular compartment, no such restraint holds for body electrolytes, which move freely between the plasma, intracellular, and interstitial fluids. Inspection of the data of Table 21-II, however, shows marked differences between the ionic contents of the extracellular and intracellular fluids. Thus, sodium is the major extracellular cation, with concentrations of about 145 meq/L, and potassium is the major intracellular cation, with concentrations of about 150 meq/L. Similarly, calcium (Ca^{++}) is high in plasma and interstitial fluid, while Mg^{++} is much higher in intracellular fluid. These large ionic gradients are actively maintained by

TABLE 21-II

ELECTROLYTE CONCENTRATIONS IN BODY COMPARTMENTS OF THE HORSE

Electrolyte	Symbol	Plasma	Interstitial Fluid	Intracellular Fluid
Sodium	Na^+	142	147	15
Potassium	K^+	3.5	3.5	150
Calcium	Ca^{++}	5.0	2.5	—
Magnesium	Mg^{++}	2.0	2.0	30
Bicarbonate	$H_2CO_3^-$	27.0	30	10.0
Chloride	Cl^-	102.0	114	1.0

NOTE: All concentrations expressed as Meq/Liter

specialized membrane pumps, such as the sodium-potassium and calcium pumps, and the energy needed to drive these pumps and maintain these electrolyte gradients contributes a substantial part of the basal metabolic rate of an animal. The principal electrolytes that we will consider in our discussion are sodium and potassium, magnesium and calcium, and the ions of acid-base balance, bicarbonate and carbonic acid, and hydrogen ion.

Sodium Ion

Among the electrolytes, sodium ion is the most abundant ion in extracellular fluid and is responsible for both the osmotic pressure of extracellular fluids and nerve activity. As will be made clear later, the horse does not have any great reserves of sodium, and a horse that is not receiving a sodium supplement can be rather easily thrown into negative sodium balance. In the horse, this occurs most readily with heavy sweating or acute diarrhea. If, in addition, fluid is replaced in these horses without the sodium, the hyponatremia (reduced blood sodium) may become severe. Because the concentration of sodium in the extracellular fluids is lowered, the kidney will excrete more water in an attempt to increase the concentration of sodium in body fluids, leading to a further reduction in blood volume. This leads to decreased circulatory blood volume and may result in hypotension, hypothermia, muscle weaknesses, and renal failure.

There are no clinical signs that are characteristic of hyponatremia beyond simple dehydration, muscle weakness, and mental depression.

Potassium

Horses used for endurance rides may be affected by hypokalemia, hypocalcemia, and alkalosis due to loss of electrolytes during competition. A condition called "synchronous diaphragmatic flutter" may also occur in these horses, which appears to be due to electrolyte imbalance causing hyperirritability of the phrenic nerve. Extremely low or high levels of potassium in the extracellular fluid are usually associated with other electrolyte and acid imbalances. Potassium is necessary for normal electrical activity in nerve and muscle, and hypokalemia causes depression, muscle weakness, recumbency, intestinal atony, and coma. Hyperkalemia usually causes bradycardia and arrythmias, with death occurring due to cardiac arrest.

Calcium Ion

Of the normal serum calcium, about 55 to 60 percent is ionized or charged, 5 to 10 percent is non-ionized but diffusible, and about 35 percent is bound to serum proteins, mainly albumin. As is the case for any drug or ion, the bound fraction is pharmacologically inactive, and serum proteins should ideally be estimated in concert with serum Ca^{++}.

The short-term significance of Serum Ca^{++} levels depends on its role in neuromuscular transmission. Calcium is a membrane stabilizer, and if Ca^{++} levels drop, so does the threshold for excitability of nerve and muscle, which therefore become hyperexcitabile. Synchronous diaphragmatic flutter, where contractions of the diaphragm are seen in hypocalcemic animals, is typical of the pattern of neuromuscular excitability when plasma Ca^{++} levels are reduced. Reduced plasma levels of Mg^{++} similarly tend to produce increased neuromuscular excitability while increased levels induce a sleeplike state, and some of the older anesthetics and sedatives used in the horse contained added Mg^{++}.

Acid-Base Balance

The normal pH of the blood in the horse is about 7.4, and pH values of below 6.8 or above 7.8 are not compatible with life. When the pH of the plasma falls, the horse is said to be in acidosis, and the acidosis may be either respiratory or metabolic. A respiratory acidois is due to inadequate respiration or gas exchange in the lungs and retention of carbon dioxide (CO_2). Metabolic acidosis results from a decrease in bicarbonate in the blood and is due to a loss of bicarbonate (HCO_3^-) or an increase in acid. Metabolic acidosis may be due to excessive loss of fluid into the gut, as in diarrhea, high intestinal obstruction, or colitis X. Other causes of metabolic acidosis are inadequate tissue perfusion as in shock, grain engorgement, starvation, or myositis. A rapidly reversible acidosis normally follows strenuous exercise, as the lactic acid formed during muscular work moves from the muscles to the bloodstream.

As is obvious from this discussion, the normal pH of the blood is maintained within fairly narrow limits by the ratios of bicarbonate (HCO_3^-) to H_2CO_3, or dissolved carbon dioxide, in the blood. These constitute what is called a buffer system, and when the ratio of bicarbonate to dissolved CO_2 is 20:1 (see Appendix B), the pH of the blood is about 7.4 or normal. Shifts from this 20:1 ratio are associated with the changes of acidosis and alkalosis, and these are usually named by describing their cause. Further, in real life, the causes of acid-base disturbances are never simple, and there are always compensating changes. Accurate determination of changes in the acid-base status of an animal requires blood gas determination and as such is often outside the reach of most horsemen and practitioners. Therefore, rules of thumb to guide practitioners in clinical situations in which they do not have laboratory backup are necessary. The objective of therapy is to restore the blood electrolyte values outlined to as close to normal as possible.

The optimal treatment for respiratory acidosis is to increase pulmonary ventilation and "blow" off the excess CO_2. On the other hand, the optimal treatment for metabolic acidosis is usually sodium bicarbonate given IV or, under some circumstances, lactate ions, which are converted to bicarbonate ions in the liver.

The estimated base deficit in horses with a metabolic acidosis varies from 1500 mEq or 125 gm of biocarbonate in mild diarrhea to about 3750 mEq of bicarbonate to correct the deficit in severe diarrhea. Therefore, with the usual 5% $NaHCO_3$ solution, between 2½ and 6 liters of bicarbonate solution may be needed to correct a base deficit. Because practitioners are often faced with acute situations or other circumstances under which they must guess as to the acid-base status of the animal, general guidelines are necessary for such circumstances. Other workers have suggested 2 to 4 liters of 5% $NaHCO_3$ administered relatively rapidly in acidosis, followed by spiked lactated Ringer's solution containing 204 gm/L of $KHCO_3$.

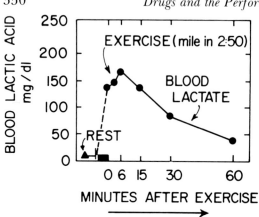

Figure 21-2. Blood lactic acid levels at rest and after exercise in Standardbred horses. Four Standardbred horses that had been in training for nine weeks were used. For these experiments, blood lactic acid levels were measured in the horses immediately prior to exercise (solid triangle, ▲) and the horses then trained for one mile in about two minutes and fifty seconds (solid bar on horizontal axis). The solid circles (●—●) show plasma levels of lactic acid during the hour following exercise. Modified from Krazyanek (1976).

The Alkalotic Diet

During strenuous muscular activity, incomplete combustion of muscle fuels takes place, giving rise to increased blood levels of lactic acid. This increase occurs very rapidly during the type of exercise output that may be expected of Thoroughbred or Standardbred horses, does not peak until about six minutes after the exercise ends, and then declines slowly (Fig. 21-2). During this marked (up to fortyfold) increase in blood lactic acid levels, the pH of the blood drops (Fig. 21-3), the blood becoming increasingly acid. Then, as the animal recovers from his exercise, the blood becomes progressively less acidic and is back to close to normal within one hour of the exercise (Fig. 21-3).

As horses are trained and become increasingly fit, they adapt better to the stress of exercise, and the peak blood lactate levels of trained horses are less than in untrained horses (Fig. 21-4). This lower peaking of blood lactate levels is part of the adaption to exercise that we call fitness, and conversely, the increase in acidity of the blood (decrease in pH) that we see during strenuous exercise plays an important part in the development of fatigue.

Because the change in blood pH to the very acidic values shown in Figure 21-3 appears to be one of the major causes of fatigue, it is thus a limiting factor in performance. The possibility has therefore been suggested that by increasing what is called an athlete's base or alkali reserve, his performance might be im-

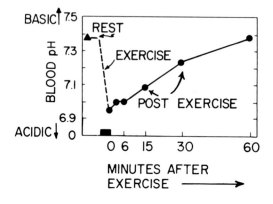

Figure 21-3. Blood pH values at rest and after exercise in Standardbred horses. The blood pH of four Standardbred horses was measured at rest (solid triangle, ▲) and after exercise as outlined in Figure 21-1. The solid circles (●—●) show blood pH (acidic values) during the first hour after exercise. A low pH value represents a high blood acidity. Modified from Krzyanek (1976).

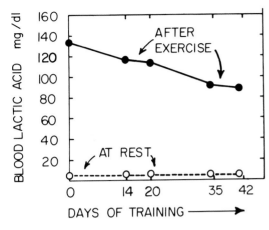

Figure 21-4. Effect of training on peak blood lactic acid levels after exercise in Standardbred horses. The solid circles (●) show the peak blood lactic acid levels in horses postexercise. As training progressed, the peak blood lactate levels fell, presumably as the horses became fitter. Modified from Milne (1976).

proved. Thus an athlete might be fed a diet rich in alkali, such as a fruit diet, or he might be administered a base, such as bicarbonate, prior to an event. Theoretically, this might be expected to give him an advantage with respect to the duration of maximal muscular effort. While little experimental work has been done in this area, what has been reported seems to suggest a positive effect of alkalosis on prolonging endurance in athletes.

Water Balance

The first comprehensive studies on water and electrolyte balance in the horse were carried out by Tasker in the late 1960s. In the normal 1,000 lb. stalled horse, kept under moderate climatic conditions, Tasker found that the average daily intake of water is about 26 liters (7 gallons) a day, or about 54 ml/kg body weight. These horses produced about 5.5 liters (1.5 gallons) of urine per day and about 19 kg of feces, of which about 14 liters (3.6 gallons) was water (Table 21-III). The balance of the water intake, amounting to a little less than 2 gallons, was presumably lost from the lungs and skin. In the normal horse, therefore, a substantial portion of his water intake is lost through the lungs and skin, and one can readily appreciate that under conditions of heat stress a much greater proportion of water is likely to be lost through the lungs and skin by sweating.

TABLE 21-III
WATER BALANCE IN THE HORSE

Intake (Liters)		Output (Liters)	
Drinking	25.3	Urine	5.5
Metabolic water	2.7	Feces	14.0
		Respiration (skin)	8.5
	28.0		28.0

NOTE: These figures are for normal horses in a cool environment. Fluid loss can be greatly increased in fever, diarrhea, with profuse and prolonged perspiration, and simply due to an increased respiratory rate. Under these circumstances, if water intake is not correspondingly increased, dehydration may occur. Since different electrolytes may be lost in different circumstances, electrolyte replacement varies depending on the precipitating cause.

As well as studying water balance in his horses, Tasker also studied electrolyte balance. In the 10 kg of good quality alfalfa-timothy hay that he fed his horses, the sodium intake of these horses was just 320 mEq/day, while the loss of Na^+ in urine and feces was 123 mEq/day. Because these horses were considered to be in sodium balance, the balance of the sodium was probably being lost via the sweat or other routes. It is, however, important to remember that this daily turnover of sodium is equal to the amount of sodium in 3 liters of plasma, and since the bulk of a horse's sodium is found in the extracellular fluid, increased sodium loss for any reason can easily result in rapid depletion of body sodium. This, of course, is the reason that most horses are provided with salt licks, to insure that they get sufficient sodium in their diet to balance any unusual losses.

In contrast with sodium, most horses get more than sufficient potassium in their diet, and in fact, one of the problems that a horse has is excreting his excess K^+. Hay and other plant products are particularly rich in potassium, and in their 10 kg of hay Tasker's horses got almost 4,000 mEq of K, most of which (3,200 mEq) they excreted through the kidneys. Potassium balance is therefore not usually a problem in horses.

Dehydration

Dehydration is caused either by failure of water intake or, more commonly, by excessive water loss. The most common forms of excessive water loss are due to diarrhea or sweating. In many forms of dehydration the lesion that most urgently needs correction is not the fluid loss but the associated electrolyte deficit.

The most important clinical finding in dehydration is dryness and wrinkling of the skin. The simplest test of this is to pick up the skin into a fold. In the normal horse, or at the mildest level of dehydration (i.e. a 3 to 4 per cent fluid deficit), the skin rapidly falls back into place on the body. In more severe dehydration (6 to 8 per cent) the fold of skin remains "tented" for from 2 to 4 seconds. If the level of dehydration is 8 to 10 per cent, the skin fold will remain elevated from 6 to 10 seconds, and beyond 11 per cent dehydration the fold remains elevated for up to 45 seconds. It is important to remember that if the dehydration has occurred rapidly, skin tenting will underestimate the severity of dehydration, as water will still be moving from the subcutaneous tissues into the central fluid compartments. It is also important to remember that the actual final volumes associated with these percent changes are about 3.0 liters/percent dehydration in a 450 kg horse. A moderately (5 percent) dehydrated horse therefore needs about 15 to 20 liters of fluid to replaced his volume deficit, while a severely (10 percent) dehydrated horse will need about 30 to 40 liters or more of replacement fluids.

Other clinical signs of dehydration which have been reported include listlessness and depression, sunken eyes, dryness of the mucous membranes, and reduced urine volume. Such signs should be taken into account when assessing the clinical condition of a dehydrated animal.

Carlson and his colleagues studied the water and electrolyte changes in eight horses deprived of food and water for three days during a period of high environmental temperatures. These horses suffered an average weight loss of 51.5 kg, or almost 11 percent of their body weight, more than half of which was lost in the first twenty-four hours. This substantial degree of dehydration was

In severe dehydration the skin remains "tented" for several seconds after a fold is picked up.

distributed between the extracellular fluid (ECF) compartment and the intracellular fluid compartment (ICF), so the water deficit was distributed throughout the entire body. There was no significant change in the PCV throughout the process of dehydration. However, the total plasma protein (TPP) increased by 10 gm/L, although this increase was only about half of what one would expect based on the observed decrease in plasma volume. Thus, although TPP is a more useful guide than PCV as to changes in plasma volume, it is not an absolute guide, as shifts of protein into and out of the vascular system occur in association with volume changes.

Among the plasma cations, only Na^+ showed increases in Carlson's study, with no changes observed in K^+, Ca^{++}, Mg^{++}, and P. The increase in Na^+ concentration was significant, although again the hypernatremia was smaller than one would predict from the contraction in EDF volume. Thus, the clinicopathological picture seen was that of a hypertonic fluid volume contraction* with elevated plasma Na^+ and TPP. For this pattern of simple dehydration, provision of drinking water is the obvious treatment. Because electrolyte deficits in this condition are minimal, parenteral fluid replacement should consist largely of isotonic or hypotonic dextrose solutions.

Carlson and his coworkers have also made a detailed study of fluid and electrolyte changes in endurance trained horses during the course of endurance races. In this study, they sampled nineteen horses prior to, during, and immediately after a 100-mile endurance ride. Since the temperature at the midpoint rest stop was 105° in the shade, these horses were both exercise and heat stressed. On the other hand, most horses in the test group had received some form of electrolyte supplementation prior to or during the ride.

Carlson divided the horses into two groups, those that completed the ride and those that were retired at the halfway point, in the hope of identifying a pattern of plasma or electrolyte changes in the group that retired. Both groups of horses were dehydrated, but it turned out that the majority of the horses that had to retire were more severely dehydrated than the horses that continued.

The acid-base status of these horses was of considerable interest in that most of the horses that completed the course developed a moderate metabolic alkalosis. Carlson felt that this was because most of the exercise that these horses were performing was below the anerobic threshold and the apparent chloride depletion contributed to this unexpected effect. Similarly, all the horses that withdrew had a positive base balance, and Carlson concluded that the common practice of sodium bicarbonate therapy in such horses was unwarranted in the absence of chemical evidence for a metabolic acidosis.

In conclusion, Carlson noted that both groups of horses in this trail ride study showed evidence of fluid and electrolyte losses, with relatively greater losses of electrolytes, giving rise to a hypotonic fluid volume concentration. Under these conditions, electrolytes as well as water are required to restore fluid balance, and balanced electrolyte solutions such as Ringer's may be beneficial in severe cases.

In an earlier report, Carlson studied horses under the same conditions, but there the mid-ride samples were taken before the horses were watered. In this case, he found the major changes in PCV and TPP mid-ride, with PCV returning toward control by post-ride and TPP fully recovered post-ride. These observations of maximal changes at mid-ride with partial to complete recovery by post-ride presumably reflect an early initial fluid loss, with later recovery of extracellular fluid volume both from drinking water and movement of tissue water into the plasma compartment.

Plasma phosphorus, presumably as inorganic phosphate, rose markedly throughout the ride and was the only electrolyte value to increase during the ride.

---

* Reduced blood volume with an increased concentration of sodium and protein.

All other serum electrolyte values fell, from Mg^{++}, which decreased minimally, to all the other values tested, for which declines were significant, at least at the .05 level or less. The drop in plasma chloride was most marked, being statistically significant at the 1 percent level of probability.

In contrast with the PCV and TPP values, which recovered after the midpoint in the ride, serum electrolyte levels tended to fall throughout the ride. This is apparently due to the continued losses of electrolytes in the sweat, which the horses were not able to replenish so readily. Chloride appears to be the major anion in the sweat of horses, and this was the electrolyte most severely depleted.

The decreases in serum Ca^{++} seen were considered by Carlson and Mansman to amount to almost 50 percent of the exchangeable Ca^{++} pool. Decreases of this magnitude have reportedly been implicated in muscle spasms of lactation and transit tetany in horses.

Based on their observations in these studies, these authors concluded that horses used on endurance rides may be able to replenish their water losses at rest stops and streams, but that electrolyte losses with declining serum levels of electrolytes would continue throughout the ride. Oral or intravenous supplementation of electrolytes for horses during the ride was suggested, with the supplements to contain calcium, potassium, magnesium and sodium chloride, with a special emphasis on chloride.

Synchronous diaphragmatic flutter (SDF), or thumps, is another condition that is not unusual in endurance horses with electrolyte imbalances. It so happens that in the horse the right phrenic nerve, which activates the diaphragm, passes over the right atrium and is closely allied with it. Because of this anatomical relationship, the heartbeat is under some circumstances able to initiate a sharp contraction of the diaphragm, which contraction occurs at the same time as, and is therefore synchronized with, the heartbeat. Because of the role of Ca^{++} in stabilizing nerve cell membranes these events are particularly likely to occur in hypocalcemic animals. The actual flutter itself is rather like a hiccup, with the difference that its occurrence is synchronized to the heartbeat. That its occurrence is not uncommon is demonstrated by the fact that about 10 percent of horses that were voluntarily withdrawn from trail rides were eliminated for thumps.

Acute Diarrhea

Under normal conditions, fecal water loss is the largest component of water loss. In the normal horse, the fluid contents of the intestine amount to about 35 liters, 75 percent of which is found in the large bowel. The water content of the bowel is likely to be less during anorexia and substantially higher during diarrhea.

The only quantitative data on diarrhea in the horse are those of Tasker et al., who induced diarrhea with aloin. In his experiments, the most substantial water loss observed was in one horse which put out 40 kg of feces containing an estimated 37 liters of water. Meagher has suggested that horses in acute diarrhea may lose between 50 and 100 liters of water a day, and other estimates range as high as 80 liters a day. Other conditions that are therapeutically equivalent to diarrhea are early colitis X and high intestinal obstruction. In both of these conditions there is a rapid and substantial loss of fluid and electrolytes into the intestine without any overt diarrhea. As in diarrhea, there are substantial losses of gastric and pancreatic intestinal secretions which contain Na^+, K^+, and HCO_3^- ions.

Substantial K^+ deficits are likely to develop in horses with acute diarrhea. Since horses with acute diarrhea are often anorectic, their potassium intake is greatly reduced, while fecal losses are greatly increased. In addition, changes in the acid-base balance of these horses may affect the potassium balance, a decrease in plasma pH being associated with a movement of K^+ from intracellular to extracellular sites. Serum potassium levels of less than 3.0 mEq/L are suggestive of severe hypokalemia in the horse, and Carlson suggests that K^+ deficits of horses with acute diarrhea and hypokalemia may range up to several thousand mEq. Since attempts to relace K^+ deficits of this magnitude intravenously are not advisable,* oral administration of K^+ chloride is the only logical approach, with serum K^+ levels being used to guide the replacement therapy.

According to Tasker, horses with profuse diarrhea tend to have significant decreases in the concentrations of all important electrolytes. In treating these horses, Tasker found the best results by using Ringer's lactate fortified with additional salts as needed. These workers used Ringer's lactate with either 5 gm of $NaHCO_3$ or 5 gm of $KHCO_3$ or, in some cases, 5 gm of each added per liter. Tasker recommends a total of 40 liters of this fluid in twenty-four hours, the first 10 liters I.V. and the remainder orally at twelve-hour intervals.

The rapid administration of solutions with such high concentrations of K^+ and bicarbonate is not without danger, and this danger is greatly increased if renal function is impaired. Tasker et al. suggest the initial treatment of horses with suspected renal failure with the less dangerous Ringer's lactate to be followed with more potent corrective solutions when evidence of good kidney function is obtained.

Shock

If the circulating blood volume becomes substantially reduced, either from fluid loss to the exterior or "pooling" in tissues, hypovolemic shock arises. When this cycle starts, reflex adrenergic activity closes arteriolar and venular sphincters to maintain blood pressure. Blood becomes sequestered in the capillary bed, and the resulting inadequate tissue perfusion causes tissue anoxia and a resulting metabolic acidosis.

Because the existence of shock indicates a substantial loss of circulating blood volume, by definition a large volume of replacement fluid is required, and since shock is an acute condition, the fluids should be administered rapidly. A large diameter indwelling IV catheter should be introduced and therapy started at the rate of 1 ml/kg/minute. In severe shock, Meagher considers that it may be necessary to administer 50 ml/kg, or about 20 liters, to a 1,000 lb. horse during the first three hours. With the necessity of administering fluids at this rate, laboratory measurements of Na^+, K^+, and HCO_3^- are very helpful. In their absence,

---

* This is because high concentrations of potassium, which may be obtained during IV injection of potassium, may cause cardiac irregularities, depression, and death.

Meagher suggests 0.25 gm/kg of $NaHCO_3$ in 3 liters of 5% dextrose as a slow IV drip over a two to three hour period. Based on the consideration that animals in shock can be relatively low in plasma K^+, Meagher suggests that additional K^+ at the rate of 10 mEq/liter may be added after the first 12 liters of fluid have been administered. Thirty to 100 liters of IV fluid may be needed in the first twenty-four hours when treating an equine shock patient, which creates considerable economic and logistic problems for the clinician.

Other considerations in shock therapy in the horse include the monitoring of central venous pressure, which provides accurate information on the animal's circulatory status. If the shock is due to massive blood loss or pooling of blood in capillary beds, plasma expanders may be useful. The most satisfactory expander is plasma from healthy horses, which may be stored frozen and thawed before use. Commercially available plasma expanders may also be used, particularly if plasma protein has decreased below 4.5 gms/dl. They are, however, expensive in the volumes required and tend to leave the plasma readily.

Colics

In obstructive colics of the small intestine, intestinal fluids build up in the gut, which leads to the accumulation of Na^+, Cl^+, K^+, and HCO_3^- ions in the gut. In simple obstructive colics, blockade of the bowel is not complicated by necrotic damage to the bowel wall. Blockade of the bowel causes distension of the gut proximal to the obstruction, and pain. If the obstruction is high in the gastrointestinal tract, passage of the stomach tube will allow regurgitation of large amounts of acidic fluid. In this case the predominant loss is of water and H^+ ions into the upper GIT, so the most appropriate treatment in this case consists of a balanced electrolyte solution containing extra chloride.

If the obstruction is lower down in the gastrointestinal tract, the signs of colic develop more slowly, with depression, inappetence, and mild abdominal pain being the presenting signs. In these cases the ususal clinical picture is that of dehydration, as fluid intake is reduced, with metabolic acidosis and shock developing if the condition is not relieved. Sweating can also add to the fluid loss. In such circumstances, Mason recommends 1 liter of equine plasma as a volume expander, and 8 to 10 liters of lactated Ringer's to be infused IV during the first hour. During surgery, this infusion is continued, with the addition of bicarbonate as required to combat the acidosis, with dosage controlled by serial HCO_3^- determination where possible.

In summary, therefore, proper fluid and electrolyte balance are of vital importance to the performance horse, and in most cases his performance is limited by his ability to maintain his internal environment constant during exercise stress. While most horses start their performance with good fluid, water, and electrolyte balance, they deviate from this balance during the course of their exercise, and the horses that can delay this deviation are usually the most successful performers.

The role of blood cells and blood doping in performance is not experimentally clear, but careful investigations may suggest a positive role. Since one of the limiting factors in performance is the transport of oxygen to the tissues, an increased hematocrit would seem to be a logical mechanism of improving performance. Recent experimental evidence suggests that it may be possible to do this in man, but whether or not it will be possible to do so in the horse remains to be seen. Nature, or more accurately, the evolutionary process, has provided the horse with his own blood doping mechanism, where under stress he can sometimes double his hematocrit by ejecting red blood cells from his spleen. While this mechanism suggests that blood doping might very well be effective in man, who does not have a contractile spleen, whether or not it would work in the horse, which is already well equipped in this area, remains to be seen.

Another potential mechanism of improving performance in horses is increasing their base reserve and thus delaying the onset of lactic acid induced fatigue. Again, there is some slim experimental evidence that this may be a factor in man, but whether or not it would work in the horse is unknown.

A distinct fluid balance problem occurs in trail ride horses which are exercised over long periods in hot temperatures. In these horses metabolic acidosis does not appear to occur, but rather a metabolic alkalosis due to chloride losses in sweat. In such instances, supplementation with bicarbonate is not advisable, but rather supplementation with potassium, calcium, magnesium, and sodium chloride, with special emphasis on the chloride to replace the losses caused by sweating.

SELECTED REFERENCES

Archer, R. K. and Clabby, J.: The effect of excitation and exertion on the circulating blood of horses. *Vet Rec, 77*:689-690, 1965.

Amdur, R. A.: Functions of the equine large intestine and their inter-relationships in disease. *Cornell Vet 65*:303, 1975.

Carlson, G. P.: Fluid therapy in horses with acute diarrhea. *Vet Clin North Am, 1*:313-329, November, 1979.

Carlson, G. P., Harrold, D., and Rumbaugh, G. E.: Volume dilution of sodium thiocyanate as a measure of extracellular fluid volume in the horse. *Am J Vet Res, 40*:587-589, 1979.

Carlson, G. P. and Mansmann, R. A.: Serum electrolyte and plasma protein alterations in horses used in endurance rides. *J Am Vet Med Assoc, 165*:262-264, 1974.

Carlson, G. P. and Ocen, P. O.: Composition of equine sweat following exercise in high environmental temperatures and in response to I.V. epinephrine administration. *J Equine Med Surg, 3*:27-32, 1979.

Carlson, G. P., Ocen, P. O., and Harrold, D.: Clinicopathologic alterations in normal and exhausted endurance horses. *Theriogenology, 6*:93-104, 1976.

Carlson, G. P., Rumbaugh, G. E., and Harrold, D.: Clinicopathologic alterations in the horse produced by food and water deprivation during periods of high environmental temperatures. *Am J Vet Res, 40*:982-985, 1979.

Donawick, W. J.: Metabolic management of the horse with acute abdominal crisis. *J S Afr Vet Assoc, 46*:107-110, 1975.

Hinton, M.: On the watering of horses. A review. *Equine Vet J, 10*:27-31, 1978.

Kohn, L. W.: Preparative management of the equine patient with an abdominal crisis. *Vet Clin North Am, Large Animal Practice, 1(2)*:289-311, 1979.

Krzyanek, H., Milne, D. W., Gabel, A. A., and Smith, L. G.: Acid base values of Standardbred horses recovering from strenuous exercise. *Am J Vet Res, 37*:291-294, 1976.

Mason, I. A.: A practical approach to fluid therapy in the horse. *Aust Vet J, 46*:671, 1972.

Meagher, D. M.: Clinical evaluation and management of shock in the equine patient. *Vet Clin North Am, 6*:245-255, 1976.

Milne, D. W., Skarda, R. T., Gabel, A. A., Smith, L. G., and Ault, K.: Effects of training on biochemical values in Standardbred horses. *Am J Vet Res, 37*:285-290, 1976.

Schaepdryver, A. E. and Hebbelinck, M.: *Doping.* New York, Pergamon Pr, 1965.

Tasker, J. B.: Fluid and electrolyte studies in the horse. I. Blood values in 100 normal horses. *Cornell Vet, 56*:67, 1966.

———: Fluid and electrolyte studies in the horse. II. An apparatus for the collection of total daily urine and feces from horses. *Cornell Vet, 56*:77, 1966.

————: Fluid and electrolyte studies in the horse. III. The intake and output of water, sodium, and potassium in normal horses. *Cornell Vet, 57:*649, 1967.

————: Fluid and electrolyte studies in the horse. IV. The effects of fasting and thirsting. *Cornell Vet, 57:*658, 1967.

————: Fluid and electrolyte studies in the horse. V. The effects of diarrhea. *Cornell Vet, 57:*668-677, 1967.

————: Electrolyte therapy in gastrointestinal disease. *VM SAC, 61:*765-772, 1966.

Waterman, A.: A review of the diagnosis and treatment of fluid and electrolyte disorders in the horse. *Equine Vet J, 9:*43, 1977.

Section V

THE CONTROL OF MEDICATION IN PERFORMANCE HORSES

IN THIS SECTION we will review the regulation of medication in performance horses as it is currently handled in North America. This process starts with the drawing of blood and urine from horses, either pre- or post-race, and the delivery of the samples to the testing laboratory. In the laboratory the chemist analyzes these samples for the presence of drugs, using highly technical and specialized procedures. When the chemist has identified a prohibited drug or drug metabolite in one of these samples, he then reports his findings to the stewards, who may or may not take action on the report. The first chapter of this section basically describes the sampling and testing processes used in a good modern laboratory and how the chemist comes to the conclusion that he has unequivocally identified a drug or drug metabolite in a sample. When a chemist makes such an identification and reports it to his commissioners, he has completed his section of the regulatory process, and the act of reporting such a finding is known as "calling a positive."

While the identification of a drug in a biological sample is a challenging and tedious process, the next two steps are even more ambiguous and challenging. The stewards must take the data from the chemist, which heretofore has almost always been simply an identification, and fit it into the context of their rules. More recently, the inherent weakness of time rules and the importance of the concentration of drugs in blood and, to a lesser extent, urine has been recognized in the formulation of rules. In particular, the drafting of these rules in such a way that the medication policies of a jurisdiction can be effectively and fairly enforced is a major undertaking and is discussed in detail in the second chapter of this section.

One approach to the problem of medication control, which became very popular in the United States during the 1970s, was that of controlled medication programs. The administrative basis for these programs is set forth in the second chapter of this section, and a number of the perceived and actual problems with these programs are outlined. One of the major charges against controlled medication programs is that they may lead to a change in the "nature of the breed," and a discussion of the problem is presented in the final section of the second chapter.

The third chapter in this section deals with legal problems and the medication of racing horses. These usually start at the level of the hearing, which is commonly the first point at which disciplinary action may be taken, and can presumably proceed all the way to the appropriate Supreme Court. For a review of this area, Richard Heard, as a practicing attorney, takes over for the last chapter and explains some of the legal pitfalls in wait for those who become involved in the problems of drugs in performance horses.

361

CHEMICAL TESTING FOR DRUGS AND CALLING "POSITIVES": HOW THE ANALYST DOES (OR SHOULD DO) IT

T HE TESTING OF BODY FLUIDS from horses for the presence of drugs was first introduced into racing in Europe about 1910. In the year 1912, a horse called BOURBON ROSE won the gold cup at Maisons Lafitte in France but was disqualified because it yielded the first "positive" dope test. Following a pattern that has since become all too familiar, the owners sued but lost their case. Routine testing for drugs in horses had arrived and had been supported in the courts.

Seventy years after these events, the "test barn" or "spit box"* and the analytical chemist remain the basic tools by which the improper use of drugs in performance horses is controlled. This is because, for essentially all the drugs that we have discussed to date, the clinical signs of their actions are not sufficiently clear-cut or distinguishable to allow improperly medicated horses to be picked out pre-race. Occasionally, if an animal is overdosed with a tranquilizer, the clinical signs of penile protrusion and depression are sufficiently clear-cut to draw attention to the animal's condition, but these cannot give more than a general indication of the class of drug that may be involved. Therefore, even in the unlikely event that suspicious clinical signs are seen pre-race, it is still necessary to take a blood or urine sample to unequivocally confirm the presence of a drug and allow disciplinary action to be taken.

One of the very few circumstances under which the detection of "clinical" signs of medication prior to an event may be possible is that of the "gingering" of saddle horses. A "gingered" saddle horse is one that has had ginger applied beneath his tail, which is thought to encourage him to hold his tail up from his haunches and thus produce good "tail carriage" for the judges. Speaking on this problem, Doctor John Lengel, of the American Horse Shows Association, stated that "I do not intend to be facetious when I state that it appears that the only way to approach the problem of ginger control from a legal and practical point of view is to have the stewards sniff for it under the horse's tail." While any information obtained by sniffing under a horse's tail is likely to be highly subjective, most medication control procedures rest on rigorous chemical identification of the drug, and this is a highly sophisticated area.

The most comprehensive pattern of medication testing is pre-race testing. In a pre-race testing system all the horses are stabled in a secure area at least one hour before the race; blood samples are then drawn from each of these horses and analyzed immediately for drugs in an adjacent laboratory, usually trackside. If evidence for the presence of a forbidden substance is found, a report is made to

---

* The title "spit box" for the test barn presumably dates back to the days when saliva or "spit" was the principal sample taken in drug testing.

The only way to approach ginger control in show horses from a legal and practical point of view is to have the stewards sniff for it under the horse's tail.

the stewards and further samples are drawn. The stewards will usually scratch the horse and, depending on the medication rules in the particular jurisdiction, may or may not hold a hearing. Once the horses have run the race, urine samples are taken from them and tested in the same way as is done for post-race testing. Pre-race testing in this country always uses blood samples, although at one time a pre-race testing scheme in Singapore used urine samples. Pre-race testing is now used in harness racing in New York, New Jersey, Pennsylvania, and Ohio and has just recently been introduced in Thoroughbred racing in New York.

The major advantage of pre-race testing is that it is the only mechanism that can actually prevent the running of illegally medicated horses. It is equitable in that all horses running are tested, and in the event that a suspicious sample is found, further samples can be taken to confirm or deny this suspicion. It acts to nip illegal medication in the bud, for the horse is disqualified before he starts in the race rather than after he may have won a large purse. For this reason, pre-race testing acts to remove some of the financial incentive to legal challenge of the testing process. Finally, pre-race testing is a highly visible and elaborate procedure, and as such it represents substantial evidence of the racing authorities' commitment to medication control.

Weighed against these advantages, however, pre-race testing has a number of disadvantages. The very short period available in which to test and confirm the presence of the drug imposes technical limitations on the testing process. Further, because the pre-race testing laboratory must be located at the actual track, neither the amount nor the quality of the analytical equipment is usually the same as that available at a central post-race laboratory. These constraints in time and instrumentation are inevitably reflected in the quality of the information available to the analyst when he makes his decisions on the presence or absence of drugs in the pre-prace testing samples.

The use of blood as the testing medium in pre-race testing may impose further constraints on the testing process. While blood can be very easily and rapidly obtained from horses, the volume of blood available for use in a pre-race test is usually about one or two test tubes full (20 ml), less than a tenth of the volume usually available. This small volume means that the quantity of drug available to the analyst is correspondingly reduced. Further, some drugs or drug metabolites are usually found in lower concentrations in blood than in urine, which further adds to the difficulty of testing blood samples for drugs. Indeed, some drugs used in racing are sufficiently potent that they are pharmacologically effective in the horse at blood levels that are currently either difficult to detect or are only marginally detectable.

On the other hand, blood testing has a number of advantages, which will become more important as analytical methods improve. If a drug is found in the bloodstream, it is usually found as the unchanged drug and not in the changed or metabolized form in which it is usually found in horse's urine. If a drug is found in the blood, it is much more likely to be pharmacologically active and actually to have affected the horse's performance than if just a metabolite were found in the urine. If the pharmacology of the drug has been characterized, one should be able to tell, with some accuracy, from the concentration of the drug in blood whether or not the horse was affected by the drug. This, of course, is what happens in the human, where a certain blood level of alcohol is taken as legal evidence of drunkenness. Finally, diuretics such as Lasix® do not act to dilute or reduce the concentration of any drug in the bloodstream, which means that Lasix® cannot be used to dilute drugs in the blood in the same way as it can dilute some drugs or drug metabolites in urine.

Pre-race testing is, however, relatively expensive, and this is the major limitation on its implementation. Holding facilities for the horses have to be made available, and laboratory space and a complete set of instruments have to be provided at each track to process the sample. Highly trained personnel have to be available at each track, usually at some distance from their homes, for the period of the meet, which may be difficult to arrange. These operational considerations and expenses make an extensive pre-race testing program a substantial administrative and logistic task as well as scientific challenge.

The more usual pattern of testing in racing around the world is post-race testing, most commonly of a urine sample taken post-race. In post-race testing only a fraction of the horses running are selected for testing, the horses usually selected being winners, beaten favorites, and any horses that may have aroused the suspicions of the stewards or commission veterinarians. Once selected, these

BUNKUM STATE TESTING PROGRAM

The inclusion of blood sampling in all post-race testing schemes is now recommended.

horses are sent immediately from the track to the test barn area (Fig. 22-1). In the test barn area the horse is cooled out, identified, and then put in box stall with an attendant who waits for the horse to urinate. As soon as the horse urinates, the test barn attendant catches a sample in a cup on a long handle and brings it to the commission veterinarian (Fig. 22-2). The trainer's assistant or other representative witnesses this procedure and signs a number docket attesting (Fig. 22-3) to the fact that the urine sample bearing that number did indeed come from his horse (Fig. 22-4). This code number is then attached to the sealed jar in which the urine sample is placed for transportation to the laboratory (Fig. 22-5). In some jurisdictions, a blood sample is also drawn, sealed, and transported with the urine sample to the laboratory. Since blood samples are easily and rapidly drawn (Fig. 22-6) at minimal extra cost, and since they may be quite valuable to the analyst, the inclusion of blood sampling in all post-race testing schemes is now recommended (Fig. 22-7).

The collection of urine samples is slow and difficult compared with collection of blood samples. The attendant has to wait for the horse to void a urine sample

Figure 22-1. The equipment and transportation box for equine forensic samples. The collected samples are stored and transported in a secure metal box, which is padlocked during transportation. The box is lined with Styrofoam® insulation and contains space for about twenty urine jars. The box also contains the Vacutainer® tubes and sterile needles for collecting the blood samples and the sample tags to be attached to the blood and urine samples. It also contains a number of frozen gel-packs, to keep its contents cool during transportation.

spontaneously, and although most horses will void within an hour, some may take considerably longer. In some jurisdictions, furosemide (Lasix®) is administered to horses to facilitate the collection of a urine sample, but this can give rise to detection problems with certain drugs. This slow pace of collection of urine samples means that only a small number of the horses in a race can have urine collected from them post-race unless the track is equipped with a large horse holding facility.

Urine testing has a number of advantages over bood testing for the detection of drugs or drug metabolites post-race, and for these reasons it is currently the backbone of drug testing in horses. Urine is available in relatively large quantities compared with blood, the average sample delivered to a post-race testing laboratory being on the order of 150 to 250 ml, or about a coffee mug full of urine. A further major advantage is that drugs and drug metabolites are often concentrated in urine. Because of the larger volume of urine obtainable, sufficient samples for split tests and confirmatory tests by other laboratories are often available.

There are, however, a number of problems with urine testing that work to the detriment of the horseman and, indeed, create problems for the industry as a whole. The principal problem is that drugs may show up in urine samples for long

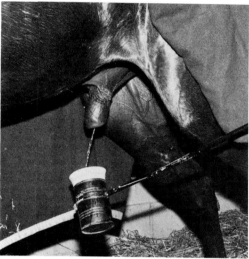

Figure 22-2. Urine sampling. Urine samples are "caught" as spontaneously voided urine post-race. Once the horse has been cooled out and blood sampled, he is brought to the urine testing stall. The veterinarian's assistant is provided with a plastic cup and a long-handled holder for the cup. When the horse voids, a urine sample is caught in the plastic cup by the assistant and brought to the veterinarian's office. About 90 percent of horses provide a urine sample within one hour, the bulk of the remainder provide a sample within two hours, but a small number of horses will fail to provide samples within the allotted time. Courtesy of Steven Ballard, University of Kentucky.

after they were administered to the horse and long after their pharmacological effects have disappeared (Table 22-I). For example, if a dose of Lasix® is given intravenously, its pharmacological effects in the horse are essentially over within two hours, and the drug can no longer be detected in plasma after five hours. Because Lasix® is pumped directly into the urine, however, it is found in high concentrations in urine and is found there for up to three days or longer. Lasix® can, therefore, be detected in horse urine for at least twenty times longer than its period of pharmacological action, which means it is possible to call Lasix® positives on horses that had Lasix® in their urine but not, for all practical purposes, in their bloodstream at the time of racing.

This situation also holds for other drugs. The pharmacological effects of pentazocine are short lived in the horse, not lasting more than about four hours, while the drug is detectable in plasma for only about eight hours. In contrast with these relatively short time periods of drug action and detection in blood, however, is the finding that metabolites of pentazocine can still be detected in equine urine for up to five days after a dose. Similarly, the pharmacological effects of fentanyl are over within one hour after it is injected, but the drug can be detected in plasma

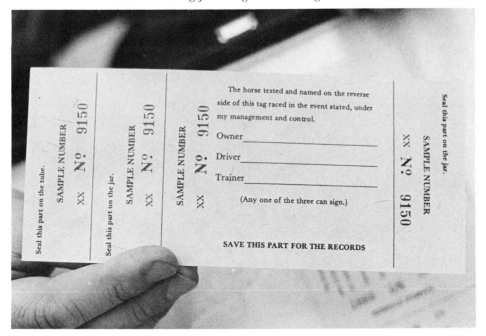

The horse tested and named on the reverse side of this tag raced in the event stated, under my management and control.

Owner_____

Driver_____

Trainer_____

(Any one of the three can sign.)

SAVE THIS PART FOR THE RECORDS

Figure 22-3. The sample tag. A sample tag, with portions to be attached to the blood samples, the two urine jars for the split tests, and the witness portion, which may be signed by the owner, trainer, or driver.

Figure 22-4. Witnessing the sample. The trainer or his representative signs the sample tags to witness the fact that the sample tested actually came from the horse in question. Courtesy of Steven Ballard, University of Kentucky.

22-5A

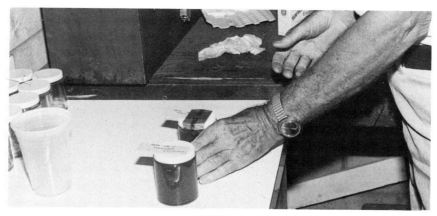

22-5B

22-5C

Figure 22-5. Splitting and sealing the urine samples. In Standardbred racing in Kentucky, the urine sample is divided into two equal portions and each sealed independently with paired tags and evidence tape. One half of the "split" is sent to the commission analyst, while the other half is retained by the commission. Courtesy of Steven Ballard, University of Kentucky.

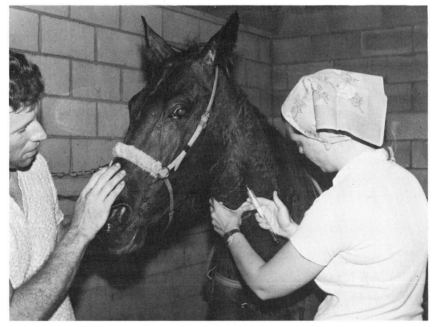

22-6A

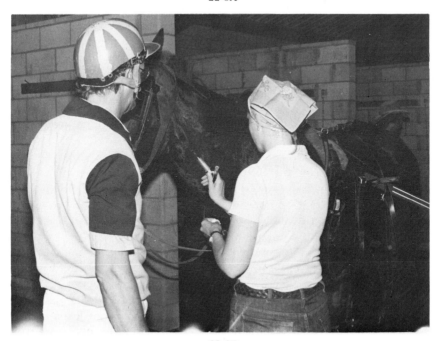

22-6B

Figure 22-6. Drawing of a blood sample from a horse. Blood is easily and rapidly obtained, either pre- or post-race, from Thoroughbred or Standardbred horses. The site is first swabbed with disinfectant and the venipuncture needle introduced into the vein. The Vacutainer® tube is then placed into the needle holder and the blood is automatically drawn into the evacuated tube. Usually about two 20 ml tubes of blood are drawn. Courtesy of Steven Ballard, University of Kentucky.

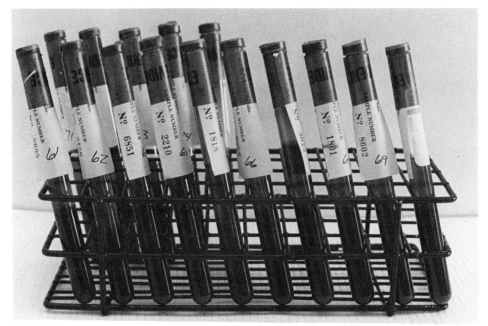

Figure 22-7. Blood samples. Blood samples sealed with evidence tape, which encloses both the stopper and the sample tag. These blood samples have been opened, and laboratory numbers have been added to the sample tags.

for twelve hours and in urine for ninety-six hours after a single dose. The bottom line on urine testing, therefore, is that simple detection of a drug in urine has no bearing on the possibility of it having a pharmacological effect at the time of racing. Further, given the prolonged "clearance times" of some drugs, the use of urine testing is likely to "skew" the detection picture in favor of drugs that are cleared slowly and that appear in urine for long periods.

This problem is further compounded by the fact that it is essentially impossible from single urinary concentrations to tell within anything but the very broadest of limits when a drug was administered to a horse. This is because both the volume and acidity of urine are varied by the horse as he holds his internal environment constant. As pointed out earlier, the concentration of procaine in a horse urine can vary by up to 9,000-fold depending on the acidity of the urine, let alone any changes caused by volume or individual variation among animals. A further complication reported recently in discussions among my colleagues is that the concentration of drug detected in a single urine sample may vary by ±50 percent, depending only on the portion of the urine sample selected for analysis. This huge range of possible drug concentrations in horse urine leads me to the conclusion that anyone who tries to estimate a time of drug administration within the context of a forty-eight or seventy-two hour rule from a single identification of a drug in urine may well be just making guesses against tremendous odds.

It is also, as will be made clear later (Chapter 23), essentially impossible to determine from blood data when a drug was administered. However, one can

One advantage of urine as a forensic sample is that it is available in relatively large quantities.

usually relate the blood levels to pharmacological effect. Similarly, blood levels of drugs are easy to determine and confirm between labs, whereas measurements of urinary levels of drugs can be poorly repeatable from lab to lab, because of the uneven distribution of drug in urine samples.

The other biological samples that have been used in testing programs are saliva and sweat. To my knowledge, sweat is only rarely if ever taken as a drug testing sample. Sweat is not usually available pre-race, which rules it out as a pre-race test.

TABLE 22-I

RELATIONSHIP OF PHARMACOLOGICAL EFFECT TO CLEARANCE TIMES
FOR DRUGS IN BLOOD AND URINE

| Drug | *Approximate Duration of Pharmacological Effect* | *"Clearance Times"* | |
		Plasma	*Urine*
Furosemide	4 hours	5-12 hrs	3 days
Procaine	4 hours	<12 hrs	13 days
Apomorphine	<4 hours	N/A	2 days
Phenylbutazone	36 hours	9 days	14 days?
Pentazocine	<4 hours	8 hrs	5 days
Morphine	12 hours	—	5 days
Fentanyl	1 hour	12 hrs	4 days
Reserpine	10 days	5 days	—

Further, only very limited information is available on the excretion of drugs in sweat, which makes it difficult to estimate its value as a forensic sample. Finally, it can be very difficult to refute a defense that substances detected in sweat were only surface contaminants and were never actually present in the horse. For these reasons, sweat is not considered a satisfactory sample by most forensic authorities and is now rarely used in equine forensic chemistry.

Saliva is still used as a forensic sample in equine drug testing in some jurisdictions. Saliva samples are collected by swabbing the horse's mouth with a gauze pad held in a forceps, and the pad is occasionally moistened with dilute acetic acid to encourage the secretion of saliva. These procedures usually yield between 3 and 15 ml of dilute saliva, and saliva samples taken in this way are rapidly and easily collected. Unfortunately, however, the concentrations of many drugs in saliva are low, and the volume of the sample obtained is also usually quite small.

The concentrations of drugs in saliva are low because that fraction of the drug which is protein bound in blood does not pass into the saliva. Thus, acidic drugs such as phenylbutazone, the other non-steroidal anti-inflammatory drugs, and furosemide are found in saliva only in quite low concentrations. Because saliva is basic, relative to plasma, the entry of basic drugs, which includes narcotics and other central nervous system stimulants, is also restricted. On top of this, the small volumes (2 to 3 ml) of undiluted saliva, which occasionally may be all that is obtainable, can cause further problems. For these reasons saliva is not, to our knowledge, routinely used as a biological fluid in most drug testing programs in the United States.

Whatever the nature of the forensic sample, however, the identification, care, and handling of all samples, once drawn, is essentially similar. In order for the "positive" called by the analyst to be based on a valid sample from the animal, the security of the sample — the so-called "chain of evidence" — must be secured and be defensible. This is an extremely important area, as it is one that is highly likely to be challenged in the event of litigation. The horse must therefore be properly identified, the taking of the sample properly witnessed, and the sample jar sealed with evidence tape. Evidence tape is a special tape applied to the lids of the jars in which the glue is stronger than the tape. Any attempt, therefore, to remove the tape in one piece is doomed to failure, and evidence tape is difficult to tamper with without leaving obvious signs of such tampering (Fig. 22-8). Further, the sample container should be secure and solid and not of a nature that might easily be pierced with a fine hypodermic needle and a contaminant introduced into the system.

Once taken, sealed, and witnessed, the samples should be held in a cooled, secure container and transported to the laboratory as rapidly as possible (see Fig. 22-1). Their receipt in the laboratory should be recorded in a bound laboratory log, the page dated for that day. The log should record the code numbers of the samples received, their approximate volume, and any comments on their appearance. Once the sample is opened, the pH and specific gravity of the urine sample should be noted and recorded, as both pH and specific gravity may be related to the amounts of some drugs found in urine.

If the procedure of the International Olympic Committee is followed, as it is by

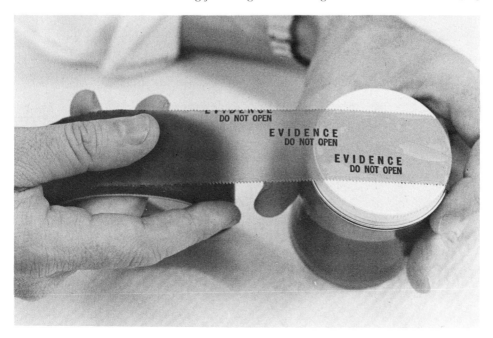

22-8A

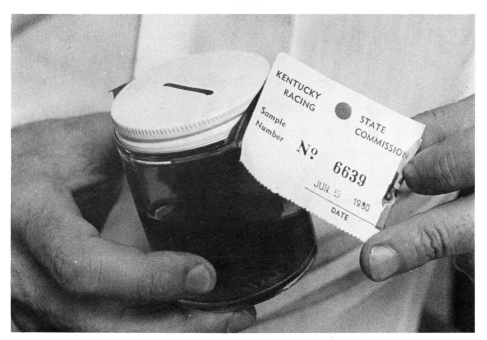

22-8B

Figure 22-8. Evidence tape. Evidence tape is applied to the sides of the jar and over the lid, enclosing the urine sample portion of the tag as shown in the lower panel. When firmly attached, the evidence tape cannot be removed without destroying the tape.

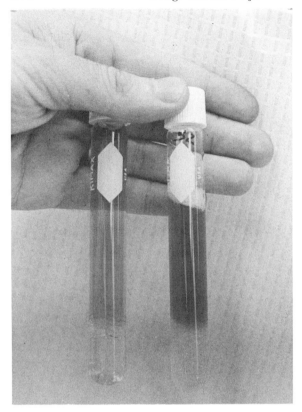

Figure 22-9. Solvent extraction. Samples of blood and urine have been diluted with buffer to adjust the pH and added on top of an organic solvent layer. These samples are then rotated on the Rotorack to allow extraction of the drug into the organic solvent layer.

many European laboratories, split samples are taken, which arrive in the laboratory in two bottles, labelled "A" and "B." The analysis is started on the A sample and the B sample is stored frozen. In the event of a "positive," the B sample is then available for confirmatory analysis, either in the presence of a referee or by an independent laboratory. This procedure safeguards the interests of the horseman, and willingness to take part in such a system is a clear-cut measure of the analyst's confidence in his own ability. In fact, in some European laboratories an analysis will not be started in the absence of a referee's sample. This system has proven its worth in Europe because at least one "positive" called recently was not confirmed by an unquestionably competent refereeing laboratory in another country. Unfortunately, in the United States, many jurisdictions do not require a referee sample, and it is all to easy to dispose of, consume, or allow to deteriorate the remains of a test sample, and with it the only possibility of independent verification of the analytical work on which the "positive" was called.

In addition, the laboratory should have an up-to-date loose-leaf manual on the testing procedures in use on that particular day, as methods in all laboratories change with time, and sometimes quite rapidly. As part of this manual the laboratory should have clear-cut written criteria set up in advance to be used for differentiating between data points. For example, in the thin-layer chromatographic work by Sunshine, all Rf values differing by more than ±0.05 were considered distinguishable. Similar criteria also need to be established for gas chromatographic retention times and other quantitative data. In the absence of such written criteria, the analyst makes his judgments based on how he feels at the particular time that the sample appears in front of him. If such criteria are not established, the analyst's decision on the interpretation of data points may be influenced by his forthcoming summer vacation or a recent interview with his commissioners in ways that cannot be described as scientific.

The first step in an actual drug analysis is usually the taking from the sample of two portions of about 10 to 20 ml each. One of these portions is made acidic with about 5 ml of saturated acid phosphate buffer, and one is made basic with sodium tetraborate. Then an equal volume of a solvent, such as benzene or dichloromethane (Fig. 22-9), is added to each system and the whole shaken up together (Fig. 22-10). When the organic solvent settles out, the acidic drugs will have migrated into the organic solvent under acidic conditions, while basic drugs migrate into the solvent under basic conditions. In this way, acidic drugs such as phenylbutazone, furosemide, naproxen, and so forth will tend to predominate in the acidic extract, while basic drugs such as amphetamine, methylphenidate, cocaine, and the local anesthetics will tend to predominate in the basic extract. This process is technically called solvent extraction. Other drugs, such as caffeine and reserpine, which do not carry any dominant electrical charge, are called neutral drugs and are not easy to separate from other drugs at this stage.

Once the organic solvent has settled out, it and the drugs it contains are drawn off and evaporated down to a very small volume. A small portion of these concentrated extracts is then spotted on a "thin-layer plate" and chromatographed by a process called thin layer chromatography (TLC). Other common

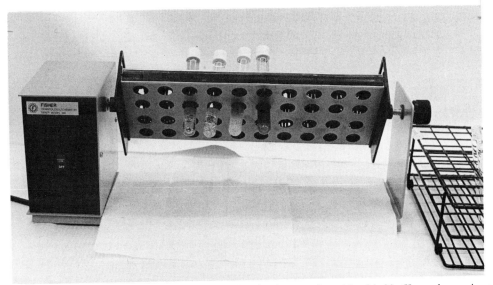

Figure 22-10. The extraction process. The blood and urine samples, with added buffer and organic solvent, are rotated on a Rotorack for about ten to twenty minutes. During this process transfer of the drug to the organic solvent occurs. At the end of this period the tubes are centrifuged to separate the aqueous and organic layers, and the organic solvent, now containing the drug, is removed.

maneuvers with acidic extracts include ultraviolet spectrometry (UV analysis), gas chromatography (GC), and, occasionally, high performance liquid chromatography (HPLC). If positive indications for the presence of a drug appear in any or all of these test systems, the extract may be examined by gas chromatography-mass spectrometry (GC-MS).

The same general procedure is followed with the basic extract. While a portion of the extract may be subjected to thin-layer chromatography, an increasingly common procedure is to react the extract with a highly reactive "marker" chemical such as pentafluoropropionic anhydride (PFPA) and examine the result by gas chromatography (GC). This method is useful for picking up very small quantities of central nervous system stimulants such as amphetamine and methylphenidate. Again, if suspicious peaks are found, the material may be subjected to gas chromatography-mass spectrometry. A general flow sheet for drug analysis is presented schematically in Figure 22-11.

Horses excrete some drugs, such as apomorphine, morphine, Valium®, and pentazocine, in their urine by linking these drugs to highly water soluble sugar molecules such as glucuronic acid (see Chapter 4). Before analysis for these drugs can commence, the drug portion of this complex must be split out by incubating the urine with hydrochloric acid, sodium hydroxide, or a specific enzyme called

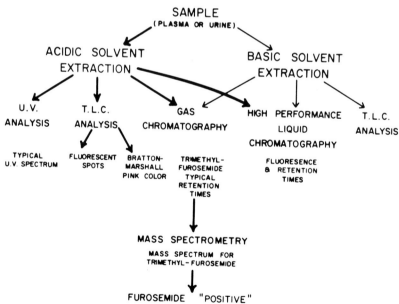

Figure 22-11. General drug testing scheme. The blood or urine sample is extracted under acidic or basic conditions and the extracts subjected to analysis as indicated. The heavy arrows show a typical pattern for furosemide. As an acidic drug it is recovered in the acidic extract, and typical screening tests for its presence would be thin-layer chromatography (TLC), where it shows up under UV light, and a color test called the Bratton-Marshall reaction. Furosemide can also be detected by UV scanning and by high performance liquid chromatography. For unequivocal confirmation of furosemide in a urine sample, it may be methylated to yield trimethylfurosemide and the product analyzed by mass spectrometry.

glucuronidase. Once this process, which takes from two to three hours, is complete, testing for these drugs proceeds by acidic or basic extraction as previously described.

The essence of all these procedures is that they give varying kinds of evidence about the presence of a drug. Although analytical testing for drugs in horses has been with us now for about seventy years, most horsemen, veterinarians, and commissioners know little about the actual techniques that the analyst uses to determine whether or not a medication violation exists. In the remainder of this chapter we will briefly outline some of the methods used in the testing process and show how the analyst arrives at the decision that he has identified a given drug in a horse with sufficient certainty to "call a positive" for that drug.

Generally speaking, a "positive" is called when an analyst reports the presence in a sample of a drug that violates a medication rule. In some jurisdictions the finding of any foreign substance in a blood or urine sample is cause for substantial penalties against a trainer. In other jurisdictions, such as California, the drug found must be a stimulant, depressant, or narcotic, and the discovery of other agents does not necessarily elicit substantial sanctions. In this chapter, therefore, when we speak of a "positive" we are concerned with the identification and reporting of a drug in a sample under circumstances that may give rise to a substantial penalty against an owner, trainer, or veterinarian and result in court review of the proceedings.

As well as not being defined in law, the concept of a positive is not well defined in chemistry either. While it is usually assumed to mean that the drug that is called positive is present in the urine sample, many drugs are not found in horse urine in significant quantities but rather are found in metabolically changed forms. The analyst then manipulates the urine, for example by acidic or enzymatic hydrolysis, until he can split out the parent drug from its metabolite in the urine sample. He may then call a "positive" for the drug in question, even though the urine sample contains no detectable levels of anything but metabolites of the drug on which he called the positive.

An analyst calls a "positive" when he believes he has sufficient evidence to unequivocally identify a specific drug or foreign chemical substance in the sample. At the first sign of something suggesting the presence of a drug, the analyst has what he calls a "suspicious sample." As he continues to gather evidence, he must ask himself how good or useful the evidence is and at what point he should pronounce it "positive." Before we can understand how he arrives at this important judgment, we will have to look more closely at the analytical techniques* that the analyst uses and the quality of information that they provide to him.

Ultraviolet Spectrometry

In ultraviolet (UV) spectrometry, light of wavelengths shorter than the human eye can detect is directed through the suspected solution. If a drug is present in

---

* The definitive text on analytical techniques in equine drug testing is the *Proceedings of the Third International Symposium on Equine Medication Control*, which was held in Lexington, Kentucky in 1979. Copies of this Proceedings are available at $39.50 each from the author at the Department of Veterinary Science, University of Kentucky, Lexington, Kentucky 40546.

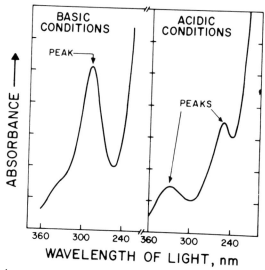

Figure 22-12. UV absorbance patterns of flunixin. The right panel shows two absorbance peaks for flunixin at 250 nm and 330 nm under acidic conditions, while the left panel shows a single peak at 290 nm under basic conditions. Reproduced with permission from Tobin, *J Equine Med Surg, 2:*518, 1978.

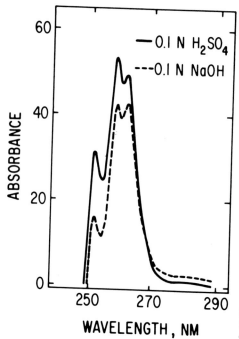

Figure 22-13. UV absorbance curves for fentanyl under acidic (solid line) and basic (dashed line) conditions.

sufficient concentrations, and if the drug absorbs UV light, the instrument will plot out a graph of the drug's absorbance of light at each wavelength. A typical UV absorbance spectrum for the non-steroidal anti-inflammatory drug flunixin, extracted from horse urine, is shown in Figure 22-12. From the shape of the UV curve and the wave lengths at which the peaks occur, the analyst will often be able to guess at the identity of the drug. He will then change the solution in which the drug is suspended from acidic to basic, and if the shape of the curve changes in a way that supports his opinion as to which drug is present, he will have made a tentative drug identification.

There are two principal problems with UV data as a basis for drug identification. The first is that many compounds share broadly similar UV absorption spectra, so the test cannot distinguish between many agents. For example, amphetamine, atropine, and fentanyl have broadly similar UV absorption curves despite being very different both structurally and pharmacologically (Fig. 22-13).

The second problem is that the portion of the UV region used by analysts is relatively small, which means that there are at most about 200 different values for UV absorption peaks. If only about 20 per cent of known compounds absorb in the UV, then there are about 4,000 different candidate compounds for each UV peak. This problem is further complicated by the fact that extacts of horse urine will contain unknown compounds that also absorb in the UV and tend to confuse the picture. Because no control (drug-free) sample is available, it is not possible to run matched controls. For these reasons UV data may suggest the presence of a compound but cannot positively identify it. UV is therefore considered a screening technique by most forensic experts.

Thin-Layer Chromatography (TLC)

Thin-layer chromatography is another extremely useful screening technique. It gets its name from the fact that the experiment is performed on a thin layer of silica gel or other adsorbent coated on a glass or metal plate. The drug extract is spotted about 1 cm from the edge of the plate (Fig. 22-14) and the plate stood on edge in a solvent system (Fig. 22-15). As the solvent system migrates up the plate, the compounds in the spot move along the plate at varying speeds, depending on their affinity for either the solvent (which is moving) or the gel (which is stationary). Compounds that spend about half their time in each phase will migrate about one-half the way up the plate and are spoken of as having an Rf of about 0.5. Other compounds may spend most of their time absorbed to the silica gel and barely move at all from the point of origin. Others may spend most of their time in the solvent and migrate close to the "solvent front"* and thus have an Rf in the region of 0.9 to 1.0 (Fig. 22-15).

When an analyst sees spots that suggest the presence of a drug, he makes an educated guess as to which drug it might be. He then reruns the experiment with his best guess running right beside his unknown. If the spots clearly do not migrate the same distance relative to the solvent front, he can be quite sure that the drug and the unknown are not the same substance. If the spots do migrate

---

* The solvent front is the leading edge (front) of the solvent as it moves up the TLC plate.

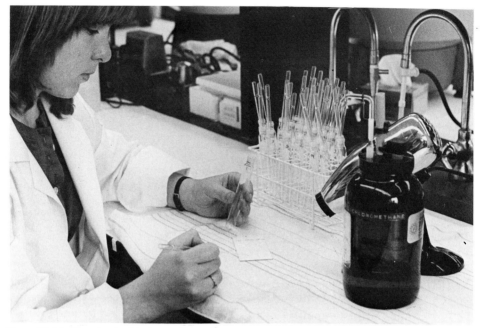

Figure 22-14. "Spotting" a thin-layer plate. The organic solvent extract of the blood or urine sample is concentrated and then spotted from a micropipette on a thin-layer plate under a stream of air from a hair dryer. The plate will then be placed in a thin-layer tank, as shown in Figure 22-15, chromatographed, and then developed to yield a typical TLC plate as shown in Figure 22-16.

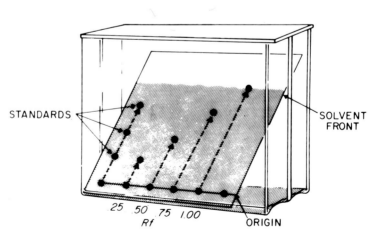

Figure 22-15. Thin-layer chromatography. Drug standards and unknowns are spotted at the origin and the plate stood on end in the solvent. The fraction of the distance migrated by the drug in comparison with the distance migrated by the solvent front is the Rf of the drug. Reproduced with permission from Tobin, *J Equine Med Surg, 2:*518, 1978.

together (within the somewhat elastic limits of his experimental error), they may be the same substance, but they are not necessarily the same substance (Fig. 22-16).

The reason one can never be sure about identify with TLC is statistical. The maximum number of spots that one can hope to separate physically on a TLC plate is about twenty. With 4.2 million chemical candidates,* one has about 210,000 possible chemicals for each spot. A 99 percent specific color or other marker reaction would reduce this number 100-fold and leave only 2,000 possible candidates for each spot. "Specific" extraction conditions might possibly reduce this number even further, but a considerable probability of overlap in TLC systems still exists. This is the basic problem with trying to use TLC for definitive identification. TLC simply does not have the resolving power necessary to generate a specific identification in the context of forensic chemistry. Similarly, high performance TLC (HPTLC), which under optimal conditions is only about twice as good as regular TLC, is also unable to generate specific identification data.

Since most forensic chemists are aware of the lack of specificity of TLC, they usually elect to compare the drug and the unknown in a number of different TLC systems. If both spots again migrate the same distance, the chances that the analyst is right are improved. In an experimental test of this procedure, Sunshine and his coworkers chromatographed 138 drugs in four solvent systems. They were unable to separate twenty-five of these drugs in four solvent systems, and in experiments with even seven TLC systems, overlaps were still found. A reasonable conclusion from these experiments is that the number of solvent systems required to separate pure solutions of just the 4,000 drugs in common use without risk of overlap is both astronomic and unlikely to be run by the average drug testing laboratory.

It is also very important to remember that this 20 percent overlap rate seen in Sunshine's experiments with four TLC systems was found with pure solutions of single drugs. In real life, running multiple TLC systems for drug identification in complex biological samples leaves one open to another source of error, that due to "partial" false positives. In this mechanism, the occurrence of a drug or endogenous biochemical in a plasma sample that will run with the standard in only two of the four systems, along with another substance or drug that can co-migrate with the standard in the other two systems, will lead to a "false positive." This "false positive" will occur due to the coincidence of two different substances in a plasma sample, neither of which alone could give rise to a "false positive" in the four TLC systems. Because of this inherent problem, multiple TLC systems analysis of biological samples cannot be considered specific for even a sub-class of chemicals that would run with the standard in four systems, as there is no way of telling whether or not four spots obtained from a blood or urine sample are due to one single substance or four different substances. In its current form, therefore, TLC is a test that can readily prove the absence of a drug but cannot, even with the use

---

* There are about 4,000 active drug ingredients in common use, 63,000 chemicals in everyday use, and, as of November, 1977, about 4,000,000 chemical entities, a number that was increasing at the rate of about 6,000/week.

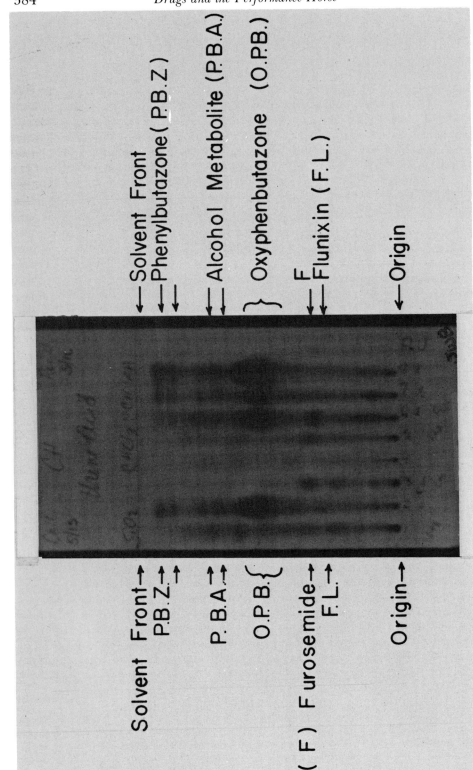

of multiple systems, prove its presence. It is consequently not considered a specific test by most forensic authorities.

Gas Chromatography

Gas chromatography (GC) functions on the same principle as TLC with the difference that the mobile phase is a gas and the stationary phase may be any one of a huge variety of materials. Because the mobile phase is gaseous, the substance to be chromatographed must be volatile, which restricts GC analysis to the approximately 400,000 volatile chemicals and perhaps another 400,000 that can be volatilized after appropriate treatment.

Gas chromatography is like TLC in that some drugs will flow right along with the gas and others will stick to the column (stationary phase) near the origin and never come out. However, if one has chosen the right column pack (stationary phase), mobile phase (gas), temperature, gas flow, and so forth, one can arrange for a nice separation of drugs by GC. To start the experiment, the unknown is injected onto the column and allowed to percolate through the system (Fig. 22-17). Given a suitable detector at the end of the column, one can record the exit from the column of everything the detector will detect. Some typical gas chromatographic records for procaine in horse urine are presented in Figure 22-18.

Inspection of Figure 22-18 or any GC record obviously raises the question of how one can know what each peak the pen writes represents, and for that matter, how can one know that a peak does not contain two or more drugs? The answer to this question is the same as before, i.e. you guess at what a peak may be and then test your guess by running a pure (authentic) sample of the drug you suspect. If the pure sample and the unknown come off the column at close to the same time and the peaks look exactly the same shape, you may have guessed right. If, on the other hand, the pure standard and the suspect peak come off at clearly different times, you know for sure that you are wrong and will have to try another guess.

With respect to the problem of specificity, exactly the same principles apply to GC as aply to TLC. On a 200 meter capillary GC column, one can separate about 400 compounds in about a four-hour experimental run. However, most drug detection laboratories, and especially pre-race laboratories, do not have this kind of time, so they use short columns (1 to 2 meters) and short experimental times, on the order of minutes. With these systems one cannot hope to separate more than about 100 compounds. Since there are about 800,000 compounds that can be volatilized, there are 8,000 possible candidates for each peak. Because of this problem, the usual procedure at this stage is to further test one's guess by

←

Figure 22-16. Thin-layer chromatograms of acidic urine extracts. Urine samples from eight horses were extracted under acidic conditions, spotted at the indicated points on the origin, and then chromatographed in a chloroform-cyclohexane-acetic acid system. When the solvent system reached the horizontal line at the top of the plate marked solvent front, the plate was withdrawn from the developing tank, air-dried, and viewed and photographed under short-wave UV light. Urine samples #2, #5, #7, and #8 contain major spots of oxyphenbutazone (O.P.B.), doublet spots of the alcohol metabolite of phenylbutazone (P.B.A.), and, close to the solvent front, doublet spots of phenylbutazone (P.B.Z.). At the extreme right of the plate is a flunixin (F.L.) standard, and urine #6 contains a flunixin spot in the corresponding position. Urines #1, #3, and #5 have furosemide (F) spots, running slightly ahead of the flunixin spots. All the other materials on the plates are normal urine constituents. Thin-layer plate courtesy of Professor Jerry Blake, University of Kentucky Drug Testing Program.

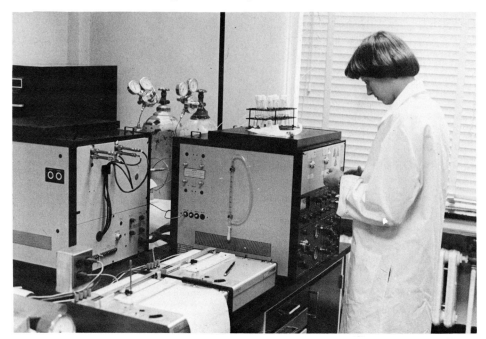

22-17. Gas chromatography. A minute amount of a concentrated drug sample is being injected into a gas chromatograph. The record of the chromatograph is drawn out on the strip chart in the lower left corner of the illustration; a typical gas chromatographic record is presented in Figure 22-18.

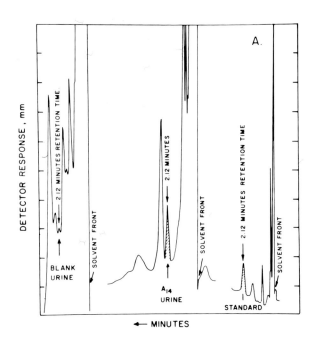

22-18. Gas chromatographic analysis of procaine derivatives in horse urine. The right chromatogram is that of a standard solution of 10 ng/ml of procaine derivatized with heptafluorobutyric anhydride (HFBA); the center chromatogram is that of a urine sample from a horse pretreated with procaine HCl and similarly treated; the left chromatogram is that of urine from a control horse similarly derivatized. Reproduced with permission from Tobin and Blake, *J Equine Med Surg,* 1:188, 1977.

changing the column temperature once or twice to see whether or not the material continues to cochromatograph with the analyst's best guess. Then the pair (suspect and authentic) are usually run on a different GC column at three different temperatures. If the unknown and suspect continue to chromatograph together, many analysts will conclude that they have identified the drug.

A helpful test of identity that is rarely used is to mix an equivalent amount of the suspect and authentic material and chromatograph them together. If they are indeed the same substance, the suspect peak should double in size, remain symmetrical, and show no tendency to "split," no matter what the chromatographic conditions. This is a particularly useful test, because in its absence one is relying on stopwatch timings of peaks by a person whose principal joy and accomplishment in life may well be to match unknown peaks that he finds in urine samples with peaks caused by prohibitied drugs. While such enthusiasm is highly commendable, it can also lead to errors, and I, personally, very much like to see combined samples in every GC run where an unknown is being compared with an authentic for forensic identification.

Again, because GC only produces a small number of data points at best indirectly related to overall chemical structure, one cannot conclude from GC that one has identified a drug. All that one can say is that the unknown and the authentic compound are indistinguishable in the systems and under the conditions in which they were compared. While GC is usually considered more accurate than TLC, just how accurate it is is not clear. To my knowledge, there is no study on the resolving power of GC which compares with the Sunshine study on the resolving power of TLC. Some analysts suggest a 10 percent error rate in drug identification based on TLC and GC, while other authorities hold that cochromatography on three different and distinct column systems is a very good evidence for identity and that the most important factor is the skill and ability of the analyst.

The Gas Chromatograph-Mass Spectrometer

In the gas chromatograph-mass spectrometer (GC-MS), the unknown materials forming the peaks that come off the gas chromatograph are fed directly into a mass spectrometer, which functions as a detector for the gas chromatograph (Fig. 22-19). However, as well as simply detecting a drug peak, the mass spectrometer can measure its molecular weight and determine its "fragmentation pattern." This gives what is sometimes called a molecular "fingerprint" for each drug, and a good mass spectrum is considered to be among the best evidence available as to the identity of a drug (Figs. 22-20 and 22-21).

The principle of mass spectrometry is relatively straightforward. The drug peak from the gas chromatograph is introduced into a vacuum chamber, where it is bombarded with electrons. The electrons charge the drug molecules and, depending on their energy, may fragment the molecules. These charged fragments are then forced through a magnetic field, which separates them on the basis of their size and the electrical charge that they carry. At the end of the analysis tube, the impact of the ions is recorded on an ion detector, and the number of each mass is tallied. Changing the strength of the magnetic field changes the mass/

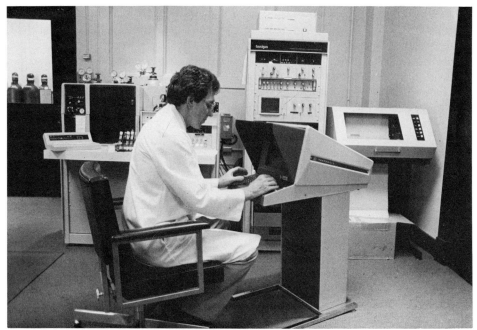

22-19. Gas chromatography-mass spectrometry. This apparatus consists of a gas chromatograph, which is to the left behind the operator, the mass spectrometer and computer, which is in the center, and a printout unit to the right. The operator, Professor Jerry Blake, is sitting at the control console in front of the apparatus.

charge ratio of the ions hitting the detector and in less than a second yields a mass spectrum for a drug.

Some typical mass spectra are shown in Figures 22-20 and 22-21, one of which is a laboratory standard of dipyrone and one of which is a urine sample identified as containing dipyrone (A). In these experiments, dipyrone (molecular weight 351.4) broke down to yield a fragment of molecular weight 217.2, present in quite small amounts and series of smaller fragments, all of which are represented essentially equally in both spectra. It is this kind of detailed evidence of similar chemical structures that makes mass spectrometry such a useful tool for identify-

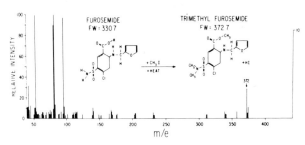

Figure 22-20. Mass spectrum of trimethyl furosemide. Furosemide (Lasix®) was methylated to convert it into trimethyl furosemide, a form of furosemide that "runs" well on a gas chromatograph. This furosemide derivative was then subjected to gas chromatography-mass spectrometry. Reproduced with permission from Roberts, *J Equine Med Surg*, 2:185, 1978.

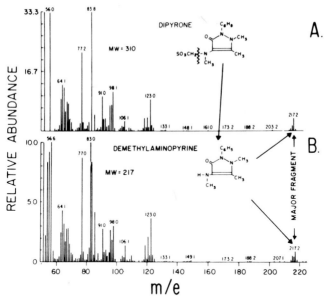

Figure 22-21. Mass-spectrometric analysis of dipyrone in horse urine. *A* shows the mass spectrum of a dipyrone standard, while *B* shows the spectrum of an unknown recovered from horse urine. The largest fragment present in both spectra is of mass 217.2, consistent with breakdown of dipyrone to methylaminopyrine in both samples. Many other ions of similar m/e are present in similar abundances, suggesting that sample B does indeed contain dipyrone. Reproduced with permission from Tobin, *J Equine Med Surg,* 2:518, 1978.

ing drugs. Since each known chemical, and thus its fragmentation pattern, is unique, this type of information yields a virtual "fingerprint" of the chemical in question. Equally important, the mass spectrometer is able to detect nanogram quantities of drugs and as such is sufficiently sensitive to be useful for drug detection in body fluids of horses.

High Performance Liquid Chromatography

High performance liquid chromatography (HPLC) is broadly similar to GC except that the mobile phase is a liquid under very high pressure. Because liquid solvents for most chemical compounds are available, the potential field of application of HPLC is much wider than that for GC, which requires volatile compounds. Further, the theoretical efficiency of HPLC is very much higher than that of GC, although HPLC columns do not appear to withstand the contamination problems of routine screening of biological samples as well as GC columns. However, at this time, HPLC is only beginning to be used in routine drug testing.

Microcrystal Tests

The microcrystal test is one of the oldest, simplest, and relatively sensitive tests used in analytical and forensic chemistry. In this test the suspected drug is allowed to interact with a reagent (usually a heavy metal salt) to yield crystals of a shape and color characteristic for that drug. If microcrystal evidence is used, more than one microcrystal test should be run and color photographs of both the standard and unknown microcrystals should be made available for use in court.

The identification of microcrystals is usually based on their shape and color. However, another simple test is the classical melting point test. Since every crystal has a specific melting point, the melting points of authentic crystals, unknown crystals, and crystals composed of a mixture of the authentic and the unknown would add further evidence of identity. However, for reasons that remain unclear, melting point tests on crystals are rarely done.

Radioimmunoassay

In radioimmunoassay (RIA), a "specific" antibody to a drug molecule is used to bind both a sample of radiolabeled drug and whatever unlabeled drug may be added with the unknown plasma or urine sample. If a significant amount of nonradioactive drug is added to the system, enough drug is displaced for the reduction of radioactivity in the system to be measurable. Given a supply of the "specific" antibody, RIA is rapid, inexpensive, sensitive, and sufficiently specific to make a good screening test. However, since only a poorly defined portion of the drug binds to and interacts with the antibody, RIA can never be a specific *chemical* test.

"CALLING" A "POSITIVE"

Having briefly reviewed the chemical methods available to the analyst, we can now look over his shoulder as he examined his data. The average analyst will have in his laboratory about 200 to 300 samples of authentic drugs (standards) with which he will try to match any suspect peaks or spots in his test systems. Because the 200 standards cover many of the drugs commonly used on the track, he will be able to match them up successfully much more often than odds of 200 knowns against the 4,000 drugs in common use, the 63,000 chemicals in common use, or the 4.2 million chemicals might suggest. If the analyst has GC-MS with a computerized library, he will have access to about 40,000 chemical spectra, which improves the scope of his search 200-fold.

At some point in this matching procedure, the analyst may decide to call a "positive." He will do this when he is satisfied that he has attained certain analytical criteria for the presence of a prohibited drug. In some jurisdictions these criteria are explicitly stated. For example, to call a "positive" in Canadian racing, the analyst must present evidence of identity in three distinct and independent analytical systems. The Association of Official Racing Chemists also has a policy that a positive should not be called without, in general, a minimum of three independent analytical methods, and they have issued an absolute recommendation that two be the minimum number of independent tests employed to call a positive.

The problem of deciding when an analyst has accumulated sufficient information to call a positive is a very real one and is a critical problem in the area of drug identification. The problem arises because the analyst will usually have a number of pieces of evidence generated by quite different methods, and the methods used and thus the quality of the evidence on which he bases his identification will vary from drug to drug, from analyst to analyst, and also, of course, from laboratory to laboratory. How, then, is the analyst to introduce some order into his methods and assure that the quality of the evidence upon which he calls a positive is at least reasonably consistent from drug to drug?

The commission chemist in a given jurisdiction is rather like a ship's captain; what he says goes in that jurisdiction, and he can base his "positive" calls on the phases of the moon if he wants to. In a more serious vein, however, an analyst may report an analytical method as a "screening"* method and change his mind and decide to call "positives" on it. He is also free to make his decision based on what other analysts might consider partial data or incomplete analytical work. If he is wise, however, he will take good care to consume all of the samples under such circumstances, for sooner or later incomplete analytical work will catch up with him if the jurisdiction has a referee system. Anyone who chooses to make judgments on only a part of the available evidence in any circumstance is sooner or later going to be in error. Doctors bury their mistakes, scientists publish their mistakes, and analysts who are, after all, only human, "call" theirs.

Until very recently, there was no way of comparing the quality of evidence obtained by different methods and judging the amount of evidence needed to call a positive. More recently, however, Doctor Wayne Duer, of Florida, has devised a process in which he determines the number of "distinguishable regions" afforded by a method and from these generates a score for a method. These scores yield a direct measure of the quality of a method and show how these methods may be compared and weighed against each other. Further, quantitation of the information yield of each method allows the contribution of each individual method to be evaluated and thus yields a solid scientific statement on the overall weight of the analytical data (Table 22-II). It is quite clear from this analysis that GC-MS provides a most powerful analytical method, and this is the method that is usually considered "specific" in the forensic sense by most drug testing laboratories.

A very real problem arises in "calling positives" when GC-MS data is not available for either economic or technical reasons. If GC-MS data is not available, positives called on TLC, GC, or other empirical methods are "positives" called on evidence with a distinct probability of error. Data from the Cornell University Drug Testing Program, which has the longest experience with GC-MS confirmation of analytical data, suggests that up to 10 percent of tentative drug identifications obtained with TLC and GC may turn out to be incorrect when tested by GC-MS. Analysts who call positives in the absence of good GC-MS data should keep such estimated error levels in mind and only "call positives" on the very best of empirical evidence.

Calling positives on empirical or any other kind of evidence means that the analyst should be prepared to present all his physical evidence for examination if required. This should include all chart records such as presented in Figures 21-12, 12-18, and 12-21, and all actual physical evidence such as thin-layer plates and microcrystals, or good quality color photographs of these if the evidence

---

* A screening method is a method that will suggest the presence of a drug in a sample but which carries too high an error rate for "positives" to be called based on the method.

TABLE 22-II

NUMBER OF DISTINGUISHABLE REGIONS AFFORDED BY ANALYTICAL METHODS

Method	Regions
Thin-layer chromatography	5
Ultraviolet spectrophotometry	14
Fluorescence emission	44
Fluorescence excitation	40
Liquid chromatography	30
Gas chromatography	10
Selected ion monitoring	10
Mass spectrometry	360
Infrared spectrophotometry	168
Color test (Marquis)	1 to 7
Crystal test	81

NOTE: The basis of Duer's scheme is that the number of distinguishable regions afforded by a group of tests must be greater than the number of known compounds, which is currently estimated as 5 million. By using a number of different tests, the products of the number of distinguishable regions in each test may readily exceed 5 million. For example, observations on sulfamerazine might include five corresponding maxima in ultraviolet spectra (one maximum in methanol, two maxima in aqueous acid, and two maxima in aqueous base), one corresponding R_f in thin-layer chromatography, and one correspondence in retention volume in liquid chromatography. The number of distinguishable regions from the ultraviolet spectra is $(14)^5$ or 537, 824. The number of distinguishable regions from the thin-layer chromatogram is 5. The number of distinguishable regions from the liquid chromatogram is 30. Therefore, the total number of distinguishable regions in the analytical scheme is 537,824 $\times$ 5 $\times$ 30 $\times$ 30, or 80,673,600, which exceeds 5,000,000.

SOURCE: Adapted from Duer et al. (1980).

cannot be preserved. If a subjective judgment of color is involved, the analyst's color vision should be certified,* which should help avoid testimony about colors that are not generally associated with certain chemical reactions. All physical evidence should be presented with accompanying evidence from suitable controls, matched as closely as possible with the test samples and run *simultaneously* with the tests in question. Just producing typed statements that "UV spectra typical of drug X" were observed is good evidence of an ability to type but is totally useless as chemical evidence of the presence of drug "X." Similarly, statements made under oath may be good evidence of a command of the English language, and possibly also body language, but they again do not constitute scientific evidence. Though affidavits and sworn statements carry considerable weight in law, they carry no weight in science, where physical evidence and an *ability to reproduce the evidence or events described* are the only criteria. Therefore, the remains of the original duplicate sample should be preserved at all costs for independent analysis. Only in this way can the potential for error inherent in any human process be reduced and all concerned be assured that the matching process, on which drug detection depends, has been as good as possible.

The requirement for meticulous care and conservative interpretation of data

---

* In this regard, the requirements for a steward in Kentucky include the necessity to have "corrected twenty-twenty (20-20) vision and ability to distinguish colors correctly." Clearly, concern exists in the industry that stewards do not get colors confused, but no precautions are currently taken with analysts in this regard. Stewards, of course, are likely to make their errors in public and become the subjects of massive ridicule. An analyst, however, makes his color errors in private and thus has much greater deniability.

and the use of referee samples are of paramount importance in drug testing in horses. At the outset, it should be quite clearly understood that analytical methods that may be quite acceptable in experimental work may be of very limited value in forensic work. In an experimental situation, where one administers a known drug to a horse, relatively simple analytical methods will often suffice. This is because these horses can be tested before and after the experiment to insure that they are not yielding "false positives." In the forensic situation, however, no control (i.e. predrug or postdrug) samples are available from the horse, and samples are being drawn from a large number of horses under widely differing conditions. These horses will have been treated with many different drugs, feed additives, and domestic remedies, exposed to many different varieties of plant life, and may have been exposed to any one of the approximately 4.2 million known chemical entities. On scientific grounds, therefore, scrupulous care must be taken in any forensic test merely to insure accuracy, quite apart from the consideration that personal and professional reputations and livelihoods are usually involved. Because of these considerations, drug "positives" should be "called" only on the strongest scientific grounds and with adequate independent confirmaiton of the presence of the drug by referee analysts.

Among the most important reasons for this stringency are the huge analytical odds against which equine forensic testing operates. These statistical odds are far more demanding than is realized by most laymen and also, unfortunately, by some scientists in this field. For example, one sometimes finds groups of investigators in this field exchanging "blind"* studies consisting of small numbers of test samples, usually on the order of ten to twenty samples. While successful completion of these "tests" may be reassuring to the investigators involved, the results of these tests are not helpful in analyzing the error rates likely to occur in routine testing. The reasons for this discrepancy are twofold and depend on both the error rate in the testing process and the very large numbers of horses involved in routine equine drug testing.

In this regard, the first point that must be clearly understood about forensic testing is that the error rate,† or rate at which false positives are called, does not depend simply on the quality of the test, but also on the rate at which the drug is used in the population being tested. To illustrate how this can be, let us first consider two specific circumstances in which a drug test with a small probability of error is being used to control drug use.

The first hypothetical circumstance that we will consider is one where every horse in the population being tested is on the drug. Under these conditions, the requirement for accuracy in the test being used is nil. You can simply walk up to any horse, declare it "positive" for the drug, and it will, by definition, be "positive." Under these circumstances, the error rate or rate of "false positives" is nil and cannot be anything else.† This rate is, of course, quite independent of the quality of the test in question. This circumstance is rather like asking a marksman to hit the gound, for no matter where he points his rifle, he cannot miss.

---

* A blind study is one in which an investigator sends a number of samples to another lab and the lab has to pick out the samples which contain the drug and those which do not. It is called "blind" because the investigator is "blind" to which samples contain the drug and which do not.

† For the purposes of this discussion, an error is defined as calling a "false positive," while simply missing a "positive" does not count.

For the second circumstance, let us assume that we have an excellent test for another drug but that particular drug is not being used at all in the population being tested, If, given the human condition, an analyst makes any errors in applying this excellent test, the rate at which false positives are called on this second test will be 100 percent. To use the analogy of the marksman, he cannot hit a target that does not exist, and any shots that he fires must be counted as misses. The message from these two limiting, albeit somewhat unusual, circumstances is that the accuracy of drug testing depends not only on the quality of the drug test but also on the frequency with which the drug is present in the population being examined.

While these two circumstances are quite clear, they are obviously not common circumstances in drug testing. To show how the principles outlined above apply to the real world, let us take a third circumstance of the type that one occasionally runs into in this field.

Let us suppose that I develop a test for a drug, one that I think is a useful and needed test. Let us further suppose that I want to check the quality of this test with a small study of the error rate of this test. I might therefore go out and find about twenty convenient horses, dose one with the drug in question, and then see if I can pick out the drug-treated horse. In this test I pick out the treated horse and find no "false positives" in the untreated horses. If I am not a thoughtful man, I may then feel that my test has been validated, and I might proceed to "call positives" on it, in the belief that I have conducted a useful statistical study. Beyond that, I might even present my studies to laymen in the belief that they constitute scientific validation of the method, and the studies may be accepted as such.

Now, the problem with a "validating study" such as the one described above is that when this test is put into practice, the numbers involved will almost certainly change in such a way as to make a twenty-horse study statistically worthless. If the test is used on just 100 horses in an event, and the testing procedure yields, let us say, five positives, I might be led to conclude that the test has produced five "positives." But has it? The little twenty-horse "blind study" only shows that the incidence of false positives will be less than one in twenty, which is perfectly consistent with five false positives in every 100 horses tested. So, are the "positives" I seen in actual practice real or false? Based on the evidence outlined here, principally my hypothetical study, I can never know.

The generally accepted level of error for stringent scientific work is a 1 percent rate of error due to chance. It is clear, therefore, that for a study such as the one outlined above to be valid, I would have to screen more than 10,000 horses in an experimental trial to allow me to call positives on a population in which the incidence of drug use is 1 percent and to be accurate at the 1 percent level of error. If I were dealing with the more usual "positive" call rate of about 0.1 to 0.2 percent, then I would have to screen more than 100,000 horses, clearly an impractical approach.*

These simple calculations, therefore, show that the approach of seeking to validate an equine forensic test for individual use by screening by a small number

---

* The rigorous mathematical treatment of this type of problem was worked out by an English clergyman called Bayes in the eighteenth century and is presented in Appendix D.

of horses is both futile and demonstrates a lack of understanding of the quantitative aspects of drug testing. Similarly, interlaboratory studies where investigators exchange small numbers of test samples are very unlikely to allow statistical validation of drug testing procedures. These tests do, however, operate in the reverse, in that a laboratory or individual who fails a small blind test is highly unlikely to be able to screen large numbers of forensic samples with an acceptable degree of accuracy. To go back to our analogy with the marksman, just becaue he can hit a barn door does not necessarily mean that he can hit a bullseye. On the other hand, however, if he cannot hit a barn door, it is highly unlikely that he will be able to hit a bullseye under any circumstances.

For these reasons, equine forensic testing has relied on only the highest quality analytical procedures and the use of independent confirmatory tests. The importance in the drug testing process of independent confirmatory tests cannot be overemphasized. While the necessity for these independent tests was apparently arrived at intuitively by the Association of Official Racing Chemists, it is relatively easy to demonstrate their importance mathematically. Given a number of independent tests it can be shown that though their individual accuracy is quite low, in the aggregate the conclusions from a battery of such independent tests is statistically highly reliable.*

The critical point, therefore, in any analysis is determining what constitutes an independent test. The answer to this question is quite simple. If the tests in question are subject to the same type of error, or to error from the same source, then they are not independent tests. To take a simple example, if I developed a thin-layer test for a drug in which the final endpoint is a particular color, then I

---

* See Appendix D.

Experiments that have not been published are like wines that have not been tasted — nobody knows if they're any good!

could not simply run the test in three different solvent systems or on three different plates and claim that they are three independent tests. This is because I might possibly make the same mistake in identifying the color in all three variations of the test, and all the tests would be wrong due to the same error. Similarly, minor variations on a theme such as running a gas chromatographic analysis at a different temperature cannot be accounted as independent tests.

As well as being independently tested, the suspected compound should also be subjected to mass spectrometric or infrared analysis. This is because these methods, properly carried out, provide the most compelling evidence for the chemical identity of a substance. Finally, in the last analysis, the only scientifically acceptable evidence that a sample contains a certain drug is the ability to repeat the experimental work, and the importance of this requirement should not be underestimated.

In assuring the repeatibility of a piece of scientific work, the role played by publication is vitally important. If the scientist does not publish his methods and results, nobody can be quite sure what he is claiming or what he did to support his claims. Experiments that have not been properly published, then, are an unknown quantity and cannot be judged. They are like wines that have never been tasted — nobody can ever know how good they are, and they may, in fact, be much less than one has been led to believe.

The most important and fundamental safeguard in forensic science is the split sample, independently analyzed.

On the other hand, if the methods by which the experiment was performed and the results that were obtained are published, the experiment can be repeated (i.e. the wine tasted) and the validity of the claim evaluated. The importance to the scientific process of the "repeatability" of an event is absolutely fundamental. Although a procedure or test may be "performed" in a scientist's laboratory and the results published in very prestigious scientific journals, a scientific report is not accepted as a scientific fact until the events reported are repeated by what is known in science as an "independent investigator." An independent investigator is a scientist who is clearly not in any way tied or beholden to the investigator who made the original scientific contribution, and he should preferably have a solid scientific reputation. Until this is done, a report remains just an unconfirmed report and has no standing as fact in science. Forensic chemists, attorneys, and adjudicators who take it upon themselves to review scientific problems would do well to keep the standards of science in mind when they judge science.

The final, most important, and most fundamental safeguard in forensic science, therefore, is the "referee" sample. In the absence of a "referee sample," sanctions are meted out on the basis of "unconfirmed" reports. Given a referee sample, "splits" can be sent out from the lab "calling the positive" to laboratories recommended by both the prosecution and the defense. This is the system currently in use by Mr. John MacDonald of the Illinois Racing Board, and it is one that speaks of the laboratory's confidence in its work. When properly used, it leads to independent confirmation of analytical findings and in the face of such evidence leaves no reasonable doubt that, given the current state of the analytical art, every precaution was taken to protect the rights of the accused. In a word, to paraphrase an old saying, a good analysis should not only be done but should also be seen to be done, and referee samples are the only way to ensure this.

SELECTED REFERENCES

Atti Della Conferenza Internazionale sul Doping: Stampa Degli Atti a Cura Dello Studio Ega Congressi, Viale Tiziano, Roma, Italia, 146-147.

Blake, J. W. and Tobin, T.: The gas liquid chromatograph and the electron capture detector in equine drug testing. *Br J Sports Med, 10:*129-132, 1976.

Duer, W. C., DeKanel, J., and Hall, T. D.: A necessary condition for drug identification. *Proceedings of the Third International Symposium on Equine Medication Control,* Tobin, T., Blake, J. W. and Woods, W. E., Eds. Dept. of Veterinary Science, University of Kentucky, 1979, pp. 489-497.

Maugh, T. H., III: Speaking of science: Chemicals: How many are there? *Science, 199(13):*162, 1978.

Maylin, G. A.: Pre-race testing. *Cornell Vet, 64:*325-334, 1974.

Shapiro, R. H.: Chemical defenses in drug cases. *J Crim Def, 2:*131-144, 1976.

Stein, B., Laessig, R. H., and Indriksons, A.: An evaluation of drug testing procedures used by forensic laboratories and the qualifications of their analysts. *Wis Law Rev, 3:*726-789, 1973.

Sunshine, I., Fike, W. F., and Landesman, H.: Identification of therapeutically significant organic bases by thin layer chromatography. *J Forensic Sci, 11:*428-439, 1966.

Tobin, T.: A review of the pharmacology of reserpine in the horse. *J Equine Med Surg, 2:*433-438, 1978.

Tobin, T.: Pharmacology review: Testing for drugs in horses. *J Equine Med Surg, 2:*518-524, 1978.

Tobin, T., Blake, J. W., Sturma, L., Arnett, S., and Truelove, J.: Pharmacology of procaine in the horse. Pharmacokinetics and behavioral effects. *Am J Vet Res, 38:*637-647, 1977.

Tobin, T., Roberts, B. L., and Miller, J. R.: The pharmacology of furosemide in the horse. I. Effects on the disposition of procaine, methylphenidate, phenylbutazone and pentazocine. *J Equine Med Surg, 1:*402-409, 1977.

Tobin, T., Maylin, G. A., Henion, J., Woodward, C., Ray, R. S., Johnston, J., and Blake, J. W.: An evaluation of pre- and post-race testing and blood and urine testing in horses. *J Equine Med Surg, 3:*85-90, 1979.

Chapter 23

APPLYING THE ANALYST'S DATA: THE DRAFTING OF RULES, CONTROLLED MEDICATION PROGRAMS, AND THE EFFECTS OF DRUGS ON BREEDING

THE GOAL OF THIS CHAPTER is to integrate the pharmacological and analytical sections of this book into the rule-making process before beginning the legal chapter. In the first section of this chapter, we will deal with the realities of analytical chemistry and pharmacology and show how they affect the drafting of rules. The second section of this chapter will then review those rules on which pharmacological distinctions must be made, i.e. the rules of controlled medication programs. Further, now that the reader has had the opportunity to review the classes of drugs other than the controlled medications available to horsemen, the actions and effects of phenylbutazone and furosemide will be put into perspective. The third and final section will point out what little we know about the action of controlled medication programs on the "breed" and will again try to put this problem in perspective.

THE DRAFTING OF MEDICATION RULES

The first problem that rule makers have to come to grips with in drafting their rules is to decide which, if any, of the various therapeutic medications currently available they are going to allow to be used. In this regard, the list of permitted medications may be quite limited and consist of just furosemide and/or phenylbutazone (see Table 23-I), or the list of permitted drugs may be much more extensive (see Table 23-II). While a variety of approaches to this problem are viable, as was demonstrated in the United States in the 1970s, in the last anaysis this decision comes down to a value judgment on the part of the rule makers and the racing community that they serve.

Irrespective of the decision on which drugs to permit, the simplest and most logical way of approaching this problem is to make the presence in blood or urine samples of drug substances* "foreign to the natural horse" a violation, with specific stated exceptions if the rule makers so desire. For example, the proposed guidelines for a national medication rule prepared by the National Association of State Racing Commissioners (Appendix E) permit certain levels of phenylbutazone and furosemide to appear in the blood and urine of racing horses, and the presence of any other medications constitutes a violation of this rule. There is, however, little point in attempting to list prohibited medications, for, as indicated earlier, there are about 63,000 chemicals in common use today. Furthermore, outside of this large number of chemicals in common use, the number of known chemicals grows by about 6,000 a day.

---

* Including drug precursors and drug metabolites.

Having defined their rule with respect to which drugs to permit, the next problem with which the regulators are faced is that of drafting their rule and applying it. Their easiest decisions come when the drugs the analysts find in a horse have no legitimate use in equine medicine and fall into the stimulant, depressant, narcotic analgesic, tranquilizer, or local anesthetic groups. Examples of such drugs might be apomorphine, some of the very potent narcotic analgesics, or some of the amphetamine-type stimulant drugs. Since there is not much likelihood of there being good and valid reasons for the presence of these drugs in the blood or urine of racing horses, the authorities will have little trouble interpreting the forensic significance of such findings. This is because the identification of these substances in the blood or urine of a horse will generally be evidence of a rule violation, most likely with intent.

A more difficult situation arises when the drug in question has legitimate medical uses in the treatment of racing horses and can be shown to have been used recently in the medical treatment of a horse. Examples of such drugs would be the narcotic analgesic pentazocine (Talwin®), which may be used in the treatment of colics, or procaine, which may be administered either as a local anesthetic or as procaine penicillin. Both of these drugs have legitimate uses in equine medicine, yet both are prohibited substances under the rules of racing and may have been administered to the horse in question with the intention of influencing his performance. Both also have the ability to appear in urine for long periods after the last dose, up to five days after the last dose for Talwin® and up to thirteen days for procaine. At this point the adjudicators have a problem on their hands. They have to decide whether or not these drugs were administered for legitimate medical reasons a number of days before the event or whether they were administered close to the race to affect the performance of the horse. When faced with this problem, adjudicators will usually look to their analyst for an opinion as to when the drug in question was administered to the horse.

This problem of pinpointing the time of drug administration has become more acute with the recent rapid increase in sentiment against controlled medication programs. It is a fact of life now in American racing that many horses that race are "cooled out" after a race on medications such as phenylbutazone. What this means is that horses are given a full therapeutic dose of phenylbutazone immediately after a race and then maintained on the drug for a period. This treatment prevents the horse from "cooling out" sore and is a substantial help toward keeping him fit and sound for the next race. This is considered good medical practice in racing circles and is frequently used by the most conservative of horsemen on the soundest of horses. The problem, of course, comes for the horseman when he has to decide when the treatments should stop so that the horse can run "drug-free" during the next race. The problem for the authorities comes in deciding what they should consider to be a "drug-free" horse.

At this point both the regulators and the regulated run into the technical problem of "clearance times" for drugs in horses. As pointed out in Chapter 5 and Appendix A, drugs are only very slowly "cleared" from a horse, so in theory at least they continue to be detectable for weeks or months after they are administered to horses. As a practical matter, therefore, a drug becomes "cleared" only when an analyst can no longer find it, and this period unfortunately has little or no relationship to the period of pharmacological action of a drug. Therefore, the periods for which most drugs are detected are usually determined quite arbitrarily by the analyst, his abilities, and by the methods available to him, and not at all by the rule makers or the period of the pharmacological action of the drug.

This technical problem of "clearance times" is a very real regulatory problem, and during the 1960s and 1970s two major solutions to this problem were developed. One solution was to allow medication with phenylbutazone up to the day before racing, or later, which meant that horses could race with readily detectable concentrations of phenylbutazone or other drugs in their bodies. This solution to the problem was called a controlled medication program. The other solution to the problem was to impose a time rule such as a forty-eight-hour or seventy-two-hour rule, so that horses racing should not have been treated with any agents within this time period (see Table 23-I) and would, at least in the opinion of the drafters of these rules, be racing without effective levels of drugs in their systems. This solution to the problem is the time rule solution, and it is, for technical reasons, a less than satisfactory solution to the problem.

The problem with rules that specify a given time limitation is that if the adjudicators wish to use analytical data and their analyst's expertise to enforce a time rule, their analyst will have to swear in court that he can tell, from what is usually a single qualitative analytical determination in a urine sample, whether or not a drug was given at a certain time before the race. This period may be within hours of the race, if the drug in question is Lasix®, or it may be twenty-four to forty-eight hours before the race in the case of phenylbutazone or other drugs. To do this the analyst will have to look at his data, make whatever mental or other calculations he feels are necessary, and then swear under oath that the substance was administered to the animal within the forbidden period.

If the analyst is uninformed about the movements of drugs through horses (pharmacokinetics),* he may be prepared to make such statements. One of the most brazen claims I have ever heard in this regard was that of a certain western testing lab, which had convinced at least some horsemen that it could determine to within eight minutes when a dose of furosemide had been administered to a horse! Whether or not the lab believed it could do this is not clear, but it certainly appeared to have the horsemen in this jurisdiction convinced, although how such a bluff could be maintained is another question. In the long run, however, bluffs of this nature will be found to be just that, and when perceived as such, they will lead to further doubt and distrust of the authorities and analysts.

If the analyst is knowledgeable, however, he will know that it is essentially impossible to determine the time of drug administration from a plasma or urinary drug concentration with any degree of accuracy, and he will avoid trying to bluff horsemen into compliance with time limits that may be written into medication rules. He will know that a single plasma or urinary level of a drug does not provide enough information to determine the time of drug administration with any

---

* Most analysts tend to be trained in chemistry and generally have no formal training whatsoever in the field of drug movements through horses or any other species.

accuracy. The reason for this is that there is no way of telling whether or not a given blood or urine level of a drug has resulted from a small dose of a drug given just minutes before the sample was taken, a normal dose given twenty or twenty-four hours previously, or a very large dose given forty-eight hours previously. Obviously, the analyst can make an estimate within some very broad limits, and it may be reasonable for him to say that it was highly likely that drug "X" was administered within the last four days, but it is usually not possible for him to say, with any certainty, that a drug such as phenylbutazone was or was not administered within twenty, twenty-four, or twenty-eight hours of post time.

The principal reason that the analyst usually cannot make a useful time determination from analytical data is presented graphically in Figure 23-1. In this example, we follow the rate of decline of either blood or urine levels of a hypothetical drug. The blood or urine levels that we may expect to find can vary anywhere between the very highest levels, associated with toxicity, and the lowest levels that the analyst can detect. For this particular example we have chosen a hypothetical drug whose blood or urine levels fall in a log-linear manner with time, and we will assume that we are dealing with the hypothetical average horse.

In Figure 23-1 we have assumed that the analyst has detected and quantitated 100 ng/ml of a prohibited drug in the sample from the horse. He has, however, no way whatsoever of knowing whether or not this blood or urine level resulted from a small dose of the drug administered intravenously just before the sample was taken or a very large dose administered several days before. Any estimates of the time of administration that he might make would be purely speculative, and their accuracy would be essentially nil. It should also be kept in mind that these constraints hold even if the behavior of the drug is ideal and does not show any horse-to-horse variation. As we will see later, blood levels of a given drug in horses can show significant variation between horses, and urinary levels of drugs, as pointed out earlier, are highly variable. These variables, overlaid on the basic

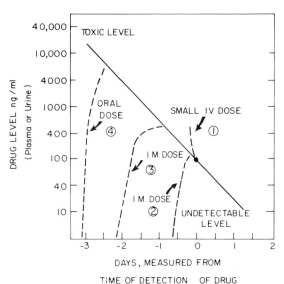

Figure 23-1. Impossibility of administration time determination from concentration data. The solid line shows the rate of decline of blood or urine levels of a hypothetical drug against time. The upper limit from a drug level is that associated with a toxic response, while the lower level is the minimum level that the analyst can detect. For this particular drug, the analyst has detected 100 ng/ml at a known time. He cannot, however, determine whether or not this blood level was due to a small dose given IV immediately before the sample was drawn (1), or a small IM dose a few hours earlier (2), or larger doses by other routes (3, 4) much earlier. All that the analyst can say is that he found a certain drug in the biological sample at a certain concentration, and any time estimate would be highly speculative.

problems set forth in Figure 23-1, make it clear that by and large, analysts cannot make useful statements about times of drug administration from single plasma or urinary concentrations.

It would, of course, be perfectly reasonable and proper for the analyst, looking at data such as Figure 23-1, to swear that the concentration of the drug in the urine was *consistent* with, let us say, treatment #2, an IM dose of the drug given within twenty-four hours of the sample being taken. However, if asked, he would also have to swear that the blood or urine level that he found could just as well be due to a larger oral dose given earlier, or to any one of a number of different dose, routine, and time combinations. In other words, he has only a single data point, and his ability to make explicit exclusionary statements about the prior history of the drug in the animal is very limited indeed.

Despite having been the basis on which medication violations were prosecuted for years,* the inability of analysts to determine times of drug administration is now generally accepted in the field. This change in position is typified by the following exchange between two analysts at the Second Symposium on Equine Pharmacology at the Ohio State University in 1978, Doctors Ray and Sams both being analysts at the Ohio State University Drug Testing Laboratory.

Doctor Ray: I am involved with the drug testing for the racing commission. In testifying before these commissions, often I am asked the question, "Doctor, did you quantitate the drug in the urine?" Answer: "yes."

Question: "From this, can you predict when the drug had been administered?" These questions arise because most jurisdictions have rules that state that medication can't be administered less than twenty-four, forty-eight, or seventy-two hours before the race. The accused person may respond, "Yes, indeed, I did administer the medication, but it was given one hour before the deadline." I'm wondering if it's a practical assumption that we can use the information from urinary concentrations to extrapolate back to predict administration times?

Doctor Sams: I think it is very difficult to do because of the variability in horses, variability in their rate of urine production, and so, as a consequence, there is a substantial amount of variability that we just don't know about when we measure urinary concentration or a blood concentration. I think that variability is sufficiently great that it is almost impossible for us to predict either the time of administration or the size of the dose.

Doctor Ray: All right, then, one question to follow up on that. How about that same question in the case of plasma drug concentration? Could we do any better job of estimating either the quantity or, better yet, the time of this medication?

Doctor Sams: I think we can do a little better because we eliminate that variability due to rate of urine flow and pH.

Although one may be able to do a little better in plasma than in urine because of the reduced variability, the basic problems outlined in Figure 23-1 still hold for plasma levels of the drug. Time rules, then, are difficult to enforce based on analytical data, and drafters of rules must look elsewhere in their efforts to control medication use.

The simplest way to enforce a time rule is to isolate the treated horses for the period of the rule. If this period is short, and if the number of horses to be

---

* For years, analysts who were making only qualitative determinations of the presence of a drug were making time of administration estimates to enable the prosecution of medication violations. Since such estimates cannot be made from good quantitative data, it requires even more imagination to make them from qualitative information.

supervised is small, then a detention or security barn system is feasible. A typical example of such a system is that proposed in the 1980 National Association of State Racing Commissioners (NASRC) guidelines for the control of furosemide.* Under this rule, the horses are stabled in a secure area a number of hours before the race, and both the dose of furosemide and its time of administration can be controlled. Under a system such as this, very good control of medication programs is obviously possible.

Unfortunately, systems such as this are only practical if the number of horses involved is small and the time periods are short. What, then, are regulators to do if the need is for a forty-eight-hour rule for all horses? The only practical answer, if the required control period is longer than a couple of hours, is to frame the rule in terms of concentration and to make the finding of more than a certain concentration of drug in a horse grounds for penalty. Enforcement of this rule is relatively straightforward, since analysts can accurately measure and testify to the concentrations of many drugs in equine blood.

When discussing concentration rules, the superiority of blood over urine as a forensic sample is remarkable. As pointed out earlier, urine volume and pH, and therefore its drug content, can vary enormously over quite short periods of time.† However, the horse must, if he is to remain alive, maintain his blood plasma volume and pH within quite narrow limits, and for these reasons plasma levels of drugs are much less variable than urinary levels. Plasma drug concentrations, therefore, provide much more satisfactory, equitable, and reliable forensic information than urinary data. The only trick with this solution to the problem is determining the blood level of the drug at which a violation will be declared.

One approach to determining the blood level at which a medication violation should be declared was presented by the experimental work of the NASRC Committee on Medication. During the formulation of this group's proposed guidelines, an experiment was carried out to determine the blood levels of phenylbutazone in horses twenty-four hours after the last dose of a typical therapeutic regimen of this drug. To this end, forty-nine horses were dosed with 4 gm of phenylbutazone orally for three days, then dosed IV with 2 gm phenylbutazone on the fourth day, and blood samples were drawn at twenty-four hours after the last dose of phenylbutazone. Based on determinations in four different laboratories, the average plasma level of phenylbutazone after these doses was determined to be 4.13 μg/ml at twenty-four hours after the last dose. Approximately 4.13 μg/ml, therefore, would be the expected level of phenylbutazone in the average horse that had trained on phenylbutazone and from which the drug had been withdrawn twenty-four hours prior to racing. This figure, therefore, provides one with a beginning basis for the drafting of the equivalent of a "no race day medication rule" in terms of blood levels of phenylbutazone.

Having determined the mean or average level of phenylbutazone that one will find in racing horses complying with a no race day medication rule, the next problem is to determine the blood level at which one is going to declare a medication violation. Obviously, 4.13 μg/ml is not a violation level for a "twenty-

---

* See Appendix E.
† See Appendix B for an outline of some of the problems with urine as a forensic sample.

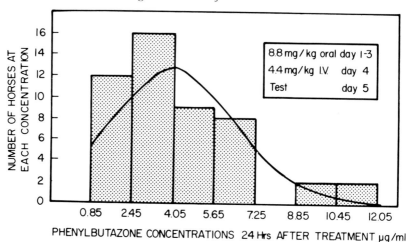

Figure 23-2. Phenylbutazone levels in forty-nine horses twenty-four hours after therapeutic doses of phenylbutazone. Forty-nine horses were dosed with 8.8 mg/kg (about 4.0 gm/1000 lb.) of phenylbutazone orally for three days and then given 4.4 mg/kg (2 gm/1000 lb.) on the fourth day. Twenty-four hours after the IV dose, blood samples were drawn from each and assayed for phenylbutazone. The vertical bars show the number of horses found with the indicated blood levels of phenylbutazone, while the solid line represents a population curve fitted to these data. These data are reproduced with the permission of the National Association of State Racing Commissioners. The experimental protocol was prepared by the NASRC Blue Ribbon Medication Committee. The horses were dosed and analytical facilities were provided by Doctor George Maylin, Cornell University; Doctor Cliff Woodward, Pennsylvania; Doctor Richard Sams, The Ohio State University; and Doctor Thomas Tobin, University of Kentucky. Data analysis was performed at Cornell and Kentucky. These experiments were completed in the spring of 1980.

four-hour" rule, for about 50 per cent of the horses will have blood levels of phenylbutazone below 4.13 µg/ml, 50 per cent will also have blood levels higher, and a small number may be expected to have much higher blood levels. The actual spread of the data from this experiment is shown in Figure 23-2. In this illustration, each hatched bar represents the number of horses found to have blood levels within a particular range. While the "average" horse had a blood level of about 4.13 µg/ml, the blood levels in some horses were much higher, and two had blood levels of between 10.5 and 12.05 µg/ml. If two horses in forty-nine can show these high blood levels, it is obvious that the number of horses in a population of 10,000 that show high blood levels of the drug is going to be substantial. The problem, then, becomes where to put the cutoff for the higher blood levels, or conversely, how one determines whether one has an unusual blood level or a medication violation.

To do this, one measures the variability in the population by determining what is called the standard deviation for the data. Within plus or minus of what is called one standard deviation of the mean of the population, one finds 67.4 percent of the population, and within 1.96 standard deviations of the mean one has about 95 percent of the population. Therefore, if one sets the limit at the mean plus 1.96 standard deviations, one is going to catch a certain percentage of horsemen who overmedicate, along with the about 2.5 percent of all horsemen who comply with the rules. While a 2.5 percent level of error does not sound like much, it means that in 10,000 samples a year, 250 horsemen who stayed within the rules are going to be "called."

If one sets the limit at the mean ± 2.33 standard deviations, one may expect that about 1/100 will be outside these limits. However, since half of these will be low levels, the number of high "overages"* due to chance in this population will be 1/200. If the jurisdiction screens 10,000 samples per year, then it is going to have fifty innocent "overages" a year. It is, however, important to recognize that the analyst will never be able to distinguish between these innocent "overages" and the horseman who administers too large a dose or a dose too close to race time. Care must be taken, therefore, that any penalties rendered are not overly severe, as a certain proportion of these penalties will be inflicted on innocent people.

Based on the data of Figure 23-2, a blood level of phenylbutazone of about 16.5 μg/ml may be expected to encompass all but 1/200 of the population measured. While this may sound like a high blood level, and the figure of a 1/200 probability of calling a positive on an innocent man sounds small, in most jurisdictions this will amount to more than one "innocent positive" a week, which is a substantial rate. As pointed out in Chapter 22 and Appendix D, the rate of error in any large scale screening process has to be very small, because even a very small error rate is magnified by the large numbers of horses screened in most medication testing situations.

An alternate way of determining what levels of a drug are permissible is the pharmacological method. In this method one simply determines the blood level of a drug at which its pharmacological effects are lost, and this becomes the highest permissible blood level of the drug. This approach is the basis of the blood alcohol test in humans. In the blood alcohol test it is recognized that small levels of blood alcohol have no significant effect on driving performance, and an offense is not committed until a certain level of blood alcohol is exceeded. Similar critical drug levels can easily be determined for most common therapeutic agents in the horse, and these levels written into the medication rules.

It is very important that upper limits for legal blood levels of the drugs in common medical use in racehorses be set. In the absence of such limits, any rule that one writes is arbitrary in both its structure and application. Such rules tend to be written by purists, who hold that horses should run absolutely medication-free, and these are commonly called "hay, oats, and water" rules.

The sense of a "hay, oats and water" rule is that horses running with any detectable level of a substance foreign to the natural horse in them should be disqualified. This is the equivalent of saying that anyone who has any detectable level of blood alcohol is guilty of drunken driving. While the simplicity of the "detectable level" concept is appealing, its rigorous implementation would certainly put a halt to all racing. While easy to draft and apply, such rules are inherently less equitable and more open to arbitrary application than any other. The problem, as always in this area, is that the dividing line between what is and what is not a "hay, oats and water" horse is not very easy to define.

A typical "hay, oats, and water" rule would appear to be the recent Florida

---

* An "overage" is a blood level of a drug above the limit set for that drug.

medication statute.* This law states that "the racing of an animal with any drug, medication, stimulant, depressant, hypnotic, narcotic, local anaesthetic, drug-masking agent, or any substance foreign to the natural horse or dog is prohibited." It further goes on to say that "it is a violation of this section for a person to administer or cause to be administered any drug, medication, stimulant, depressant, hypnotic, narcotic, local anaesthetic, drug-masking agent, or any substance foreign to the natural horse or dog to an animal *which will result in a positive test* for such a substance based on samples taken from the animal immediately prior to or immediately after the racing of that animal."

This act then continues with a statement that rules may be promulgated that "identify (a) unacceptable levels of substances existing naturally in the untreated dog or horse, but at abnormal physiological concentrations; (b) acceptable levels of trace elements or innocuous substances in test samples."

The sense and intent of this law is that if the analyst can find any substance foreign to the natural horse in a sample, than the law has been violated. Once a foreign substance has been detected in a horse, at no matter what level, or presumably no matter what the nature of the material, then the rule has been violated.

The effect of rules of this type is to put the horseman in the type of box described at the end of Chapter 5. This is because the sensitivity of the tests used, or the criteria for calling a positive, are totally unstated in such a rule. The implementation and enforcement of the rule, therefore, is entirely in the hands of the chemist. To go back to our speeding analogy, the chemist, by choosing the sensitivity of the test, arbitrarily sets the speed limit. He can change the speed limit without notice, simply by changing the sensitivity of the test or his interpretation of the test. Finally, because the application of this rule depends to a large extent on the talents and abilities of the chemist, the same rule may be applied with quite different levels of stringency in different jurisdictions or from laboratory to laboratory within the same jurisdiction, depending on which chemist selects the analytical method and does the analytical work.

Such quantitatively undefined rules may be enforced in ways that have little relationship to reality. This is because there is little relationship between periods for which drugs are detectable in horses and the duration of their pharmacological activity. For example, the pharmacological action of phenylbutazone only lasts for about twenty-four to thirty-six hours, but the drug can be detected in plasma and urine for up to nine days. Therefore, a horse can be in violation of a "hay, oats, and water rule" for nine days, while the actual violation of running the horse "on bute" took place about seven days previously.

The sense, then, of "hay, oats, and water" rules is incorrect. The actual problem of a medication violation only arises when the horse has an effective level of a pharmacologically active agent in his blood. "Hay, oats, and water" rules, in their enthusiasm to attack medication violations, are open to unwise use and in some circumstances may compel authorities to act in situations where discretion would be more appropriate.

---

* State of Florida Race Medication Statute, 1980.

The impropriety of calling positives on trace, or nonsignificant, or noneffective levels of drugs has been clearly recognized by many authorities. The old-style time rules, i.e. twenty-four, forty-eight, or seventy-two-hour rules, were an implicit recognition of this problem and an attempt to cope with it. More recently, the proposed NASRC medication guidelines, which have set residual levels of phenylbutazone below which no action is taken, have also, in principle, recognized the impracticality of trying to run horses without trace levels of legitimate medications in them.

Similarly, the proposed federal bill to control the use of medication in racehorses also recognizes these facts of life. In drafts* of this proposed act, the term "wrongfully drugged" is defined as meaning the application of a drug or foreign substance to a horse in such a way as to make it "possible for a horse with a physiological injury, soreness, pain, depression, or any other physical or psychological unsoundness to race as though it were sound, or for the purpose of improving or impairing the performance of the horse."

The act then goes on to specify that the biochemical analysts shall report "samples which contain *sufficient levels* of chemicals or other foreign substances so as to indicate, in accordance with the regulations promulgated by the administrator, the probability that the horse producing the sample had been wrongfully drugged."

Under these drafts of this act, then, the term "wrongfully drugged" only applies to horses containing "sufficient levels" of drugs to be pharmacologically active. The proposed federal bill, then, is not a "hay, oats, and water" bill but a "no pharmacological effect" bill. While not likely to be easy to administer, this bill at least attempts to tackle the actual problem and is a bill that recognizes some of the nuances of medication control in racehorses.

A further problem in the area of medication control is the concept of trying to call positives on endogenous substances. This thought is also expressed in the Florida law, which holds that "unacceptable levels of substances existing naturally in the untreated dog or horse, but at abnormal physiological concentrations" may be banned. Under rules such as this, if unusually high levels of certain hormones or hormone metabolites were found in blood or urine samples, then the analyst would be empowered to call "positives" for an endogenous substance in that animal.

The problem with such rules is that it is likely to be very difficult to determine at what blood level of an endogenous hormone a "positive" should be called. Just like the wide range of the blood concentrations of phenylbutazone in Figure 23-2, blood or urinary levels of endogenous substances are also likely to vary widely. Screening 10,000 or more samples a year, then, is a good way of finding the biochemically atypical horses in a population. Without further study of the individual horse and its biochemistry, it is impossible to distinguish between a biochemically atypical horse and one that has been treated with hormones or other endogenous substances.

The classic case of a biochemical abnormality in a horse giving rise to an

---

* Draft of the proposed "Corrupt Horse Racing Practices Act of 1979."

"inadvertent" positive was the so-called HILL HOUSE case in England. In early 1967, HILL HOUSE won the Schweppes gold trophy hurdle at Newbury, and he won it by twelve lengths over his nearest rival. Because this performance was considerably better than might have been expected from his previous form, the stewards ordered a urine test. The urine samples were reported to contain abnormally high concentrations of cortisol, and on the basis of this information the National Hunt Committee suspended the owner and the trainer.

The owner and trainer, however, claimed that no steroids had been administered to HILL HOUSE, but that the high level of cortisol in his urine was normal for this horse and had been manufactured by the horse. This claim on the part of the owner was supported by independent scientific evidence. Because of this the stewards ordered HILL HOUSE sent to the Equine Research Station at Newmarket, where he was given food and exercise and periodically reexamined. These studies showed that HILL HOUSE had much higher levels of urinary cortisol than most horses, and that these levels were equivalent to those found in HILL HOUSE by the analyst after the race. The stewards accordingly dismissed the case, presumably on the assumption that HILL HOUSE was a biochemically atypical horse and that the "positive" was the horse's "fault."

In summary, therefore, medication rules are best drafted in terms prohibiting all drug substances foreign to the natural horse, with stated exceptions if the jurisdiction so requires. Unless direct supervision of the horses is envisioned, rules should be drafted not in terms of time but in terms of concentrations of the drugs in blood. This is because analysts can confidently testify concerning blood concentration data but can, in general, only speculate as to times of administration. The drug concentrations at which violations occur should be specified in the rule, because in their absence the analyst arbitrarily determines the violation level when he selects his method. As a forensic medium, urine is, in general, much less satisfactory than blood because of the inherent variability of drug and drug metabolite concentrations in urine. Finally, it should be kept in mind that though the analyst can be confident about the concentration of a drug that he finds in blood samples, he cannot, on the basis of a single pre- or post-race sample, distinguish between random overages caused by a horse and intentional overages caused by the horseman. Care must be taken, therefore, with the setting of the "overage" level that the level selected is not too low nor the penalty for exceeding it too high, as a certain percentage of innocent horsemen will inevitably be convicted under any rule, no matter how well drafted or carefully enforced the rule is.

CONTROLLED MEDICATION PROGRAMS

A generation ago, when almost all of the drugs available to horsemen fell into the categories of stimulants, depressants, narcotics, or local anesthetics, most medications were clearly not suitable for use in racing horses. Since then, however, the development of drugs such as phenylbutazone and furosemide has given rise to a new category of drugs, which are clearly beneficial to racing horses and which carry with them none of the problems associated with the types of medication previously available. These drugs are legitimate therapeutic agents, and horsemen can clearly see the benefits to their horses of these drugs. They are thought to allow horses to run "up to form" but not to exceed their "form," and they also appear to allow horses to run more consistently from day to day. Phenylbutazone is an aid to training in that it helps to condition a horse, and furosemide appears to aid horses with respiratory or "wind" problems. The popularity and effectiveness of these agents led to pressure on racing authorities to allow the use of these drugs in the late 1950s and early 1960s, and by the mid-1970s many states had gone to what are called controlled medication programs (Table 23-I).

A controlled medication program is a program under which certain drugs are approved for use in horses at times most often including the last day before racing and occasionally including medication on race day (Table 23-II). Before instituting its controlled medication program, the California Horse Racing Board made a careful study of the problem, and this board has also developed the most complete statistics in this area. The California Horse Racing Board approved phenylbutazone for use in horses up to the last day before racing in 1970 and approved furosemide for use in bleeders in 1975. There were very good reasons for the California Horse Racing Board taking this more liberal approach to the use of medication; these reasons remain valid today and form the scientific and legal foundations of any controlled medication program.

The first problem the California Horse Racing Board encountered was the increased sensitivity of drug testing. As testing increased in sensitivity and the legitimate therapeutic use of relatively innocuous drugs such as phenylbutazone increased, the Board found itself in the position of calling positives on drugs such as phenylbutazone which the trainers claimed had been given more than twenty-four hours before race time. Since the Board had little information on this subject at the time, it found itself in the position of not being able to refute this defense. Further, the California Penal Code has a criminal statute that prohibits the administration of any drug to racing horses, and the statute defines a "drug" for racing purposes as any narcotic, stimulant, or depressant. Since phenylbutazone fell outside this classification, the horsemen also had the defense that the Horse Racing Board was exceeding the statutory provision against drug use set forth in the Penal Code.

Another problem that concerned the California Horse Racing Board was the necessity that they preserve the trainer/insurer rule. This rule, which imposes on the trainer strict responsibility for the presence of medication in the biological fluids of a horse, was considered by the Board as absolutely vital for the protection of horse racing. In the opinion of the Board, however, the trainer/insurer rule was only barely surviving in the courts, and the Board felt that overuse of the rule and attempts to apply it in the control of relatively innocuous drugs, or in cases where the Board did not have the necessary scientific data to back up its position, would inevitably lead to its loss. As pointed out by the Board, "bad cases make bad law," and the Board hoped that by establishing carefully drafted and liberal medication rules, the trainer/insurer rule could be retained for use in serious drug (in the Penal Code sense) related cases.

The Board elected to call their new rules a program, inasmuch as all the rules were coordinated and shaped to yield a satisfactory, workable medication situa-

Table 23-I

SUMMARY OF RESTRICTIONS GOVERNING USE OF PHENYLBUTAZONE AND FUROSEMIDE IN VARIOUS STATES

State	Phenylbutazone					Furosemide			
	Bute allowed on race day	No bute within 18-24 hrs of race	No bute within 48 hrs of race	No bute within 72 hrs of race	No bute allowed	Lasix allowed on race day	Lasix must be adm. 3-5 hrs before race	No Lasix within 48 hrs	No Lasix allowed
California		x				x	x		
Colorado		x				x	x		
Connecticut			x					x	
Florida	x					x			
Idaho					x				x
Illinois Thoroughbred	x								x
Harness				x					x
Kentucky Thoroughbred	x						x	x	
Harness					x		x		
Louisiana	x					x	x		
Massachusetts	x								x
Montana					x				x
New Hampshire	x					x			
New Jersey		x					x		
New York			x					x	
Ohio	x						x		
Pennsylvania Thoroughbred	x								x
Harness				x					x
South Dakota	x								x
Washington	x						x		
West Virginia	x						x		

SOURCE: Poppell, Carolyn F. (Assistant Science Advisor): *Issue Brief: Phenylbutazone and Furosemide in Race Horses in Maryland.* Maryland General Assembly, 1979.

TABLE 23-II

A CONTROLLED MEDICATION LIST FROM A MIDWESTERN STATE, 1974

A. The administration of only the following list of drugs, classes of drugs, and medicaments is permitted by this rule and considered for the purposes of this rule to be controlled medication:
1. Vitamins
2. Minerals & Electrolytes
3. Sugars
4. Proteins & Protein Hydrolysates
5. Sex Hormones
6. Anabolic Hormones
7. Salicylates
8. *Dipyrone
9. *Antibiotics & Sulfonamides (containing no local anesthetics)
10. *Furosemide
11. *Chlorothiazide
12. ACTH (adrenocorticotropic hormones)
13. Adrenocorticosteroids (natural & synthetic)
14. *Phenylbutazone
15. *Oxyphenylbutazone
16. *Indomethacin
B. Controlled medication may be administered to a horse that is entered to race on a particular day no later than four (4) hours prior to post time of the first race of that day.

NOTE: While this may look like a very extensive list, in actual fact most of these substances are endogenous to the horse. The asterisks (*) mark the substances "foreign to the natural horse" which most laboratories can test for and are thus amenable to control.

tion. It was called controlled, inasmuch as all substances recognized as being medication were controlled. The program called for detailed reporting of all medications administered, dispensed, or prescribed within the racing enclosure. All race-day medication was prohibited, and if any unreported medication was detected, it would be an improper medication. However, such an "improper medication" violation only incurs lesser penalties and is not considered by the Board to be a "positive."

Under the California rule, an infringement resulting in a "positive" would be use of the drugs defined under the Penal Code, i.e. the narcotics, stimulants, depressants, and local anesthetics, and to these infringements the trainer/insurer rule applies. Thus, the California controlled medication program clearly distinguished between two classes of drugs, the Penal Code drugs, whose detection constituted a "positive," and other medications, whose use was permitted within narrowly controlled conditions and concerning which the penalties for improper use were considerably less rigorous.

This, then, is the background and current status of California's controlled medication program, which served as the prototype for many of the controlled medication programs in the United States. These programs have been very successful in that they met with good acceptance among the racing community and became widespread in the United States during the 1970s. Recently, however, these programs have come under strong attack from a number of groups, and it is probably appropriate at this point to review the charges made against controlled medication programs and, more importantly, the evidence on which these charges are based.

Furosemide has been charged with being toxic to horses, improving the performance of horses, allowing horses to be run hot and cold, flushing drugs out of horses, and being used to keep "pulmonary criples" running. The facts, however, are much less dramatic. Furosemide does *not* flush drugs out of the bloodstream of horses, despite what backstretch "experts" may say on national television programs. Lasix® is not toxic to horses and is, in fact, a very safe drug both in horses and humans, being the fifth most commonly prescribed drug in humans. Lasix® does not improve the performance of horses and therefore does not "move horses up." Because it does not "move horses up," Lasix® cannot be used to run horses hot and cold. While Lasix® will dilute some drugs and drug metabolites in equine urine, the effects are transient, lasting for as little as three hours when the dose of furosemide is the dose used in the treatment of epistaxis.

Just how small the diluting effect of furosemide is in post-race urine samples is shown in Figure 23-3. In this study, the concentration of phenylbutazone and its metabolites in the urine of racing horses was measured and compared with the concentrations in horses that had been treated pre-race with furosemide. Even though there was no supervision of the dosage of furosemide or the time when it was administered, the urinary concentrations found in the furosemide-treated horses were bracketed by the concentrations found in the untreated horses. The mean concentration of "phenylbutazone" in the furosemide-treated horses was about 100 µg/ml, compared with about 181 µg/ml in the control horses.

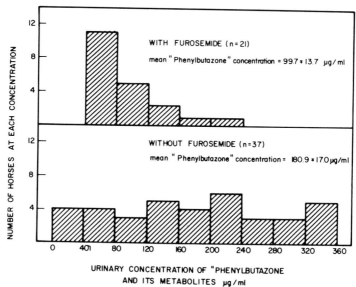

Figure 23-3. Urinary concentrations of phenylbutazone and its metabolites in furosemide-treated and untreated horses. Urine samples from horses racing in a midwestern state were analyzed for their content of phenylbutazone or phenylbutazone metabolites by measuring the absorbance of acidic extracts of these urines at 258 nm. The upper panel shows urinary concentrations of "phenylbutazone" or its metabolites in furosemide-treated horses, while the lower panel shows the urinary concentrations in horses not treated with furosemide. The mean "phenylbutazone" concentration in the furosemide-treated horses was more than 50% of that in the control horses, and a number of untreated horses had phenylbutazone concentrations below those of the control horses.

Furosemide treatment, therefore, produced less than a 50 per cent reduction in the urinary concentration of this drug and is unlikely to have a greater effect with other drugs or drug metabolites. The use of furosemide in performance horses, therefore, threatens neither horses, owners, analysts, nor the integrity of racing and appears to produce its most bizarre responses in the minds of antimedication folk.

Like the charges against furosemide, the charges against phenylbutazone levelled by opponents of controlled medication programs are often substantially in error. From the discussion of the mechanism of action of phenylbutazone in Chapter 6, it is clear that the action of phenylbutazone is to prevent the *hyper-*algesic effects induced by the inflammatory response and prostaglandins. The much-vaunted analgesic effect of these agents, therefore, is simply an action to return pain perception in an inflamed area to normal, and the action of these drugs is certainly not to "kill" pain sensation in that area. On a comparative basis, phenylbutazone is no more effective, unusual, or exotic an analgesic in the horse than aspirin is in man, and it has no more capacity to stimulate unusual performance in the horse than aspirin can in man. It is absolutely incorrect, therefore, to think of these drugs as numbing an area in the manner of a local anesthetic block, or as reducing the general awareness of pain by the brain as a narcotic will. Phenylbutazone cannot do either of these things and, as most veterinarians are well aware, will not make a horse with more than minimal musculoskeletal problems run sound.

The claim that phenylbutazone "masks" other drugs depends entirely on the concentration of phenylbutazone, the drugs that are being tested for, the diligence with which the search for other drugs is pursued, and to some extent on the experience and attitudes of the analyst. In this regard the authoritative 1977 report of the Veterinary Chemists Advisory Committee to the National Association of State Racing Commissioners concluded that medication with phenylbutazone on race day may make the detection of illegal medication more difficult. Similarly, in 1980, this committee concluded that if medication with phenylbutazone on race day is withheld, then the masking effect of phenylbutazone is minimal.

The relative unimportance of the masking and diluting effects of phenylbutazone and furosemide are borne out by the experience of three of the major racing states that first developed and implemented the tests for fentanyl (Sublimaze®). These states (Colorado, Illinois, Florida) are states in which the use of phenylbutazone and furosemide were then permitted, and their supposed diluting and masking effects were available to horsemen. Nevertheless, analysts in all three of these states were able to detect, confirm, and prosecute a large number of fentanyl positives and to effectively eliminate the use of fentanyl in these states. In sharp contrast with this record stands New York, where phenylbutazone and furosemide are not allowed and, as of this writing, no fentanyl positives have been called. Clearly, the use of phenylbutazone and furosemide in no way interfered with these states' efforts to detect, control, or prosecute the use of a potent narcotic, fentanyl.

The charge that phenylbutazone is overused or abused in the states where its use is permitted is also not supported by the data. Figure 23-4 shows the blood levels of phenylbutazone found after various dosage schedules and drawn from the data of a number of different workers. The data show that blood levels of phenylbutazone in horses at about twelve hours after dosing (i.e. at optimal drug effect) are about 10 μg/ml. Similarly, if one studies plasma levels of drugs in a population of horses racing under a controlled medication program, one finds (Fig. 23-5) that the mean blood level of phenylbutazone in these horses is also about 9 to 10 μg/ml, with a fairly tight range around the mean. These data suggest no evidence for abuse or overusage of the drug and do not support widespread claims that phenylbutazone is abused under controlled medication programs.

The last and most emotional charge against phenylbutazone is that its use results in an increased number of breakdowns. In the layman's mind this charge has a certain plausibility, since phenylbutazone is thought of as being a powerful painkiller that enables injured horses to run "sound." Inspection of the available data, however, is not consistent with this hypothesis and is more consistent with

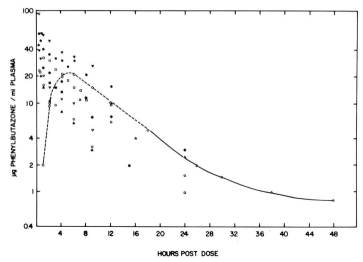

Figure 23-4. Plasma levels of phenylbutazone after different dosage schedules. The symbols show the plasma levels of phenylbutazone observed after administration of different dosage schedules of this drug to horses by different workers, as indicated below. The data show that therapeutic dosage schedules of phenylbutazone are associated with blood levels of this drug of about 10 μg/ml at the time of optimal therapeutic effect, which occurs at about twelve hours after dosing. The key presented below gives the data source, dose of phenylbutazone, and method of dosing.

○ Tobin, unpublished data 1/80; n = 2, 4 mg/kg IV, GC method.
● Tobin, *Am J Vet Res, 38:*123, 1977; n = 4, 6.6 mg/kg IV, spectrophoto. method.
□ Tobin, *Am J Vet Res, 38:*123, 1977; n = 4, 6.6 mg/kg IV, GC method.
■ Maylin, *Proc 20th Meeting AAEP,* 1974, pp. 243-48; n = 3, 4.4 mg/kg IV, GC method.
△ Maylin, *Proc 20th Meeting AAEP,* 1974; same experiment, multiple doses (0 hr, 24 hr, 48 hr, 72 hr); data from 72 hr injection.
▲ Piperno et al, *J Am Vet Med Assoc, 153:*195, 1968; n = 6, 4.4 mg/kg IV, spectrophoto. method.
▽ Piperno et al, *J Am Vet Med Assoc, 153:*195, 1968; n = 1, 8.8 mg/kg IV, spectrophoto. method.
▼ Piperno et al, *J Am Vet Med Assoc, 153:*195, 1968; n = 1, 17.6 mg/kg IV, spectrophoto. method.
◇ Piperno et al, *J Am Vet Med Assoc, 153:*195, 1968; n = 1, 4.4 mg/kg IV, spectrophoto. method.
◆ Tobin et al, *J Equine Med Surg, 1:*402, 1977; n = 7, 6.6 mg/kg IV, GC method.

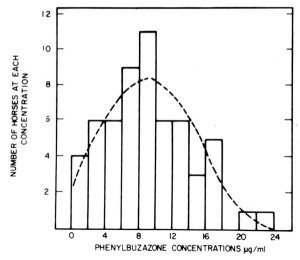

Figure 23-5 Phenylbutazone concentrations in the blood of fifty-eight racing horses. In a study in a midwestern racing state, blood levels of phenylbutazone in fifty-eight racing horses were measured. The vertical bars show the numbers of horses with blood levels of phenylbutazone in the indicated ranges. The dotted line represents an approximate distribution curve drawn by eye. The data show that the median blood level of phenylbutazone in the blood of these horses was about 9 µg/ml, with no blood levels above 24 µg/ml. The blood levels of phenylbutazone in these horses, therefore, cluster around the level to be expected in the blood of horses after therapeutic doses of this drug.

what is known of the pharmacology of phenylbutazone in the horse and, to bring the point home to the layman, of its human equivalent, aspirin.

The first point that has to be borne in mind when analyzing breakdown data is that the term "breakdown" has never been defined. Because of this, one man's definition of breakdown may be an injury severe enough to require destruction of a horse, while another man's breakdown may be the horse pulling up lame. Because there is no agreed operational definition as to what constitutes a breakdown, a more reasonable approach is to use the figures of accidents either fatal or leading to horses being "put down" on the track. This is because the circumstances under which horses are put down are fairly clearly defined and thus are likely to be consistent from track to track and from year to year.

As a drug, phenylbutazone in the horse is the approximate equivalent of aspirin in man.

As of this writing, three sets of "statistical" data on the effects of phenylbutazone on the incidence of breakdowns are available. The most clear-cut data are those from California racing, which are presented in Figure 23-6. As shown in this illustration, the rate at which horses broke down or had to be destroyed was not changed by the advent of racing on phenylbutazone in California. The data on horses destroyed on the track over this period are particularly convincing, since the indications for destruction are relatively unambiguous and not likely to vary much between different veterinarians or different tracks. On the other hand, "breakdown" is a poorly defined term, and the types of conditions described by this term are more likely to vary from track to track and from veterinarian to veterinarian. The relative stability of the number of horses destroyed in California racing, which has held steady at about 100 per year or about one in 500 starters over the decade of the 1970s, speaks very strongly against an increase in the injury rate of horses racing on phenylbutazone.

Further, comparison of the figures for the percent of starters on phenylbutazone against the percent of winners on phenylbutazone shows that the percentages of horses in both categories are approximately equal (Table 23-III). Horses running on phenylbutazone, therefore, do not appear to have any significant advantage over untreated horses, and these data, of course, suggest that they are not any less likely to finish (i.e. to break down) than untreated horses.

These data and conclusions from California Thoroughbred racing are well supported by data from Colorado Thoroughbred racing. According to Doctor

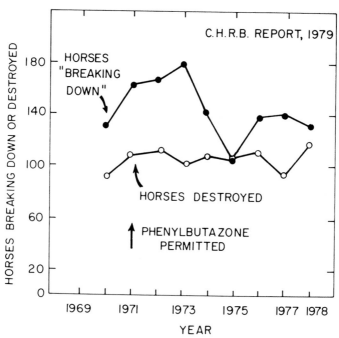

Figure 23-6. Breakdowns and horses destroyed in California racing. The open circles (o—o) show the number of horses destroyed in California racing, corrected for the number of starters, from 1970 to 1978, while the solid circles (•—•) show the number of breakdowns occurring over the same period.

TABLE 23-III
CONTROLLED MEDICATION STATISTICS
CALIFORNIA

Year	Starters on "Bute" %	Winners on "Bute" %
1971	47	43
1972	50	49
1973	52	50
1974	55	56
1975	61	62
1976	65	66
Six-Year Average:	55	54.33

Gene Bierhaus of the Colorado Racing Commission, the probability of a horse having an accident that requires his destruction is independent of whether or not the horse is on phenylbutazone. Further, the overall destruction rate of horses running in Colorado during the 1970s was a relatively low (1/1020), even though about 60 per cent of these horses were on phenylbutazone (Table 23-IV). This rate was less than half the rate at which breakdowns requiring destruction occurred prior to the advent of medication and has led Doctor Bierhaus to conclude that in his experience the incidence of breakdowns requiring destruction has not been increased by the advent of controlled medication programs.

These data from California and Colorado Thoroughbred racing are well sup-

TABLE 23-IV
COLORADO THOROUGHBRED RACING BREAKDOWNS
1954-1979

Year	Days of Racing	# Destroyed (Butazolidin was not available)
1954	45	12

In 1954 all of the racing was during the summer and track conditions were better, compared to 1971-77. 1/444 starters had to be destroyed.

		Destroyed		
Year	Days of Racing	On "bute"	No "bute"	Total
1971	60	4	2	6
1972	60	2	3	5
1973	67	5	4	9
1974	92	6	3	9
1975	84	3	2	5
1976	88	4	3	7
1977	99	5	2	7
1978	96	5	2	7
1979	44 (completed)	1	0	1
Total		35	21	56
% Breakdowns		62.5%	37.5%	100%

% of horses running on "bute" varies between 60 and 65%.

SOURCES: Doctor Gene Bierhaus, Chief Commission Veterinarian, Colorado, personal communication, 1979; Poppell, Carolyn F. (Assistant Science Advisor): *Issue Brief: Phenylbutazone and Furosemide in Race Horses in Maryland.* Maryland General Assembly, 1979.

ported by a careful pilot study carried out by workers from the University of Pennsylvania at Pennsylvania National Racetrack and reported at the Jockey Club Round Table conference, 1979. This study extended over a period of four months and covered forty-five days of observation. In this study, a breakdown was defined as an injury severe enough to prevent a horse finishing a race. Out of 3,910 horses at risk in this meet, they found 19 breakdowns, or a rate of about 1 in 206. These workers were very careful to point out that this breakdown rate was *"not higher than the incidence of injuries occurring at tracks in New Jersey and New York, which have restrictions on the use of phenylbutazone."* These observations would appear to deny claims that tracks allow the use of phenylbutazone become dumping grounds for unsound horses that can only run on "bute." Whatever the circumstances that brought horsemen and their horses to Pennsylvania National Racetrack, and whether or not they ran on phenylbutazone, these horses were not any more likely to break down than supposedly "sounder" horses racing without the benefit of phenylbutazone at neighboring tracks.

It appears, therefore, that at this point the weight of the evidence available suggests that the use of phenylbutazone is not associated with an increase in the breakdown rate. It must be emphasized, however, that the available data are far from complete and that the analyses performed on these data have, in general, been quite unsophisticated. The only detailed study in this area has been the University of Pennsylvania study, and more studies of this caliber would be very useful.

A number of other arguments have also been advanced against the use of phenylbutazone and furosemide in horses, which arguments have been repeated at the highest levels of government. It has been argued, for example, that the FDA has not approved furosemide for use in the treatment of epistaxis. The FDA however, has explicitly approved furosemide for use in the treatment of pulmonary congestion or lung edema in the horse. Since it is this action against pulmonary congestion which appears to be the basis of its action against epistaxis, a good case can be made that this approval covers its use in "bleeders."

The argument that these drugs are being put to uses for which they were not "intended" betrays ignorance of the whole human experience with drugs. This argument appears to suppose that somewhere, perhaps under the care of some incredibly ancient and learned university professor, is a large book, full of lists of intended uses for drugs. Furthermore, since nobody knows where these lists come from or whether the lists just spring into existence, there must therefore exist lists of "intended" and proper uses for those drugs that man has not yet discovered.

This whole concept of "intended" uses for drugs so dear to the hearts of certain people is, of course, just so much rubbish. There are no "intended" uses for drugs. All but one of the 4,000 drugs in common use today were discovered by chance, and *all* drug actions and effects have been discovered by trial and error. There are no "intended" uses for drugs, there never have been, and there never will be. The uses for drugs in man and horses have been discovered by man by careful observation, and the clinical use of phenylbutazone and furosemide in performance horses certainly comes under that heading.

The final argument, presented to cap all arguments about phenylbutazone and furosemide, is that these medications do not cure any of the conditions that they treat. However, one must remember that in this imperfect world there are no drugs that "cure" anything. For example, if the reader is unfortunate enough to catch an infectious disease, he or she may be left with the feeling that the doses of penicillin cured it. Well, you are, of course, cured, as long as you stay away from the cause of the problem, but if you are reexposed to the infection, the chances are that you are going to have to keep taking penicillin. Similarly, the horse on phenylbutazone will heal and cure, spontaneously, with or without phenylbutazone, but if you run him to the point that brought on the condition in the first place, then it is going to recur. Which brings us to the last point. The alternative to phenylbutazone that is commonly suggested is to "lay up" the horse. Laying up, of course, does not cure anything either, because the condition will only recur when the horse is returned to the track, the environment in which the condition developed in the first place.

In summary, therefore, controlled medication programs represent one approach to the substantial technical and regulatory problems that are involved in medication control. These programs were carefully thought out and implemented and were well accepted in the racing community. When used in conjunction with good pre-race examinations and good laboratory support, they represent a very workable approach to the problem of medication control. Controlled medication programs are, however, peculiarly susceptible to attack from individuals and groups who feel that it is basically wrong to allow horses access to modern therapeutic medication during a competitive event.

THE LONG-TERM EFFECTS OF MEDICATION

The final problem, and by far the most difficult question to answer is what the use of medication is going to do to what is rather loosely called the "breed." The prophets of doom hold that permissive medication will give rise to a "breed" of horses that will only be able to run on "bute." The essence of this position was put forward by the stewards of the turf authorities of Ireland, Great Britain, and France, who issued a joint statement on this problem in 1971, which read as follows:

> It has been suggested that the Rules of Racing in our three countries should be relaxed to permit the use of phenylbutazone and similar anti-inflammatory drugs.
> In a number of American states the use of phenylbutazone is permitted, but only under strict supervision, and it is significant that, where this happens, a horse once given the substance must continue to receive it throughout the season, whether its physical state requires it or not, in order to prevent any possibility of discrepancies in form.
> This practice we consider completely undesirable and we are advised that the use of phenylbutazone can seriously jeopardise the soundness of our blood lines and would be liable to have a most damaging effect on the breeding industry.
> We wish to make it absolutely clear that under no circumstances should this situation be allowed to occur and we therefore reaffirm our intention to adhere strictly to the existing Rules of Racing and will severely penalise those responsible for any breach of the rules.

Responding promptly to this statement from the powers that be in European Thoroughbred racing, the Royal College of Veterinary Surgeons immediately endorsed this lay opinion and advised all its members to study its implications as follows:

> The Royal College of Veterinary Surgeons endorses fully the statement published on October 21st in the RACING CALENDAR by the Turf Authorities of Great Britain, Ireland and France. The attention of all veterinarians is drawn to the implications of this statement for the profession. Any veterinarian who prescribes, supplies or administers such drugs for horses in a period prior to racing must be aware that the discovery on testing by the Turf Authorities of any residue of any such drug or its metabolites will have very serious consequences for the trainer, and indeed for the veterinarian, in the light of paragraph 58 of the Royal College's Guide to Professional Conduct.
>
> In the absence of precise information regarding elimination times, it is suggested that a veterinarian who is asked to prescribe treatment for racehorses in situations where anti-inflammatory drugs appear to be appropriate, should advise the trainer of the dangers involved in the use of such drugs when the horse is due to race in the forseeable future. It should be made clear to the trainer, in writing, that there are no certain elimination times, as such times depend upon a great many variable factors such as the route of administration of the drug and its excretion rate in the individual animal. In addition, improved techniques now enable laboratories to detect the presence of smaller and smaller residues at periods more and more remote from the time of administration. There must therefore be the chance that any test on a horse which has had administered to it an anti-inflammatory drug may prove positive and since this will place the trainer at risk with the Turf Authorities, the trainer must decide whether or not to run this risk in the light of such advice as the veterinarian is able to offer.
>
> It is appreciated that in the light of the foregoing, veterinarians will wish to receive guidance regarding the elimination times of the various anti-inflammatory drugs. Serious inquiry has been made of the possibility of providing such information but it is unfortunately the position that in the present state of scientific knowledge precise elimination times cannot be given. It must be recognized that this lack of certain information cannot be used in any way as an excuse for indiscriminate use of such drugs. If a veterinarian recommends the discontinuance of any such drug *not less than eight days before racing* (even although such a period may be longer than is necessary in many instances) he should be able to feel sure that he has catered for all but the most exceptional case.

Whatever else may be said about the Jockey Club statement, the spectacle of a professional body promptly and unquestioningly endorsing a lay opinion, based on anonymous advice and expressed in a turf publication, says very little for the professional independence of that body.

The first comment that any scientist might have about the Jockey Club statement is "what on earth is a 'sound bloodline'?" Presuming that a useful, objective, operational definition of a "sound bloodline" could be developed, the next step would be to measure the "soundness" of these "bloodlines" and compare them. Only in this way can a scientist hope to come up with a definitive answer to the Jockey Club statement, which certainly covers a broad area.

Contrary to the opinion of the Royal College of Veterinary Surgeons and the Jockey Club stewards, it has been suggested that since all breeding and bloodline decisions of interest in the equine world are made by humans, phenylbutazone is not going to in any way affect the breeding of bloodstock. On the whole, the first argument that controlled medication is going to change the "breed" — is most likely true. If experimental biology has taught us anything, it has taught us that altering the selective pressures on a biological system changes the system, or alternatively, that biological systems adapt to the situation in which they find themselves. Perhaps the most dramatic example of this, and one that is certainly close to home, has been in our own species. Since the introduction of insulin, the incidence of diabetes in the human population has increased manyfold, and it is estimated that by the end of this century a substantial fraction of the North American population will be diabetic. The introduction of insulin, therefore, has changed the selective pressures on the human population, and individuals who were previously strongly selected against are now to some extent protected from these selective pressures, particularly through their reproductive years. Similarly, if racing horses are selected for breeding primarily on the basis of their running performance, then phenylbutazone may affect the pool of animals from which we breed and thus inevitably what horsemen call "the breed" or "bloodlines." Conversely, if phenylbutazone prevents the elimination of certain animals from the pool of runners, it will also affect the pool we breed from and thus, inevitably, the "breed."

It is clear, therefore, that in principle, controlled medication is certainly capable of "changing the breed." The next question is the important one, which is, Is it doing so in practice? The answer to this depends on whether or not phenylbutazone is influencing the pool of animals from which we breed.

It is not possible at this time to answer the question as to whether or not medication programs will change the "breed." This is partly because no one can measure what they mean by "the breed," and also because the influence of phenylbutazone on the pool of animals that we breed from is small. The best

"Bute or shoot" has been suggested by some to be the bottom line of the medication dilemma.

horses, with the best bloodlines, are raced essentially drug-free, and these, of course, are the horses that dominate in breeding. On the other hand, it is the less expensive horses, racing for smaller purses at smaller tracks, that tend to be on medication. These horses are, of course, the workhorses of the racing world, and their future as breeding stock tends to be small. For these horses the alternative to controlled medication is either medication with illegal drugs or retirement from the track. Since horses are expensive to keep, retirement from the track may lead to retirement from life, presenting the owner of the horse with the classic "bute or shoot" dilemma. Under these circumstances, the use of phenylbutazone is, from the point of view of all concerned — and not the least the horse — a very practical and humane practice.

In analyzing this problem it is also important to put medication in perspective, for medication is only one of a large number of interferences that man has visited on the horse. Most performance horses are bred under highly artificial conditions, some being kept under lights to get them into heat out of season. Horse breeders, who may often decry the use of medications on the track, will use antibiotics, hormones, releasing factors, tranquilizers, and prostaglandins to get their mares in foal and enable them to carry their foals to term. The stallion that breeds their mares is a stallion that has "won his spurs" through a small number of sprints at top speed before his fourth year, rather than being selected by years of competition with his fellow stallions, equine predators, and the elements. As a foal he will have been treated with antibiotics to maneuver him past the foalhood diseases of the horse, he may well have had surgery to correct deformities or errors of conformation, and he will have been vaccinated against the diseases of foals.

If the horse does not handle well and adjust to humans, and although his behavioral patterns may be those that would make him successful in the wild, he may not have much of a career ahead of him as a racehorse. If he does, he will never race on nature's hooves, but on steel or aluminum or perhaps even plastic racing plates. He will be wormed throughout his racing career to ensure that he carries a minimal number of uninvited guests in his gastrointestinal tract. If this horse gets dosed with the equine equivalent of aspirin during the peak trials of his working career, one could quite reasonably argue that it is hardly anything to get excited about. Ballet dancers do it all the time, for they too, like racehorses, are prone to musculoskeletal problems. Controlled medication is only one of the many variations that man has introduced into the life of the horse, and it is probably one of the least dramatic from the point of the future of the "breed."

The use of the human equivalent of phenylbutazone by ballet dancers brings us to one of the most clear-cut justifications for use of these drugs, i.e. in the highly trained show or eventing horse. The long and expensive training of these horses, the age they have attained by the time their training is complete, and the vigorous and complicated nature of the exercise makes it reasonable on both economic and humanitarian grounds to allow the judicious medication of these animals. In the last analysis, drugs are just another one of man's tools in his control of his environment, and they are no better or worse for either man or horse than most of the other tools that man's ingenuity has put at his disposal.

SELECTED REFERENCES

A Report on Four Years of Controlled Medication in California, and Controlled Medication Statistical Report. California Horse Racing Board, January 30, 1974.

Controlled Medication in California. California Horse Racing Board, February 9, 1979.

Gabel, A.: The medication problem: facts and recommendations. Personal communication, 1979.

Goldstein, A.: *Biostatistics, An Introductory Text.* New York, Macmillan, 1964.

Maylin, G. A.: Disposition of phenylbutazone in the horse. *Proc 20th Annual Convention AAEP*, 243-248, 1974.

O'Dea, Joseph C.: A reasoned approach to medication. *The Thoroughbred Record,* 776-770, March 13, 1976.

Phenylbutazone and similar anti-inflammatory drugs. *Vet Rec,* 537-538, Vol. 89, November 13, 1971.

Piperno, E., Ellis, O. J., Getty, S. M., and Brody, T. M.: Plasma and urine levels of phenylbutazone in the horse. *J Am Vet Med Assoc, 153:*195, 1968.

Poppell, C. F., Assistant Science Advisor: *Issue Brief: Phenylbutazone and Furosemide in Race Horses in Maryland.* Maryland General Assembly, 1979.

Proceedings of Second Symposium on Equine Pharmacology. The Ohio State University, 35-36, 1978. Golden, CO, American Association of Equine Practitioners, 1979.

Proposed National Medication Rule Guidelines. *Proc NASRC Annual Meeting,* Lexington, KY, 1980.

Pryor, D. H.: *The Congressional Record — Senate.* May 1, 1980, pp. s4454-s4455.

Reasoner, H.: "60 Minutes" investigation of drugs in horse racing. Reprinted in *The Horseman's Journal,* 4-8, July, 1979.

Soma, L., Solow, R., and Fregin, G. F.: Track Survey — Pennsylvania National Race Track — Pilot Study — Summary of Results. Presentation by G. F. Fregin at the Jockey Club Round Table, August, 1979.

Tobin, T., Blake, J. W., and Valentine, R.: Drug interactions in the horse: Effects of chloramphenicol, quinidine, and oxyphenbutazone on phenylbutazone metabolism. *Am J Vet Res, 38:*123, 1977.

Tobin, T., Roberts, B. L., and Miller, J. R.: The pharmacology of furosemide in the horse. I. Effects on the disposition of procaine, methylphenidate, phenylbutazone, and pentazocine. *J Equine Med Surg, 1:*402, 1977.

Chapter 24

LEGAL ASPECTS OF MEDICATION RULE ENFORCEMENT

RICHARD HEARD

Grant and Heard
Columbus, Montana

THE FIRST QUESTION that any attorney representing an owner or trainer should ask when inquiring into the legal aspects of medication in parimutuel racing is, "Where does the racing commission get its authority to make rules allowing or prohibiting the use of any substance administered to a horse in racing?" The statutes that authorize parimutuel racing in a state also create a racing commission, which is vested with authority of the type shown in the following language:

> The Board is vested with the full power to promulgate reasonable rules and regulations for the purpose of administering the provisions of this Act and to prescribe reasonable rules, regulations and conditions under which all horse race meetings in the State shall be held and conducted. Such reasonable rules and regulations are to provide for the prevention of practices detrimental to the public interest and for the best interests of horse racing and to impose penalties for violations thereof.[1]

From this statutory authority commissions adopt medication and other rules that govern the conduct of persons licensed to participate in racing. The wording of the medication rules in the various states has evolved since the 1930s through a series of definitions and criteria designed to prevent a breach of the medication policy of that jurisdiction.

Some medication rules prohibit the use of certain categories of substances, such as narcotics, stimulants, depressants or local anesthetics, analgesics, or any derivative or compound thereof. This is contrasted with the uniform rule proposed by the NASRC in the early 1960s, which prohibited the use of any substance that was of a character as could affect the speed of a horse in a race. Rules of both types were subject to court challenges and legal arguments based on expert testimony as to whether the particular substance discovered in the test fell within the prohibition contained in the particular medication rule. As the state of the medication art became more advanced, the rules were continually amended to try to keep pace with new substances, both artificial and natural, which were being administered to horses in racing.

At any medication hearing the trainer and/or owner is entitled to expect that the commission, through its veterinarian, chemist, and other witnesses, can show a proper chain of evidence for the sample in question.

The evidence should show that the horse was continuously observed from the finish line to the test barn area, where it was assigned to a state veterinarian or one of his assistants for urine and/or blood sample collection. The evidence should then show that the horse was properly identified, that the resulting sample was

---

[1] Illinois Horse Racing Act of 1975, §37-9(b).

tagged showing the basic identification of the horse, and that the sample was gathered in the presence of the trainer or his authorized representative. Some states by rule and the rest by accepted practice do not disclose the name of the owner or trainer on the laboratory's portion of the sample identification card. However, by code on the card the stewards can correlate the sample with the signed portion of the test ticket retained by the state veterinarian. The state veterinarian is charged with the responsibility of protecting the samples until such time as they are delivered to the official testing laboratory. Absent this chain of evidence, and the question of improper medication becomes mute.

After the sample, properly taken and properly protected, is delivered to the testing laboratory, the laboratory will follow its standardized procedures for testing. Upon a report of a drug positive from the laboratory, a myriad of legal procedures and processes will be triggered.

The usual sequence of proceeding on a positive drug test would be an informal stewards hearing, followed by a formal commission hearing, which would be the last step at the administrative level. If the matter were pursued further, it would go to the appropriate trial court and from there on through the various levels of appellate courts.

One of the first things that a trainer can expect after a report of a positive test by the laboratory to the stewards in any jurisdiction is the resulting search of the trainer's stables, tack room, vehicle, living quarters, and other places within the racetrack enclosure.

All persons who make application to participate in parimutuel racing complete a multiple-page license application form, which in the fine print either at the bottom or on the back side of the form contains a consent to the type of search described above. Therefore, the owner, trainer, veterinarian, or other licensee participating in racing will ask, "Can my person and property be searched without my consent? Does the Constitution protect me and my property from unreasonable searches?"

The problem the courts have faced in this area has been in trying to strike a proper balance between the rights of the persons participating in racing, such as owners, trainers, and veterinarians, as opposed to the protection of the betting public and preserving the integrity of the sport of racing from corrupt practices.

Basically, we are talking about the application of the Fourth Amendment of the United States Constitution, which says —

> The right of the people to be secure in their persons, houses, papers and effects against unreasonable searches and seizures, shall not be violated, and no warrant shall be issued but upon probable cause, supported by oath or affirmation, and particularly describing the place to be searched and the person or things to be seized.

The Fourth Amendment protection for the individual, then, has been in the requirement of probable cause and the impartiality of the magistrate issuing the search warrant.

The usual practice in racing is that of a trainer, veterinarian, or other licensed person being searched, together with the stable area and vehicles under his control, without a warrant, without a showing of probable cause, and without specifications of the items being searched for. Generally, the search is made to detect illegal medication or related paraphernalia.

The usual search at the racetrack occurs upon a report of illegal medication or apparatus being used. The search is generally carried out by racetrack security personnel or state security personnel without further justification or application for authority to search. The average person licensed to participate in racing is not aware that he has consented to a search of his stable, vehicle, living quarters, and other areas within the racing enclosure until he is asked to consent to a search of those areas. The constitutional variance in the typical search conducted at a racetrack and resulting seizure of medication substances or paraphernalia has been justified to the courts by racing commissions on the grounds that the search conducted was of an administrative nature on behalf of an administrative agency and does not pertain to a typical criminal proceeding under the state or federal criminal codes.

The courts have then had the difficult task of balancing the constitutional rights of the individual and the protection of the integrity of the industry and the betting public. Some recent cases in this area are worthy of consideration at this point. The first two cases involved searches conducted on persons licensed to participate in racing. The third case involved a person who was participating in racing but who was unlicensed in the state where the search took place. The end result of the three decisions indicates that the rights of the individual have been watered down to protect the rights of the betting public and the integrity of the industry to a point that must be worrysome to constitutional scholars and persons holding a license to participate in racing.

The first case arose in the state of Pennsylvania, where a licensed trainer was asked by officials of the Pennsylvania Racing Commission for permission to search his stable, tack and feed rooms, and other areas under the control of the trainer.[2] Consent was given, and nothing was found. The officials then asked for permission to search the trainer's vehicle, which was parked on the grounds. The trainer declined unless a search warrant was produced, whereupon the officials forced entry into the truck without a warrant in reliance on the consent executed by the trainer on the license application. Various drugs and devices were discovered in the truck, and the trainer was subsequently suspended. The trainer filed suit, alleging that the warrantless search was a violation of the guarantee against unreasonable searches and seizures contained in the Fourth Amendment. The Pennsylvania Supreme Court approved the search and upheld the penalty of twelve months suspension of license. The Pennsylvania Court relied on several United States Supreme Court decisions allowing warrantless administrative or regulatory searches. The court allowed the warrantless search to stand on the reasoning that the requirement of a warrant would allow the trainer time to dispose of the drugs or related paraphernalia, and secondly, the court determined that horse racing was a highly regulated field and that the trainer had consented to abide by the rules of that particular field when he executed an application for a trainer's license.

---

[2] Lanchester v. Pennsylvania State Horse Racing Commission, 325 A.2d 648 (1974).

A suspension of a veterinarian's license to participate in parimutuel racing was upheld by the United States Supreme Court in an appeal from a decision of the Illinois Racing Board.[3] A licensed veterinarian was approached by agents of the Illinois Racing Board based on a report from the state racing chemist that the veterinarian might have been dispensing a prohibited substance. The veterinarian was advised that he would not have to allow a search of his vehicle or person but that such a refusal would constitute a violation of the Illinois Racing Rules. The veterinarian consented to a search of his automobile but refused to allow a search of his person. Immediately thereafter a stewards hearing was held, and the veterinarian's continued refusal to allow a search of his person caused his license to be suspended and the matter to be referred to the Illinois Racing Board. Thereafter, the veterinarian filed suit in Federal Court challenging the constitutionality of the Search and Seizure Rule. The three-judge federal court upheld the Illinois rule. The decision was then appealed to the United States Supreme Court, and that court affirmed the lower court's judgment.

The fact that distinguishes the Illinois case from the Pennsylvania case was that the suspension in Illinois was based on the licensee's refusal to consent to the search under the language contained in the license application and the Illinois Racing Rules.

The conclusion of the courts at this time is that the regulation of betting, the legitimacy of competition, and the control of the use of drugs to effect the outcome of races establishes a compelling interest that necessitates the quick action accomplished by a warrantless search and that this action balances the public interest as against the invasion of the right of privacy of the individual licensee being searched.

A third and different case involved the search of an unlicensed veterinarian at 11:00 PM at Bowie Race Track.[4] The veterinarian was licensed in Pennsylvania but not licensed as a veterinarian in Maryland, nor was he licensed by the Maryland Commission to practice veterinary medicine at the Maryland racetrack. The veterinarian and his vehicle were searched by agents of the TRPB, and he was found to be in possession of a prohibited Schedule II narcotic drug. Evidence from this warrantless search was used as a basis for criminal indictment for violation of the federal drug rules.

The federal court refused the veterinarian's Motion to Suppress the evidence obtained in the warrantless search, stating that by treating a horse at a Maryland racetrack the veterinarian had subjected himself to the Maryland Rules of Racing, and therefore, the Fourth Amendment challenge to the search failed. The interesting point in the court's decision is the statement by Judge Watkins in answering the veterinarian's challenge that only persons licensed by the Maryland Racing Commission were subject to the rules of the racing commission:

> I repeat, again, that I find it a little difficult to feel that a person who is disqualified, generally, is entitled to greater protection than one who had made every effort to comply with the formal requirements, but I think that when you read .04 in connection with .01 that it is quite clear that the rule was intended to apply to those who participated in track meetings, as such, or those who

---

[3] *Wilkey v. The Illinois Racing Board, et al.,* Cause No. 74C3524 U.S. District Court, Northern District of Illinois (1975) Affirmed U.S. Supreme Court (1975).

[4] *United States v. Baudin,* Cause No. 75-0297-W, U.S. Dist. Ct. for Dist. of Maryland (1975).

participated in racing, and Dr. Bodin was participating in racing at the time, not merely by his presence, but by the treatment of horses.

The impact of this decision would cause one to wonder whether the veterinarian would suffer less sanctions and penalties had he been licensed to treat horses in the state of Maryland and had ended up appearing before the stewards at Bowie Race Track or the Maryland Commission on a license suspension or revocation proceeding. Also in question would be whether such action would have been deemed by the federal authorities to be sufficient penalty to avoid prosecution for violation of the federal drug rule.

The area of search and seizure at the racetrack seems to be one of the few areas in racing law in which there are unanimous judicial opinions at the present time. Warrantless administrative searches will be upheld on the basis that they are in the best interest of racing and its participants and therefore are reasonable under the requirements of the Fourth Amendment.

In conjunction with the search of the trainer's person and stable area, he will receive a notice of a stewards hearing charging him with a violation of the medication rule which resulted from the positive drug test on the animal under his care, control, and supervision. What can a trainer and/or owner expect when he attends a stewards hearing on a medication violation that could result in a suspension or revocation of his license? The stewards hearing should be held in such a manner as to afford due process to the individual charged with the violation of the racing statute and to protect the integrity and interest of the sport in promptly conducting the hearing and arriving at a just and fair determination of the matter. Due process has been defined by the United States Supreme Court as —

> The "due process of law" clause of Fourteenth Amendment requires that action by state through any of its agencies must be consistent with fundamental principles of liberty and justice.[5]

Due process in the context of a stewards or commission hearing should be a notice to the accused of the medication violation, an opportunity to prepare for the hearing, the right to have counsel present at the hearing, the right to cross-examine witnesses presented in support of the medication charge, and the right of the accused to present evidence on his own behalf.

Generally, a stewards hearing is an informal proceeding at which the trainer, owner, or other licensee who has been charged with a violation of the racing act first responds to the charges. In many instances the individual has been notified of the time and the place of hearing verbally and waives any further time to prepare for the hearing or to have counsel present if the infraction carries a fine or other minimum penalty. However, in those instances where a stewards hearing on a positive drug test can result in a suspension of a license for any period of time, the formality of the hearing should be carefully looked at to see that the person accused of breaching the racing rules receives a proper notice of the time and place of the hearing, which notice contains a statement defining the rule that was allegedly violated, both by rule number and definition, and some statement as to the time and place of the violation and horse involved. The accused should have a

---

[5] Buchalter v. People of State of New York, 63 S.Ct. 1129, 319 U.S. 427 (1943).

notification of his rights at the stewards hearing. The notification should make it clear that the accused has the right to have counsel present at the hearing, sufficient time to prepare for the hearing and to respond to the charges made, and the further right to cross-examine the witnesses testifying against him and to adduce testimony in support of his innocence.

The passage of time has seen a great shift in the attitudes of persons participating in racing. Years ago when a licensee appearing before the stewards was summarily fined and/or suspended, he often left the stewards hearing feeling that the matter was ended without further possible recourse. Over the years, more and more decisions made by stewards were appealed to the racing commission itself, and oftentimes the decisions of the racing commission were then appealed to the courts. Several explanations could be made for the change in attitude by persons licensed to participate in racing. One could be the recognition that the stewards had in some instances been heavy-handed and trod on the person's rights. Also, the stewards may not have afforded a fair hearing in that they were prejudiced or biased before the hearing ever commenced. On the other hand, the liberal tendency of the courts to intervene in the administrative process by issuing Temporary Restraining Orders and other stay proceedings before either the stewards or the commission have had an opportunity to conduct a proper administrative hearing into the alleged violation has had a tendency to encourage people not to follow the orderly administrative process involved in meeting a challenge to an alleged medication rule violation.

More recently, if any medication violation claim has been defeated, it has been on the basis of procedural defects in the gathering or preserving of the evidence in support of the medication violation or failure to afford a fair hearing to the accused at the administrative level. Time after time the courts never reached the issue of the quality and accuracy of the testing procedures or the applicability of the racing rule to the medication in question. Rather, the cases are often decided on some procedural defect separate and apart from the major issue of the medication rule. Many good cases have reached bad results because of procedural defects in the gathering of evidence or in the adequacy of the hearing held after the alleged violation. Administrative hearings must be properly conducted before the severe penalty of a suspension or revocation of a racing license is imposed for a medication or other like violation.

The next major issue facing an owner or trainer charged with a medication violation is the Absolute Insurer Rule. Suppose after the report of a positive test that the search of the trainer's living quarters, tack room, vehicles, and stable area fail to disclose any illegal medication or medication paraphernalia. What then is the basis for the commission authority to suspend or revoke the trainer's license? The usual basis is the racing rule that makes the trainer of a horse absolutely responsible for the condition of the horse entered in a race, regardless of the actions of third parties. The trainer will contend, either at the administrative hearings or in the court proceedings, that the state or the racetrack did not meet their responsibility due to the lack of security on the back side of the racetrack, making the trainer's responsibility virtually unbearable or unmeetable due to the ease with which unlicensed persons are able to gain access to the stable area. These arguments have been less than persuasive with the courts and administrative agencies as evidenced by the decisions upholding the Absolute Insurer Rule.

The traditional arguments waged in court hearings contesting the validity of the Absolute Insurer Rule have claimed that the individual's constitutional right to equal protection and due process of law prohibit the taking of a trainer's license without a full hearing and substantial proof being made to the commission. The Absolute Insurer Rule has been pictured as punishing a trainer without requiring proof that the trainer had any "knowledge" that the horse's body contained a prohibited substance at the time it was entered in the race. Actually, the legal theory of "scienter" or "guilty knowledge" on the part of the trainer has not been deemed a necessary element to the validity of the Absolute Insurer Rule, since the rule was adopted for the protection and general welfare of the wagering public, who cannot protect themselves from drugged horses.

Some of the earlier court decisions construing the Absolute Insurer Rule determined the rule unconstitutional on the basis that the conclusive presumption stated in the rule created an irrebuttable presumption in law which could not be used to cancel a trainer's license to participate in racing. The courts considered the license to be a "property right," which could not be revoked under the Absolute Insurer Rule. Conversely, those courts that determined that a license to participate in racing was a mere "privilege" and that it was within the police power of the state to regulate public racetracks (since partimutuel wagering is not constitutionally guaranteed but rather falls within the regulatory powers of the state and its agencies) determined that the Absolute Insurer Rule was constitutionally sound. The difference in judicial attitudes between the contrasting decisions in the Absolute Insurer Rule cases seems at times to arise over whether the court was offended by the medications used, such as morphine or other prohibited substances, in contrast with some of the permissive medications.

Most racing jurisdictions today have adopted the Trainer Responsibility-Absolute Insurer Rule. This rule has been upheld in most parimutuel jurisdictions by the highest appellate court of the respective states. Therefore, the majority rule at this time is that a trainer can have his license suspended or revoked based on a violation of the Trainer Responsibility Rule, even if the trainer can submit evidence adduced from a lie detector test or other sources showing that he had absolutely no part in medicating the horse and had no knowledge that the horse was, in fact, medicated. This type of decision again reflects the attitude of the courts in serving the state's interest in preventing fraud at the racetrack while maintaining public confidence in the integrity of the sport, at the expense of the constitutional rights of the individual trainer or other license holder.

How, then, should an owner or trainer respond to a charge of a medication rule violation? As in all legal disputes, the best time to win any lawsuit is in the first instance. Therefore, any owner or trainer faced with a suspension or revocation of a license should approach the stewards hearing with a serious attitude. He should be represented by legal counsel and should be prepared to take any and all steps necessary to prove his innocence.

If a trainer appears at the stewards hearing on a charge of alleged medication violation and takes a passive role by just listening to the state's witnesses, almost surely the decision of the stewards will be that the medication violation did, in fact, take place, and by application of the Trainer Responsibility Rule the trainer's license will be suspended. If at that point the trainer believes that he has been aggrieved and wishes to appeal the matter to the State Racing Commission, he then will have the burden of being the appellant in the matter, asking the commission to overrule a decision reached by their stewards. Even if the administrative law in the state in question provides that the commission hearing will be a de novo type of hearing, with the burden again placed on the commission to prove the alleged violation, the trainer stands in the first light before the commission as having been found guilty by the stewards. This in and of itself places a burden, whether legal or not, on the trainer to rebut the decision reached by the stewards. The proceedings before any racing commission are generally much more formal in nature than the proceedings conducted at the stewards hearing. The defendant should make all reasonable explanations for the situation and call in whatever expert witnesses he can avail himself of to explain his side of the matter.

There are two very sound reasons why a trainer charged with a medication violation should have the assistance of counsel and prepare fully and diligently for the hearing before the racing commission. First, if the accused can convince the commission that there is a defect in the testing collection or other proceedings involved with the medication violation, then, in fact, the proceedings should be dismissed. Second, if the state meets the requirement of showing that all of the proper procedures were followed and all the testing procedures were accurate, then the trainer should still have all mitigating evidence of which he can avail himself to justify or excuse why the violation arose. If the decision of the commission is then favorable, the matter is ended. However, if the racing commission upholds the stewards' decision that a medication violation did occur and that the trainer's license is to be suspended for a period of time or revoked, then the accused must recognize that in most jurisdictions the administrative procedure acts of the respective states limit the scope of the hearing that will be conducted in the courts if the trainer appeals the commission's decision to the appropriate reviewing court.

Generally no new evidence can be introduced at the reviewing court level, but rather the court will look at the transcript from the commission hearing with the only possibility of overturning the commission's decision being based generally on one of two challenges: a constitutional challenge to one of the statutes or rules involved, or the traditional challenge that the finding of the administrative agency, in this case the racing commission, was arbitrary and not supported by substantial evidence. This rule was brought out in the famous 1968 Kentucky Derby case, wherein the horse, DANCER'S IMAGE, was disqualified from first place on a report of the racing commission's testing laboratory that the urine sample taken from the horse after the race contained the prohibited substance phenylbutazone.[6]

After a lengthy stewards hearing, which was subsequently appealed to the Kentucky State Racing Commission, and an even more extensive and lengthy

---

[6] Kentucky State Racing Commission v. Peter Fuller, 481 S.W.2d 298 (1972).

commission hearing, the decision to disqualify DANCER'S IMAGE from first place was upheld. Thereafter the matter was appealed to the Franklin Circuit Court, which held that the commission and stewards' decision should be set aside for lack of substantial evidence to support the decision. The racing commission then appealed to the Court of Appeals, which affirmed the decision of the stewards and the commision. The appellate court held that on an appeal from the racing commission, no additional evidence could be introduced except as to fraud or misconduct of some party engaged in the administration of the act and effecting the order appealed from. The court otherwise would hear the case upon the hearing as attested by the commission. Upon the appeal, the reviewing court was limited to determining whether or not (a) the commission acted without or in excess of its power; (b) the order appealed from was procured by fraud; and (c) if questions of fact were an issue, whether or not substantial evidence in the record supported the Order appealed from.

Therefore, an owner or trainer charged with a medication violation who has pursued the full administrative process of both a stewards hearing and commission hearing takes a very limited appeal to the reviewing court in almost all racing jurisdictions that have an administrative procedure act or statute similar to that in Kentucky. Courts traditionally have been reluctant to overturn a decision of an administrative agency absent of showing of abuse of discretion, lack of substantial evidence, fraud, or valid constitutional issue. Generally, courts follow the standard rule relied upon by the Kentucky Court in the DANCER'S IMAGE case:

> In determining whether the findings of the Commission challenged by plaintiffs are arbitrary or capricious or unsupported by substantial evidence, the Court is not free to substitute its judgment for that of the Commission as to the weight of the evidence or the inferences to be drawn from the evidence.

After the completion of the stewards hearing, if the decision is adverse to the license holder, the question then is should the licensee follow the administrative process and appeal the decision to the racing commission for a prompt hearing, or should the licensee at that point attempt to depart from the administrative process and file suit to prevent the imposition of the stewards' ruling on a claim of error, or on constitutional grounds?

Numerous cases can be cited wherein a trainer, owner, jockey, or other licensed person in racing has gone to court seeking a Temporary Restraining Order alleging irreparable damage if his or her license is suspended. One very interesting case concerning this position arose in Illinois, where a driver of a harness horse won a permanent injunction in the Illinois Circuit Court prohibiting the Illinois Racing Board from hearing charges alleging violations of the state medication rules.[7]

The trainer claimed that to allow the commission to hear charges against him would severely damage his reputation and thus impair his earning power in conducting a racing stable. The state of Illinois countered, claiming that the trainer had failed to exhaust his administrative remedies, and the Illinois Supreme Court agreed. The Supreme Court decision rendered by Judge Goldenhersh stated that —

---

[7] Graham v. Illinois Racing Boad, 394 N.E.2d 1148 (1979).

The administrative proceedings and the available judicial review provide ample opportunity to determine the admissibility into evidence of the urine specimens, and we are not persuaded that plaintiff was without an adequate remedy at law.

Further the court held in response to the plaintiff's contention that his reputation and earning power would be damaged in that —

The proceedings commenced against the plaintiff by the Board would result in no greater harm to his reputation than that suffered by one required to defend against a criminal prosecution brought lawfully and in good faith.

The long-standing rule in administrative law has been that the party charged with violating an administrative rule must exhaust his administrative remedies before being able to seek the intervention or relief of the judicial system. However, in numerous cases, the courts failed to exercise the restraint established in law and on a minimal showing of possible harm have issued Temporary Restraining Orders preventing stewards or commissions from conducting hearings into certain matters or from suspending a license pending completion of the court process.

The reason that so many licensees have sought the haven of the court process at the earliest time is the fact that court calendars are clogged, and once a case is filed, it oftentimes drags on for months or years, while the trainer continues to race under the authority of the Temporary Restraining Order.

Probably the most pressing question to any owner or trainer involved in a medication issue is whether his license to participate in racing can be summarily suspended on a report of a positive test prior to a hearing either before the stewards or the commission. A 1975 West Virginia case answered this question in the affirmative.[8] The West Virginia Racing Rules provided that the stewards at any race meeting could suspend a license and such suspension would be effective immediately. The rule then made the obligation on the person affected to demand a hearing but provided that such a demand for hearing did not operate to stay or suspend the execution of any Order suspending or revoking the owner-trainer license.

The owner-trainer appealed to the commission, and when the commission refused to stay the suspension the owner-trainer then filed suit in Federal District Court seeking a determination that the No Stay Rule was unconstitutional. The Federal District Court ruled against the owner-trainer's contentions, and an appeal was made to the United States Court of Appeals Fourth Circuit. The parties agreed in federal court that the owner-trainer's license was a "property right" and that due process required the owner-trainer be given notice, a hearing, and an opportunity to defend his interests if the license is to be suspended or revoked. The narrow issue presented to the court on appeal was whether the license suspension could *precede* the notice and hearing which due process required.

The appellate court examined decisions from other administrative areas where prior notice and hearing were not mandated before a suspension was imposed. The court's final decision was again based upon a balancing of the normal and

---

[8] Hubel v. West Virginia Racing Commission, 513 F.2d 240 (1975).

usual right to notice and hearing before disciplinary sanctions were imposed versus the humanitarian interest in protecting the health of the horse and the broader and the more weighty interest in protecting the purity of the sport, to protect the revenues derived from parimutuel operations and for the protection of the betting public. The court in its ruling said in part —

> The combination of strict liability, imposed by Rule 793, (Trainer Responsibility Rule) and immediate suspension without the possibility of stay, deters tampering and promotes care. The combination also removes from racing those who would have proved either unable or unwilling to protect their horses from unauthorized drugs.

This decision was widely followed in racing circles.

The right to suspend a license prior to hearing was subsequently affirmed in a 1979 United States Supreme Court decision. A Mr. Barchi was a trainer of Standardbred horses, and a horse that he raced at Monticello Raceway tested positive for the presence of Lasix®.[9] To substantiate his innocence in administering any prohibitive substance to the horse in question, Mr. Barchi took two polygraph tests, which confirmed his innocence in the matter. However, his license was suspended for fifteen days by the racing officials at the track. Mr. Barchi thereafter sued claiming infringement of his constitutional rights and denial of due process and equal protection.

Mr. Barchi made three major contentions, the first being a due process question in that he was suspended prior to a hearing. Secondly, he claimed that the harness racing statutes did not provide for administrative stays whereas the Thoroughbred racing law in New York did provide for such stays. Thirdly, as in all medication lawsuits, Mr. Barchi also challenged the constitutionality of the Trainer Responsibility Rule. The United States District Court upheld Mr. Barchi's first two contentions and denied the third. Thereafter, the New York Racing and Wagering Board appealed to the United States Supreme Court.

Justice White, speaking for the majority of the court, stated that due process as it pertained to the facts of the Barchi matter required an opportunity for Barchi to be heard at a meaningful time and in a meaningful manner. In general, a state is entitled to impose an interim suspension of the license of a horse trainer without affording the trainer an evidentiary hearing prior to suspension, whenever it has been satisfactorily established that there is probable cause to believe that a horse handled by a trainer has been drugged and that the trainer has been at least negligent in connection with the drugging. Thus, a horse trainer is afforded all the process that is due to him prior to the interim suspension of his license without a presuspension hearing, as authorized by state law on the basis of a post-race urinalysis test revealing the presence of drugs in the system of a horse handled by the trainer, provided there are statutory or administrative rules that guarantee the trainer a prompt postsuspension judicial or administrative hearing that will definitely determine the issues.

The justices affirmed the concept that the trainer's license could be suspended without an evidentiary hearing being conducted, provided there was a prompt postsuspension hearing conducted into the full matter. The court stated that during the interim suspension stage, an expert's affirmance of the positive drug

---

[9] Barry v. Barchi, 61 L. Ed.2d 365 (1979).

test, although unsubstantiated and not beyond error, would appear sufficiently reliable to satisfy constitutional requirements. The Supreme Court did hold that it was necessary in this instance that Barchi be assured of a prompt postsuspension hearing, one that would proceed and be concluded without appreciable delay. The court determined that the New York statutes at that time as applied to Barchi's case were deficient in that respect, and the suspension was constitutionally infirm under the Due Process Clause of the Fourteenth Amendment. The court went on to uphold the state's right to prohibit administrative stays in harness racing, even though such stays were available under Thoroughbred racing rules.

Additionally, the court upheld the constitutionality of the New York Trainer Responsibility Rule disallowing Barchi's constitutional challenge to that statute.

Again we see a case that was not decided on the actual merits of the rule wording itself but rather on the administration of the rule, in that the court determined that there was no assurance that there would be a prompt postsuspension hearing held in that the commission had a period of at least thirty days in which to render a decision after the commission hearing.

Many trainers have found themselves in the position where they have served the suspension time meted out by the stewards before the validity of their claim was decided either by a racing commission or by a court after a hearing and decision. Many racing jurisdictions have now amended their statutes to provide for the type of prompt postsuspension hearings and decisions referred to by the United States Supreme Court in the Barchi case.

As a result of a final hearing, administrative or judicial, determining that the trainer was guilty of a violation of a medication rule, the next ruling in conjunction with that decision is a ruling placing the medicated horse last in the order of finish and redistributing the purse money in the race. This situation has caused some great concern and criticism to all officials and licensees in racing due to the fact that the public has already been paid on the parimutuel decision that the medicated horse won the race, yet, in fact, some other owner will receive the purse money awarded to the adjusted order of finish in that race.

Recently several owners have filed challenges to the purse redistribution sanction resulting from a medication violation. The court decisions seem to unanimously support the authority of the stewards and the racing commissions to redistribute purses.

A group of owners in Illinois filed suit after a rash of apomorphine cases when they received notice that the purses would be redistributed. The contention of the owners was that such a redistribution was unconstitutional in that it deprived them of money earned without evidence that the owners had been personally liable for the violations.[10] The Federal District Court ruled that the plaintiffs' defense was not substantiated in that the court determined that fixing of responsibility for drugging is not an unnecessary precondition for the denial of prize money. There is a sufficiently rational relationship between the rule as written and the legitimate government purpose that the Due Process Clause is not offended. Similar reasoning would satisfy any equal protection claim lodged by the owner.

In a 1977 Kentucky case, William C. Jacobs sued the Kentucky State Racing

---

[10] Edelberg v. Illinois Racing Board, Cause No. 75C951, U.S. Dist. Ct. for Northern Dist. (1975).

Commission as a result of a ruling by the commission that the purse money from Mr. Jacobs' horse, who was a winner at Keeneland on April 26, 1973, but later tested positive for a phenylbutazone derivative, would be redistributed to the susequently placed horses.[11] Mr. Jacobs challenged first the authority of the Kentucky State Racing Commission to enact and enforce a rule that would prohibit participation in the purse distribution by a horse that tested positive for a prohibited medication. The Kentucky Appellate Court answered the challenge in the following language:

> That statute provides that it is in the interest of the public . . . to vest in the Commission forceful control of thoroughbred racing. . . . Moreover, the statutes permit rules which condemn the presence of prohibited substances which affect the speed or health of a race horse. . . . The record indicates that the subject animal had a history of chronic ankle trouble. The medication was prescribed to reduce pain. The ultimate affect of the alleviation of such pain on the outcome of the race or the speed of the horse is clearly within the purview of the Commission's authority as enunciated by the statutes. . . .

Mr. Jacobs then raised the question that seemed to cause the courts more concern: the testing of winners only in a race without testing the horses that would be advanced to first position as a result of a positive test on the winner. Although the court disallowed the owners' challenge due to the action being a legitimate classification based on long-standing custom and practice, the court did indicate that the racing commission might consider an amendment to the testing procedures to test at least the second and third place horses, who would have an increased share in the purse monies if the first place horse were disqualified.

As we enter the decade of the 1980s, persons holding an owner's, trainer's, or other racing license must recognize that even though the courts may hold such a license to be a valuable property right protected by constitutional guarantees, recent court decisions have diminished the constitutional rights of the license holders, especially in the area of medication violations, where the courts seem to be offended by the type of violation charged when the court is called upon to balance the interests of the public against the rights of the individual license holder.

---

[11] Jacobs v. Kentucky State Racing Commission, Ky. App., 562 SW2d 641 (1977).

ACTUAL "CLEARANCE TIMES" FOR DRUGS IN HORSES

WHILE THE PRACTICAL MATTER of "clearance times" for drugs in horses depends on the analyst's methods it is also possible to quite easily calculate the actual clearance times for drugs in horses. This is because manipulations such as are presented in Figure 4-3 deal with the abstract concept of concentrations. In actuality, however, if a horse continues to excrete a drug, its concentration must at some point drop to one drug molecule per horse, and even that single drug molecule will eventually be excreted in most horses. It is relatively easy to calculate what this time period is likely to be for individual drugs, and in this example we do so for phenylbutazone in a horse.

Before we can perform this calculation, we need to know how many drug molecules we inject into a horse with a dose of phenylbutazone. Avogadro's number tells us that 6×10^{23} is the number of molecules contained in the gram molecular weight of any substance, and 308 grams is the gram molecular weight of phenylbutazone. The usual 3 gm/1000 lb. horse dose of phenylbutazone therefore

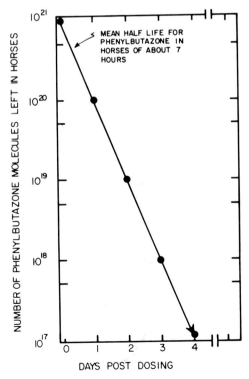

Figure A-1. Actual clearance time for phenylbutazone in horses. The solid circles (●) show the daily decline in the blood levels of phenylbutazone in horses, in which its plasma half-life is about seven hours. About 10^{21} molecules are injected into the horse, and only 10^{20} are left after the first day. If this process continues at about the same rate, the horse will be excreting the last of its phenylbutazone on the twenty-first day postdosing.

contains about 6×10^{21} molecules of phenylbutazone, and this is the number of phenylbutazone molecules that we inject into a horse with each 3 gm dose.

If we assume that the half-life of phenylbutazone in our average horse is about seven hours, then in twenty-four hours the horse will clear 90 percent or 1 log unit of this dose of phenylbutazone from his system (Fig. A-1). In the next twenty-four hours he will clear another 90 percent or so, and by twenty-one days after the dose he will be clearing the last of the phenylbutazone from his system. Therefore, a drug with about a seven-hour half-life will "clear" the system of the horse within about twenty-one days.

Since the number of drug molecules injected into a horse is not likely to be less than about 10^{16} for even the most potent drugs, the time taken for any drug to clear a horse is about sixteen to twenty times the number of days that it takes the horse to clear a log unit of the drug. For example, if a drug has a urinary half-life of about twenty-four hours, it will then take about 3.3 days to clear a log unit of the drug and therefore about sixty-six days for the drug to actually clear the horse. Alternatively, a simple rule of thumb (Tobin's rule) is that it takes about 6 half-lives for any drug to clear a horse.

WHY URINARY pH AFFECTS THE DISTRIBUTION OF SOME DRUGS

THE DRUGS WHOSE DISTRIBUTION in the body depends on whether the body fluid is acidic or basic are themselves weak acids or weak bases. Acidic drugs, such as penicillin, furosemide, and many of the non-steroidal anti-inflammatory drugs, tend to carry negative charges under physiological conditions (Fib. B-1). On the other hand, basic drugs such as procaine, amphetamine and pentazocine tend to carry positive charges (Fig. B-2). There also exists a group of neutral drugs, such as caffeine and reserpine, which carries no predominant charge. Analysts usually classify drugs as either acidic, neutral, or basic drugs, depending on the charge they carry, for the very good reason that this classification determines the way they analyze them.

The charge that a drug carries is important to the horseman and the analyst

ACIDIC DRUGS CARRY GROUPS SUCH AS COOH, WHICH EASILY LOSE A H⁺ TO GIVE A NEGATIVELY CHARGED MOLECULE. EG. LASIX

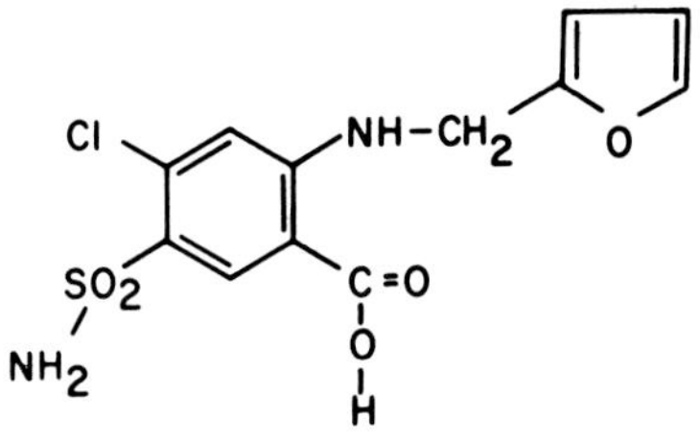

UNDER ALKALINE CONDITIONS, WITH A LOW CONCENTRATION OF H⁺, THIS BECOMES:

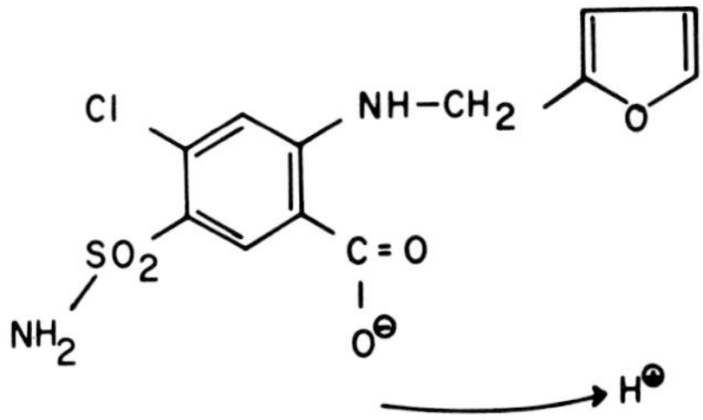

AND THE NEGATIVE CHARGE BINDS LASIX TO WATER MOLECULES.

Figure B-1

BASIC DRUGS EASILY PICK UP A H$^+$ TO GIVE A POSITIVELY CHARGED MOLECULE. EG. PROCAINE

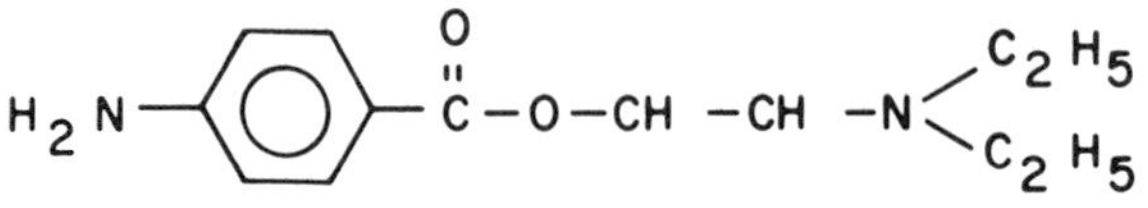

UNDER ACIDIC CONDITIONS, WITH HIGH CONCENTRATION OF H$^+$, THIS BECOMES:

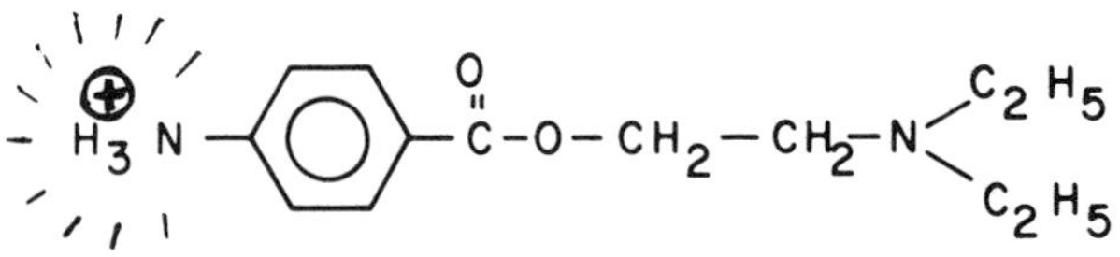

AND THE POSITIVE CHARGE BINDS PROCAINE TO WATER MOLECULES.

Figure B-2

because it can profoundly affect distribution of the drug between urine and the kidney in a horse, or between urine and an organic solvent in the analyst's laboratory. The experiment of Figure B-3 shows how procaine distributes between the organic solvent benzene and water as the acidity (pH) of the water changes. If the water is acidic, and therefore contains an excess of hydrogen ions (H$^+$), the procaine stays in the water and will not move into the benzene. Under these conditions, the procaine is essentially trapped in the water. On the other hand, if the system is basic (alkaline), the procaine moves into the benzene and can easily be extracted by the analyst. To get basic drugs such as procaine out of a blood or urine sample, the analyst makes the blood or urine basic (alkaline), and under these conditions the procaine moves rapidly from the aqueous solution into the organic solution.

The reason procaine stays in the blood or urine under acidic conditions is that it picks up a H$^+$ readily in acidic solution (Fig. B-2). This H$^+$ makes the procaine molecule positively charged, and it binds more tightly to the water molecules, each of which carries a negative charge on the oxygen and a positive charge on the hydrogen. Under acidic conditions, therefore, it is very difficult to get procaine to move out of water, blood or urine, and this is the reason that procaine tends to trap in acidic urines (Fig. B-3). This can be very easily demonstrated experimentally (Fig. B-4), and one can also calculate what the theoretical distribution between blood and urine would be, given that horse plasma usually has a pH of about 7.4, while that of urine may vary from about pH 4.0 to pH 9.5.

These pH-dependent ratios are calculated from the following transformation of the Henderson-Hasselbalch equation:

$$\frac{(Plasma)}{(Urine)} = \frac{1 + antilog\ (pHa - pH)}{1 + antilog\ (pKa - pH)}$$

Given that the pKa of procaine is 8.7, and assuming an acidic urine of pH 4.7, a basic urine of pH 9.7, and a plasma pH of 7.4, in the basic urine:

$$\frac{(Plasma\ Drug)}{(Urinary\ Drug)} = \frac{1 + antilog\ (8.7 - 7.4)}{1 + antilog\ (8.7 - 9.7)} = \frac{21}{1.1} = \frac{19}{1}$$

Therefore, this basic urine will contain $\frac{1}{19}$ of the procaine that the plasma contains.

In the acidic urine:

$$\frac{(Plasma\ Drug)}{(Urinary\ Drug)} = \frac{1 + antilog\ (8.7 - 7.4)}{1 + antilog\ (8.7 - 4.7)} = \frac{21}{10,1001} = \frac{1}{476}$$

Therefore, this acidic urine will contain 476 times more procaine than the plasma.

DISTRIBUTION OF PROCAINE BETWEEN WATER AND BENZENE

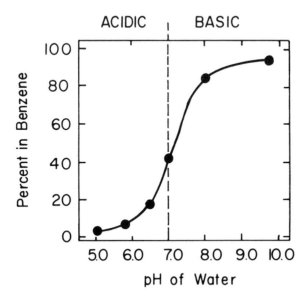

UNDER ACID CONDITIONS MOST OF THE PROCAINE
STAYS IN THE WATER. UNDER BASIC CONDITIONS
IT MOVES INTO THE BENZENE.

Figure B-3

EACH WATER MOLECULE IS CHARGED, CARRYING POSITIVE
CHARGES ON THE HYDROGEN AND NEGATIVE ON THE OXYGEN.

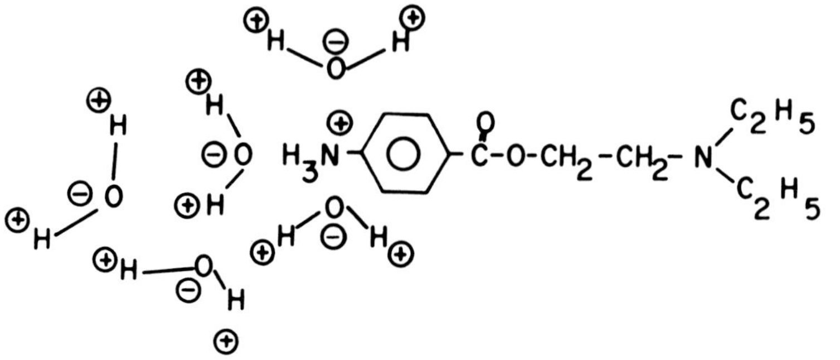

BECAUSE OF THESE CHARGES, WATER BINDS STRONGLY TO
CHARGED DRUG MOLECULES, WHETHER THEY ARE POSITIVELY
OR NEGATIVELY CHARGED.

Figure B-4

The possible theoretical range of urinary procaine concentrations given a single plasmas concentration is therefore $19 \times 476 = 9044$ or a more than 9,000-fold possible range in urinary procaine concentration. Whether or not this huge range is actually reached in practice is academic; the calculation clearly shows that urinary levels of drugs can be tremendously variable and are not useful for indicating anything more than the presence of the drug.

Much the same holds for acidic drugs, which will tend to stay in water or urine under basic conditions and move into organic solvents under acidic conditions. This phenomenon depends on the fact that every water molecule carries a small positive charge on both its hydrogens and a negative charge on its oxygens. Thus, drugs carrying a negative charge (Lasix®) will bond to the hydrogen ends of a water molecule and not move out of aqueous solution. However, if one puts Lasix® in an acidic solution, it will pick up a H^+, lose its net charge, and under these conditions move into the organic solvent. In this way, it is possible for an analyst to control the movement of many drugs between water and organic solvents (or tissues) simply by varying the acidity (hydrogen ion concentration, pH) of the drug's environment.

The analyst uses this property of drugs when he wants to extract a drug from blood or urine. If he wants to extract a basic drug, he simply renders the plasma or urine basic by adding an alkaline solution, shakes it up with an organic solvent, and the basic drugs move into the solvent, as in Figure 23-3. If he wants to extract an acidic drug, he makes the plasma or urine acidic, shakes it up with the organic solvent, and the acidic drugs move into the organic solvent. As we saw in Chapter 22, this process is usually the first step on the part of the analyst in the drug detection process.

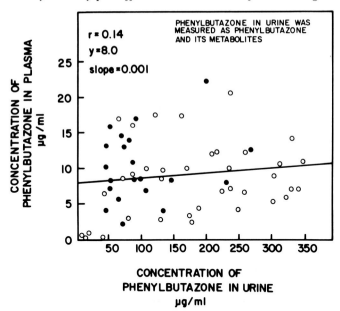

Figure B-5. Correlation between plasma and urinary levels of "phenylbutazone." Blood and urinary levels of phenylbutazone in fifty-eight racing horses were compared. Blood levels of phenylbutazone were measured by gas chromatography, while urinary levels of phenylbutazone were measured as "phenylbutazone" and its metabolites by UV analysis. The open circles (o—o) show the correlation between these levels for horses treated with phenylbutazone alone, while the solid circles (●—●) show the correlation for those urine samples in which furosemide was detected. The data show that there is essentially no correlation between blood levels of phenylbutazone and urinary concentrations of phenylbutazone and its metabolites.

A good practical example of the discrepancies that one may expect between plasma and urinary concentrations of drugs is presented in Figure B-5. In this illustration we have plotted the blood levels of phenylbutazone in fifty-eight horses against the urinary concentrations of phenylbutazone and its metabolites. The concentration of phenylbutazone and its metabolite in the urine sample was measured by the method commonly used by drug testing laboratories. If there was a direct relationship between blood and urinary levels of the drug, the line through the points would start at zero in the lower left-hand corner of the figure and slope upwards toward the opposite corner of the graph, with the points distributed closely around the line. In actual fact, however, the line of best fit to these very scattered data is almost a horizontal straight line! This means that there is essentially no correlation between these urinary concentrations of phenylbutazone and its metabolites and the blood levels of phenylbutazone. For example, inspection of the graph shows that one can have blood levels of phenylbutazone of about 9 µg/ml associated with urinary concentrations of from 70 µg/ml to 325 µg/ml. Thus, urinary concentrations of phenylbutazone and its metabolites bear no relationship whatsoever to blood levels of phenylbutazone and therefore presumably to dosage levels of this drug.

THE BUFFERING ROLE OF BICARBONATE IN BLOOD

BICARBONATE IS PRESENT in blood in three forms, and these forms are all in equilibrium as described by the following equation:

$$CO_2 + H_2O \rightleftharpoons H_2CO_3 \rightleftharpoons H^+ + HCO_3^-$$

The normal concentration of HCO_3^- in equine blood is about 26 mM/Liter, while that of H_2CO_3 is about 1.3 mM Liter, and the pKa of H_2CO_3 is about 6.1. The relationship between pH, pKa, and the concentrations of carbonate and bicarbonate in this system may be expressed by the Henderson-Hasselbach equation:

$$pH = pKa \; Log \frac{[HCO_3^-]}{[H_2CO_3]}$$

$$\therefore pH = 6.1 + Log \frac{26}{1.3} = 6.1 + 1.3 = 7.4$$

Therefore, the pH of the blood is maintained at about 7.4 as long as the ratio of HCO_3^- to H_2CO_3 is about 20:1. The pH of the blood is kept within the normal range by respiration, which can "blow off" excessive CO_2, and by the kidney, which can vary its elimination of HCO_3^- or H^+ as required. As a maneuver in fluid therapy, either acid or base or volume may be added to the horse to restore these parameters to normal.

BAYES' THEOREM AND EQUINE DRUG TESTING

O NE OF THE MAJOR PROBLEMS facing forensic chemists in adversary proceedings involving drug identification is determining the probability of error in the identification of drugs. In the equine drug testing area, forensic samples are traditionally identified as being "positive" for a named drug. Using this notation, an erroneous identification is referred to as a "false positive," and one of the problems facing all concerned in adversary hearings is to determine the probability that these classifications are correctly assigned.

Reviewing the statistical basis upon which decisions in the equine drug testing area are sometimes based, I was struck by the very substantial discrepancy between the statistical basis for these decisions and the normally accepted statistical criteria for accuracy in scientific work. Considering this problem, I discussed it with Doctor Peter Purdue, a colleague in the University of Kentucky Statistics Department. Doctor Purdue told me that what I had stumbled on was Bayes' theorem, Bayes having been an eighteenth-century English clergyman who pioneered the mathematical treatment of the probability of error in situations similar to equine drug testing. The purpose of this Appendix is to outline Bayes' theorem and show how it applies to equine drug testing and to drug testing in general.*

Bayes theorem is essentially a way of updating probabilities in the light of experimental evidence. In the present context we consider the "experiment" of selecting a horse at random from a well-defined group, subjecting the horse to a certain test, and on the basis of this test assigning the horse to one of two groups: *drug free* and *not drug free*. Because all real tests have some finite probability of error, there will be errors involved in the making of these assignments. Here we examine the impact of uncertainty due to two sources, error in the test, and the frequency of drug use in the population.

For the purposes of this analysis, let —

D + be the event that the selected horse is *not drug free*
D − be the event that the selected horse is *drug free*
T + be the event that the selected horse gives a "positive" test score
T − be the event that the selected horse is given a "negative" test score

We assume that certain frequencies or probabilities are known:

  (i) the probability of D +, i.e. P(D +) = p, say
 (ii) the probability of T + given D +, i.e. P(T +/D +), assumed to be 1
(iii) the probability of T + given D −, i.e. P(T +/D −) = Θ, say

The two parameters of the model are p, the frequency of drugged horses in the population of horses under study, and Θ, the frequency of false positives.

---

* This appendix represents a very abbreviated approach to this problem. A more detailed analysis is being developed for publication.

Since we wish to determine the probability that a positive test result is a true positive, the value we require is that of $P(D+/T+)$. The form of Bayes' theorem we need states —

$$P(D+/T+) = \frac{P(T+/D+)\ P(D+)}{P(T+/D+)\ P(D+)\ +\ P(T+/D-)\ P(D-)}$$

Letting $\pi+ = P(D+/T+)$ this can be written as —

$$\pi+ = \frac{p}{p + (1-p)\,\Theta}$$

Before the analyst will assign a horse to the "drugged" group, $\pi+$ must be very close to 1, say at least .95. As we shall see, in the present framework, Θ must be almost zero for $\pi+$ to attain such high values when p is very small.

Some indication of the joint behavior of $\pi+$ and Θ is given in Figure D-1.

The dependence of $\pi+$ upon the population parameter p can be clearly seen. For example, when $p = .01$, i.e. the pool of horses contains 1 percent drugged horses, to get a value of $+\geq.95$ we need a value of $\Theta\leq.0005$. This means only about 5 false positives per 10,000 test applications! And the problem becomes even worse when the more realistic p value of .001 is chosen. Then $\Theta\leq.00005$ is needed, i.e. 5 false positives per 100,000 test applications.

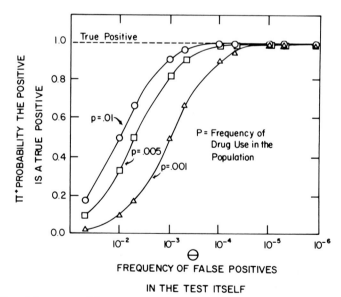

Figure D-1. Effect of frequency of drug use on the probability of a true positive. The probability that a called "positive" is a true positive is shown on the vertical axis, against inherent test accuracy on the horizontal axis. The open circles (o—o) show the probability of a false positive when the rate of drug use in the population being tested is 1%, and the accuracy of the test or tests uses is varied as indicated on the horizontal axis. Even with this relatively high rate of drug use, the test must be known to be accurate to more than 1×10^{-4} for the probability that a called "positive" is a true positive to be 99% or greater. When the ratio of drug use in the population is lower, either .05% (open squares, □—□) or .01% (triangles, ▵—▵), the accuracy of the tests used must be correspondingly increased to maintain a 99% probability that a positive is a true positive.

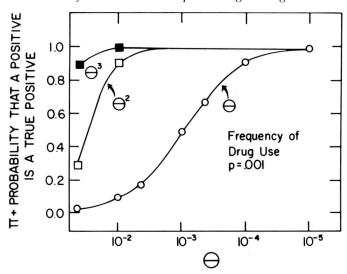

FREQUENCY OF FALSE POSITIVES IN THE TEST

Figure D-2. Effect of multiple independent tests on the probability of error in drug testing. In this illustration, the probability that a positive is a true positive is displayed on the vertical axis against the inherent error rate in the test on the horizontal axis. The open circles (o—o) show the probability of a true positive, given a population frequency of drug use of 0.001 (0.1%) using only a single test (Θ). If, however, two independent tests with the same error rate are used (Θ^2), the probability of a true positive is that indicated by the open squares (□—□). If three independent tests are used (Θ^3), the probability of a true positive is that indicated by the solid squares (■—■).

This raises very serious validation problems. To validate the test procedure, a sample of drug-free horses is chosen, the test administered, and the proportion of false positives, $\hat{\Theta}$, recorded. $\hat{\Theta}$ is an estimate of Θ. In order that a 95 percent confidence interval for $\hat{\Theta}$ be within 10 percent of the true value of Θ, a sample of size equal to approximately 1,000,000 would be needed! Clearly, such a procedure to validate forensic tests is unworkable.

The situation is much improved, however, if independent tests are available. This is because for tests of equivalent accuracy, the value of Θ is raised to the power of the number of tests. The effect of this on the probability of false positives is shown in Figure D-2. In this illustration we set the frequency of drug use in the population at .001, or 1 in 1,000, and examine the effect of an increased number of independent tests. While a single test needs to be validated at the 1 : 10,000 level, three *independent* tests with an error rate of 1 : 100 give a Θ value of 1/1,000,000 and as such are more than sufficient to reduce the probability of a false positive very substantially.

These observations and calculations, therefore, show that the approach of seeking to validate a forensic test by screening small numbers of horses in blind or other tests is futile and demonstrates a basic lack of understanding of the quantitative aspects of drug testing programs. Unfortunately, tests on such small numbers of horses are often carried out in the racing industry and may be used to impress uninformed adjudicators, who are not likely to be familiar with the probability of error when such tests are applied in routine testing.

The second conclusion to be drawn from this analysis is that if a number of completely independent tests are used, the probability of a false positive can be greatly reduced. Because the effect of independent tests is to raise Θ to the power of the number of tests, Θ can be rapidly reduced to a very useful value. Thus, while one test with an inherent error rate of 1 percent is not in and of itself a very useful test, three independent tests of the same quality can be very useful tests indeed. This is because the probability of error in a sample that has yielded a positive score in three independent tests is $(0.01)^3$ or 1×10^{-6}, i.e. the combination has a potential accuracy of one error in 1,000,000 tests.

This power of combined tests requires that the tests be absolutely independent of each other. If two tests are subject to the same type of error, this reduces the power by which Θ is raised and thus the power of the combination. This would, of course, rule out claims that running thin-layer tests in different solvent systems or GC systems at different temperatures constitutes independent tests when, for example, an error in the visualization of such tests could render all the tests incorrect.

The second consideration about the power of such combined tests is that the sample must pass all the tests to which it is subjected. If, for example, a given sample yielded a positive for a drug on three tests but failed a fourth, failure on the fourth would automatically negate the previous three "positives." This is a rigorous requirement of the "step" testing approach, and analysts who find a sample positive in three tests for a drug but negative in a fourth test must keep this requirement in mind and not call a positive based on the three positive tests.

A third conclusion from the value of multiplicative tests is that it may be possible to experimentally validate individual tests at a low level of accuracy. To validate tests at the 0.01 percent level of error, relatively modest numbers of horses are required. Thus, experimental tests would serve to validate individual tests at that level, and use of this method could allow one to validate a sequence of tests on a relatively small number of horses.

SELECTED REFERENCES

Duer, W. C., DeKanel, J., and Hall, T. D.: A necessary condition for drug identification. *Proc Third International Symposium on Equine Medication Control*, Lexington, KY, 1979, in press.

Parzen, E.: *Modern Probability Theory and Its Application*. New York, Wiley, 1960.

Ray, R. S., Sams, R. A., and Huffman, R.: Detection, identification and quantitation of reserpine and diazepam. *Proc Second Equine Pharmacology Symposium*. Golden, CO, AAEP, 1979, pp. 209-215.

The Chemical Laboratory and its Role in Racing, Second Revision. Jamaica, NY, American Association of Official Racing Chemists, 1974, p. 30.

NATIONAL ASSOCIATION OF STATE RACING COMMISSIONERS PROPOSED NATIONAL MEDICATION GUIDELINES, APRIL 1980

Rule 1.01. It shall be the intent of these rules to protect the integrity of horse racing, to guard the health of the horse, and to safeguard the interests of the public and the racing participants through the prohibition or control of all drugs and medications or substances foreign to the natural horse. In this context:

(a) No horse participating in a race shall carry in its body any substance foreign to the natural horse except as hereinafter provided.

(b) No foreign substance shall be administered to a horse entered to race by injection, oral administration, rectal infusion or suppository, or by inhalation within 24 hours prior to the scheduled post time for the first race, except as hereinafter provided.

(c) No person other than a veterinarian shall have in his/her possession any equipment for hypodermic injection, any substance for hypodermic administration, or any foreign substance which can be administered internally to a horse by any route, except for an existing condition and as prescribed by a veterinarian. The supply of such prescribed foreign substance(s) shall be limited by ethical practice consistent with the purposes of this rule.

(d) Notwithstanding the provisions of Rule 1.01(c) above any person may have in his possession within a race track enclosure any chemical or biological substance for use on his own person, provided that, if such chemical substance is prohibited from being dispensed by any Federal law or law of this state without a prescription, he is in possession of documentary evidence that a valid prescription for such chemical or biological substance has been issued to him.

(e) Notwithstanding the provisions of Rule 1.01(c) above, any person may have in his possession within any race track enclosure any hypodermic syringe or needle for the purpose of administering a chemical or biological substance to himself, provided that he has notified the state steward: 1) of his possession of such device, 2) of the size of such device, and 3) of the chemical substance to be administered by such device, and has obtained written permission for possession and use from the state steward.

Rule 1.02. The terms and words used in these rules are defined as:

(a) *Hypodermic Injection* shall mean any injection into or under the skin or mucosa, including intradermal injection, subcutaneous injection, submucosal injection, intramuscular injection, intravenous injection, intra-arterial injection, intra-articular injection, intrabursal injection, intraocular (intraconjunctival) injection.

(b) *Foreign Substances* shall mean all substances except those which exist naturally in the untreated horse at normal physiological concentration.

(c) *Veterinarian* shall mean a veterinary practitioner authorized to practice on the race track.

(d) *Horse* includes all horses registered for racing under the jurisdiction of the Commission or Board, and for the purposes of this regulation shall mean stallion, colt, gelding, ridgling, filly or mare.

(e) *Chemist* shall mean any official racing chemist designated by the Commission.

(f) *Test Sample* shall mean any body substance including but not limited to blood or urine taken from a horse under the supervision of the Commission Veterinarian and in such manner as prescribed by the Commission for the purpose of analysis.

(g) *Race Day* shall mean the 24-hour period prior to the scheduled post time for the first race.

(h) *Test Level* shall mean the concentration of a foreign substance found in the test sample.

(i) *Bleeder* shall mean a horse which hemorrhages from within the respiratory tract during a race or within one hour post-race, or during exercise or within one hour of such exercise.

(j) *Bleeder List* shall mean a tabulation of all bleeders to be maintained by the Commission.

(k) *Furosemide* shall mean 4-chloro-N-(2-furylmethyl)-5-sulfamoylanthranilic acid.

(l) *Security Stall* means the stall assigned by the Racing Commission to a horse on the Bleeder List, for occupancy as a prerequisite for receiving bleeder medication. Sometimes called the detention stall.

(m) *Security Area* means the area surrounding the security stall delineated by the Racing Commission and controlled by it.

Rule 1.03. No horse participating in a race shall carry in its body any foreign substance except as provided in Rule 1.04 of these Rules and Regulations.

(a) A finding by the chemist that a foreign substance is present in the test sample shall be prima facie evidence that such foreign substance was administered and carried in the body of the horse while participating in a race. Such a finding shall also be taken as prima facie evidence that the trainer and his agents responsible for the care or custody of the horse has/have been negligent in the handling or care of the horse.

Rule 1.04. A foreign substance of accepted therapeutic value may be administered as prescribed by a veterinarian when test levels and guidelines for its use have been established by the Veterinary-Chemist Advisory Committee of the National Association of State Racing Commissioners and approved by the Racing Commission.

Rule 1.04.1. Only one (1) approved non-steroidal anti-inflammatory drug (NSAID) may be present in a horse's body while it is participating in a race. The presence of more than one NSAID at any test level is forbidden.

Rule 1.04.2. The test level of phenylbutazone under this rule shall not be in excess of 2 micrograms (mcg) per milliliter (ml) of plasma. The test level for oxyphenbutazone under this rule shall not be in excess of 2 micrograms (mcg) per milliliter (ml) of plasma.

Rule 1.05. The administration of furosemide shall be permitted for the prophylactic treatment of a confirmed bleeder under the following conditions and guidelines and with the approval of the Commission Veterinarian.

Rule 1.05.1. In order to obtain approval for the administration of furosemide the bleeder horse must be placed on the Bleeder List.

Rule 1.05.2. Only the following horses shall be placed on the Bleeder List:

(a) A horse which during the race or within the first hour immediately following a race is observed by the Commission Veterinarian or Stewards to be shedding blood from one or both nostrils or is found to have bled internally. The Commission Veterinarian may require an endoscopic examination of the horse in order to confirm inclusion on the Bleeder List;

(b) A horse which bled during exercise on the race track or within the first hour following such exercise is subject to the same conditions as in Paragraph (a) above.

Rule 1.05.3. The endoscopic examination provided for in Paragraph 1.05.2(a) above shall be conducted by a veterinarian licensed by the Commission and employed by the owner or his agent, and shall be conducted in the presence of and in consultation with the Commission Veterinarian. Such endoscopic examination must be conducted within one (1) hour of the finish of the race or exercise in which the horse has participated and bled, and must reveal hemorrhage in the lumen of the respiratory tract. Endoscopic examination under this rule shall be at a time and place set by the Commission Veterinarian and shall be conducted in his presence.

Rule 1.05.4. The confirmation of a bleeder horse must be certified in writing by the Commission Veterinarian and entered by him on the Bleeder List. A copy of such certification shall be issued to the owner of the horse or his agent upon request.

Rule 1.05.5. Every confirmed bleeder regardless of age shall be placed on the Bleeder List. An up-to-date Bleeder List shall be maintained by the Commission.

Rule 1.05.6. A horse shall be removed from the Bleeder List only upon the direction of the Commission Veterinarian, who shall certify in writing to the Commission Steward his recommendation for removal.

Rule 1.05.7. Once a horse is placed on the Bleeder List he must be assigned to a pre-race security stall not less than five hours prior to scheduled post time for the race in which it is entered to start. Once placed in the security area, a horse will remain there until it is taken to the paddock to be saddled or harnessed for the race.

Rule 1.05.8. Horses qualified for medication and so indicated on the official

Bleeder List must be treated at least five (5) hours prior to post time. Immediately prior to treatment, a blood sample shall be taken by the Commission Veterinarian and delivered to the testing laboratory under the standard procedure for collection, identification and transmittal as is used in routine testing.

Rule 1.05.9. Bleeder medication shall be administered by a veterinarian licensed by the Racing Commission and employed by the owner of the horse or by his agent and at a dose level recommended by the manufacturer and approved by the Commission Veterinarian. The administration of bleeder medication shall be witnessed by the Commission Veterinarian or an inspector assigned by him.

Rule 1.05.10. While in the security area, the horse shall be in the care, custody and control of the trainer or a licensed person assigned by him. The trainer shall be responsible for the condition, care and handling of the horse while it remains in the security area.

Rule 1.05.11. A bleeder horse shipped into this state from another jurisdiction must comply with the procedure outlined above. However, a bleeder horse shipped into this state from another jurisdiction may be automatically placed on the Bleeder List provided that the jurisdiction from which it was shipped qualified it as a bleeder using criteria satisfactory to this state. A current certificate setting forth his qualifications as a bleeder must be transmitted to the Commission Steward at the track in this state to which it is shipped.

Rule 1.06. Each and every horse entered to race shall be subjected to a veterinary examination for racing soundness and health on race day, not later than two hours prior to official post time for the first race.

Rule 1.06.1. Such an examination shall be referred to as the "Racing Soundness Exam."

Rule 1.06.2. All such examinations shall be conducted in or near the stall to which the animal is assigned and shall be conducted by a veterinarian employed by the Racing Commission or approved by it.

Rule 1.06.3. The veterinarian stipulated in Paragraph 1.06.2 above shall keep or cause to be kept a continuing health and racing soundness record of each horse so examined.

Rule 1.07. Every horse which suffers a breakdown on the race track, in training, or in competition, and is destroyed, and every other horse which expires while stabled on the race track under the jurisdiction of the Racing Commission, shall undergo a postmortem examination at a time and place acceptable to the Commission Veterinarian to determine the injury or sickness which resulted in euthanasia or natural death.

Rule 1.07.1. The postmortem examination required under this rule shall be conducted by a veterinarian employed by the owner or his trainer in the presence of and in consultation with the Commission Veterinarian.

Rule 1.07.2. Test samples must be obtained from the carcass upon which the postmortem examination is conducted and shall be sent to a laboratory approved by the Commission for testing for foreign substances and natural substances at abnormal levels. When practical, blood and urine test samples should be procured prior to euthanasia.

Rule 1.07.3. The owner of the deceased horse shall make payment of any charges due the veterinarian employed by him to conduct the postmortem examination. The services of the Commission Veterinarian and the laboratory testing of postmortem samples shall be made available by the Racing Commission without charge to the owner.

Rule 1.07.4. A record of every such postmortem shall be filed with the Racing Commission by the owner's veterinarian within 72 hours of the death and shall be submitted on a form supplied by the Commission.

Rule 1.07.5. Each owner and trainer accepts the responsibility for the postmortem examination provided herein as a requisite for maintaining the occupational license issued by the Commission.

Rule 1.08. The Racing Commission has the authority to direct the official laboratory to retain and preserve by freezing samples for future analysis.

Rule 1.08.1. The fact that purse money has been distributed prior to the issuance of a laboratory report shall not be deemed a finding that no chemical substance has been administered, in violation of these rules, to the horse earning such purse money.

NOTE: These guidelines were amended at the April 1981 meeting of the National Association of State Racing Commissioners Meeting in New Orleans to delete all references to furosemide. The deletions include 1.02 k, l, m, and all of rule 1.05.

INDEX